FOURTH EDITION

Advertising Media Planning

Jack Z. Sissors
Lincoln Bumba

NTC Business Books
a division of *NTC Publishing Group* • Lincolnwood, Illinois USA

Library of Congress Cataloging-in-Publication Data

Sissors, Jack Zanville
    Advertising media planning / Jack Z. Sissors, Lincoln Bumba. —
4th ed.
      p.   cm.
    Includes index.
    ISBN 0-8442-3508-3
    1. Advertising media planning. I. Bumba, Lincoln. II. Title.
HF5826.5.S57   1992
659.1′11—dc20   92-11405
                                           CIP

Published by NTC Business Books, a division of NTC Publishing Group
4255 West Touhy Avenue, Lincolnwood (Chicago), Illinois 60646-1975, U.S.A.
© 1993 by Jack Z. Sissors and Lincoln Bumba.
Manufactured in the United States of America.
2 3 4 5 6 7 8 9 0 VP 9 8 7 6 5 4 3 2 1

Contents

Foreword

Few people are better qualified to author a definitive book on media planning and strategy than Jack Sissors. Jack and I first met when I was in charge of the media department at the Leo Burnett Company. The lure of academe pulled Jack away from a promising career. Leo Burnett's loss was Northwestern University's gain.

Jack's close association with practitioner colleagues has kept him current in the field of media planning. He created Northwestern University's annual "Media Symposium" for planners, and works on the Advertising Research Foundation's media research committees. In addition, he created and ran the *Journal of Media Planning,* a periodical written especially for media planners, which has made its mark in our business.

Jack's coauthor has a fine reputation at the Leo Burnett Company and in the media world, in general. He is Lincoln J. Bumba, who is Senior Vice President and International Media Director at Burnett. Linc has worked in the media department for twenty-nine years, and brings to the book a wealth of media knowledge and experience acquired by working for sophisticated clients such as Procter and Gamble, Kellogg's, Pillsbury, McDonald's, and other leading marketers.

Sissors and Bumba have written the most comprehensive text I have seen on the complex world of modern media planning. Very few areas of the communications business have changed more in the past ten years than media, as mass media has given way to targeted media. Students and practitioners alike will find this book up to date; it leaves few, if any, questions unanswered. As media planning becomes more complex, the need to have a firm grasp on changing concepts and practices becomes more important than ever. This new edition is must reading for anyone who wants to understand the theory and practice of advertising media planning.

Leonard S. Matthews
Former President of the Leo Burnett Company,
and Past President of the American Association
of Advertising Agencies

Preface

This book is an introduction to advertising media planning—a major activity in the advertising industry, especially in advertising agencies and client organizations. Because media plans can involve enormous expenditures of money, a good plan can help advertisers achieve their communication goals and, at the same time, avoid wasting money, time, and effort.

This book emphasizes consumer media rather than industrial media, and national advertising planning rather than local planning. Since consumer media concepts are basically similar to the other media, one can learn media planning concepts from this text and make relatively easy transitions to other, more specialized media.

Originally, this book was written for students majoring in advertising in colleges and universities. However, it also has been widely used as an introduction to media planning in advertising agencies and corporate marketing departments.

This edition has some major differences from its predecessor. It describes dramatic changes that have occurred in the advertising industry and their effects on media and media planning. Such changes include new measuring techniques, such as passive peoplemeters; single source research data; new kinds of media strategies, such as cross media planning; and the increasing use of non-traditional media. New ideas in targeting consumers (such as database marketing) are also discussed. This edition also introduces and explains integrated marketing communications and how it may affect media planning. The chapter on using the computer has been eliminated because it is no longer needed. Most colleges require computer literacy of all advertising majors, and advertising companies often provide computer orientation for new staff members.

This book also covers the use of media strategies that can help resolve marketing and media problems, so the reader knows how and why certain strategies are chosen and how they work.

Basic mathematical concepts of media planning are included. We think that knowing this math affects the degree of understanding and appreciation of media plans by agencies or consultants. The math may look formidable, but is relatively simple to understand.

The reader will find that this is a book that emphasizes media *concepts* rather than how-to-do-it explanations. We want the reader to be able to "think media" and understand the complexities behind all decisions that go into media planning. Knowing these concepts can help people find jobs in advertising agencies as well as other places in the industry. Many professionals who do work besides media planning in the advertising industry need to know how media is planned, and this book also can help them do a better job.

In essence then, the book urges readers to develop a mental set that helps them understand ideas and concepts, and appreciate what planners have in mind when they create a media plan.

Jack Z. Sissors
Lincoln Bumba

1
Introduction to Media Planning

How to Think about Media

Media exist primarily to deliver entertainment, information, and advertisements to a vast audience throughout the country. Media should be thought of as both a carrier and a delivery system. They carry advertisements and deliver them to individuals who buy or choose media first on the basis of the kind and quality of entertainment and information, and secondly on the kinds of advertisements they carry. Advertisers find media a convenient and relatively inexpensive delivery system. It could be more expensive to deliver advertisements to a mass audience by buying media that did not carry entertainment and information.

It is important to recognize that consumers have specialized needs that media can meet, such as wanting to know more about certain kinds of products and brands. At times, audiences may browse a print medium, stopping to look at or read any advertisements that seem interesting. At other times, they may deliberately search a medium looking for a certain kind of product. Print media therefore tend to serve as a catalog for readers. Broadcast media audiences also pay attention to many commercials, but not the same way as print audiences.

Advertisers often want to reach both mass and specialized audiences (such as women aged 25 to 54), and find that it is more expensive to buy media that reach specialized audiences.

However, no matter which kind of audience advertisers want to reach, it is imperative that they plan the purchase of media as far ahead of publishing or broadcast dates as possible. Advertisers cannot afford to buy media impulsively or capriciously. Therefore, the planning function is a major operation in advertising agencies and at client companies. There is too much money involved to *not* plan ahead of time. This book concentrates on the planning function.

The Difference Between "Media" and "Vehicles"

There are two words that are sometimes used as if they meant the same thing: *medium* (the plural is media) and *vehicle*. They are not the same.

A *medium* should refer to a "class" of carriers such as television, newspapers, magazines, etc. In other words, it should refer to a group of carriers that have similar characteristics.

A *vehicle* is an individual carrier within a medium. The *Chicago Tribune* is a carrier within the newspaper group. The *10 o'clock news* or *60 Minutes* are vehicles within television. *Ladies Home Journal* and *McCalls* are vehicles within the magazine group.

The problem for students learning media planning is that some persons in the advertising business use both *medium* and *vehicle* interchangeably. That practice should be avoided.

Media Planning

Media planning consists of the series of decisions made to answer the question for advertisers: "What are the best means of delivering advertisements to prospective purchasers of my brand or service?" (Advertisements are delivered by media such as newspapers, magazines, or television.) While this definition is rather general, it provides a broad picture of what media planning is all about.

Some specific questions that a media planner attempts to answer are:

- How many prospects (for purchasing a given brand of product) do I need to reach?
- In which medium (and vehicles) should I place ads?
- How many times a month should prospects see each ad?
- In which months should ads appear?
- In which markets and regions of the United States should ads appear?
- How much money should be spent in each medium?

These are only a few of the questions that must be asked. Each one requires a specific answer and decision.

When all questions have been asked and decisions made, the recommendations and rationales are organized into a written document called a *media plan*. The plan, when approved by the advertiser, becomes a blueprint for the selection and use of media. Once the advertiser has approved the plan, it also serves as a guide for actually purchasing the media.

It would be a mistake, however, to think of media planning as nothing more than finding answers to a list of questions about media. Such a view is too narrow to provide the necessary perspective. Rather, it is better to assume that each question represents certain kinds of problems that need to be solved. Some problems are relatively simple, such as, "On which day of the week should television commercials be shown?" Other problems, however, are much more difficult, such as, "In which media will ads most affect the prospect's buying behavior to result in sales?"

Media planning should be thought of as a process or a series of decisions that provides the best possible answers to a set of problems. A planner may find that a solution to a given problem does not guarantee that it will work when other factors are considered. Finding the *best* solutions to a set of problems represents the main task of planners, and this is what makes media planning such an intellectually challenging activity.

The Changing Role of Media Planners

The role of media planners has changed in advertising agencies. Today, media planning ranks in importance with marketing and creative planning, but in the early days of advertising agency operations, media planning consisted of simple, clerical-type tasks. There were fewer media available in those days, and little research on media audiences had been done to guide planners in decision making.

Planning today is an executive function because it has become so much more complex and important than it was years ago. Today's planners must have a greater knowledge base from which to formulate media plans. The planners must not only know more about media, which have increased tremendously in number, but also know more about marketing, research, and advertising than did their predecessors. Most important, planners are called upon not only to make decisions, but to defend those decisions as the best that could be made after considering the many alternatives.

What brought about this change? Foremost was the rise of the marketing concept, which changed media planning from an isolated activity to one closely related to marketing planning. In fact, one way to evaluate a media plan is to measure how effectively it helps to attain marketing objectives. Another cause of the change was the development of new and more definitive media audience research techniques. As a result, there are more research data available to help planners choose from among a myriad of alternatives.

The change was also due to the increase in advertising expenditures by companies with smaller profit ratios to selling expenses. Quite simply, companies of all sizes now spend many more dollars for media. Also, the prices for purchasing ads in the various media have accelerated rapidly—media are very expensive for advertisers to buy. As a consequence, company managements want better proof than ever before that their money is well spent. The media planner is the one who is responsible for providing detailed and valid explanations for the media decisions.

Media planning, then, is not so much a matter of being able to answer such relatively simple questions as where to place advertisements or how many advertisements to run each week, as it is a matter of proving that optimal decisions were made under a given set of marketing circumstances. Advertisers demand such explanations, and media planners must be able to provide them. Today's media planners have changed as requirements for planning have changed. The new planner must have breadth of knowledge, marketing understanding, research familiarity, creative planning awareness, and media acumen to do the job competently. It is within this framework that media planning now takes place.

Classes of Media

Mass Media

Mass media, such as newspapers, magazines, radio, and television are especially well suited for delivering advertisements—as well as news, entertainment, and educational material—to a widespread general (or mass) audience. (See Figure 1–1.) Planners find mass media valuable because (1) such media may be able to deliver large audiences at relatively low costs, (2) they can deliver advertisements to special kinds of audiences who are attracted to each medium's editorial or programming, and (3) they tend to develop strong loyalties among audiences who return to their favorite medium with a high degree of regularity. If a planner wants to reach a special kind of audience repeatedly within a certain time period, some media vehicles will be better suited for this purpose than others. Recent research suggests, for example, that certain types of broadcast programs create higher degrees of viewer interest than other program types, thus offering better environments for commercials.

Media planners, however, also know that mass media (like other media) have their limitations in delivering advertising messages. The most serious is that mass media audiences do not see, hear, or read a medium solely because of the advertising content. Media vary in their ability to get both editorial and advertising material exposed.

Newspapers have news, entertainment, information, and catalog values for their readers. A newspaper generally has excellent readership of both editorial and advertising material, serving as a buying guide for readers who are looking for many different kinds of products. Housewives, for example, often check newspaper ads immediately before their regular food shopping day to find the best grocery bargains. For frequently purchased products, where prices are prominently displayed, newspapers can be a very effective selling medium.

Magazines, on the other hand, are much different in their ability to get ads read. Although some people buy a magazine because they are looking for specific product information on a car or a piece of furniture, most magazine readers are looking for interesting editorial material rather than product information.

Broadcast media, such as radio and television, are least sought out by consumers for the advertisements alone. Broadcast commercials have an intrusive character, breaking into the play or action of a program and compelling some attention to the advertising message. Whether any given viewer will or will not watch a particular commercial is determined more by the ingenuity and value of the message than by its appearance on an interesting program. Audiences could seek them out for making buying decisions, and complete the sale via the media.

The effectiveness of the commercial or advertisement to communicate obviously affects the impact it will have on the consumer and the number of consumers who will read, see, or hear it. This is true regardless of which medium is used.

Traditional versus Non-Traditional Media

Traditional Media. Another way of categorizing media is by dividing them into groups of either (1) traditional or (2) non-traditional media. When planners talk about traditional media they usually mean mass media such as newspapers, magazines, radio, television and outdoor, or media that have been traditionally used for reaching mass audiences. Cable television, while relatively new, is often viewed as a traditional medium because it has become so popular. Pay-per-view cable television is newer, and some planners may also call it a non-traditional medium.

Non-traditional media. But non-traditional media consists of almost any innovative way of delivering ad messages to consumers. Non-traditional media is also sometimes called the *new media*. Furthermore, it consists of methods of disseminating advertising messages through means not usually called media. For example, the combination of magazines and sales promotion is sometimes called non-traditional media even though sales promotion has not historically been categorized as a medium.

The need for non-traditional media is based on the need for finding better ways of reaching consumers who have either changed their living habits, or who belong in marketing categories that are new and different from the traditional ways of categorizing consumers. In the past consumers usually were categorized by demographics such as women aged 18–49 or men with incomes over $50,000 a year. Now, however, there are data learned from new kinds of research that show who most often buys a given brand of product, and also at the same time, measure which medium they see most often. If that medium is crowded with other kinds of advertising, the media planner may assume that consumers will have little inclination to look at his product or brand. This is called "clutter" and planners seek to avoid it if possible. Non-traditional media are often less cluttered than established traditional media.

In addition, non-traditional media may consist of a combination of advertising delivery and sales incentives (through sales promotion or public relations).

While many media planners have recommended that the client use non-traditional media, there have been some difficult problems in determining what the advertiser receives for his money. The problem is caused by not having any continuing measurements of the audience sizes delivered by these less established media. In most instances planners have to "guesstimate" the sizes of audiences. Without such measurements it is difficult to calculate a cost-per-thousand number that represents the value of the money spent for advertising related to the number of audiences delivered. (See pages 76–77 for a further discussion of cost per thousands.)

Because there are so many non-traditional media, only a sample are shown on Figure 1-1.

Specialized Media

Special interest consumer magazines appeal to specific reader interests such as skiing, money management, photography, or antiques. These magazines are read as much for their advertising as they are for their editorial content. Therefore, these magazines often attract readers who purchase the magazine not only for the editorial material, but also for information on the kinds of products advertised. Such media are often referred to as niche media because of their special interest focus.

A large category of media also exists to meet the specialized needs of industrial manufacturers, service companies, wholesalers, retailers, and professional workers such as physicians, attorneys, and teachers. These media may take the form of publications that contain editorial matter, as well as advertising pertaining to the specialized market, but they may also include films, trade shows, convention exhibits, and phonograph records. Business-to-business advertisers are typically the advertisers most interested in these publications.

Other specialized media exist exclusively for the purpose of delivering advertising messages. They carry no editorial matter and are not sought after by readers as are other forms of media. Such advertising-oriented media include handbills, direct mail, outdoor billboards, car cards that appear on buses or trucks, and free-standing inserts in newspapers (called FSI).

Another specialized medium is the catalog. Although catalogs are often requested by consumers, they may not be looked at with the same degree of frequency as are mass media. At the same time, many advertisers find catalogs productive since consumers use them as shopping guides. One form of catalog is the telephone book, which carries advertising but also carries editorial matter—telephone numbers. Plumbers, for example, might justifiably use telephone book advertising exclusively because plumbers aren't needed until emergencies arise. On such occasions, the consumer will search ads in the Yellow Pages to find a plumber, but probably will not notice such ads at any other time.

FIGURE 1-1. Media Most Often Used for Advertising

There are many options open for delivering advertising messages to potential buyers. Some of these media have been widely used for many years, such as "Traditional Media." Others, however, either are very specialized, or are so new that they have not been widely used, but are being considered.

Traditional Media (Mass Media)

Print media
  Newspapers
  Magazines
  Supplements (newspaper distributed magazines)
  Shoppers (local newspapers carrying mostly ads)
  Direct mail
  Handbills
  Freestanding inserts (FSI) in newspapers and magazines

Broadcast media
  Television programs (network or local)
  Spot television (commercials placed between programs or in local programs)
  Radio programs (network or local)
  Spot radio (commercials placed between programs or in local programs)
  Cable (basic)
  Pay cable
  Pay-per-view cable

Other
  Outdoor (printed, painted)
  Car cards and smaller posters

Specialized Media

Yellow Pages of phone books
Business publications (including professional journals)
Directories and membership listings
Event programs (including concert, theater, and sporting programs)
Handbills
Catalogs

Non-Traditional Media

Ads on parking meters, on back of bus transfers, etc.
Ads in grocery baskets: on vidscreen or mini-billboards (Actmedia)
The Airport Channel, or Ted Turner's private network

Non-Traditional Media (cont.)

Putting a client's name on balloons at a sporting event
Value Added incentives:
  CBS: conducted a mall tour to promote coverage of NCAA basketball tournament.
  NBC: Cooperated with McDonald's hamburgers by running a "watch and win" prize game (called McMillions).
Special Reports. Example: Christopher Whittle's magazines delivered to 16,800 doctor's office reception areas.
Special Reports TV. Example: Whittle's original family-oriented TV programming delivered on a videodisk-driven 27 inch TV set in the same doctor's offices as Special Reports magazines.
Educational network. Example: Chris Whittle's TV program and magazine combination delivered at junior and senior high schools throughout the country for students and teachers. Part of this program is called *Channel One*, and is a daily 12-minute news/information program for teenagers; and *The Educator Channel*, a professional TV development program for teachers
Customized Comic books: one is called "Captain America Meets the Asthma Monster," distributed in doctor's offices and promoting Allen & Hanbury's inhalers.
The Floor Board, a process that affixes miniature billboards to the floors of grocery stores.
Cross media (combinations of in-store with traditional media). Example: GuidePosters, a combination of maps and ads showing best restaurants in a market, and advertising from those restaurants. Or a promotional blitz featuring a sport like soccer and American Airlines. A world-wide soccer tournament is held, and the competition is to be held in eight to 12 American cities.
On-line in-flight advertising on airlines' video programming. Some airlines are adding additional video monitoring to gain additional attention
Ad placements at ski resorts for the skier market. It uses movie trailers (ads before or after a movie)
Ads on video cassette jackets

General Procedures in Planning Media

Marketing considerations must precede media planning. Media planning never starts with answers to such questions as "Which medium should I select?" or "Should I use television or magazines?" Planning grows out of a marketing problem that needs to be solved. To start without knowing or understanding the underlying marketing problem is illogical because the use of media is primarily a tool for implementing the marketing strategy. So the starting point for a media plan should be an analysis of a marketing situation. This analysis is made so that both marketing and media planners can get a bird's-eye view of how a company has been operating against its competitors in the total market. The analysis serves as a means of learning what the details of the problem are, where possibilities lie for its solution, and where the company can gain an advantage over its competitors in the marketplace.

After the marketing situation has been analyzed, a *marketing strategy and plan* is devised that states marketing objectives and spells out the actions to accomplish those objectives. When the marketing strategy calls for advertising, it is usually to communicate some information to consumers that affects the attainment of a marketing objective. Media are the means whereby advertisements are delivered to the market.

Once a marketing plan has been devised, an *advertising creative strategy* must also be determined. This consists of decisions about what is to be communicated, how it will be executed, and what it is supposed to accomplish. A statement of advertising copy themes and how copy will be used to communicate the selling message is also part of that strategy. Media planning decisions are affected by advertising creative strategy because some creative strategies are better suited to one medium than to any other. For example, if a product requires demonstration, television may be the best medium. If an ad must be shown in high-fidelity color, magazines or newspaper supplements may be preferable. Creative strategy also determines the prospect profile in terms of such demographic variables as age, sex, income, or occupation. These prospects now become the targets that the planner will focus on in selecting media vehicles.

It should be noted that up to this point persons other than the media planner have been making decisions that will ultimately affect the media plan. The marketing or marketing research people were responsible for the situation analysis and marketing plan, though media planners are, at times, involved at the inception of the marketing plan. Copywriters and art directors are generally responsible for carrying out the creative strategy. Sometimes a marketing plan may be as simple as a memorandum from a marketing executive to the media planner, or even an idea in an advertising executive's mind. In such informal situations, media planning may begin almost immediately with little or no marketing research preceding it. Figure 1–2 summarizes the preplanning steps.

The media planner begins work once a marketing strategy plan is in

FIGURE 1–2. The Scope of Media Pre-planning Activities

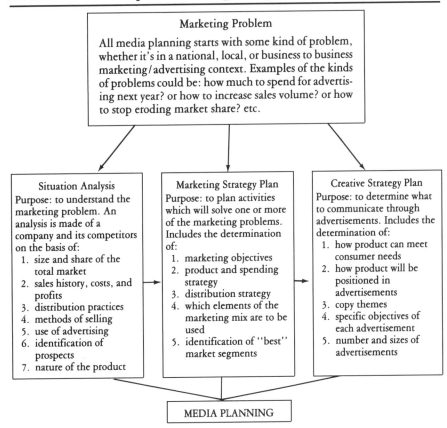

hand. This plan sets the tone and guides the direction of the media decisions to follow.

The first thing to come out of such a plan is a statement of media *objectives.* These are the goals that a media planner believes are most important in helping to attain marketing objectives. Goals include determination of which *targets*—those persons most likely to purchase a given product or service—are most important, how many of those targets need to be reached, and where advertising should be concentrated at what times.

Media strategies develop out of objectives. A media strategy is a series of actions selected from several possible alternatives to best achieve the media objectives. Media strategies will cover such decisions as which kinds of media should be used, whether national or spot broadcast advertising should be used, how ads should be scheduled, and many other decisions.

After the strategy is determined, the implementation of the media plan begins. Some planners call all these subsequent decisions *tactics.* Whatever they are called, many decisions still have to be made before tactics culminate in a media plan. As indicated in Figure 1–3, these decisions might include the selection of vehicles in which to place ads, the number of ads to be placed in each vehicle, the size of each ad, and the specific position within each vehicle that an ad will occupy.

Principles of Selecting Media Vehicles

Of all the media decisions made, one of the most important is selecting individual vehicles. Planners tend to select one or more vehicles that effectively reach an optimum number of prospects (a) with an optimum amount of frequency (or repetition), (b) at the lowest cost per thousand prospects reached (called cost efficiency), (c) with a minimum of waste (or nonprospects), and (d) within a specified budget.

These principles apply most when selecting vehicles for mass-produced and mass-consumed products such as food, clothing, or automobiles. Yet even though they may be more difficult to execute, the principles should be the same in selecting vehicles for such products as noncommercial airplanes or yachts where prospects are distributed unevenly throughout the population. It may be less cost efficient to reach those prospects than it would be to reach prospects for mass-consumed products because planners may have to select vehicles that contain large amounts of waste to reach such selective markets. There are other times when the principles may have to be modified. For example, if a creative strategy calls for certain kinds of media such as those that produce ads in high-fidelity color, then cost or waste may have to be disregarded in favor of meeting creative goals. Most often, however, these principles are followed consistently in planning.

When planners apply media selection principles, they use media delivery statistics as one piece of evidence that they have achieved the reach required. *Delivery* simply means the number of audience members reached by, or exposed to, a vehicle or a combination of media vehicles.

With the goal of obtaining the highest possible exposure, the planner starts by looking among the many media alternatives that will reach prospects. A planner does this through using media audience research data for individual vehicles. The data are in the form of numbers classified by audience types, and the numbers listed for each medium may be used as proof of audience delivery. In other words, the planner may use this statistical evidence to prove that the best vehicle(s) for reaching the targeted prospects has been selected. Obviously there are other considerations in making this decision. Costs of media may be so high per prospect reached that the planner may have to reject the first choice in favor of other media that reach smaller numbers of prospects but at lower costs.

Once audience delivery numbers have been found, they are related to the total number of prospects in the market. If a market consists of 35 million women in the United States who purchased a given kind of product within the last month, then the size of the market is 35 million. The planner may select certain magazines that reach 17$\frac{1}{2}$ million purchasing women, or 50 percent of the market. Is 50 percent enough? It depends on the market-

FIGURE 1–3. Kinds of Questions That Lead to Decisions about Media Objectives and Strategies

The following is an overview of some of the many questions that lead to media objectives and strategies. Note that strategies grow out of objectives.

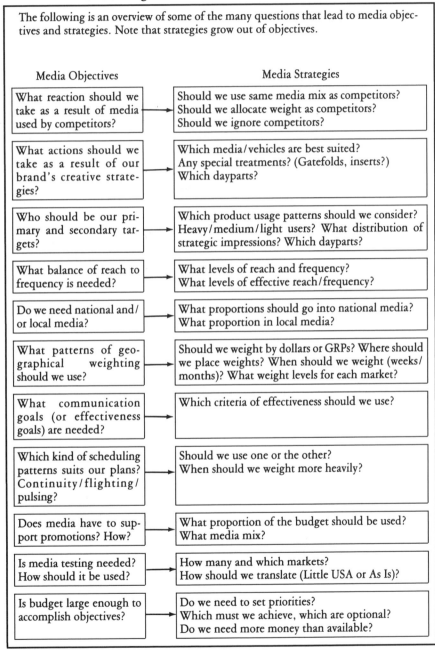

Media Objectives	Media Strategies
What reaction should we take as a result of media used by competitors?	Should we use same media mix as competitors? Should we allocate weight as competitors? Should we ignore competitors?
What actions should we take as a result of our brand's creative strategies?	Which media/vehicles are best suited? Any special treatments? (Gatefolds, inserts?) Which dayparts?
Who should be our primary and secondary targets?	Which product usage patterns should we consider? Heavy/medium/light users? What distribution of strategic impressions? Which dayparts?
What balance of reach to frequency is needed?	What levels of reach and frequency? What levels of effective reach/frequency?
Do we need national and/or local media?	What proportions should go into national media? What proportion in local media?
What patterns of geographical weighting should we use?	Should we weight by dollars or GRPs? Where should we place weights? When should we weight (weeks/months)? What weight levels for each market?
What communication goals (or effectiveness goals) are needed?	Which criteria of effectiveness should we use?
Which kind of scheduling patterns suits our plans? Continuity/flighting/pulsing?	Should we use one or the other? When should we weight more heavily?
Does media have to support promotions? How?	What proportion of the budget should be used? What media mix?
Is media testing needed? How should it be used?	How many and which markets? How should we translate (Little USA or As Is)?
Is budget large enough to accomplish objectives?	Do we need to set priorities? Which must we achieve, which are optional? Do we need more money than available?

ing objectives. If it isn't enough, the planner may select one or more other media vehicles to increase the percentage reached. Because no decision is made in a vacuum, the planner must also take into consideration the creative, promotional, and executional goals of the marketing strategy while evaluating the vehicle's ability to deliver prospects.

Media Plans Are Custom Tailored

A media plan is designed expressly to meet the needs of an advertiser at a given point in time for specific marketing purposes. Today's media plan is usually not a copy of last year's plan, nor is it simply a blank form with spaces that can be filled in quickly with selected dates or times for running ads. Each media plan should be different from preceding ones for the same product.

Why, then, are plans custom tailored? The answer is that the marketplace is a dynamic center of activity that is rarely the same from year to year. Competitors rarely stand still in their marketing activities. They may be changing their messages, changing their marketing expenditures, introducing new brands, or discontinuing distribution of old brands. Consumers, too, change—moving to different geographical areas, getting new jobs, retiring, getting married, adopting different leisure-time activities, or buying new kinds of products.

As a result, the marketing situation of an advertiser presents new opportunities as well as new problems. The result is a need for a tailor-made media plan to fit a specific marketing situation.

Media planning is not a science with hard and fast rules that can be easily implemented. Because marketing situations change, new approaches to planning are constantly needed to keep up with, or ahead of, competitors. Media planning is also affected by the new kinds of research or analysis needed to keep abreast of a changing business world. Media planning requires a great sensitivity to change. See Case Study 1–1.

Problems in Media Planning

Although media planning has become very important within advertising agency operations, it is not performed as efficiently as one might suppose. The planner is faced with many different kinds of problems that make it difficult to arrive at objective decisions.

Media Proliferation

One of the most significant problems facing a media planner these days is media proliferation, which means that the number of media is growing fast and the number of media options is therefore increasing. On the one hand, this may make it easier for a planner to find just the right vehicle in which to

CASE STUDY 1–1
Is There a *Best* Media Strategy?

Competitive Media Expenditures for Selected Retail Companies
(in annual percentages)

	Network TV %	Spot TV %	Cable TV %	Syndi- cated TV %	Maga- zines %	News- papers %	Sunday Magazines %	Outdoor %	Spot Radio %	Network Radio %	Total %
Bloomingdales	0	4.3	0	0	4.8	88.5	1.3	0	1.1	0	100
Macy's	0	9.9	0	0	1.2	88.3	0.4	0	0.2	0	100
K mart	20.3	9.5	1.9	1.1	9.9	33.8	6.1	9.5	7.9	0	100
Wal-Mart	0.1	68.9	1.4	0	10.6	3.9	14.9	0	0.3	0	100.1
Sears	29.9	9.8	1.7	0.6	3	32.5	3.2	0	8.1	11.2	100

Source: Brand Report No. 172: "Service Please," in *Marketing & Media Decisions*, 1990, p.79.

Comments:

1. Media selection strategy is shown in the above chart. Media expenditure often provide more insight into strategy than any other data.
2. From the data one may conclude that there is no one best media strategy for all advertisers. The reason is that each advertiser perceives the market in slightly different ways, based on its own marketing needs. Some marketers want to increase market share, while others want to simply maintain their present position. Such differences play a role in media selection. Also, some advertisers see one or another media as being more effective for them than others.
3. Two of the competitors (Bloomingdale's and Macy's) spent more money (proportionately) in newspapers than others. Newspapers have often been the primary and traditional medium used by department stores.
4. But Wal-Mart spent a larger percentage of its money in spot TV.
5. Occasionally, one sees all competitors in a category using the same or similar media selection strategies.

place ads because the new media are highly specialized, having been created to meet the interests of a relatively small, selective group of people.

On the other hand, the planner faces two major problems with this approach. The first problem was mentioned earlier: namely that many of these media do not have measurements of their audience sizes. So a planner only has a rough idea of how many potential customers he could possibly reach if he places ads in one of these media. Therefore a planner must use whatever information is available to make a calculated guess of the audience size, but it is still a guess. Traditional media usually have their audiences measured continuously by an outside research company. So when a planner needs evidence of how large an audience could be, the planner may feel safer in buying a traditional rather than a non-traditional medium.

The second major problem is that as the number of media have increased, so has the opportunity for advertising clutter. There are so many advertisements in so many different media that its effect may be to reduce the number of ads actually seen. Many planners feel that the audience sizes of any media are less important than the number of persons who sees these ads. They tend to feel that non-traditional media offer the advertiser a better opportunity to see ads than traditional media since non-traditional media tend not to carry as many competitive advertisements.

When there are periods of economic recession, media proliferation tends to decrease as some of these media go out of business, having not been able to maintain enough advertising to make it profitable. During times of economic prosperity the number of media tend to grow faster.

Insufficient Media Data

Media planners almost always require more data about markets and media than are available. Some data never will be available, either because audiences cannot be measured or the data are too expensive to collect. For example, no continuing research service measures the audience exposure to outdoor advertising, or to AM or FM radio listening in every market in the United States, or to portable television viewing. Why? Because such services are too costly to provide and because there is no adequate way of measuring these audiences. Both outdoor exposure and local radio listening have been measured—but not on a continuing basis in all cities so as to give the planner comprehensive and up-to-date information. There are also inadequate research data showing the amount of money that competitors spend yearly for outdoor advertising, for local radio advertising, and for newspaper ads.

In television planning, measurements of the audience size for commercial messages are not available. Most television rating services measure the audience size only in terms of individuals or homes tuned in to programs. This does constitute exposure measurement even though there is no assurance that those who press people meter buttons are paying attention to a program. Even if there is an audience in front of the television sets watching a given program, there is no guarantee that they would watch the commercials. How, then, can the media planner know with any degree of certainty how many people will view or hear a commercial on any given program?

Furthermore, while it may be possible to estimate the size of the audience for a given commercial, there is no way to measure the degree of attention audiences pay to that commercial. For example, suppose the media planner wants to know the audience size of a 15-second spot that airs at 7:00 p.m. on any given night in a market like Chicago. No company actually measures that audience size. The general practice is to measure the audience during the last 15 minutes of a program broadcast *before* 7:00 p.m. and the first 15 minutes of a program *after* that period and then average the two. One could hardly say that this practice is an accurate measurement yet this is the way that television commercials have been measured for more than 30 years. It is likely to continue until a breakthrough in measurement techniques is discovered.

Measuring network audience sizes of commercials inside programs is even more important. Despite the invention of people meters, there also has not been a breakthrough in this significant measurement. If such data were available, the planner would be able to make decisions about television with a greater degree of confidence than is now possible.

Another problem in television planning is that decisions about the future performance of television programs must be based on data that represent past performance. If the future is radically different from the past, then the data on which a decision is based may be worthless.

The problem of obtaining sufficient information is especially acute for small advertisers, many of whom cannot afford to buy research data. These companies often do not know how large their own retail sales are because they sell only to distributors or wholesalers. The media planner, then, must guess at the client's sales position in any given market.

Measuring how people read newspapers and magazines is another problem. How much of any given magazine or newspaper is read? How many advertisements are read? How thoroughly are they read? What is the value of placing an advertisement in one vehicle versus another? How does each vehicle affect the perception of an advertisement that it carries? Answers to these and many other questions are not available on a continuing basis, so the media planner must make decisions without knowing all the pertinent facts.

Time Pressures

A problem that affects media planning in an entirely different way is that of the time pressure involved in making decisions. When the agency and advertiser are ready to start their advertising program, the planner often is faced with a lack of sufficient time to solve problems thoroughly. For example, in many cases the planner requires competitive media expenditure analyses showing how much each competitor spends in major markets throughout the country. Gathering such information is a time-consuming task for media analysts, and the planner may have to bypass this investigation in order to write a media plan quickly.

Another time-related problem is the limited number of broadcast times and programs available to be purchased by advertisers at any given time. This problem is compounded if the client is slow to approve the budget, in which case the most desirable broadcast time periods and/or programs may be spoken for before the advertiser enters the marketplace.

In other situations, new research data are so plentiful that there is neither personnel nor time to analyze them. This is especially true for the large amounts of computerized data on media audiences and brand usage. The computer is able to produce masses of cross tabulations at lightning speeds, but often such data may go unused because there is insufficient time to analyze them.

External Influences on Media Decisions

There are at least two external influences on media planning decisions besides the directions that numbers provide. Whether these influences result in *better* media plans is not clear. But because of their subtle nature, there is a danger that they could exert negative influences on the best judgments of planners. Those who favor these kinds of influence think otherwise. The two influences are:

The Pressure to Produce "Creative" Media Plans. An established tradition in most advertising agency media departments is to provide clients with statistical proof that media decisions are the best alternative action that could be taken under budget and other constraints normally required for media planning. Therefore media plans are usually given to clients in statistical formats, composed of many pages of numbers.

But it seems as if a growing number of planners are developing an antagonism toward these kinds of plans. Some persons have a feeling that media plans for brands within the same product category are beginning to look too much alike. Media plans that are similar may tend to nullify each other's best efforts at reaching and communicating with consumers. Therefore, a brand may suffer.

Alan Goldin, media director, House of Seagram, and Kathy Neisloss, advertising director of *Vanity Fair,* wrote about young assistant media planners who are CPM driven. They grow weary of numbers-only accusations and look for opportunities to accelerate their rise in the profession by standing out and supporting some "out-of-ordinary" media opportunities. But their motivation may be further inspired by agency and account managers who dread the typical, mundane media plans. They "continually encourage something new in the name of imagination, creativity, or innovation."[1]

A better way to proceed, these planners suggest, is to make media plans "creative." This approach may suggest that quantitatively based plans are not creative, which is questionable. The definition of what creative means, however, is not universally agreed upon. On one hand, a plan that is different from other plans would probably be called creative. On the other hand, some planners would object, saying that "just being different" is not enough. The latter persons feel that the term "creative" means innovative, or doing things in novel and unusual ways.

One problem with the creative idea, therefore, is that the meaning of "creative" may need better definition. In fact, at least two approaches to achieving a "creative" media plan exist. First, some planners prefer a media plan that starts with a sound basic set of quantitative data, and then proceeds beyond the data innovatively, at no extra cost. Placing a pet food commercial within a TV program that features pets might be one example. Sec-

---

1. Goldin, Alan and Neisloss, Kathy, "Evaluating Print Qualitatively: A No-Nonsense Guide," in *Inside Print,* November 1986, pp. 27–29.

ond, other planners feel that the numbers are relatively unimportant and that decisions for or against vehicles simply have to be innovative. These people might want a plan that is much different than plans for other products in the category, one that stands out because it represents an innovative way to communicate with people.

How many planners in this country support the concept of "creative" media plans? There are no data available. But there is a feeling that the idea is growing. The subject has been part of speeches given at various media planning conventions. Planners have discussed the need for creativity in their speeches and articles. One speech that was very well received in the industry was made by Philip Gerber, media director of Tatham-Laird, Kudner, Chicago.[2]

Another reason for a call for creativity is the feeling that media numbers are not as precise as many people assume them to be. Numbers such as ratings and audience sizes are not measures of everyone in the universe; they are projections based on samples. But once numbers get printed on paper, especially computer paper, or appear in plan reports, they seem to have a credibility that may not be warranted. In the last analysis, they are only estimates, and perhaps rough estimates at that.

In addition, "creative" media plans may be used by advertisers and their agencies in an attempt to reach increasingly fragmented and difficult-to-target audiences. The increasing number of working women, for example, may force more creative and selective daypart/program selection or add a nontraditional publication to a "women 25–54 schedule" which typically would consist only of daytime TV and women's service books.

The call for creativity in planning also comes from some media salespeople who do not have the largest or most acceptable media audience numbers for their vehicles as compared to their competitors', and who ask planners to make decisions on a subjective rather than objective basis. Perhaps the vehicle they are selling has a "something" that can't be measured very well. Therefore, these people tend to be among the groups advocating more planning on a subjective and creative basis.

The need to be different also seems to have its roots in more than a simple rejection of quantitative values. It may be related to planners' performance as persons in need of self-expression. Media planners who work on the same product group team with creative people may be stimulated by the apparent freedom that the latter people have and wish they too could have that opportunity. Creative media plans may be an avenue for self-expression.

Goldin and Neisloss argued for a balanced point of view when they wrote that

> there is no such thing as a purely qualitative media opportunity. Everything can and must be accompanied by some supporting data

---

2. Gerber, Philip, "Looking Behind the Numbers," speech given at the 1985 Media Symposium, Northwestern University, June 1985.

or sound reason and logic. Every recommendation should be prudent, not frivolous, defendable, not impulsive.

A media pro who goes only by the numbers *or* by ''gut'' feelings is no pro at all.[3] *(See pages 248–249 for more on creative planning.)*

Institutional Influences on Media Decisions. One of the less obvious sources of influence on media decisions is the effect of client pressures to use or not use certain media vehicles, or to use them in certain ways. Often these pressures are well known by everyone working on a client's account; the client may continually remind everyone of the restrictions. But there are times when these influences are known by relatively few persons, perhaps only those who regularly visit the client and are constantly communicating directly with him or her.

But there are other subtle influences that affect planners. There may be people, such as directors or assistant directors in the media department, or in account executive positions, who may in some way, influence decisions.

The problem with these institutional influences is that little or no information is available concerning the extent to which they exist, or how much they affect decisions. These influences probably vary from client to client, too.

It seems self-evident that both sources of influence need to be studied in greater detail so that we can speak more authoritatively about them than we can at present.

Lack of Objectivity

One of the continuing problems in media decision making is the sterility of thinking about strategy. Planners are not always objective. For example, an overdependence on numbers may affect objectivity. Media executives often feel that when a decision is substantiated by numbers, such as television ratings, the decision must be valid because the numbers prove it so. It is often difficult to argue with decisions proved by numbers, yet the numbers can be misleading. The methods of measurement may be imprecise, the sample size may be too small, the technique of measurement may be biased or too insensitive to really measure what it is supposed to, or there may be a set of numbers of major significance not available to the media planner—all of which may affect the objectivity of the decision maker. Uncritical acceptance of numbers can be a dangerous practice and may lead to a decision that common sense indicates is wrong. The planner should be wary of overreliance on numbers.

Objectivity is also affected when a planner accepts relative data as absolute. For example, the sizes of television audiences reported through ratings are not absolute measurements. When a television rating service shows that 15 million homes tuned in to a given television program, this does not nec-

---

3. Goldin and Neisloss, ''Evaluating Print Qualitatively,'' p. 27.

essarily mean that precisely 15 million homes actually tuned in to the program. Since the sample of homes measured was only about 4,000, projections from 4,000 to a total of about 23 million homes means that the margin of error may be quite large. It may be plus or minus a million homes. Such data are to be used for relative purposes only, and the data merely show that Program A probably has a larger audience size than Program B.

On the other hand, a planner cannot ignore the numbers and make decisions entirely on the basis of experience. Clients are certain to challenge the basis upon which media decisions are made.

Measuring Advertising Effectiveness

Because there is no valid way of measuring advertising effectiveness, it is often difficult to prove that media decisions were effective. Consequently, decision making has not been able to advance to the point where there is always substantive proof that one medium is much better than another. Often a media planner has biased preferences in favor of one media class over others and will favor that medium regardless of what statistics or other objective evidence might indicate.

Notwithstanding these problems, decision making is improving and will undoubtedly improve as long as the people in charge realize there are problems that need solutions and make attempts at improving the situation. The Advertising Research Foundation (ARF) and the Association of National Advertisers (ANA) have attacked some of the more pressing problems of research data and methodology. Furthermore, new and more highly qualified personnel within both agency and client organizations have shown a dissatisfaction with traditional methods of decision making and have demanded new and better evidence for decisions. They are critical of the misuse of statistics and have a broad enough background in research, marketing, advertising, and media to set high standards of performance. The era of accountability in which many large companies now operate also will act to improve the decision-making function by demanding better research data and the removal of major obstacles that stand in the way of such data.

QUESTIONS FOR DISCUSSION

1. What marketing questions should be answered before media planning begins?
2. What do media planners want to know most about audiences of non-traditional media?
3. Explain the term *media delivery*.
4. Explain why a media plan that reaches a large number of people is not necessarily the best media choice.
5. Explain why media plans should be custom-made rather than repetitions of older plans.
6. What can an advertiser learn from an analysis of competitors' spending habits last year?

7. What is meant by *waste* in media selection?
8. Explain *accountability* in media planning.
9. While consumers like television and radio, what is one of their main dislikes of the advertising media?
10. While clients want to know the number of targets delivered by a media plan, what would they prefer to know, if possible?

SELECTED READINGS

Abrams, Charles, "Facts, Figures and Fantasies," *Journal of Media Planning*, Spring 1991, 17–23.

Beggs, William, "The Future of Advertising Media," *LINK*, September 1991, 11 + .

Coen, Robert, "Changes in Advertising in the Twentieth Century and the Implications for Media Planning," *Journal of Media Planning*, Fall 1991, 58–67.

Cohen, Stanley, "The Dangers of Today's Media Revolution," *Advertising Age*, September 30, 1991, 30.

Hume, Scott, "Whittle: Future Belongs to New Media," *Advertising Age*, August 26, 1991, 3.

Hume, Scott, "Special Report: Traditional Media," *Advertising Age*, August 19, 1991, 27 + .

Hume, Scott, "Bounty in Most Unusual Places: Unexpected Media Hard to Measure. Often Startlingly Effective," *Advertising Age*, August 27, 1991, S–1.

Katz, Helen, "The Personal Touch: Media Planning in the 1990s," *Journal of Media Planning*, Fall 1990, 39–45.

"New Media Scare Agencies," *Advertising Age*, "Letters to Editor," August 9, 1991, 22.

Martin, Steve, "Taking the Guesswork Out of Media Planning, *Marketing and Media Decisions*, May 1991, 196–198.

"Media Buying and Planning," *Advertising Age*, September 22, 1991.

Murdock, Gene, and Anthony McGann, "Audience Reactions to a New Advertising Medium," *Journal of Media Planning*, Spring 1991, 29–37.

"Ostrow on Media: Support Refocus from CPMs, Human Judgment is the Key," *Advertising Age*, October 16, 1987.

Premier, August, "Finding the Forest in Media Planning," *Journal of Media Planning*, Fall 1990, 7–12.

Selwitz, Robert, "Clients Are Taking a More Active Role in Deciding Where Their Advertising Dollars Should Go," *Madison Avenue*, May 1985, 72–76.

Wang, Paul, Hazry Nelsen, and John Bace, "Integrating Media Planning and Marketing Communication Strategies: An Exploratory Case Study in a Business to Business Context," *Journal of Media Planning*, Spring 1991, 47–52.

2

Integrated Marketing Communications, Database Marketing, and Media Planning

Integrated Marketing Communications

In Chapter 1, we discussed how media planning has drastically changed with the expansion of purchasing data, the increase of media audience data, and the proliferation of media options available to planners. However, there are other recent changes in the advertising industry that we have not yet covered. The changes include the kinds of marketing communications tools that advertising agencies use to communicate with consumers or measure their responses to advertising on their clients' behalf.

Although advertising has been the popular choice of marketing communication executives for years, other forms of communication may now be required *in addition to advertising in its traditional forms* for an advertiser to effectively talk to the target audience. Evidence supporting this trend shows that advertisers are spending increasing amounts of their marketing budgets on other communication forms *in conjunction with their traditional advertising efforts.* Included are elements such as public relations, direct marketing, sales promotion, and combinations of the above. Essentially, marketers are using a wider variety of communication tools today than ever before. This concept of broadening an advertiser's communication mix to include a full variety of tools is part of the concept known as integrated marketing communications. One key element is that integrated marketing communications entails coordination of all marketing efforts into a single, unified plan, with one cohesive message for consumers to understand, regardless of which communication tool is used to deliver this message. Often this is referred to as speaking to consumers with "one voice"—just part of the concept. There's more.

Integration is a term that suggests the blending of different tools to deliver a unified message, and that the blend should be perceived by consumers as "seamless." The word seamless means that the messages coming from any or all of the communication tools used should appear to be part of the total picture, and not separate entities. The concern is that if each communication element is not integrated with others, then each may deliver a somewhat different message that potentially could confuse consumers and/or weaken the entire marketing effort.

One may wonder why a topic such as integrated marketing communications should be discussed in a media text. The reason is that integrated marketing communications has media implications that are not yet understood by everyone in the marketing and/or advertising business. Some professionals believe that it will impact all aspects of marketing and advertising. Still others call it a buzzword, suggesting that the terms are bandied about too casually and not everyone means the same thing when they use the phrase. The discussion that follows will clarify some of the more important concepts associated with integrated marketing communications and will illustrate its potential influence within the realm of media.

Dimensions of integrated marketing communications

The starting place for integrating marketing communications is a diagnosis of marketing problems facing a brand and then looking for the best solutions regardless of whether the solution uses traditional advertising or something else.

This suggests that the solution to some marketing problems must include any communications that will help solve the problem. In the past, advertising alone was usually felt to be sufficient. Now public relations, sales promotion, and/or direct marketing should also be considered as viable alternatives.

Integration means blending the different communication forms into "a seamless" totality. Literally this means presenting different messages in such a way that consumers perceive one basic idea coming from different forms of communication that are used. Each form is part of the same overall communication. The net affect of all these forms should not be contaminated by radically different ideas that make it difficult for consumers to understand the messages.

Most consumers perceive all forms of marketing communication to be advertisements. While professionals understand the differences between public relations, sales promotion, direct marketing, and advertising, many consumers do not. They tend to believe that almost any form of marketing communication is an advertisement. As a consequence, professionals can easily see the need for blending messages into a single entity.

Communication companies working independently for the same client and brand do not necessarily integrate their communications with that of other companies who are also working for the same client and brand. Simply because a company is competent to produce marketing communications does not mean that it will integrate its communications with those of other companies working on the same marketing problem. This situation calls for some person or group to supervise the overall efforts of different communication companies and bring about seamless communications. Clients, not advertising agencies, have usually provided such control.

Advertising agencies who own the public relations, sales promotion, or direct marketing departments, or subsidiary companies do not necessarily do a better job of integrating communications simply because they are part of one company. Many advertising agencies have bought separate communication companies in order to offer their clients all different communication services under one roof. This is called "one-stop shopping," implying that a client can buy different kinds of communication from one agency. Therefore, as an example, an agency may now offer a public relations operation, or a direct marketing operation to their clients. Sometimes advertising agencies have bought public relations companies or other ancillary communication services and allowed them to be located in different buildings and to have their own unique name, operating as an agency subsidiary. But there is no guarantee that these departments (or subsidiaries) can do a better job of integrating messages than if they were unified.

The reason is that each department or subsidiary may perceive the problem in a different way, and implement a solution according to its own unique perceptions. Furthermore, since each department is usually a profit center, then each may compete with other departments for business or power, and for part of a total operating budget. Thus "turf wars" may be created that can defeat integration efforts. Personnel of these other services may be paid less, and command less respect than advertising personnel in the same agency. The result may affect morale and perhaps the entire integration process.

Under the integrated marketing communications concept, the clients rather than advertising agencies usually want to control the integration process. They want to be able to select specialized communication companies that meet their needs, and not have only one advertising agency in control.

One additional thought about this concept is that integration may go beyond the various methods of marketing communication and require that even sales personnel, switchboard operators, office clerks, and mail and shipping departments personnel to speak with one voice as they talk to consumers about a particular brand or product. The point here is that almost everyone in a company may be involved in the communication process. Interpersonal communications therefore may also help attain marketing goals as well as public communications.

How Media Planning Fits into Integrated Marketing Communications

(One Scenario)

Integrated marketing communications could have an effect on media and media planning for two major reasons. (1) Each of these four communication concepts may require different kinds of media, used in different ways than ever before. For example, when advertising is used alone, it may only have required the use of mass media. But when public relations are added, then different very specialized media may be required because the targets are now more specialized. And if sales promotion and direct marketing (direct mail or telemarketing) are added to public relations and advertising, then media planning can become complex. (2) The number of media available for consumers to choose from has grown to such large proportions that it will require more attention to planning than ever before. The problem is that consumers may suffer from semantic satiation (or too much communication). Which communication medium is necessary and which should not be chosen? Perhaps that already happened when cable advertising began to grow, or many new magazines were started to meet the highly specialized interests of small groups of consumers. A planner must determine how to avoid this problem.

As a consequence, the media departments of agencies may play a much more important role in the future than ever before. This could require the use of new ways to analyze consumers. In the past consumers were selected to receive advertising on the basis of demographics and product usage only. Now there are newer ways of analyzing consumers that determine which media are seen most often by buyers of specific brands. Even the time of day that consumers are exposed to media may play a more important role in planning.

Future media planners may work more closely with advertising copywriters than they have in the past. Copywriters will write special ads for different kinds of consumers, and *different kinds of media*. This is different from the days of mass marketing, when advertising copy was written first and then given to media planners to find the best media in which to place ads. Often ads were placed only in national media like network television or national magazines. That procedure was relatively simple. Now media may have a distinctly local character (rather than national), and may be based on using more of the new media alternatives.

(Another Scenario)

A different scenario that may affect media planning could be for magazines or some other medium to create integrated marketing programs. The magazine would first make sure that it has a clear idea of its editorial program and how it affects its readers' lives. It would also do an intensive study of readers' lives and the products they buy. The research would concentrate on demographics, psychographics, products purchased most often, and depth of reading. This information would be placed in databases that could be easily accessed for market and media planning. Attention would focus on changes that are occurring in readers' lives and in terms of products that better meet their needs. Eventually the magazine would consider whether the present magazine is the best one to meet consumers' needs or whether new ones should be developed for special market segments.

Armed with the research, the magazine would go to clients and sell not only marketing but media plans and creative services to advertisers. They could offer advertisers creative work at relatively low prices and at the same time show that they knew more about the consumer and meeting his needs than advertising agencies are now doing. As Don Schultz, professor of the Integrated Advertising/Marketing Communications department at Northwestern University noted, ". . . a *Time-Warner* could say, why pay an agency $250,000 to do a commercial when we've got these production facilities and creative people? We'll *give* you the creative to get you into our media."[1]

The key to bringing about the scenario described above is to have a better relationship between magazines and advertisers than they now have. The essence of this relationship is for magazines to better explain the editorial basis for their publication. As Schultz noted, "the content is the critical factor in winning and keeping readers and advertisers. . . ."[2]

The Driving Force behind Integration

As discussed earlier, the impact of integrated marketing communications is not fully understood. Some in the industry believe it will simply pass as a fad, however, this is not the belief of John O'Toole, president of the American Association of Advertising Agencies. O'Toole is an industry leader who believes in the concept of integrated communications and has called for ad agencies to change their operations to accommodate other forms of marketing communications in addition to advertising. This holistic approach to communication encompasses all types of "promotion" as part of the "marketing mix concept."[3] O'Toole believes so firmly in the concept of integration that he has warned "the future success of the advertising agency business will belong to those that can make that change." But what has happened to fuel the conviction of John O'Toole and others to the concept of integration? The answer lies within an examination of consumers and how they are responding to advertising messages.

Today consumers are inundated with thousands of advertising messages each day. This number has grown dramatically over the last 30 years. As a result, consumers are not as responsive to traditional forms of advertising as in days gone by. In addition, the increase in the use of interactive devices such as toll-free numbers and mail order catalogs has made it easier for consumers to gather product information they want *when they want it*. Essentially, this has made consumers smarter and allows them to make their pur-

---

1. Lukovitz, Karlene, "Get Ready for One-on-One Marketing, *FOLIO,* October 1991, p.69.
2. Ibid., p.68.
3. See discussion of the marketing mix in Chapter 3.

chasing decisions more independently of advertising than in the past. This means that advertisers have had to adapt their means of communicating to accommodate this changing environment. Integrated marketing communications is one solution that advertisers are turning to in greater numbers to meet the challenges of the changing environment.

Implications of Integrated Marketing Communications for Media Planning

To date, little has been written or discussed on how integrated marketing communications should affect media planning. Furthermore, among those who have expressed their opinions, there appears to be no consensus. The general direction isn't clear because the new version of integrated marketing communication is still in an early stage of development. However, even though there are some new planning principles that will probably move into prominent positions as media planning evolves in future years, the older media planning principles will continue to play an important role in future planning decisions. Based on developments to date, let's take a look at how media planning will change to accommodate the new tools emerging from the advent of integrated marketing communications.

1. **Reliance on mass media will be reduced as more highly targeted media are integrated into media plans.** Through the use of database analysis and single source data, media planners will know more precisely who to target and which media best reaches those targets. This scenario is based on the ability of marketers to know more precisely who their consumers are and where they live. This kind of targeting is different than it was in the past. Whereas demographics could pinpoint *prospects,* these new research techniques may be able to pinpoint *buyers.* There are clear advantages to reaching buyers rather than prospective buyers, even though actual buyers are fewer in number than prospects.

   Reaching buyers may work as long as consumers and data about them do not change often. But the history of consumers and media preference suggests that consumer loyalties do change over time and their media habits also change. Furthermore, competitive media strategies also change. Therefore database analysis may have to be conducted quite often to keep up with such changes. Will marketers or their agencies be willing to maintain these expenditures?

2. **Numerical data will be needed to compare media alternatives.** The need for numerical data to compare alternative media vehicles will remain a requirement, just as it has for many years. However, the numbers will be different. Instead of using media exposure data there will be a movement to find ''impact'' data that proves that one or more media are better than other media

because they sell more of a given brand. Without such proof, however, planners may return to traditional planning techniques.

Finding these kinds of numbers will not be easy, despite the potential for new data from new scanning services such as BehaviorScan or Home*Scan. The problem was expressed in an article in *Advertising Age* about the use of non-traditional media.[4]

Media comparisons made on ''gut feelings'' or on word descriptions of one medium versus another cannot be acceptable, because words usually are a poor means of expressing details about an object. Even our legal system has had extreme difficulty in knowing and interpreting the precise meaning of words.

Most likely, two kinds of data will have to be mixed. One kind of data will cover media exposure as it has in the past. Although exposure data does not tell anything about the ability of the medium to sell, *it does tell a planner which medium offers the greatest opportunity for exposure to advertisements,* which is much better than guesswork or gut feelings. Sales data will be a good addition, if it is valid. Only time will tell how useful scanner sales data will be.

3. **Reach and frequency will continue to be used. Reach data will be used whenever possible to show the pattern of communication delivered.** Dispersion patterns of alternative media will be as important as ever depending on how buyers themselves are distributed throughout the country. For those brands with wide distribution, a reach measurement is an important part of planning media strategy. Even in local markets it will be important to know delivery patterns as shown by local reach.

Frequency will also be important as a means of controlling communication delivery without waste. It is assumed that buyers may react differently to different amounts of repetition. Some buyers may respond immediately to one ad exposure, while others may need different amounts of repetition to achieve an adequate total response. But planners will still need to know how much frequency a media plan delivers.

4. **Costs per thousand will continue to have a role in media planning.** Some planners have revelled in the possibility that now costs per thousand (CPMs) are less relevant. One of the big changes in media planning within the last 10 years has been to place a more moderate value on costs per thousand in planning. Whereas once they were one of the main criteria in selecting me-

4. Radding, Alan. ''Execs Resort to 'Gut Feelings.' Despite Hunger for Data, Ad Recommendations Often Guesswork.'' *Advertising Age* August 27, 1990, p.S–4.

dia, they have changed to being one of several criteria for deciding to buy or not buy a medium. This trend will probably continue.

On the other hand, cost per thousand comparisons may rise again in importance, albeit on a different basis. If data becomes available that records target delivery of new media, then CPMs again can play a key role in making plan comparisons. The CPM may be used in considering various alternative new media having similar response data. Sellers of media often disparage CPMs as being old-fashioned and out-of-date. However, the ridicule has to be at least partly caused by their inability to create selective media with low CPMs.

5. **Planners will need to know more about other marketing communication tools than they traditionally have used.** The planning of event marketing, direct marketing, sales promotion, and public relations requires more than a casual understanding of these communication tools.

How does each affect communication effectiveness? In writing media objectives, planners cannot use the same language and ideas they used for planning advertising with all other forms of communications. Media planners have not traditionally been involved with event marketing or other public relations tools. Planners may have to sit in creative meetings while communication objectives are being discussed to be able to integrate advertising.

One of the most significant needs will be to know the synergy of two communications forms like public relations and advertising. Is the sum of those two greater than the addition of the two, or less than the sum of the two? The fact that duplication synergies may now exist could be a problem for both a client and media planner to recognize.

6. **The control of seamless communication will be necessary to implement the integrated communication process.** It is important for the industry to attain seamless integration effectively. This may not be an easy task. Who will make the ''seamless'' judgments in an agency? The media planner? The copywriters? In a seminar on integrated marketing communication at Northwestern University in 1991, one speaker called attention to the need for a quarterback who would oversee integration in an agency. The quarterback is not necessarily the creative head, nor the account representative, nor the media planner, but someone who understands the entire scope of the integration process. On the other hand, where does a media planner stand in the process? Perhaps the planner will not be involved very much. Or, the planner may be the key player and require special training to obtain experience before handling the entire integration process.

It's also conceivable that the client may control the "seamless" feature. If so, will the client also control the work of the media planner?

7. **Creative media planning will need to fit within the integrated concept.** Are integration and creative media planning part of the same thing? No one has answered this question yet. It is assumed, of course, that there will always be pressure for media planning to be more creative in the next planning cycle than it was in the current one. A problem may be that achieving greater creativity may interfere with the integration process.

8. **Media planners will need to evaluate the value of offbeat communication tools in relation to the more traditional media.** A question arises about whether any form of communication is the equivalent of an advertisement. There has been much talk in the trade press and among marketers that every form of communication is perceived as an advertisement. Therefore, balloons with printing on them, small ads on the back of bus transfers, stadium signs, and benches in parks with messages on them may be viewed as advertisements. The method of displaying these messages has been seen as the media. In-store advertising techniques also are offered as advertising media. Are these different forms equal in value and, if not, what criteria will be used to make comparisons of effectiveness? What proportion of communication from in-store media directly affects sales of a given brand? All these forms of media are certainly not of comparable value at present. The danger here is that perhaps media planning will turn into an activity where anything goes. It may lose its standards of reasonableness and turn to any one communication form as the equivalent of any other. If the planner acknowledges that there is a difference, it is necessary to find those criteria that make it reasonable to compare one with another on a logical basis.

Database Marketing and Media Planning

Database marketing is the use of computerized lists that show the purchasing histories of consumers who have bought a given brand of product. The list, however, is the foundation of which consumers with the best sales potential are selected for marketing communication efforts. The assumption underlying the use of a database is that if consumers have purchased your product and have been satisfied with it in the past, they will be good candidates for your future communication efforts. In other words, it's easier to sell more product to your current users than it is to gain new users. Furthermore, product users now know the brand, so marketing efforts can proceed beyond the typical need for building brand awareness that is so often the main advertising objective when advertising in mass media.

Today the use of database marketing has grown as the direct marketing industry has grown. Direct marketers were among the first to see its value and use it in selling directly to consumers. Advertisers have also appreciated direct marketing's abilities to predict sales on a more objective basis than with any other marketing tools. The use of databases have improved target market identification so that it is better than it was before when done by SMRB or MRI.

Today database marketing is characterized by a number of features such as:

(1) It is a means of finding consumers who already know the value of a brand because they purchased it in the past.

(2) The data of databases, however, are much more complete than found by syndicated research companies. Of most importance is the fact that this can create what might be called one-on-one marketing (or the seller communicating directly with a buyer who has a name and an address). Contrast this with the use of mass media where the advertiser only has a vague or general idea of whom he is talking to.

(3) Information about the relationship of the individual consumers with the company, called "relationship information," is gathered and available to be used to maintain customer loyalty and company concerns about consumers.

(4) Whereas databases were mostly used to help predict who was most likely to buy a certain product, today there are the added uses of helping to identify and change consumer behavior. This is made possible when the more precise needs of consumers have now been catalogued on the computer.

(5) Databases were formerly identified with only direct marketers, but today they have a much broader usage, including advertising agencies, retailer chains, and product manufacturers (who can know the purchase product differences from store to store, allowing them to supply each individual store with specialized products to meet the needs of consumers in that area).

Basic Information of the Database

Essentially a database is a list of personal information about consumers that have been entered into a computer. Each person on this list is known by name, address, phone number, and/or his other family members' purchasing history. Purchasing information would list the names, model numbers, prices, quantities purchased and dates when purchased over a long period of time as part of a purchasing history.

In essence, the advertiser, using the computer as a "search and find" operation, can quickly build a new, special list of former buyers who have been satisfied with the products and the company that sells those products. Advertising now can be written precisely for the kinds of people in the database. Furthermore, these consumers can be located geographically, and communicated with directly. On the other hand, mass media communication has been somewhat indirect. As a result of database marketing, media communication can take on a "personal tone" and manner, and reach targets at the consumers' homes. Persons who have not purchased the products would not be on the database list. Therefore media dollars are not wasted on low potential prospects.

Some ways information for a database is acquired:
(1) Purchasing behavior measurements are recorded and entered on a list. Data such as individuals' names, addresses, phone numbers, and other private information are obtained from surveys conducted by the advertiser. Other information is found at the time of purchase, or by questionnaires sent to purchasers afterwards. *All of this information is offered voluntarily.*
(2) Questions that consumers ask of the company headquarters about the product. Companies often use 1-800 phone numbers and ask consumers to phone if they have problems with their products, or if they simply want to know more.
(3) Many companies ask each new purchaser to fill out an information card (found in the box in which the product was packaged). These cards may be part of a warranty, or simply be questions that buyers are asked to supply.
(4) Whenever products are returned for repair or replacement, information about the purchaser may become available.

The marketer can now place all of this information into a computerized database, and when the company wants to know who buys, where they live, their telephone number, or what they think of a certain product, the information is there to make it possible to communicate *directly* with buyers. Media used may be direct mail, personal letters, telephone calls, and media chosen that represent consumers' favorites.

How database data are used. The data can be used for marketing programs to build loyalty, and/or stimulate trial. Brand users may be offered merchandise, event tickets, newsletters, and discounts to keep consumers loyal. Database advertising is also used when there is a feeling that mass media cannot be as direct as a database program. Miller brewing company used direct response TV and print ads urging customers to call a toll-free number and receive a T-shirt and a free "Miller-Time Card." They also received a newsletter called *Creative Loafing* that contained sports, entertainment and lifestyle features, discount offers at record stores, and Ticketmaster outlets. The newsletter also included a $1 check good on Miller products, enabling the company to keep track of responses to the offer. Print ads and posters in bars and restaurants featured ''Now it's Miller Time'' and ''Get the best deals on the best times'' slogans. All of this database usage was supplemental to Miller's regular media schedule.

Database is a technique that avoids waste in media planning because it allows targeting to be more precise. Since data comes from ''former buyers'' only rather than from broad demographic classes, there should be less waste.

Also since the names and addresses of users are known, media buying can become cost efficient—smaller advertising expenditures should be able to produce more sales. It is like using a rifle rather than a shotgun to hit targets.

Furthermore, advertising copy can talk to consumers about their own needs as opposed to broader group needs as is now being done in mass media advertising. The advertiser therefore can operate as an interested friend of users and not as an adversary trying to push non-users to buy. The direct communication aspect is quite important in all database programs.

Some problems of database planning. One of the objections to building a database is that it may overstep the right of privacy. One consumer said: ''it bothered him that certain businesses know where he lives, the name of his wife, his children, and where his children went to school . . . when the bottom line is that someone is attempting to sell him something.'' Others counter-reply by saying ''that consumers gave this information out willingly, therefore they should not fear that their privacy is being invaded.''

Another problem arises when a company compiles a database for its own use and then sells the list to some other marketer. Some people feel that database information should be used by *only* one company.

Finally, databases may need to be updated constantly as people move around and/or change their interests. This represents an upkeep cost and effort that must be maintained. An outdated database cannot be of much value. But companies might want to cut back on upkeep expenditures, and the data may lose its freshness.

Conclusions

Database marketing is growing in this country as more direct marketers, retailers, manufacturers, and advertising agencies find uses for it. The most significant media outcome of it will be the selection of ''direct'' media as opposed to mass media. This should eliminate waste and make it more cost effective. Secondly, responses to advertising and media will now be measured. This has been a situation that marketers have longed for over many years. Such responses in turn can now enable marketers to better predict the outcomes of advertising communications.

Now media planners can also get away from ''vehicle exposure'' measurements with all of its inadequacies to ''advertising exposure and response,'' with all of its potential for making logical and reasonable media plans. One consequence of this potential change is that the audience sizes of media selected may be smaller than they were when mass media were used almost exclusively. The smaller sized audiences reached through direct media, however, are much more valuable to the advertiser than ever before. Probably as important as any of the advantages that databases will allow is the opportunity for businesses to turn consumers into friends who want to satisfy customers, and not adversaries who want to sell products no matter how badly consumers may feel later. The opportunity for relationship marketing can only develop when sellers feel affinity towards consumers' needs, and make it possible to keep in close touch with each other.

QUESTIONS FOR DISCUSSION

1. Explain the reasons why advertisers are spending an increasing amount of money on other forms of communication than advertising.
2. Why is a "seamless totality" one of the objectives for integrated marketing communications?
3. Why is "sales promotion" considered a form of marketing communication?
4. Who, in an advertising agency, was recommended to "control" the team efforts of integrated marketing communications?
5. Why do some consumers object to having their names on a database list?
6. Ideally, what can databases do for marketers that they could not do in prior years?
7. In what ways can database target identification be better than SMRB or MRI target identifications?
8. What is so different about the starting place for integrated marketing communication and traditional advertising communication?
9. Marketers talk about "relationship marketing." Explain what it is and why it is necessary.
10. Why do many clients want to control integrated marketing operations rather than allow advertising agencies to control it?

SELECTED READINGS

Bergold, Roy, "Integrated Marketing Communications: McDonald's McLean DeLuxe," *Integrated Marketing Communications,* June 1991, Northwestern University, 24–29.

Caruso, Thomas, "Kotler: Future Marketers Will Focus on Customer Database to Compete Globally," *Marketing News,* June 8, 1992, 11,22.

"The Database Revolution," *Target Marketing,* May 1992, 16 + .

Eisenhart, Tom, "Going the Integrated Route," *Business Marketing,* December 1990, 24–32.

"Get Ready for One-on-One Marketing," *Folio,* October 1991, 64 + .

Harris, Thomas, "The Integration of Advertising and Public Relations," speech to the Association for Education in Journalism, August 8, 1991, Boston, MA.

Hume, Scott, "McD's May Be Fried by Database Rental," *Advertising Age,* March 30, 1992, 1, 58.

"Integration and Reality, *PROMO,* March 1991, 6 + .

Kalish, David, "The New Advertising: A Full Menu of Integrated Services," *Agency,* Winter 1991, 44–45.

Koelle, Mary, "Integrated Marketing Communications," *Integrated Marketing Communications,* June 1991, Northwestern University, 6–14.

Levin, Gary, "Database Draws Fevered Interest," *Advertising Age,* June 8, 1992, 31.

Levin, Gary, "Databases Loom Large for the 90s," *Advertising Age,* October 21, 1991, 22–24.

Levin, Gary, and Ira Teinowitz, "Databases Add Up for Brewers," *Advertising Age,* February 17, 1992, 12.

"Lintas Groups Units Under 'Integrated' Umbrella," *PROMO,* March 1991, 8.

Myers, Jeff, "What Integrated Marketing Communications Is/Is Not/ Could Be," *Integrated Marketing Communications,* June 1991, Northwestern University, 30–35.

Neavill, Michael, "Communications from the Real Customer's Viewpoint," *Integrated Marketing Communications,* June 1991, Northwestern University, 16–22.

O'Brien, Richard. "Can Agencies Deliver Integrated Marketing Communications?" *Integrated Marketing Communications,* June 1991, Northwestern University, 46–52.

"Recession Not Hurting Database Growth: Exec," *Advertising Age,* January 13, 1992, 25 + .

Reilly, James, "The Role of Integrated Marketing Communications in Brand Management," *A.N.A. The Advertiser,* Fall 1991. 32–38.

Reinhard, Keith L., *The New Creativity in Brand Building,* presentation to Association of National Advertisers annual meeting, Naples, Florida, October 24, 1990, 18.

Reitman, Jerry, "Integrated Communications: Fantasy or the Future?" *Integrated Marketing Communications,* June 1991, Northwestern University, 54–59.

Robinson, William A., "How to Integrate Media Advertising and Promotion," *Promotion Marketing,* March 1991, 31.

Schultz, Don and William Badger, "The Status of Integrated Marketing Communications in Client Organizations," *Integrated Marketing Communications,* June 1991, Northwestern University, 36–45.

Urbanski, Al, "Dawn of Integrated Marketing," *Food and Beverage Marketing,* 1991, 18–19.

3

The Relationship between Media, Advertising, and Consumers

The purpose of this chapter is to help the reader think about the relationship of media, advertising, and consumers. This relationship affects the manner in which consumers perceive media as well as advertising. It also affects the manner in which media is measured, planned, and delivered. This chapter sets the stage for Chapter 4, "Basic Measurements and Calculations."

How Consumers Choose Media

Consumers Want Entertainment and Information

Most advertising is delivered to consumers by mass media such as newspapers, television, magazines, or radio. Audiences are not, however, waiting for mass media to come to their doors. They have many other activities that compete for their time and interest, such as bussiness, family, church, and leisure.

Audiences become interested in certain subjects because a need or want is met. The television programs they watch and the magazines they read are chosen because they expect to see certain subjects that satisfy their interests quickly. Sometimes they are willing to waste a bit of time as they watch television programs of little interest while waiting for their favorite programs to come on. In the same manner, they may leaf through a newspaper or magazine casually as they wait to go on to some other activity. It is probable that they pay less attention to these intervening media than they do to their favorites.

What audiences usually want from media is either entertainment or information. (Information would include education as well.) To what extent does any media vehicle provide what audiences want? There must be different degrees of intensity among audiences in evaluating media contents. To say that television is sought because it features sports programming does not mean that all sports are watched with equal intensity. Again, this difference in intensity will most likely affect the difference in degrees of attention paid to advertising or to the programming itself. Audiences will usually choose vehicles that represent the level of intensity that correlates with their interest in the subject.

Cost of Vehicles May Affect Choices

Media that audiences must pay for—such as pay cable or magazines—tend to be evaluated a bit more critically than media they get for free, such as television and radio. Expensive media vehicles are probably evaluated more critically than free media. In times of prosperity, the cost of buying media is usually not perceived to be high regardless of what is charged. In times of economic recession, however, these same costs are perceived differently. If the price is too high for the benefits provided, audiences may move to less costly media or choose only those that are free.

Magazine publishers who reacted to a prosperous economy in the 1980s created many new and specialized media, and helped create media proliferation. During the recession of the early 1990s, some of those specialized publications went out of business and others lost money as circulation and income dropped. *ADWEEK* reported that 45 percent of all magazines lost circulation, an indication that the need for entertainment and information varies with how much money audiences are willing to spend on specialized interests.

Audiences Have Strong Feelings about Media

Many audience members have strong or very weak feelings about a medium. Some of the feelings are expressed by adjectives that describe what it is they like, such as being a leader, being authoritative, provocative, warm, cold, strong, weak, etc. Some media are difficult to describe, suggesting that the relationship between audience members and the media is confusing, negative, or indifferent. Measurements are sometimes made of media images, and feelings often show up for some media. Media that take political stands are usually perceived to have clear cut images. An image represents feelings, attitudes, opinions, and facts about a medium.

Some Consumers Develop Loyalties to Certain Vehicles

Audiences often like some media vehicles so much that they develop loyalties that go beyond economic constraint. If they favor newspapers or magazines, they may cut back expenses somewhere else in their budgets to afford their favorite medium.

Loyalty to media vehicles, however, does not necessarily mean that media advertisements will be perceived frequently or that the audience will buy more of the advertised products. Other factors affect buying, including the need to have more information about a brand. If the audience already has a great deal of brand knowledge, it may respond to the advertising. Generally, when any changes have been made in the brand, or there have been changes in contents or creative styles of advertising, then the message may influence buying behavior to some extent.

Media Usage and Subsequent Behavior

Some magazine subscribers do not read their latest copies immediately, and may have back issues of the magazine lying somewhere in their homes that have not even been opened. If a typical audience member were asked: ''Why haven't you read your magazine, since you are paying for it?'' the answer may be something like this, ''Well, I intend to get around to reading them some day. But I am simply too busy now.'' Advertisers who bought space in those magazines may think they are reaching all the persons measured by survey companies and reported as readers of those magazines. This is not so. The potential for reaching these people may exist, but the audience may never fulfill its potential.

There is a widespread assumption that television—as a medium—sells better than print media. Perhaps the number of magazine readers who have delayed reading current issues do not respond to ads immediately, and this may account for the problem. Television, however, is intrusive and its audiences tend to react to (watch) the medium in a more regular manner than they read magazines. Added to this is the fact that television, being an excellent teaching tool (using audio plus visual), may also account for this assumption.

Different media vary in their abilities to draw large audiences. Television programs featuring famous persons or interesting events such as the Olympics or the Superbowl may draw large audiences. Yet audience response varies greatly to ads carried in these programs. Some seem to sell their products well; others don't. All of this suggests that there is more to selecting media vehicles than finding those that deliver large size audiences. It is difficult, however, to assess the effectiveness of one media vehicle's ability to sell the advertised products on the basis of advertisements carried by the vehicle. Large audiences don't automatically sell more than smaller sized audiences.

One of the problems in determining a response to television advertising has been the continuing research made with telephone coincidental surveys. In these surveys, audiences all over the country are questioned by callers who ask: (a) Are you listening to program X? (b) Did you just hear a commercial (within the last five minutes)? (c) Do you remember the name of the brand being advertised? (d) Do you remember the main part of the message? The responses to these questions are usually negative even though the number of people who heard the commercial was great. These findings suggest that often consumers simply don't pay much attention to the commercials because they don't need the brand or product and they already know a lot about the brand. Furthermore, audiences have developed the ability to see and hear a message, and then forget it. Perhaps this is caused by an overload of communication—"semantic satiation."

Sometimes audiences pay attention to commercials or print ads but don't respond immediately. In one study of response to a retailer's coupon promotion, some buyers came to the store with their coupons a month after the ad appeared. Yet they had cut coupons out and kept them until they found the time to bring them in. Response was not immediate.

Relationships between Audiences and Media Vary

Relationships between audiences and media run the gamut from very casual to very intense. When national football conference teams are playing, the reason for watching any game may depend on how much of a chance a team has in making the playoffs. If there is a good chance, an audience may return each week with a sense of loyalty and anticipation for the game. If a team has a losing record, however, then the number of viewers may drop.

Even if a vehicle has a large, interested audience, the numbers may not be the critical determination of its effect. Relationships today are not very strong, especially among certain demographically defined audiences. Teenagers seem uninterested in reading newspapers, and all the techniques that have been used to attract them still have not changed the very loose relationship between the two.

Mass media are rejected by some media planners in favor of more specialized media with smaller, more selective audiences. Data from single source research often indicates that small market segments account for a large proportion of sales. This may not be accurate. The relationship between audiences and media, however, is more important. If they are casual, then advertising may not be effective. If the relationships are close, then smaller audiences may account for a large proportion of sales. Media planners should think about these relationships as they plan media.

How Audiences Process Information from Media

Much of the information received from media is transferred to the brain and is called *short-term memory storage*. Such information, like the last few words of a sentence just heard or read, or a telephone number found in the phone book, may be recalled for a very short time, but is soon forgotten. Advertisers have observed that audiences who want to remember some part of an advertising message can do so by spending time and effort in rehearsing the message. They can repeat it mentally by reviewing it in their minds until it is learned. If this rehearsal is repeated often, the message is remembered because it has been transferred to long-term memory storage in the brain.

The point is that media often do not do any more than deliver advertising to consumers. Media planners sometimes may be called on to help consumers remember a message by buying media vehicles repeatedly (containing an ad) within a given time period. If audiences are not interested, they will not pay attention and the repetitions will be wasted. Audiences can be very selective in choosing what they want to hear or see.

Can a media planner do any more to deliver advertising messages? There is widespread disagreement among media professionals about the answer to this question. Some say much can be done by strategic media planning. By careful media selection and timing, by placing ads in markets where sales opportunities are best, by repeating the advertising, and by other strategic activities, a planner can help the advertiser achieve his goals. Others say that a media planner's job is done when the message is delivered to the right targets, at the right time, and in sufficient quantities. This subject will be discussed again later in the chapter on the media planning process.

It is clear that media work with the creative message and the appeal of a product to get the message through to consumers. When a product is wanted or needed for any reason, the audience tends to pay attention to an ad for that product. They may not notice an ad the first time it is broadcast or printed, but their attention will presumably alert them to find that ad inevitably. The point is that audiences are not waiting for an ad to appear. They may have higher priorities, at least for a time. Perhaps more important is the creative impact of the words, sounds, color, and pictures of that ad. Creative effort can take ordinary ideas and dramatize them to such an extent that the audience will pay attention to the ad for a short time at least. Yet great creative effort for products that are not wanted are likely to have little effect on audiences. The general public believes otherwise—they tend to believe that any product can be sold by clever advertising.

It seems clear, however, that media planners should know more about consumers, their needs, and perceptions, than they have historically known. Planners will have to use their knowledge of consumer behavior research findings in addition to traditional planning techniques to do a competent job in the future.

Where Media Becomes Important in the Buying Process

It is assumed that the power of media to deliver and provide influence and impact for advertising messages may also depend on where in the purchasing process a consumer happens to be. If we use the Engel/Kollats model of the buying process, we find that the order of purchasing looks somewhat like the following:

1. Problem recognition (e.g., auto needs new tires or individual wants a new suit of clothes).
2. Search for alternatives to solve a problem (e.g., consumer reads,

hears, or sees advertising; talks to a friend about the problem; or goes shopping for product or brand).

3. Alternative evaluation of different brands (e.g., consumer has found two or three brands that could solve a problem). Which one should be chosen?

4. Purchases made through choice of a brand. This is the buying action.

5. After buying, the consumer evaluates whether the product and brand meets expectations of solving the problem. This is the postpurchasing evaluation.

6. Feedback to the brain about how satisfying the purchase was. Unsatisfactory purchases may be returned or consumer may keep the product/brand and look for confirmation that a good buying decision was made. Frustration in the quality of the purchase may result in anger or indignation against the brand or the store where the purchase was made.[1]

If consumers do not perceive that they have a problem, then presumably, they will not react much to either media or advertising. On the other hand, when consumers do have a problem, they may be very receptive to both. Some problems are very simple, such as finding that there is no catsup in the house when hamburgers are being served; others, such as buying a new home, or deciding on a new career, are complex. The latter two problems may require great attention to media and, thus, advertising.

When consumers are trying to decide which brand to buy to resolve a problem they tend to be receptive to both media and ads. Different media measurement techniques have been considered as possible means for comparing audience sizes so that the best vehicles can be selected on behalf of a client.

Table 3–1 shows that there are many ways that media audiences are measured, however, the one that has been used for over 30 years is vehicle "exposure."

Media Planning and the Marketing Mix

It is important for anyone studying media planning to understand the relationship between media planning and the marketing mix. The marketing mix is a group of elements that a firm uses to sell a product. This mix was once called the "four Ps" product, place (or distribution), price, and promotion—and is a shorthand method for discussing these selling tools. For example, price—which has always been part of the marketing mix—can

---

1. Engel, J. F. and R. D. Blackwell, *Consumer Behavior*, Chicago: Dryden Press, 1982, 25–33.

be manipulated to sell by lowering it below competitors' prices, or, at times, by raising it.

It has been suggested that the four Ps are dead. However, this is not true for the elements that comprise the marketing mix. The marketing mix is as important as ever. There always were more elements than the four Ps that marketers could use in marketing. Listed below is a fuller account of the four modified Ps:[2]

Product	*Place*	*Price*	*Promotion*
Quality	Distribution	List price	Advertising
Features	channels	Discounts	Copy and art
Options	Coverage	Allowances	Media
Style	Locations	Payment period	Personal selling
Brand name	Inventory	Credit terms	Sales promotion
Packaging	Transportation		Public relations
			Direct marketing
			Integrated marketing
			Event marketing
			Local area marketing

Although media is not always considered to be a fundamental element of the marketing mix, there are many times that it should because it plays a significant role in the selling process when advertising is required.

The key to understanding the relationship between media and the marketing mix is that *media does not work alone*. It is part of a team of selling variables, which are helpful in the selling process. Planners often get so involved with the complexity of their work that they tend to forget this. In addition, media's role is important because it *controls the efficient delivery of advertisements* to those who will probably buy. Therefore, targeting correctly is one way that the marketing-media team effort is fulfilled. Inefficient targeting means wasted effort and money. Media *adds a qualitative value to an advertisement* because of some quality in the medium. An example is *Good Housekeeping*'s "Seal of Approval" that helps consumers make better buying decisions. Other qualitative values may exist for specialized media that contribute to the medium's integral role in the advertising message.

How Important Is Each Marketing Mix Element? To appreciate the marketing mix, every student should assign a value to each of the marketing mix elements listed above in selling a product of some kind. To do this, distribute 100 points among all of the elements in any way that helps to visualize how important each element is in selling. Note that some marketing mix elements may not be appropriate for the product you select. There may not be total agreement among all class members, however, many students will agree about most of the marketing mix's values.

---

2. Modified from Kotler, Philip, *Marketing Management*, Prentice–Hall, 1984, p. 69.

Exposure: The Basic Measurement of Media Audiences

Industry leaders have chosen a measurement of media audiences—exposure—that is less than desirable, but one that can differentiate media vehicles on the basis of their audience sizes. The audiences also can be measured at a reasonable cost.

Technically speaking, the meaning of exposure is "open eyes (or listening ears) facing the medium." Practically (as will be explained in detail in Chapter 4), it is a measurement of people who either say they are sure that they have looked into a vehicle; or say they read a vehicle within a given time period (yesterday, for newspapers; within the last thirty days, for a monthly magazine); or that they were looking in the direction of the TV set or listening to the radio, when a program was being broadcast.

Exposure measurements are different for each medium. In magazines, for example, persons exposed to a publication are counted if they say they read the publication. But persons exposed to a television program are counted only if they press a button on a people meter measuring device. Not every home will have such a device. But even when the device is available, and even though a person may be watching a program, the failure to press a certain button on the device will mean that a viewer is not counted. (See Chapter 5 for explanation of people meters.)

Media Exposure Does Not Indicate Whether an Audience Saw Advertisements

Persons who are not acquainted with measurements of media audiences are always surprised when they are told that audience sizes numbers obtained from media research such as *Simmons Market Research Bureau* or *A. C. Nielsen* do not count the number of people or households who have been exposed to advertisements in the vehicles. The term exposure literally means "open eyes facing the medium."

Even some experienced professionals who have worked in the advertising business for many years have either forgotten or never knew that media exposure measurements do not show how many persons have read advertisements. And it cannot be assumed that because a media vehicle has a large audience it will automatically have a large number of individuals who saw any given ad.

The reason for this is that *if* the industry should start measuring readership of ads rather than exposure to vehicles, the numbers would be inaccurate because they would miss persons who actually saw many ads, *but because they have poor memories, they will have forgotten. Therefore the numbers produced by such measurements will grossly underestimate the true count of a media vehicle audience size.* Sometimes, the measurements will be inaccurate because audiences indeed have seen ads, but because of other interests and activities, they have forgotten. On the other hand, media

TABLE 3-1. Various Ways That Media Vehicles Could Be Measured

Media Measurement	What It Measures	What It Means
Vehicle exposure	Exposure to TV or print media	Open eyes facing a vehicle (or opportunities-to-see ads)
Print media circulation	Number of copies distributed	People/families receiving newspaper vehicles (no exposure counted)
Advertising exposure	Number of ads exposed per issue or per TV program.	A gross (or crude) counting of total number of ads exposed in a vehicle
Advertising perception	Number of ads that consumers remember having seen in a vehicle	The smallest amount of communication remembered of ads in a vehicle
Advertising communication	The total amount of recalled material from ads in a vehicle	Counts the feedback from ad messages in vehicles
Response function: *media effectiveness*	The number of responses to advertising in a vehicle	Measures the effects of advertising on consumers of responses such as sales, brand awareness, attitude change, and recall of messages

Source: Audience Concepts Committee. Modified from *Towards Better Media Comparisons*, Advertising Research Foundation, 1961, p. 18.

exposure measurements will cover all those people and be related to advertising in a certain way:

> It is necessary to be exposed to a vehicle before anyone can see an advertisement. Therefore media exposure measurements represents an *opportunity to see advertisements*. There is a world of difference between being exposed and not being exposed, just as there is a great difference between 0 and 1 (1 meaning being exposed).

Therefore one of the most widely used measurements of media vehicle audiences (reach) is based on the idea of counting people who have been exposed to a television program at least one (or more times), within a given time period, such as four weeks. The four week reach of a television program is a very important statistic in planning.

The Need for Better Media Vehicle Measurements

Meanwhile, planners need a better measurement that can help them find the best medium or vehicle to help sell a client's product brand or service. If it could be shown that one medium sells more of a brand than any other media, and if the cost were not prohibitive, then that medium would be the one in which to place advertising. Unfortunately, there is no measurement available today that can provide precisely that kind of information. There are planners who have conducted custom-made research to guide them in finding a medium that has the greatest sales potential. The problem with that kind of research is that it is difficult to parse out a medium's contribution to a sale.

After all, media are not the only factors contributing to sales. Every element of the marketing mix may contribute a little, and some contribute a great deal. For example, sometimes the thing that is most responsible for selling a product is a reduced price. Media that carry news of the price reduction in an ad play a secondary role in the sale, while the price, and the advertising message, play a major role. Other media mix factors that contribute to a sale are distribution, positioning, personal selling, sales promotion, public relations, and packaging. (It is assumed that the most important element in the selling of a brand are its product quality and uniqueness.)

But many planners are dissatisfied with using exposure for media comparison purposes. They argue that media are *not* passive carriers of ads. Each medium has some power to affect an audience in some way, and this power should be measured. In technical terms, this power may be called the *response functions of media*.

Table 3–1 shows a response function called *effectiveness*. Measurements are called *effective frequency or effective reach*. These measurements use exposure as a basis for, first of all, determining a vehicle's audience size. Planners then modify exposure, using research to determine how many exposures to ads (or vehicles) to bring about such things as increased sales, brand awareness, and attitude change.

At this time, the use of *effective* frequency and reach are not objectively measured; they usually represent response data extrapolated from media comparisons. In other words, general research on responses to advertising may be used as if it applied to a particular brand being advertised. Many times this practice is not valid. If research were done on responses to ads for television sets, it may not be applicable to ads for margarine, or cake mixes.

Although there is disagreement in the industry about how to use this frequency and reach information, it is used a great deal. Special research for specific product categories is being done in an attempt to make this measurement valid and lay better theoretical foundations for it. In any case, effective frequency and reach are relatively new measurement ideas for the media planner's use. (See Chapter 6 on "Reach and Frequency" for further discussions on this subject.)

It is important to note that media planning should not be a mechanistic activity limited only to delivering media. Good media planners perceive consumers' needs and wants, and how consumers view advertising as an aid in helping them make buying decisions. As time goes on, media planners will expend additional efforts to better know and understand consumers. (See Case Study 3–1.)

CASE STUDY 3-1
How Consumers Could React to Our Media and
Our Advertising

How can a planner think about the effect of a media plan in terms of the ultimate sales response? One answer that may help is to estimate what happens after the ads appear in the media vehicles. The following is a hypothetical example of such an estimate:

		Target Audience
1. Number of targets in the U.S.		10,000,000
2. Percent of U.S. targets that were exposed to media vehicles (this is the *reach* of our media plan)	50%	5,000,000
3. Percent of those reached who saw any ad in vehicles (called ad exposure)	25%	1,250,000
4. Percent of targets who saw any ad, who read ''our'' ad(s)	25%	312,500
5. Percent of those who read our ads who bought our brand because of our ad(s)	10%	31,250
6. Percent of those who bought our brand once, who also bought it a second time (a rough measure of brand loyalty)	10%	3,125

Question at this point: Is there anything that a media planner can do through planning procedures to increase the size of responses?

Two considerations should be made about these estimates:

1. These criteria are not the only ones that could be developed. Various stages of information processing could be incorporated into the model, and estimates could be made for each.

2. There is no precise way to make all these estimates, but experience with a brand over time should help planners improve their accuracy.

Measurements of Responses to Advertising in Vehicles

Some media planners believe that vehicles are nothing more than passive carriers of ads to consumers. A simple measurement such as exposure, therefore, may be considered adequate for comparing audience sizes of media vehicles. In other words, the vehicle (or vehicles) that deliver the largest number of exposed targets at the most efficient cost may be a good enough criterion for selecting media.

QUESTIONS FOR DISCUSSION

1. How much of a magazine would an individual have to read to be considered a reader of a magazine?
2. What is the significance of opportunity-to-see (OTS) measurements for media planners?
3. Why is it so difficult to measure the number of consumers who bought a particular brand of product because they claim to have seen television commercials for that brand?
4. Do consumers ever use media as a catalog? Explain.
5. Explain why audience measurement research does not show how many people were watching commercials or advertisements?
6. Essentially, what do consumers want most from media?
7. What kind of audience measurements would be better than vehicle exposure?
8. Media are considered to be "active" and "passive." Explain in what ways they are active.
9. What is the role of the marketing mix in media planning.
10. What is one limitation of magazine advertising?

SELECTED READINGS

ADFORUM, "An Overview of TV Commercial Impact Studies," September 1982, 50–52.

Audience Concepts Committee, *Toward Better Media Comparisons*, Advertising Research Foundation, NY, 1961.

Banks, Seymour, "Considerations for a New ARF Media Evaluation Model," *Journal of Media Planning*, Fall 1989, 8–12.

Burnett, John J., "Examining the Media Habits of the Affluent Elderly" *Journal of Advertising Research*, November 1991, 33–41.

Lamond, "The Impact of Channel Switching on Commercial Audiences," *Journal of Media Planning*, Fall 1987, 27–32.

Maroney, Denman, "A New Model of Marketing Communication," *Journal of Media Planning*, Fall 1989, 20–24.

Murdock, Gene W. and Anthony F. McGann, "Audience Reactions to a New Medium," *Journal of Media Planning*, Spring 1991, 29–37.

Newspaper Advertising Bureau, *The Search for Information in the Daily Newspaper*, Newsprint Information Committee, Newspaper Advertising Bureau, 1988, 6.

Phelps, Steven, "A Reconsideration of the ARF Media Model," *Journal of Media Planning*, Fall 1989, 2–3.

Schiavone, Nicholas P., "Lessons from the Radio Research Experience for All Electronic Media," *Journal of Media Planning*, Spring 1989, 15–22.

Solomon, Debbie, "Children's Saturday Viewing Habits in the People Meter Era," *Journal of Media Planning*, Spring 1988, 5–10.

Warrens, Robert, "Seeing What the Viewer Sees," *Journal of Media Planning*, Fall 1986, 51–52.

Weilbacher, William M., "How Consumers' View of Media Can Lead to Better Media Planning," *Journal of Media Planning*, Fall 1990, 19–24.

Zeller, Joseph P., Interactive Media— Playthings of the 90s, or Path to Better Plans?" *Journal of Media Planning*, Fall 1990, 25–30.

4

Basic Measurements and Calculations

The purpose of this chapter is to describe and explain basic measurements and calculations used in media planning. These explanations serve as the foundation by which media strategy decisions, to be discussed later, can be understood. The measurements and calculations discussed in this chapter are by no means all that are available. They simply represent those used most frequently. Throughout the chapter, the reader also will be introduced to media terminology not generally found in everyday speech. Terms such as *reach, gross rating points (GRPs),* or *cost per thousand* are examples of unique media language.

The importance of understanding how media audiences are measured and what those measurements mean should be obvious. Media planners can, and sometimes do, make strategy decisions without using measurement data as a guide, but such decisions may be difficult to defend because they tend to be too subjective. Measurement data, on the other hand, provide a degree of objectivity that is hard to refute.

How Media Vehicles Are Measured

Most media audiences are measured through sample surveys, using data about a small group to find out about a larger universe. The chief reason for measuring samples rather than a vehicle's entire audience is that samples are less expensive to measure. But even if a vehicle's entire audience could be measured, it is doubtful that it would produce data that would justify the extra cost and time.

Sample sizes may vary from as little as 200 to as many as 30,000 individuals. Measurements are usually made at specified intervals, not every day of the year.

Network television audiences are measured through national samples of households whose program preferences are recorded by an electronic peoplemeter.

Since September 1987, the A. C. Nielsen Company has employed a single sample of 4,000 peoplemeter homes to produce all national television ratings. These meters automatically record the time of day, day of week, and channel numbers tuned in. Audience composition is collected when household members indicate that they are watching TV by "logging in" to the peoplemeter using a hand-held remote device. Thus, there is only one sample used for both national household and persons' ratings. The transition to the electronic peoplemeter involved more than a change in data collection device. It also included a larger sample (4,000 homes versus 1,700 metered homes and 2,400 diary homes under the old system); a younger, more representative sample of the entire population; new editing rules for processing data; and a heightened research awareness on the part of all users.

Local television viewing is measured in 25 metered markets with a combination of meters and diaries. Meters provide continuous household data, while the diaries provide demographic data. The two samples are "wedded" together 4–7 times/year. The 25 metered markets cover about 50% of the U.S. population. The remaining 186 local markets are measured by diary method only. By November 1992, there will be 28 metered markets.

Radio measurements are also made through the use of diaries. However, the number of markets measured is smaller than for television. Furthermore, only large markets are measured relatively often (about 70 percent of the time).

At least three different techniques are commonly used to measure newspaper and magazine audiences. They are:

Through-the-book technique for magazines. A sample of readers is selected and interviewed personally. The interviewer shows each respondent a *stripped-down copy*—one in which all the ads have been eliminated, leaving only editorial material—of the magazine to be measured. After qualifying the respondent by making sure that he or she remembers having seen the cover page, the interviewer slowly turns the pages and asks whether each story looks interesting. The ostensible purpose of asking whether a respondent is interested in each article is to subtly determine whether the respondent really did read (or was exposed to) the magazine in question. After examining each article, the interviewer eventually asks, "Now that we have gone through the entire magazine, are you sure that you have looked into it?" Only those respondents who still say that they were sure they had looked into the book are counted. Those who are not quite sure and those who reply that they had not looked into the magazine are not counted. Those who say they are sure they have looked into the magazine are then asked demographic questions.

Recent-reading technique for magazines. A sample of respondents is visited by an interviewer who has a specially designed procedure to elicit responses. On individual cards are pasted the logotypes of magazines. Respondents are shown one card at a time and then asked if they read the magazine within the last month and where they read it. After this questioning, respondents are asked for demographic information. The interviewer also leaves behind a questionnaire that asks respondents to fill out details about various products they have used and how often they used them. The interviewer returns later to pick up this special questionnaire. On this second visit, the interviewer again asks questions about which magazines have been read over a period of time.

Yesterday-reading technique for newspapers. Respondents in a selected sample are asked which newspapers they read yesterday. The procedure is much the same as the recent-reading magazine technique. Because there are relatively few newspapers read in any given market, this interview is relatively short.

These techniques are not used equally. The through-the-book and recent-reading techniques for magazines have been combined in the Simmons Market Research Bureau (SMRB) Report. Mediamark Research Inc. (MRI) uses recent reading.

Outdoor advertising audiences are measured by asking a sample of drivers to trace their day's travel on a map, indicating routes traveled and destinations. Then a plastic overlay sheet is placed on top of the respondent's map to indicate which billboards have been passed. Tabulations are made showing the numbers and demographics of audiences. These measurements are simply exposures to, or opportunities to see, the billboards.

Planners are always looking for better ways to measure audiences. Changes in measuring technology are continually being made as new ideas or methods are developed.

General Uses of Vehicle Audience Measurements

The most significant problem facing media planners is that of deciding in which medium to place advertisements, because there are so many alternatives to choose from, and the numbers available are growing. The size and cost of target audiences in these alternatives are very important measurements for comparison purposes.

The result of all these attempts at measurements is a large volume of numerical data, produced at regular intervals. However, the effect of such a quantity of data on media planners and others involved in marketing/media operations may sometimes be to provide a sense of confidence that is perhaps unwarranted. Despite the quantitative aspect, media planning is not scientific in the same manner that physics is. Media audience numbers are the best that can be attained at a reasonable cost, but they do not represent the kind of measurement data planners would ideally like to have, such as information about which media vehicle produces the most sales. Because the numbers may take on an importance that is not warranted, users of measurement data are warned that while the numbers are necessary, they are not absolutes, but rough estimates that need interpretation.

Planners use audience measurement data for the following comparative purposes:

1. To learn the demographics of product or brand users
2. To learn the audience demographics of various kinds of media vehicles—who reads, sees, or hears the vehicles
3. To learn the way purchasers use a product or brand (Are they heavy, medium, or light users?)
4. To learn whether audience members of a particular media vehicle are heavy, medium, or light users of the product
5. To learn how many people were exposed to vehicles

All of the above information has one basic purpose: to help the planner match media with target markets. The market for any product, from margarine to automobiles, can be identified in terms of certain demographics. What the planner wants is to find media vehicles that best reach the demographic target. Two main concepts guide planners in their use of measurement data. The first is to find vehicles that reach the largest numbers of prospects for a product category or a brand within that category. But planners do not always select the vehicle that delivers the largest number of prospects; sometimes they choose the vehicle that delivers the optimum number of prospects. An *optimum number* means that the number of prospects reached is sufficiently high to achieve some marketing/media goal and yet at the same time allow the planner to attain another goal, such as frequency. The vehicle that delivers the largest number of prospects represents large target reach, while the vehicle that provides a sufficient level of reach with a desired level of frequency would be the optimum. (For a more detailed discussion of the relationship of reach to frequency, see Chapter 6.)

Table 4–1 shows how media might be matched with a market using measurement data. Which medium is best according to the matching process of Table 4–1? A tentative answer is the one with the largest audience of prospects. Later analysis may or may not confirm this conclusion, because cost, as well as audience size, is also a consideration. But the first step in making a selection decision will probably center on the matching process.

Various Concepts of Audience Measurements

One of the difficulties in matching markets with media is that no single measurement can be used to determine the audience sizes for all media. Therefore, it is difficult to make intermedia comparisons (such as compari-

TABLE 4-1.   An Example of Matching Media with Markets (Cola Market)

Key Demographics (Adults)	Time		Reader's Digest		Popular Mechanics		Demo-graphic Base
	Readers (000s)	Cover-age*	Readers (000s)	Cover-age*	Readers (000s)	Cover-age*	
Ages 18–34	8925	15.0%	8188	13.7%	2025	3.4%	59851
Live in metro suburban	9722	13.7%	14530	20.5%	2185	3.1%	70781
Regular cola drinkers	20583	13.7%	30124	20.1%	4724	3.2%	149938

Source: Simmons Market Research Bureau, 1992. Reprinted by permission.
* Coverage = Readers ÷ Demographic Base.

sons between the audience sizes of a television program and a magazine). Audience size numbers do not mean the same thing from medium to medium because they are measured on different bases.

Actual or Potential Audience Size Measurements

Those who use media audience research should be careful not to confuse data that show the actual size of a vehicle's audience with other data that look similar, but show only potential audience size. The division of audience measurement data into classifications of actual versus potential, or vehicle distribution versus vehicle exposure, is the result of new measuring techniques. Before statistical sampling was widely accepted, media owners simply used distribution counts of their vehicles as evidence of audience size. Circulation of print media is one of these older measurements. It represents only potential audience size of the measured vehicle because it does not measure how many people will actually read a given copy of the periodical. As media research techniques have become more scientific, print media have been able to define their readership in terms of numbers of people who actually read the publication, in addition to just pure circulation or distribution counts.

Print Measurements

Print Circulation Measurements. Measurements of circulation are available for most newspaper and magazine vehicles, but these data are of limited use in selection decisions because they do not provide the planner with precise enough information.

   Circulation data also do not accurately reflect the number of readers in a vehicle's audience. One unit of circulation means one copy of a periodical distributed, but for every copy distributed, there may be as many as six different readers. One cannot know the size of a vehicle's audience simply by looking at its circulation, yet it is the audience size that is one of the major considerations in newspaper media selection. Furthermore, circulation data tell the planner nothing about the demographics of the audience—crucial information when planning is based on reaching precise demographic targets.

As a result, circulation data are seldom used alone in selecting magazines in which to place ads. However, such data still are often used in making decisions about newspapers because little other audience data are available. Circulation data, while admittedly limited, are still valuable.

When circulation data must be used, measurements verified by the Audit Bureau of Circulation (ABC), as shown in Figure 4–1, are the most reliable. The accuracy of ABC audits is widely accepted throughout the advertising industry. The ABC is a nonprofit, cooperative association of about 1,100 advertisers and advertising agencies; and 2,800 daily and weekly newspapers, business publications, magazines, and farm publications in the United States and Canada. It audits and reports circulations of these publications at regular intervals.

ABC data will include paid circulations categorized for newspapers by city zone, trading zone, and outside areas. In addition, circulation is categorized for newspapers by Metropolitan Statistical Areas (MSA), making it possible to determine how the distribution of circulation matches selling and marketing areas of advertisers.

Magazine data from ABC show circulation categorized by size of metropolitan areas, by states and regions of the United States, and by other geographical divisions, all aimed at helping the planner choose the medium that best reaches geographical targets. No demographic data of the reading audience are available from ABC.

FIGURE 4–1. ABC Checklist for Evaluating Magazine Publisher's Statements

The following is an eleven-point checklist for evaluating data provided on an ABC Publisher's Statement. These statements are used by media planners and buyers to help them make decisions in selecting magazines. The data shown here is simulated, but valid data is found in a typical Magazine Publisher's Statement.*

1. AVERAGE PAID CIRCULATION FOR 6 MONTHS ENDED DECEMBER 31, (YEAR)	
Subscriptions:	295,069
Single Copy Sales:	109,721
AVERAGE TOTAL PAID CIRCULATION	404,790
Advertising Rate Base—Paid Circulation	400,000
Average Total Non-Paid Distribution 12,050	

1. **Are you getting what you paid for?** If the magazine guaranteed a rate base, was it met? If not, compensation could be claimed.

   Check to make sure you know the ratio of subscriptions versus single-copy sales. Publications with a high percentage of single-copy sales tend to fluctuate more dramatically in circulation from issue to issue and this might have an impact on a client's seasonal requirements. Some-

---

* *Checklist for Media Planners and Buyers.* Audit Bureau of Circulation, Schaumburg, Illinois, 1990, 4 pages.

times a magazine that has strong newsstand circulation is considered to have more "vitality" than those with a large percentage of subscription circulation. Some planners view high subscription circulation, especially long-term subscriptions, as a strong commitment on the part of subscribers to read a magazine because they are willing to pay their money in advance.

2. PAID CIRCULATION total of subscriptions and single copy sales (BY ISSUES)

Issue	Subscriptions	Single Copy Sales	Total Paid	Issue	Subscriptions	Single Copy Sales	Total Paid
July	285,960	116,637	402,597	Oct.	301,738	105,764	407,502
Aug.	297,181	107,749	404,930	Nov.	290,590	109,495	400,085
Sept.	300,315	102,700	403,015	Dec.	294,630	115,979	410,609

2. **Did the Magazine Meet Rate Base Every Issue?** Check the delivery of the specific issues used to make sure the rate base, as reported on the Publisher's Statement, was achieved. If not, perhaps compensation could be negotiated. Did the circulation fluctuate dramatically? If so, find out why. Was it price-driven or was there a special promotion? Maybe it was the editorial content. Look to see which issues have the highest single-copy sales, then check the cover and editorial content of that issue. It may give you insight into what is most appealing for readers. You may want to schedule your ad into future issues with similar content.

ANALYSIS OF TOTAL NEW AND RENEWAL SUBSCRIPTIONS
Sold during 6 Month Period Ended December 31, (Year)

3. AUTHORIZED PRICES

    (a) Basic Prices: Single Copy: $1.50.
        Subscriptions: 1 yr. $12.00; 2 yrs. $22.00; 3 yrs. $30.00 19,431
    (b) Higher than basic prices: None .... None
    (c) Lower than basic prices: 1 yr. $7.00, $8.00, $8.99; 2 yrs. $13.99 78,924
    (d) Association subscription prices .... None

        Total Subscriptions Sold in Period 98,355

4. DURATION OF SUBSCRIPTIONS SOLD:

    (a) One to six months (1 to 6 issues) 600
    (b) Seven to twelve (7 to 12 issues) 143
    (c) Thirteen to twenty-four months 1,021
    (d) Twenty-five to thirty-six months 85,669
    (e) Thirty-seven to forty-eight months 9,100
    (f) Forty-nine months and more 1,822

        Total Subscriptions Sold in Period 98,355

5. CHANNELS OF SUBSCRIPTION SALES:

    (a) Ordered by mail and/or direct request 68,501
    (b) Ordered through salespeople:
        1. Catalog agencies and individual agents 8,644
        2. Publisher's own and other publisher's salespeople 590
        3. Independent agencies' salespeople 14,100
        4. Newspaper agencies .... None
        5. Members of schools, churches, fraternal and similar organizations 6,317
    (c) Association memberships .... None
    (d) All other channels, See Par. 11(a) 203

        Total Subscriptions Sold in Period 98,355

3. What is the magazine's selling strategy? Evaluate the percentage of circulation sold below basic price. When comparing two or more magazines, make sure you are aware of how they relate in terms of the basic price and number of issues. This paragraph reveals the strength and quality of subscriptions sold. A large percentage sold at rates lower than the basic price may indicate problems in maintaining circulation levels. Some advertisers assign less importance to lower-than-basic subscriptions.

However, lower-than-basic subscription selling prices are often introductory, trial and experimental offers. Reduced rate subscriptions are part of direct mail methods and many believe that direct mail subscriptions are good quality circulation. Subscriptions are discounted for the same reason as are advertisers' products—to stimulate sales.

4. How many issues are subscribers buying? Evaluate the length of subscriptions. The duration of subscriptions sold may indicate the ''value'' of these subscriptions. Subscriptions sold for one to six months may not be considered very ''solid'' because the subscriber is only committing for a brief time. Longer term subscriptions may signal a loyal reader.

However, weekly publishers frequently sell for a shorter term. Every publisher looks differently at the value or desirability of selling subscriptions for varying lengths of term. In order to retain flexibility for future price increases, or to introduce their magazine to new subscribers, some publishers will sell subscriptions for less than a one-year term.

5. How are subscriptions sold? This paragraph can further identify the ''value'' of subscriptions. What percentage of subscriptions has been requested by mail and/or direct request versus associations, catalog agencies, etc.? Depending on advertisers' needs, some channels of selling subscriptions may be considered less appropriate than others.

Subscriptions sold through direct mail agents, such as Publishers Clearing House and American Family Publishers, are also included in the ''direct to publisher'' category.

---

6. USE OF PREMIUMS

   (a) Ordered without premium 92,434
   (b) Ordered with material reprinted from this publication, See Par. 11(b) 2,891
   (c) Ordered with other premiums, See Par. 11(c) 3,030
      Total Subscriptions Sold in Period 98,355

---

6. Are premiums used in subscription selling? Evaluate the percentage of circulation sold with premiums. If a publication sells subscriptions using a large number of premiums, the value of those subscriptions could vary.

Was a premium used? If so, what was it, and what was its value? Do you think it might be incentive enough to purchase a subscription that otherwise might not be wanted? Or, has the publisher found a natural marketing tool for giving subscribers extra value?

ADDITIONAL CIRCULATION INFORMATION

7. POST EXPIRATION COPIES INCLUDED IN PAID CIRCULATION (PAR 1):
   (a) Average number of copies served on subscriptions not more than three months after
      expiration 12,060

7. Are post expiration copies notably high? Check the number of post expiration copies. If they seem to be notably high, it could be a signal to ask a publication about the health of the circulation. Publishers sometimes use arrears as a circulation renewal strategy.

How many copies are included in paid circulation even though the subscription has expired? Subtract this number from the average total paid circulation in Paragraph 1. Compare the result with the rate base. Are they carrying these arrears simply to disguise rate base shortcomings?

8. BASIS ON WHICH COPIES WERE SOLD TO RETAIL OUTLETS:

Fully returnable 93.15%
Nonreturnable 6.85%
100.00%

8. Are copies sold to retail outlets fully returnable? Are the magazines fully returnable? Most publishers sell their magazines to wholesalers and retailers on a fully returnable basis. Special interest magazines may sell to specialty stores such as ski shops and bridal salons on a non-returnable basis. If there is a high percentage of non-returnable copies, you may wish to ask a publication where they are sold.

9. U.S. PAID CIRCULATION BY ABCD COUNTY SIZE based on October, (Year) Issue

May, Year issue used in establishing percentages.
Total paid circulation of this issue was 0.67% greater than average total paid circulation for period.

County Size	No. of Counties	% of U.S. Population	Subscription Circulation		Single Copy Circulation		Total Circulation	
			Copies	% Total	Copies	% Total	Copies	% Total
A	177	41%	106,572	36.57	39,397	40.57	145,969	37.57
B	408	30%	90,690	31.12	33,871	34.88	124,561	32.06
C	496	15%	52,572	18.04	14,867	15.31	67,439	17.36
D	1,993	14%	41,585	14.27	8,973	9.24	50,558	13.01
	3,074	100%	291,419	100.00	97,108	100.00	388,527	100.00
Alaska-Hawaii Unclassified	27		1,483		891		2,374	
TOTAL U.S.	3,101		292,902		97,999		390,901	

EXPLANATION OF ABCD COUNTY SIZES*

A—All counties which are, in whole or in part, within the boundaries of Census Metropolitan Areas.

B—All remaining counties which are, in whole or in part, within the boundaries of Census Agglomerations of 25,000 population or over and other counties containing a place of 25,000 or more population not officially designated as Census Agglomerations.

C—All remaining counties which are, in whole or in part, within the boundaries of Census Agglomerations of less than 25,000 population and other counties containing a place of 10,000 or more population.

D—All remaining counties.

*See another definition of ABCD county size.

9. Where is the circulation concentrated? This information is used primarily as an indication of a magazine's urban or rural skew. A magazine can be evaluated based on its geographic strengths and weaknesses in A, B, C and D counties. Similar to a Brand Development Index (BDI) or a Category Development Index (CDI), a Magazine Development Index (MDI) can be calculated for each magazine on a county-size or state-by-state basis. Magazines' MDIs can be compared to determine strengths and weaknesses in specific areas. This provides the ability to measure a magazine's strength in specific marketing/geographic areas that are important to the product or brand being advertised.

10. EXPLANATORY:

Latest Released Audit Report Issued for 12 months ended June 30, (Year).
Variation from Publisher's Statements

Audit Period Ended	Rate Base	Audit Report	Publisher's Statements	Difference	Percentage of Difference
6-30-(Year)	400,000	403,384	402,833	+ 551	+ 0.14
6-30-(Year)	375,000	394,666	396,709	− 2,043	− 0.51
6-30-(Year)	(a)	381,446	385,207	− 3,761	− 0.98
6-30-(Year)	350,000	373,611	372,912	+ 699	+ 0.19
6-30-(Year)	350,000	358,402	359,601	− 1,199	− 0.33

(a) Effective 1/1(Year) changed from 350,000 to 375,000.

(a) Par. 5(d): Represents subscriptions sold through Prototype catalogs, hobby shops and libraries.

(b) Par. 6(b): A book with no advertised or stated value titled *Prototype's Greatest Articles* which consisted of articles reprinted from previous issues was offered free in connection with a 1 year subscription at $12.00.

(c) Par. 6(c): A dufflebag with no advertised or stated value was offered free with subscriptions sold at basic prices.

(d) Par. 8: A Sweepstakes Collection Contest was conducted during the period covered by this statement in which prizes were offered to subscribers who paid in full.

(e) During the period covered by this statement a Sweepstakes was run in which prizes worth $10,000.00 were awarded.
Total expirations during 12 months May 1, (Year)—April 30, (Year) 236,219
Total renewals of these expirations 171,602
12 month renewal percentage 72.65%

10. What is the renewal rate? Publishers have the option of showing their renewal rate in their Publisher's Statements. If the renewal rate is high relative to similar publications, it may indicate a more loyal audience or it could also mean lower prices. It could be sweepstakes-induced. It could also indicate a stagnant readership for your advertiser.

However, if the renewal rate is low, it could signal a change in editorial direction, or the editorial may have a short-term audience interest, such as a bridal or teen magazine.

11. GEOGRAPHIC ANALYSIS OF TOTAL PAID CIRCULATION for the October, (Year) Issue

Total paid circulation of this issue was 0.67% greater than average total paid circulation for period.

STATE	Subs.	Single Copy Sales	TOTAL	% of Cir.	% of Pop.
Maine	2,144	619	2,763		
New Hampshire	2,016	588	2,604		
Vermont	1,037	352	1,389		
Massachusetts	6,750	2,512	9,262		
Rhode Island	1,087	432	1,519		
Connecticut	4,907	1,345	6,252		
NEW ENGLAND	17,941	5,848	23,789	6.09	5.45

STATE	Subs.	Single Copy Sales	TOTAL	% of Cir.	% of Pop.
New York	18,594	6,688	25,282		
New Jersey	8,834	3,121	11,955		
Pennsylvania	15,153	4,502	19,655		
MIDDLE ATLANTIC	42,581	14,311	56,892	14.55	16.24
Ohio	14,500	4,017	18,517		
Indiana	7,598	2,178	9,776		
Illinois	17,086	3,531	20,617		
Michigan	12,654	3,882	16,536		
Wisconsin	8,402	2,189	10,591		
EAST N. CENTRAL	60,240	15,797	76,037	19.45	18.40
Minnesota	8,018	1,916	9,934		
Iowa	6,341	1,345	7,686		
Missouri	5,470	1,630	7,100		
North Dakota	1,393	356	1,749		
South Dakota	1,287	317	1,604		
Nebraska	2,344	507	2,851		
Kansas	3,914	973	4,887		
WEST N. CENTRAL	28,767	7,044	35,811	9.16	7.59
Delaware	857	248	1,105		
Maryland	5,013	1,638	6,651		
District of Columbia ..	426	338	764		
Virginia	5,520	2,376	7,896		
West Virginia	1,994	580	2,574		
North Carolina	5,889	1,586	7,475		
South Carolina	2,616	941	3,557		
Georgia	5,106	1,753	6,859		
Florida	10,803	5,289	16,092		
SOUTH ATLANTIC	38,224	14,749	52,973	13.55	16.31
Kentucky	3,166	774	3,940		
Tennessee	4,383	1,420	5,803		
Alabama	3,012	899	3,911		
Mississippi	1,729	735	2,464		
EAST S. CENTRAL	12,290	3,828	16,118	4.12	6.47
Arkansas	2,060	447	2,507		
Louisiana	3,733	1,374	5,107		
Oklahoma	4,922	1,533	6,475		
Texas	16,243	6,845	23,088		
WEST S. CENTRAL	26,958	10,219	37,177	9.51	10.48
Montana	1,479	491	1,970		
Idaho	1,587	503	2,090		
Wyoming	1,056	330	1,386		
Colorado	5,470	2,222	7,692		
New Mexico	1,964	753	2,717		
Arizona	4,047	1,452	5,499		
Utah	1,665	886	2,551		
Nevada	1,371	610	1,981		
MOUNTAIN	18,639	7,247	25,886	6.62	5.02

STATE	Subs.	Single Copy Sales	TOTAL	% of Cir.	% of Pop.
Alaska	815	436	1,251		
Washington	6,272	2,549	8,821		
Oregon	3,353	1,252	4,605		
California	36,154	14,264	50,418		
Hawaii	668	455	1,123		
PACIFIC	47,262	18,956	66,218	16.95	14.04
Miscellaneous					
Unclassified					
UNITED STATES	292,902	97,999	390,901	100.00	100.00
U.S. Cir. Percent of Grand Total				95.93	
Poss. & Other Areas	284	38	322	0.08	
U.S. & POSS., etc.	293,186	98,037	391,223	96.01	
Canada	7,438	6,327	13,765	3.38	
Newfoundland	99	22	121	0.88	
Nova Scotia	250	266	516	3.75	
Prince Edward Island ..	31	26	57	0.42	
New Brunswick	130	152	282	2.05	
Quebec	849	634	1,483	10.77	
Ontario	3,446	2,499	5,945	43.19	
Manitoba	298	223	521	3.78	
Saskatchewan	347	202	549	3.99	
Alberta	874	1,011	1,885	13.69	
British Columbia	1,078	1,267	2,345	17.04	
Northwest Territories ..	23	13	36	0.26	
Yukon Territories	13	12	25	0.18	
CANADA	7,438	6,327	13,765	100.00	100.00
Foreign	873	1,236	2,109	0.52	
Unclassified					
Military or Civilian Personnel Overseas	241	164	405	0.09	
GRAND TOTAL	301,738	105,764	407,502	100.00	

10a. CANADIAN PAID CIRCULATION BY ABCD COUNTY SIZE based on October, (Year) Issue

Size	County No. of Counties	% of Canadian Pop	Subscription Circulation Copies	% Total	Single Copy Circulation Copies	% Total	Total Circulation Copies	% Total
A	56	62%	4,382	58.91	4,198	86.35	8,580	62.33
B	57	18%	1,416	19.04	1,013	16.01	2,429	17.65
C	46	9%	909	12.22	648	10.24	1,557	11.31
D	106	11%	731	9.83	468	7.40	1,199	8.71
Total CANADA	265	100%	7,438	100.00	6,327	100.00	13.765 100.00	

11. Is the publication going to the regions you require? This paragraph can be used to compare and contrast a magazine's regional strengths. Regional strengths that correspond to an advertiser's priorities might indicate a valuable vehicle for a print campaign.

Regional or state circulations are often important for determining feasibility of test markets, as well as estimating costs or regional or state issues (which are often based on circulation CPMs). Circulation strengths and weaknesses in certain regions also may be used in selecting a magazine schedule for products with regional distribution. A magazine can be evaluated based on its geographic strengths and weaknesses on a state-by-state basis, similar to BDIs and CDIs.

Print Audience Measurements. Measurements of the actual size of print audience vehicles can be made by first sampling readers to find an average number of *readers per copy*. This figure then is multiplied by the circulation to provide an estimate of the total audience of readers. Most media planners are not interested in the total audience, per se, but only in the numbers of those demographic targets who are the best prospects to purchase their products.

The Concept of Audience Accumulation

Audience accumulation is the buildup of total audiences over time. The time element, however, varies by medium. A major part of the accumulation concept is that audience members are counted only once, no matter how many additional times they are exposed to a particular vehicle. This is called *reach*. Another measurement, called *frequency*, accounts for average repeat exposure. Both reach and frequency will be discussed in more detail in Chapter 6.

Audience Accumulation in Magazines. In magazines, audience accumulates in three ways:

1. Over the issue life of the publication, as the magazine is read by more and more people, passing it along from one reader to another
2. When advertising is placed in successive issues of the same magazine
3. When advertising is placed in the same month's issue of different magazines

The first method of audience accumulation is measured by various researchers who report on the *total audience* of the average issue of a publication. The amount of time it takes for this audience buildup has no bearing on the measurement. A person reading a magazine a month or more after its issuance is counted as a reader to the same extent as the person who reads the magazine the first day it is issued.

The second method of accumulation takes place over different issues such as the January, February, and March issues. New readers may read a given issue each time it appears.

Quick accumulation is possible when the same ad is run in a given month's issues of different magazines. Some who read one magazine will not read others.

Within a magazine's total audience, researchers distinguish between *primary readers* (either those who have purchased the magazine or the members of the purchaser's household), and *pass-along readers* (those not in the purchaser's household). Typical pass-along readers are the purchaser's friends, and/or people reading in doctors' offices, beauty salons, and on airplanes.

In addition to the type of reader (primary or pass along), a second designator of exposure is also researched: *place* of reading. Syndicated research companies provide data showing where people read magazines. Simmons Market Research Bureau and MRI cite in-home and out-of-home readership for all the publications in their reports.

Several isolated research studies have indicated that the in-home reader, whether a primary or pass-along reader, reads more pages of a magazine and spends more time reading than the person outside of the home. Media planners sometimes use this information to give different values, or weights, to each type of reader in order to compare one media vehicle to another.

Audience Accumulation in Broadcast. Audiences also build in broadcast media. Although the concept of accumulation is the same as with magazines, the mechanics differ widely. A television program, with the exception of those recorded on a video cassette recorder, does not have a life beyond its broadcast time. Unlike tangible magazine copies, once a TV or radio program is broadcast, it is finished. Those people who viewed/listened to the show are the only audience the program will have. There is no pass-along audience as with magazines. Time *is* a major element in broadcast accumulation.

Nevertheless, TV and radio programs do accumulate audience in three ways:

1. Within the program while it is being broadcast
2. With successive airings of the same program within a four-week period
3. With the airing of different programs within the same four-week period

TV viewers are counted by peoplemeters if they press the buttons designating them as viewers of a given program. If new viewers watch a program after the first telecast, they are added to those who viewed it previously. Radio listeners are so designated if they listen to five minutes or more of the program. Therefore, if ten people are viewing a program during the first five minutes, then an additional ten people tune in the program in the next five minutes and stay tuned for at least five minutes, the program has accumulated a total audience of twenty people.

Each week that a program is aired, new audience members will tune in for the first time, and thus the accumulation grows. Another way accumulation grows is by advertising on different programs that appeal to the same audience such as women aged 18–49.

In the real world, people tune in and tune out programs at different times during the program broadcast. While ten people might tune in a particular

TABLE 4–2. Comparison of Program Ratings: Average Quarter Hour versus Total for Entire Program

Program	Date of Telecast	Households Viewing (%)	
		Average Quarter Hour	Total Program
60 Minutes	Sunday	18.2	24.8
Beverly Hills 90210	Thursday	12.9	16.2
ABC Monday Night Movie	Monday	9.7	17.4

Source: Nielsen Media Research, NTI, April 20–26, 1992. Reprinted by permission.

program in the first five minutes, some of them will tune out and some new people will tune in. This phenomenon occurs throughout the program.

Table 4–2 shows how the accumulated total audience of a single episode varies for several programs compared with the audience who viewed the program during an average fifteen-minute segment. The tune-in audience in every case is greater in number than those who tuned out. The bucket, therefore, was being filled faster than it was being emptied. This results in a gradual buildup of audience over the entire program.

The Coverage Concept

Audiences can be analyzed in two broad ways: in total numbers of people (e.g., the evening news audience) and as a percentage of the demographic universe of which they are a part (e.g., all women aged 35–49). One might compare the audience size of ten magazines or television programs on the basis of which delivers the greatest number of people in a target audience, or on the basis of which delivers the highest percentage of the total population in that target audience. Either method will reveal the same relative differences between the media vehicles.

Coverage is a convenient statistical term used to assess the degree to which a media vehicle delivers a given target audience. The higher the coverage, the greater the delivery. Coverage is usually expressed as a percentage of a market population reached.

To calculate coverage, the delivery of a specific demographic group (or target audience) by a given media is divided by the total population of that demographic group (the market size). If Magazine X, for example, is read by 2¹/₂ million women 35–49, and the total population of women 35–49 is 25 million, then Magazine X has a 10 percent coverage of this target audience.

Unfortunately, the term *coverage* may be confusing because it is used in different ways for different media forms. See Table 4–3 for a summary of its meanings.

In magazines, coverage is used in an ideal manner. If there are 12 million households in the United States that own cats and Magazine A reaches 6 million of them, then Magazine A's coverage is 50 percent. This 50 percent represents actual exposure to the vehicle.

TABLE 4–3.   Different Meanings of the Term "Coverage"

Kind of Coverage	Meaning	Uses
General Concept (more accurately called "Market Coverage")	The number of prospects delivered (exposed) by a given medium. Coverage expressed as a percent of the universe of prospects.	Serves as a goal in planning. Used to determine whether media selected are delivering enough prospects.
Newspaper Coverage	The number of circulation units as a percent of the number of households in an area. If the readers of newspapers in a local market are measured, then coverage is the number of readers in a demographic segment (such as men 18–24) as a percent of all men 18–24 in the local market.	For local markets. A goal to determine whether enough households are reached with one or more newspapers. This represents *potential* audience size.
Magazine Coverage (sometimes called "Reach")	Same as the general concept. Prospects are demographically defined.	Same as the general concept. This represents *estimated actual* audience size.
Spot TV and Radio Coverage (local market)	The number of TV (or radio) homes within the signal area of station that can tune in to that station.	Serves as a basis for potential delivery in planning. Indicates the maximum size of the *potential* audience of radio or TV homes.
Spot TV Coverage for a national campaign (also for spot radio)	Total number of TV homes in selected markets that are part of a campaign, that can tune in (or can be reached).	It can show how much of the country's TV homes may be *potentially* delivered by a spot plan. Maximum number and percent of potential exposure.
Network TV Program Coverage	The number and percent of all stations in a network carrying a given program compared to total TV homes in U.S.	An indication of the maximum *potential* of TV homes that a TV program can reach.
Outdoor Advertising and Transit Coverage	The number of people who pass, and are exposed to a given showing of billboards in a local market, expressed as a percent of the total of all people in the market.	To determine the size of an audience that might look at each showing of billboards.

But in newspapers and television, coverage may only represent potential for exposure, not actual exposure (or reach).

Because coverage can mean a number of different things, it is important for anyone who uses this term to know and understand its alternative meanings. Following is a discussion of how coverage is defined in specific media.

Newspaper Coverage. Most newspapers measure the number of copies sold or distributed and call this "circulation." Newspaper coverage represents the number of copies circulated compared to the number of households in the circulation area.

If the circulation of a newspaper is 500,000 and the number of households in the area is 2,000,000, then the coverage is 25 percent. The assumption is made that each unit of circulation equals one household covered. Coverage represents potential rather than actual exposure since everyone who *receives* a copy of a newspaper *does not read it*. No exposure to the medium is necessarily assumed. So coverage based on circulation is only a rough comparison of newspaper audience size related to the market size as measured by the total number of households in that area.

Coverage in newspaper planning, therefore, is not the same as for magazines and other media. The limiting factor is the kind of research that is available.

When using newspaper coverage, planners sometimes suggest that a minimum coverage level in any individual market should be no less than 50 percent. If it can be assumed that not all persons in all households will be exposed to any given edition of a newspaper, then 50 percent is the lowest level that seems practical. Perhaps only two-thirds of that 50 percent will be exposed. Some media planners often set much higher limits on local market coverage, such as no less than 70 percent. In such situations, it may take two or even three newspapers in that community to attain a 70 percent unduplicated coverage.

When a newspaper has research of its readership and provides a breakdown of that audience by demographic segments, then coverage will mean something different. It will mean the number of individuals exposed to newspapers compared to the total number of *individuals* (rather than households) in the market. Because such measurements are not always available on a regular basis, newspaper coverage usually means potential exposure.

Magazine Coverage. Magazine coverage, already defined, is the simple ratio of the number of prospects delivered compared with the size of a target market. An example of magazine market coverage is shown in Table 4–4. In Table 4–4, the market is defined as all principal shoppers who used paper napkins within the last month, or 75,953,000 shoppers. Each magazine reaches a proportion of that market, representing its market coverage. If a market is defined demographically, then coverage by a magazine represents a proportion of a demographic segment base.

Another way to look at magazine market coverage is to look at total users of a given product class. If, for example, one of the syndicated research compan-

TABLE 4-4.   Market Coverage of Paper Napkin Users of Selected Magazines*

Used Paper Napkins within Last Month	Number (thousands)	Coverage (%)
Total Users	75,953	100.0
Family Circle	10,992	14.5
Ladies' Home Journal	9,347	12.3
McCall's	8,528	11.2

Source: Simmons Market Research Bureau, 1991. Reprinted by permission.
* For principal shoppers.

ies reported that 75,953,000 principal shoppers used paper napkins within the last month, then that figure would represent the size of the total market. If 8,528,000 readers of *McCall's* used paper napkins within the last month, then that number would represent 11.2 percent market coverage by *McCall's*.

It should be clear from the preceding discussion that planners may define market sizes differently. A market may be defined as all female homemakers aged 18–49, or it may be defined as all product users. The subject of defining markets will be discussed again in Chapter 7.

Local Television and Radio Coverage. For local radio and television, coverage means the number (or percent) of homes with radio or television sets within the signal area of a given station that *can* tune in to that station because they can pick up the station's signal. Whether or not they choose to tune in depends on a number of factors such as (a) whether the programming of the station is interesting enough to attract them; (b) the power of the station, since more powerful stations can cover more homes than weaker stations; (c) the height of a station's antenna and the pull of the home's antenna, which affect reception of signals; and (d) the number and nature of obstructions that may prevent the television signal from being received, such as bridges, tall buildings, or mountains.

Television stations produce an engineering contour map based on their signal strength in a market to indicate how wide an area the station's signal covers. The strongest signal is designated "Grade A" (or one that covers the primary market area surrounding the station). The next strongest signal is "Grade B" (or secondary area coverage). These measurements, however, are not as useful in determining coverage as those that estimate the number of homes covered regardless of whether they are in Grade A or B areas. Research has also shown that some homes outside of the A or B areas can and do receive certain stations.

In order to learn the coverage of a station, research companies send out mail questionnaires to a carefully selected sample of homes located inside and outside the A and B signal areas. These questionnaires ask respondents to list the stations they view regularly. From the returns, estimates are made of how many homes in each county are covered by a station's signal. Such measurements are the starting place for determining the maximum potential audience for a given station. The criterion for being included in a station's coverage statistics is that the home must be able to receive the signal.

TABLE 4-5. Coverage of Top U.S. Markets by
Using Spot TV

Markets	Coverage (%)
Top 10	31
Top 20	45
Top 30	54
Top 40	61
Top 50	67
Top 60	72
Top 70	76
Top 80	80
Top 90	83
Top 100	86

Source: Leo Burnett 1992 Media Costs and Coverage.

Spot Radio or Television Coverage in Multiple Markets. An advertiser who buys spot announcements in a number of markets located in various geographical regions of the United States may be interested in knowing what percentage of all television (or radio) homes in the country the commercial may potentially reach. Perhaps a planner has selected fifty of the largest markets in the country in which to advertise. In order to determine the percentage of coverage, it is only necessary to learn the coverage of each station in a plan and add the figures to find the coverage of the entire plan. For example, by buying spot announcements in the largest fifty markets, planners can potentially reach nearly 70 percent of the television homes in the country. The planner knows, then, that the maximum audience size (expressed in terms of homes than can tune in to a station's signal) is no larger than 70 percent. Since not everyone in those fifty markets will see the commercials, the exposure will be lower than 70 percent. Table 4–5 lists the percentage coverages of the largest markets.

Network Television Coverage. In network television, coverage is defined as the number and percentage of all U.S. television households that are able to receive a given program. Generally speaking, the degree of coverage is affected by the number of stations in a network lineup. The more stations, the more coverage. Table 4–6 indicates the coverage of several network programs.

In broadcast, the term *circulation* is sometimes used to mean the same thing as coverage, but properly used it has a different meaning. Circulation means the number of radio or television households that *can* and *do* tune in

TABLE 4-6. Network Program Coverage

Network	Program	Household Coverage (%)	Number of Stations in Network Lineup
ABC	20/20	99	225
NBC	Unsolved Mysteries	97	219
CBS	Rescue: 911	96	207
FOX	Married with Children	94	166

Source: Nielsen Pocketpiece, April 20–26, 1992.

TABLE 4-7.   **Reach and Frequency of Outdoor Showings for Adults**

100 Showing		50 Showing		25 Showing	
Reach	Frequency	Reach	Frequency	Reach	Frequency
91.5%	27.9	90.6%	14.3	87.4%	7.7

Source: Simmons Market Research Bureau, Inc., 1991. Reprinted by permission.

to a station a minimum number of times, whether once a month, once a week, or once during a part of the day. Therefore, circulation describes the potential audience size of a network or a station over a period of time. Circulation is a potential audience measurement in that the minimum tune-in required for counting is generally spread over a broad time period, rather than a specific day and time. It is important, then, to remember that both coverage and circulation are measurements of the gross potential audience. *Gross* refers to a crude estimate, and *potential* means that the numbers deal with opportunities rather than actual audience tune-ins to a program. Opportunities for tune-in vary by time of day.

Out-of-Home Media Coverage.   Out-of-home media include all media that are located outside a person's home, such as billboards, posters in shopping malls, advertisements in and on buses, and so forth. Coverage for out-of-home media is the percentage of the population that *passes* the advertisement. Coverage for out-of-home media, therefore, represents the potential for advertising exposure.

Out-of-home media, such as billboards, are generally purchased by advertisers on the basis of daily GRPs. GRPs are equivalent to a 100 showing in thirty days. A *100 showing* is the number of billboards needed in a given market to produce the equivalent of 100 percent coverage of the market potentially exposed in a single day. Suppose a market has 100 different billboards erected in and around the city, each of which is passed by an average of 1,000 people each day. If an advertiser purchases ten of these billboards, the equivalent of 10,000 people will pass these boards. If the market has a population of 10,000, then these ten boards would constitute 100 GRPs, or a 100 showing. Other showing sizes can also be purchased, such as a 75 (comprising 75 percent as many boards as in a 100 showing), a 50 showing (half as many boards), and so on. They may also be expressed as 100, 75, 50, and 25 GRPs.

The outdoor medium is able to generate very high coverage, and therefore high reach, over time. Table 4-7 shows the accumulated reach over a thirty-day period for different size outdoor showings.

Households Using Television (HUT)

One important television measurement that is frequently used in planning is *households using television (HUT)*. It is a coverage figure and represents the percentage of homes tuned into television at a given point in time. Because it includes a *time* consideration, HUT may be classified as a measurement of *net* potential audience size.

FIGURE 4–2.   Hour-by-hour % of TV Usage Among Households

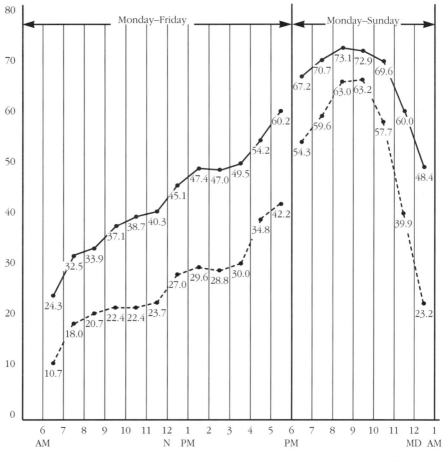

Source: A.C. Nielsen Co. Jan–Feb 1989. Reprinted by permission of Nielsen Media.

Modifying Coverage Data by HUT Data. Coverage data in television represent only audience potential. If a station covers 1,410,000 TV homes, this does not mean that an advertiser will reach all of those homes with a commercial on that station. But what determines how many homes will be reached? To a great extent, the HUT at any time of day will provide a clue to the possible tune-in. As a measure of the net potential audience, HUT indicates what percentage of households with a television set have it turned on at any given time of day, such as morning, early afternoon, late afternoon, prime time, or late evening. The statistics are reported by fifteen-minute segments to allow a closer examination of tune-ins during various times of the day. Figure 4–2 shows how audience sizes vary by time of day.

Television viewing is affected by living habits. In the morning, tune-in tends to be low, with many men and women at work and children in school. Primary viewers are mothers and small children. When children return

TABLE 4–8. Variations in Viewing by Daypart and Season

Daypart	Total TV Households Tuned In (%)			
	Spring	Summer	Fall	Winter
Daytime (Mon.–Fri.)	25	27	27	30
Early Fringe (Mon.–Fri.)	41	40	47	50
Prime Time (Mon.–Sun.)	55	53	61	62
Late Fringe (Mon.–Fri.)	28	28	29	29

Source: Nielsen Media Research, Households Using TV Summary Report, 1991. Reprinted by permission.

home from school about 4:00 p.m., the tune-ins rise dramatically, and after 6:00 p.m., when many people have returned home from work, the rise in tune-ins is even greater. After 10:00 p.m., viewing drops again. Table 4–8 indicates the variations in viewing for different time periods, as well as by seasons of the year.

The planner can study HUT data and estimate potential audience size better than by studying coverage figures alone. In the evening hours there are more viewers available than at any other time of day, since both children and adults are usually at home. But there are variations in viewing not only during a single day, but during a given week, and month. During the summer, for example, when persons spend more time out-of-doors, television viewing is much lower in some viewing periods than it is in winter. These variations affect the size of audience that can be obtained.

The media planner, knowing that variations in viewing patterns exist, refines the coverage data to learn the approximate size of an audience that can be reached at various times. Table 4–9 gives an example of how the potential audience size in the Chicago area may vary by county and by time period. The advertiser who selects Station A can never hope to reach all of the 2,930,390 households at one time because some of them will prefer other local stations.

From Nielsen or Arbitron, however, it is possible to determine how large the net potential audience is. Table 4–10 shows these data for Station A. These figures would probably be lower if the planner were studying data for

TABLE 4–9. Potential Audience Size in Chicago Metropolitan Area for Station A

Chicago Metro Area Counties	Daytime (Mon.–Fri.)		Prime Time (Mon.–Sun.)	
	Avg. Qtr. Hr. Households	Percent of County	Avg. Qtr. Hr. Households	Percent of County
Cook (Illinois)	66,689	13	207,276	17
DuPage	5,338	10	31,444	18
Kane	1,620	7	10,585	16
Lake	3,333	11	15,796	16
McHenry	954	7	5,557	14
Will	2,315	7	11,306	16
Lake (Indiana)	7,432	13	19,172	16
Porter	1,589	13	4,304	15

Source: Nielsen Station Index, County Coverage Study, 1991. Reprinted by permission.

TABLE 4-10. Average Number of Homes Reached at Least Once by Station A

Morning (Mon.–Fri.) 6:00 A.M.–12:00 P.M.	Afternoon (Mon.–Fri.) 12:00 N–7:00 P.M.	Evening (Sat.–Sun.)	
		7:00–10:00 P.M.	10:00–10:30 P.M.
1,221,000	2,810,000	2,438,000	1,508,000

Source: Nielsen Station Index, Viewers in Profile, November 1991. Reprinted by permission.

the months of July or August, because fewer persons watch television during these months. Furthermore, there are also differences between the net potential audience of Station A and other Chicago stations. In any case, these figures help the advertiser learn about his potential audience size.

After potential audience sizes are examined, program ratings are used to learn the estimated audience size for a given program.

Broadcast Ratings

A *broadcast rating* (television or radio) represents an estimate of audience size of the audience that has viewed a program, or has tuned in during a specific time period. This rating is determined through sampling procedures. It is financially and physically impossible to measure the viewing habits of every person in the United States, but it is possible to measure a small sample of viewers. This information, however, is only an *estimate* of the size of the actual viewing audience.

These estimates are reported in the form of percentages of an audience base. For households tuned in to a network television program, the base figure usually includes all households in the United States that have at least one television set. For local television markets, the base is all TV households in the metropolitan area, or some other specially designated area.

Ratings are made for both households and individuals. The people base for network television consists of all persons of a given age group in network television households. For example, for women aged 18–49, the network program base would be all women aged 18–49 in television households in the United States.

A local radio rating is usually expressed in the form of an average quarter-hour tune-in, and as a percentage of either the people in the Metropolitan Statistical Area (MSA) or some other specific geographical area.

Rather than talk about a rating of 18 percent, it is common practice to talk only about a program having an 18 rating. The fact that a rating is a percentage is always assumed to be understood.

The Average Audience Rating. The A. C. Nielsen Company provides an average audience rating, obtained through a people meter device, which represents the percentage of homes (and people) tuned in to the average minute of a program. Data provided in the Nielsen Television Index shows average audience ratings tuned in for each half-hour or quarter-hour segment.

TABLE 4-11.   Computing an Average Audience Rating

Minutes in a Program	1	2	3	4	5	6	7	8	9	10	11	12	13	14	15
Percent Tuned in	30	30	30	31	31	31	31	32	32	32	33	33	33	33	33

Total Tuned in for 15 minutes = 475
475 ÷ 15 = 31.7 (the average percentage tune-in for 15 minutes)

To learn how many households (or people) have tuned in to a program one need only multiply the rating times the total number of TV households in the United States. This is called a "projection." For example, if a program had a 16.0 average audience rating, and the total number of households in the United States were 93,100,000, then 93,100,000 × .16 = 14,896,000 households tuned in. On a local market level, the base would be relatively smaller, but the procedure for projection would be the same.

Table 4–11 illustrates the method by which the average audience rating is calculated for a fifteen-minute segment of a program.

Share of Audience Rating. The *share of audience rating* reflects the percentage of homes tuned in to a program based *only* on those homes that had their sets turned on, rather than on all television homes, as in the average audience rating. If all average audience ratings for a fifteen-minute time period were added together, the sum would represent the HUT, which always is a proportion of all television homes and is always less than 100 percent. But the sum of all share of audience ratings represents only those homes tuned in at a particular time and theoretically equals 100 percent since homes that had their sets turned off are never figured in the base. The formula for computing share is as follows:

$$\text{Share} \ = \ \frac{\text{Rating}}{\text{HUT}}$$

A comparison of share data with average audience ratings is illustrated in Table 4–12. In Table 4–12, 40 percent of the sets were *not* turned on. When this 40 percent is added to the HUT, the total is 100 percent. Share was computed by dividing the average audience rating by the HUT. The sum of all average audience ratings equaled the HUT, or 60 percent. But the sum of share of audience ratings is 100 percent.

The value of a share statistic is that it enables the media planner to compare two programs broadcast at radically different times of the day, week, or

TABLE 4-12.   Difference between Average Audience Rating and Share

Programs Being Broadcast during Same 15-Minute Period	Average Audience Rating (%)	Share of Audience Rating (%)
A	20	33.3
B	10	16.7
C	30	50.0
Total	60 (HUT)	100.0

TABLE 4–13. Program X, Ratings versus Share

Month of Year	Average Audience Rating	HUT	Share of Audience Rating
January	15.2	66.5	22.9
April	14.6	63.6	23.0
July	12.5	49.8	25.1

year, or any time where the HUTs for different programs are radically different. To illustrate the use of share data, Table 4–13 shows ratings for a sample program and its shares at different times of the year. If a media planner had made decisions about Program X based only on the average audience rating, he or she might have concluded that this program was losing its audience. After all, ratings were declining. But a study of HUTs shows that they, too, were declining, as might be expected when comparing HUTs for January and July. When shares were computed, however, the numbers showed that the program was not only doing well, but actually improving from January to July.

Share is best used when making comparisons based on radically different HUTs. In other words, when the bases for ratings differ, share may be the most appropriate measure.

Figure 4–3 shows sample pages from Nielsen Television Index to illustrate the various kinds of ratings used by media analysts. The reader should note the ''Average Audience'' and ''Share'' for each program listed.

It is important to remember that while ratings may be reported for households, they are also reported for people viewing programs. Such ratings usually are broken down by various demographic groups such as age and sex. Furthermore, Nielsen also can show viewer data of programs cross-tabulated by sex and age and other demographic breakdowns. These cross-tabulations allow a media planner to have a better perception of who views each program so that it is possible to better match markets with media.

Measurements of Message Weight

When planners want to know the audience size for a single TV program, they use either a program rating or a calculation of the number of viewers exposed to the program. For a single ad in a magazine, they use either a target audience measurement, or a percent coverage of the market figure. But many times, planners want to discuss audience sizes for more than one program. To do that they simply add ratings or audience size numbers and disregard the duplication that results.

The sum of ratings (percentages) is called *gross rating points*. The sum of audience sizes for more than one ad is called *gross impressions*. Both numbers are *duplicated*, that is, they are sums of other measurements that may overlap. Gross rating points are often called GRPs.

FIGURE 4–3. *Nielsen* National TV Audience Estimates—Eve. Thurs. Apr. 30, 1992

TIME		7:00	7:15	7:30	7:45	8:00	8:15	8:30	8:45	9:00	9:15	9:30	9:45	10:00	10:15	10:30	10:45
HUT		52.8	53.2	54.4	56.3	60.3	62.1	63.7	64.6	64.7	66.4	66.4	65.9	63.8	62.4	61.2	58.8
ABC TV							◀— COLUMBO (R)(PAE) —▶							◀— PRIMETIME LIVE —▶				
Hhld Audience % & (000)	%					7.4	6.820		6.6*		8.1*		8.3*	16.0	14.740		16.2*
TA%.Avg. Aud. 1/2 Hr.	%					13.6	6.8*		10*		12*		13*	22.9	15.9*		27*
Share Audience	%					12	11*							26	25*		
Avg. Aud. by 1/4 Hr.	%					7.2	6.4	6.5	6.7	7.9	8.3	8.1	8.4	15.1	16.7	16.3	16.1
CBS TV						◀— TOP COPS —▶				◀— STREET STORIES —▶				◀— HUMAN FACTOR —▶			
Hhld Audience % & (000)	%					7.8	7.180		7.9*	11.8	10.870		12.3*	6.6	6.080		6.7*
TA%.Avg. Aud. 1/2 Hr.	%					11.3	7.7*		12*	16.8	11.3*		19*	9.8	6.6*		10*
Share Audience	%					12	13*			18	17*			11	11*		
Avg. Aud. by 1/4 Hr.	%					7.7	7.6	7.9	7.9	10.6	11.9	12.7	11.9	6.9	6.4	6.5	6.8
NBC TV						◀— BILL COSBY SHOW —▶				◀CHEERS▶		◀WINGS▶		◀— L.A. LAW —▶			
Hhld Audience % & (000)	%					28.0	25.790		29.7*	19.9	18.330	15.5	14.280	13.2	12.160		13.4*
TA%.Avg. Aud. 1/2 Hr.	%					34.4	26.4*		46*	22.9	10.3*	17.6		17.6	13.0*		22*
Share Audience	%					45	43*			30		23		21	21*		
Avg. Aud. by 1/4 Hr.	%					24.9	27.9	29.7	29.7	20.2	19.6	15.8	15.2	13.1	12.9	13.6	13.2
FOX TV						◀— SIMPSONS SPECIAL (R) —▶				◀— BEVERLY HILLS 90210 —▶							
Hhld Audience % & (000)	%					8.8	8.100		9.1*	10.8	9.950		11.3*				
TA%.Avg. Aud. 1/2 Hr.	%					12.4	8.5*		14*	14.1	10.3*		17*				
Share Audience	%					14	14*			16	16*						
Avg. Aud. by 1/4 Hr.	%					8.0	8.9	8.8	9.3	10.0	10.7	11.3	11.2				
INDEPENDENTS (Incl. Superstations except TBS)																	
Average Audience		11.8 (+F)		12.6 (+F)		4.9		4.8		5.6		6.1		14.8 (+F)		12.6 (+F)	
Share Audience	%	22		23		8		7		9		9		24		21	
PBS																	
Average Audience		1.5		2.2		1.8		1.5		2.2		2.2		1.2		1.1	
Share Audience	%	3		4		3		2		3		3		2		2	
Cable Orig. (Including TBS)																	
Average Audience		8.6 (+F)		9.8 (+F)		9.7		9.9		12.2		14.2		13.9 (+F)		12.3 (+F)	
Share Audience	%	16		18		16		15		19		21		22		21	
Pay Services																	
Average Audience		1.0		1.3		0.9		1.1		1.8		1.6		1.8		1.7	
Share Audience	%	2		2		1		2		3		2		3		3	

U.S. TV Households: 92,100,000

Using gross rating points, or gross impressions, enables the planner to use a single number to describe the effect of *message weight*. Message weight is a number that quickly tells the planner the duplicated audience sizes for many programs within a given time period. In spot television, planners often deal with the number of gross rating points per week or per month. But one also can discuss the message weight of an entire year using either gross rating points or gross impressions. The user of these numbers, however, must always remember that they represent duplicated audiences.

Gross Rating Points in Broadcast Media

In planning for television, gross rating points are often used to describe the message weight of a week or a month. Shown below is an example of commercials that constituted 90 gross rating points a week:

Two commercials each with a 15 rating	=	30 GRPs
Five commercials each with a 10 rating	=	50 GRPs
Two commercials each with a 5 rating	=	10 GRPs
Total weekly GRPs	=	90

For television planning, one might also want to know how many GRPs per month would be needed to attain a 70 reach. There are appropriate tables and formulas to make such reach estimates once the number of GRPs is known.

Gross Rating Points in Other Media

In recent years, planners have extended the GRP concept to other media such as magazines, newspapers, and outdoor. In magazines, for example, gross rating points equal the percent of market coverage of a target audience times the number of ad insertions. An example would be as follows:

McCall's target reach of paper napkin users	=	22.2%
Number of ads to be placed in *McCall's*	=	× 5
Gross rating points		111

Another way of using gross rating points for magazines (or newspapers) is to add the target coverage for one insertion in a number of magazines as shown below.

Target coverage for *McCall's*	=	22.5%
Target coverage for *Good Housekeeping*	=	20.6
Target coverage for *Time*	=	14.2
Target coverage for *Woman's Day*	=	22.5
Gross rating points	=	79.8 (rounded to 80 GRPs)

One last way to calculate GRPs is to multiply reach times frequency for a given time period.

The Outdoor Advertising Association of America adopted as its basic unit of sale the term "100 gross rating points daily." This basic standardized unit of poster sales is the number of poster panels required in each market to produce a daily effective circulation equal to the population of the market. Other units of sale would be expressed as fractions of the basic unit: 75 gross rating points daily, 50 gross rating points daily, and 25 gross rating points daily. This change in no way alters the thirty-day period of sale and measurement.

Gross Impressions

Use of gross impressions (or gross weight of media). Gross impressions are the new numbers of media audiences, in duplicated form. The purpose of gross impression analysis is to get a quick look at the total audience size of one or more media, thus the gross weight of a plan. Through this one number a planner can make comparisons with other plans and other groups of vehicles that might have been selected. Gross impressions are an alternative to accumulated audience data or reach, which shows the unduplicated audience size. Thus gross impressions represent the weight of a select group of media vehicles.

There are two methods of finding gross impressions. One method is to multiply GRPs by a target audience base. For example, if a planner intended to buy 130 target GRPs a month (for men 18–49 in the U.S.) then multiply 1.3 × 59 million U.S. market base. The product of these numbers are 76,700,000 gross impressions.

The other method of calculating gross impressions is to add the target audience sizes delivered by each vehicle, as follows:

Program A:	5,160,000	targets reached
Program B:	6,990,000	'' ''
Program C:	4,320,000	'' ''
Program D:	6,180,000	'' ''
Gross impressions	22,650,000	targets reached

Another use of broadcast gross impressions might occur when someone wants to know the weight of nine commercials that may be purchased on any one program. The gross impressions for nine commercials on Program A (above):

$$9 \quad \times \quad 5,160,000 \quad = \quad 46,440,000$$

The use of gross impressions for print media is much the same as it is for broadcast. The following examples shows how total gross impressions would be calculated for three magazines with varying numbers of ads:

Magazine	No. of targets reached	No. of ads to be purchased	Gross impressions
A	5,000,000	× 5	= 25,000,000
B	2,100,000	× 3	= 6,300,000
C	7,000,000	× 2	= 14,000,000
Total gross impressions			45,300,000

The number of impressions delivered by a media plan usually runs into the millions, and because the number is so large, it is called a *boxcar* figure. Its value, however, is debatable. Alone, gross impressions have limited meaning. But if they can be related to some measure of campaign effectiveness such as sales volume, brand awareness levels, or competitive media plan effectiveness, they can be used to compare media.

Gross impressions also are useful in comparing the weight given to geographic areas or demographic segments of a market. For example, if the planner wants to be sure that a given media plan reaches a number of different geographic areas in the correct proportions, the gross impressions could be added for each vehicle in the plan and then the proportions of each compared with a weighted goal. Table 4–14 gives an example of how this works. This table indicates that the gross impression distribution of the vehicles selected comes fairly close to the goals set for the plan. It may not be worth extra effort to make the gross impression totals come any closer to the stated goals.

Other impression analysis could have been made for targets by age, sex, income, or any other demographic segment desired.

TABLE 4–14. Distribution of Gross Impressions in Media Plan for Brand X

County Size	Gross Impressions Delivered (thousands)				Target (%)	Goal Set for Plan (%)
	Vehicle 1	Vehicle 2	Vehicle 3	Total		
A	308,582	246,972	471,342	1,026,896	51.0	47.0
B	276,980	151,370	471,342	582,331	24.1	26.7
C	187,752	72,764	78,798	339,312	17.3	15.5
D	156,150	60,016	18,796	234,962	7.6	10.8
					100.0	100.0

Measures of Cost Efficiency

One of the principles of media planning stated earlier was that media should be selected on their ability to reach the largest audience of prospects at the lowest unit cost. Matching markets with media helps accomplish one part of this principle. The search for media with large audiences of prospects rather than large total audiences recognizes that media costs are too high to permit advertising to those individuals who are not likely to buy the product.

But the other portion of the principle is equally important. This requires that media be selected that reach the largest number of prospects at the most efficient cost. Cost efficiency simply means that audience size must be related to media costs.

Cost per Thousand

Rather than compute a single unit cost, the advertising industry prefers to compute a cost per thousand targets reached. Cost per thousand may be computed for a printed page or broadcast time, and the audience base may be either circulation, homes reached, readers, or number of audience members of any kind of demographic or product usage classification.

Cost per thousand is a comparative device. It enables the planner to compare one medium or media vehicle with another to find those that are the most efficient, and it may be used for either intramedia or intermedia comparisons.

Shown below are various formulas that may be used for making comparisons on the basis of cost per thousand (abbreviated as CPM):

1. *For print media (when audience data are not available)*

$$\text{CPM} = \frac{\text{Cost of 1 page (black-and-white)} \times 1000}{\text{Circulation}}$$

Because many print media do not have audience research data, this formula is often used. But it tells nothing about the audience.

2. *For print media (when audience data are available)*

$$\text{CPM} = \frac{\text{Cost of 1 page (black-and-white)} \times 1000}{\text{Number of prospects reached}}$$

3. *For broadcast media (based on homes reached by a given program or time period)*

$$\text{CPM} = \frac{\text{Cost of 1 unit of time} \times 1000}{\text{Number of homes reached by a given program or time period}}$$

4. *For broadcast media (when audience data are available)*

$$\text{CPM} = \frac{\text{Cost of 1 unit of time} \times 1000}{\text{Number of prospects reached by a given program or time period}}$$

5. *For newspapers (when cost of ad is known)*

$$\text{CPM} = \frac{\text{Cost of ad} \times 1000}{\text{Circulation}}$$

6. *For newspapers where only circulation is the base, and the agate line rate is used to establish the milline rate*

$$\text{Milline rate} = \frac{\text{Cost of 1 agate line} \times 1 \text{ million}}{\text{Total circulation}}$$

The procedure for using any of the above formulas is to compare media on the basis of the two variables: audience and cost. *The lowest cost-per-thousand medium* is the most efficient, other things being equal.

Media planners should be wary about automatically accepting or rejecting media vehicles on the basis of the lowest cost-per-thousand number. A difference of 10 percent one way or another is meaningless, and there are people such as David Poltrack, director of research at CBS who noted that the range of error in television sample audiences is so great that a true calculation of the room for error would "tell us that even a CPM variation of *a dollar or more* may not be real." (emphasis added)[1]

It is obvious that wherever precise demographic classifications of the audiences are available, these data should be used in the denominator of the formula. Generally, the medium (or media) with the lowest cost per thousand is selected, but not always. Whenever a very special kind of target audience is required, and there are few or no media which reach them exclusively, then the cost-per-thousand comparisons may be ignored. In the latter situation, media selections are based on the principle of reaching the largest number of targets, regardless of cost.

For example, there are times when individuals with very high incomes (over $100,000 annually) are target audiences. A few media vehicles reach a small proportion of these audiences, but even if many such vehicles were used, the total number of persons reached might be relatively small. On the other hand, a very large number of these persons might be reached with mass media such as a network television program or a national magazine. It is obvious that either of these two media would also include a large amount of waste, so that when costs per thousand are computed, they will seem unduly high. Yet the waste and the high costs per thousand might have to be ignored in order to maximize the size of target audiences reached.

Mass produced and consumed products, such as cigarettes, breakfast cereals, and automobiles, usually have target audiences for whom media are selected primarily on a cost-per-thousand basis. Specialized products such as yachts, private airplanes, and classical recordings have specialized target audiences that may require less attention be paid to cost efficiencies and more to audience sizes.

---

1. Larson, Erik, "Watching Americans Watch TV," *Atlantic Monthly*, March 1992, 72.

Cost per Rating Point

Another method of comparing the cost efficiency of vehicles is that of the *cost per rating point* (CPRP). Essentially, a CPRP is a method of comparing alternative broadcast vehicles; relating cost to a rating rather than to an audience number such as in a cost-per-thousand comparison. Both are measurements of relative value, but each uses a different base. The formula for calculating CPRP is as follows:

$$\text{Cost per rating point} = \frac{\text{Cost of a commercial}}{\text{Rating}}$$

If the cost of a prime-time spot commercial was $1,000 and the rating for that spot was 10, then the CPRP would be $100.

How does a CPRP compare with a CPM for the same station and commercial? The following shows the differences:

CPRP	CPM
Cost of thirty-second commercial: $110	Cost of thirty-second commercial: $110
Metro rating, 2:00 P.M.: 8	No. H.H. delivered, 2:00 P.M.: 77,000
$110 + 8 = $13.75	$110 × 1000 ÷ 77,000 = $1.43

Is there any preference for using one over the other? Generally, costs per thousand are most often used to compare any vehicle efficiency, while CPRP is a tool most often used for quick cost comparisons in broadcast planning.

QUESTIONS FOR DISCUSSION

1. What is the significance of two measurements: the number of readers of magazine X, and the coverage of magazine X?
2. Does the coverage of a given network television program indicate how many viewers it will have?
3. Will 100 gross rating points a week in a given market equal 100 reach?
4. What is the difference, generally, between newspaper and magazine coverage?
5. What, precisely, is the meaning of the following? "We will have a 75 percent coverage in a spot television buy, if we buy the top sixty markets in the United States."
6. What is the relationship between GRPs and gross impressions?
7. Why are television ratings not an accurate measurement of the audience size for commercials broadcast within a program?
8. Is it proper to talk about the four-week reach of *Reader's Digest*? Briefly explain.
9. Of what value is it to know the readers per copy of a magazine?
10. Briefly explain why HUT figures for a given time period (such as a Monday evening in February) do not change very much from year to year.

11. Many newspaper columnists who are television critics tend to disparage broadcast ratings with a statement such as, "Well, no one ever called me to ask which program I was watching." Is this statement valid? Briefly explain.

SELECTED READINGS

Advertising Age, Who's Watching What and Where," April 6, 1992, S–16.

Chicago Advertising and Media, "The Numbers Game: How Scarborough and ABC Measure Circulation," June 16–30, 1991, 19.

Dubin, Wes, "The Worst of Times . . . the Best of Times," *Journal of Media Planning,* Fall 1990, 13–18.

DuPress, Scotty, "The Numbers of New Technology and Media," *Mediaweek,* March 30, 1992, 14.

Economist, "American Television Ratings: Wheel of Misfortune," June 23, 1990, 68.

Faber, Neil, "Efficiency Is Not Really That Unless Based on Target Demographics," *Media Decisions,* October 1978, 84.

Kaatz, Ron, "Toward Even Better Media Comparisons," *MRCC Review,* (Media Research Club of Chicago), March 1992, 1–2.

Killion, Kevin C. "Using People Meter information," *Journal of Media Planning,* Spring 1987, 47–52.

Larson, Erik, "Watching Americans Watching TV," *Atlantic Monthly,* March 1992, 66–80.

Levine, Steven R. and Rick Heller, "Overestimating Primetime Break Position Ratings," *Journal of Media Planning,* Spring 1988, 1–4.

Mandese, Joe, "Groups Propose TV Rating Changes," *Advertising Age,* September 9, 1991, 33.

Mandese, Joe, "Arbitron Tries to Tune Up Ratings," *Advertising Age,* September 9, 1991, S–11.

Media Decisions, "What Is Best for Buying—CPGRP or CPM?" February 1973, 48–49.

Mediaweek, "Research: Advertising Execs Think Network TV Still Works," January 10, 1992, 33.

Nielsen, A.C., "Superbowl History 1967–1991" *Media News,* January 1992, 2.

Rutens, W.S., "A Guide to TV Ratings," *Journal of Advertising Research,* February 1978, 11–18.

Sims, Jonathon B., "People Meters: Implications for Media Planning and Buying," *Journal of Media Planning,* Fall 1987, 13–18.

Walley, W., "Big 3 Nets Put Heat on Nielsen to Change Rating System," *Advertising Age,* June 25, 1990, 60.

5

New Media Measuring Tools

This chapter discusses recently developed media measurement tools that may have major effects on media planning processes. Some are already widely known because of their stunning addition to our knowledge about how audiences watch television. Others, such as single source measurements, have provided more accurate knowledge about the relationship between media exposure and purchasing. New measurements, such as the passive people meter, may provide the most needed kind of information for advertisers: who really watches their commercials. All of this will likely change the scope and power of media planning in the future.

People Meters and the New Passive People Meters

Probably no measuring tool in media history has generated as much interest and discussion as people meters, a device for measuring the number of people watching television programs. These meters first were used in the United States in September, 1987 by the A. C. Nielsen Company. However, their introduction resulted in protests by the three networks because they produced lower ratings and smaller audience sizes than were expected. Now, a new kind of measuring instrument has been developed, called the "passive" people meter, and the interest and discussion may be even greater than for the original meter, but for different reasons.

Neilsen expects the passive people meter to be on the market in about three years and provide measurement data with values that far surpasses that of the original meter. Although the first people meters provided the most accurate measurements, the passive people meters will provide something new and better: *measurements of how many persons watched the commercials*. Media planners have always wanted to know how well audiences watched commercials but had to settle for only knowing audience sizes of television programs. There has been plenty of evidence to refute the assumption that audiences who watched programs also watched all the commercials within. Currently, media planners have very limited ways to measure how many people read ads in print media. Passive people meters allow planners to obtain commercial audience measurements, which will not require special behavior by respondents, thus avoiding bias. Perhaps now there will be more motivation for print media ads to be measured and more investment in finding a print solution.

The Value of Passivity

The *passivity* aspect of the people meter is the basis for a near-ideal measurement. Passivity means that respondents do not have to behave in a certain way as they did when using the original meters.

When using the original people meters, each member of a family was assigned a specially-numbered button on the meter, which sat on top of the set (See Figure 5-1). Guests were assigned special buttons that also had to be pushed. Each person who watched television had to press the special button to show that they were going to watch television. Later, they had to press the same button before leaving the viewing room. If they did not perform these actions, their measurements could not be used. In other words, the people meter—an improvement over previous television audience measurements—was by no means perfect.

In fact, at least two segments of a television audience tended *not* to push all the buttons at all of the required times: the very young and the aged. Audiences soon became tired of pushing the required bottons. The invention of the passive people meter solved the problem of button-pushing behavior.

How Passive People Meters Work

Essentially, the passive meter works like a sonar detecting device, noting the presence of people by their body heat. It can count persons present, although when first tested, dogs were also counted. (This problem has now been solved.)

The following is one description about how the meter works:[1]

> The machine and I had already been introduced—that is, it had scanned me and then stored four images of my face: three head-on portraits and one quarter-profile. It was now ready to try matching the real me to these digital mug shots.
>
> If it succeeded, it would display on a nearby video screen my name and a number indicating how confident it was about the identifica-

---

1. Erik Larson, ''Watching Americans Watch TV,'' *Atlantic Monthly*, March 1992, 77–78.

tion. A number and no name would mean it had failed. I did not want a zero. A zero would be a pretty good indicator that I had died or at least stopped breathing. A number from 63 to 83 would mean that I was a person, although not someone the meter knew. Anything higher would mean that it knew me well enough to display my name.

The meter scans the room every two seconds, looking for signs of life. It compares each fresh image in a given location with its predecessor to produce a digital likeness of humanness.

. . . The system next locates the melange of digits most resembling those for a human head, a search program that may at least help Nielsen separate the men from the dogs. The machine notices every departure and return. Its reliance on head-on or nearly head-on views, moreover, means that it will not count people who are present, but involved in other activities such as reading a newspaper or making love on the floor.

Implications of Passive Meters for Media Planning

Passive people meters will enable a planner to choose the media vehicle that delivers the largest number of commercial-watching demographic targets. If a company knows the day and time that each commercial is broadcast, then it can know how many individuals saw them. Later, they can relate commercial watching with responses, such as sales or other communication goals. That alone represents a great improvement over present day planning techniques, however, it may change other criteria for selecting vehicles. For example, now it will be possible to measure the four-week reach of *commercials*, a vast improvement over measuring the reach of programs.

The position that a television commercial program occupies may now become more important than ever before. Should a commercial be placed in the front, middle, or end of a half-hour program? In the past, it was assumed that the first and last slots were best and the middle slots were poorest. The networks and local stations may start charging for premium positions.

We may find that many programs will lose a substantial portion of their audience as it gets closer to ending; the commercials at the end may suffer.

If audience sizes today are much smaller than ever before, there could be a disenchantment with advertising and companies may search for less expensive forms of communication vehicles. In fact, many professionals believe that integrated marketing communications will become more important.

But now that commercials can be measured, advertisers can turn their attention to making random survey research measurements more accurate. When random samples turn out to be not very random, then passive meter ratings can be just as inaccurate. Perhaps advertisers will demand more care-

ful selection of samples and more attention to keeping the percent of responses high. When sample households do not respond to research, then
the household's value to the research finding is reduced.

There is the issue of whether audiences will object to the passive people
meter because it intrudes on their privacy. Perhaps the government may in-
tercede and not allow passive meters in homes. All of these ideas may affect
media planning to a greater or lesser degree.

Single Source Data

Another major development in media planning measurement is called single
source data. It can hardly be called brand new because some companies have
been using it since 1979. Single source means that household television viewing data has been gathered, and that measurements of packaged goods purchased have been measured from the *same* families. Thus, the term "single
source." Students must remember that media has been planned to match
viewing measurements and purchasing from two *different* samples. Even passive people meter data will come only from a sample of viewing audiences. As
it now stands, purchasing data will have to be measured from a different sample.

The value of research data coming from a single sample is that it provides
an idea of how much media advertising affects purchasing. Since measurements will come from a single family, it will presumably be more accurate
than if it came from two different samples. In fact, product purchases verified with the use of the uniform product code (UPC) is generally agreed to
be very accurate. If measurements of both television viewing and buying of a
specific brand like Coca Cola should rise, it may suggest that advertising has
caused Coke sales to rise. However, statistical correlation of two numbers
both rising at the same time does not prove that one caused the other. There
is, however, a relationship that—if verified by other measurements—may
indeed prove it is valid.

The following material discusses some of the work of leaders in the single
source data field.

BehaviorScan

One of the early leaders in single source measurement has been Information
Resources, Inc. (IRI), which started BehaviorScan in 1979.

IRI created a proprietary household panel of 3,000 households in each of
its six test markets scattered throughout the United States. Panel members
shop with a special ID card that they present at the checkout counter in grocery and drugstores that have special scanners. Data from these scanners not
only show which brands, sizes, and prices were paid, but also show when the

FIGURE 5-1. Nielsen's People Meter (with Hand-Held Remote Unit)
Reprinted courtesy of Nielsen Media Research.

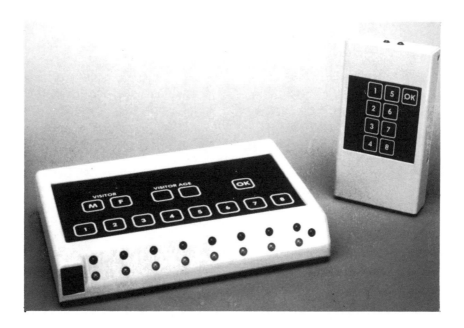

products were bought. The demographic descriptions of household purchasers are recorded along with the purchases so that it is possible to know who bought what, and when.

With such recording of household purchases possible, a marketer can manipulate variables such as prices, sales promotion, advertising, or other elements of the marketing mix to see how each affects purchasing. In fact, BehaviorScan panels can be split into two or more subgroups that are perfectly matched on the basis of past purchases of a particular product, or on demographics, or kinds of stores shopped.

For advertising, commercials can be controlled so that one group sees a particular commercial, but the other groups see a different or control commercial. The comparison potential of alternative marketing mix elements makes it possible for an advertiser to try various promotional schemes in test markets before starting to distribute nationally. One of the significant elements of BehaviorScan for media planners is the ability to match television programs, or dayparts, with product/brand sales.

BehaviorScan is also used for planning media where 1,000 special families in each of its six markets are equipped with television meters to monitor set usage and channel selection on a continuous basis. Viewing data is collected nightly and sent automatically to a computer facility for processing. This viewing data can be linked to purchasing data. For example, BehaviorScan uses an advertising exposure measurement that matches advertising frequency with sales. (Media planners have long used vehicle exposure frequency in planning rather than advertising exposure frequency and tried to relate vehicle frequency to sales.) Advertising exposure is a more useful measurement for determining how much frequency is needed to affect sales. Now that data is available for planners, BehaviorScan can also be used to determine which daypart is best for advertising certain product categories and/or brands.

The ultimate goal of media planners is to have sales matched to alternative media so it will be possible to find the best media options. By allowing planners to add other media measurements, such as those from magazines and newspapers, BehaviorScan testing is coming closer to measuring the real world.

There are seven magazines that have established "sub-regional" editions for testing within the BehaviorScan markets. BehaviorScan magazine insertions are a separate buy from regional advertising placed in these magazines. For magazines that get most of their circulation through newsstand sales, a special BehaviorScan issue that contains the client's test advertising is produced for the stores within the test market. Subscription magazines have special editions designated by zip codes.

BehaviorScan also allows advertisers to conduct newspaper tests in each BehaviorScan market. The local daily paper in a market will insert weekday split-run advertising for BehaviorScan clients on a specified "BehaviorScan Drop Day." BehaviorScan newspaper drops are targeted to individual subscriber homes within the test markets.

Here is a sample of questions that BehaviorScan can answer:

1. How many consumers try my brand and how many buy it a second, third, or more times afterwards?
2. What volume level will my brand achieve in one year? Two years?
3. What affects sales more—increased advertising or new copy?
4. Who are my brand's buyers and what other product categories do they buy?
5. What television programs (or dayparts) reach the largest number of purchasers of my brand?

Nielsen Home*Scan

This is a new single source measurement that incorporates a database that can be used for marketing and media planning. The database measures a large number of U.S. households and records who they are demographically and which brands they buy.

By the end of 1992, Nielsen Home*Scan—through NPD-Nielsen, Inc.—will scan purchases in a sample of 40,000 households, and measure 1,000 packaged goods categories and 9,000 brands. Like BehaviorScan, Home*Scan will measure magazine and newspaper reading and television viewing and correlate that data with purchase data. Two of the big differences between Nielsen Home*Scan and BehaviorScan are (1) Nielsen will require consumers to do their own scanning by using small UPC portable hand scanners, while BehaviorScan uses store scanners and requires consumers to have identification cards that alert the store personnel to keep buying data separate from other data that scanners record. With Nielsen, the number of different kinds of products recorded will be wide—coming from a variety of retail outlets, convenience stores, food stores, department stores, drug stores, discount stores, liquor stores, and toy stores. (2) Nielsen's sample is national while BehaviorScan's covers six markets: Pittsfield, Massachusetts; Marion, Indiana; Eau Claire, Wisconsin; Grand Junction, Colorado; and Cedar Rapids, Iowa. (See Figure 5.2.)

The kinds of questions that Home*Scan will answer are similar to those of BehaviorScan, including media planning questions.

ScanAmerica

ScanAmerica is owned by Arbitron and had been planning for a single source measurement for some time. In 1991, it was finally launched with customers such as CBS, Young & Rubicam, and Bristol-Myers Squibb, but in September 1992 the national ScanAmerica gave up on its national TV ratings service. This service combined network TV ratings with product purchase measurements. While advertisers talked about a single-source measurement, they apparently were not willing to pay enough for Arbitron to make a profit.

FIGURE 5–2. Nielsen's Home*Scan.

Photo showing a package being scanned by hand with Nielsen's Home*Scan.

Geodemographic Measurements

A technique that is about twenty years old, and is still being developed, is that of correlating precise geographic and demographic data with media audience data. The idea behind this kind of measurement is that people with the same life-styles and income tend to live in the same geographic vicinity. Areas can be identified by zip codes and product purchases. They also can be identified by correlating purchasing data with census tract data in areas as small as a city block. Therefore, a media planner may be able to select media that will reach them precisely, with little or no waste. If measurements are not available for every single block or zip code area, then mathematical procedures are used to refine the data.

FIGURE 5-2. Continued.

Once a week panel members who make scans transmit information directly to Nielsen's computers via telephone.

Some of the companies who are involved in selling this kind of information are Claritas' PRIZM, using zip code data; C.A.C.I. Company's ACORN, which analyzes life-styles on a census block; and Arbitron, which has a measurement called Product Target AID. Much of the analysis made by these companies, including charts, maps, and tables, is made by computer.

A new player in this arena is National TV Conquest, a subsidiary of Donnelley's ClusterPlus Workstation. ClusterPlus assigns each of the nation's neighborhoods (often defined by Zip + 4 code) to one of 47 clusters, with each cluster representing many neighborhoods across the United States that share key demographic and socioeconomic features. National TV Conquest connects Nielsen ratings with those clusters identified as having a high propensity to own or use a product and/or who have a high composition of users, based on syndicated or proprietary product user information. Although the ratings are not true user ratings, the cluster analysis does provide a powerful way to examine the media habits of lifestyle groups who tend to use or own a particular product.

To this date, geodemographic measurements have not been widely used, at least not by advertising agencies. Some clients, however, have used these techniques with varying degrees of success. Questions have been raised about whether it is economically possible to upgrade data as time passes; whether television programs, for example, can be classified by life-styles; and whether data collected over time will be valid.

Other New Measurement Ideas

The Weinblatt Measurements

This era seems to have spawned many ideas for measuring media in ways not thought of before. Lee Weinblatt, chief executive officer of the Pretesting Company, Englewood, New Jersey, has created a wristwatch and a pair of reading glasses that measure magazine and television audiences. The watch measures readership by recording transmissions from microchips placed in magazine ads. The glasses, coupled with an infrared transmitter in the TV set, can record who is watching television.

These two are called "passive" measuring devices because the wearer does not have to respond in any way. No buttons need be pushed, and no records made by writing.

The wristwatch looks like any other wristwatch, but is equipped with a recorder that reads signals from the microchips embedded in ads that are to be tested. When the watch comes within nine inches of the magazine, it begins recording the name of the magazine, and how long the respondent looked at it. It stops when the respondent puts the magazine aside.

The glasses require a recorder that sits atop a TV set and tells whether a respondent is looking at the screen. When the user looks away, it stops recording.

The A.C. Nielsen Company is testing the idea at present. Both devices are so new that no records of adoptions have been recorded at this time.

Conclusions

All of these new measurement ideas should have some effect on the quality of media planning because they can provide better insights into media audiences; some of these measurements even provide insights into the consuming behavior of these audiences. In fact, it seems clear that what media planners want more than anything is to be able to prove that any medium chosen will sell more of a product than any other medium. This idea goes back to the Audience Concepts Committee of the Advertising Research Foundation's 1961 model of the ultimate media comparison: to show that there *is* a direct relationship between a media vehicle and sale. Perhaps these new measurements won't quite reach the ultimate comparison; certainly they will move media planning closer to the goal than it has ever been before.

Ron Kaatz, formerly senior vice president and director of media resources and research at J. Walter Thompson, and now a professor of advertising at Northwestern University's Medill School of Journalism, asked an assembly at Chicago's Marketing and Media Workshop, "While a move to people-meters would improve our national TV rating system, in the long run, would product usage ratings be a more useful improvement?" The response to this question was that 64 percent agreed and 36 percent disagreed. This result suggests that planners want both improvements, but some want something more than better ratings.

The implication for students and those entering the world of media planning is that it is important to know what is going on in the area of new measurements, and to be prepared to use innovations in the most efficient ways.

QUESTIONS FOR DISCUSSION

1. Essentially, what is the advantage of a passive people meter over a non-passive meter?
2. What is the main concept underlying single source measurements?
3. What are the main differences between BehaviorScan and Home*Scan measurements of products that consumers purchased?
4. What advantages would single source measurements have over simple demographic measurements for media planning?

SELECTED READINGS

ACORN, *ACORN Market Segment Descriptions*, C.A.C.I., Market Analysis Division, 1982, 1–18.

Broadcasting Staff, "1987 Ushers in the People Meter Era," *Broadcasting,* January 5, 1987, 59–63.

Cebrzynski, Gregg, "New Research Tools Provide 'Accurate' Attention Data," *Marketing News,* April 11, 1986, 5ff.

Gay, Verne, "Automatic Metering Service Signs JWT," *Advertising Age,* November 17, 1986, 6.

Gay, Verne, "AGB May Resurface: Percy Stops Service," *Advertising Age,* August 8, 1988, 2, 43.

Gullen, Phil, and Hugh Johnson, "Relating Product Purchasing and TV Viewing," *Journal of Advertising Research*, December 1986/January 1987, 9–19.

Kaatz, Ron, "Mediology: Feedback '85," *Marketing and Media Decisions*, November 1985, 88–89.

Larson, Erik, "Watching Americans Watch TV," *Atlantic Monthly,* March 1992, 66–80.

Papazian, Edward, "More People-Meter Games: What Constitutes Viewing?" *Media Matters,* September 1986, 5.

Papazian, Edward, "Reservations about Single Source," *Marketing and Media Decisions*, October 1986, 104.

Phelps, Stephen P., "Media Planning . . . The Measurement Gap," *Marketing and Media Decisions*, July 1986, 148–149.

Staff, "ScanAmerica Tells You Precisely Who's Watching, Who's Buying," *Beyond the Ratings* (Arbitron), March 1986, 7.

Staff, "Can Geodemographics Simplify Media Planning?" *Marketing and Media Decisions*, August 1984, 66–82.

Staff, "Reducing Costs and Increasing Efficiency with ERIM TESTIGHT," *Nielsen Researcher,* No. 2, 1985, 2–7.

Staff, "Networks and Ad Agencies Battle over Estimates of TV Viewership," *The Wall Street Journal,* January 7, 1987, 1.

Walley, Wayne, "Arbitron Folds National ScanAmerica," *Advertising Age,* September 7, 1992, 36.

.

6

Reach, Frequency, and Effective Frequency

The preceding chapter introduced the concept of audience accumulation along with other measurements. This chapter amplifies the subject of accumulation in terms of reach and frequency, two of the most important considerations in planning media. Reach and frequency are parts of strategy planning and can be manipulated to attain certain marketing and media objectives. Generally, when broad message dispersion patterns are needed, then high levels of reach will be planned. But when a great deal of repetition is needed, then high frequency or effective frequency levels will be planned. Sometimes planning will have to attain both high reach and high frequency.

What Is Reach (in Broadcast Media)?

Reach (formerly called "coverage" in the early days of media planning) is a measurement of audience accumulation (See Chapter 5 for a review of the accumulation concept). Reach measurements tell planners how many different prospects or households are in a media vehicle's audience over a period of time, originally measured over four weeks, but now examined over any number of weeks the planner feels are relevant. The term "different" is meant to indicate that no one is counted more than once, in a reach measurement.

Frequency is a measurement that provides planners with the average number of times in a given period a vehicle or vehicles were exposed. Note that at present "exposure" is the key measurement concept, but in a few years, this is expected to change from exposure of the vehicle to exposure to the average number of commercials seen in a specific period.

Reach is usually expressed as a percentage of a universe with whom a

TABLE 6–1.   An Example of a Four-Week Reach Measurement for Program X

Person	Week 1	Week 2	Week 3	Week 4
1	—	—	—	—
2	—	—	—	—
3	⊕	×	—	×
4	—	—	—	—
5	⊕	—	×	—
6	—	—	⊕	×
7	—	⊕	×	—
8	⊕	—	—	—
9	⊕	×	—	×
10	—	—	—	⊕
Ratings Each Week	40	30	30	40

For a weekly evening program: × = Viewed the program;
⊕ = Counted only in reach measurement.
GRPs = 140, reach = 70, frequency = 2.

planner is trying to communicate. If the universe is women aged 18 to 49, then all women 18 to 49 represent the universe.

Reach is unduplicated and is different from GRPs which are duplicated. The following example illustrates the difference:

> A weekly television program has an average weekly rating of 25. Therefore its four-week gross rating points are 100 (25 × 4 = 100). The same television program may have a four-week reach of 65 percent (or 65). Since reach is unduplicated, that number will be smaller than the gross rating points. To find this reach, the audience of the television program would have to be measured over a 4-week period.

The reason that audience members are counted only once in a reach measurement lies in the history of media research. When early planners were trying to decide what kind of measurement ought to be used to count the size of a vehicle's audience, some felt that an audience member would have to be exposed about three times to a vehicle before ads within that vehicle would have any effect. Other planners disagreed, saying that it could not be known how many exposures would be required. Planners decided to compromise and to count one exposure to a vehicle as evidence of reach, because whether or not the ad was seen, there was a large difference between being exposed and not being exposed. To be exposed at least once meant that audiences then had an opportunity to see ads within the vehicle. There obviously would be no opportunity to see ads if there were no exposure.

Another historical reason for the development of reach concerned the invention of a statistic for radio and television that would parallel the audience reach of a monthly magazine. Planners realized it would be unfair to compare a one-week broadcast rating with the reach of a monthly issue of a magazine. Obviously the magazine reach would be higher, but by using a four-week reach for broadcast media, the planner now had a statistic that was fairly comparable to that of a monthly magazine in terms of audience size.

Table 6–1 illustrates the measurement of reach, using a sample of ten persons. The sample size for measuring reach is actually much larger, but ten was used to simplify the concept. While four weeks is the usual measuring period, reach can be measured for almost any period of time. Four weeks happens to have become a standard measuring unit, easily conforming to a monthly accounting period.

Table 6–1 is interpreted this way. Persons 3, 5, 8, and 9 saw the program in week 1, so the one week rating is 40% or 40 (four out of 10). Since viewers are counted only once, the one-week reach is the same as the one week rating. In week number two, only one *new* person was added to the audience so the second week rating was 10 and the two week reach was 50 (or 40 for week one and + 10 for week two). In week three, only one new viewer was added so the rating was 10, but the three week reach was 60. In week four, again, only one new viewer was added (Viewer No. 10) and the four week reach was 70. Note that persons 3, 5, 6, and 9 viewed the program more than once, in the four week period but were counted only once for the purpose of calculating reach. Also note that the one week rating is unduplicated, so it would be correct to call that rating the one-week reach, though common practice usually refers to it as a rating.

Kinds of Reach

There are two different kinds of reach that a planner would like to know about in broadcast planning: (a) the four-week reach of an individual vehicle such as a television program, or (b) the combined reach of four or five television programs that would be used as a single package in an ad campaign.

No matter which the planner is interested in, the same principles apply, namely, that audience members are counted only once, no matter how many times they may see the vehicle within a four-week period. In situation (b) where four television programs are being considered for one campaign package, some audience members may be exposed three or four times to only one television program, while other audience members may be exposed to all four television programs a different number of times. But if they see any one of the four programs at least once, they are counted as having been reached in a four-week period.

Suppose, for example, that the reach of four programs was 35 million men, aged 18–34. This means that if the planner places a commercial in each of the four television programs, it is estimated that 35 million men, aged 18–34, will have an opportunity to see at least one of those four vehicles and, hopefully, one of the four commercials within the vehicles. The word ''hopefully'' is a reminder that reach is concerned only with vehicle exposure, not ad exposure. Other measurements can provide ad exposure, but they are not yet available on a syndicated basis.

Table 6–2 shows how the reach of four television programs is calculated. Eight people viewed one of the four programs (called Program A, B, C, or D) at least once in a four-week period. A person is counted only once regardless of

TABLE 6-2.   Calculating the Combined Reach of Four Television Programs

Person	Program A	Program B	Program C	Program D	Total (four programs)
1	⊕	×	—	—	⊕
2	⊕	×	—	×	⊕
3	—	—	—	⊕	⊕
4	—	⊕	×	×	⊕
5	—	—	⊕	—	⊕
6	—	—	⊕	—	⊕
7	⊕	×	×	×	⊕
8	—	—	—	—	—
9	⊕	×	—	×	⊕
10	—	—	—	—	—
Reach	40%	50%	40%	50%	80%

× = Viewed program at least once; ⊕ = Counted in reach measurement.

how many programs were viewed. Therefore Person 1, who watched both Programs A and B, is counted only once, as is Person 7, who watched all four programs. The combined reach of the four programs is 8 or 80 percent. Each of the programs also had a reach of its own for the four weeks. The combined reach of all four programs is more properly known as the *net reach* of the four. Other terms that are sometimes used to describe the net reach of four television programs are "cumulative audience," or "audience accumulated by four television programs," or "net unduplicated audience." Each is correct, but in popular usage people are more likely to say, "The reach of four programs is. . . ."

Relationship of Reach to Coverage

Students and others are sometimes confused about whether to use the term coverage or reach when referring to audience accumulation data. The terms can be interchangeable because coverage sometimes is synonymous with reach. A better answer is that coverage and reach are quite different because coverage *could mean potential* to be exposed to the advertising, while reach refers to those people who *actually are* exposed. (See Chapter 4 for complete explanations of coverage for each advertising medium.)

TABLE 6-3.   How to Use the Terms Reach and Coverage

Use Reach	to express a whole number or percentage of different people actually exposed only once to a media vehicle or combination of vehicles. Example: Television program X reaches 9 million men aged 18–34 within a four-week period. Example: Magazine Y has a reach of 25 percent of men aged 18–34 with an average issue.
Use Coverage	to express the potential audience of a broadcast medium *or the actual audience* of a print medium exposed only once. Example: A network television program may have a coverage of 95 percent of TV homes in the U.S. Example: Magazine Y has a 25 percent coverage of men aged 18–34. (Means same as reach.)

FIGURE 6-1. The Shape of a Typical Reach Curve

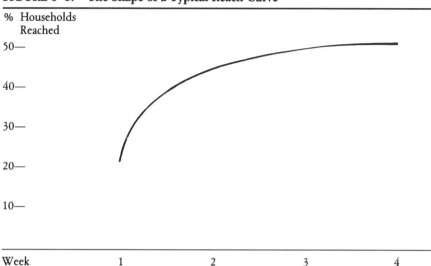

Popular usage of these terms provides the basic answer. Coverage *usually* refers to potential audience for broadcast media and to actual delivered audience for print media. Reach *always* refers to the audience actually delivered by any advertising vehicle. Table 6-3 treats the distinction in capsule form.

How Reach Builds Over Time

Reach for television programs accumulates, or builds, in a fairly consistent pattern over time. The first time a program is telecast, it accumulates the largest number of viewers. The second time it is telecast, most of the viewers are repeat viewers, although some new viewers are accumulated. The third and subsequent telecasts accumulate even fewer new viewers. If viewing over a four-week period were plotted on a graph, the curve drawn would look similar to that in Figure 6-1. If the same program were telecast over a long period of time, the curve eventually would flatten out and become almost horizontal, though it would never become perfectly horizontal because there would still be some persons, somewhere, tuning in the program for the first time.

An interesting aspect of the reach curve is that when the curve for any single program is compared with that for another program, the curves are similar in shape even though one curve may be higher or lower on a graph than another. Figure 6-2 shows reach accumulated for two television shows over a period of four consecutive telecasts.

Study of the reach curves for multiple television programs or commercials over a period of twenty-six weeks shows basically similar curves with only slight variations. Figures 6-3 and 6-4 plot reach curves for a period of twenty-six weeks for different parts of the day (called *dayparts*) and for different weight (GRP) levels.

FIGURE 6–2.   Reach Curves of Two Television Programs

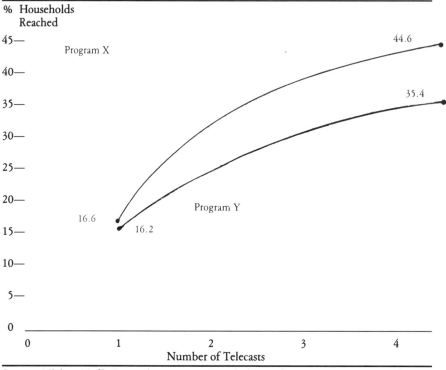

% Households
Reached

Source: Nielsen Media Research, Program Cumulative Audiences Report. Reprinted by permission.

FIGURE 6–3.   Net Reach Curves of Multiple Programs for Twenty-Six Weeks*

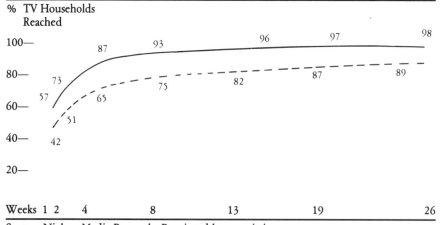

% TV Households
Reached

Source: Nielsen Media Research. Reprinted by permission.
KEY: ————— Prime time; ————— Monday–Friday daytime.
*Heavy weights of GRPs are used in each.

FIGURE 6–4   Net Reach Curves of Multiple Commercials for Twenty-Six Weeks with Different Weight Levels*

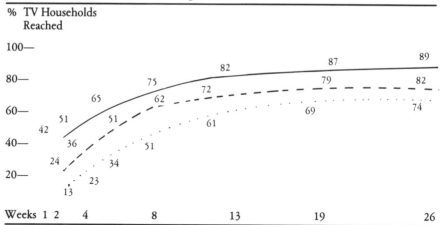

Source: Nielsen Media Research. Reprinted by permission.
Note: The more messages telecast, the more gross rating points they will accumulate. Therefore there is a direct relationship between the number of gross rating points achieved in a four-week period, and the degree of frequency that develops.
KEY: Light Schedule ············8 Messages/4 Weeks;
       Moderate Schedule ———— 16 Messages/4 Weeks;
       Heavy Schedule ———— 48 Messages/ 4 Weeks.
*Monday–Friday daytime schedules only.

What Is Reach (in Print Media)?

An issue of a magazine or newspaper, not time as in broadcast media, provides the basic measuring unit for reach measurement in print media. One does not usually speak of the four-week reach of Magazine A, although there are measurements that estimate audience accumulation over time for an average issue of a magazine. Generally speaking, monthly magazines have a longer issue life than weeklies and general content magazines a longer life than news-oriented magazines.

Magazine reach can be expressed in a number of ways:

1. Audience reach of one issue of a magazine, for example, the reach of the July 1 issue of *Newsweek* (may also be called the total audience of *Newsweek*)
2. Target audience reach of multiple issues of the same magazine, for example, the reach (or net unduplicated audience) of the July 1, July 8, July 15, July 22, and July 29 issues of *Newsweek*
3. Target audience reach of single issues of different magazines within the same month, for example, the reach (or net unduplicated audience) of July issues of *McCall's, Ladies Home Journal, Reader's Digest,* and *TV Guide*
4. The reach of single or multiple issues of different magazines oc-

TABLE 6–4.   The Meaning of Reach, Summarized

Reach is
1. A measurement of audience accumulation
2. An unduplicated statistic
3. Measured, although it can sometimes be estimated
4. Measured for a single vehicle, or a group of different vehicles
5. Measured for subsequent issues of the same magazine, e.g., the seven-issue reach of *TV Guide* is . . .
6. Reported for a four-week period of television watching
7. Reported for almost any period of time in broadcast measurements
8. Reported by the issue in print media
9. Reported either as a raw number or as a percentage of some universe
10. Reported for households, or for individuals in a demographic category
11. Another term for coverage in print media
12. Measured on the basis of exposure to a vehicle or vehicles
13. Not measured on the basis of exposure to ads in vehicles, but commercial exposure is expected to be measured by passive people meters
14. A measurement that tells how many different people had an opportunity to see ads in vehicles
15. A media strategy that shows dispersion of audiences

curring throughout the advertising campaign, for example, the reach of *Popular Mechanics* in June and August, *Field & Stream* in July and August, and *Sport* in June and July

Because there are many qualities expressed in a reach measurement, it becomes important to know them all. Table 6–4 summarizes these qualities.

Frequency in Broadcast and Print Media

Frequency is a companion statistic to reach that tells the planner the average number of times that audience members were exposed to a broadcast program within a four-week period, or were exposed to issues of different print media. Reach is a measure of message dispersion, indicating how widely the message may be received in a target universe. Frequency is a measure of repetition, indicating to what extent audience members were exposed to the same vehicle or group of vehicles. Both reach and frequency are valuable decision-making tools because they give the planner different options for arranging message delivery in a media plan.

Frequency is usually calculated from measurement data. The formula is the same for broadcast and print media:

$$\text{Frequency} = \frac{\text{GRPs or total duplicated audience}}{\text{Reach}}$$

Example in broadcast: Program X telecast once each week has an average rating of 20 for each week. It has a four-week reach of 43. The frequency is as follows:

$$\text{Frequency} = \frac{20 \times 4}{43} \text{ or } 1.9$$

Example in Print: *TV Guide* has a reach of 54 for six consecutive issues. Its one-issue reach is 29.5.

$$\text{Frequency} = \frac{29.5 \times 6}{54.0} \text{ or } 3.3$$

Frequency Distribution

Persons who use measurement data sometimes forget that frequency is an average and not an absolute number. It is subject, therefore, to the characteristics of all statistical averages. Averages, for example, are affected by extreme scores in a distribution. A few very high numbers may bring up the average of all other scores while a few very low ones may drag down the average. The only way to guard against being deceived by a frequency statistic is to look at a frequency distribution and see whether some segments of a sample are getting disproportionately more frequency than others.

Table 6–5 shows a sample divided into fixed quintiles and each group's reach and frequency. (*Fixed quintiles* means that the sample of audience members exposed was divided into five equal groups, each with 20 percent of the total number exposed.) The distribution of frequency is obviously unequal in Table 6–5. Some of the quintiles received much more frequency than others. This phenomenon is known as *skew*.

Figure 6–5 dramatizes the skew by showing the frequency distribution in graphic form. While Program X had a 5.2 average frequency in Figure 6–5, some segments were receiving more frequency than others. The average frequency of 5.2 does not indicate the disparity. The planner may be deceived by the average frequency level of Program X, thinking that every home in the sample tuned to the program 5.2 times during a four-week period. The illustration shows otherwise. Frequency distributions with a large skew are called *unbalanced*.

Frequency distributions can be arranged according to quintiles, but they can also be arranged according to single increments of exposure, giving the planner a more detailed picture of exposure. Table 6–6 shows a frequency dis-

TABLE 6–5.   Quintile Analysis of Tune-ins for Program X

Divisions of Viewer Sample	Reach (%)	Frequency	GRPs
Heaviest 20%	17	11	187
Next 20%	17	6	103
Third 20%	17	5	85
Next 20%	17	3	51
Lightest 20%	17	1	17
Totals*	85	5.2 avg.	443

*Reach of entire sample, 85; frequency of entire sample, 5.2; gross rating points, 443.

FIGURE 6-5. Frequency Distribution for Program X

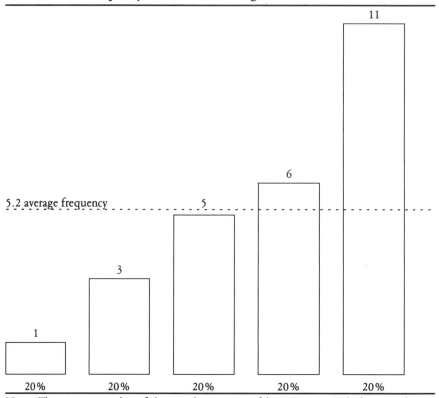

Note: The average number of times each group tuned in to Program X is shown at the top of each column.

TABLE 6-6. Frequency Distribution of a Media Plan

		Frequency of Exposure	Number Exposed (thousands)
		0	8,227
		1	3,125
		2	2,269
		3	3,632
Reach	71.97	4	5,235
Frequency	4.01	5	2,474
Gross Impressions	84,749	6	1,201
Number Reached	21,129	7	1,462
Universe	29,356	8	771
		9	622
		10	135
		11	104
		12	98
			21,129 = 71.97%

TABLE 6–7.   Four-Week Reaches and Frequencies of Two Media Plans

Frequency of Exposure	Plan A	Plan B
1	24%	20%
2	16	15
3	9	12
4–5	6	13
6–8	5	10
9–12	5	4
13 +	5	1
Average Frequency	4.0	3.6
Total Reach	70	75
Reach at 3 + Frequency	30	40

tribution of exposure for all media in a given plan. Subtracting the number reached from the universe size shows that 8,227,000 of the universe of 29,356,000 did not see any of the vehicles used. Some 3,125,000 were exposed only once out of the twelve opportunities for exposure, and 2,269,000 were exposed to any two out of the twelve exposures. The number exposed at any frequency is unduplicated, meaning that these people are counted only once. A person receiving twelve exposures would not be counted at any other frequency level.

Frequency distributions therefore provide planners with a method of determining the pattern of repetition that the plan provides. Alternative plans may provide more or fewer repetition patterns. More important, however, is that the distribution will show whether repetition is spread widely, or only among a very few prospects.

The example in Table 6–7 shows how a frequency distribution can help a media planner decide among alternative plans. Plan A has a 4.0 frequency and Plan B, a 3.6. If frequency is important, then Plan A would seem to be the better plan.

Upon studying a frequency distribution such as the one in Table 6–7, however, the planner learns something that could change the decision: Plan A delivers more audience members at exposure levels 1 and 2. But for exposures 3–8, Plan B is superior. Plan B reaches more persons than does Plan A at the 3 or higher exposure level. If the advertising effort requires that people receive high levels of exposures (higher levels of frequency), then Plan B is the obvious choice. But only a frequency distribution made it possible for the planner to see why B was better than A.

The Relationship of Reach to Frequency

It is necessary to understand that reach and frequency occur at the same time, but at different rates and in an inverse relationship. Within a given number of gross rating points, as one goes up, the other goes down. Let us first look at the mathematics to understand how these companion terms relate to each other:

$$\text{Reach} \times \text{Frequency} = \text{Gross Rating Points}$$

An advertising schedule composed of a 50 reach with a 2.0 frequency yields 100 GRPs. If these same 100 GRPs were obtained in a different mixture of media, the reach might increase, but the frequency would decline. Conversely, a 100 GRP schedule in still other media mixtures might produce higher frequency, but less reach.

Seymour Banks, formerly vice president of Leo Burnett Company, explained the dynamics of reach and frequency relative to rating size and number of telecasts, as follows:

> Reach is not directly proportional to either ratings or the number of telecasts. Rather, as ratings increase or as the number of telecasts used increases, reach also rises but at a decreasing rate. This is more easily understood when we consider that the companion of reach is frequency. And when the rating or the number of telecasts increases, some of this increase goes towards boosting reach, while some of it contributes toward an increase in frequency.[1]

Up to a certain point, it is relatively easy to build reach. By selecting television programs of a different nature in which to place commercials, it is possible to reach different kinds of people. But there is a point of diminishing returns, where each attempt to build more reach by selecting more and different kinds of programs results in reaching the same persons over and over again, with an increase in frequency rather than in reach. Some homes may never tune in their television sets over an entire month, so they are impossible to reach with TV in that month. Reach will increase as ratings and number of telecasts increase, but it will begin to decline in rate (not total) over time.

The point of diminishing returns mentioned in the previous paragraph occurs at about 70 percent and varies somewhat because some target audiences are easier or more difficult to reach. Then frequency begins to rise much faster than reach as additional media vehicles are added to the schedule. The problem can be seen in the following illustration:

Suppose that a media planner has devised a plan requiring the attainment of an 80 percent reach level. The planner selects a number of media vehicles, with a net reach of 75 percent. The question now facing the planner is how to reach the remaining 5 percent. When another vehicle is added to the list, reach may go up perhaps 1 percent, while frequency may go up a great deal. So it may take a large number of additional vehicles to reach the total of 80 percent. Meanwhile, as vehicles are added, frequency rises very fast because every new vehicle adds only a miniscule amount to reach and a large amount to frequency.

---

1. Banks, Seymour, "How to Estimate Reach and Frequency," Leo Burnett Company, 1960, p.5.

To summarize: reach and frequency are inversely related. As reach rises quickly, frequency tends to be low. Conversely, as frequency rises quickly, reach tends to be low.

Programs That Develop Reach or Frequency

Programs that develop reach are those whose contents tend to change during a given telecast or from week to week. As the contents change, so do audience types. When movies are broadcast, with a drama one week and a comedy the next, two different audiences are likely to develop (with some overlap, of course). Movies, therefore, tend to develop more reach than frequency. But a soap opera broadcast five days a week, or twenty times a month, will tend to draw a relatively smaller audience but one with greater frequency of viewing. An increase in the number of messages delivered also increases the potential for higher frequency.

Table 6–8 indicates that the drama had a much larger reach than did the soap opera, but the soap opera had a much larger frequency than did the drama. Part of the reason for the larger frequency was the frequency of telecasts. The more often a program is broadcast, the more likely it is that it will have a higher frequency.

Roadblock versus Scatter Strategy

Planning media to build reach can be accomplished in the ways just discussed, but there are two other ways: (a) purchasing commercials on all three networks during the same half hour, called a *roadblock*, or (b) buying a *scatter plan* that places commercials within a number of different program types and time periods, thus bringing in new audience members. Figure 6–6 on the following page shows the differences. The chart shows that when the number of GRPs is low, the roadblock produces more reach. When the number of GRPs is high, either technique will produce about the same reach.

TABLE 6–8. Comparison of Frequencies for Two Different Kinds of Programs

	Daytime Soap Opera (broadcast twenty times a month)	Nighttime Drama (broadcast once a week)
Total Audience Rating per Telecast	9.7*	19.4
Four-Week Reach	25.4	40.0
Frequency	7.6	1.9
	$\dfrac{9.7 \times 20^*}{25.4} = 7.6$	$\dfrac{19.4 \times 4}{40.0} = 1.9$

*The 9.7 rating is the average rating for a program broadcast 5 times each week (from Monday to Friday) and 4 weeks a month, or 20 telecasts.

FIGURE 6–6.   Difference between Roadblock and Scatter to Build Reach *

Reach %	114	111	104	104	101	101

Source: Nielsen Media Research (Prime time, Nov.–Dec. 1977). Reprinted by permission.
*Roadblock indexed to scatter.

Frequency:						
Roadblock	1.0	1.5	2.0	2.5	3.0	3.5
Scatter	1.2	1.7	2.1	2.6	3.0	3.5
GRPs	50	100	150	200	250	300

Effective Frequency and Reach

One of the most significant changes in media planning in recent years is the development of the concepts of *effective frequency and reach*. These concepts help planners understand a number of important facts that affect media planning such as which of two plans is better, or how much repetition is needed to achieve communication objectives. Strategically, these concepts are also attempts by planners to go beyond and improve regular reach and frequency data (as described in Chapter 6), and result in better planning.

This chapter explains in detail what effective frequency and reach are, how they are used, some continuing problems with both the theory and practice, and a discussion of the role that both may play in the future.

The Underlying Need for Effective Frequency

For many years advertising practitioners have been trying to answer some important questions about advertising repetition—questions, such as the following, whose answers are all related to the effective frequency concept.

1. How much advertising is enough?
2. How many times must an advertising message be repeated for it to effectively communicate?

3. How much reach and frequency are ideal for a media plan?
4. How can planners improve the art of media planning?

Most of the research on these questions was directed toward answering the second question.

The Essence of Effective Frequency

Effective frequency may be defined as the amount of frequency (or repetition) necessary for advertisements to be effective in communicating. The underlying assumption, of course, is that average frequency used in most media plans is *not* effective. Therefore, effective frequency may represent a great improvement over ordinary reach and frequency numbers used in traditionally created media plans.

The problem with ordinary reach and frequency is that they are not directly related to the effects that media plans may produce. They do not help a planner determine the adequacy of alternative plans. An ordinary reach number simply represents opportunities for audiences to see advertisements. There is no guarantee that those who are reached actually see any of the ads because exposure measurements used to compare media do not cover exposure to ads. Even if audiences see ads in a vehicle, there is no way to know whether the ads were effective or not simply by noting the reach of a media plan. Ordinary frequency generated by a plan is an average number of target audiences exposed to the media vehicles selected. Average frequency, too, is not related to the plan's effectiveness.

But planners who use effective frequency attempt to correct both situations by estimating the number of repetitions that are needed to attain communication goals such as achieving brand awareness, attitude changes, brand switching, and recall of messages, to name a few.

If, for example, someone sets a communication goal of building 70 percent brand awareness, a media planner should ask, how much repetition will help accomplish the task? Through test marketing, or studying responses to advertising done in the past, an estimate may be made of the vehicle frequency level needed. One unusual aspect of making an effective frequency decision is that it represents a technique of media planning that is different from those used in the past.

In the first place, building brand awareness is usually thought to be a communication goal—not a media goal. So by using effective frequency, planners are enlarging the scope of their work, combining media and creative activities. That combination in itself is a relatively new idea in media planning.

Second, there often is no data by which to determine objectively how much repetition is necessary to accomplish the task. Therefore the answer to the planner's question mentioned earlier may have to be based on either experience, or specialized research. If experience is used as a basis for the

FIGURE 6–7: S-Shaped Response Curve

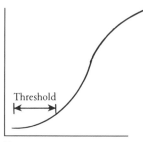

Frequency

answer, then it may be rather subjective, because it is difficult to parse out a media vehicle's contribution to building brand awareness.

If research is used to find the answer to the awareness problem, then it will take both time and money, and the end result may not be conclusive, because it is difficult to prove that research findings are applicable to all plans equally.

The key point to be made is that it is not easy to prove the relationship between effective frequency and a 70 percent goal of brand awareness; the relationship is a subtle one, not a simple cause and effect relationship.

Response Curves and Effective Frequency

An important point in understanding the meaning of effective frequency is that the number at which point frequency is called ''effective'' is based on ideas of how much repetition is needed to communicate with consumers. This number has been found or estimated by observing what has happened at varying repetitive levels to achieve communication goals in the past. The results, plotted on a graph, have been called ''response functions'' or ''response curves.''

A response function is a measurement of advertising effect (as is a response curve). Over a period of many years, practitioners have hypothesized about how advertising works. Most have felt that advertising does not work immediately. According to Herbert Krugman, author of the ''three hit theory,'' the first time an advertisement is perceived may result in audiences raising questions about the brand such as, ''What is it?'' After audiences have perceived the same ad a second time, they may ask, ''What of it?'' The second exposure, then, is where consumers react to the commercial and begin to compare alternative brands. The third exposure is a reminder of the other two, and is the beginning of a time where consumers pay little or no attention. Krugman hypothesized that when audiences are in the market to buy a product, they may return to that second repetition. Therefore, effective frequency begins after the second repetition, *but only when a consumer is ready to buy a given product.*

Many other practitioners have hypothesized that audiences begin to respond to advertising at about the third repetition. Beginning with the third

FIGURE 6–8: Convex Response Curve

Response

Frequency

repetition, the number of responses begin to grow with each additional repetition. In fact, response rises, but at a declining rate. If this hypothesis is plotted on a graph it will have an "S shape." (See Figure 6–7.) The first two repetitions are a "threshold" which audiences have to pass before advertisements become effective.

Most researchers of advertising responses curve, however, have not found the S-shaped curve to occur very often. In fact, a different kind of curve, often called a "convex-shaped" or "convex" curve, has been found more often. Nevertheless, many media planners, who have adopted the effective frequency concept, believe that a convex curve represents a graphical picture of how repetition works in advertising. (See Figure 6–8.)

Effective Frequency Numbers

Effective frequency is expressed as a number. This number may vary from one repetition to as many as ten or more. Some planners, at first, thought the optimum effective frequency number was from three repetitions on. This was called the "three-plus" concept. Later, however, there was much agreement that the optimum effective frequency number could be as low as one or as many as nine (or more), or that the number could even be a range, such as a frequency level from two to seven. To date, this question has not been resolved, and more research on response functions may be needed to settle the argument.

What Is Effective Reach?

Effective reach is the second part of the concept. It represents the percent of a vehicle's audience reached at each effective frequency increment. If the effective frequency is believed to be from two to seven repetitions, then the reach is the sum of individual reach percentages for each frequency level. This can best be seen by the example in Table 6–9.

TABLE 6-9. How Effective Reach Is Calculated*

Frequency, or Number of Impressions	Percent Reached at Each Frequency Level		Percent Reached at Least One or More Times
1	19.4		67.2
2	13.9		47.8
3	10.4		33.9
4	7.8		23.6
5	5.8	28.1%**	15.8
6	4.1		10.5

*A frequency distribution for a reach of 67.2 and a frequency of 3.1.
**If effective frequency is from 3 to 6 repetitions, then effective reach is the sum of all percentages reached from 3 to 6 or, in the example, 28.1%.

This table shows that the effective reach number is dependent on effective frequency numbers. In this example, because effective frequency is defined as being from a three to a six frequency, then effective reach is found in the sum of percentages in the second column for frequencies 3, 4, 5, and 6, or 28.1 percent. Both effective frequency and reach are a necessary part of the same concept. They are not independent of each other.

A Brief History of Effective Frequency

Effective frequency, as an idea, existed prior to being given that name. In 1957, Brown, Lessler, and Weilbacher, in their book *Advertising Media,* wrote:

> It should be pointed out that there exists for every brand or product, a theoretical number of impressions required to convert each individual prospect into a purchaser.[2]

The authors gave an example of what their version of effective frequency was when they wrote:

> In order to maintain cigarette brand loyalty, it is necessary for the average smoker to receive sixteen television commercial messages for his usual brand, if the competitive copy claims are all roughly equivalent.

> And even though the notion of an average number of impressions required for action may be abstract, it does indicate the direction in which measurement must develop.[3]

This kind of measurement did not exist in 1957, but researchers ran many different kinds of experiments to learn if there was an optimum amount of repetition that could be called "effective."

---

2. Brown, Lyndon O., Lessler, Richard S., and Weilbacher, William M., *Advertising Media,* New York: The Ronald Press, 1957, p. 343.
   3. Ibid.

Two British researchers, S. Broadbent and S. Segnit, contributed to the development of effective frequency when they won a prize for a paper entitled, "Response Functions in Media Planning," as part of the 1967 Thomson Medals and Awards in London. They devised a technique for evaluating media plans by using response function data. They offered ideas on how alternative media plans might be compared on an effective frequency basis, even if they did not use the terms effective frequency. They also hypothesized about the nature of response curves.

In the United States, the person who first started to publicize the need for effectiveness measures in media planning was Alvin Achenbaum, who was then director of corporate planning and marketing services at J. Walter Thompson, New York. Achenbaum did not advocate the use of effective frequency as we know it now, but recommended the use of effective rating points (ERPs). ERPs were a combination of effective frequency and reach as a replacement for gross rating points (GRPs).

Probably the greatest impetus to establishing the concept in this country was the publication, in 1979, of *Effective Frequency: The Relationship between Frequency and Advertising Awareness* by Michael J. Naples.[4] This book, published by the Association of National Advertisers, became required reading for almost every planner in this country. After 1979, the concept spread throughout advertising agency media departments in the United States and is now used widely. Much of the background research that had been done on the concept was summarized in Naples's book. What follows is a brief summary of material in Naples's book covering significant research on the effective frequency concept.

Research That Underlies the Effective Frequency Concept

General Findings

The studies cited by Naples were performed by different persons for different reasons, but, in essence, they concluded that it takes at least two to three repeated exposures for a message to be learned. Some studies, like that done by Robert C. Grass for DuPont, found that some messages were effective from the third to the eighth exposure per month. Krugman's "three hit" theory was also discussed in these research projects. Most of the studies found that the effect of frequency increases, but at a declining rate. In essence, their conclusions correspond to the convex response curve. One of the studies, that done by Ogilvy & Mather, found that at the one frequency level, advertising effectiveness during different dayparts was relatively the same, but a higher frequency level at night was more effective than it was during other dayparts. Product category and brands also made a difference

---

4. Naples, Michael J., *Effective Frequency,* New York: Association of National Advertisers, Inc., 1979.

TABLE 6–10. Relationship of Frequency Levels and Purchasing the Same Brand Again

	Media Exposure (various number of repetitions)			
	0	1	2	3
Percent of brand's purchases repeated at the next purchase	54.4	58.4	62.6	63.1
Percent of gain		+ 4.0	+ 4.3	+ .04

in frequency effects. Two researchers (Appel and Jacobovits) found that too much frequency had negative effects, although they did not indicate how much repetition brought these effects about.

The McDonald Study

The most significant study reported by Naples in terms of motivating media planners to adopt the concept was done by Colin McDonald in 1971.[5] The study, commissioned by the London office of J. Walter Thompson, was analyzed and reported by Colin McDonald of the British Market Research Bureau. A report on that study appeared in Naples's 1979 book. The subsequent widespread publicity helped it become one of the leading pieces of research that underlie the effective frequency concept.

The methodology used in this study involved having a panel of consumers in Great Britain keep two kinds of records: the number of television, magazine, and newspapers that they were exposed to each day for thirteen weeks, and the number of brands (in nine product categories) they had purchased in the same time period. The specific time unit that was analyzed, the purchasing cycle for nine brand categories, ranged from an average of $1^{1}/_{2}$ to $2^{1}/_{2}$ weeks. The media exposures that McDonald measured were really vehicle exposures or opportunities to see (OTS) and not exposures to advertisements. In Naples's book, McDonald used terms that seemed to indicate that advertising exposure was being measured, but subsequent explanations made it clear that it was really OTS.

McDonald counted the panel's OTS for every brand in each purchase interval, and compared this with purchasing behavior, noting whether successive purchases at the beginning and end of each interval were of the same brand or a different brand.

On one hand, Jeremy Elliott, senior associate director of J. Walter Thompson, London, commenting on McDonald's study, wrote that "the first OTS increased retention of advertising and that a second OTS increased it as much again." But the third and any additional OTS in the purchase interval had little effect. (See Table 6–10.)

On the other hand, Elliott noted that OTS also had a different effect, the second OTS was about twice as effective as the first in bringing about brand

5. McDonald, Colin, "What Is the Short-Term Effect of Advertising?" in *Effective Frequency*, 1979, pp. 83–104.

TABLE 6–11. Relationship of Frequency Levels and Purchasing of Different Brands

	Media Exposure (various number of repetitions)			
	0	1	2	3
Percent of competitive purchases in which consumers switched to a different brand at the next purchase	17.2	20.91	27.4	27.9
Percent of gain		+ 3.7	+ 6.5	+ 0.5

switching. Elliott noted that brands that had two or more OTS in a purchasing interval were making gains at the expense of brands that had only one OTS. He concluded that "it takes greater stimulation to overcome inertia and change behavior than it does to maintain it."[6] Nevertheless, the third OTS still had no incremental value. (See Table 6–11.)

McDonald's study was important because it showed that it took at least two OTS to bring about brand switching, and that media plans ought to have at least as many to make frequency effective. Of course, the study was also well done, and that contributed further to its acceptance. Elliott also pointed out that J. Walter Thompson has undertaken another study, similar to McDonald's, to determine which levels of frequency are effective. The results of this study concluded that effective frequency should be defined as four-plus coverage.[7]

Naples's Conclusions about Effective Frequency Studies

After presenting many research studies that supported the idea of effective frequency, Naples arrived at some conclusions about the implications for media planners. The following is a summary of each of his conclusions:

1. One exposure of an advertisement to a target consumer group (within a purchase cycle) has little or no effect.
2. Because one exposure is usually ineffective, the main thrust of media planning should be on emphasizing frequency rather than reach.
3. Most of the research studies suggested that two exposures within a purchase cycle is an effective threshold level.
4. Three exposures within a purchase cycle, however, is felt to be optimal.
5. After three exposures within a purchasing cycle, advertising becomes more effective as frequency is increased, but at a decreas-

6. Elliott, Jeremy, "How Advertising Frequency Affects Advertising Effectiveness: Indications of Change," *ADMAP*, October 1985, pp. 512–515.

7. Cullen, Phil, and Johnson, Hugh, "Relating Product Purchasing and TV Viewing," *Journal of Advertising Research*, December 1986–January 1987, pp. 9–19.

ing rate. If this were drawn on a graph, it would appear as a convex curve rising from a zero point.

6. Wear-out of an advertising campaign is not caused by too much frequency *per se*. It is caused by copy and content problems.

7. Generally, small and less well-known brands will benefit most by increased frequency. Larger and well-known brands may or may not be helped by increasing frequency "depending on how close they are to advertising saturation levels."

8. Different dayparts on television are affected by different frequency levels. A similar idea applies to thin versus thick magazines, with the thinner ones having better response effects than the thicker ones.

9. Frequency responses are affected by the amount of money an advertiser spends as a percentage of the product category total. Those brands with the greatest proportion of exposures within their categories should also gain great effect when frequency is increased.

10. The responses due to increased frequency are not affected by different media. What is true for one medium is true for others.

11. Each brand may require a different level of frequency of exposure. One cannot generalize from a given brand's experiences to some other brand. Specialized research is required to find the unique frequency level for a brand.

12. Two brands spending the same amount of money for advertising may have different responses to their frequencies.[8]

Problems with the Effective Frequency Concept

When McDonald's study was published in Naples's book it was widely accepted among media planners. But as time went on, a number of questions began to be asked, not only of McDonald's study, but of other aspects of effective frequency research. These problems are summarized and discussed in the following paragraphs.

The Need for Product Category Differentiation

One of the major problems of effective frequency research was that most of it did not show much difference between frequency effects for various product categories. This lack of differentiation tended to mislead planners into thinking that effective frequency is the same for all product categories. Now, a growing number of planners have said "that idea cannot be correct." There *should* be differences between various product category frequency levels.

8. Naples, Michael, *Effective Frequency: The Relationship between Frequency and Advertising Effectiveness,* New York: Association of National Advertisers, 1979, pp. 63–82.

Unfortunately, no measurements exist to show just which levels are needed for different kinds of products. Until this problem is resolved, media planners will have to make subjective decisions about how much frequency is necessary. There is, however, some speculation that high-involvement products may need less frequency and low-involvement products may need more. The same idea may apply to frequency levels between interesting and noninteresting products. The role of frequency, then, may be to help break through the perceptual inertia of consumers for certain kinds of products.

Is There a Threshold?

Another problem with the concept is whether or not a "threshold" always exists before consumers begin to respond to advertising messages. Most of the research on the subject suggested that there were relatively few responses to the first few impressions of an advertising campaign. Advertising began to work with the second or third impression. Those who believed in the three-plus frequency concept felt that advertising began to be effective with the third impression. But many direct marketing practitioners objected, noting that, in their business, the first impressions often drew tremendous responses. Gus Priemer, then director of advertising service and media at S. C. Johnson, also noted that in his experience of new product introductions, the first impression had been able to generate noteworthy responses.

Members who attended a "Symposium on Effective Frequency" held in April, 1986, at Northwestern University also questioned whether a threshold was realistic. The consensus at that meeting was that most response curves are convex, not S-shaped. The S-shaped curve was the one that indicated there was a threshold. Nevertheless, many planners still believe in a threshold.

The Relationship between Good Advertising and Effective Frequency

There have been a great many questions asked about whether effective frequency could be affected by the quality of advertising messages. Why, for example, shouldn't the ad message play a more important role in determining how much frequency is effective? Dull, uninteresting copy may require a great deal more frequency than scintillating creative messages. But most of the research did not address that question. In fact, some planners believe that the role of media frequency in bringing about consumer responses has been grossly overstated.

Does Advertising Wear Out When There Is Too Much Frequency?

Some of the research cited by Naples showed that there were negative responses that occurred after using too much repetition. Some consumers may even forget an advertising message because of high levels of frequency. The research of Valentine Appel and L. Jacobovits (also reported in Naples's

TABLE 6-12.   Differences between Homes Tuned-in, Viewing, Exposed, and Re-
calling Commercial Content in St. Louis and Chicago

	St. Louis Index	Chicago Index
Homes tuned in to program	100	100
Homemakers viewing program	59	50
Viewers possibly exposed to commercial	36	38
Viewers recalling content of commercial	16	20

Source: Gomer, Frank G., and Vedder, Blair B., "Another Look Beyond the TV Ratings,"
A. N. A. Television Advertising Workshop, New York, June 17, 1964.

book), suggested that. (The shape of a wear-out curve was considered to be like an inverted U.) But there seems to be no wide-ranging concern about this potential problem among media planners.

In 1968, Robert C. Grass of DuPont, through his research, found that there were satiation effects on attention and learning levels as a result of increased advertising frequency.[9] After two or three exposures, attention and learning declined. Nonetheless, Grass also found, through a different piece of research, that favorable attitudes toward a company developed because of increased advertising frequency, and there were no diminishing returns.

The main problem, then, is when, and under what circumstances, does frequency affect wear-out? It should be remembered that those who use the three-plus concept assume that there is no wear-out, at least no wear-out caused by too much repetition. But some persons in the industry feel that there may be a range of wear-out, and after the range has been passed, wear-out begins. Achenbaum said that the range may be from three to ten, or perhaps, from two to seven, but he could not say with assurance (based on existing research) where the optimal range was.

Thus the problem exists. Planners will simply have to use judgment in answering this question until research provides a more definitive answer.

How Much Vehicle Exposure Equals Advertising Exposure?

One of the difficult things to know about effective frequency is how to translate vehicle exposures into advertising exposures. Much research on effective frequency has been based on advertising exposure. But media planners still use vehicle exposure as a basis for planning. Certainly, there is no one-to-one relationship between the two. The number of advertising exposures is assumed to be less than vehicle exposures simply because every audience member does not look at every advertisement. During a television program broadcast, people do many other things than watch commercials. Perhaps the best known research studies on the differences between vehicle and advertising exposure were done by the Foote, Cone & Belding and Needham, Louis & Brorby agencies in 1962 and 1963.

---

9. Grass, Robert C., and Wallace, Wallace H., "Satiation Effects of TV Commercials," in *Journal of Advertising Research*, September 1969, pp. 3–8.

As Table 6–12 shows, the number possibly exposed is considerably fewer than the number who viewed the program, and the recall level is even less than that, for both Chicago and St. Louis. If the "possibly exposed" group is considered the equivalent of "exposed" (and there is no reason to disagree with that assumption), then there is strong evidence that vehicle and audience frequency are very different.

The effective frequency concept for media planners relates most importantly to this point: How much media vehicle frequency is necessary to achieve the advertising exposure frequencies found in most of the research studies? Radio and television ratings and magazine audience exposures represent only exposures to vehicles. To go beyond vehicle frequency, we need research that either relates vehicle frequency to advertising frequency, or directly shows the effects of vehicle exposure frequency to a given response. Some research studies have tried to do the latter, but more research is obviously needed.

Some research, such as McDonald's, was devised to get around this problem by measuring opportunities to see the correlation between purchasing and brand switching. But it is doubtful that media planners can assume that McDonald's findings are directly translatable to a media plan based on vehicle reach and frequency. Members who attended the 1986 Effective Frequency Symposium recommended that media planners use rules of thumb in converting vehicle exposure to advertising exposures. One might, for example, reduce television vehicle exposures to 35 percent of the total because various research studies done over the years have suggested that of those who were exposed to a television program, an average of 35 percent would see the commercials within the program.

Such generalized rules of thumb tend to make media planning less accurate than it is now, and their use is obviously going to raise more questions about the validity of effective frequency than are being raised now. Adjustments of vehicle exposure cannot be a simple mathematical computation because marketing creative, media, and sales promotion strategies are too different for each brand to make such generalizations.

Should Media Planning Be Based on Purchasing Cycles?

Historically, a considerable amount of media planning was based on a four-week period. Today, reach and frequency are typically expressed in terms of periods of advertising and for the total media plan. But one of Naples's recommendations about effective frequency is to use the purchasing cycle instead. McDonald's study found purchasing cycles to be important in analyzing his data. Therefore, purchasing cycles have been recommended by McDonald and others as well.[10]

---

10. McDonald, Colin, "Individual Respondent Analysis Made Better with Complete Single Source Records," in *Effective Frequency: State of the Art,* New York: Advertising Research Foundation, 1982, pp. 181–194.

If they are used in media planning, reach and frequency may have to be calculated for time periods as short as one or two days, such as the cycle for milk, or for as long as one year, for products such as tire chains and grass seed. This practice could be problematical because the time span between purchases for any individual may not match the span for all the people who are product category users. If, for example, a product has a purchase cycle of one month, one individual may buy that product at the first day of the month, and others at the last. The average user may buy somewhere in between. Therefore an advertiser, trying to use a purchase cycle in media planning, would have to advertise all during the month in order to maximize opportunities for consumers to see advertisements for a given brand. What then would be the advantage of using a purchase cycle?

At present, there have been relatively few attempts to plan reach and frequency on the basis of purchase cycles, although some attempts have been made experimenting with flighting patterns.

Where Effective Frequency Stands Now in Media Planning

Despite all the problems and questions that have been raised about effective frequency as a technique for media planning, it seems as if it is here to stay. Often it is used in its most simple form, the three-plus version. At other times, it is imaginatively used.

The consensus seems to be that even though there are problems with the concept, it is worth using. It is, potentially, very useful to planners. If it is used moderately, over time, as more research becomes available, the concept will be improved a great deal. As a result, media planning will also be improved. Therefore its use ought to be continued.

Case Study 6–1 shows one approach to using effective frequency. (See Chapter 9 on how to set effective frequency levels.)

CASE STUDY 6–1
Using the Effective Frequency Concept to
Determine the Impact of Alternative Media Plans

The following is a practical example of how effective frequency might be used to judge the impact of three alternative media plans. Impact is defined as providing the largest number of responses to advertising at various frequency levels.

1. Reach, frequency, and target GRPs of three media plans:

	Monthly GRPs	Reach	Frequency
Daytime only plan	296	52	5.7
Nighttime only plan	142	71	2.0
Day + magazine plan	296	80	3.7

2. Subjective judgments are made about effectiveness of three media:

Daytime network TV	65 index of value
Nighttime network TV	100 index of value
Women's magazines	50 index of value

3. GRPs are multiplied by index of values:

Daytime plan		296 × .65 =	192 net delivery	
Nighttime plan		142 × 1.00 =	142 net delivery	
Day	(157 GRPs)157 × .65 =		102 net delivery	} Total: 172
Magazine	(139 GRPs)139 × .50 =		70 net delivery	

4. Gross reach and frequency are converted to net delivery:

Example: Daytime network TV

Gross Delivery			Net Delivery		
GRPs	Reach	Frequency	GRPs	Reach	Frequency
296	52	5.7	192	48	4.0

Effective frequency has been determined to be from 2 to 7 exposures. Therefore, a frequency distribution has been given an index of effective response for every frequency level. These indices are subjectively made here, but they could be objectively measured in test marketing situations.

5. Subjective judgments about indices of responses:

Frequency levels	Index of Response
From 1 to 3 exposures	50
From 4 to 7 exposures	100
From 8-plus exposures	100

A frequency distribution (from computer analysis) is now performed to show percentage of net delivery reach for each frequency level. These reaches are multiplied by the index of responses.

6. Frequency distribution × Index of Responses:

Example: Daytime network TV

Frequency Levels	Net Reach	×	Index of Responses	=	Net Impact
1 to 3 exp.	28.8%	×	50	=	14.4
4 to 7 exp.	11.8	×	100	=	11.8
8 + exp.	7.2	×	100	=	7.2
Totals	47.8%				33.4

7. Now, all net impacts for three alternatives are calculated:

Media Plan Alternative	Net Impact	Original Gross	
		Reach	Frequency
Daytime plan	33	52	5.7
Nighttime plan	39	71	2.0
Day + magazine plan	39	80	3.7

8. *Results:*

1. The nighttime plan and the day plus magazine plan are equivalent in impact. This was not evident by studying reach and frequency alone.
2. The daytime plan is clearly the one with less impact potential.
3. The most critical points in these analyses were the subjective judgments of media values, and index of responses. These judgments can be improved by taking a consensus vote and averaging scores of a number of media experts within an organization. Or, they can be measured objectively through test marketing where variable weights can be determined.
4. Although this technique seems somewhat arbitrary, especially in the value judgments that have to be made, such judgments are usually made in media planning outside the confines of the data. In other words, data is collected on reach and frequency, cost-per-thousand, etc., but eventually someone has to make judgments about their values. This technique formalizes the judgment process.

Source: Fine, Jules, *Sex and Sanity in Media Planning,* A.N.A., March 21, 1979.

QUESTIONS FOR DISCUSSION

1. If a planner wanted to build reach quickly using magazines alone, which of the three magazine methods of building reach should be used?
2. Which kinds of magazines tend to develop large reach, and which develop large frequency?
3. Why can't one add the ratings for each week in a four-week period to find that program's four-week reach?
4. Which kinds of television programs tend to develop large reach?
5. Which kinds of television programs tend to develop high frequency?
6. Why is it likely that a television program with a high initial rating (in Week 1) will probably also have a high four-week reach?
7. Briefly explain: Is a rating for one telecast of a television program equivalent to a one-telecast reach?
8. If a television program were measured for fifty-two weeks (consecutively) what would the shape of the reach curve for that program probably look like?
9. Briefly explain: Of what value is a frequency distribution analysis of a television program's tune-ins?
10. Explain whether all advertising has a threshold that it must go through before it becomes effective.
11. Why did so many media planners adopt the "three-plus concept" in their advertising media planning?
12. Can too much frequency in advertising have negative consequences?
13. What are the most significant problems with the effective frequency concept?
14. Explain why effective frequency is felt to be superior to average frequency, normally used in media planning.

15. Explain the meaning of a response curve. Which response curve is found most often in advertising research?
16. Explain how effective frequency might be used to compare two alternative media plans.

SELECTED READINGS

Achenbaum, Alvin, "Effective Exposure: The Subversion of a Useful Idea," *Journal of Media Planning,* Fall 1986, 11–12.

Batra, Rajeev, and Michael L. Ray, "Situational Effects of Advertising Repetition: The Moderating Influence of Motivation, Ability, and Opportunity to Respond," *Journal of Consumer Research,* March 1986, 432–45.

Behrmann, William V., "Putting Effective Frequency Strategies to Work in Media Planning," *Effective Frequency: The State of the Art,* New York: Advertising Research Foundation, 1982, 103–28.

Benz, William, "The Road to Better Use of Effective Frequency," *Journal of Media Planning,* Fall 1986, 13–16.

Cannon, Hugh M. and Norman Goldring, "Another Look at Effective Frequency," *Journal of Media Planning,* Fall 1986, 29–36.

Cannon, Hugh M., "A Theory Based Approach to Optimal Frequency," *Journal of Media Planning,* Fall 1987, 33–44.

Cannon, Hugh M., "Reach and Frequency Estimates for Specialized Markets," *Journal of Advertising Research,* June/July 1983, 45, 53.

Cole, Don, "Hidden Reach," *Marketing and Media Decisions,* June 1986, 92.

Douglas, Stephen A., "The Integrated Metered Data Base: Why Is It Needed?" *Journal of Media Planning,* Fall 1986.

Elliott, Jeremy, "How Advertising Frequency Affects Advertising Effective-

ness: Indications of Change," *ADMAP,* October 1985, 512–515.

Evans, Cynthia, "Estimates of Reach and Frequency for Non-Standard Media, *Journal of Media Planning,* Spring 1989, 35–39.

Evanson, Donald, "Media Plans Frequently Don't Effectively Use Effective Reach," *Journal of Media Planning,* Fall 1986, 43–46.

Goldring, Norman, "Shifting Focus: Another View of Frequency," *Journal of Media Planning,* Spring 1988, 19–26.

Knowlton, Archa, "Effective Frequency: Why Is It Important?" *Effective Frequency: The State of the Art,* New York: Advertising Research Foundation, 1982, 1–12.

Krugman, Herbert E., "Next Steps—A Productive Approach to Measuring Effective Frequency," *Effective Frequency: The State of the Art,* New York: Advertising Research Foundation, 1982, 129–38.

Lancaster, Kent M., and Thomas C. Martin, "Estimating Audience Duplication Among Consumer Magazines, *Journal of Media Planning,* Fall 1988, 22–28.

Leckenby, John D., and Kishim Shizue, "How Media Directors View Reach and Frequency Estimation," *Journal of Advertising Research,* June/July 1982, 64–69.

Lonning, Stephen, "Effective Frequency: A Planner's Perspective," *Journal of Media Planning,* Fall 1986, 47–50.

McDonald, Colin, "Individual Respondent Analysis Made Better with

Complete Single Source Records,'' *Effective Frequency: State of the Art,* New York: Advertising Research Foundation, 1982, 181–94.

Naples, Michael J., *Effective Frequency,* New York: Association of National Advertisers, Inc., 1979.

Ostrow, Joseph W., ''Setting Frequency Levels,'' *Effective Frequency: The State of the Art,* New York: Advertising Research Foundation, 1982, 89–102.

Papazian, Edward, ''The Frequency Fracas,'' *Marketing and Media Decisions,* June 1986, 85, 86.

Priemer, August, ''New Alternatives to Effective Frequency in Media Planning,'' *Journal of Media Planning,* Fall 1986, 25–28.

Rice, Marshall, '' A Practical Method for Estimating Reach and Frequency,'' *Journal of Media Planning,* Fall 1988, 29–39.

Rice, Marshall, ''Errata: A Practical Method for Estimating Reach and Frequency,'' *Journal of Media Planning,* Spring 1989, 51.

Samuels, Gabe, ''Why This Approach Will Produce Better Inputs than Awareness to GRP Models,'' *Effective Frequency: The State of the Art,* New York: Advertising Research Foundation, 1982, 155–66.

Schloss, Ira J., ''How Important Is Effective Frequency to Advertisers and Media Planners?'' *Effective Frequency: The State of the Art,* New York: Advertising Research Foundation, 1982, 13–20.

Schultz, Don E., and Martin Block, ''Empirical Estimation of Advertising Response Functions,'' *Journal of Media Planning,* Fall 1986, 17–24.

Seagram, Joseph E. & Sons, Inc., ''A Study of the Effectiveness of Advertising Frequency in Magazines,'' *Time, Inc.,* 1982.

Sissors, Jack Z., ''Advice to Media Planners on How to Use Effective Frequency,'' *Journal of Media Planning,* Fall 1986, 3–9.

Spaeth, James, ''An Industry Data and Information Bank: How to Make It Work,'' *Effective Frequency: The State of the Art,* New York: Advertising Research Foundation, 1982, 139–54.

Sprague, Jeremy D., ''Estimating Newspaper Turnover Rates,'' *Journal of Advertising Research,* June-/July 1983, 9–14.

Steiner, Robert L., ''Point of View: The Paradox of Increasing Returns to Advertising,'' *Journal of Advertising Research,* February/March 1987, 45–52.

Wenzel, Wilfred, and Rolf Speetzen, ''How Much Frequency Is Enough?'' *Journal of Media Planning,* Spring 1987, 5–16.

7

Marketing Strategy and Media Planning

There are many ways to start the media planning process, but the best way is by analyzing the situation of a brand in the marketplace. The reason for making such an analysis is to learn how successful a brand has been against its competition, with the objectives of finding "opportunity" areas to exploit or "problem" areas to correct. Ultimately, the findings of a situation analysis should lead to the establishment of marketing objectives and strategies, which in turn lead to the establishment of media objectives and strategies. Although the responsibility for making a marketing situation analysis usually does not rest with a media planner, someone from the agency media department, such as a media researcher, may be involved to some extent in the research activities. Media planners often are involved in the marketing situation analysis, particularly the examination of the consumer, the competitive weight, and geographic and seasonal sales analysis.

What a Media Planner Needs to Know

To develop a successful media plan the planner must know as much as possible about the marketing background of the brand being advertised. This background includes product quality, product use, pricing, distribution, packaging, sales promotion, personal selling activities, public relations, and advertising. From a practical standpoint, planners may not need to know every detail, but they should know those pieces of information that contribute to the best planning. Those elements in a marketing situation analysis that most interest a planner are:

History of the market. This deals with sales of all brands in the market, including the brand for which planning is to be done. The analysis includes geographic sales distribution, market size in dollars/units, market shares, seasonal effects, and price effects. The goal is to find out where brands are now in terms of share of market and how they got there. An important item, for example, might be pricing history. What happened to prices for various brands over the years, and how did these price manipulations affect sales? Another concern might be an analysis of cost history and profit related to sales, both for the brand under consideration and for competitors' brands, if known.

Distribution channels. The objective here is to learn how a brand and its competitors distribute products. This includes the following information about each distribution channel: shelf-facings, inventories held, out-of-stock situations, methods of selling, display and advertising allowances, and how and why promotions are used. Problems of selling are sometimes caused by poor distribution, not advertising. Distribution information often affects media strategy because it may help the planner decide where to advertise.

The consumer of the product. This profile of users of the generic product type includes personal demographics such as age, sex, income, and occupation, as well as geographic location. Psychographics—life-styles and attitudes—should also be included. A consumer profile of those who buy a specific brand versus those who buy competing products is important. Buying habits should also be analyzed in terms of when products are purchased; in which kind of retail outlets; and which sizes, models, and colors are purchased most often. How and when consumers use these products also ought to be known. Finally, it would be helpful to know about the *buyer,* the *user,* and the *persons who motivate buyers/users.* All of this information helps the media planner select targets for media.

The product. A history of the product and how it was developed is included in the product section of the analysis. When and why product changes were made and the effects of such changes on each competitive brand could be important. Consumer perceptions of the values of various brands are also important background information for the media planner.

Advertising and media analysis. An analysis of media expenditures for competing brands would probably be the most important information that a media planner would like to know. This would include media classes used, names of individual vehicles, number of ads used, when advertising ran, and dollar and percentage allocation to each medium and market.

The Marketing Strategy Plan

Once the facts about a marketing situation have been gathered, the data then should be analyzed to learn where problems and opportunities lie. An *opportunity* may be defined as a marketing activity which, if adopted, may result in an advantage over the competitor. Such an opportunity might take place in a situation in which a manufacturer has improved a brand so that it is superior to competing brands, but this advantage may be known by only 10 percent of the potential consumers. If the manufacturer is able to communicate this advantage to 50 percent or more of potential consumers, increased sales may result.

Problem areas, on the other hand, are those that demand some action to correct the situation. A problem area might be a situation in which a brand does not have a competitive advantage or one in which a brand has been steadily losing its share of market for any number of reasons. Finding the causes for the decline is a first step toward changing the situation. Most situation analyses turn up more problem areas than opportunities, but the delineation of each problem area is a necessary preliminary step to marketing and media planning.

Marketing strategy planning consists of planning marketing actions that will solve the major problems and take advantage of the opportunities. In effect, a *marketing strategy and plan* is a blueprint for action geared to selling the product, with the ultimate goal of gaining an advantage over a competitor who, in a sense, is the enemy.

Perhaps the weakest part of many advertising campaigns is the lack of a sound selling strategy. Arthur Tatham, formerly chairman of the board of Tatham-Laird & Kudner advertising agency, once said, "Brilliant copy and art will never make a weak selling strategy succeed. But . . . once there is a sound selling strategy, then good copy and art will multiply its effectiveness." Tatham's statement also applies to media selection and use. Without a sound selling strategy, media planning may represent wasted effort. Media planning does not exist as an activity unrelated to marketing; it is a service function of marketing and selling. The fact that media are often selected and used without being based on a sound selling strategy demonstrates poor logic and inefficient modes of operation. Selling strategy is the heart of a marketing strategy and plan.

In summary, the major goals in a marketing strategy and plan are as follows:

1. Setting objectives that will help solve existing problems and take advantage of opportunity and problem areas
2. Deciding how the product should be sold
3. Determining to whom the main selling effort should be directed
4. Determining what role various elements of the marketing mix should play in the sale of a brand

5. Determining what adjustments should be made in package shapes or sizes
6. Determining how much should be spent

Most often, the marketing plan is written by someone other than the media planner. Yet, even though the latter may not be directly involved in drawing up the plan, there are a number of reasons why the marketing strategy plan is a significant document to media planners.

The foremost reason is that the marketing plan serves as a unifying and organizing force for all activity within an agency on a given brand's marketing and advertising plans. This means that the market researchers, account executives, and creative people, as well as media planners, are all working from a single source of information. Thus, the plan serves to coordinate all efforts toward the same goals. Large advertising agencies often have so many persons working on so many different accounts that communication becomes difficult. The media planner, especially, needs to know that his or her decisions will be directed toward the same objectives as those of others on the agency team.

Once the plan has been written, it becomes easier to visualize the whole scheme of operations for a given brand. All proposed plans can be evaluated for their logic and completeness to avoid information gaps or contradictions. If a marketing plan exists only in someone's mind or in bits or scraps of memoranda, then errors are hard to locate because no one has an overview of the entire operation.

Perhaps the key to the success of a marketing plan is the degree to which all tactics are spelled out. Herbert Zeltner, marketing consultant, cautioned that many marketing plans are "either glossed over in the rush of hammering together a marketing program, or merely slapped together as a collection of ponderous cliches." He noted:

> To be truly useful, the market strategy statement should not merely reflect some happy generalities about an increase in volume or share of market for the coming fiscal period.

> But establishing the requirement that a specific percent volume increase is to be achieved—through the expenditure of a precise sensible sum of money—and that this increase can most realistically be expected through more aggressive development of certain stated territories or segments of the market . . . is the type of statement which gives a properly astute media planner the challenge he needs to create both a perspective and workable media recommendation.[1]

The media planner needs specific direction, explicitly stated, in order to begin decision making. The media plan grows directly out of the marketing

1. Zeltner, Herbert, "Marketing Strategy Statement," *Media/Scope,* August 1964, p. 10.

strategy whenever it requires that advertising be used. The various segments of the strategy statement, however, are not all equally significant to the media planner. Foremost in importance are the marketing objectives, the basic selling idea, sources of business, overall sales strategy, and spending strategy. Each of these will be discussed in more detail on the following pages. Figure 7–1 shows an outline of a basic strategy statement.

Marketing Objectives

The marketing goals that the company and agency agree upon may, if achieved, result in the solution of a marketing problem. Marketing goals are measurable in most cases and provide a means of determining whether the strategy employed has been effective. For the media planner, the objectives will undoubtedly affect the kinds of media selected and how media is used. In a sense, then, marketing objectives serve as controls for media planning.

Most marketing objectives relate directly to achieving share of market for a brand; others relate to communication objectives. Here is a sample of marketing objectives for different brands (taken from various strategy statements):

- To increase share in an expanding segment of the X market
- To regain lost volume—increase sales a maximum of 5 percent and, in turn, shoot for a 14 percent share of market
- To acquire a 20 percent share of market the first year after national introduction, 25 percent the second year, and 30 percent the third year
- To introduce the product so that we have at least 5 percent share in each sales division
- To increase share of market and increase the morale of the sales force in the face of many competitive new product introductions
- To find and persuade new customers for our product
- To maintain national coverage
- To provide regional and local impact where two-thirds of sales are made
- To increase the overall visibility of the product name against the potential customers and the trade across the country

Whenever marketing objectives require advertising in specific geographical areas, then media must be selected that best reach those areas. Sometimes the objectives call for added promotional effort in a geographical region such as the West Coast, or the East Central part of the country. Other times, the objectives may call for a special advertising effort in a given market such as Los Angeles or Cincinnati. Such objectives may limit media choices because few media vehicles are available in some specified areas. The marketing objectives provide direction for the planner in selecting media, but it is up to the planner to find media that best *deliver* the target audience specified.

FIGURE 7-1. Outline for Basic Marketing Strategy Statement

I. *Major Strategy*
   This should be the briefest possible statement of the major one or two strategies you are going to recommend for the planning period, with just enough statement of the problem to explain the strategy. If you can write this section in one or two sentences or paragraphs, do so. If it takes you more than a single-spaced page, it is probably too long.

II. *Basic Objectives*
   A. Short Term (applies to next fiscal twelve months, unless otherwise stated, e.g., six months):

1. Increase share of total market	4. Increase total market
2. Arrest decline in share	5. Profit goal
3. Develop added volume	6. Reduce losses

   Translate objectives into approximate sales and/or profit goals.
   B. Long Term (applies to any prescribed period beyond the next planning period):
      1. Increase share of total market
      2. Increase total market
      3. Increase profits
      4. Position goal, i.e., gain leadership
      5. Develop and establish a brand or corporate image
      6. Expand line of service or products
   Translate objectives into approximate sales and/or profit goals.

III. *The Basic Selling Idea*
   A one- or two-sentence statement of the key selling idea. This is the base from which the creative strategy evolves.

IV. *Presentation of the Basic Selling Idea*
   This is the creative strategy in its briefest form.

V. *Use or Uses for Which the Product Will Be Advertised*
   A. Major   B. Minor

VI. *Sources of Business and Relative Importance of Each*
   A. Consumer Sources—What are the characteristics of the people who are the best prospects?

1. Regional factors	6. Occupation of head of household
2. City size	7. Family size
3. County size	8. Seasonal
4. Income groups	9. Sex—men, women, children
5. Age of housewife	10. Who is principal purchaser?

   B. Dealer Sources—What is relative importance of various types of outlets?
   C. Competitive Sources—Important competitive brands or companies—national, regional, local

VII. *Overall Sales Strategy*

A. Relative importance of price	C. Relative importance of dealers
1. To the consumer	D. Relative importance of advertising
2. To the trade	E. Relative importance of promotion
B. Relative importance of personal salesmanship	F. Relative importance of publicity

VIII. *Product Strategy*
   A. The need for product improvement—Analysis of product superiorities and weaknesses compared to competitive products
   B. The need for related products
   C. The need for adding new sizes or deleting unprofitable sizes
   D. The need for improving: 1. Packaging   2. Package design

IX. *Spending Strategy*
   A. Is there a need for higher or lower margins? What effect will this have on price, quality, quantity of the product?
   B. What is the proper amount to spend:
      1. On introduction?   2. On re-introduction?   3. On on-going basis?
   C. Is an extended payout plan indicated, and if so, what is the optimum time?

X. *Facts and Documentation*
   The pertinent facts needed to define the problems and to document the strategies outlined in the strategy sections

When marketing objectives call for increases in share of market with special effort directed only at prospects, the media planner may be called upon to increase the number of messages to known prospects. In such cases, media selection becomes secondary to methods of using media. One such method may be to increase the frequency of exposure of advertising messages to prospects.

Occasionally, objectives deal with some area other than market share; for example, the requirement may be "to increase the image of authority among adults." In this situation, it might be felt that adults, especially those aged 21–44, are good prospects, yet they are not buying the product. The marketing objective influences the selection of adult-appeal media, such as magazines and Sunday supplements, and perhaps the use of well-known, authoritative television announcers whose personality images are strong in the 21- to 44-year-old age group.

The Marketing Mix and Strategy

The tools that marketers use for implementing strategy are discussed in Chapter 3 in a discussion of the marketing mix. Each element of the mix is a selling tool. A good product that meets consumers' wants and needs is one of the best selling tools. Price is a selling tool, as is distribution. If a grocery store does not carry a given brand of product, many customers will ask for some other brand instead. They usually *will not* go to some other store in search for the brand. Promotion, in general, and sales promotion specifically are each selling tools. Other forms of promotion are public relations (including event marketing), direct marketing and advertising copy and art, and media.

The idea of a marketing mix is that it takes a number of different marketing mix elements to sell a product. Selling canned peas may require a good product, price, distribution, advertising, and sales promotion. But selling automobiles may require a different mix: product, price, distribution, sales promotion, public relations, and advertising. So the idea of a "mix" is important in terms of finding the optimum elements for selling.

The use of many marketing mix communication elements usually requires integration because each element may be conveying a different message and thereby reduce the effectiveness of communication. Integrated marketing communication for seamless effects has become a goal in building marketing strategy. (See Chapter 2 for a discussion of integrating marketing communication.)

The Budget

Once the marketing objectives have been stated, it is necessary to know how much money will be required to attain them. It is not realistic to make a grandiose marketing plan and then find that the advertiser is unwilling or unable to provide sufficient funds to make the plan successful. (Budgeting and allocations to markets and media will be discussed in a later chapter.) At this point, the media planner may be called in to help estimate the costs of the media strategy even before the main portion of the plan has been started. If enough money is not available to accomplish a given set of objectives, then the objectives may have to be reduced or revised.

Estimating the cost of a marketing plan usually involves two separate activities: estimating media costs and estimating production costs. Media costs may be ascertained by checking published reference books that show media rates or by phoning media representatives to obtain general costs. Production costs may be estimated either by arbitrarily allocating a given percentage of the total budget for that purpose or, if the advertising is relatively simple, by obtaining estimates on specific kinds of production pieces that are needed, such as art work, typography, videotape, or film. Generally, the media planner is responsible for estimating only the media cost portion of the marketing plan.

The main problem in estimating marketing costs is determining whether any given amount of money spent for advertising will attain a given set of objectives. Marketing and media planners most often rely on their experiences with other brands and products as a basis for making these estimates. But other factors also enter in. A new product introduction may require very heavy investments to get it off the ground. Competitors' advertising—where and how much—also may influence the marketing budget. Brands that have to defend their shares of market against the inroads of competitors, or those that aspire to increase market share, may have to spend heavily. Determining the exact amount is by no means a scientific matter. It is based mostly on experience, although there are mathematical models that estimate the effect of various spending levels. Past experience may show, for example, that an advertiser increased its national share of market by three percentage points by spending $10 million. It could then be roughly estimated that it would cost $3,333,333 to raise the share one percentage point. This linear relationship of spending and share of market, however, is seldom witnessed in the real world.

Sometimes the planner recommends spending an amount of money beyond the means of the advertiser. In such cases, either the objectives have to be changed or the advertiser must realize that spending the available budget will not produce the results desired. Sometimes, no matter what sum is recommended, the advertiser has a preconceived notion of the maximum amount that can be profitably spent and will not entertain requests for larger amounts. It behooves the planner, therefore, to establish budget parameters *before* full media plans are devised.

Creative Strategy

A major part of the marketing strategy plan is an explanation of how the product will be sold or a statement of the basic selling idea. From that basic selling idea comes the creative strategy, possibly the single most important influence on the planner during the media selection process. Many times the creative strategy directs the planner in choosing one medium over another or in selecting a combination of media.

Where color is an integral part of the creative strategy, then magazines, direct mail, newspaper supplements, or color television may be required. Newspapers accepting free-standing color inserts (FSIs) offer additional alternatives to the media planner. Where the creative strategy calls for the use of cartoon characters, then either comic strips or television may be most appropriate. Again, direction is given to the selection process.

Where a strategy calls for demonstration, one might first think of television; yet it is possible to demonstrate the use of a product in print media through the use of sequential panels showing the various steps in the use of the product. Radio also is capable of demonstration through the use of words that play on the listener's imagination.

Sometimes the creative strategy may call for the use of an announcer or salesperson who can exude a feeling of warmth and sincerity. Either television or radio may be required here, because each excels at conveying emotional impact.

If the creative strategy calls for music, media choices may be limited to radio or television. An alternative is to record the music and advertising message on thin vinyl records and have them inserted into magazines. In this case, however, the creative strategy may have to give way to the budget, which may not tolerate the expense of recording and inserting the record.

Occasionally, creative strategy calls for large and dominating illustrations. This suggests billboards to the media planner, although direct mail or a two-page center spread in newspapers or magazines may be equally acceptable.

Some advertising messages may seem to have more impact on consumers in one medium than they do in another. It should be noted, however, that *impact* is a hazy concept. It is generally assumed to mean that advertising does something to audience members, such as make the message memorable, change attitudes toward the brand, impart significant bits of information, or perhaps serve as a motivating factor in buying. The assumption is not always valid, because there is often little proof that what is claimed to happen actually does. In any case, where creative strategies call for traditional media because of their perceived impact, the planner may find it difficult to break tradition.

So, the creative strategy is an integral part of media planning, perhaps the most important of all. The planner cannot start work without first knowing what is to be said and how it is to be presented to consumers. Only then can media alternatives begin to be considered.

Dealers and Distribution

A major factor in media decision making is distribution to dealers, as it only makes sense to limit advertising to areas where the product is distributed. To do otherwise is to waste effort and money. There are, of course, exceptions, such as when a manufacturer will advertise in an area where the product is not distributed in an effort to "force" distribution on the dealers in that area. Perhaps dealers have refused to handle a new brand because they feel they already have too many similar products on their shelves. Some grocery chains even practice a *one-for-one policy* in which they refuse to take on a new brand unless the manufacturer removes an existing brand from the shelves. By advertising in an area where a product is not yet distributed, the manufacturer hopes that the advertising will create such a demand for the product that the dealers and distributors will be forced to carry the brand. This strategy, however, might sometimes backfire, because consumers who seek the brand and cannot find it might be alienated as future consumers of the brand.

For most products, however, advertising is limited to areas where the product is distributed, and even then, only to the markets that produce the most sales or have the greatest potential for sales.

Because dealers are important sources of business, the ability to select media that best communicate with dealers represents another aspect of the planner's job. Most frequently used is the trade press, but a planner may also choose to communicate with dealers through direct mail or trade shows and conventions or even mass media.

In some cases, the major problem in selling a product is not advertising to consumers, but to dealers. Such a case was discussed by T. Norman Tveter, a marketing expert:

> The problem was to sell a top-quality model train to fathers through boy salesmen, or the sons of those fathers. A sales analysis by the media director, based on sales for the two previous years, was the basis for planning advertising and promotion. Only then did strong points as well as weak show up concerning such factors as availability and rate of sales.

> Using a state-by-state breakdown of two boy age groups . . . as measures of potential, the analysis showed that sales were radically out of line with market potential. Also a breakdown in dollars of shipments to various outlets—such as department stores, specialty chains, and premium distributors—showed that 50 cities accounted for 78 percent of the shipments. Seventeen better-producing cities alone accounted for 62 percent of the shipments, and the two best producing areas, 28 percent to 30 percent. This left about 135 metropolitan areas accounting for approximately 22 percent of the shipments, simply because there were not enough dealers handling the product.

> From this it was concluded that more effective use of media to develop dealers' business was needed. Fewer publications with larger, dramatic advertising to impress dealers was indicated. There were

more than 100 metro areas where just one act of getting the right dealer with the proper cooperation could swing all negative factors to positive and score many hundreds of thousands of dollars in new retail sales. In other words, an impressive, primary dealer merchandising campaign in general media was indicated to take precedence over smaller-copy, more frequency, straight-consumer type of sell.[2]

This case illustrates the role of dealers in getting products sold, and also indicates how media can be used in communicating with dealers.

Dealers also influence media decisions because they are so important in selling at the local level. They are at the firing line and often know which medium works best in their markets. At times they may communicate with the agency indirectly through distributors, wholesalers, or salespeople. Their influence may be very important for their own markets. Furthermore, they often dislike agency media choices, feeling that the media planner is too distant from the scene of action to know which local or national medium works best. In any case, the media planner must pay a great deal of attention to both dealers and importance of distribution in the media plan.

Overall Sales Strategy

The media planner should examine each element of the marketing mix to determine how it might affect media selection and use. Foremost, of course, is the role to be played by advertising. Although one can conceive of a situation where sales promotion, for example, might be more important in attaining objectives, advertising usually plays a significant role in the marketing strategy, and its role should be defined. The more specific this definition is, the better the media planner can plan strategy. Generally, advertising is assigned a communication task that must be accomplished before a product can be sold effectively.

When pricing tactics are important in marketing strategy, a special media effort may be needed either to announce the price or keep the news in front of the consumers. Special prices to dealers may require special trade media selections and use.

Sales promotion, too, has special significance to media planners. Many promotions call for inserts in magazines or newspapers, such as coupons, booklets, samples of fabrics, tinfoils, or even vinyl records. All of these inserts require careful planning, especially in estimating their cost and timing. Marketing or creative plans might also require gatefolds, diecuts, or special inks, all of which require additional media considerations. Furthermore, the media planner must often select media to announce and keep a special promotion in front of consumers. Contests, cents-off deals, and premiums may

2. Tveter, T. Norman, "What the Media Expert Gains from Studying Markets," *Media/Scope,* May 1964, pp. 96, 100.

lose their impact if they are not noticed by consumers. The general media strategy in such a case is to buy media so as to get the largest reach possible.

For other promotions, it may be necessary to tie in local store information with national advertising so that the audience in any given market knows where to buy an advertised national brand. The names and addresses of stores carrying the product are usually listed at the end of commercials or next to or near newspaper or magazine ads.

Other parts of the marketing mix such as personal selling, public relations, or packaging are of less importance in media planning. But the planner should know as much as possible about the whole marketing strategy to maximize the effectiveness of media decisions.

Test Marketing

Whenever a marketing strategy plan calls for test marketing, there is likely to be media involvement. For example, a test marketing situation might use three markets to test whether the following objectives can be attained: (a) to gain a substantial share of each market's sales, (b) to determine whether the total market for the product can be expanded, (c) to determine how many repeat purchases will be made, (d) to accomplish the above objectives within a reasonable length of time at a reasonable profit. Special media planning will be required in this situation.

To carry out the test, the new brand may be introduced in each of the three markets using different marketing tactics. In Market A, 50 percent of the households may be given a free sample; in Market B, 100 percent of the households may be given a free sample; while in Market C, local newspapers could carry a coupon redeemable for a free sample at local stores. In each case, local advertising may be required to call attention to the offers, especially to the coupon offer. Measurements of sales would then be made and compared market by market to see which performed best.

As another example, test marketing could affect media planning if media weight varied in each of the three test markets. (*Weight* refers to the number of dollars spent, or GRP levels, in each market.) Market A might receive 100 television GRPs per week; Market B, 150 per week; and Market C, 200 per week. Sales would then be measured to see how the different weights affected volume.

Still another way to test media weights in several markets would be to give each market a specified advertising weight for a limited period of time. Sales would be measured for that period, then a heavier weighting might be applied to each market equally or in different proportions and sales again measured. (Test marketing strategy affects media planning in ways ranging from simple dissemination of advertising to special testing situations within all or portions of the test markets. For more details on test marketing, see Chapter 17.)

In summary, then, the marketing strategy plan will affect the media planner's operation in many ways. The media plan itself will grow out of a marketing plan. It is inconceivable for the media planner to operate without first having some kind of marketing strategy as a basis on which to select and use media. The ideal situation occurs when the marketing strategy plan is written and available for all personnel who work on a product or brand within the agency. The plan then serves as a unifying force and directs action toward a common goal.

Competitive Media Expenditure Analysis

Once the planner has scrutinized the marketing strategy plan to determine how media will be involved, it is time to consider the kinds of media and the way they are used by competition. Sometimes competition varies so much that the planner may have to sort out local and regional competitors as well as those on the national level. The planner's first job is to know just who the competitors are, and, his or her second, to know to what extent competitors affect sales.

There is little problem in finding such information if the advertiser or agency subscribes to Nielsen or various other syndicated research sources. But there is quite a problem in discovering who competitors are when such research services are not purchased. Some information may be obtained from news in the trade press about competitive media expenditures, but products produced and sold locally may not be identified very well, especially if they do not advertise much. Other sources of information may be local media salespeople, media representatives, local media research departments, or the company's own sales staff.

In determining the effect of competitors' media plans and devising strategies to counter such effects, the key piece of information is the share of market held by each competitor as compared with the advertiser's brand. Brands that lead or are close behind the advertiser may pose a threat. As far as media planning is concerned, the question is: "Should we use the same media our competitors use, or make special efforts to use different media?" Another question is, "How much advertising should we put into a market to counter competitors' advertising effects?"

The answers to these and other questions about competitors depend to a great extent on an advertiser's marketing objectives and an evaluation of what effect competitors may have in preventing the attainment of such objectives. Each situation may be different. Whether to use the same media competitors use may not be as important as answering the question, "Which medium or combination of media best reaches the kind of prospects who are likely to buy my brand?" The media that best reach prospects for "my" brand may happen to be identical with the media used by competitors. But the media planner, although considering competitors, should not necessarily imitate them simply because they happen to have larger shares of markets.

Planners should try to assess weaknesses in competitors' media tactics. Perhaps a competitor is not using a medium properly, or has dissipated advertising money in too many media, or is missing an important segment of the market. These errors represent opportunities in media selection and use and should be exploited. The analysis of a competitor's activities and its effects on a brand is not done in order to copy its tactics, but rather to assess its strengths and weaknesses in light of the marketing objectives. Plans for attaining objectives are made on the basis of problem as well as opportunity situations.

In essence, then, the planner must know at least the following information about competitors before making plans:

- Which media are used? Which are most significant?
- How much is spent in each medium? Total for all media?
- In which markets are media concentrated?
- How much weight is placed in each market?
- Which issues, broadcasts, times of year are used? In other words, when do competitors use various media and how are they used?

We will see in the next section that the compilation of competitive media information is very much an inexact science.

Major Expenditure Data Sources

Media spending information can be purchased from regular reporting services, although these services have limitations. They do not provide a perfect picture of competitive media expenditures because it is economically unfeasible to measure every dollar spent in every medium for every product. The task is simply too great. Expenditure analyses are therefore never quite complete. Furthermore, such analyses are not precise, because the dollars reported do not incorporate the discounts earned when each competitor purchased space or time. There may be large variations between what the syndicated services report and what competitors actually spent. Finally, competitive reporting companies often do not accurately break down spending allocations when two or three brands appear in a single ad. In other words, the entire cost of the ad may be credited to one of the three brands to the exclusion of the other two. The best way to assess the accuracy of competitive media use reports is to compare the findings of these reports to the actual media use for the product you have planned and placed in media.

These limitations do not render competitive media expenditure analyses invalid, but the data are not to be interpreted literally. Coupled with other marketing and media information, such data will help provide a more complete picture of a competitor's spending activities than would be possible otherwise.

Following is a brief description of the information provided by major media expenditure data sources. It should be noted that the data generally report expenditures of large national advertisers only; neither small national advertisers nor retail advertisers of any size are represented. Users of such data should be aware that often they may be missing significant information simply because it is not reported by any of the services. In such cases, it would be necessary to estimate spending.

Leading National Advertisers (LNA)—Newspaper Service. Leading National Advertisers Newspaper Services reports advertising expenditures in daily and Sunday newspapers in 82 cities. Actual measured advertising has been multiplied by the one-time rate (general open inch rate) of every newspaper measured. It also uses rates for premium space portions of a newspaper such as group supplements (*USA Weekend* and *Parade*), preprinted inserts, color comics, and rotogravure and color advertising.

The contents of a typical LNA newspaper service report are divided into three sections: (a) alphabetical product index and their classifications; (b) current quarter and year-to-date "projected 125 markets" totals for each product and class; and (c) brand detail—LNA reports expenditures within parent company within subclass for each brand spending $25,000 or more. Detailed spending data includes monthly, quarterly, and cumulative spending. (See Figure 7–2)

Because most daily newspapers in this country have converted to standard advertising units (SAUs) from agate lines, it is necessary to make conversions from one to the other. LNA measures advertising in agate lines, but reports this information in SAU inches. The technique they use is as follows:

1. Measure a printed page, both width and depth in inches.
2. Calculate the square inches (multiply width times depth).
3. Divide the square inches by 2.0625 (2.0625 equals agate lines in an SAU inch).
4. Measure total agate lines of a page by multiplying one column depth in agate lines times the number of columns on a page.
5. Calculate the factor for converting agate lines to SAU inches by dividing the total agate lines for a page by the MRCS/SAU inches on a page.

Leading National Advertisers (LNA)—BAR/LNA Multimedia Service. The Leading National Advertisers publishes multimedia reports that cover 10 media: magazines, supplements, newspapers, network television, spot television, syndicated television, network radio, national spot radio, cable television networks, and outdoor. (See Figure 7–3).

These reports are prepared quarterly and are available 18 weeks after the end of a quarter. The brand data is derived from BAR, Publisher's Information Bureau (PIB), and LNA Outdoor.

1. Ad Summary lists brands, and shows total spending in 10 media, including parent company and classification codes.
2. Company/Brand shows companies, and dollars spent for the year to date (YTD) in the 10 media. A 10-media total is also shown.

FIGURE 7–2.　LNA Newspaper Brand Detail January–September 1990

CLASS/PARENT/ BRAND/CITY	NEWS PAPER		JUL	AUG	SEP	QTR	YTD
＊＊ T432 RESORT PROMOTION (AREA)							
LAKE GEORGE REGION OF (NY)/							
LAKE GEORGE REGION NY RESORT PROMOTION							
(CONTINUED)							
BERGEN CTY	R	S			836	836	2037
BOSTON	G	S					5297
BOSTON	H	S					1683
HARTFORD	C	S			3346	3346	3346
NEW YORK	N	S					5150
NEWARK	SL	S					1898
TOTAL NEWSPAPERS					4182	4182	19411
OTHER SUNDAY MAGS.							22249
TOTAL SUNDAY MAGS.							22249
TOTAL BRAND EXP.					4182	41660	
NEWSPAPERS PROJ. 125 MKTS.						5403	23570
SUNDAY MAGS. PROJ. 125 MKTS.							23584
LAKE HAVASU CITY/LAKE HAVASU ARIZONA RESORT PROMOTION							
DENVER	P	S					1653
LOS ANGELS	T	M	2852		2852	5704	8336
LOS ANGELS	T	S	3312	3384	3312	10008	11942
ORANGE CTY	R	S		953		953	1808
TOTAL NEWSPAPERS			6164	4337	6164	16665	23739
TOTAL BRAND EXP.						16665	23739
NEWSPAPERS PROJ. 125 MKTS.						17665	25577
LAKE LANIER ISLAND/LAKE LANIER ISLAND GEORGIA RP							
GWINNETT	N	M			415	415	415
TOTAL NEWSPAPERS				415		415	415
TOTAL BRAND EXP.						415	415
NEWSPAPERS PROJ. 125 MKTS.						17743	29829
LAKE TAHOE VISITORS AUTHORITY/LAKE TAHOE RESORT PROMOTION							
CNTRA COSTA	T	S	1911		2484	4395	4395
LOS ANGELS	T	S	69732			69732	235921
SAN FRAN	C	M					2562
SAN FRAN	E&C	S	8154	1091		9245	9245
SAN JOSE	MN	S	5947			5947	5825
TOTAL NEWSPAPERS			85744	1091	2484	89319	261872
TOTAL BRAND EXP.						89319	261872
NEWSPAPERS PROJ. 125 MKTS.						101142	286148
LANCASTER COUNTY OF/PENNSYLVANIA DUTCH COUNTRY RESORT PROMO							
ALLENTOWN	C	S					1176
ASBURY PK	P	S					2229
BALTIMORE	S	M					1402
BALTIMORE	S	S					4664
BERGEN CTY	R	S					2358
BOSTON	G	S					4191
BOSTON	H	M					2823
BOSTON	H	S					4284
COLUMBUS	D	S					1862
HARTFORD	C	S					3994
LONG ILAND	N	S					4363
NEW YORK	P	AD					5449
NEW YORK	T	M					3733
NEW YORK	T	S					4607
NEWARK	SL	M					4450
NEWARK	SL	S					5611
PHILA	I	M					13780
PHILA	I	S	2129			2129	9554
PHILA	N	E					7010
PITTSBURGH	P	S					5453
WSTCH RCKL	RD	S					286
TOTAL NEWSPAPERS			2129			2129	103259
USA WEEKEND							21622
PARADE							9595
TOTAL SUNDAY MAGS.							31217
TOTAL BRAND EXP.					2129	134476	
NEWSPAPERS PROJ. 125 MKTS.						2725	165663
SUNDAY MAGS. PROJ. 125 MKTS.							31217
LAS VEGAS CITY OF/LAS VEGAS NEVADA RESORT PROMOTION							
DALLAS	N	S					8965
LA·SFV	N	S					5787
LOS ANGELS	T	S	3168	3240	4320	10728	123341
ORANGE CTY	R	S					8777
PHOENIX	AR	S	92412	81501	73604	247517	251018
TOTAL NEWSPAPERS			95580	84741	77924	258245	397888
TOTAL BRAND EXP.						258245	397888
NEWSPAPERS PROJ. 125 MKTS.						362262	548969
MAINE STATE OF/MAINE RESORT PROMOTION							
BOSTON	G	S			2940	2940	104779

CLASS/PARENT/ BRAND/CITY	NEWS PAPER		JUL	AUG	SEP	QTR	YTD
MAINE STATE OF/MAINE RESORT PROMOTION							
(CONTINUED)							
BOSTON	H	M					2015
BOSTON	H	S					23756
HARTFORD	C	M					2252
HARTFORD	C	S					6259
TOTAL NEWSPAPERS					2940	2940	139061
OTHER SUNDAY MAGS.			6550	16692	23242		8470c
TOTAL SUNDAY MAGS.			6550	16692	23242		84706
TOTAL BRAND EXP.						26182	223767
NEWSPAPERS PROJ. 125 MKTS.						14756	199279
SUNDAY MAGS. PROJ. 125 MKTS.						31377	114353
MALAYSIA FEDERATION OF/MALAYSIA RESORT PROMOTION							
LA TIMES MAGAZINE							28590
TOTAL SUNDAY MAGS.							28590
TOTAL BRAND EXP.							28590
SUNDAY MAGS. PROJ. 125 MKTS.							28590
MANATEE COUNTY OF (FL)/							
MANATEE COUNTY FLORIDA RESORT PROMOTION							
NEWSPAPERS PROJ. 125 MKTS.						85859	153052
MANITOBA PROVINCE OF/MANITOBA CANADA RESORT PROMOTION							
COLUMBUS	D	M					3709
MILWAUKEE	S	M					3201
MINNEAPOLS	ST	S					5825
MINNEAPOLS	ST	AD					6099
ST LOUIS	PD	M					2661
TOTAL NEWSPAPERS							21495
TOTAL BRAND EXP.							21495
NEWSPAPERS PROJ. 125 MKTS.							38725
MARYLAND STATE OF/MARYLAND RESORT PROMOTION							
ALLENTOWN	C	S					450
ANNAPOLIS	C	S					23573
BALTIMORE	S	E					977
BALTIMORE	S	M					988
BALTIMORE	S	S	12221			12221	128485
TOTAL NEWSPAPERS			12221			12221	154473
OTHER SUNDAY MAGS.							3164
TOTAL SUNDAY MAGS.							3164
TOTAL BRAND EXP.						12221	157637
NEWSPAPERS PROJ. 125 MKTS.						15643	561358
SUNDAY MAGS. PROJ. 125 MKTS.							4050
MASSACHUSETTS COMMONWEALTH OF/MASSACHUSETTS RESORT PROMOTION							
BOSTON	G	S					174983
BOSTON	H	M					2745
NEW YORK	T	S					21927
TOTAL NEWSPAPERS							199655
NY TIMES MAGAZINE							52350
TOTAL SUNDAY MAGS.							52350
TOTAL BRAND EXP.							252005
NEWSPAPERS PROJ. 125 MKTS.							263175
SUNDAY MAGS. PROJ. 125 MKTS.							52350
MAUI COUNTY OF/MAUI HAWAII RESORT PROMOTION							
DENVER	P	S			2584	2584	2584
DENVER	RMN	S					2561
LA/LNG BCH	PT	S			1475	1475	1475
LA·SFV	N	S					1890
LOS ANGELS	T	M					1342
LOS ANGELS	T	S					10077
ORANGE CTY	R	S					2945
SAN FRAN	E&C	S					5742
SEATTLE	T	PI S			3444	3444	6888
TOTAL NEWSPAPERS				7503		7503	35504
TOTAL BRAND EXP.						7503	35504
NEWSPAPERS PROJ. 125 MKTS.						9736	43088
MCA INC/YOSEMITE RESORT PROMOTION							
CNTRA COSTA	T	S					3849
LOS ANGELS	T	S					58428
ORANGE CTY	R	S					8340
SAN FRAN	E&C	S					29739
SAN JOSE	MN	S					5613
TOTAL NEWSPAPERS							105969
TOTAL BRAND EXP.							105969
NEWSPAPERS PROJ. 125 MKTS.							125263
MEXICO REPUBLIC OF/ACAPULCO MEXICO RESORT PROMOTION							
DALLAS	N	S					1246⌐
HOUSTON	C	S					23352
LOS ANGELS	T	S					75020

380

FIGURE 7–3. LNA/ARBITRON Multi-Media Service January–September 1991

AD $ SUMMARY
BRAND INDEX

BRAND/PARENT COMPANY	CLASS CODE	10-MEDIA YTD $ (000)	MEDIA USED	BRAND/PARENT COMPANY	CLASS CODE	10-MEDIA YTD $ (000)	MEDIA USED
VIDEO LIBRARY VIDEO STORE	G715	0.4	O	VILLIARD PRESS BOOKS	B410	77.9	CR
BLOCKBUSTER ENTERTAINMENT CORP				VILLIARD PRESS			
VIDEO LIQUIDATORS VIDEOS	G61V	33.2	S	VIM LIQUID CLEANSER	H431	0.3	S
VIDEO LIQUIDATORS				UNILEVER NV			
VIDEO MAGAZINE SUBS	G618	45.1	C	VIMCO PASTA	F125	15.3	D
REESE PUBLISHING CO				BORDEN INC			
VIDEO REVIEW MAGAZINE SUBS	G618	50.3	MR	VINEYARD NATIONAL BANK CONSUMER SERVICES	B151	53.1	W
VIARE PUBLISHING				COMPANY UNKNOWN			
VIDEO SALES RECORDINGS	H331	48.0	S	VINTAGE BOOKS	B410	190.4	MPW
VIDEO SALES				ADVANCE PUBLICATIONS			
VIDEO SENSATIONS VIDEOS	G61V	110.0	M	VINYLINE WINDOWS HOME	H514-5	44.1	S
VIDEO SENSATIONS				RAF INDUSTRIES INC			
VIDEO TECHNOLOGY MURDUCK TALKING DCK	G421	228.4	SY	VIP REALTY GROUP	B230	25.2	O
VIDEO TECHNOLOGY INDUSTRIES INC				VIP REALTY GROUP INC			
VIDEO TECHNOLOGY SOCRATES EDUC VIDEO SYS	G421	7.8	S	VIPCO VINYL SIDING	H512-5	43.5	S
VIDEO TECHNOLOGY INDUSTRIES INC				CRANE PLASTICS CO			
VIDEO TELECOM MEDIA CONFERENCING	B149	36.2	M	VIPONT PHARMACEUTICALS DENTAL PRODUCTS	D121	41.0	D
VIDEO TELECOM				COLGATE-PALMOLIVE CO			
VIDEO TUTORIAL SERVICES	H332	30.9	C	VIRGIN ATLANTIC AIRLINES PASSENGER	T413	3,869.7	WONSD
VIDEO TUTORIAL SERVICES INC				VIRGIN ATLANTIC			
VIDICOMP DISTRIBUTORS INC	G715	59.9	W	VIRGIN AUDIO RECORDINGS	H331	106.4	MOS
VIDICOMP DISTRIBUTORS INC				VIRGIN GROUP THE			
VIEWERS CHOICE CABLE TV PROGRAM	B442	39.8	W	VIRGIN MASTERTRONIC GAME SOFTWARE	G421	102.0	M
VIEWERS CHOICE				VIRGIN MASTERTRONIC INTL INC			
VIEWMASTER PRODUCTS	G423	6.1	N	VIRGIN MASTERTRONIC INTL SOFTWARE DIST	B340	30.6	M
TYCO TOYS INC				VIRGIN MASTERTRONIC INTL INC			
VIGORO FERTILIZER	T630	32.0	D	VIRGINIA BEACH RESORT HOTEL VIRGINIA BCH	T431	136.0	W
GREAT AMERICAN MANAGEMENT & INVESTMNT CO				VIRGINIA BEACH RESORT HOTEL & TENNIS CLB			
VIKANE HOUSEHOLD INSECTICIDES	H241	72.1	W	VIRGINIA BEACH VIRGINIA RESORT PROMOTION	T432	1,602.4	MPWS
COMPANY UNKNOWN				VIRGINIA BEACH			
VIKING COMPUTERIZED SEWING MACHINE	H219	78.4	PWS	VIRGINIA CREDIT UNION LEAGUE	B159	43.3	W
ELECTROLUX AB				VIRGINIA CREDIT UNION			
VIKING HEALTH SPA	D241	33.5	W	VIRGINIA DEPT OF AGRICULTURE & CONSUMER	B162	54.4	W
COMPANY UNKNOWN				VIRGINIA COMMONWEALTH OF			
VIKING MILLWORK	B111	51.0	W	VIRGINIA EDUCATION ASSOCIATION	B119-9	97.6	SC
COMPANY UNKNOWN				VIRGINIA EDUCATION ASSOCIATION			
VIKING PENGUIN INC BOOKS	B410	599.7	MPWD	VIRGINIA FUND	B153	30.1	W
PEARSON PLC				COMPANY UNKNOWN			
VIKING PRESS	B410	84.1	MW	VIRGINIA INDUSTRIAL DEVELOPMENT	B620	16.4	M
PEARSON PLC				VIRGINIA COMMONWEALTH OF			
VIKING RANGES	H212	313.2	MP	VIRGINIA METALCRAFTERS GALLERIES	G612	25.3	M
VIKING RANGE CORP				SPRIGG LANE INVESTMENT CORP			
VIKING STUDIO BOOKS	B410	14.5	M	VIRGINIA PENINSULA VIRGINIA RESORT PROMO	T432	33.4	M
PEARSON PLC				VIRGINIA PENINSULA AREA OF			
VILLA JULIE COLLEGE	B133	67.7	W	VIRGINIA POWER	B141	636.4	MWOS
COMPANY UNKNOWN				DOMINION RESOURCES INC			
VILLA ROMA COUNTRY CLUB CALLICOON	T431	249.5	W	VIRGINIA POWER MINORITY VENDOR PGM	B141-8	5.6	W
VILLA ROMA COUNTRY CLUB				DOMINION RESOURCES INC			
VILLA VERA HOTEL & RACQUET CLUB MEXICO	T431	99.9	M	VIRGINIA RESORT PROMOTION	T432	2,041.2	MWOSC
VILLA VERA HOTEL & RACQUET CLUB				VIRGINIA COMMONWEALTH OF			
VILLAGE AT BRECKENRIDGE RESORT BRECK	T431	41.3	MWO	VIRGINIA SLIMS 100 CIG RG FL	G111	5,585.0	MPWO
VILLAGE AT BRECKENRIDGE				PHILIP MORRIS COMPANIES INC			
VILLAGE BANK	B151	49.2	W	VIRGINIA SLIMS 100 CIGS MN FL	G111	1,217.4	M
COMPANY UNKNOWN				PHILIP MORRIS COMPANIES INC			
VILLAGE BATH BATH TABLETS	D131	184.4	M	VIRGINIA SLIMS 100S FIL MEN LIG MEN CIG	G111	29.0	M
COLGATE-PALMOLIVE CO				PHILIP MORRIS COMPANIES INC			
VILLAGE FASHION OUTLET APPAREL M & W	G711-3	0.3	O	VIRGINIA SLIMS CIG ADV	G111	389.1	PW
BIG M INC				PHILIP MORRIS COMPANIES INC			
VILLAGE GREEN (HOUSEHOLD)	G714	43.5	M	VIRGINIA SLIMS CIGARETTES	G111	62.3	M
VILLAGE GREEN				PHILIP MORRIS COMPANIES INC			
VILLAGE HOMES REAL ESTATE	B230	29.7	W	VIRGINIA SLIMS CIGARETTES SPORTING EVENT	G111	252.1	MO
VILLAGE HOMES				PHILIP MORRIS COMPANIES INC			
VILLAGE INN PANCAKE HOUSE RESTAURANTS	G330	443.8	SD	VIRGINIA SLIMS LIG 100S FILTER & MEN CIG	G111	45.8	W
VICORP RESTAURANTS INC				PHILIP MORRIS COMPANIES INC			
VILLAGE INN RESTAURANT	G330	338.0	OS	VIRGINIA SLIMS LIGHTS CIGARETTES	G111	1,008.2	MP
TECTON MANAGEMENT SERVICES INC				PHILIP MORRIS COMPANIES INC			
VILLAGE OPTICAL	G71E	34.6	W	VIRGINIA SLIMS LT 100 CIG MN FL	G111	168.4	M
COMPANY UNKNOWN				PHILIP MORRIS COMPANIES INC			
VILLAGE PANTRY FOOD STR	G715	128.2	S	VIRGINIA SLIMS LT 100 CIG RG FL	G111	5,105.7	MP
MARSH SUPERMARKETS INC				PHILIP MORRIS COMPANIES INC			
VILLAGE RV	T130	94.2	W	VIRGINIA SLIMS LT 120S CIG RG FL	G111	304.2	M
COMPANY UNKNOWN				PHILIP MORRIS COMPANIES INC			
VILLAGE SHOPPING DISTRICT	G719	32.3	W	VIRGINIA SLIMS SUPERSLIMS 100 CIG MN FL	G111	472.3	M
UNIVERSITY VILLAGE ASSOCIATION				PHILIP MORRIS COMPANIES INC			
VILLAGES AT KILLINGTON RESORT	T431	51.0	M	VIRGINIA SLIMS SUPERSLIMS 100 CIG RG FL	G111	2,764.2	M
VILLAGES AT KILLINGTON				PHILIP MORRIS COMPANIES INC			
VILLAGES AT PORTS O CALL	G329	61.7	PW	VIRGINIA SLIMS ULTRA LTS 100 CIG MN FL	G111	1,367.8	M
COMPANY UNKNOWN				PHILIP MORRIS COMPANIES INC			
VILLARD BOOKS	B410	672.9	MPWRD	VIRGINIA SLIMS ULTRA LTS 100 CIG RG FL	G111	149.4	M
ADVANCE PUBLICATIONS				PHILIP MORRIS COMPANIES INC			
VILLAS PLAZA CANCUN RESORT MEXICO	T431	3.9	M	VIRGINIA STATE LOTTERY	B163	6,115.7	WS
FIESTA AMERICANA HOTELS				VIRGINIA COMMONWEALTH OF			
VILLEROY & BOCH CHINA	H111	0.9	O	VISA CHARGE CARD	B121	19,368.2	MPWNSYCRD
VILLEROY & BOCH				VISA INTERNATIONAL			
VILLEROY & BOCH GALLERY	G712	50.7	W	VISA CHARGE CARD & CORPORATE CARD	B121	436.5	M
VILLEROY & BOCH				VISA INTERNATIONAL			

M = MAGAZINES	O = OUTDOOR	C = CABLE TV NETWORKS
P = SUNDAY MAGAZINES	N = NETWORK TV	R = NETWORK RADIO
H = NEWSPAPERS	S = SPOT TV	D = NATL SPOT RADIO
A = ALL	Y = SYNDICATED TV	

3. Class/Brand YTD shows brands grouped by PIB classes. Within each class, brands are listed by their parent companies. Data includes dollars spent for the year to date in 10 media.
4. Class/Brand QTR shows brands grouped by PIB classes. Brands are listed by parent company, and data shows dollars spent for the current quarter in the 10 media, plus totals for each.

The main advantage of these reports is that brand spending information is available in one source.

LNA Outdoor Advertising Service. This is a service that reports national and regional poster and painted outdoor signs in markets with a 100,000 population or more. Brand market-by-market expenditure data represents gross sales volume for those plant operators who participate. (See Figure 7–4.)

The service has five reports as follows:

1. Outdoor Contributors by Market shows which plant operators have contributed advertising expenditure data for each quarter's report.
2. Classification Totals shows expenditures listed by industry, major, subclass, and special classes.
3. Brand Index lists all brands that bought outdoor during the reporting period. It also shows parent company and classification code.
4. Parent Company Index summarizes spending by quarter for each brand and parent company.
5. Outdoor Brand Detail shows brands by parent company within classification subclasses and total dollars spent for the year to date and each quarter.

Publisher's Information Bureau (PIB/LNA)–Publisher's Advertising Reports (PAR). This is a monthly report showing expenditures in over 100 magazines and two supplements (*Parade* and *USA Weekend*). PIB publishes five volumes. The first four volumes cover expenditures by brand within specific product classes. (See, for example, Figure 7–5). The fifth volume covers total revenues by magazine and product class. It also covers parent companies and brand expenditures.

Costs are estimated by using the one-time rates for each insertion. Seasonal rates are used if all the usual frequency and volume discounts are earned by an advertiser. Regional one-time rates reflect discounts for use of more than one edition, where applicable. Advertisers who buy a great deal of magazine advertising may show overspending because they earned volume discounts that were not reported. Not all magazines are covered.

Mediawatch. Arbitron's Mediawatch reports advertising expenditures for broadcast media using computer digitized video and audio data. The fol-

FIGURE 7–4. Outdoor Advertising Service Brand Detail January–December 1991

CLASS COMPANY BRAND STATE - MARKET	CURRENT QUARTER $ (000)			YEAR-TO-DATE $ (000)		
	TOTAL	POSTER	PAINT	TOTAL	POSTER	PAINT
F310 BEER (CONT'D)						
STROH BREWERY CO (CONT'D)						
OLD MILWAUKEE BEER(F3100)						
OH FINDLAY	0.0	0.0	0.0	10.0	10.0	0.0
PA BERKS-SCHUYLKILL & MONTGOMERY	0.0	0.0	0.0	6.9	5.4	1.5
PA ERIE	0.0	0.0	0.0	2.4	2.4	0.0
PA HARRISBURG	2.7	0.0	2.7	24.5	0.0	24.5
PA PITTSBURGH	0.0	0.0	0.0	3.0	3.0	0.0
PA YORK-LANCASTER	10.9	10.9	0.0	61.7	61.7	0.0
TX BEAUMONT-PORT ARTHUR-ORANGE	0.0	0.0	0.0	1.5	1.5	0.0
WV HUNTINGTON-ASHLAND	1.2	1.2	0.0	1.2	1.2	0.0
BRAND TOTAL	198.6	191.4	7.3	724.2	693.5	30.7
OLD MILWAUKEE LIGHT BEER (F3100)						
NY UTICA-ROME	0.0	0.0	0.0	1.3	1.3	0.0
NY WATERTOWN-OSWEGO	2.5	2.5	0.0	4.7	4.7	0.0
BRAND TOTAL	2.5	2.5	0.0	5.9	5.9	0.0
PIELS BEER (F3100)						
NY BUFFALO	0.0	0.0	0.0	12.7	12.7	0.0
PA WILLIAMSPORT	0.0	0.0	0.0	2.2	2.2	0.0
BRAND TOTAL	0.0	0.0	0.0	14.9	14.9	0.0
SCHAEFER BEER (F3100)						
LA LAKE CHARLES	0.0	0.0	0.0	17.8	17.8	0.0
TX BROWNSVILLE-HARLINGEN-SAN BENIT	0.0	0.0	0.0	8.0	8.0	0.0
BRAND TOTAL	0.0	0.0	0.0	25.8	25.8	0.0
SCHLITZ BEER (F3100)						
TN NASHVILLE-DAVIDSON	0.0	0.0	0.0	0.9	0.9	0.0
SCHLITZ MALT LIQUOR (F3100)						
AL TUSCALOOSA	0.0	0.0	0.0	0.5	0.5	0.0
CA LOS ANGELES METRO MARKET	12.8	12.8	0.0	38.5	38.5	0.0
CA SAN DIEGO	0.0	0.0	0.0	5.6	5.6	0.0
CA SAN FRANCISCO-OAKLAND-SAN JOSE METRO	9.9	9.9	0.0	16.6	16.6	0.0
FL FT MEYERS	1.8	1.8	0.0	5.5	5.5	0.0
FL PENSACOLA	0.0	0.0	0.0	3.6	3.6	0.0
GA ALBANY	2.0	2.0	0.0	10.0	10.0	0.0
GA AUGUSTA	0.0	0.0	0.0	5.6	5.6	0.0
IN LAFAYETTE-WEST LAFAYETTE	2.3	2.3	0.0	7.0	7.0	0.0
LA ALEXANDRIA	4.1	4.1	0.0	8.1	8.1	0.0
LA MONROE	9.3	9.3	0.0	13.9	13.9	0.0
MI GRAND RAPIDS	0.0	0.0	0.0	2.0	2.0	0.0
MN ST CLOUD	0.0	0.0	0.0	2.0	2.0	0.0
NC WILMINGTON	3.8	3.8	0.0	7.7	7.7	0.0
NY BUFFALO	2.7	2.7	0.0	16.7	16.7	0.0
NY SYRACUSE	0.0	0.0	0.0	1.9	1.9	0.0
OH CINCINNATI	0.0	0.0	0.0	3.3	3.3	0.0
OR PORTLAND & SALEM	0.0	0.0	0.0	24.2	24.2	0.0
PA HARRISBURG	0.0	0.0	0.0	6.3	6.3	0.0
PA PITTSBURGH	0.0	0.0	0.0	18.2	18.2	0.0
TN CLARKSVILLE-HOPKINSVILLE	0.0	0.0	0.0	0.5	0.5	0.0
TN NASHVILLE-DAVIDSON	1.9	1.9	0.0	7.5	7.5	0.0
TX AUSTIN	3.5	3.5	0.0	7.0	7.0	0.0
TX BEAUMONT-PORT ARTHUR-ORANGE	6.0	6.0	0.0	10.0	10.0	0.0
TX HOUSTON	15.7	15.7	0.0	20.9	20.9	0.0
BRAND TOTAL	75.9	75.9	0.0	242.9	242.9	0.0
STROH BREWERY CO GENERAL PROMOTION (F3108)						
AL MONTGOMERY	0.0	0.0	0.0	1.6	1.6	0.0
FL PENSACOLA	0.0	0.0	0.0	7.6	7.6	0.0
GA ALBANY	0.0	0.0	0.0	3.6	3.6	0.0
BRAND TOTAL	0.0	0.0	0.00	12.8	12.8	0.0
STROH BREWERY CO MINORITY VENDOR PROGRAM (F3108)						
AL MONTGOMERY	0.0	0.0	0.0	4.8	4.8	0.0
STROHS BEER (F3100)						
AL BIRMINGHAM	0.0	0.0	0.0	1.4	1.4	0.0
AL HUNTSVILLE	0.0	0.0	0.0	3.5	3.5	0.0
AL MOBILE	0.0	0.0	0.0	5.5	5.5	0.0
AL MONTGOMERY	0.0	0.0	0.0	4.8	4.8	0.0
AL SHOALS	0.0	0.0	0.0	1.7	1.7	0.0
AZ PHOENIX	0.0	0.0	0.0	2.3	0.0	2.3

FIGURE 7-5.   Leading National Advertisers 1992 Brand Detail Report as of March 31

APPAREL

LORALIE ORIGINALS
REDDING, CA 96001
SEVENTEEN   8 OC   134.1
Y-T-D%
Y-T-DP   TOT NEO PCS 134.1
                  TOT PG   8.00

LORRIE KABALA COLLECTIBLES
CANOGA PARK, CA 91303
BRIDE'S   2 OD   37.2
Y-T-D%
Y-T-DP   TOT NEO PCS 37.2
                 TOT PG   2.00

LOUIS FERAUD INC
NEW YORK, NY
ELLE   2   0 64   56.7
                  19.9
Y-T-D%
Y-T-DP   TOT NEO PCS 78.5
                  TOT DOL   2.64

LOUIS FERAUD INC
NEW YORK, NY
ELLE   1   0 00   29.9
Y-T-D%
Y-T-DP   TOT NEO PCS 29.9
                  TOT DOL   1.00

LUBIAM USA INC
NEW YORK, NY
GENT QLTY   1 00   53.9
                   13.3
Y-T-D%
Y-T-DP   TOT NEO PCS 67.1
                   TOT DOL   3.00

MARINA BRIDALS INC
BROOKLYN, NY 11223
BRIDL GO   2 00   16.2
Y-T-D%
Y-T-DP   TOT NEO PCS 16.2
                  TOT DOL   2.00

MARIONAT BRIDAL VEILS
NEW YORK, NY
BRIDL GO   7 00   63.3
Y-T-D%
Y-T-DP   TOT NEO PCS 63.3
                  TOT DOL   7.00

MARIONAT BRIDAL VEILS
NEW YORK, NY
BRIDL GO   3 00 48
BRIDL GO   3 00 45
MOD BRIDE 2 00 48
MOD BRIDE
Y-T-D%
Y-T-DP   3 00   TOT NEO PCS 46.7
                  TOT DOL   13.00

MARISSA COLLECTIONS
NEW YORK, NY 10018
BRIDE'S   2 67   47.7
Y-T-D%
Y-T-DP   TOT NEO PCS 47.7

lowing reports, showing brand, product and parent company, schedule detail, and estimated expenditures, are prepared:

- Network TV (See Figure 7–6.)
- Cable TV networks
- Network radio
- National syndicated TV
- National spot TV cumulative reports (See Figure 7–7.)
- Full-time spot TV monthly reports in 75 BAR spot TV markets

Specific program and brand information is obtained by Mediawatch's system of "pattern recognition technology" whereby computers recognize a given commercial by its unique digitized electronic code. Videotapes of commercials are no longer necessary. However, for syndication and the Fox network, Arbitron will continue to videotape their satellite feeds and manually record the commercial activity. The most significant benefit of Mediawatch is its ability to monitor all 75 BAR spot TV markets continuously, thus improving the accuracy of both activity and cost estimates.

In addition, Mediawatch has a "Checking Service" that reports commercial placement irregularities, such as product conflicts, overcommercialization, and multiple spotting, to subscribing agencies.

To estimate brand spending, Mediawatch assigns a dollar value to each program and applies this rate to each brand television commercial monitored. Network costs estimates are developed from information provided by the networks. Syndicated program rates are based on cost data supplied by advertisers and agencies. Spot TV rates are provided by a few agencies and buying services and are adjusted to agree with station revenue information compiled by the Television Bureau of Advertising. The entire reporting process is done manually.

Gathering and Assembling the Data

The first of two major tasks involved in studying competitive expenditures is to gather and assemble the data. The second task is to analyze them.

What kinds of data should the media planner seek? The most obvious answer is to find the amount of money that each competitor spends annually in each medium. Such data provide a bird's-eye view of the competitor's media activities. To make such data more meaningful, the planner should analyze expenditures for individual brands, rather than total expenditures for a company. Because each brand is competing with others for a proportion of total market sales, specific expenditures by brands are most meaningful. In gathering expenditure data by brand, it is advisable to include the planner's brand as well as competitors' brands so that all are compared on the same research basis.

Furthermore, in analyzing expenditure data, it is important not only to show dollars spent in each medium, but what percentage that comprises of

FIGURE 7-6. Section 2—Brand Detail within Parent Company

PARENT COMPANY BRAND/PRODUCT PROGRAM	NETWORK AND DAY	CLASS CODE & TIME	JANUARY			FEBRUARY			MARCH			1ST QTR # YEAR TO DATE		
			NO OF COMM	MINUTES SECONDS	DOLLAR EST (000)	NO OF COMM	MINUTES SECONDS	DOLLAR EST (000)	NO OF COMM	MINUTES SECONDS	DOLLAR EST (000)	NO OF COMM	MINUTES SECONDS	DOLLAR EST (000)
3M COMPANY														
3M PDTS-CORP PROMO		C561												
60 MINUTES	C SUN	702P	1	:30	124.1							1	:30	124.1
PRIME TIME TOTALS			1	:30	124.1							1	:30	124.1
CBS MORNING NEWS	C WED	600A	9	4:30	26.1							9	4:30	26.1
CBS THIS MORNING	C THU	700A	9	4:30	64.8							9	4:30	64.8
M/F DAYTIME TOTALS			18	9:00	90.9							18	9:00	90.9
NCAA BSKB GM-SAT 1/CBS	C SAT	100P	1	:30	20.8							1	:30	20.8
NCAA BSKB GM-SAT 2/CBS	C SAT	403P	1	:30	20.8							1	:30	20.8
NCAA BSKB GM-SAT/CBS	C SAT	148P	1	:30	20.8	1	:30	27.3				2	1:00	48.1
NCAA BSKB GM-SUN 1/CBS	C SUN	1230P	1	:30	20.8							1	:30	20.8
NCAA BSKB GM-SUN 2/CBS	C SUN	238P	1	:30	20.8							1	:30	20.8
NFC CHAMPIONSHIP GAME	C SUN	400P	1	:30	325.0							1	:30	325.0
NFC PLAYOFF GAME-SAT	C SAT	400P	1	:30	185.5							1	:30	185.5
NFC PLAYOFF GAME-SUN	C SUN	400P	1	:30	185.5							1	:30	185.5
OLYMPIC WINTERFEST	C SAT	230P	1	:30	40.0							1	:30	40.0
SUNDAY MORNING	C SUN	900A	3	1:30	52.8							3	1:30	52.8
AFC CHAMPIONSHIP GAME	N SUN	1230P	1	:30	323.0							1	:30	323.0
AFC PLAYOFF GAME-SAT	N SAT	400P	1	:30	173.0							1	:30	173.0
AFC PLAYOFF GAME-SUN	N SUN	1230P	2	1:00	346.0							2	1:00	346.0
NBA BSKB GME-SUN 1/NBC	N SUN	1200N	1	:30	55.0							1	:30	55.0
NBA BSKB GME-SUN 2/NBC	N SUN	325P	1	:30	169.0	2	1:00	113.0				3	1:30	169.0
NBA BSKB GME-SUN/NBC	N SUN	1223P	1	:30	20.8							1	:30	20.8
S/S DAYTIME TOTALS			19	9:30	1901.8	3	1:30	140.3				22	11:00	2042.1
CBS EVENING NEWS-SUN	C SUN	600P	1	:30	24.1							1	:30	24.1
CBS LATE NEWS-SUN	C SUN	1103P	3	1:30	20.1							3	1:30	20.1
E/L FRINGES TOTALS			4	2:00	46.2							4	2:00	46.2
PRODUCT TOTALS			42	21:00	2163.0	3	1:30	140.3				45	22:30	2303.3
800 FLOWERS LTD														
1-800-FLOWERS FLORIST		V361												
TODAY SHOW	N THU	700A				4	2:00	51.6				4	2:00	51.6
M/F DAYTIME TOTALS						4	2:00	51.6				4	2:00	51.6
SUNDAY TODAY	N SUN	800A				1	:30	9.0				1	:30	9.0
S/S DAYTIME TOTALS						1	:30	9.0				1	:30	9.0
TONIGHT SHOW	N MON	1136P				1	:30	24.0				1	:30	24.0
E/L FRINGES TOTALS						1	:30	24.0				1	:30	24.0
PRODUCT TOTALS						6	3:00	84.6				6	3:00	84.6
ABBOTT LABORATORIES														
CLEAR EYES EYE DROPS		D215												
ALL MY CHILDREN	A THU	100P				1	:15	9.2				1	:15	9.2
GENERAL HOSPITAL	A MON	300P				2	:30	17.8				2	:30	17.8
LOVING	A WED	1230P				1	:15	3.7				1	:15	3.7
ONE LIFE TO LIVE	A MON	200P				1	:15	8.0				1	:15	8.0
M/F DAYTIME TOTALS						5	1:15	38.7				5	1:15	38.7
LATE NIGHT CBS 1	C TUE	1233X				1	:15	4.5				1	:15	4.5
E/L FRINGES TOTALS						1	:15	4.5				1	:15	4.5
PRODUCT TOTALS						6	1:30	43.2				6	1:30	43.2
MURINE PDTS-EYE DROPS		D219												
ANOTHER WORLD	N M-F	200P	2	:30	9.8	1	:15	4.9				3	:45	14.7
CLASSIC CONCENTRATION	N FRI	1130A	1	:15	1.4							1	:15	1.4
CLOSER LOOK	N THU	1230P	1	:15	.2							1	:15	.2
DAYS OF OUR LIVES	N WED	100P	2	:30	13.0							2	:30	13.0
ONE ON ONE	N MON	1100A				1	:15	1.4				1	:15	1.4
SANTA BARBARA	N M-F	300P	2	:30	6.8	1	:15	3.4				3	:45	10.2
M/F DAYTIME TOTALS			8	2:00	32.6	3	:45	9.7				11	2:45	42.2
NBC NIGHTLY NEWS	N M-F	630P	1	:15	20.0	1	:15	22.8				2	:30	42.8
NBC SATURDAY NGT NEWS	N SAT	634P				1	:15	11.2				1	:15	11.2
E/L FRINGES TOTALS			1	:15	20.0	2	:30	34.0				3	:45	54.0
PRODUCT TOTALS			9	2:15	52.5	5	1:15	43.7				14	3:30	96.2
SELSUN BLUE PDTS-EXTRA MED SHAMPOO		D142												
GRASS ROOTS-PART 1	N MON	900P	1	:15		1	:15	43.5				1	:15	43.5
L A LAW	N THU	1000P	1	:15	75.0							1	:15	75.0
NIGHT COURT	N WED	930P	1	:15		1	:15	53.5				1	:15	53.5
REASONABLE DOUBTS	N FRI	1000P	1	:15	30.0							1	:15	30.0
TORKELSONS	N SUN	730P	1	:15	31.0							1	:15	31.0
WALTER & EMILY	N SAT	830P	1	:15	30.0							1	:15	30.0
PRIME TIME TOTALS			4	1:00	166.0	2	:30	97.0				6	1:30	263.0
COTTON BOWL GAME	C WED	130P	1	:15	28.0							1	:15	28.0
M/F DAYTIME TOTALS			1	:15	28.0							1	:15	28.0
CLLG BSKB GM 1-SUN/ABC	A SUN	130P				3	:45	10.2				3	:45	10.2
CLLG BSKB GM 2-SUN/ABC	A SUN	344P				1	:15	3.1				1	:15	3.1
CLLG BSKB GM POST 1	A SUN	334P				2	:30	6.8				2	:30	6.8
CLLG BSKB GM POST 2	A SUN	551P				1	:15	3.1				1	:15	3.1
CLLG BSKB OVTM 2/ABC	A SUN	332P				1	:15	3.1				1	:15	3.1
NCAA BSKB GM-SAT 1/CBS	C SAT	100P	1	:15	10.4							1	:15	10.4
NCAA BSKB GM-SAT/CBS	C SAT	400P	1	:15	10.4							1	:15	10.4
NFC PLAYOFF PRE-SAT	C SAT	1200N	1	:15	18.0							1	:15	18.0
TWIN 125 AUTO RACE	C SAT	1200N				1	:15	12.1				1	:15	12.1
S/S DAYTIME TOTALS			3	:45	38.8	9	2:15	38.4				12	3:00	77.2
LATE NIGHT CBS 1	C M-F	1130P	2	:30	11.0	2	:30	9.0				4	1:00	20.0
LATE NIGHT CBS 2	C THU	1230X	1	:15	.6							1	:15	.6
E/L FRINGES TOTALS			3	:45	11.6	2	:30	9.0				6	1:15	20.6
PRODUCT TOTALS			11	2:45	244.4	13	3:15	144.4				24	6:00	388.8
SELSUN BLUE PDTS-REGULAR SHAMPOO		D142												
NFC CHAMPIONSHIP POST	C SUN	706P	1	:15	30.0							1	:15	30.0
SUPER BOWL POSTGAME	C SUN	1012P	1	:15	76.7							1	:15	76.7
GRASS ROOTS-PART 2	N TUE	900P				1	:15	40.0				1	:15	40.0
HOT COUNTRY NIGHTS	N SUN	800P	1	:15	31.0							1	:15	31.0
IN THE HEAT OF/NIGHT	N TUE	900P				1	:15	41.0				1	:15	41.0
LAW & ORDER	N WED	900P				1	:15	41.0				1	:15	41.0
NIGHT COURT	N WED	930P	1	:15	55.0							1	:15	55.0
QUANTUM LEAP	N WED	1000P				1	:15	56.5				1	:15	56.5
REASONABLE DOUBTS	N TUE	1000P				1	:15	34.5				1	:15	34.5
TORKELSONS	N SUN	730P				1	:15	52.0				1	:15	52.0
UNSOLVED MYSTERIES SPC	N WED	800P				1	:15	51.0				1	:15	51.0
WINGS	N THU	930P	1	:15	77.5							1	:15	77.5
PRIME TIME TOTALS			6	1:30	321.2	8	1:30	237.0				12	3:00	558.2
CLLG BSKB GM 1-SUN/ABC	A SUN	130P				1	:15	3.4				1	:15	3.4
CLLG BSKB GM 2-SUN/ABC	A SUN	345P				1	:15	3.1				1	:15	3.1
CLLG BSKB GM POST 1	A SUN	328P				1	:15	3.1				1	:15	3.1
CLLG BSKB GM POST 2	A SUN	551P				1	:15	3.1				1	:15	3.1
NCAA BSKB GM-SUN 2/CBS	C SUN	238P	1	:15	10.4							1	:15	10.4
NCAA WMNS BSKB GAME	C SAT	200P				1	:15	4.2				1	:15	4.2
NCAA WMNS VOLLEYBALL	C SUN	230P	1	:15	3.6							1	:15	3.6
NFC PLAYOFF GAME-SUN	C SUN	400P	1	:15	92.7							1	:15	92.7
NFC PLAYOFF POST-SAT	C SAT	551P	1	:15	18.0							1	:15	18.0
NFC PLAYOFF PRE-SUN	C SUN	330P	1	:15	18.0							1	:15	18.0
SUPER BOWL PREGAME 1	C SUN	230P	1	:15	76.7							1	:15	76.7
S/S DAYTIME TOTALS			6	1:30	219.4	5	1:15	17.2				11	2:45	236.6
LATE NIGHT CBS 1	C 1130P	1130P	2	:30	11.0							2	:30	11.0
LATE NIGHT CBS 2	C M-F	100X	1	:15	.5	1	:15	.5				2	:30	1.1
E/L FRINGES TOTALS			3	:45	11.6	1	:15	.5				4	1:00	12.1
PRODUCT TOTALS			15	3:45	552.2	12	3:00	254.7				27	6:45	806.9
PARENT CO. PRIME TIME TOTALS			10	2:30	487.2	8	2:00	334.0				18	4:30	821.2
PARENT CO. M/F DAYTIME TOTALS			9	2:15	60.5	8	2:00	48.4				17	4:15	108.9
PARENT CO. S/S DAYTIME TOTALS			9	2:15	258.2	14	3:30	55.6				23	5:45	313.8
PARENT CO. E/L FRINGES TOTALS			7	1:45	43.2	6	1:30	43.5				13	3:15	91.2
PARENT CO. TOTALS			35	8:45	849.1	36	9:00	486.0				71	17:45	1335.1
ABINGTON SHOE CO														
TIMBERLAND BOOTS		A131												
WIDE WORLD/SPORTS-SAT	A SAT	430P				1	:30	25.0				1	:30	25.0
S/S DAYTIME TOTALS						1	:30	25.0				1	:30	25.0
PRODUCT TOTALS						1	:30	25.0				1	:30	25.0
ACE HARDWARE CORP														
ACE HARDWARE STORE		V345												
48 HOURS	C SUN	1000P				1	:15	38.9				1	:15	38.9
CBS FRIDAY MOVIE SPCL	C FRI	917P	1	:15	18.5							1	:15	18.5
HEARTS ARE WILD	C FRI	1000P	1	:15	28.5							1	:15	28.5
JAKE & THE FATMAN	C WED	900P	1	:15	31.0	1	:15	29.6				2	:30	60.5
OLYMPIC GAMES-NITE	C FRI	800P				3	:45	207.9				3	:45	207.9
P.S.I. LUV U SPECIAL	C THU	900P	1	:15	14.6							1	:15	14.6
BRAND/PRODUCT CONTINUES														

FIGURE 7-7. Section 2—Brand/Product Market Expenditures

BRAND/PRODUCT MARKET(S)	ESTIMATED EXPENDITURES (000) APR	MAY	JUN	QTR
F163				
COOKIES & CRACKERS				
************** CONTINUED **************				
NABISCO-RITZ CRACKERS&RITZ BITS---------CONT				
SEATTLE		.3	.*	.3
SHREVEPORT		.2		.2
ST LOUIS		.7	.3	1.0
TAMPA		.*	.2	.2
WASHINGTON			.*	.*
WEST PALM BCH			.2	.2
WICHITA			.1	.1
WILKES BARRE			.*	.*
TOTALS		10.7	5.3	16.0
NABISCO-SPRINKLED CHIPS AHOY----------				
CHICAGO	.1			.1
DALLAS		.1		.1
LOS ANGELES	.4	.7		1.1
MIAMI	.2			.2
MINNEAPOLIS	.3	.7		1.0
NEW YORK	.8			.8
RALEIGH	1.0			1.0
SAN FRANCISCO		.3		.3
TULSA	.1			.1
WASHINGTON	.2			.2
TOTALS	3.2	1.8		5.0
NABISCO-TEDDY GRAHAMS BEARWICHES----------				
ATLANTA		.4	.2	.5
BALTIMORE		.2	.1	.4
BOSTON		.2	.9	1.1
BUFFALO			1.3	1.3
CHARLESTON			.5	.5
CHARLOTTE			.1	.1
CHICAGO		.8	.5	1.3
CINCINNATI			.6	.6
CLEVELAND		.1	.3	.4
COLUMBUS		.8	.4	1.2
DALLAS		.3	.7	1.0
DENVER		.4	.1	.6
DES MOINES			.2	.2
DETROIT		.2	1.0	1.2
FLINT			.*	.*
FRESNO			.4	.4
GREEN BAY		.3		.3
GREENSBORO		.6		.6
HARRISBURG			.2	.2
HARTFORD		.7	.5	1.3
HOUSTON		.3	.3	.5
JACKSONVILLE		.1		.1
KNOXVILLE			.3	.3
LITTLE ROCK		.3	.2	.5
LOS ANGELES		.9	2.9	3.8
MEMPHIS			.*	.*
MIAMI		.4	1.1	1.5
MINNEAPOLIS		.7	1.3	2.0
NASHVILLE			.2	.2
NEW YORK		1.8	7.0	8.8
NORFOLK			1.8	1.8
OKLAHOMA CITY		.5	.1	.6
OMAHA		.3		.3
PHILADELPHIA		.5	1.5	2.1
PHOENIX		.1	.7	.8
PITTSBURGH		.1	.4	.5
PORTLAND OR			1.1	1.1
RALEIGH			.3	.3
RICHMOND		.6		.6
ROCHESTER		.9		.9
SACRAMENTO			.3	.3
SALT LAKE CITY		1.3		1.3
SAN ANTONIO			.4	.4
SAN FRANCISCO			1.5	1.5
SEATTLE		.3	1.0	1.2
ST LOUIS		4	1.0	1.4
SYRACUSE			.3	.3
TAMPA		.3	.4	.8
TOLEDO			.2	.2
WASHINGTON			1.5	1.5
WEST PALM BCH			.2	.2
WILKES BARRE			.*	.*
TOTALS		14.7	34.4	49.0
NABISCO-TEDDY GRAHAMS SNACK----------				
ALBANY		.3		.3
ALBUQUERQUE		.2	.5	.7
ATLANTA	.1	.1	.8	1.0
BALTIMORE		.1	.3	.4
BIRMINGHAM			1.5	1.5
BOSTON		.1	.6	.7
BUFFALO	2 1	1.7	.1	3.9
CHARLOTTE		.1	.4	.5
CHICAGO		.8	.7	1.5
CINCINNATI		.7		.7
CLEVELAND	.2	.6	1.7	2.5
DALLAS	.2	.7	.6	1.4
DAYTON			1.2	1.2
DENVER		.3	.7	1.0
DETROIT	.3	.5	.6	1.5
FLINT	4	.3		.6
FRESNO		.2		.2
GRAND RAPIDS		.6		.6
GREEN BAY			.5	.5
GREENVILLE			.9	.9
HARRISBURG		.1	.4	.5
HOUSTON		.4	.8	1.2
INDIANAPOLIS			.5	.5
JACKSONVILLE			.5	.5
KANSAS CITY		.4	.6	.9
LEXINGTON		.5	.1	.5
LOS ANGELES	.4	2.6	1.3	4.3
LOUISVILLE		.3	.6	.9
MEMPHIS		.4		.4
MIAMI		1.5	1.3	2.8
MILWAUKEE	.3	.3	.6	1.2
MINNEAPOLIS	.3	.9	3.2	4.4
NASHVILLE		.4	.*	.4
NEW ORLEANS		.2		.2
NEW YORK	2.7	7.1	7.6	17.4
NORFOLK	.3	1.1		1.4
OKLAHOMA CITY		.6	.1	.7
OMAHA		.1	.1	.1
PHILADELPHIA		.9	.8	1.7
PHOENIX		.1	.1	.3
PITTSBURGH	.*	.3	.6	.9
RALEIGH		.3		.3
RICHMOND			9	.9
ROCHESTER			1.0	1.0
SALT LAKE CITY	.4		.8	1.2
SAN ANTONIO	1.6	1.6	2.5	5.8
SAN DIEGO		2	.3	.5
SAN FRANCISCO	.3	1.9	1.0	3.2
SEATTLE	.1	.8	.6	1.5

BRAND/PRODUCT MARKET(S)	ESTIMATED EXPENDITURES (000) APR	MAY	JUN	QTR
ST LOUIS		.6	1.1	1.6
SYRACUSE		.3		.3
TAMPA		.3	.5	.7
TOLEDO			1.5	1.5
TULSA		.3	.3	.6
WASHINGTON	.4	1.9	1.2	3.5
WICHITA		.1		.1
WILKES BARRE		.3	.5	.8
TOTALS	10.1	33.8	42.5	86.3
NABISCO-WHEAT THINS----------				
ALBUQUERQUE		.1		.1
CINCINNATI		1.1		1.1
NASHVILLE	.1			.1
SEATTLE		.2		.2
TOTALS	.1	1.4		1.4
NABISCO-WHEAT THINS & OAT THINS----------				
ALBUQUERQUE		.1		.1
ATLANTA	.7	.3		1.0
BIRMINGHAM	1			.1
BOSTON	.2	1.4	.1	1.6
CHARLESTON	1.7			1.7
CHARLOTTE		.4	.3	.6
CHICAGO	.9	.3		1.2
CLEVELAND	6	.2		.8
DALLAS	3	.6		.9
DAYTON		.2		.2
DENVER	4.9	8.2	8.9	22.0
DETROIT	.3	.6		.9
GRAND RAPIDS	3.0	1.5		4.5
HARRISBURG		1.2		1.2
HARTFORD			.1	.1
HOUSTON	.2	.3		.5
LOS ANGELES	31.5	34.5	32.3	98.3
LOUISVILLE	8	.4		1.2
MEMPHIS	1	.8	.*	.9
MIAMI	.4	.4	.2	1.0
MINNEAPOLIS	.8	.4	.1	1.3
NASHVILLE		.8		.8
NEW ORLEANS		1.0		1.0
NEW YORK	.5	2.2		2.7
ORLANDO		.6	.2	.8
PHILADELPHIA	.6	.8		1.4
PHOENIX		6.6	9.7	16.3
PITTSBURGH	.3	.9		1.3
RALEIGH		3.0		3.0
RICHMOND	1.1			1.1
SACRAMENTO		5.8	5.5	11.3
SALT LAKE CITY	6.8	7.0	5.2	18.9
SAN DIEGO	2.9		3.6	6.5
SAN FRANCISCO	15.2	22.6	22.7	60.5
SEATTLE	.3	.3	.1	.6
SPRINGFIELD		.1	.2	.4
ST LOUIS	.1	.6		.7
SYRACUSE	.5			.5
TAMPA		.5		.5
TULSA	.6	.5		1.1
WASHINGTON		1.9		1.9
WICHITA	1.0		.3	1.3
WILKES BARRE			.*	.*
TOTALS	76.4	106.8	89.5	272.7
NABISCO-WHEATSWORTH CRACKERS----------				
PITTSBURGH			.*	.*
PEPPERIDGE FARM-WHOLESOME CHOICE CKS-------				
BUFFALO		.5		.5
PORTLAND OR		1.5		1.5
TOTALS		2.0		2.0
RY KRISP CRACKERS----------				
CHICAGO	26.7	15.8	9.0	51.5
LOS ANGELES	70.3	45.2	32.1	147.6
MINNEAPOLIS	15.9	7.6	10.4	33.9
PORTLAND OR	6.6	10.8	11.2	28.6
SAN FRANCISCO	36.9	19.0	20.2	76.1
SEATTLE	13.0	6.4	6.5	25.9
TOTALS	169.4	104.8	89.4	362.6
STELLA DORO-VARIOUS----------				
MIAMI	*			.*
WASHINGTON		.2		.2
TOTALS	*	.2		.2
SUNSHINE PDTS-CHEEZ-ITS----------				
BALTIMORE			34.6	34.8
BOSTON			47.3	47.3
BUFFALO			.6	.6
DALLAS			19.6	19.6
DETROIT			11.6	11.6
HARTFORD			24.4	24.4
HOUSTON			31.3	31.3
KANSAS CITY			37.5	37.5
LOS ANGELES			184.2	184.2
MIAMI			52.7	52.7
MINNEAPOLIS			42.1	42.1
NEW YORK			144.9	144.9
ORLANDO			26.7	26.7
PHILADELPHIA			73.2	73.2
PHOENIX			37.6	37.6
PITTSBURGH			28.2	28.2
SACRAMENTO			35.8	35.8
SAN ANTONIO			17.3	17.3
SAN DIEGO			81.7	81.7
SAN FRANCISCO			87.5	87.5
ST LOUIS			27.5	27.5
TAMPA			37.3	37.3
WASHINGTON			45.8	45.8
TOTALS			1129.5	1129.5
SUNSHINE PDTS-COOKIES&CRACKERS----------				
MIAMI			.9	.9
SUNSHINE PDTS-CRACKERS----------				
BOSTON			4.7	4.7
BUFFALO			20.4	20.4
CHICAGO			93.5	93.5
DALLAS			25.2	25.2
HARTFORD			16.5	16.5
HOUSTON			16.9	16.9
MIAMI			9.5	9.5
MINNEAPOLIS			10.5	10.5
NEW YORK			25.2	25.2
PITTSBURGH			4.3	4.3
SACRAMENTO			16.5	16.5
SAN ANTONIO			10.1	10.1
SAN FRANCISCO			10.8	10.8
TOTALS			264.1	264.1
SUNSHINE PDTS-HYDROX COOKIES----------				
BALTIMORE			40.1	40.1
BOSTON			72.4	72.4
BUFFALO			29.8	29.8
CHICAGO			96.8	96.8
DALLAS			47.7	47.7
DETROIT			29.7	29.7
HARTFORD			68.3	68.3
HOUSTON			67.6	67.6
KANSAS CITY			27.2	27.2
LOS ANGELES			198.6	198.6

BRAND/PRODUCT MARKET(S)	ESTIMATED EXPENDITURES (000) APR	MAY	JUN	QTR
MIAMI			54.0	54.0
MINNEAPOLIS			47.1	47.1
NEW YORK			236.1	236.1
ORLANDO			24.7	24.7
PHILADELPHIA			70.2	70.2
PHOENIX			37.7	37.7
PITTSBURGH			35.7	35.7
SACRAMENTO			61.0	61.0
SAN DIEGO			45.6	45.6
SAN FRANCISCO			103.4	103.4
ST LOUIS			30.1	30.1
TAMPA			38.5	38.5
WASHINGTON			45.3	45.3
TOTALS			1497.8	1497.8
VIVA PUFFS COOKIES----------				
BUFFALO	4.7			4.7
F171				
COFFEE, TEA, COCOA & MILK ADDITIVES				
4 C FOOD-INSTANT ICED TEA MIX----------				
BOSTON		38.0	78.7	116.7
HARTFORD		40.7	1.5	42.2
NEW YORK		90.3	156.2	246.5
PITTSBURGH		15.4	35.4	50.8
PORTLAND ME			.6	.6
PROVIDENCE		15.6		15.6
TOTALS		200.0	272.4	472.4
BOYDS COFFEE-REGULAR----------				
PORTLAND OR		130.2	94.0	224.2
SEATTLE	10.5	47.4		57.9
TOTALS	10.5	177.6	94.0	282.1
BOYDS COFFEE-WHOLE BEAN----------				
PORTLAND OR			24.2	24.2
CAINS FOOD-INSTANT TEA&TEA BAGS----------				
OKLAHOMA CITY		.3	.4	.7
CAINS FOOD-ONE STEP FILTER PACK----------				
OKLAHOMA CITY	.5			.5
CHOCK FULL O'NUTS-GOURMET REG&DCF RG-------				
PORTLAND ME	3.5			3.5
CHOCK FULL O'NUTS-REGULAR&DECAF REG-------				
ATLANTA	44.7	26.0		70.7
CINCINNATI	30.2			30.2
CLEVELAND	1.7			1.7
COLUMBUS	27.4			27.4
DAYTON	21.1			21.1
HARRISBURG		6.4		6.4
HARTFORD	12.8			12.8
MIAMI	84.6	16.6	.2	101.5
NORFOLK	27.0	27.1		54.1
SYRACUSE		.8		.8
WILKES BARRE	5			.5
TOTALS	250.0	77.0	.2	327.2
CHOCK FULL O'NUTS-RICH FRN RST RG&DC-------				
ALBANY	14.7	2.5		17.2
BOSTON	94.8	74.0		168.9
CLEVELAND	30.8	25.1		55.8
HARRISBURG	31.3	27.2		58.5
HARTFORD	37.8			37.8
NEW YORK	255.3	141.8		397.1
PORTLAND ME	12.0	18.5		30.5
SYRACUSE		15.9		15.9
WILKES BARRE	15.6			15.6
TOTALS	492.2	305.0		797.2
CHOCK FULL O'NUTS-VAR COFFEES----------				
ATLANTA	.7			.7
COFFEE OF COLOMBIA----------				
NEW YORK			.6	.6
CRYSTAL LIGHT-FRUIT TEA----------				
DALLAS		.1	.*	.2
HOUSTON		1.0	1.0	2.0
TOTALS		1.1	1.1	2.2
FOLGERS COFFEE-AUTOMATIC DRIP----------				
ATLANTA	.2			.2
BALTIMORE		2.2		2.2
BOSTON			.2	.2
CHICAGO	25.9	3.6		29.5
CINCINNATI	7.1		.1	7.1
CLEVELAND	11.8	2.1	9.5	23.4
COLUMBUS	11.6			11.6
DALLAS	.6		1.9	2.6
DAYTON	11.3			11.3
DENVER			1.2	1.2
DES MOINES	6.2			6.2
DETROIT	11.2	2.1		13.3
FLINT	2.0			2.0
GRAND RAPIDS	5.6	6.3		11.9
GREEN BAY	.8			.8
GREENSBORO			2.7	2.7
HOUSTON			10.5	10.5
INDIANAPOLIS	5.8		1.1	6.9
MILWAUKEE	9.7			9.7
MINNEAPOLIS	10.9	3.3	.2	14.4
NEW YORK	29.3	6.4	22.1	57.9
OKLAHOMA CITY	7.2		1.8	9.0
PITTSBURGH	8.1	1.9		10.0
ROCHESTER			1.7	1.7
SPRINGFIELD	3.0			3.0
ST LOUIS	11.3			11.3
SYRACUSE			1.5	1.5
TOLEDO	3.0	3.0		6.0
TULSA	4.0	3.2		7.2
WICHITA	4.0	3.8		7.9
TOTALS	190.8	38.0	54.5	283.3
FOLGERS COFFEE-COFFEE SINGLES----------				
ALBANY	6.1	10.5	14.6	31.3
BOSTON	34.5	38.3	41.1	113.9
BUFFALO	.3	14.2	22.8	37.2
CHICAGO	41.9	56.9	83.1	181.9
CINCINNATI		25.4	28.8	54.3
CLEVELAND	35.1	34.4	46.3	115.8
COLUMBUS	22.3	23.2	18.8	64.2
DAYTON	14.3	14.7	13.8	42.7
DETROIT	31.3	29.1	49.4	109.9
FLINT	8.3	10.5	8.6	27.4
GRAND RAPIDS	11.5	15.4	21.9	48.7
HARTFORD	17.3	20.2	15.2	52.8
INDIANAPOLIS		14.8	17.7	32.5
KANSAS CITY	18.0	22.0	24.9	64.9
LEXINGTON	11.1	7.1	9.0	27.2
LOUISVILLE	10.1	12.7	31.8	54.6
MILWAUKEE	12.5	14.2	14.1	40.9
OKLAHOMA CITY	5.2	11.6	10.6	27.4
PITTSBURGH	23.6	24.3	29.6	77.5
PORTLAND ME	2.0	4.1	5.8	12.0
PROVIDENCE	10.1	8.9	12.2	31.2
ROCHESTER	9.0	11.4	20.0	40.3
SPRINGFIELD	4.5	3.5	4.4	12.5

BARCUME · NATIONAL SPOT TV · SECOND QUARTER, 1991

BAR - BC001S/BC002S

TABLE 7-1.   Competitive Media Expenditure Analysis for a Product Class

Brands	Magazines (%)	Supple- ments (%)	News- papers (%)	Network TV (%)	Spot TV (%)	Outdoor (%)	Totals (%)
A	9.8	12.8	50.3	19.8	—	7.3	100
B	36.7	11.5	43.1	8.7	—	—	100
C	0.5	5.9	47.8	45.3	—	0.5	100
D	5.4	2.9	5.9	80.6	5.2	—	100
E	0.5	—	9.6	20.2	69.6	—	100

each competitor's annual expenditures. (See Table 7-1.) The proportion of each competitor's total expenditures in each medium makes comparisons easier, though problems can occur in making comparisons on the basis of percentages when the bases differ widely. Ten percent of one brand's total budget spent in newspapers, for example, may not be equivalent to a competitor's 10 percent spent in newspapers if the base of one was $3,000 and the base of the other, $3,000,000.

The study of annual expenditures is only one approach in analyzing competitors' marketing and media strategies. Another useful analysis may be made by comparing expenditures of a brand with its competitors on a market-by-market basis. This technique may be helpful in learning which markets were most important to competitors, and the analysis may serve as one basis for weighting media in a given market. It is easy to locate these markets in Media Records but difficult in LNA Network Television Service or LNA Magazine Analysis Service. It may be possible, however, to estimate which markets were used and the relative weights placed in these markets.

Still another kind of analysis may be made of the dollars spent in each medium by a brand and its competitors, correlated with the audience delivered for the dollars spent. This technique makes possible a quick analysis of the relative delivery effectiveness of competitors' media expenditures. Plans for a brand's reach and frequency often come from such an analysis.

Finally, it is important to learn how much was spent in each medium during each month of the year. Most brands have peak selling seasons and vary the weight of their advertising accordingly. This kind of analysis helps to establish timing and scheduling plans for the media selected later in the planning process.

Analyzing the Data

One worthwhile use of media expenditure figures is to examine spending by advertisers who lead in share of market. Those with smaller shares might want to learn which media, markets, and audiences are most important to the leaders. Sometimes it is possible to find that leading competitors ignore one or two media entirely. In such a case, it may be possible for those with lesser shares to preempt a medium for themselves. For example, all of the share leaders may emphasize network television. Then, a planner may select radio as a medium in which a brand could be very significant because no others are using radio. The planner should keep in mind, however, that if a competitor avoids a medium, there may be good reason to conclude that the medium is not appropriate for the product's advertising.

There are, of course, problems in analyzing media expenditure data. Most such data are incomplete, do not show any discounts earned in a medium, and cover only large advertisers. An additional problem is the age of the data. It is rare that any data are less than one month old, and, as a result, the nature of the data is historical rather than contemporary. The question arises whether such data have very much meaning, especially if a competitor is not currently using the same media in the same ways as in the past. Yet if a competitor uses media in a predictably consistent pattern, then additional data may be of little value. Probably the best use of an expenditure analysis is as part of an organized intelligence system including other kinds of marketing information to provide a clear picture of competitors' strategies. Although some advertising agencies tend to deprecate the use of expenditure analysis as not being worth the investment in money or time, most large agencies feel that it is valuable if used properly as an indication of spending strategy.

Probably the greatest danger in analyzing expenditure data may come from simply copying the leaders in a blind fashion. If a leading share competitor places 10 percent of its budget in Market A, then other competitors may follow the leader. But the followers' products and market strategies may not lend themselves to such weight in Market A. Furthermore, the share leader may establish its weight proportions for reasons quite different from those that followers ought to use.

An expenditure analysis is helpful as a means of knowing what competitors have done, but not necessarily as a means of knowing what to do as a result. These analyses may show, for example, that a competitor is test marketing a product, and this information may call for a revised market strategy to combat the situation. Intelligently used, expenditure data may be well worth the time and money invested.

Using Competitive Media Expenditure Analyses

Following is a list of uses of a competitive media expenditure analysis devised by the staff of *Media Decisions*.[3] It reviews the most important uses and values to be obtained by completing such an analysis:

1. The expenditure figures can show you the regionality and seasonality and how these factors are changing for all competitive and potentially competitive brands.
2. The data can give you a fix on ad budget size and media mix market by market.

---

3. *Media Decisions,* "Do You Know Your Competitive Brand Data?" August 1975, p. 60.

3. You can use the data to spot new product tests and to track new brand roll-outs.
4. You can infer from where the money is being spent how competitors view their target audiences, how they profile their brands, and where they seek to position themselves in your marketplace.
5. You can watch spending patterns of the opposition—TV flighting, radio station rotation, position practices in magazines, or day of week in newspapers.
6. Once you have complete knowledge of what your enemies are up to, you can make better decisions as to where to meet them head-on and when to outflank them.
7. In new-product and line-extension planning, expenditure data are essential to estimate how much it will cost to get into a market, who's already there, and which competitive product types are growing fastest in the new product's market segment.

Sources of Marketing Data

Size and share of market for a brand and its competitors, and other information that comprise a situation analysis, may be obtained from a number of syndicated research services. Other data may be obtained from periodicals, association reports, government, and media.

Major Data Services

The most widely used syndicated research services are those of the A. C. Nielsen Company, the Market Research Corporation of America (MRCA), Audits and Surveys, Inc., Selling Areas-Marketing, Inc. (SAMI), Mediamark Research, Inc. (MRI), and the W. R. Simmons Company (SMRB). Numerous other research companies also exist.

The A. C. Nielsen Company. Nielsen provides a national brand, store-audited service covering almost every product sold in food and drug stores. Each of these product categories is audited in a national sample of retail stores every sixty days. The service provides share-of-market data based on sales to consumers at the retail level, in addition to average retail prices, wholesale prices, inventory, out-of-stock, dealer support (displays, local advertising, and coupon redemption), and major media advertising. The sample data are then projected in order to obtain national and regional data. The figures are further broken down by county size, store type (chain and independent), brand, package size, and product type.

   The method of making an audit is to count a store's inventory of a given product no matter where it is stored. Sales for a given period are found by subtracting the total stock on hand at the close of a period from the total available for sale at the beginning. Because only a sample of stores is audited, it becomes necessary to project average per store sales to a national figure and to geographical regions, city-size groups, and so forth.

Market Research Corporation of America. MRCA maintains a consumer panel of 7,500 families who keep continuous diaries of their purchases. The panel members record food, grocery, and personal care items purchased during any given week and then mail their diaries to the company for tabulation. Diaries include quantities purchased, package sizes, prices paid, and the kind of retail outlet through which purchases were made. Other information includes effects of promotional activities such as coupons, one-cent sales, or combination sales of different products. Through such tabulations it is possible to learn the share of market for many different brands and varieties of food products.

Audits and Surveys, Inc. This service measures the national total market based on a sample of the client's product class distribution. The sample of stores to be audited is drawn only from the types of outlets in which the client has distribution. Information is provided on sales, inventory, distribution, out-of-stock, and the number of days stock is on hand. These data are projected to the total U.S. and the client's sales regions. Audits and Surveys telephones a flash report to the client at the close of the audit followed by a formal report two weeks later, compared to Nielsen's forty-five to sixty days for reports to reach a client.

Selling Areas-Marketing, Inc. (SAMI). This company reports warehouse withdrawals to food stores in defined marketing areas. Specifically, SAMI provides information on the sales movement of all dry grocery and household supplies. Frozen food, health and beauty aids, fresh meat, perishables, milk, bread, and soft drinks are not included. An "Executive Review" is especially important because it summarizes individual brand shares for all SAMI markets and provides category sales volume and brand share for the total U.S. market.

Mediamark Research, Inc. (MRI), and W. R. Simmons (SMRB). These companies provide marketing as well as media data on a regular basis. Each company reports how often products and/or brands are used so that a planner can identify heavy and light users demographically. In addition, each company reports how heavy and light users were exposed to either network television programs or national magazines. As a result, the planner can select media that not only have the largest audiences, but the largest audiences of heavy users of a given product or brand. Special studies are also available on a custom basis.

Zip Code Marketing. There are two major concerns in this area: PRIZM and ACORN. PRIZM provides marketing data at every microgeographic level including zip codes, census tracts, census block groups, compiled list cells, and postal carrier routes.

ACORN provides a classification for residential neighborhoods. It classifies all U.S. neighborhoods into forty-four distinct, homogeneous, "lifestyle" types or market segments, for example, "middle-income, post-war suburbs, older populations, etc." (For further discussion, see Chapter 5, "New Media Measuring Tools.")

Other Sources of Data

The preceding sources of data provide specific and pertinent data for a situation analysis, but are relatively expensive. The cost may be too high for many small manufacturers or agencies, so it becomes necessary to find substitute sources of data. There are a number of relatively inexpensive sources, though they do not provide the same amount of detail, especially about competitors' sales and distribution practices. When the information is incomplete, assumptions will have to be made about the missing data. These assumptions, however, can often be checked by astute observers of the marketing action of both their own company and competitors. The following list, meanwhile, may be helpful in locating data for the situation analysis.

Sales & Marketing Management Survey of Buying Power. Marketing and media planners often find the *Sales & Marketing Management Survey of Buying Power* a convenient source of three kinds of data about markets:

1. Population and household data for all major geographical markets in the United States.
2. Effective buying income and spending statistics about markets.
3. Retail sales data by broad product classes. The classes reported are: (a) food stores; (b) eating and drinking places; (c) general merchandise stores; (d) automotive dealers; (e) furniture, home furnishings, and appliances; (f) drugstores; (g) apparel and accessory stores; (h) gasoline service stations; (i) building materials and hardware stores.

No individual brand sales are shown, and there are no classifications of consumers other than by population and income. However, the periodical is convenient in locating and evaluating geographical markets by state, by Metropolitan Statistical Area, by county, or by city. Furthermore, the three factors (population, income, and retail sales) have been combined into a multiple factor index number for each market that makes comparisons among markets easier. Convenient tables ranking markets by sales potential also facilitate comparisons by each of the nine retail product categories. A user trying to find and evaluate markets for a drug product, for example, will find a table that ranks markets from best to poorest on the basis of sales of drugs. *Sales Management & Marketing Survey of Buying Power* is published annually.

Standard Rate and Data Service (SRDS). The Standard Rate and Data Service publishes media rate books for all major media. In its local media books (newspaper, spot radio, and spot television) are market data sections similar to those in the *Survey of Buying Power.* SRDS also shows geographical markets by state, Metropolitan Statistical Areas, counties, and cities, but not in as much detail as the *Buying Power* book. Retail sales, too, are shown by seven different categories: (a) food, (b) drugs, (c) general merchandise, (d) apparel, (e) home furnishings, (f) automotive, and (g) service stations. Ranking tables are also provided, showing markets for the seven product types. Local media rate books are published monthly, and the market data are revised annually.

Editor and Publisher Market Guide. This annual publication contains geographical market data similar to that of the preceding two. Markets are also ranked by population, total income, total retail sales, total food sales, and by household income. The text also provides individual descriptions of markets.

Census Data. The U.S. Department of Commerce publishes many census analyses that are helpful in marketing planning. Most useful have been the "Census of Business" and "Census of Population." But other census data, too numerous to list here, are available for special industries. The *Statistical Abstract,* published once a year, has been considered helpful as a quick source of data for media market planning.

Media Studies of Special Markets. Often local and national media conduct special market studies that may be quite helpful in learning about geographical as well as special markets. Although the purpose of these reports is to show a given medium in a favorable light, the researcher should not assume that all such studies are biased. Often a medium will sponsor a study that represents a significant contribution to the understanding of markets and media. Many times the only research available on a special market or medium is to be found in these studies.

Among the most widely used sources of market data and among the few that show brand share of markets are brand preference studies conducted by local newspapers and provided free of cost to agencies. Different newspapers use different names for these studies, but they are essentially home inventories of the many different product brands that have been recently purchased. Because there are many such studies in existence, it is possible to get some idea of the relative share of market for a brand in various parts of the country by comparing data from a composite selection.

Unfortunately, most studies are conducted only once a year and some newspapers do not repeat their studies each year. Furthermore, there may be differences in the degree of control exercised in the collection and reporting of such data, so that it is difficult to know how precise the data are. Then, too, because the data are collected only once a year, there is no measure of total volume purchased, because an individual may just happen to have purchased a given brand only at the time the study was made.

There are a number of publications that offer market and media data on a regular basis. The more useful ones are: *Advertising Age, Marketing Communications, Adweek, MediaWeek, Broadcasting, Editor & Publisher, Magazine,* and *Television/Radio Age.* Information can be obtained from the publications by either subscribing to them or by contacting their libraries to determine what studies were published in their past issues.

Associations. There are many trade associations that report market data for their members. In some cases, these data show sales by brands, but others tend to be rather general. Because there are so many different trade associations in the country, it is advisable to determine whether they can be of aid in compiling the situation analysis.

Miscellaneous Sources. There are yet other sources of data that are available at relatively low cost to the market/media planner. Federal, state, and local governments all produce various kinds of research that may be helpful. Federal data may be found by writing to the Government Printing Office in Washington, D.C.

Chambers of Commerce, both national and local, may be helpful in finding the right kinds of data needed for marketing situation purposes. Obviously this kind of data will be rather general but may be useful for preliminary portions of the analysis.

Finally, for analysis of products and product values, both *Consumer Reports* (published by the Consumer Union of U.S., Inc.) and *Consumer Bulletin* (published by Consumer Research, Inc.) provide monthly and annual publications for a small cost. Both of these organizations put various brands of products through rigorous tests to determine quality and the best buy for the money. Not all brands or models are tested, but many of the most popular brands on the market are analyzed. Ordinarily, this kind of information is difficult to obtain except by special research services, so these two publications make the job of finding product values relatively easy.

In conclusion, then, the situation analysis is a very important document in the media planning area. To the extent that it is done thoroughly and accurately, it can help the media planner make more effective decisions by providing a complete picture of the marketing situation not only for the client's brand but for the competitors'.

Use of Single Source Marketing Data for Media Planning

There are a number of single source measurement companies whose marketing information data will affect media planning more than ever before. These will come from single source measurements like BehaviorScan and Nielsen's Home*Scan. When product purchasing data is combined with media exposure data, there will be greater opportunities than before to make media selection and media usage decisions more accurately. These kinds of research, however, are still in the development stage despite the fact that many large national advertisers have used the data for special planning occasions. (The advantages are also discussed in Chapter 5.)

Listed below are still a number of stumbling blocks to the daily use of scanner data.

1. Not all the data represents the national marketplace. The use of selected markets such as those BehaviorScan measures cannot be used as a generalization that applies to all markets. Nielsen, of course, does have a national market measurement. Both national and extensive local market single source data is needed to cover many different marketing opportunities.

2. Not all media are matched with purchasing. It is important to see how alternative media fare in selling a given product. At present, network television has been most often correlated with purchasing. But newspapers, magazines, radio, and cable also need to be measured and matched. As time goes on, additional media will be measured. To make single source data most valuable, it is necessary to have all major media represented in the measurement.

3. Even then it will be important to use the passive peoplemeter measurements to best match media against purchasing. It is doubtful that all of the companies doing single source measurements will have the passive meter available. However, commercial exposure will be better than program exposure measurements, and the more alternative media is measured, the more likely it will enable a planner to cover all the bases in making comparisons.

4. It remains to be seen whether even commercial exposure measurements will provide the kinds of marketing/media data planners need to make media planning a truly scientific endeavor. There is a great need for better sample selection and better cooperation of respondents in using measurement techniques to make the data valid. If consumers do not fully cooperate in the single source measurements, the data will have limited usefulness.

QUESTIONS FOR DISCUSSION

1. What should a planner look for when analyzing the situation analysis of a brand?
2. Give an example of a marketing objective and a related marketing strategy for any brand of product.
3. Explain the difference between a marketing objective and the basic selling idea.

4. Why may it be advisable to place more advertising dollars in markets where a brand has been selling well, rather than in a new, undeveloped market?
5. Why can't a manufacturer of cereals look at its sales records and know how well the brand is selling at any local (retail) level?
6. Why may it not be a good idea for a national advertiser to select local markets in which to advertise only on the basis of shipments to those markets?
7. Should media planners select the same media that most of their competitors select? Briefly explain.
8. How can an advertiser ''force'' distribution sometimes in a market where its brand is not distributed?
9. In what ways does a sales promotion plan affect media planning?
10. What are the main roles of media in the selling process?

SELECTED READINGS

Advertising Age, ''Know Market Goals, Then Pick Media, AMC Exec Says,'' May 8, 1972, 32.

Clancy, Kevin J., ''The Failure of Marketing Programs,'' *Marketing and Media Decisions*, May 1986, 160.

Harris, Thomas, ''To Cut Through Ad Message Clutter, Add Marketing Public Relations,'' *Advertising Age*, April 29, 1991.

Horton, Cleveland, ''Mazda's Amati Embraces Target-Media Idea,'' *Advertising Age*, August 26, 1991, 4.

Journal of Small Business Management, ''Guidelines for Advertising Media Management,'' January 1978, 34–40.

Kleinfield, N.R., ''Targeting the Grocery Shopper: The Laser Scanner and the Mag-Striped Card are Altering Grocery Marketing,'' *The New York Times*, May 26, 1991.

Robinson, William A., ''Managing Your Marketing System for Better Results,'' *Potentials in Marketing*, September 1991.

Sansolo, Michael, ''Focusing on the Whole Store,'' *Progressive Grocer*, November 1991, 29–32.

Brunelli, ''The New Math of New Brands,'' *Mediaweek*, March 9, 1992, 12–15.

PROMO, ''Retailers and Scanning, What They Know, What They Don't,'' May 1988, 10–24.

Ryan, Nancy, ''Marketers Are Playing Consumer Match Game,'' *Chicago Tribune*, December 22, 1991, business section, 1–4.

8

Strategy Planning I:
Who, Where, and When

Among the most important decisions that must be made early in the media planning process are:

1. To whom should we target our advertising?
2. Where, geographically, should we advertise?
3. When should we advertise?

The answers to these questions comprise three of the most important parts of media strategy. Other parts of strategy will be discussed in subsequent chapters.

Once made, these decisions will control other decisions. For example, if it has been agreed that advertising should be directed primarily to women 18–34, then media alternatives such as sports magazines or TV programs directed primarily to men would not be appropriate. (Obviously there are some exceptions—but not many.) To control later decisions, target decisions must be made early.

Sometimes the media planner makes these decisions alone, but more often the process includes creative and marketing planners as well as input from the client. It is most often a team process.

Answers to each of the three big questions rely most heavily on numerical analysis of marketing and media data, but they also involve judgment and subjective appraisal. Numbers that are evaluated literally may be subject to error. One must know where the numbers came from—how they were obtained or calculated. The best planners know the value of research methodology as well as how to analyze the numbers. The search for objectivity in planning requires both abilities.

To Whom Should We Target Our Advertising?

Mass Markets Versus Target Markets

Prior to World War II, America was perceived as a mass market to national advertisers. Therefore, many such advertisers tried to reach almost everyone in the country. By 1947, however, the idea of a target market was advanced because consumer research became available and showed differences in purchasing by media audiences with different demographic classifications. Every product class had a slightly different demographic profile of heavy, medium, or light users. Until then, there had been few measurements available that classified purchasers demographically.

As a consequence of having such research available, the marketing industry began to use segmentation techniques, by which they divided a market into smaller segments of high potential product users. These smaller segments cost the advertisers less money to reach, and were perceived to have higher sales potential than did other consumers in the total market. Segmentation proved to be easy to use and made marketing and media planning more successful than was possible with mass marketing techniques.

The media chosen to reach these demographic target groups tended to be mass media. This tactic may have confused some marketers into believing that by using mass media, they were still practicing mass marketing. That was not true.

Mass media were selected to reach demographically defined market segments because the largest *target audiences were in the mass audiences.* So media planners had to ignore the total audiences of media vehicles and concentrate on the demographic target segments only. The net effect of this tactic was that planners sometimes had to buy a great deal of "waste"— audience members who have a low propensity to buy a given product. For example, if the targets were defined as women aged 18 to 49, any other media audience demographics such as women 50 on up, or men of any age, represented waste. But many advertisers are still selecting mass media because it delivers more precisely defined targets than do other media audiences. Marketers can tolerate waste if they reach more targets for the same amount of money.

Target Selection for Media Planning

Target selection usually starts with information from the client about the best targets, using the client's experience as a base. But the planner should then check audience data from either Simmons Market Research Bureau or MRI to study product category usage data arranged demographically. (A sample of a page from SMRB is shown in Figure 8–1.)

The goal is to identify the targets—those who are most likely to buy. Targets will most often be identified on the basis of one or more of the market's demographic characteristics. Which demographic characteristics? Those typical of consumers who have purchased the product/brand in the past and who resemble past purchasers in terms of age, income, occupation, education, and so forth. Custom-made research can provide this kind of information, but it is usually quite expensive and time-consuming.

One of the first media planning actions is to decide whether to concentrate on all users or a narrower product usage category. A great deal will depend on whom the advertiser wants to reach. This is a marketing as well as a creative and media decision. Most likely, the creative personnel and the agency account representative will recommend who they believe can be convinced to buy the brand. Sometimes the goal is to convince consumers to switch to our brand. Other times it will be to convince new persons not using the product category to try it and buy it. But once the buying category has been decided (a planner may choose combinations such as heavy and medium users, or medium and light users) the targets will then be found by studying demographic data. The use of index numbers will help the planner make that final target decision.

Lifestyle descriptions may also be used instead of demographics, or combined with demographics, to arrive at a target audience definition. At times, custom-made audience research may show that lifestyle characteristics are better at defining target markets than simple demographic characteristics. An example could be in analyzing a target market for high fidelity stereos that showed the best target to be adults aged 18 to 54 years old. But subsequent research may show that a somewhat different target also exists, of adults 25 to 54 years old skewed to the older ages, and with a lifestyle description of "liking classical music better than any other." Presumably there could be other and different lifestyle segments with different musical tastes.

Today many advertising planners tend to use only the age–sex classification for media planning because it is relatively simple to use and a valid descriptive category. Other planners prefer much more narrowly defined targets, and use media that reach such narrow segments of the market.

Using Index Numbers to Analyze Markets

In analyzing numerical data, there are three commonly used bases: raw numbers, percentages, and index numbers. Raw numbers are used least often because they are so large and because it is difficult to compare the raw numbers of one brand with those of another brand, each of which may have radically different bases. Percentages are a means of equalizing the bases of numbers from two or more companies, and thus are usually preferred over raw numbers for comparison purposes. Index numbers are special kinds of percentages that are most preferred for comparison purposes.

An index is a number that shows a relationship between two percentages

FIGURE 8-1. Page from Simmons Market Research Bureau *

0244
P-18

CAFFEINATED INSTANT & FREEZE-DRIED COFFEE: USAGE ON AVERAGE DAY IN LAST 30 DAYS
(FEMALE HOMEMAKERS)

0244
P-18

	TOTAL U.S. '000	ALL USERS A '000	B % DOWN	C % ACROSS	D INDX	HEAVY USERS FIVE OR MORE A '000	B % DOWN	C % ACROSS	D INDX	MEDIUM USERS TWO-FOUR A '000	B % DOWN	C % ACROSS	D INDX	LIGHT USERS ONE OR LESS A '000	B % DOWN	C % ACROSS	D INDX
TOTAL FEMALE HOMEMAKERS	82531	24347	100.0	29.5	100	6022	100.0	7.3	100	10760	100.0	13.0	100	7565	100.0	9.2	100
18 - 24	8060	1943	8.0	24.1	82	*393	6.5	4.9	67	968	9.0	12.0	92	*582	7.7	7.2	79
25 - 34	19731	5571	22.9	28.2	96	1441	23.9	7.3	100	2355	21.9	11.9	92	1776	23.5	9.0	98
35 - 44	16107	4660	19.1	28.9	98	1081	18.0	6.7	92	2284	21.2	14.2	109	1295	17.1	8.0	88
45 - 54	11491	3386	13.9	29.5	100	948	15.7	8.2	113	1384	12.9	12.0	92	1054	13.9	9.2	100
55 - 64	11584	3698	15.2	31.9	108	934	15.5	8.1	111	1555	14.5	13.4	103	1208	16.0	10.4	114
65 OR OLDER	15558	5089	20.9	32.7	111	1223	20.3	7.9	108	2215	20.6	14.2	109	1651	21.8	10.6	116
18 - 34	27791	7514	30.9	27.0	92	1834	30.5	6.6	90	3322	30.9	12.0	92	2357	31.2	8.5	93
18 - 49	49721	13752	56.5	27.7	94	3256	54.1	6.5	90	6301	58.6	12.7	97	4195	55.3	8.4	92
25 - 49	47328	13618	55.9	28.8	98	3471	57.6	7.3	101	6022	56.0	12.7	98	4125	54.5	8.7	95
35 - 49	21930	6238	25.6	28.4	96	1421	23.6	6.5	89	2979	27.7	13.6	104	1837	24.3	8.4	91
50 OR OLDER	32810	10595	43.5	32.3	109	2766	45.9	8.4	116	4459	41.4	13.6	104	3371	44.6	10.3	112
GRADUATED COLLEGE	12730	3694	15.2	29.0	98	673	11.2	5.3	72	1642	15.3	12.9	99	1380	18.2	10.8	118
ATTENDED COLLEGE	14775	4351	17.9	29.4	100	1031	17.1	7.0	96	1764	16.4	11.9	92	1555	20.6	10.5	115
GRADUATED HIGH SCHOOL	34358	9448	38.9	27.6	93	2231	37.0	6.5	89	4378	40.7	12.7	98	2859	37.8	8.3	91
DID NOT GRADUATE HIGH SCHOOL	20668	6834	28.1	33.1	112	2087	34.7	10.1	138	2976	27.7	14.4	110	1771	23.4	8.6	93
EMPLOYED	42595	12198	50.1	28.6	97	3091	51.3	7.3	99	5380	50.0	12.6	97	3728	49.3	8.8	95
EMPLOYED FULL-TIME	34314	10059	41.3	29.3	99	2605	43.3	7.6	104	4584	42.6	13.4	102	2870	37.9	8.4	91
EMPLOYED PART-TIME	8281	2139	8.8	25.8	88	*485	8.1	5.9	80	796	7.4	9.6	74	858	11.3	10.4	113
NOT EMPLOYED	39936	12149	49.9	30.4	103	2931	48.7	7.3	101	5380	50.0	13.5	103	3838	50.7	9.6	105
PROFESSIONAL/MANAGER	11254	3339	13.7	29.7	101	756	12.6	6.7	92	1312	12.2	11.7	89	1271	16.8	11.3	123
TECH/CLERICAL/SALES	20325	5887	24.2	29.0	98	1407	23.4	6.9	95	2786	25.9	13.7	105	1694	22.4	8.3	91
PRECISION/CRAFT	1151	**157	0.6	13.6	46	**9	0.1	0.8	11	**113	1.1	9.8	75	**35	0.5	3.0	33
OTHER EMPLOYED	9865	2815	11.6	28.5	97	919	15.3	9.3	128	1170	10.9	11.9	91	727	9.6	7.4	80
SINGLE	10026	2800	11.5	27.9	95	633	10.5	6.3	87	1275	11.8	12.7	98	892	11.8	8.9	97
MARRIED	51804	14546	59.7	28.1	95	3682	61.1	7.1	97	6385	59.3	12.3	95	4479	59.2	8.6	94
DIVORCED/SEPARATED/WIDOWED	20700	7000	28.8	33.8	115	1706	28.3	8.2	113	3100	28.8	15.0	115	2194	29.0	10.6	116
PARENTS	32158	9187	37.7	28.6	97	2433	40.4	7.6	104	4112	38.2	12.8	98	2642	34.9	8.2	90
WHITE	71508	20857	85.7	29.2	99	4985	82.8	7.0	96	9111	84.7	12.7	98	6761	89.4	9.5	103
BLACK	8998	2960	12.2	32.9	112	821	13.6	9.1	125	1432	13.3	15.9	122	707	9.3	7.9	86
OTHER	2025	*530	2.2	26.2	89	**215	3.6	10.6	146	**218	2.0	10.8	83	**97	1.3	4.8	52
NORTHEAST-CENSUS	17926	6186	25.4	34.5	117	1348	22.4	7.5	103	2879	26.8	16.1	123	1959	25.9	10.9	119
MIDWEST	20733	5525	22.7	26.6	90	1332	22.1	6.4	88	2328	21.6	11.2	86	1865	24.7	9.0	98
SOUTH	28151	8443	34.7	30.0	102	2360	39.2	8.4	115	3826	35.6	13.6	104	2257	29.8	8.0	87
WEST	15723	4193	17.2	26.7	90	982	16.3	6.2	86	1727	16.1	11.0	84	1485	19.6	9.4	103
NORTHEAST-MKTG.	18407	6470	26.6	35.1	119	1402	23.3	7.6	104	3134	29.1	17.0	131	1934	25.6	10.5	115
EAST CENTRAL	11926	3835	15.8	32.2	109	1100	18.3	9.2	126	1414	13.1	11.9	91	1321	17.5	11.1	121
WEST CENTRAL	13778	3297	13.5	23.9	81	716	11.9	5.2	71	1478	13.7	10.7	82	1104	14.6	8.0	87
SOUTH	24337	6965	28.6	28.6	97	1892	31.4	7.8	107	3186	29.6	13.1	100	1888	25.0	7.8	85
PACIFIC	14084	3780	15.5	26.8	91	913	15.2	6.5	89	1549	14.4	11.0	84	1319	17.4	9.4	102
COUNTY SIZE A	34003	10266	42.2	30.2	102	2277	37.8	6.7	92	4625	43.0	13.6	104	3364	44.5	9.9	108
COUNTY SIZE B	24548	6906	28.4	28.1	95	1579	26.2	6.4	88	3096	28.8	12.6	97	2231	29.5	9.1	99
COUNTY SIZE C	12690	3838	15.8	30.2	103	1253	20.8	9.9	135	1578	14.7	12.4	95	1007	13.3	7.9	87
COUNTY SIZE D	11270	3338	13.7	29.6	100	913	15.2	8.1	111	1461	13.6	13.0	99	964	12.7	8.6	93
METRO CENTRAL CITY	25244	7807	32.1	30.9	105	1621	26.9	6.4	88	3773	35.1	14.9	115	2412	31.9	9.6	104
METRO SUBURBAN	37633	10659	43.8	28.3	96	2506	41.6	6.7	91	4570	42.5	12.1	93	3583	47.4	9.5	104
NON METRO	19654	5841	24.2	29.7	101	1894	31.5	9.6	132	2417	22.5	12.3	94	1570	20.8	8.0	87
TOP 5 ADI'S	18670	5525	22.7	29.6	100	1292	21.5	6.9	95	2459	22.9	13.2	101	1774	23.5	9.5	104
TOP 10 ADI'S	26125	7906	32.5	30.3	103	1862	30.9	7.1	98	3705	34.4	14.2	109	2339	30.9	9.0	98
TOP 20 ADI'S	37308	11147	45.8	29.9	101	2458	40.8	6.6	90	5048	47.3	13.6	105	3402	47.6	9.7	105
HSHLD INC. $60,000 OR MORE	6423	2123	8.7	33.1	112	*532	8.8	8.3	114	805	7.5	12.5	96	786	10.4	12.2	134
$50,000 OR MORE	10293	3276	13.5	31.8	108	*802	13.3	7.8	107	1345	12.5	13.1	100	1129	14.9	11.0	120
$40,000 OR MORE	19142	5628	23.1	29.4	100	1331	22.1	7.0	95	2532	23.5	13.2	101	1765	23.3	9.2	100
$30,000 OR MORE	32190	9295	38.2	28.9	98	2101	34.9	6.5	89	4177	38.8	13.0	100	3017	39.9	9.4	102
$30,000 - $39,999	13048	3666	15.1	28.1	95	771	12.8	5.9	81	1644	15.3	12.6	97	1252	16.5	9.6	105
$20,000 - $29,999	17313	4934	20.3	28.5	97	1271	21.1	7.3	101	1995	18.5	11.5	88	1668	22.0	9.6	105
$10,000 - $19,999	18416	5475	22.5	29.7	101	1358	22.6	7.4	101	2519	23.4	13.7	105	1598	21.1	8.7	95
UNDER $10,000	14412	4643	19.1	31.8	108	1291	21.4	8.8	121	2070	19.2	14.2	109	1282	16.9	8.9	97
HOUSEHOLD OF 1 PERSON	12984	4008	16.5	30.9	105	956	15.9	7.4	101	1711	15.9	13.2	101	1341	17.7	10.3	113
2 PEOPLE	26960	7830	32.2	29.0	98	1717	28.5	6.4	87	3452	32.1	12.8	98	2661	35.2	9.9	108
3 OR 4 PEOPLE	31657	9225	37.9	29.1	99	2263	37.6	7.1	98	4235	39.4	13.4	99	2727	36.0	8.6	94
5 OR MORE PEOPLE	10930	3285	13.5	30.1	102	1085	18.0	9.9	136	1362	12.7	12.5	96	837	11.1	7.7	84
NO CHILD IN HSHLD	47582	14409	59.2	30.3	103	3337	55.4	7.0	96	6358	59.1	13.4	102	4714	62.3	9.9	108
CHILD(REN) UNDER 2 YRS	7212	2028	8.3	28.1	95	*495	8.2	6.9	94	902	8.4	12.5	96	*632	8.4	8.8	96
2 - 5 YEARS	12718	3434	14.1	27.0	92	964	16.0	7.6	104	1526	14.2	12.0	92	944	12.5	7.4	81
6 - 11 YEARS	16339	4826	19.8	29.5	100	1269	21.1	7.8	106	2142	19.9	13.1	101	1416	18.7	8.7	95
12 - 17 YEARS	15497	4569	18.8	29.5	100	1234	20.5	7.9	108	2118	19.7	13.5	103	1217	16.1	7.8	85
RESIDENCE OWNED	56505	16723	68.7	29.6	100	4099	68.1	7.3	99	7333	68.2	13.0	100	5291	69.9	9.4	102
VALUE: $60,000 OR MORE	29835	8845	36.3	29.6	100	2151	35.7	7.2	99	3786	35.2	12.7	97	2909	38.5	9.8	106
VALUE: UNDER $60,000	26670	7878	32.4	29.5	100	1949	32.4	7.3	100	3548	33.0	13.3	102	2382	31.5	8.9	97

(continued)

Source: Simmons Market Research Bureau, 1987. Reprinted by permission.

FIGURE 8-1.   (continued)

*How to Read This Data:

Top Row: There were an estimated 82,531,000 female homemakers in the U.S.

Column

A—24,347,000 homemakers used caffeinated instant and freeze-dried coffee (within the last 30 days).

B—Column A represents 100% of users.

C—29.5% of all homemakers used caffeinated instant and freeze-dried coffee (24,347,000 ÷ 82,531,000 = 29.5%).

Second Row: There were an estimated 8,060,000 female homemakers who are aged 18–24 in the U.S.

A—1,943,000 homemakers used caffeinated instant and freeze-dried coffee.

B—8.0% of all users are aged 18–24 (1,943,000 ÷ 24,347,000 = .079 or 8.0%).

C—24.1% of all homemakers aged 18–24 are users (1,943,000 ÷ 8,060,000 = 24.1%).

D—The index of usage (users compared to the population base) is 82 (24.1% ÷ 29.5% × 100 = 82). This means that female homemakers aged 18–24 drink 18% less than the average female homemaker (100 equals average).

or between two raw numbers. Generally index numbers are printed as whole numbers, though they can be printed as percentages. The value of an index number is that it relates population demographics to sales or product usage for many different demographic segments, enabling one to have a convenient common method for comparison. If the population segment is considered to be "average," then an index number for sales tells how much above or below average sales are, in absolute terms. An average index number is 100, while 125 is 25 percent above average, and 80 is 20 percent below average. An example of how index numbers may be used is shown in Tables 8–1 and 8–2.

Which demographic segments should be selected as target markets for

TABLE 8-1.   Use of Ground Coffee by Age Segment

Age Segment	No. of Homemakers in U.S. (thousands)	U.S. Homemakers (%)	No. of Homemaker Users (thousands)	Homemaker Users (%)
18–24	9515	11.6	4204	8.9
25–34	19317	23.5	10588	22.5
35–44	15210	18.5	9526	20.2
45–54	11398	13.9	7397	15.7
55–64	11663	14.2	7278	15.5
65 +	15171	18.4	8102	17.2
Total	82274	100.0	47095	100.0

Source: Simmons Market Research Bureau, 1985. Reprinted by permission.

TABLE 8-2.   Calculating Index Numbers (based on Table 8-1)

Age Segment	Calculation	Index
18–24	8.9 ÷ 11.6	77
25–34	22.5 ÷ 23.5	96
35–44	20.2 ÷ 18.5	109
45–54	15.7 ÷ 13.9	113
55–64	15.5 ÷ 14.2	109
65 +	17.2 ÷ 18.4	93

media to reach? The usual answer is: Select those demographic segments with the largest volume of sales, or the largest number of users. In other words, advertise where the brand has a history of success. According to the traditional point of view, then, three age segments of homemakers in Table 8–1 might be the prime targets for ground coffee—those aged 25–34, 35–44, and 45–54. Of course, 45–54 and 55–64 are also relatively high. Obviously, income, occupation, education, and other demographic categories would also have to be checked before a final decision could be made.

However, there is another way to look at the data in Table 8–1, and that is to compare the percentage of usage in each age segment to the percentage of population in that segment. (One could compare the raw numbers of usage and population distribution in each segment, but such comparisons are more difficult than those made using percentages.)

When the percentage of usage is compared with the percentage of population distribution in each segment, an index number may be calculated to make the comparisons easier to analyze. The formula for calculating such numbers is as follows:

$$\text{Index number} = \frac{\% \text{ of users in a demographic segment}}{\% \text{ of population in the same segment}} \times 100$$

Using the formula to calculate index numbers for the data in Table 8–1 yields the index numbers in Table 8–2. The index numbers in Table 8–2 show how much the product is being used compared with the potential (or population proportion) for use in each segment. An index number above 100, as seen in the 35–44, 45–54, and 55–64 age groups, indicates higher than average usage. Now one can see that the potential for usage has shifted a bit to older age segments. In this sense, *index numbers more accurately indicate potential for usage or sales.* One cannot easily see this kind of relationship, however, without first calculating the index numbers.

It may be helpful to think of index numbers as measures of central tendency, just as ''averages'' or ''means'' are in the statistical world. An average does not describe any one person in a group, only the group as a whole.

Likewise, an index number over 100 means that the usage of the product is proportionately greater in that segment than one that is average (100) or below average (any number below 100). Segments with index numbers over 100 do not necessarily have numerically more users in them than in other segments; they may only have proportionately more. Theoretically, the segment with the highest index number represents the best potential for usage. In analyzing marketing data, one should calculate index numbers for all demographic groups such as age, sex, income, occupation, and education.

Although the technique of calculating index numbers shown in Table 8–2 can be used, there is a simpler way of computing the numbers that is often preferred by planners. This method is shown in Table 8–3. Briefly stated, the method starts with a measurement of the total number of users in a market. A percentage of the universe is then computed. This percentage indicates that of the total population, X percent are users. The number of users is compared with the number of individuals in each population segment and percentages are calculated. Finally, each of these segment percentages is divided by the total percentage of users. Note that the index numbers obtained by this method are identical to those obtained in Table 8–2.

A note of caution about using index numbers: One may be easily misled into believing that the demographic segment with the highest index number *always* represents the best potential. This is not true. Aside from the fact that one segment may have some other qualification that is of great marketing value, there is also the possibility that a segment with a high index number may have a low degree of product usage or sales or a low population size for that segment. If so, the segment with the highest index number may not represent the best potential for continued usage.

TABLE 8–3.   Another Method of Calculating Index Numbers

Step One: Find the total number of users compared with the total population in the market as follows:
   a. Total number of users in all segments: 47,095,000
   b. Total number of homemakers in the U.S.: 82,274,000
   c. Percentage of total homemakers that are users: 57.2%

Step Two: Find the percentage of users in each demographic segment (from Table 8–1):

	No. of Users		Population Size		Percent Users/ Population
18–24	4,204	÷	9,515	=	44.2%
25–34	10,588	÷	19,317	=	54.8
35–44	9,526	÷	15,210	=	62.6
45–54	7,397	÷	11,398	=	64.9
55–64	7,278	÷	11,663	=	62.4
65 +	8,102	÷	15,171	=	53.4

Step Three: Divide each of the percentages in Step Two by the percentage in Step One:

	Percent Users/Pop.		Percent of Homemakers/Users		Index
18–24	44.2	÷	57.2	=	77
25–34	54.8	÷	57.2	=	96
35–44	62.6	÷	57.2	=	109
45–54	64.9	÷	57.2	=	113
55–64	62.4	÷	57.2	=	109
65 +	53.4	÷	57.2	=	93

To illustrate, Table 8–4 shows marketing data for a fictitious brand, showing that, although the 18–24 age segment has the highest index number (134), it also has the lowest percentage of product usage and the lowest population percentage of any segment. It would not be very meaningful, therefore, to limit the selection of media to those reaching the 18–24 segment and ignore the other segments, especially since 85 percent of the usage is in the 25 and older segment.

One should first examine the volume of usage or sales in each demographic segment to determine whether the volume warrants inclusion as a media target. Only then will index numbers help locate good potential target segments.

It is also important to note that differences in comparing index numbers that are less than 10 are generally insignificant.

Using Psychographic and Lifestyle Analysis

The term *psychographic* is an adjective used to describe psychological characteristics of consumers. Psychographics are used to differentiate among prospects with the same demographic characteristics.

Psychographic descriptions of purchasers are sought because demographic descriptions do not discriminate well enough between consumers. For example, a janitor may be in the same income class as a college professor, but their lives and purchasing habits are likely to be vastly different. Two adults may have graduated from college, but their life-styles could be radically different. Two men may be working in the same profession, but demographic analysis would not show that they tend to buy different kinds of products. Market researchers, therefore, have long felt that the best way to go beyond demographics is to use some kind of psychological description of consumers.

In the past, many different kinds of psychological descriptions were tried and discarded. Social class categorization was one of the first attempts at psychological-sociological discrimination, but it was only minimally helpful. Later researchers used findings from various psychological tests to help find better discriminators, but without success. Even intelligence quotients (IQs) were tried. In addition to the attempts of market researchers to find psychological discriminators, media publishers also sought a similar mea-

TABLE 8–4.   An Example of Misleading Index Numbers

Age Segment	Population in Each Segment (%)	Product Usage in Each Segment (%)	Index
18–24	11.1	15.0	134
25–34	19.3	17.8	92
35–49	30.2	29.2	97
50+	39.4	38.0	96
Total	100.0	100.0	

sure as a means of differentiating media audiences. *Better Homes & Gardens* conducted some well-known research in 1956 showing that the magazine's audience contained many venturesome persons—those who were first in a social group to try new products. Yet researchers were generally dissatisfied with most attempts to provide psychological descriptions of consumers.

Another method of psychological analysis called *life-style research* has caught the attention of many marketing and media planners. Joseph T. Plummer, of the McCann-Erickson advertising agency, is one of the leaders in this research. Plummer describes life-style research as follows:

> Lifestyle is designed to answer questions about people in terms of their activities, interests, and opinions. It measures their activities in terms of how they spend their time in work and leisure; their interests in terms of what they place importance on in their immediate surroundings; their opinions in terms of their stance on social issues, institutions, and themselves; and finally, basic facts such as their age, sex, income, and where they live.[1]

In order to find consumers' life-styles, samples of individuals are selected and administered questionnaires which ask respondents to check such things as:

_____ I like gardening.
_____ I do not get enough sleep.
_____ I enjoy going to concerts.
_____ A news magazine is more interesting than a fiction magazine.
_____ There should be a gun in every home.
_____ Instant coffee is more economical than ground coffee.
_____ I stay home most evenings.
_____ There is a lot of love in our family.[2]

These questions cover activities, opinions, and interests as well as media usage and preferences, and product and brand usage. Life-style analysis has shown that media audiences differ a great deal and can be used to predict who will prefer one medium over another.

Simmons Market Research Bureau also reports psychographic data as well as demographic research. To obtain a psychographic breakdown of users, Simmons asks each respondent to evaluate a list of fourteen personality traits in terms of "how you would like to be." Then each respondent is asked to indicate from the same list "how you feel you are." Each of these fourteen characteristics is cross tabulated for each product category, for heavy users (in those categories where usage rates are 10 percent or higher), for magazine audiences, and for demographics. Listed below are the fourteen characteristics:

---

1. Plummer, Joseph T., "Life Style Patterns," *Journal of Broadcasting*, Winter, 1971–72, p.79.
2. Plummer, p.81.

Trait	*Meaning*
Energetic	Usually energetic, active, and on-the-go
Courteous and cooperative	Always courteous, polite, and cooperative
Self-controlled	Cool-headed, even-tempered, and calm
Venturesome	Adventurous and willing to risk trying new things
Happy and outgoing	Cheerful, happy, and outgoing
Pragmatic	Practical, down-to-earth, and well-organized
Not anxious	Not worried or distressed
Influential	Able to persuade, convince, and influence others to accept your ideas
Benevolent	Always considerate, sympathetic, and kind
Not domineering	Not bossy, domineering, or stubborn
Inquisitive	Intellectually curious about others' opinions
Self-confident	Self-assured and poised
Spontaneously decisive	Able to make decisions on the spur of the moment
Not egocentric	Not self-centered, egotistical, or conceited

One way in which such data may help planners in selecting target markets is to compare regular with heavy users. Table 8–5 shows some psychological differences between regular and heavy users of cigarettes. One might weigh this information subjectively using the demographic information already obtained to get a more definitive picture of regular versus heavy users. Or one might evaluate media selected on the basis of demographic segments on their ability to reach desired psychographic segments in order to find which media provide the best reach of both targets. The special needs of planners may also dictate other uses for psychographics.

Media planners who are looking for better target audience definitions will certainly find psychographic definitions radically different from those

TABLE 8–5. Some Psychographic Differences between Male Regular and Heavy Smokers

Traits	Regular Smokers			Heavy Smokers*		
	Index Self-Image	Index Ideal Image	Total	Index Self-Image	Index Ideal Image	Total
Energetic	96	101	197	144	88	232
Courteous and cooperative	97	112	209	119	169	288
Not anxious	127	106	233	156	50	206
Benevolent	98	89	187	181	113	294
Not domineering	96	105	201	75	50	125

Source: Simmons Market Research Bureau. Reprinted by permission.
*Heavy smokers—11+ packs per week.

of demographics. But being different does not necessarily make psychographics better. The important question is: How useful are psychographic target definitions?

The answer is that psychographics can be used in media planning when certain conditions are met. If a market has been identified demographically, yet there is reason to believe that the demographics do not segment the market precisely, then psychographic analysis may discover new dimensions of the target audience. If such new dimensions are found, however, it is important to have available an analysis that shows which alternative media reach large numbers of the psychographic categories that are shown to be important for the given brand. This may be difficult, because syndicated research services such as Simmons provide only a limited analysis of psychographic categories. It may mean that the planner will require custom-made research in order to find which alternative media reach the required psychographic categories. If the data are available and if categories such as those provided by Simmons give the planner more insight about who the best target is, then psychographics may play a large role in media selection.

After the data have been analyzed, the planner should decide on one or more demographic and psychographic segments that constitute the target audience. If the planner has access to a computer, it may be possible to have as many as three or four demographic segments all cross tabulated as a single target audience. An example of a cross tabulated single target is women 18–49 years of age whose household incomes are more than $25,000 a year, who have achieved a high school or higher level education, and whose households consist of five or more people.

If such cross tabulation is not available, the planner will then have to take the top two or three mutually exclusive segments as targets and determine to what extent each is to be reached in the media plan. The reason for requiring mutually exclusive segments is to enable the planner to reach each segment separately, and then measure gross impressions delivered to each without the confusion of one segment being part of another. For example, women 18–49 is an exclusive segment. But once one adds the demographic segment "total women with incomes of more than $25,000 a year," there is bound to be some duplication. Some women will be earning less than $25,000 but still be in the 18–49 category, and some will be earning more than $25,000 who are not aged 18–49.

Only cross-tabulated data can bring the two segments together. Table 8–6 shows an example of cross tabulation.

Where to Advertise

There are a number of answers to the question of where to advertise. The simplest, of course, is to advertise wherever the brand is distributed. Obvi-

TABLE 8-6.   Cross Tabulation of User Demographics for a Product Category

	Adult Female Usage Patterns			
	Average No. Times Used per Week	Women in Group (%)	Total Usages per Week (%)	Index of Usage
Total U.S.	4.95	100	100	100
Household size 1–4; children 6–17 or none; B, C, D counties; college; $3,000+ income	6.54	6.2	8.2	132
Household size 1–4; children 6–17 or none; B, C, D counties; grade or high school; $8,000+ income	6.18	7.2	9.0	125
Same as above except income $3,000–$7,999	5.30	13.0	13.9	107
Household size 1–4; children 6–17 or none; income $3,000+ ; A counties	5.14	22.0	22.9	104
Household size 5+ ; high school or less	4.83	18.2	17.8	98
Household size 1–4; children 6–17 or none; income under $3,000	4.58	14.4	13.4	93
Household size 1–4; children under 6	4.27	13.1	11.2	86
Household size 5+ ; some college	3.03	5.9	3.6	61

Source: Reprinted by permission of J. Walter Thompson Company.

ously, it is usually a waste of money to advertise in a geographical market where the brand is not distributed. Occasionally, however, the objective may be to "force" distribution by creating a demand for a brand through advertising, even though the brand is not distributed in the market. When the planner has this objective, it makes sense to advertise before distribution is available.

Beyond the obvious answer, however, is the question of whether it is better to advertise in geographical markets where sales for a given brand have been good, or where sales *have not* been good.

Some planners feel that to advertise where sales have been good is a good defensive strategy—one should protect what one has and also try to build on it. Additionally, one should ask, Have sales in the good markets been fully exploited? If not, why not spend more money there, rather than going to some other market where the risks would be greater? After all, many customers like the brand well enough to buy it repeatedly and their word-of-mouth influence may well prompt sales to people who have not purchased the brand in the past.

Choosing where to advertise is really a matter of risks. Despite the observation that "it is always good sense to fish where the fish are," is an advertiser missing productive new markets by placing most advertising in the best markets? Yet can the advertiser afford the risk of losing the best markets to sound out new, unknown markets? The "defensive strategy" minimizes risks and maximizes potential.

Advertising in markets where a brand's sales are low is called an "offensive strategy'' because success may require heavier advertising expenditures than previously used. Again, the risks must be carefully weighed. If competitors have been selling well in these markets but the brand in question has not, the question is, why? Is it due to poor distribution? Is it due to insufficient advertising expenditures in the market? Some other reason? Can these problems be corrected?

A planner selecting a market with a low-sales history should be able to answer the following question: Is there any evidence that increased advertising in this market will produce a corresponding increase in sales? This is a difficult, but necessary, question. Students in practice exercises often want to increase advertising because they believe that ''advertising sells.'' But they usually cannot find any other strong reason for doing so except that competitors are selling well in the market. One must understand, however, that once a competitor becomes entrenched in a market with a good brand that meets the needs of consumers, there may be no reason for consumers to switch brands. In fact, it may be impossible to get them to switch brands, unless the new brand has some superior attribute that, if publicized, will cause consumers to switch. The risks of trying to exploit such a market are great and the likelihood of success is, at best, indeterminable.

Finally, the greatest risk is to select new markets where neither the designated brand nor competitive brands have been exploited through advertising. These markets may have great sales potential, but may also be difficult places to sell a given product. It also might be assumed that if these markets really had great potential, competitors would have known about it too, and would have made efforts to exploit them.

Aside from these basic guides for market selection, there are other factors that should be taken into consideration. One of the foremost involves selecting one or perhaps more markets in each of the client's sales territories. Almost all companies with nationally distributed products divide the country into sales territories, and these in turn may be subdivided into smaller groups. The names of such territories vary somewhat from company to company. Some use the terms ''divisions and districts,'' others use ''regions and divisions'' or other designations. No matter what they are called, it may be necessary to include at least one market in each of these divisions, depending on the needs of the company. The *weights* (or quantity of advertising used) in these areas may vary a great deal, however, so that the better markets receive more dollars of advertising than the poorer markets.

Thus, to answer the question of where to advertise, planners study distribution, sales records, or brand/product usage. Simmons provides data on usage, while Nielsen and other similar companies provide data on sales.

Classification of Geographical Areas

Sales should be analyzed by different geographical patterns, from the largest, that is, regions of the country, to the smallest neighborhoods, although analysis by neighborhood may not be possible because of the lack of research data. The idea behind geographical analysis at all levels is to learn precisely where prospects live. This information serves as a guide in media selection. The following are the most commonly used geographical categories:

- Regions
- States
- Counties
- Metropolitan or nonmetropolitan areas
- TV market delineation such as DMA (designated market area), or ADI (area of dominant influence)

In studying marketing and media research data, the analyst will find a number of different methods used to divide the country geographically. The Census Bureau divides the country into four regions and nine divisions. The Media Audience Research Committee of the American Association of Advertising Agencies recommends that the country be divided into four areas. The A.C. Nielsen Company, however, uses a division consisting of ten geographical territories, although it will divide the country in almost any way most suitable for a specific client. A comparison of these divisions is shown in Table 8–7. Figure 8–2 maps the states in Nielsen's ten territories.

What is a local market to a media planner? A *market* is a group of people living in a certain geographic area, who are likely to buy a given product or brand. But that definition is unsatisfactory for planners when it comes to determining the nature of a local market because definitions vary depending on the research company providing the data for a given area. Different research companies define markets differently to meet the needs of their users. A local retailer who advertises exclusively in newspapers in a given city may prefer to think of its market as a *retail trading zone* which includes the central city and surrounding suburbs. But a national advertiser who uses all media may prefer that a market be defined in terms of the entire metropolitan area, and would use the Census Bureau's Metropolitan Statistical Area definition. Another manufacturer who uses television almost exclusively,

TABLE 8–7.   Comparison of Geographic Divisions

4As Media Audience Research Committee Divisions	Nielsen's Basic 10 Territories	Census Bureau's Nine Divisions	Census Bureau's Four Regions
1. North East	1. New England	1. New England	1. Northeast
2. North Central	2. Middle Atlantic	2. Middle Atlantic	
3. South	3. Metro New York	3. East N. Central	2. Midwest
4. Pacific	4. East Central	4. West N. Central	
	5. Metro Chicago	5. South Atlantic	3. South
	6. West Central	6. East S. Central	
	7. South East	7. West S. Central	
	8. Metro Los Angeles	8. Mountain	4. West
	9. South West	9. Pacific	
	10. Remaining Pacific		

FIGURE 8-2.   Nielsen Territories

Source: Reprinted by permission of Nielsen Media Research.

however, may prefer to use Arbitron's area of dominant influence. Each of these local market definitions is somewhat different.

As a result, it becomes important for the planner to know the various definitions of what constitutes a local market when planning media. Which definition is most suitable? There has been some agitation from media planners to standardize definitions, but without much success. Until standardization becomes acceptable, the differences should be clearly understood. The following list explains the most often used definitions:

Area of Dominant Influence (ADI). All counties in which the home-market stations receive a preponderance of total viewing hours. This definition was conceived by Arbitron. The ground rules for the ADI allocations are relatively simple. Once the estimated total viewing hours for a county and the percentage of such estimated total for each station are known, Arbitron adds up the station percentages by market of origin. The market of origin having the largest total percentage is deemed by Arbitron to be the "dominant influence" in the county under consideration, and thus the county is allocated to that market for ADI purposes. The total number of ADI markets in the country may change from year to year as research on them is updated.

Designated Market Area (DMA). This definition, used by the A. C. Nielsen Company for a television market, includes counties in the metropolitan area of a market provided that at least one station in that area is estimated to have the largest average quarter-hour audience share from 9:00 A.M. to midnight, plus the remainder of counties in which this market's station are estimated to have the largest average quarter-hour share.

Metropolitan Statistical Area (MSA). The MSA has replaced the Standard Metropolitan Statistical Area definition used in the past. An MSA is a population area with a large nucleus at the center and adjacent areas that have a large degree of economic and social integration with the center. The MSAs may be classified on the basis of the following levels:

Level A—population of 1,000,000 or more
Level B—population of 250,000 to 999,999
Level C—population of 100,000 to 249,999
Level D—population of less than 100,000

Note the difference between the MSA classifications and A. C. Nielsen's classifications on page 173.

PMSAs and CMSAs. Within the metropolitan areas of one million or more population, separate component parts of an MSA are defined if certain criteria are met as follows:

Primary Metropolitan Statistical Area (PMSA)—The MSA defined by counties

Consolidated Metropolitan Statistical Area (CMSA)—Large metropolitan complexes that contain PMSAs

The following analysis is shown to better explain how these new designations would look for the Chicago SMA:

Chicago PMSA
    Cook County
    DuPage County
    McHenry County

Chicago, Gary, Ind., Lake County, Ill., Illinois, Indiana, Wisconsin CMSA
    Chicago, Ill., PMSA
    Aurora, Ill., PMSA
    Gary-Hammond, Ind., PMSA
    Joliet, Ill., PMSA
    Kenosha, Wisc., PMSA
    Lake County, Ill., PMSA

City Zone and Retail Trading Zone. These terms are used by newspapers in defining their markets. A *city zone* represents the corporate city limits plus heavily populated areas adjoining a city in which the newspaper is sold, as designated by an agreement between the publisher and the Audit Bureau of Circulation. A *retail trading zone* is an area beyond the city zone from which retailers draw sufficient customers to warrant spending advertising dollars to reach them. This area is also determined by the agreement of the publisher and the Audit Bureau of Circulation.

Newspaper Designated Markets. This is another newspaper classification and covers the geographical area in which the newspaper provides primary editorial and advertising services. Decisions about which areas are to be included and the boundary lines are made by the Audit Bureau of Circulation in consultation with the publisher. Publishers who report their circulations by newspaper designated markets usually eliminate city and retail trading zone circulation data.

Newspaper market definitions may also be made by counties in which coverage percentages are computed. Data show where newspapers have at least 50 percent coverage, 20 percent coverage, and so forth.

To illustrate how market definitions vary, even within one geographical market, a map of the city of Chicago and outlying areas is shown in Figure 8–3. It shows the ADI (with nineteen counties in Illinois, Wisconsin, Indiana, and Michigan), the MSA (three counties), and the newspaper desig-

FIGURE 8–3. ADI, MSA, and Newspaper Designated Markets of Chicago—by Counties

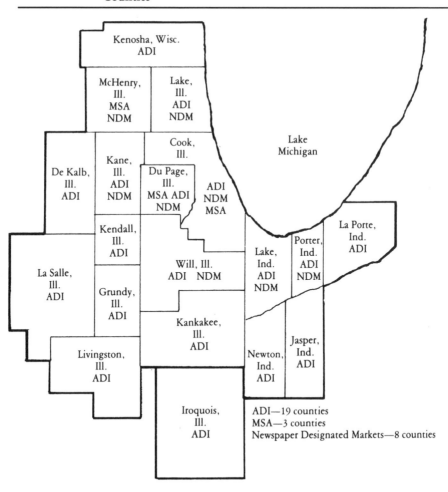

nated markets of the *Chicago Tribune* (with eight counties in Illinois and Indiana).

Sales Analysis

After sales volume information about a brand and its competitors has been gathered, it is possible to start making decisions about where to advertise. One approach is to select geographical markets on the basis of sales or market share produced in the past. In this situation, the volume of past sales, rather than the index of potential sales, is the deciding factor. Without a doubt, the volume of sales produced by a geographic market in the past has to be the first consideration in making the selection. The question of whether to go to high-index potential markets depends to some extent on whether sales have been optimized in the existing high-volume markets. Perhaps an increase in advertising in current markets will result in an equivalent increase in sales.

Table 8–8 shows the sales of a company and its competitors reported on the basis of seven regions, plus three large metropolitan areas: New York, Chicago, and Los Angeles. In this table, index numbers were computed by comparing sales percentages for each brand with total industry sales by region.

Does Table 8–8 tell the planner precisely where to advertise? No, but it tells where the brand is doing well as compared with competitors: in New England, East Central, West Central, Chicago, and the Southwest. Obtaining and understanding this kind of information is necessary before the planner proceeds to more specific information that will help pinpoint markets in which to advertise.

Sales analysis by regions usually is followed by a county analysis that pro-

TABLE 8–8.   Sales of Brand X and Competitors—by Regions

	Total Industry Sales			Brand X		Brand Y		Brand Z	
Region	U.S. House-holds (%)	Sales (%)	Index	Sales (%)	Index	Sales (%)	Index	Sales (%)	Index
New England	5.8	3.4	59	3.5	103	3.5	103	2.4	71
New York	8.4	5.0	60	4.6	92	4.5	90	6.5	130
Middle Atlantic	11.4	10.8	94	11.0	102	10.1	94	12.9	119
East Central	15.8	17.6	111	19.5	111	16.8	95	18.3	104
West Central	14.0	16.0	115	17.5	109	16.2	101	16.4	103
Chicago	3.7	5.4	144	7.1	131	5.4	98	5.3	98
Southeast	15.7	13.3	85	13.1	98	12.1	91	14.0	105
Southwest	9.9	8.8	89	9.4	104	9.2	105	7.5	85
Los Angeles	5.1	7.0	138	4.7	67	9.1	130	5.8	83
Remaining Pacific	10.2	12.7	124	9.6	76	13.2	104	10.9	86
Total	100.0	100.0		100.0		100.0		100.0	

Source: Data provided by a major advertiser.

vides another dimension for the media planner to consider in selecting media to reach markets.

To deal with county sizes conveniently, Nielsen and Arbitron use an A, B, C, D classification system:

A counties—all counties located within the twenty-five largest metropolitan areas
B counties—all counties not included under A that have more than 150,000 population
C counties—all counties not included in A and B that have more than 40,000 population
D counties—all remaining counties

Table 8–9 shows a sales breakdown by county size for liquid and powdered forms of a given product. For the total market, county size C has the best potential. For the liquid market segment, county A shows the best potential, followed closely by C Counties. For the powdered market segment, C counties have the best potential. Once again, note the potential for sales shown by index numbers and the actual sales volume shown for the total market and its segments. In all cases, county size A has the highest percentage of sales. Both volume and potential will have to be weighed before a decision is made.

Heavy User Data

Although a geographic analysis may be a start in answering the question of where to advertise, an examination of heavy user data may provide additional insights. Often, a small percentage of heavy users account for the largest percentage of product usage. This is true for many product categories, but not for all.

Studying heavy users gives a different dimension of where the market is located. If the marketing strategy calls for heavy users, then their whereabouts becomes important. Table 8–10 shows that heavy users of international flavored instant coffee tend to be in metropolitan central city areas, whereas light users are within the metropolitan suburban area.

TABLE 8–9.   Sales of Total Market and Segments—by County Size

County Size	Population Distribution	Total Market Sales (%)	Index	Powdered Market Segment Sales (%)	Index	Liquid Market Segment Sales (%)	Index
A	41.4	42.3	102	39.1	94	45.4	110
B	27.2	26.9	99	27.6	101	26.2	96
C	16.3	19.2	117	20.6	126	17.9	109
D	15.1	11.6	76	12.7	84	10.5	70
Total	100.0	100.0		100.0		100.0	

Source: Data supplied by a major advertiser.

TABLE 8-10.   Heavy and Light Users of International Flavored Instant Coffee

	Index			
	All Users	Heavy Users	Medium Users	Light Users
Metropolitan (central city)	103	127	103	94
Metropolitan (suburban)	107	104	88	120
Nonmetropolitan	81	60	118	70

Source: Simmons Market Research Bureau, 1986. Reprinted by permission.

The Brand Development Index (BDI)

One of the most useful tools available to a media planner in deciding where to advertise is the *brand development index (BDI)*. The BDI is quite simple in structure, and calculated from data for each individual market in which the brand is sold according to the following formula:

$$\text{BDI} = \frac{\% \text{ of a brand's total U.S. sales in Market X}}{\% \text{ of total U.S. population in Market X}} \times 100$$

Here's an example of how the BDI would be calculated for a brand in Seattle:

$$\frac{\text{Sales of the brand in Seattle (\% of U.S.)}}{\text{Population in Seattle (\% of U.S.)}} \quad \frac{3.09}{1.23} \times 100 = 251$$

The BDI is an index number representing sales potential. It conforms to the same basic characteristics of index numbers discussed earlier. The larger the sales in a market relative to population percentage, the higher the BDI in that market.

The Category Development Index (CDI)

The *category development index (CDI)* is similar to the BDI except that it is based on the percentage of sales of a product category in a given market rather than a brand. The method of calculating the CDI is as follows:

$$\text{CDI} = \frac{\% \text{ of a product category's total U.S. sales in Market X}}{\% \text{ of total U.S. population in Market X}} \times 100$$

Example of the CDI in Seattle:

$$\frac{\text{Category sales in Seattle (\% of U.S.)}}{\text{Population in Seattle (\% of U.S.)}} \quad \frac{2.71}{1.23} \times 100 = 220$$

Both the BDI and CDI are useful in decision making. One tells the planner the relative strengths and weaknesses for the brand and the other, the relative strengths and weaknesses for the category. Any market where the brand is sold should have these indices calculated for it.

The following are the possible results (see Figure 8–4):

High BDI and high CDI. This kind of market usually represents good sales potential for both the brand and the category.

High BDI and low CDI. Here the category is not selling well, but the brand is. Probably a good market in which to advertise, but surely one to watch to see if the brand's sales decline in time.

Low BDI and high CDI. This kind of market shows potential for the category but demands that someone study the reason why the brand is not doing well here. Is it because of poor distribution? Not enough advertising dollars, GRPs, or reach in the market? To advertise in this market without knowing the answer would be a risk.

Low BDI and low CDI. This kind of market represents a risk for any brand. Here, too, a planner might want to know why the category doesn't sell well. Such a market would probably not be a good place to advertise under most circumstances.

In using the BDI/CDI data for each market in decision making, the planner has a number of ways to proceed. One is to set arbitrary parameters for each market. For example, a planner could decide that for a market to be selected it would have to meet at least one of the following requirements:

- It would have to have a BDI of 125 or higher.
- It would have to have a BDI at least ten points higher than the CDI.
- It would have to have a certain percentage sales increase over a previous year in that market, and/or a sales volume of X dollars in the market.

Market selection on such a basis may seem arbitrary, but it could be based on the experience of a planner who, over a period of years, simply knows which market characteristics have been the most profitable.

Weighted BDIs and CDIs. Another method of selecting markets might be to weight the BDI and CDI to arrive at a single combined index. Before this weighting is done, however, a marketing strategy decision must be made to guide the media planner in the proper weighting of the two indices. A mar-

FIGURE 8–4. BDI/CDI Relationships

	High BDI	Low BDI
High CDI	High share of market Good market potential	Low share of market Good market potential
Low CDI	High share of market Monitor for sales decline	Low share of market Poor market potential

keting strategy that calls for X dollars of advertising spending in direct proportion to sales (a basically defensive posture) requires that the BDI be used exclusively in allocating media expenditures to each market. At the other extreme, a marketing strategy that requires that brand advertising be allocated only on the basis of category development (a basically offensive posture that is generally used for new brands that have not developed a sales pattern) would force the media planner to use only the CDI in deciding spending by market. Any mixture of these two strategies requires a mixture of weights for the BDI and the CDI. For example, if the marketing strategy states that brand sales should be protected in all high sales areas, but that spending should be increased where category development is high and brand development is low, the planner might elect to weight the BDI 75 percent and the CDI 25 percent. The following illustrates how the calculation would be made in a typical market:

$$\begin{aligned} BDI &= 165 \times .75 = 124 \\ CDI &= 140 \times .25 = 35 \end{aligned} \quad 124 + 35 = 159 = \text{Weighted BDI/CDI}$$

All markets would be evaluated on the basis of a similar weighting and only those that reach a certain level would be selected. Weighting, however, may be a risky procedure unless the planner knows exactly what each weighting signifies. A safer procedure might be to weight the BDI and CDI 50 percent each and then combine them. Nevertheless, some kind of arbitrary decision would have to be made. The cut-off point might be set at 125. Any markets indexed at over 125 would be selected and any under 125 rejected, at least until experience dictates otherwise.

Using Buying Power Indices

There are times when an advertiser may not know its product's sales volume in each geographical market, possibly because the advertiser sells through distributors and wholesalers. Although many manufacturers in the food, drug, and appliance fields know, from their own records, how large their sales are to wholesalers or distributors, they often do not know how well sales are going at the retail level. The factory is separated from the consumer by what is called the *pipeline* (composed of wholesalers and retailers). What happens at the consumer level is eventually reflected in activity at the factory, but the time lag can be exceedingly long. Sales to wholesalers may be high, but wholesalers may have large inventories in their warehouses because the product hasn't been selling well at the retail level.

Furthermore, even if a manufacturer should eventually learn how consumer sales are going, this information may not be indicative of a brand's share of total sales compared to its competitors'. The best that these advertisers can do is to examine the number of wholesale shipments into each market and prepare their media plans on such a basis. The weakness of this technique should be apparent, though; the relative number of shipments into a given market may not be equivalent to the sales potential of that market. Lack of sales volume and share, market by market, handicaps the media planner in deciding where to place advertising. Nevertheless, many small advertisers simply cannot afford to purchase sales volume and share data from the syndicated research services. Shipments or sales potentials determined through other ways may then have to be used.

One source available to almost all advertisers and agencies is *Sales & Marketing Management*'s "Survey of Buying Power," which can help determine the sales potential of geographic markets. The "Survey of Buying Power" is published annually and is available to anyone at a relatively low cost. The data are based on census measurements plus updated projections.

The survey uses a multiple factor index that is computed for every major metropolitan area in the country. A *factor* is a market quality that affects sales. Therefore, it is possible to examine the general sales potential of every geographical market. Generally, the more people there are in a market, the greater the sales potential; so population is a factor. Effective buying income based on total income after taxes (similar to disposable income), is another market factor. A third factor in the survey's index is total retail sales.

The three factors are arbitrarily weighted to indicate that some factors are more important than others in making sales. Population is weighted twice, total retail sales are weighted three times, and effective buying income is weighted five times.

On one hand, the indices described help the planner determine the relative value of each market. These values in turn may be used to determine budgets or media weights. On the other hand, the indices may be too general for certain kinds of products. Some specialized products may need additional or more specific marketing data. However, the information in the "Survey of Buying Power" may be used with data from other sources to provide a better and more selective index. The market for air conditioners could be used as an example. It would be possible to combine survey data with information on average maximum annual temperature and average annual humidity to create a special index number for each market. Furthermore, factors could be weighted in any way necessary to get a better perspective of the relative value of each market.

One can use the buying power indices for a quick evaluation of alternative geographic markets.

The question of where to advertise is based on an analysis of sales and product usage or general sales potential, plus consideration of whatever marketing objectives must be met. The users of the buying power data will find that the index numbers are an easy way to compare a large number of categories. If raw numbers or percentages are needed, they are usually provided so that users need not make any further preliminary calculations.

Determining Cut-Off Points

In selecting markets for advertising, it is often difficult to judge at which point to drop markets that are at the bottom of the list. The place at which the list is divided into those markets that are selected and those rejected is called the *cut-off point*.

One way to establish a cut-off point is to select markets on the basis of some arbitrary number, usually in multiples of 10, 25, or 50. This is a widespread practice in industry. So whatever markets are listed as Number 51 or lower may be eliminated. Yet most media planners would agree that there isn't always much difference between the 50th market and the 51st market.

A more logical way to cut off is to determine how much weight (in terms of dollars) should be assigned to the best markets. Once these dollars have been allocated, then all remaining money may be distributed to the poorer markets based on a weighting system. Usually such weighting would be based on spending a minimum amount of money in a market. If a market's potential does not justify such an expenditure, then it may not be worthwhile to advertise. Weighting systems divide markets into groups titled A, B, C, and so on. A markets might receive a given number of dollars of advertising, B markets receive somewhat less, and C markets receive much less.

At times a system of gross rating points is used to determine how much money will be spent in a market. The money is allocated from the top of the list down, until it runs out, thereby automatically establishing the cut-off point.

In many cases, media planners and client representatives have, through experience, developed a minimum number of markets that must be on any list. Additional markets may be added if there is money left after allocating money to the basic list.

One of the problems in establishing cut-off points is that often a small number of markets account for a very large percentage of sales. For example, twenty-five markets might account for 75 percent of a brand's sales. But the next twenty-five largest markets might only account for 8 percent additional sales. Usually media planners prefer to have fewer markets, but have enough money to fully exploit the selected markets.

Often, too, marketing objectives affect the length of a list. For example, if an objective is "to protect the brand's share of market from inroads of competitors," then more money may have to be put into markets where competitors are trying to sell against the brand. Usually these are a brand's best markets, so the list may have to be reduced somewhat in order to allocate extra money at the top of the list.

The whole process of selecting markets and determining cut-off points is not the responsibility only of the media planner, but may be shared by the account executive and a client representative. In such cases, decisions are made by compromise as well as by logic. In a personal conversation, one media planner explained:

This give and take process between the account executive, the client, and myself is often logical, but sometimes ludicrous. For example, I'll have both Rochester and Albany on my market list. The account man may take Albany off but leave Rochester in. But the client puts Albany back in and removes Rochester. Why? Well it could be that we can't afford both, or the client feels that he has to back a stronger sales force at Albany. But the whole process of selecting markets is an ''editing'' operation, in which we each edit the others' recommendations until a market list takes shape.

In summary, market lists and cut-off points are established on the basis of subjective factors as well as objective criteria. The most important criteria are the sales goals and the money needed to attain them in each market. Experience, compromise, and some arbitrary factors also influence the process at various times. Other, more sophisticated methods of selecting markets to receive advertising are discussed in Chapter 10.

When to Advertise

Decisions about when to advertise depend on a number of important considerations such as (a) when sales are greatest or lowest, (b) budget constraints, (c) when competitors advertise, (d) the specific goals for the brand in question, (e) availability of the product, and (f) promotional requirements. Each of these points deserves individual discussion, though there is one point underlying them all: Advertise when people tend to buy the product in question, because it is difficult if not impossible to make them buy at any other time. Studying sales by product category over a period of twenty or more years shows that buying takes place at fairly regular intervals and not capriciously. Therefore, it is important to learn when people tend to buy and to capitalize on these buying habits.

Analyzing Monthly Sales

The most important consideration in deciding when to advertise is to know when sales peaks occur for the product category compared with when sales peaks occur for the brand. Table 8–11 shows category sales indexed to brand sales by month. Sales for the category in question tend to be rather flat month by month, but the brand tends to have rather clear-cut highs and lows. Theoretically, the brand should advertise more heavily in those months when its sales have been higher.

However, the answer may not be quite so clear-cut. It may be that the category sells well in a particular month, while the brand does not. Thus the dilemma. Should the brand advertise more heavily in those months when the *category* is selling well or in the months when the *brand* is selling well?

TABLE 8–11.   Category and Brand Sales by Months

Month	Category Sales (%)	Brand Sales (%)	Index
January	8.5	6.9	81*
February	7.7	6.5	85
March	8.5	8.2	96
April	8.2	7.5	91
May	8.5	8.9	105
June	8.2	8.9	109
July	8.5	9.4	110
August	8.5	10.3	121
September	8.2	6.8	83
October	8.5	8.8	103
November	8.2	7.6	93
December	8.5	10.2	120

*6.9 ÷ 8.5 × 100 = 81.

Usually, one would advertise more heavily in the months when the category is selling well. Although other considerations may require a change in this strategy, some planners use only category sales as their guide in planning.

Usually a monthly sales analysis for a product category will indicate a seasonal effect. Thus a planner should keep in mind the effect of certain seasons on sales in studying monthly sales records. Back-to-school or graduation months certainly influence the sales of certain kinds of products, as do Christmas or Easter. January and August have become the "white goods" months to sell bed linens, towels, and tablecloths. If a brand belongs to a category that is affected by seasons, then monthly sales should be more carefully studied so as not to miss an opportunity.

Budget Constraints

Often the advertising budget is not large enough to permit year-round advertising. In such a situation, the planner will probably allocate the advertising dollars to the best selling months. Whether to maintain *continuity* (continuous advertising all year long) or *flights* (periodic advertising interspersed with no advertising) is dependent on other considerations that will be discussed later.

Competitive Activities

In planning a media schedule it is important to consider when competitors advertise. If their timing pattern is different than that of the overall category, then the planner will have to decide how important the difference is. Does it put the planner's own brand in a weaker position? If so, the planner may want to copy a competitor's timing. Most often, however, competitors tend to follow category sales patterns fairly closely.

Specific Goals for the Brand

At times a marketing or media objective is to react aggressively to competitive strategies. Perhaps such a strategy may be necessary to attain a market share increase. In such a situation, one might time heavy advertising to begin before most competitors start. As a result, a brand may achieve higher and quicker visibility before the normal buying season starts. Another specific goal may be to outspend competitors in some particular month. This may require withdrawing money allocated to the year-long advertising effort for the concentrated attack. Other marketing/media goals may also affect timing. New product introductions, for example, require a timing pattern of heavy initial advertising (first quarter of sales year) and relatively lighter weights later on.

Product Availability

In certain marketing situations, marketing demand outstrips a manufacturer's ability to supply the product. Even though a company may be building a new plant to keep up with demand, the added capacity may not be ready for some time. In such a case, the timing of advertising has to be related to production availability. Most often a problem with availability occurs when new products are introduced, but it occasionally happens when there is a surge in the sales of existing products.

Promotional Requirements

If an aggressive sales promotion campaign is planned for a brand preceding or during the brand's regular advertising campaign, this may affect timing. A cents-off deal, for example, may require aggressive advertising when the campaign to announce the promotion starts.

QUESTIONS FOR DISCUSSION

1. Why are counties usually preferred to cities as geographic areas for selling?
2. What other information would you need to compute an index number if you knew that 11.1% of all housewives ages 18–24 had used a product within the last month?
3. In searching for demographic target segments, is the segment with the highest index number always the best target? Explain briefly.
4. What is the value of knowing a brand development index (BDI) number of a given market?
5. Differentiate a lifestyle from a demographic segment and explain how it can help in determining media targets.
6. Can advertising be used to increase sales of our brand in low CDI markets?
7. How could the data from the *Sales & Marketing Management* "Survey of Buying Power" be used to create one's own index for selling outboard motors?

8. Percentages are easier to use than raw numbers in comparing sales or usage data for two brands. But why should the user pay special attention to the bases on which the two sets of figures were computed?

9. Consumer lifestyles are often advocated to be used as discriminators in selecting targets. Are lifestyles always necessary in selecting media targets?

10. The time to advertise is when consumers are buying. But consumers buy our product, face soap, all year long. Under those conditions, when should we advertise if we can't afford to advertise in every week of the year?

SELECTED READINGS

Advertising Age, "Newspaper Bureau Promotes Psychographics," September 10, 1973, 6.

Committee on Research (Media Research Subcommittee), *Recommended Breakdowns for Consumer Media Data*, American Association of Advertising Agencies (revised), 1973.

Editor & Publisher, "Study Indicates Psychographic Data Are Weak Media Buying Tool," September 8, 1973, 8–9.

Media Decisions, "How—Not Where," January 1968, 22.

Media Decisions, "Beyond Demographics," February 1968, 22–23.

Media Decisions, "How Nestlé Uses Psychographics," July 1973, 68–71.

Media Decisions, "What's the Competition Doing?" September 1973, 64ff.

Media Decisions, "The Campaign That Psychographics Built," April 1974, 64ff.

Media Decisions, "Timing," December 1978, 140.

Nelson Alan R., "New Psychographics: Action-Creating Ideas, Not Lifeless Statistics," *Advertising Age*, June 28, 1971, 1, 34.

Ostrow, Joseph, "Competitive Media Expenditure Analysis," *Media Decisions*, December 1971, 52.

Papazian, Edward, "Buzz Words Like Psychographics," *Media Decisions*, October 1973, 14–16.

Papazian, Edward, "Media Targeting: Like Pinning the Tail on the Donkey," *Media Decisions*, November 1977, 14–16.

Peterson, Robert A., "Psychographics and Media Exposure," *Journal of Advertising Research*, June 1972, 17–20.

Plummer, Joseph T., "Lifestyle Patterns," *Journal of Broadcasting*, Winter 1971–72, 78–89.

Shiffman, Phil, "Psychographic Data Could Be the Base for Both Copy and Media," *Media Decisions*, August 1973, 80–82.

Strong, Edward C., "The Spacing and Timing of Advertising," *Journal of Advertising Research*, December 1977, 25–31.

Teel, J. E., Bearden, W. O., and Durand, R. M., "Psychographics of Radio and TV Audiences," *Journal of Advertising Research*, April 1979, 53–56.

Tveter, T. Norman, "What the Media Expert Gains from Studying Markets," *Media/Scope*, May 1964, 94–100.

Wells, William D. (ed.), *Lifestyle and Psychographics*, Chicago: American Marketing Association, 1974.

Wells, William D., "Psychographics: A Critical Review," *Journal of Marketing Research*, May 1975, 196–213.

9

Strategy Planning II: Weighting, Reach, Frequency, and Continuity

In Chapter 8 three major strategy decisions were discussed: target audiences, geographical market selection, and timing. These decisions must be made early in the planning process because they control other strategy decisions discussed in this chapter. This chapter also contains decisions that follow those in Chapter 8; a further discussion of geographical weighting, reach and frequency, and continuity versus flighting.

Geographical Weighting

Geographical weighting is the practice of giving extra consideration to one or more markets that have more sales potential—because of location or demographics or other reasons—than other markets. A record of good sales and/or good potential for sales for the product category and the brand being advertised may make one market more important than others. If all geographical markets had an equal record of sales and/or sales potential, then there would be no need to add extra advertising weight. But markets are rarely equal in value, so weighting is necessary.

There is another reason for weighting markets. Advertisers who buy national media usually find that the gross impressions delivered by a media plan do not match differences in local sales potentials. Market A may have good sales potential but receive relatively few impressions from national media, while Market B may have weak sales potential but receive many more impressions than required.

TABLE 9–1. How Network Television Delivery of Gross Rating Points Varies by Market

	Network Prime Time GRPs (Nielsen February 1992)
National Average	100
New York	101
Miami	83
Detroit	102
Chicago	104
Denver	94
Los Angeles	81

Table 9–1 illustrates the difference in gross rating points delivered by a nighttime network TV schedule in different markets. As the table shows, the delivery of GRPs by a national medium such as network television is generally distributed unevenly among markets. If the delivery of these GRPs happened to match sales potential in each market closely, there would be no need for adjustment. Unfortunately, this rarely happens, so adjustments in advertising weight are required.

The final determination of the need for weighting is the wide variance in media costs—again, not necessarily in relation to sales potential. On one hand, a planner who allocates dollars on a proportional basis may be unable to buy as much advertising as required in the best markets because costs may be too high. On the other hand, one may be able to buy more impressions than needed in less expensive markets.

To illustrate the variation in media costs, Table 9–2 gives a cost-per-thousand analysis for several spot TV markets. The reader should recall that cost-per-thousand numbers reflect the relationship between target audiences delivered and the costs of media in delivering those targets. Table 9–2 shows that media costs per thousand for reaching women age 25–54 in various markets are not directly proportional to the size of each market. Smaller markets (e.g., Hartford, Baltimore, and San Francisco) often have a higher CPM than larger markets (e.g., New York and Chicago) to reach a given target audience.

Different Forms of Weighting

There are different techniques of weighting that will accomplish the same objectives. The simplest way, the *dollar allocation technique*, allocates proportionately more money to good markets. Therefore, if Market A accounts for 10 percent of total sales, it receives 10 percent of the advertising budget. This technique, however, does not take varying media costs into consideration.

A second technique, *gross impression weighting,* does take varying media costs into consideration. It allocates the budget on the basis of gross impressions desired: Good markets are budgeted to receive more impressions and weaker markets, fewer.

TABLE 9–2.   Cost-per-Thousand Analysis

City	B/W Cost U.S. Households	Spot TV CPM, Women 25–54 (Avg. M–F, 4–6 p.m.)
New York	7.6%	$4.42
Hartford	1.0	9.95
Chicago	3.4	4.55
San Francisco	2.4	10.61
Baltimore	1.0	9.05

Table 9–3 illustrates the differences between the first and second weighting techniques. The table shows that when dollars are allocated proportionately, gross impressions vary; when gross impressions are allocated proportionately, dollars vary.

Why do these two techniques differ? Dollar allocation does *not* take media gross impressions into consideration. Therefore, 10 percent of the available dollars buys more impressions in Market A than Market B because cost per thousand is lower in Market A. So the dollar allocation technique leaves Market B with fewer gross impressions per year than Market A, even though sales potential is equal. To equalize the number of gross impressions in A and B, the planner will tend to favor gross impression allocation. Yet each technique has different values.

Dollar allocation tends to generate:

1. More impressions in cost-efficient markets (A cost-efficient market is one where the cost per thousand is relatively low.)
2. Fewer impressions in inefficient markets or high cost-per-thousand markets
3. The opportunity for good markets to develop their potential because more gross impressions are received in these markets, presumably generating more sales
4. A slightly unbalanced advertising weight-to-sales ratio

Gross impression allocation tends to generate:

1. Proportional communication pressure regardless of cost
2. Balanced reach and frequency based on sales potential (This means that the good markets get proportionately more reach and frequency than poor markets.)

TABLE 9–3.   Differences in Weighting Methods

	Total Sales (%)	CPM	Dollar Weighting		Gross Impression Weighting	
			10% of Dollars	No. of Gross Impressions 10% Dollars Buy	10% of Impressions	Cost of 10% Impressions
Market A	10	$2.50	$100,000	40 million	32 million	$ 80,000
Market B	10	3.75	100,000	26 million	32 million	120,000
Total			$200,000	66 million	64 million	$200,000

Source: Ogilvy & Mather.

3. The opportunity for good markets to develop their potential because more gross impressions are received in these markets, presumably generating more sales

4. A slightly unbalanced advertising-to-sales ratio

In deciding which weighting technique to use, the planner has to consider which best meets the marketing objectives. In many instances, gross impression weighting is considered better because it is more directly related to communication goals. One of the main goals of media strategy planning is to reach large numbers of target audiences with a certain amount of repetition. Within a given budget, gross impression weighting accomplishes this goal best because it takes media costs into consideration. In the dollar allocation technique, costs may be directly proportional to sales, but audiences may not be reached often enough or in sufficiently large numbers.

Tables 9–4 and 9–5 provide another picture of the relationships of both processes. Table 9–4 shows again that even when dollars are matched perfectly against sales percentage, gross impressions do not match (except in Market B). Table 9–5 shows that when gross impressions are matched perfectly against sales percentages, dollar costs do not match (again, except in Market B).

Share of Voice (Message Weight Distribution)

A planning concept that is sometimes used in making media decisions is called *share of voice*. It is also more appropriately called *message weight distribution*. This concept requires a planner to determine how much advertising is being done for his brand relative to the amount being done for competitive brands. A share of voice is a percentage of total advertising weight for each brand.

The assumption underlying share of voice is that if a brand is not spending an amount equal to or exceeding the expenditures of competitors, then it may not be able to achieve its goals. This assumption is not necessarily valid because there may be many variables, other than media spending, that affect the success of an advertising campaign. The superiority of the brand, or the uniqueness of the copy, or the amount and quality of distribution, or

TABLE 9–4.   How U.S. Dollar Allocation Matches Sales Distribution

| | | | Dollar Allocation | | |
Market	Sales (%)	Cost (thousands)	Total Cost (%)	Gross Impressions That Can Be Bought (millions)	Total Gross Impressions (%)
A	45	$ 675	45	343	48
B	30	450	30	214	30
C	15	225	15	93	13
D	10	150	10	64	9
Total U.S.	100	$1,500	100	714	100

Source: Ogilvy & Mather.

TABLE 9-5.   How Gross Impression Allocation Matches Sales Distribution

Market	Sales (%)	Gross Impressions Planned For (millions)	Total Gross Impressions (%)	Cost of Gross Impressions Planned (thousands)	Total Cost (%)
A	45	318	45	$ 637	42
B	30	212	30	444	30
C	15	106	15	251	17
D	10	71	10	168	11
Total	100	707	100	$1,500	100

Source: Ogilvy & Mather.

frequency and quality of promotions are a few variables that may be more important. In fact, many planners do not use the share of voice concept at all, while others think of it as a general idea that may be of help in determining allocations and/or budgets.

If, however, one is inclined to determine share of voice, it is important to do so on other bases than comparing the percent of dollars spent. "Dollars spent" do not buy a constant number of gross impressions or target rating points. So, it would be better to first find how many gross impressions or target rating points can be purchased for a given number of dollars and then convert this information into percentages. Comparisons can be made, for example, on the basis of the actual number of messages (or commercials) delivered.

Table 9-6 shows the share of TV messages to women 18-39 for nine brands. It is important to note that the share of voice (TV messages) does not match share of TV dollars in the example shown.

It also analyzes nine competitors and their message weight deliveries. The table shows that Brand A has 35 percent of the market but spends only 25 percent of the total TV dollars and has a relatively lower percentage of message delivery than Brand B.

TABLE 9-6.   Share of Voice (Message Weight Distribution) for Nine Competitors

Brand	Share of Market (%)	Share of TV dollars (%)	Share of TV Messages to Women 18-39 (%)
A	35	25	19
B	26	25	28
C	17	16	16
D	8	8	12
E	7	4	6
F	4	3	6
G	3	2	4
H	N/A	14	8
I	N/A	3	1
Total	100	100	100

Source: Roth, Paul, "How to Plan Media," *Media Decisions,* 1976, p. 26.

The planner should ask a number of questions to determine "why" Brand A has such a high ratio of market share to message share. Is Brand A inherently superior in quality to B? Does Brand A have better distribution? Better copy? Most other brands show a high degree of consistency between market share and message share. Additional message weight analysis should be made of individual markets to see how they, too, relate to market share.

Guidelines in Geographical Weighting

There is no one formula used to determine advertising weights applied in different geographic areas. Weighting decisions are usually a result of many factors. Using one or the other of the two techniques described earlier, a planner may weight advertising in geographic markets in a number of ways. The following guidelines comprise some of the more important considerations in weighting.

A general concept is to apply extra weight to markets where sales volume or market share is high. In a market-by-market analysis, a planner might look at the brand development index (BDI) and compare it with a category development index (CDI). At times, more weight is added to markets with high BDIs. More often, however, when a CDI is high and a BDI is low for a given market, additional weight may be added to bring the market up to its potential (as shown in the CDI).

Market potential, as a basis for weighting, may depend on any one, or perhaps all, of the following considerations:

1. Past history of each market's responsiveness to advertising. If a local market has not responded well to advertising in the past, then additional weight may not help.
2. History of profitability. Although additional weighting in a local market may improve sales volume or market share, it may do so at an unprofitable level. There may be a point of diminishing returns relative to profits in adding extra weight to a market.
3. Pipeline problems. If distribution levels in a market are low, or difficult to increase, or there are other marketing channel problems, then these factors may influence the amount of extra weight to be applied.
4. Sales force input. Some companies use their salespeople as sources of marketing intelligence at the local level. Their information may affect the manner in which weighting is applied.
5. Local market idiosyncracies. Some local markets may have problems in communication and/or selling that may not be true of other markets. One advertiser may find that an equal number of GRPs applied to both large and small markets usually produces greater awareness in smaller markets, regardless of other factors. If such idiosyncracies exist, then they should be allowed for in the weighting decision.

6. Competitive noise levels. If competitors advertise heavily in a market, the net effect of the noise level may require heavier weight in that market.
7. Cost efficiency of advertising in the market. Additional weighting may cost too much or result in cost inefficiency.

Once these considerations are evaluated, the planner may want to decide on a course of action that could affect the final weighting. Does the advertiser want to defend strengths in good markets? Improve weaknesses in problem markets? Or develop opportunity markets? After this decision has been made and other factors considered, weighting decisions for local geographical areas can be made.

Case Studies 9–1, 9–2, and 9–3 are examples of how different advertisers have used weighting techniques.

CASE STUDY 9–1
Allocating Weights to Spot TV Markets on a Pro-Rata Basis

In this example, weights are shown by the amount of money allocated to each spot TV market in a media plan. While only five markets are shown, this technique could be used for over 100 markets if necessary.

A Budget Allocated Proportionately to Sales Made by Each Area

Sales Area	Sales Made by Each Area (%)	Budget Goal	Network Delivery* (%)
A	30	$1,500,000	25
B	15	750,000	15
C	10	500,000	20
D	10	500,000	10
E	35	1,750,000	30
Total	100	$5,000,000	100

Source: J. Walter Thompson Company, *Allocating Advertising Weight Geographically*, 1973, p. 9.
*Delivery is based on a number of selected network programs that cover targets.

For purposes of illustration, assume that a manufacturer sells a product in five geographic areas (or markets) of the country. Sales percentages for each of the five areas are shown in the example, as is a proportional allocation of the budget to each sales area. Also shown is the percentage of network television delivery in each sales area.

The example shows that each area received a proportional amount of dollars equal to the percentage of sales made in the area. However, a close look at the relationship of sales and network delivery percentages shows some anomalies. For example, Area A delivered 30 percent of total sales but has only 25 percent of total network delivery. As a result, it may be necessary to allocate some of the budget to local television.

The problem that arises is how to divide the television budget between network and spot so that each area receives an equitable portion of the budget. Ideally, a planner would like the percentage of network television delivery to match sales percentages in each market. Therefore, if a market provides 20 percent of total U.S. sales, then it should receive 20 percent of the budget. Unfortunately, when advertisers use network television, the delivery in some markets is more than needed, while the delivery in other markets is less than needed.

For example, if sales in Market A are 30 percent and the percentage of total U.S. network program delivery is 20 percent, then some way must be found to bring television delivery up to the 30 percent level. This may be done by adding a certain amount of dollars to local spot television. However, if a market accounts for 10 percent of sales and network television delivery is 20 percent of the U.S. total, one cannot easily cut network, market by market. So a technique has been created to take dollars from network television in certain markets and add them to spot television to bring each market up to a percentage equal to its sales.

The technique outlined step-by-step applies to the example below.

Allocation of Budget to Network and Spot TV

Sales Area	Sales Made by Each Area (%)	Budget Goal	Total Network Delivery (%)	Index: Network to Sales Delivery	Network Budget	Spot TV (Local) Budget
A	30	$1,500,000	25	83	$ 625,000	$ 875,000
B	15	750,000	15	100	375,000	375,000
C	10	500,000	20	200	500,000	—
D	10	500,000	10	100	250,000	250,000
E	35	1,750,000	30	86	750,000	1,000,000
Total	100	$5,000,000	100		$2,500,000	$2,500,000

Source: J. Walter Thompson Company, *Allocating Advertising Weight Geographically*, 1973, p. 9.

1. This table shows a national advertiser who buys network television advertising in five markets. (This is a simulated example, since it is highly unlikely that so few markets would ever be used. But the solution would work for 200 or more markets.)
2. The planner starts by allocating a pre-determined national budget of $5,000,000 for the five markets. The pro rata system would allot each market the same percent as it accounted for in sales. Market A received $1,500,000 (.30 × $5 million); B received $750,000 (.15 × $5 million); etc.
3. Now the marketer has to know how much network delivery went into each market. This will require knowing the GRPs of each program bought in each market. All the GRPs for all the markets

are added, and a percentage of delivery is calculated. This is the data in the column labeled ''Total Network Delivery.''

4. The planner now can see some anomalies. For example, Market A was under-delivered because it developed 30% of sales but only received 25% of national television delivery. It should have received 30%. Market B was right on target with 15% sales and 15% network delivery. Theoretically B does not need additional spot television. Market C is over-delivered. It had 10% sales but received 20% network delivery.

5. To clarify over- or under-delivery, an index is calculated for each market:

$$\text{Index of delivery} = \frac{\% \text{ of network TV delivery in a market}}{\% \text{ of sales in the same market}}$$

Here are indices of delivery: A = 83; B = 100; C = 200 (C is the most over-delivered market); D = 100; and E = 86.

6. At this point, the planner calculates what the total for the five markets would be based on Market C's over-delivery—which only had 10% of sales? The formula for this would be:

X (.20) = $500,000 (or, what number times 20% equal $500,000?)

The answer is $2,500,000, which now becomes the network budget; another $2,500,000 would be used for the spot TV budget. So $2,500,000 is the budget based on C's TV delivery.

7. Now each market's pro rata budget is multiplied by delivery percent to find the amount that would go into a *new* network allocation. That number has been recorded in the column labeled Network Budget and was obtained as follows: A .25 × $2,500,000 = $625,000; B .15 × $2,500,000 = $575,000; C .20 × $2,500,000 = $500,000 (this has not changed).

8. Each market's *new* network budget is subtracted from its pro rata budget and this amount is now a first estimate of how much money to allot to spot TV that will enable each market to match sales percentages with delivery. Check math for spot TV budget. Note that market C received no money for spot TV. Why?

CASE STUDY 9–2
Weighting Markets on the Basis of Minimum BDIs and CDIs

Chapter 8 discussed how BDIs and CDIs are generally used in selecting target markets. These two evaluative statistics may also be used to weight markets on the basis of minimum standards.

In this method, sales goals are first set for each individual market. Then 5 percent of the budget is cut from each market and reallocated to problem and/or opportunity markets.

A problem market is one:
1. With at least 1 percent of brand sales
2. With a CDI and BDI less than 100
3. With an unfavorable sales trend

An opportunity market is one:
1. With at least 1 percent of brand sales
2. With a CDI over 100, but BDI lower than CDI
3. With client's brand showing an unfavorable sales trend, but the product category doing well

Note: When CDI is over 100, the category is doing well. A BDI under 100 usually indicates a brand is not doing well.

The 5 percent that was cut from each market's budget is now distributed to both problem and opportunity markets. The idea underlying this practice is that problem markets may be strengthened by additional dollars, while opportunity markets need extra dollars to optimize potential. But at the same time, all markets were allocated *some* money based on potential.

Note: All markets will receive some advertising weight through the use of network television or national magazines. The weights discussed in this case are added to national weights.

CASE STUDY 9-3
Weighting Markets by Combining Quantitative and Qualitative Values for Each Market

This technique was used by an advertiser who purchased network TV to provide national coverage, and spot TV to weight the best markets. The value of each market was determined as follows:

Step 1. Calculate the cost index. The cost index is simply the average CPM for all spot TV markets in the country, related to the CPM for each individual market. If the average CPM for the country was $2.50 and it was $3.50 for Market A, then the cost index would be 140.

$$\$3.50 \div \$2.50 = 140 \text{ cost index}$$

Step 2. Calculate the CDI/CPM value for each market. If Market A had a CDI of 120, then the CDI/CPM value for each market would be 86.

$$120 \div 140 = 86$$

Market A now has less value than it had before because the CDI/CPM value is so low.

Step 3. Determine each market's responsiveness to advertising. This is primarily a qualitative judgment. If sales last year rose by more than 15 percent in a market, that market could be described as responsive. If sales rose between 3 percent and 15 percent, it might be described as somewhat responsive. If sales rose less than 3 percent, it might be described as not responsive. (An alternative method for making this decision is at the end of this section.)

Step 4. Assign extra weight on the basis of the following criteria:
   Group A Markets (Receive 50 percent more weight than average)

1. CDIs are high
2. CPMs are reasonable
3. Network delivery is low
4. Responsiveness to advertising was good in the past
   Group B Markets (Receive 25 percent more weight than average)
   Combinations of those considerations above yield a lower number, but show that the market is important
   Group C Markets (No spot TV)
   All other markets

The following example shows three sample markets assigned extra weight as described earlier:

Weighting on the Basis of CDI and CPM

Markets	Share of U.S. Population (%)	Industry Sales	Network TV Delivery	CDI	CDI/ Spot CPM	Sales Trend Last Yr. (%)	Weighting Used
Chicago	4.0	4.7	97	117	158	+ 19	A—add 50%
Seattle	1.2	1.8	85	150	117	+ 6	B—add 25%
Indianapolis	1.1	1.2	109	101	83	− 1	C—None

Note: Responsiveness to advertising could be determined differently. For example, an advertising-to-sales ratio figure could be calculated as follows: If sales in Market A were $1,450,000 and advertising in that market were $340,000, then the A/S ratio would be 0.235 (340 ÷ 1450 = 0.235). Then an index of advertising to sales could be calculated whereby the A/S index for Market A was divided by the A/S index for the entire country. For example: 0.235 ÷ 0.405 = 0.58.

These indices could be added to the CPM average for each market and the CDI for each market to provide a multiple factor index as follows:

$$
\begin{array}{lr}
\text{Market A} & \\
\text{CDI/CPM Index:} & 86 \\
\text{CDI} & 120 \\
\text{A/Sales Index} & \underline{58} \\
\text{Total} & 264 \\
& \\
\text{Average for Market A} & 88 \\
(264 \div 3 = 88) &
\end{array}
$$

Population of Market A: 5 percent of total U.S. × 88 average index = 4.4 percent of the total allocation for Market A.

This technique could be used to allocate spot dollars proportionately throughout the country.

The three case studies indicate that different advertisers use different methods of weighting. No single method is used to the exclusion of all others. Each technique meets the needs of individual advertisers.

Reach and Frequency

As explained earlier, *reach* refers to how many different people are exposed to a vehicle at least once, while *frequency* refers to how often they are reached in a given period of time (often four weeks).

When to Emphasize Reach

Almost all media plans cover the subjects of reach and frequency. But sometimes reach is emphasized more than frequency, and other times the opposite is true.

A general rule for knowing when to emphasize reach is *whenever anything new is being planned in the marketplace.* The meaning of "new" can be applied to announcing a new price, for example, because consumers usually will not respond to a message until something has been changed in the marketplace that benefits them. A new price can indeed be a benefit if it is lower than it was formerly. Old marketing practices do not need to be changed if they are judged to be successful in selling. Listed below are some other examples of new marketing factors that require a reach strategy. Each can benefit some consumers to a greater or lesser degree:

New distribution (new stores that now carry the brand)
New features of a product that meet consumers' needs
New advertising copy (new words and/or pictures)
New sales promotion incentives
New packaging
New models of the brand being introduced
New media being used for the first time
New positions in the store where brand is to be found
New servicing opportunities
New home delivery patterns
New marketing and/or advertising objectives for the brand

How Much Reach Is Necessary?

One of the most difficult decisions facing a media planner is setting the level of reach needed for a media plan. It is difficult because there is little hard evidence from research or experimentation that provides the necessary direction. What is known about how much reach to use is the product of tradition, experience, common sense, and research done for particular brands in certain market situations. But there is little evidence to indicate that a given reach level is "correct" for a given marketing situation. Therefore the guidance provided here, based as it is on widely held beliefs, has to be general. Even with all these qualifiers, there are some planners who may disagree with this approach.

It is generally held that high reach is necessary for new product introductions, the rationale being that few people know the name of the brand or what its value is. As many different people as possible need to be informed, thus the need for high reach. But determining just how much reach is necessary is difficult.

The purpose of high reach is to generate awareness of the new brand. The reach level may be decided to some extent by the brand awareness level that is needed. Is the goal to make 65 percent of the targets aware of a brand name? Some people will need only one exposure to a vehicle to become aware of that brand. Others will need multiple exposures, so a certain level of frequency will be needed in addition to reach. Some planners might opt for a reach level higher than the brand awareness level desired, on the assumption that not everyone exposed to a vehicle will be exposed to the ad and the brand name. Others will want reach *and* frequency, which for planning purposes can be expressed in gross rating points. Within a given number of gross rating points, the reach and frequency levels can be juggled to bring either one to a required level. Some available research attempts to relate GRP levels to brand awareness levels. For example, one piece of research conducted by a well-known advertising agency found that about 2,400 GRPs a year produced a 70 percent brand awareness.

Sales promotion activities also need a high degree of reach because consumers need to be made aware when certain deals or promotional options are available. In planning media to advertise a cents-off deal, a high level of awareness is a requirement and, again, the precise amount of reach needed cannot be expressed.

One media planning strategy might be to set a reach level equal to or surpassing that of competitors who are deemed to be vulnerable to attack. Presumably these competitors have products that are not as good as the brand in question, or perhaps they are not advertising enough, or to the right targets. Setting a reach level equal to or higher than that of certain competitors offers a potential advantage to the planner, and is a way to determine how much reach ought to be attained.

Another consideration in planning reach is the budget. No matter which media are chosen, a fixed budget size limits the amount of reach possible.

All the planner has to do is to calculate the amount of target reach that each medium and vehicle will deliver, plus the amount of continuity desired, to set a reach level.

There is a media strategy that stretches media dollars and therefore also stretches reach. This strategy holds that by cutting ad unit sizes, more money will be available to buy new reach. (The same strategy can be used to buy more frequency.) If the planned ad unit is thirty-second commercials or full-page ads, it could be cut to ten-second IDs or half-page ads. But there are two penalties for cutting unit sizes. First, the cost of smaller unit sizes usually is not exactly proportional to larger sizes—a ten-second ID costs 55 to 65 percent of a thirty-second commercial; a half-page ad costs 55 to 65 percent of a full-page ad. Second, there is a possible loss in communication value from the smaller ad unit.

Probably the best level of reach is determined by looking at what levels were used previously. If a brand has successfully achieved certain marketing goals in the past with a given level of reach, this same level (or proportional adjustment) should probably be used again.

In essence, then, the amount of reach needed for a media plan is based more on judgment and experience than on research evidence. Since media plans almost always require a certain amount of frequency, the combination of reach and frequency can be calculated in terms of gross rating points. But research on GRPs and communication effects is weak, and the GRP level is also a matter of judgment and experience.

When to Emphasize Frequency

Frequency is emphasized whenever repetition, not dispersion, is the key selling strategy. This has implications for reach too, because reach and frequency are inversely related. As frequency is increased, reach levels will tend to decline. It is possible to have very high frequencies and reaches as low as 10%. Can a planner tolerate only 10% of a market receiving an average frequency of 15? Shown below is an example of these relationships:

> High reach: (70: high reach and a 2: low frequency = 140 GRPs a month)
>
> High frequency: (15: high frequency and 9.3: a low reach = 140 GRPs a month)

Generally, high frequency is necessary to compete in a highly competitive market, or when a product is sold frequently.

How Much Frequency Is Necessary?

The question of how much frequency is necessary is probably the most pressing problem facing media planners. It is more important than learning how much reach or how many GRPs are necessary. A great deal of thinking and research has gone into this subject, although no clear-cut breakthroughs are yet apparent.

Frequency is needed whenever repetition of a message is necessary. Most planners feel that there are practical reasons for needing more than minimum amounts of frequency.

The first reason for needing frequency is that not everyone hears or sees an ad the first time it appears. Why? Because so many ads bombard a person each day that it is impossible for anyone to pay attention to all of them. Even if an individual has seen an ad many times, little or none of the information may have been absorbed by the person. Therefore, one goal of frequency is to surpass the *threshold*, the first few exposures, so that the audience member will absorb the message. Research has shown that there are indeed threshold levels for some advertising, although it isn't known precisely whether the threshold is one, two, three, or more exposures.

In some cases, one exposure may be sufficient. Gus Priemer, advertising director of S. C. Johnson Company, has proved through test-market research on a new product that the first impression of an ad was remembered for a certain product/brand at a given time. As he explained:

> My own evidence strongly suggests that the first ad exposure actually *can* stimulate a large proportion of total *advertising response*, even when a product is using TV where the viewer is not in control of the communication vehicle.
>
> My TV evidence comes from some 35 first-exposure tests of commercials done for 16 new products prior to test marketing.
>
> For five of these products, viewers had already memorized the new brand name at significant levels (7 to 9 percent of those exposed to the test commercial). Almost one in four had clearly understood the new product promise of the testing brands.[1]

Priemer was not, however, generalizing about all products or all brands. He simply pointed out that there are different thresholds for different brands.

Frequency in media is not the same as frequency of ad exposure. In media planning, the frequency sought is vehicle exposure. But not everyone exposed to a vehicle also sees the ads in that vehicle. So, any frequency expressed as part of a media plan overstates the size of frequency of exposure to ads in the vehicle chosen. Because there is no syndicated research measurement of ad exposure, a planner must plan for more frequency than seems necessary; this creates a cushion of loss of exposure to account for audience members who see the vehicles, but don't see the ads of a given brand.

There has been a feeling in the industry for years that high frequency (or repetition) represents a strong form of persuasion in selling a product. The more frequently a persuasive message is heard or seen, the more likely the

---

1. Priemer, Gus, "Are We Doing the Wrong Thing Right?" *Media Decisions,* May 1979, p. 64.

consumer is to see the merits of the advertised brand and be convinced to buy. At least, that is a widely held assumption. Additionally, the higher the frequency and the longer the advertising effort, the better the opportunity to reach a person when he or she is most ready to buy the product.

Some feel that every media planner should try to learn how many impressions (meaning frequency of exposure) a consumer needs before being persuaded to buy a given brand. This number is part of a cause-and-effect relationship. Planners assume that a level of impressions that will directly affect sales exists for every brand. However, this level is probably somewhat different for every brand and must be determined by experimental research. Test marketing experiments may have to be conducted, trying various frequency levels to determine which is the most productive.

Even those planners who view frequency as not necessarily a direct cause of sales see it as a necessary requirement for communicating with large numbers of disinterested consumers, or consumers who miss advertising because they are inundated by the noise level of all the competitive ads. Frequency, therefore, is a means of "getting through" to the consumer. The following quotation, from over a hundred years ago, has often been cited as a generalization about how frequency affects communications, and eventually sales.

> The first time a man looks at an advertisement, he does not see it.
> The second time he does not notice it.
> The third time he is conscious of its existence.
> The fourth time he faintly remembers having seen it before.
> The fifth time he reads it.
> The sixth time he turns up his nose at it.
> The seventh time he reads it through and says, "Oh brother!"
> The eighth time he says, "Here's that confounded thing again!"
> The ninth time he wonders if it amounts to anything.
> The tenth time he thinks he will ask his neighbor if he has tried it.
> The eleventh time he wonders how the advertiser makes it pay.
> The twelfth time he thinks perhaps it may be worth something.
> The thirteenth time he thinks it must be a good thing.
> The fourteenth time he remembers that he has wanted such a thing
>   for a long time.
> The fifteenth time he is tantalized because he cannot afford to buy it.
> The sixteenth time he thinks he will buy it some day.
> The seventeenth time he makes a memorandum of it.
> The eighteenth time he swears at his poverty.
> The nineteenth time he counts his money carefully.
> The twentieth time he sees it, he buys the article, or instructs his
>   wife to do so.[2]

2. Smith, Thomas, *Hints to Intending Advertisers* (London, 1885): quoted in Herbert E. Krugman, "An Application of Learning Theory to TV Copy Testing," *Public Opinion Quarterly*, vol. 26, 1962, pp. 626–34.

Many media planners believe that a plan should have a frequency level of at least four exposures a month. The thinking is that the first three exposures tend to be ignored, but the fourth is the threshold at which consumers begin to pay attention to the advertising message.

Other planners disagree. Some say that the frequency level must vary because certain situations may require higher or lower levels. The uniqueness of the advertising message, for example, can affect frequency. The more innovative and unusual the message is, the more likely that consumers will notice it and pay attention to it. The converse is also true. A rather ordinary ad message might need many more than four exposures to be seen and remembered. (In all discussions on frequency levels, the planner must be aware that creative executions vary from brand to brand, and the creative element can argue for more or less frequency than the competition uses.)

Another consideration affecting the frequency level is the perceived value of a brand as compared with the values of competitors' brands. When a brand has an important and easily perceivable benefit not shared by competitors, then less frequency may be called for. In other words, the brand has an easily exploited advantage over competitors. But when a brand is very much like all other brands in a product category, more frequency may be necessary for the message to be noticed or remembered.

The noise level in a product category also plays a role in deciding how much frequency is needed. On one hand, if many similar brands are being advertised simultaneously, consumers may find it difficult to recall the message for any one brand amid the confusion caused by the noise level of competitors. On the other hand, when few competitors advertise, less frequency may be required.

Some planners feel that a frequency level should be based on the level of that used by a brand's most serious competitive threat; or, that the competitor who is the most vulnerable to a brand's promotional attack efforts should be singled out. The frequency level of that competitor should be equaled or surpassed, with the objective of gaining an advantage.

Media values may also be used in conjunction with gross-rating-point planning to determine frequency (as well as reach) levels. Media value is simply the judgment that a given medium has been found, through experience, to be more effective for a brand and its creative message, thus justifying more frequency in that medium. The chief problem, however, in combining media evaluations and frequency levels is that of making too subjective an evaluation of each medium. Is daytime television always less than 35 percent as effective as prime-time television? To say that it is *always* less effective is an unreasonable assumption. For certain brands, in certain marketing situations, at certain times, the 35 percent differential may be true—but it is dangerous to generalize. The method is a good one, however, when research evidence can be used to back up a generalization about media values.

Frequency levels in media plans therefore range quite a bit. When the threatening or vulnerable competitor technique is being used, frequency levels may go to as high as fifteen average exposures a month. But these levels are not decided upon in a scientific manner in terms of a cause-and-effect relationship. Even when various frequency levels are tested in three or four local markets and one is found to be better than others, there is no guarantee that this level can be projected nationally. What is true in a test market may or may not be valid for every market. The experience of many national advertisers who have used test marketing for setting frequency levels varies from a few who have had excellent results to many who have had costly failures.

All of these considerations about where to set the frequency level are based primarily on common sense, and on unfortunately little research evidence. As a consequence, it is not surprising to find frequency levels being set somewhat arbitrarily, based on tradition plus common sense. In the future, the concepts and practices of *effective* reach and frequency may totally supplant present techniques.

One of the most important guidelines to remember in determining how much frequency is necessary is that vehicle frequency does not equal advertising frequency. The levels planned for media vehicles should not be confused with advertising frequency, which must also be planned.

Effective Frequency and Reach

The question of how to set effective frequency (and effective reach) levels cannot be answered very well, despite the fact that planners have been using the 3 + level in their plans for a number of years. There is enough agreement among the leading researchers and practitioners of media to agree that a 3 + level is not correct. The reason, as discussed in Chapter 6, is that it is oversimplified. There are too many variables in planning that the 3 + concept does not address.

However, these same people agree that there already are guidelines for setting effective frequency levels in an objective manner. We may not know objectively how much frequency is needed, but we can know that 3 + is not the correct level *unless* we have modified that number by the guideline criteria. Therefore, the best advice to date is to plan media in the same way that planners did *without* effective frequency. This procedure means that the first step in planning is to review the different variables that can affect the amount of frequency needed. Then, starting with a frequency level needed to account for these variables, add them to what is already known about effective frequency. In other words, considering all the variables that affect normal frequency, one might arrive at a 2 + level. Adding that to the 3 + level arrived at by some effective frequency research, brings one to a 5 + level. However, a planner could end up with a 1 + plan just as well, depending on these variables.

Joseph Ostrow spelled out the variables that planners should first consider in his talk at the Advertising Research Foundation Conference on Effective Frequency in 1982. (Ostrow's ideas are presented in Case Study 9–4, along with some numbers that could be applied for every consideration that Ostrow recommends which the authors have supplied.)

CASE STUDY 9-4
How to Set Effective Frequency Levels

One of the problems facing a media planner is that of deciding how much effective frequency a media plan should have. Although the research may be interpreted to suggest a 3 + level, there is great dispute about it.

One suggestion about how to set a frequency level was made by Joseph W. Ostrow, executive vice president of the Foote-Cone & Belding agency at the 1982 Effective Frequency Conference sponsored by the Advertising Research Foundation.[3] He specified a number of conditions that should influence the decision, based on marketing, media, and creative strategy considerations. He pointed out that "the right level of frequency for a media plan is the point at which effective communication takes place." For example, "getting consumers to understand the message; helping consumers become more positive about a product (or service) or influencing the purchase decisions directly."

The authors, however, have made some additional suggestions about Ostrow's model to help solve the problem of setting the correct frequency level, by asking the reader/user to add a certain amount of frequency points to a base, if the marketing, media, or creative condition meets the planner's needs. These additional frequency points are only suggestions; the user may opt for different ones.

The planner should use these additional points by starting with a base, such as a 3 + level, then adding or subtracting points as the situation dictates.

Here's an example of how to use these suggestions. Suppose a planner is faced with the following situations:

1. He or she is introducing a new product.
2. The introduction is in a highly competitive market.
3. The product has a short purchase cycle.
4. The brand will be among those that are less well known.
5. The product is not used daily.
6. Ad copy is somewhat complex.
7. Copy is more unique than competitors'.
8. Copy will be in large-size ad units.
9. There is high ad clutter in category media.
10. Media environment is compatible with product.
11. Advertising will be continuous.
12. Many media will be used.
13. There will be many opportunities for repetition.

---

3. Ostrow, Joseph W., "Setting Effective Frequency Levels," *Effective Frequency: The State of the Art,* New York: Advertising Research Foundation, Key Issues Workshop, 1982, pp. 89–102.

The planner should now consult Ostrow's considerations and note the suggested point levels that may be added for setting effective frequency levels, as follows:

Marketing Factors That Affect Effective Frequency

Marketing Factors	Frequency Needed	Comments
Established brands	Lower	Repetition helps consumers learn a message. New brands need to be learned.
New brands	Higher	
High market share	Lower	High market share assumes that brand loyalty must be high. Thus less frequency needed.
Low market share	Higher	
Dominant brand in market	Lower	Large brands may not benefit from more repetition if the market is saturated. Smaller brands can benefit from more frequency.
Smaller, less well-known brands	Higher	
High brand loyalty	Lower	An inverse relationship usually exists between frequency and brand loyalty.
Low brand loyalty	Higher	
Long purchase cycle	Lower	Consumers may do more thinking about products with longer purchase cycles.
Short purchase cycle (High volume segments)	Higher	
Product used daily	Higher	Products used daily, or more than once daily probably need higher frequency.
Product used occasionally	Lower	
Needed to beat competition	Higher	In heavy-spending-categories, more frequency may be needed above the level that achieves effective communication.
Advertising to older consumers or children	Higher	Special targets may need higher frequency levels.

Copy Factors That Affect Effective Frequency

Copy Factors	Frequency Needed	Comments
Complex copy	Higher	Copy research augmenting good copy may be needed to determine how copy is perceived.
Simple copy	Lower	
Copy less unique than competition	Higher	The assumption is that copy uniqueness is an asset that translates to less frequency.
Copy more unique	Lower	
New copy campaign	Higher	Just as a new product introduction needs higher frequency, so does new copy.
Continuing campaign	Lower	

Image type copy	Higher	Image campaigns are deemed more complex and subtle, needing more frequency.
Product sell copy	Lower	
More different kinds of messages	Higher	This covers the question of how much message variation there is, and is tied to the number of commercials in a pool of commercials.
Single kind of message	Lower	
To avoid wearout: New messages Older messages	Higher Lower	The question here is: has advertising worn out? Measurements will need to be made to learn what the situation is.
Small ad units	Higher	Advertising units either in broadcast or print may need more or less frequency.
Larger ad units	Lower	

Media Factors That Affect Effective Frequency

Media Factors	Frequency Needed	Comments
High ad clutter	Higher	This is an oddity because high clutter requires more frequency that adds to the clutter.
Lower ad clutter	Lower	
Compatible editorial environment Non-compatible environment	Lower Higher	An example of compatible environment would be a dog food ad appearing in a television pet show.
Attentiveness high	Lower	Some media vehicles have higher attentive levels than others.
Attentiveness low	Higher	
Continuous advertising	Lower	Interruptions in advertising, such as in pulsing or flighting, need more frequency.
Pulsed or flighted advertising	Higher	
Few media used	Lower	Each medium used may require a minimum level of frequency.
More media used	Higher	
Opportunities for media repetition Fewer opportunities for repetition	Lower Higher	Certain media offer better and more opportunities for repetition, and these require less frequency.

Marketing Factors That Affect Effective Frequency

Established brands	− .2	− .1	+ .1	(+ .2)	New brands
High market share	− .2	− .1	+ .1	+ .2	Low market share
Dominant brand in market	− .2	− .1	+ .1	(+ .2)	Smaller, less well-known brands
High brand loyalty	− .2	− .1	+ .1	+ .2	Low brand loyalty

Long purchase cycle	− .2	− .1	+ .1	(+ .2)	Short purchase cycle (high volume segments)
Product used daily	− .2	(− .1)	+ .1	+ .2	Product used occasionally
			+ .1	(+ .2)	Needed to beat competition
			+ .1	+ .2	Advertising to older consumers, or children

Copy Factors That Affect Effective Frequency

Simple copy	− .2	− .1	+ .1	(+ .2)	Complex copy
Copy more unique than competition	(− .2)	− .1	+ .1	+ .2	Copy less unique than competition
Continuing campaign	− .2	− .1	+ .1	+ .2	New copy campaign
Product sell copy	− .2	− .1	+ .1	+ .2	Image type copy
Single kind of message	− .2	− .1	+ .1	+ .2	More different kinds of messages
To avoid wearout: New messages	− .2	− .1	+ .1	+ .2	Older messages
Larger ad units	− .2	(− .1)	+ .1	+ .2	Small ad units

Media Factors That Affect Effective Frequency

Lower ad clutter	− .2	− .1	+ .1	(+ .2)	High ad clutter
Compatible editorial environment	− .2	(− .1)	+ .1	+ .2	Non-compatible environment
Attentiveness high	− .2	− .1	+ .1	+ .2	Attentiveness low
Continuous advertising	(− .2)	− .1	+ .1	+ .2	Pulsed or flighted advertising
Few media used	− .2	− .1	+ .1	(+ .2)	Many media used
Opportunities for media repetition	(− .2)	− .1	+ .1	+ .2	Fewer opportunities

Source: Ostrow, Joseph W. "Setting Frequency Levels," *Effective Frequency: The State of the Art.* Copyright 1982. Reprinted by permission.

The next step is to determine how many additional points beyond 3 + that ought to be added to arrive at an effective frequency level. Ostrow's criteria are the source of these considerations, and the suggested points are the authors'.

	Suggested additional points
1. He or she is introducing a new product.	+ .2
2. The introduction is in a highly competitive market.	+ .2
3. The product has a short purchase cycle.	+ .2
4. The brand will be among those that are less well known.	+ .2
5. The product is used daily.	− .1
6. Ad copy is somewhat complex.	+ .2

7. Copy is more unique than competitors'.	– .2
8. Copy will be in large size ad units.	– .1
9. There is high ad clutter in category media.	+ .2
10. Media environment is compatible with product.	– .1
11. Advertising will be continuous.	– .2
12. Many media will be used.	+ .2
13. There will be many opportunities for repetition.	<u>– .2</u>
Sum of Points	+ .5

Effective Frequency Base	3.0 +
Additional Points	<u>+ .5</u>
Modified Effective Frequency Level	+ 3.5 or 4 +

The reader should note that not all of Ostrow's criteria may be applicable to a situation at hand. However, it is conceivable that a planner's own criteria may be added to the list to make it more relevant.

Continuity, Flighting, and Pulsing

An important part of timing advertising is scheduling it so that it appears at the most propitious selling times. A major objective of scheduling is to control the pattern of times when advertising appears by plotting advertising timing on a yearly flow chart. There are three major methods of scheduling advertising, each with a somewhat different pattern, as follows:

1. *Continuity* (sometimes called straight-through advertising)

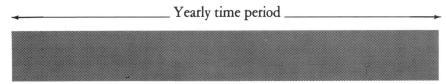

This pattern is continuous, although there may be small gaps of time, at regular intervals, when no advertising is done. One continuity pattern may be to run one ad every day for 365 days. Another continuity pattern may be one ad a week for 52 weeks. The time gaps show up in a pattern of dashes on a flow chart.

2. *Flighting* (sometimes called bursting)

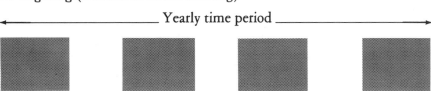

Flighting is an intermittent pattern where there are gaps of time when no advertising is done. If advertising were done once a month, this might be called flighting. Most often, however, flighting patterns are more irregular, with heavy concentrations of advertising at certain times interspersed with no advertising for shorter lengths of time.

3. *Pulsing*

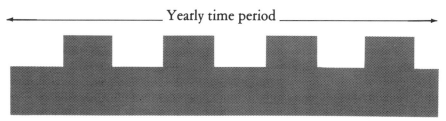

Pulsing is a form of flighting and continuity combined—where an advertiser buys continuous advertising throughout the year and "heavies up" at various propitious time periods. Pulsing is sometimes mistakenly called flighting, and when planners use either term (pulsing/flighting), they should be sure that everyone using these terms understands them.

The media planner must decide, as part of the strategy, which pattern to use.

The first step in selecting a pattern is to examine purchasing patterns for the product category. Because most product categories have unique purchasing patterns, it is important to learn what they are before thinking about a scheduling pattern. An unusual example of a purchasing cycle is the market for Christmas trees. Trees are rarely purchased at any time of the year other than November or December. But for a product such as face soap that is purchased throughout the year, though with heavier consumption in the summer, the best scheduling plan might be pulsing (year-round advertising with "heavy-up" in the summer).

Continuity

Continuity is needed when an advertiser has a message that it does not want consumers to forget. Continuous advertising works as a reminder, keeping

TABLE 9–7.   GRPs in Continuity versus Flighting

Week No. →		1	2	3	4	5	6	7	8	9	10	11	12	13	14	15	16	
Continuity pattern	GRPs	40	40	40	40	40	40	40	40	40	40	40	40	40	40	40	40	Total 640
Flighting pattern	GRPs	80	80	80	80	*				80	80	80	80	*				Total 640

Source: Ogilvy & Mather.
* Note: Higher 4-week reaches due to higher GRPs.

the message always before the consumer. That is one of the strongest arguments for continuity.

Another advantage of continuity is that the entire purchase cycle will be covered because there will be no gaping holes in time periods. This assures the planner that most of the customers are reached at all times, both when they will be purchasing and during times when they may not be buying.

Another reason for using continuity is that it makes it possible to take advantage of larger media discounts granted because so much advertising is purchased continuously. There may be cost efficiencies in such discounts, because the cost-per-target reached will tend to be lower than plans that do not contain such discounts. In addition, the advertiser may have an advantage in obtaining certain kinds of desirable positioning within media. Because the advertiser is buying a fairly large block of advertising, it may be easier to find the broadcast programs or times that are most favorable. There may also be positioning advantages in print where certain parts of the magazine or newspaper become more readily accessible to anyone who will buy a great deal of advertising over a long period of time. (See Chapter 11 on some problems in scheduling media for continuity.) But note that continuity is not a good idea for small amounts of advertising.

Flighting

An advantage of flighting over continuity is that it allows the advertiser to meet competition better by placing advertising at the most favorable times relative to competition. Advertising can be concentrated in high-sales-potential periods, either in broadcast time or print space. Advertising can be timed precisely to reach the best purchasing cycle time periods with little waste when buying is slow.

Ostensibly, flighting is used when there are budgeting limitations or sharp sales fluctuations. The advertiser buys ads only when sales are growing and drops out when sales trends are declining. This tends to save money.

Furthermore, flighting allows the planner to support advertising in one medium by using another medium simultaneously. If an advertiser plans to use television as the basic medium, then flighting allows concentration of radio and newspaper support at the same time.

Finally, flighting allows a series of ads and commercials to appear as a unified campaign rather than as a series of unrelated ads. By concentrating them at certain times of the year, the ads will appear to the consumer to be part of a single communication entity.

By concentrating advertising, an advertiser can sometimes catch competitors off guard and gain an advantage over them, especially if the competitors tend to use continuity rather than flighting in their strategy. The advantage is simply that the advertiser buys much heavier weight than competitors for a relatively short time.

But there are risks in flighting, too. The first is that so much advertising may be concentrated in one time period that the commercials could wear out before the flight is over. Great amounts of flighting in concentrated time periods tends to build high frequency.

A second drawback of flighting is that consumers may forget the essence of the advertising message between flights if too much time elapses between them. However, the effectiveness of advertising does not stop the moment advertising is stopped. There is some carry-over.

Third, competitors may take advantage of the advertiser by placing heavy ad weights at precisely the time the advertiser is not advertising. So during those times, competitors have an advantage over the advertiser.

Pulsing

Pulsing represents the best of both techniques; it is a mixture of continuity and flighting. All of the advantages of continuity and flighting are now possible, with none of the disadvantages. Pulsing is the safest of the three because it covers different marketing situations. Not all advertisers, however, would be advised to use pulsing. It best fits those product categories that are sold all year round, but have heavier concentrations of sales at intermittent periods.

Both continuity and flighting can develop the same reach and frequency over a long period of time (such as sixteen weeks), as shown in Table 9–7. However, there will be considerable differences of reach and frequency over the short run, as shown in Table 9–8. The table shows that, for a four-week period, the flighting pattern had a considerably larger reach than continuity had. The reason is the larger concentration of GRPs.

TABLE 9-8.   Reach and Frequency of Continuity versus Flighting

	Continuity	Flighting
Monthly GRPs	160	320
Reach	57	76
Frequency	2.8	4.2

Frequency Distribution No. Times Reached	Cumulative Reach	
	Continuity	Flighting
1	57.1	75.8
2	39.1	61.5
3	25.8	49.4
4 or more	15.7	39.0

Source: Ogilvy & Mather.

QUESTIONS FOR DISCUSSION

1. Which form of weighting—dollars or impressions—should be used to reach communication goals in local markets more easily?
2. What is meant by a threshold level of three impressions in a media plan?
3. Is the average frequency of a media plan equivalent to advertising exposure frequency? Explain.
4. Suppose that an advertiser plans a month-long promotion of a brand of soap, with three bars being sold for the price of two. Which would a media planner be most likely to adopt for this plan: reach or frequency? Explain.
5. In the text there is a statement about a network television program (or programs) delivering more impressions than are needed in another. Explain why that happens?
6. In the text's example of allocating an advertising budget from network to spot, which markets will be allocated more money for spot TV?
7. When is large target reach necessary in a media plan?
8. Why is it better to talk about *optimum* rather than *large* frequency in a media plan?
9. According to Joseph Ostrow, which factors affect the optimum amount of frequency needed?

SELECTED READINGS

Achenbaum, Alvin, "GRPs Can't Measure Effectiveness," *Media Decisions,* May 1977, 64–65.

Adams, S. C., S. H. Britt, and A. S. Miller, "How Many Advertising Exposures per Day?" *Journal of Advertising Research,* December 1972, 3–9.

Advertising Age, "High Cost of Advertising Got You Down? Try ERPs," November 7, 1977.

Haley, Russell I., "Sales Effects of Media Weights," *Journal of Advertising Research,* June 1978, 78.

Lippman, Stacey, "How Much Frequency," *Marketing and Media Decisions*, May 1986, 116–17.

Naples, Michael, *Effective Frequency: The Relationship Between Frequency and Advertising Effectiveness,* New York: Association of National Advertisers, 1979.

Ostrow, Joseph W., "What Level Frequency?" *Advertising Age,* November 9, 1981, S–4.

Papazian, Ed, "How Much Frequency Is Enough?" *Media Decisions*, May 1976, 12.

10
Selecting Media Classes: Intermedia Comparisons

The preceding chapters covered broad major strategy decisions comprising a part of the activities involved in media planning. This chapter and the next deal with the selection of media, covering decisions that usually follow strategy decisions. This chapter will discuss the selection of media classes—decisions on whether to use television, magazines, newspapers, or some other medium. Once media classes have been selected, then decisions about specific vehicles within classes will follow. (Vehicle choices are discussed in Chapter 11.)

Intermedia Comparisons

To make decisions about media classes the planner must make *intermedia comparisons*—comparisons among different media. Comparisons among media vehicles in the same class, such as among magazines A, B, and C, are called *intramedia* comparisons. It is obvious that intermedia comparisons should be made before intramedia comparisons.

The main problem is whether or not it is logically correct to make intermedia comparisons on a statistical basis. Although it may be valid to compare media classes statistically in some cases, in most others it is not. The reason is that the numbers for one media class may not be comparable to another class. Comparisons of readers, viewers, and listeners may aptly be likened to the comparison of apples and oranges. The definition of a reader is so different from that of a television viewer that comparisons of numbers may be misleading. For example, would it be correct to compare the cost-per-thousand viewers of a television program with the cost-per-thousand readers of a magazine? Only partially. If one vehicle delivers more audience at better cost efficiency than another in a different media class, the answer is correct to that point. But it is questionable whether a television commercial with its action and sound can be fairly compared with the static appearance of a four-color print advertisement. Yet the planner must make such comparisons whenever it is necessary to choose between two different media classes. Table 10–1 shows some of the differences between print and broadcast media.

Intermedia comparison is one of the early steps in planning after media strategies have been prepared.

Review of Consumer Media Classes

Following is a brief review of reasons for and against using major measured consumer media: newspapers, magazines, television, radio, supplements, direct response (including direct mail and telemarketing), outdoor, transit, and cable TV. The pros and cons of using a medium often grow out of a planner's perceptions and impressions rather than from objective evidence.

TABLE 10–1.   Differences between Print and Broadcast Media

Print Media	Broadcast Media
Message must be read or seen	Message must be heard, read, or seen
Message can be read at the reader's convenience	Message is viewed/heard only when it is broadcast
Message does not interfere with editorial or entertainment content, although some articles are arranged in a format that does interrupt the reader	Message often interrupts editorial or entertainment content
A reader is defined as one who was exposed to the medium	A viewer is defined as one who has tuned in to the program
Messages can be reread as often as the reader wishes	Message appears only once and viewer has no idea when the same message will be rebroadcast
Generally, one pays full or partial attention to medium while reading or even scanning	It is possible to perform other tasks while program is on, so range of attention may be from none to full
Reader can search for products of interest	Viewer has little idea when a desired product will be advertised
Color fidelity is usually excellent	Color fidelity ranges from one extreme to another depending on the TV set
Medium can be read in almost any location	Viewing is limited by the size and portability of TV or radio set
Medium is sold in space units	Medium is sold in time units
Many production variables are possible, such as gatefolds, pop-ups, Day-Glo inks	Some kinds of production variables are possible such as split-screen, cartoons, stop-motion, cut-ins

So there are some media experts who might take exception to the reasons and/or limitations stated here.

Newspapers—Reasons for Using

Sense of Immediacy. Readers tend to perceive newspapers as being the most immediate medium in the market. Every day a newspaper contains something new and with the news come new advertisements. Newspapers may be thought of as having a *now* quality at all times. This quality is important when advertisers want to communicate something immediately. When manufacturers introduce new products to the market, they usually include newspapers as part of the media mix.

Local Emphasis. Almost all daily newspapers have a local quality that is important to advertisers. Although advertisers may use a national medium such as network television, they may also want to use a medium with local impact. All selling is local and the newspaper helps emphasize that fact by advertising local merchants' names and addresses.

Flexibility. Newspapers are geographically flexible because they may be used nationally, regionally, and locally in a media plan. Even when a manufacturer's markets are widely scattered throughout the country, it is possible to reach them by using local newspapers.

Production flexibility allows copy to be changed easily and quickly. For example, some national advertisers want to have different prices for the same products in different markets. There are also special production techniques available. Perhaps an advertiser wants to include preprinted inserts in newspapers in certain geographical markets. These and other production alternatives are possible.

High-Fidelity Color Inserts. Through the use of gravure-printed inserts, newspapers can compete favorably with magazines in given markets. Gravure printing gives the advertiser brilliant, life-like colors similar to those that enhance the brand's advertisement in magazines. Furthermore, any printing technique may be used on any quality paper to provide high-fidelity color.

Mass Reach. Because newspapers are read by so many individuals in each market, total reach per market may include many individuals in each family. When a product's target audience includes Mom, Dad, and the children, then newspapers may be an ideal medium.

Catalog Value. A newspaper may serve as a catalog for consumers who are doing comparison shopping. Often consumers search their daily newspapers before they go shopping. The effect of such a search is that they are often presold before they walk into a store to buy the product. Some readers even cut out ads and bring them along as a reminder.

Ethnic Appeal. Although newspapers are considered a mass medium, they have the power to reach selective ethnic classes as well. If the local newspaper does not reach these markets, then an ethnic newspaper may do the job.

Newspapers—Limitations

Variation in ROP (Run of Press or Run of Paper) Color and Black-and-White Quality. An advertiser buying advertisements printed in ROP color may find great variations in color fidelity from market to market. This variance means that the message may be more effective in one market than in another even though all markets have the same value.

High Cost of Buying National Coverage. Although newspapers are indeed a flexible medium, the cost of buying national coverage is very high and may be prohibitive for national advertisers with limited budgets.

National Advertising Rates Usually Higher than Local Rates. Most daily newspapers charge more for national advertising than they do for local. Of course, an advertiser who must advertise in a particular local market will pay the premium rate without question.

Small Pass-Along Audience. Newspapers are rarely passed along to other audiences as magazines are. This means that advertisements in yesterday's editions have a limited time value because relatively few other persons will see the newspaper after it is read by family members.

Magazines—Reasons for Using

Selectivity. Magazines are very successful in reaching certain kinds of selected audiences. There are an increasing number of magazines being started each year to meet the interests of special groups such as tennis or chess players, cooking enthusiasts, hobby fans, or those wanting to know more about investing in the stock market. In addition, some magazines have demographic editions such as a physicians' edition, a college students' edition, or one limited to chief executive officers. Finally, there are geographic editions that enable the planner to reach broad or narrow markets. This versatility and flexibility enable the planner to use magazines in many different ways.

Fine Color Reproduction. Many magazines are able to reproduce advertisements with excellent color fidelity. The necessity for fine color reproduction is obvious for certain kinds of product advertising such as food, clothes, and cars. It is also easier to control color variations from copy to copy in magazines.

Long Life. Magazines usually have a long life, at least a week. But some last for more than a month and some for years. The effect of long life is that the advertiser can continue to build reach long after the present campaign has formally ended. Although the product featured in the ads may even have been discontinued after a number of years, the effect on a person who reads an ad years after it originally ran is to build brand awareness for long periods of time. Reach built over long periods of time, however, may not help the planner attain short-range goals.

Pass-Along Audience. Magazines usually have pass-along audiences that increase the reach. The size of the pass-along audience varies, however, from magazine to magazine.

Controlled Circulation. Because magazines are able to locate and meet the needs of special interest groups, it is possible for many of them to have controlled circulation. In a controlled circulation arrangement, the publisher is able to identify a special group of targets, mostly by profession or occupation, and then send each of these individuals the magazine free of charge. The publisher then informs advertisers that a circulation audience of a certain size can be guaranteed. Most controlled circulation magazines are in the business field.

Magazines—Limitations

Early Closing Dates. Some magazines require advertisers to have their artwork and type for four-color ads in the printing plant as much as two and a half months before the cover date. The consequence is that the marketing, creative, and production work on the campaign must be completed so far ahead of publication date that the advertiser may lose the advantage of timeliness. It is even possible for a marketing situation to have changed by the time the ad appears in print.

Lack of Immediacy. With the exception of weekly news magazines, most magazines lack a sense of urgency and immediacy. In other words, readers may not even look at the latest issue of a given magazine until some time after it has reached their homes. Even news magazines do not have the sense of immediacy that newspapers have.

Slow Building of Reach. Because some readers do not turn to their magazines quickly, reach tends to build slowly in this medium. Some readers read a small portion of a magazine immediately and then continue at later dates and times, whenever convenient. Active people who are always on the go sometimes will scan through a number of issues at one time to catch up with their reading. At other times, they just ignore a number of issues and will read only the most current one.

Newspaper Supplements—Reasons for Using

Local Market Impact with a Magazine Format. Newspaper supplements offer the advertiser the advantage of being able to reach local markets with a format that closely resembles magazines. Therefore, many of the qualities of magazines are also qualities of the supplement. Most important, however, is the ability of the planner to reach many local markets with a magazine format.

Good Color Fidelity. Newspaper supplements are usually printed on gravure presses and therefore have high color fidelity.

Depth of Penetration. Whereas magazines usually would have limited penetration in any given market, supplements have high penetration. The reason is that magazines, because of their specialized natures, might have relatively small numbers of readers in any local market. But the supplement, distributed with newspapers, would naturally have access to large numbers of individuals for whom the editorial features are of general interest.

Broadened Coverage Area. One bonus of using supplements is that it is possible to reach some markets normally covered by daily newspapers that do not carry the supplement. This is possible because large metro area newspapers will often have extensive area coverage far beyond the Metropolitan Statistical Area. Consumers in these bonus markets carrying the supplement may read their local newspapers on weekdays, but a large metro paper on Sunday.

Reach Prospects on Sunday Morning. When supplements are read, they will have little competition from other media, because Sundays typically offer freedom from other media. Many readers are more relaxed on Sundays and can spend more time reading than on other days.

High Readership. Because supplements have large penetration in individual markets, it is not surprising that they are widely read, especially by women. Working women especially tend to have the time to read this format, because it is available on Sunday, it is part of a newspaper, and because many features tend to cover women's interests.

Flexibility: Geographic and Production. It is obvious that supplements allow the planner to place advertising locally, regionally, or even nationally. But supplements also allow production flexibility such as the option of running a full-page ad in some markets, while at the same time running smaller ads in other markets.

Newspaper Supplements—Limitations

Early Closing Dates for Four-Color. Because supplements are printed by the gravure process, the material for ads must be in the printing plant as much as eight weeks before publication date. This deadline is even earlier than required for most magazines that are printed either by letterpress or offset process. Gravure is printed from copper cylinders that take an exceedingly long time to prepare. Furthermore, because it is so difficult to make corrections on gravure plates, greater care and time is taken in the preparation of the cylinders than is necessary for other printing processes.

Little Pass-Along or Secondary Readership. Because supplements come with weekend newspapers, they inherit some of the weaknesses of newspapers. One of these is that supplements rarely are passed along to others. They usually are thrown away after the family has read them. In addition, one rarely finds supplements in barber or beauty shops or doctors' or dentists' offices as one finds magazines.

Television—Reasons for Using

Sight and Sound for Dynamic Selling. Audiovisual demonstrations are one of the best teaching methods known. The combination of sight and sound gives the advertiser the benefit of a technique that comes closest to personal selling. Television selling is very dynamic. It is also one of the best methods of demonstrating the uses or advantages of a given product.

Flexibility. Network television offers broad national coverage, while spot television allows the planner to use markets in any number of combinations.

Reach of Both Selective and Mass Markets. Television may be used to attract both selective and mass markets through program selection. When professional football games are being broadcast, the audience is largely male. Children's programming on Saturday mornings, or daytime television, tends to reach selected audiences. On the other hand, some programming such as movies, comedies, or special events will attract audiences consisting of many different kinds and ages of people.

Cost Efficiency. Television can be very cost efficient at times. Daytime television, for example, usually has low costs per thousand as does fringe time. Though the overall costs are high, the audiences are large.

Television—Limitations

High Total Cost. The cost of commercial time can be beyond the means of some advertisers. The change from 60- to 30-second commercial lengths to 15-second, and even 10-second commercials reflects the advertiser's needs for lower total cost.

Short-lived Messages. Although audiovisual messages may have the potential for high recall, the nature of television commercials is such that either viewers pay attention or they may miss the message. Therefore the commercial's life tends to be fleeting.

No Catalog Value. It is evident that viewers do not search for commercials when they are in the market for a product. Although they pay greater attention to a commercial they happen to see for a product in which they are interested, they usually have little idea of the exact time such commercials will be broadcast.

Limited Availability of Good Programs and Time Slots. Because television is a widely used medium, there is a limit to the number of programs with large audience following or time slots that are available and desirable.

Radio—Reasons for Using

Reach of Special Kinds of Target Audiences. Radio is able to reach certain kinds of audiences very well. Through programming specialization a radio station becomes known for its "sound" and attracts special kinds of audiences, such as men, women, teenagers, farmers, ethnic populations, African-Americans, and the elderly. Many ethnic groups have programs dedicated to their interests. Religious groups, especially, have found radio to be an excellent communication medium.

A High Frequency Medium. Where a great deal of repetition is necessary, radio may be the ideal medium. The total cost is relatively low and there are usually many stations with time available to permit building a media plan with high frequency.

A Good Supporting Medium. Because of the low cost and good reach of special target markets, radio is often used as a supporting medium. Often when a plan uses print predominantly, radio can be added at low cost to bring sound into the plan.

Excellent for Mobile Populations. Because most Americans own and drive automobiles, radio becomes a means of reaching them while they are traveling. Many people drive long distances to and from work and the distances are getting longer as suburbs develop farther from cities. Listening to the radio in what is known as "drive time" has become a diversion to help pass the long commuting time and is an excellent means of reaching commuters.

But commuters aren't the only ones who travel every day. Homemakers often take their cars to shopping centers that may be located far from their homes. They, too, will often turn on the radio to help pass the traveling time. In fact, radio may be the last medium that homemakers are exposed to before they enter retail stores. Local retailers might very well carry on a campaign to communicate with these customers before they arrive at the stores.

Summertime Exposure. Because we are a mobile population and so many people travel during the summer months, radio is an excellent medium to reach them en route. Some experts dispute this, however, claiming that radio tune-in is no higher in the summer than it is any other time. *When* listeners tune in, however, does change during the summer, especially among teenagers who are not in school during the day.

Flexibility. Radio, like television, may be used locally, regionally, or nationally. There are a number of production advantages to radio, as well, since copy can be changed quickly, and added or eliminated from a program quickly. Despite these advantages, radio is still not highly regarded for its great production flexibility.

Local Coverage Availability. Local radio is usually purchased because it reaches a given market very well. But radio signals may be carried far from the originating market into other geographical areas. This occurs at night when the Kennelly–Heaviside layer (a natural atmospheric phenomenon) broadly disseminates signals far beyond the local market. For the national advertiser who is trying to build brand awareness in many different markets, this added feature may be perceived as a bonus when a planner buys local radio.

Radio—Limitations

Many Stations in Any One Market. In many large metropolitan markets, so many radio stations are vying for attention that only a relative few reach a large audience. If one wants to build large reach via radio, it will be necessary to buy more than one station and, in some areas, many stations. In New York City, there are 24 AM and FM stations and another 31 in the greater metropolitan area. In Chicago, there are 24 stations in the city and another 15 in the greater metro area. And the numbers are constantly changing (Arbitron Radio Market Report, New York, Fall 1991. Chicago, Spring 1991). Another consequence of the large number of stations available is the fragmentation of audiences caused by specialized programming. On the one hand, specialized programs do waste few exposures because the program structure is not attractive to everyone. On the other hand, they may fractionalize the audience too much for an advertiser who wants a mass—not class—audience.

Fleeting Messages. Like television, but even more so, radio messages are fleeting and may be missed or forgotten if only partially heard.

Direct Response

Direct response is a marketing strategy in which direct mail and/or telemarketing are often used. In our discussion of direct mail and telemarketing, we refer only to *outbound* advertising, whereby the marketer contacts the consumer. *Inbound* advertising—the consumer seeks out the marketer—(also exists e.g., calling the toll-free number on a package).

Direct Mail—Reasons for Using

Direct mail can be the most selective of all media, provided that the names and addresses of a target audience are known, and the list is up-to-date and complete. When such a list is available, there may be minimal waste, so the advertiser pays only for targets that are reached. Another list source can be a marketer's own database of names.

Response to Advertising Is Easy to Check. It is relatively easy to learn whether a direct mail piece was effective. One simply counts the number of responses to an offer. The number of inquiries from direct mail may or may not be related to sales, but inquiries from direct mailings do constitute one form of measurement. Often alternative copy treatments are sent out by direct mail and the most effective one is easily checked. Although it is very difficult to measure response functions in most other media, the same cannot be said of direct mail.

A Personal Medium. Direct mail can be a personal medium when it bears a consumer's name and address. Most advertising is very impersonal because, in most media, it is impossible to address anyone by name. Direct mail, using specific names and addresses, comes closest to overcoming this problem. Of course, not all recipients of direct mail pieces appreciate advertisers calling them familiarly by name. But many people do appreciate seeing their names in print, and may pay more attention to the offer as a result.

Geographic and Production Flexibility. Direct mail is probably the easiest of all media to tailor precisely to the geographic marketing needs of an advertiser. The beauty of this flexibility is that direct mail can be adjusted to very small markets (as small as one block or even by household), and also can be adjusted to as large an area as needed.

The medium is also flexible in terms of production. Almost any size and kind of paper and any kind of ink or special printing technique is possible. Advertisers with special creative problems may turn to direct mail because it is so versatile. Samples of a product can be mailed with ads; special die cuts can be made; special kinds of foldings and special kinds of packaging are available only in this medium.

Long Life for Certain Mailings. Consumers tend to keep catalogs for long periods of time as well as share catalogs with friends. If the advertising material has value, it tends to be kept. Some educational materials also share this quality. If the educational matter has value, such as a chart showing how to administer first aid, or a booklet on how to eliminate stains on clothing, it may be retained for long periods of time.

Savings When Advertising Is Inserted with Bills or Other Outgoing Pieces. No special envelope, special addressing, or extra postage is necessary when direct mail advertising is sent along with bills or other packages. There are creative limitations due to weight restrictions and size of the contents of an envelope and/or package. The bills have to be sent anyway, so the addition of a direct advertisement may not even cost extra postage. Printing costs, however, must be borne. Even when the total weight of the advertising enclosed with a bill is greater than the bill alone, there may still be substantial savings because there are no extra envelope and addressing costs. The addition of the advertising may increase the total cost only slightly.

Direct Mail—Limitations

Expense. Direct mail is expensive due to the cost of postage. Beyond this, there are at least two additional situations where direct mail is very expensive, perhaps more so than any other medium—when a production technique requires the use of very heavy enameled or other expensive papers or when some unusual method of engraving, artwork, or printing is used, or when very large mailings are made that cannot take advantage of bulk mailing privileges. It is unlikely that postage rates will decline in the future, and these high costs will continue to affect direct mail usage.

Inaccurate and Incomplete Lists. Without an accurate and complete mailing list, direct mail cannot do its best. In this era, when so many individuals move from one place to another, it may be too difficult or expensive to keep lists up to date or develop new ones. In the past, it was possible to buy large mass mailings at low cost and not be concerned about the accuracy of the list. But today's high postage and production costs require that accurate and complete lists be used.

Variance in Delivery Dates. Although a large mailing may be taken to the post office at one time, the pieces may be delivered to various individuals at widely different times. If time is not essential to the marketing objectives, then the lag doesn't matter. But timing of an advertising message is often critical and the direct mail user cannot control it very well. Compared with other media, direct mail comes off second best in respect to timing. When ads are placed in newspapers, they are printed on the day requested. When broadcast commercials are purchased, they are delivered not only on the day, but the hour requested. In comparison, direct mail delivery dates are unpredictable.

Telemarketing—Reasons for Using

Very Selective. Telemarketing is as selective as direct mail. The phone numbers of a target audience are derived from the same lists.

Response to Advertising is Easy to Check. Telemarketing allows immediate responses and has a quicker turnaround time than any other medium. Often, operators test out different scripts and the most effective one is easily determined.

A Personal Medium. Telemarketing is the most personal medium because it involves one-on-one verbal communication. It is also the most intrusive medium and should be targeted to the proper audience to avoid turning people off.

Geographic Flexibility. In this area, telemarketing is just like direct mail and can be adjusted to a large or a small area.

High Response Rates. Telemarketing has the highest response rates of any medium because of its "live" personal communication.

Telemarketing—Limitations

Expense. Telemarketing is expensive on a cost-per-contact basis due to the cost of callers' salaries.

Inaccurate and Incomplete Lists. Typically, 15 percent of phone numbers called are inaccurate because of people moving from one place to another.

Time. With telemarketing, there is a limit to the hours when calls can be made. For consumer programs, calls to individuals at home after 10:00 P.M. should be avoided. For business programs, calls cannot be made after 5:00 P.M., Monday through Friday.

Message Space. There is less message space in a telemarketing call than in a direct mail piece. Because time is money, only questions that are necessary may be asked.

Legislation. In recent years, both national and state legislation have been enacted and proposed to regulate the telemarketing industry. Before starting a telemarketing program, all legislation should be in compliance with state and federal laws.

Outdoor—Reasons for Using

Wide Coverage of Local Markets. Outdoor advertising is able to build large local coverage of the mobile population in many markets in a thirty-day period. However, this coverage does not represent reading of the messages, only potential exposure to them.

High Frequency. Billboards also have high frequency in reaching the mobile population of a market. It is in this area that billboards may be strongest. Although the differences in reach of a 100 versus a 50 showing are not great, the frequency levels are quite different.

Largest Size Print Ad Available. Size is a powerful attraction. Outdoor allows the advertiser to buy the largest size print ad available. The use of attractive color printing plus dramatic lighting and, at times, moving portions, all offer the advertiser great attention-getting power.

Geographic Flexibility. Outdoor may be used locally, regionally, and nationally. Even within any given market, it is possible to add emphasis wherever desired. Movable billboards enable an advertiser to concentrate messages in many places, or to increase the potential for exposure.

High Summertime Visibility. Media plans often will include billboards in the summer, because they increase the visibility of a brand name at a time when many people are traveling. Warmer weather encourages people to take to their cars, and it is possible to reach them through billboards and other outdoor signs.

Around-the-Clock Exposure. Because many billboards on main thoroughfares are lighted, anyone passing at any time of day or night can see the messages. As long as there is a mobile population, this is an opportunity for exposures.

Good for Simple Copy Theme and Package Identification. When the message is relatively short and simple and the package is distinctive, outdoor can be an excellent way to attract attention and build frequency for the message. Building brand awareness is a strength of the medium.

Outdoor—Limitations

Limited to Simple Messages. The best use of outdoor is for a simple message; complex or long messages do not work very well. This restriction means that the medium cannot be used in precisely the same manner as other print media.

High Outdoor Reach Does Not Necessarily Mean High Recall of Messages. Though outdoor may provide high reach, and sometimes good recall of ad messages, it is not necessarily true that high reach means high recall. The creativity of the message is an important criterion in assessing the ability of the message to be recalled. But because of the nature of this medium, people may often look at billboards and be unable to recall what they saw.

A High Cost Medium. Although the cost per thousand is low, outdoor is a high out-of-pocket cost medium when compared to some other media, according to the Institute of Outdoor Advertising. For a 100 showing nationally (top 100 markets), the cost is more than five million dollars for a month. Considering that outdoor is a medium often in the background, that it requires very short messages, and that drivers' interests are primarily focused on the road ahead, this cost may be prohibitive for many advertisers.

Transit Media—Reasons for Using

Transit media involve interior and exterior displays on mass transit vehicles, and terminal and station platform displays.

Transit Provides Mass Coverage of a Metropolitan Area. When an advertiser wants to reach individuals in the heart of a market, then mass transit advertising may be desirable. It is primarily a vehicle for reaching adults either on their way to, or returning from, work. But its reach is extensive.

High Frequency. Because this medium takes advantage of normal travel patterns that are duplicated many days throughout the year, there is an opportunity for a great deal of repetition of message delivery.

Relative Efficiency. Based on potential exposures, this medium can deliver large numbers of individuals at low unit costs.

Flexibility. An advertiser can select transportation vehicles in which to place ads that reach certain kinds of demographically defined groups. The advertiser does not have to select all mass transit systems, only those that are known to have large numbers of targets.

Opportunity to Position Messages to Consumers on the Way to Their Points of Purchase. Local advertisers can buy messages that reach consumers on their way to their places of purchases. Therefore, it is possible that, for some consumers, the transit ads will be the last medium they are exposed to before making a purchase. (Note that radio is often credited with the same idea.)

Transit Media—Limitations

Limited Message Space. Most often, large or complex messages cannot be disseminated in this medium because there is not enough space available to carry such messages.

High Competition from Other Media and Personal Activities. Transit is not an intrusive medium—it competes for attention with other things such as the attractiveness of scenery, the nature of the transit vehicle, or other people. The person who travels to and from work on the same transportation vehicle may be tired, bored, or interested in some other media vehicle. For exterior displays, something of extra creative pulling power is often necessary to attract attention, a requirement that may be difficult to achieve.

Cable Advertising—Reasons for Using

Cable television has shown dramatic growth in the past 10 years and is now a national medium with stature comparable to network television. Cable has 61% penetration of households able to subscribe, and the projection is that by 1995, it will have 65% penetration. The number of advertisers who have added cable to their media plans has grown enormously. In fact, cable advertising revenues grew 18% in 1991 to a total of $3 billion dollars.

Good for Reaching a National Audience. With 61% reach, and the percentage growing each year, cable is truly a national medium, whether used alone, or in conjunction with more traditional media.

Good for Adding Reach and Frequency to Network TV or Other Media. Although cable can now be used in lieu of network, it can also be *added* to network TV and any other media chosen for a media plan. The effect of this strategy is to add more reach and frequency. When cable is used this way, some of the cable homes go to increasing reach because the other media simply did not cover them. But cable homes already reached by other media add frequency to the plan.

Relatively Low Cost. Although cable's rates are rising, it is a medium that still costs less than advertising on the major television networks. Local cable is usually less expensive than local television. For example, a commercial on a Chicago television station can cost $3,000; the same commercial on cable may cost only $300.

Regional Sports Broadcasting. Cable has provided audiences all over the country with many opportunities for watching sporting events.

Respectable Ratings. There are more people watching cable than ever before. In fact, cable has been able to achieve ratings of 11 to 14 for some programs, like the Chicago Bulls' basketball team in the 1991 playoffs. The average national cable rating for all cable TV networks combined is 11.2 with a 20 share. In the last five years, ratings have grown about 11% each year for basic cable and are expected to continue growing.

Precisely Defined Target Audiences. Cable programmers have been better able to define the kinds of audiences who watch their programs, and that enables advertisers to focus more accurately on targets they want to reach.

More Upscale Audience. Cable television tends to appeal to a large upscale audience, meaning a more upper income and upper lifestyle audience. This characteristic makes companies selling more expensive products have a suitable target audience among the cable network options.

Broader Spectrum of Advertisers. When competitors are advertising on cable, it is sometimes strategically important for other competitors to be in the same medium. As more advertisers use cable, it will draw other product category advertisers, and audiences can expect to find certain kinds of products there.

Reduces Total and Average Spending Costs. Cable television, costing less than network television, can help reduce total and average spending costs for advertisers who need effective media at a lower cost. Shifting even as much as 20% of an advertising budget to cable can reduce costs.

More Specialized Targets for Advertising. The prediction is that cable will soon be able to offer as many as 150 + different channels to audiences. As a consequence, programming will have to be developed to meet many different kinds of consumers' needs. As it meets those needs, cable will become somewhat like magazines that also meet a wide array of consumers' needs.

Penetration in Major Markets Has Grown. It was not long ago when some major markets had very low cable penetration. But that has changed, and the top 20 American markets now have an average of 63% penetration with a range of 46 to 80. This is especially important for spot advertising in markets where additional weight is needed.

Cable Television—Limitations

Competition from Too Many Channels. If cable continues to grow, it is possible that there will be too much variety to choose from. If 150 channels are available to every household, the effect may be numbing for many audience members as they try to take advantage of program alternatives.

Audience Sizes May Become Too Small to Sell Effectively. Fragmentation of target audiences may simply end up in audience sizes to programs being too small. Can a small, but specialized audience buy enough of a company's product? Those who believe in micro-marketing think it can, but many advertisers disagree.

Is Not Easy to Buy. Spot cable using different cable systems is presently difficult to buy because there are little organized means of selling. When marketers choose a very selected list of markets they want to be in, the cable industry has to service the customer in a manner much like free television now does. Although plans are being made to create such a system for cable, it isn't here yet. Therefore spot cable market buying will tend to be difficult in the near future.

Home Video (VCRs)—Reasons for Using

Home video is a medium where programming is recorded and played back with advertising on it. It is also a rented videotape that contains advertising. At one time, it was thought to be a large potential market for advertisers, but now—with widespread use of cable television where movies can be rented in a pay-per-view arrangement—it is much less attractive as a class of media.

When recording programs on videotape, consumers can "zap" commercials, thus eliminating them. Consumers can also "zip" by commercials when viewing a recording and eliminate them. Seventy-eight percent of all those owning a TV set also own a videotape recorder. Fifty percent of those who own a VCR taped something within the last 30 days; 67% of those who taped zip through commercials most of the time. Seventeen percent zip through commercials all the time. Only 14% watch the entire taped program.[1]

Reaches "Hard to Reach" Audiences. Some audiences simply cannot be reached with any other medium but through home video. Generally these audiences are very selective in their choices of programs and have an opportunity through video rentals to select exactly the programs they want. They may also be the same ones who choose to tape certain kinds of programs for

---

1. "Taping and Zipping Practice," *Mediaweek*, February 10, 1992, p.13.

playback later. They do not have to be at home to do videotaping; they may simply preset their recorders to turn on and off at certain times. Then they can view these programs at almost any time.

Viewers Are Relaxed and Pay Attention. Since viewers make their own program selections and view whenever they choose, this should be an opportunity for certain advertisements to get a better viewing and/or hearing than from free television. The potential for getting the most from an advertisement is great in home video.

Opportunities for Increased Repetition (or Frequency). If audiences do not eliminate the commercials by zipping or zapping, the commercials may be kept in place continually. There are, however, videotape recorders that can automatically eliminate the recording of commercials, and if this technique should become popular, then the medium will no longer be viable for advertising.

Home Video (VCRs)—Limitations

Commercial Elimination. At this time, technology that erases commercials during recording is not widely available. Even if it becomes widely available, there is some question about how many consumers will buy the accessory, and again, there is question about how many consumers who can eliminate commercials with this technology will do so.

Cable Television May Curtail Videotaping through Pay-per-View. If that happens, then videotaping may be sharply curtailed, and again, the medium will not be viable for advertising.

Evaluating Selected "New Media Concepts"

One of the major problems facing media planners today is media fragmentation. There are so many new media available and so many ways to use them that it makes media planning difficult. In most situations, the audience sizes delivered by fragmented media are smaller than they were when using traditional mass media. On the other hand, proponents of fragmentation feel that the new media can better reach precise target audiences who have a higher potential to buy than targets in traditional media. New media have at least given planners more options than ever before in reaching target audiences. If targeting improves and goes beyond demographics (to a mixture of demographics, lifestyles, and high sales potential) then the new media are better than traditional media. Another element of the new media is that they often provide a means for making media planning more creative. Some of these techniques are innovatively new and more interesting than traditional media and may help make media more effective in delivering an advertiser's messages.

This section explains details of some of the major new media. However, there isn't enough room in this text to evaluate all such media. Those discussed here are some of the best known or most widely discussed media options.

Cross-Media (or Multi-Media)

Cross-media (also called multimedia integration) partnerships are a relatively new concept for planning media that has received a great deal of coverage in the trade press. The basic idea of cross-media planning is the assembly of a select number of different media for the purpose of reaching specific target audiences for clients. The media are put together as a package that can include network television, cable, magazines and other media, tailored to meet diverse target audience needs. The package, therefore, is an alternative to the present technique of dealing exclusively with one medium like network television or a group of media that tend not to be very selective. It is also different from having a group of mixed media in a plan that are loosely organized. The goal is to do a better job of communicating with hard to reach audiences, and to take advantage of multi-media communication advantages, especially to deal with promotions, plus advertising. But there are other appeals too, such as being a way to implement the integrated marketing communications idea, *plus value added*, and *synergy*.

Value Added is closely aligned with cross-media planning. These terms are somewhat vague but are used to describe any element of a cross-media deal beyond the actual media buy, including special events. These special events are offered at a discount rate or no charge at all. They include such things as premium positioning and bleed ads at no extra cost; tie-ins with other media such as direct mail and cable; in-store promotions or product sampling, and bonus pages, consumer custom publishing and free inventory in other media. Media, for example, will often add to a cross-media deal by printing booklets, or providing trips to tennis or golf tournaments. Clients have come to expect value added programs, and media companies are quite willing to give them.

Synergy. Costing out cross-media deals is considered to be "tricky." The reason is that cross-media deals are supposed to have synergy beyond values offered by traditional media. In other words, the totality of media values here is supposed to be greater than the sum of each medium's contribution alone. But some experts have commented on the synergy problem, "nobody yet knows how to calculate how much greater."

Cross-media deals tend to be open ended and multi-year arrangements that require constant stewardship and fine-tuning. Some media planners say that "many cross media deals are more statement than substance." The idea is so new that there is no unanimous agreement on how to use them.

Examples of Cross-Media Deals. One of the most widely publicized cross-media deals has been General Motors' combining with Time-Warner media. Phil Guarascio, head of General Motors corporate marketing and advertising, said, "automobile advertisers have the capability of using 35 to 40 different applications of non-mainline-media that Time-Warner has to offer." To date GM has implemented about a dozen. Mr. Guarascio notes that GM has used video production, graphic arts, and fulfillment capabilities and married it to magazine targeting capabilities. As a result, GM produced films and printed pieces which they distributed to their prospective customers.

More deals are expected to grow, but not of the multi-million dollar kind such as GM used.

A survey of automobile executives about cross-media deals showed that there are at least four media that were considered to be ideal for such a package (in order of preference): magazines, direct mail, network TV, and cable TV. Not quite as desirable were spot TV and newspapers.

Another highly publicized proposed cross-media deal linked magazines and cable TV; the packager had difficulty selling it. The problem was that this was a pre-packaged deal that had difficulty finding a compatible sponsor. The better idea is to design the package to meet a specific client's needs, which then makes it relatively easier to sell.

Newsweek and MTV also designed a cross-media deal targeting young adults that focused on current social and political issues. This highly publicized deal also had a problem finding a sponsor. The deal included a one-hour MTV special and a related 16-page special section in 300,000 copies of *Newsweek*, distributed to 16 to 24-year-old subscribers and presented in a special binding.

Newsweek and MTV were looking for one sponsor, most likely from the automotive, consumer electronics, or financial services businesses, or from the package goods industry. That sponsor was to get commercial time on the MTV program, eight ad pages in the 16 page special publication, and promotional and added-value elements that were not defined at the time it was planned. The program was titled: "What's Wrong with Everything?: America Out of Control in an Election Year."

The MTV special was supposed to give the results of a nationwide Gallup poll paid for by both media that surveyed young adults views on various issues including the 1992 elections. Poll results were also to be featured in *Newsweek*. (Also see an example of a cross-media plan on page 259.)

Advantages of Cross-Media. In a survey, 31% of respondents cited lower CPMs on cross media deals *as the primary advantage* and 27% cited the ability to deliver a single message in a variety of media as a secondary advantage. Low CPMs represent media cost efficiency, and in effect, those who choose cross-media for efficiency are looking for better media buys for the money. The ability to deliver specialized targets is part of using the integrated marketing communications concept (discussed in Chapter 2). This technique makes it possible to deliver "seamless" communication that will better serve the advertiser's needs.

Many agencies and clients also like the value added programs because they place the media company in a partnership role rather than simply as a seller of time and space. A problem will be that media companies may be willing to offer the value added programs in a recession, but not when the economy picks up. Nevertheless, agencies and their clients may insist on continuing the practice.

Disadvantages of Cross-Media. The jury is still out on their value. In other words, it is difficult to prove that this technique is better than using traditional media alone. However, cross-media plans certainly are more interesting communication vehicles both to the consumers and advertisers. The problem in evaluating these deals mentioned above is that it is difficult to know whether the deals will remain in the arsenal of planners for a long time, or whether they will tend to be used only in specific, selective individual situations.

As mentioned before, unless the deal is designed and tailored for a particular client's needs, it may be difficult to sell broadly.

Database Media Planning

Database media planning (also discussed in Chapter 2) is a technique of building a list of individuals who are known to be purchasers of a given brand. Each person on this list is known by name, address, phone number, and his sales potential, as a minimum. Then the data is placed in a computer to form the database. In essence the advertiser can now, theoretically, eliminate waste in advertising because he knows who the targets are and how to reach them.

Place Media

There are a large number of new media that are distinguished by the fact that they are located out-of-home and are to be found in a particular place. Listed below is a small sample of some of the best known categories of place media and a brief explanation:

Categories of place media

Aerial	Banner towing airplanes
Airport/airplane	Displays inside airports
	In-flight video programming
	Bar news network located in airport bars
	Video monitors located throughout airports and carrying entertainment and commercials
	Laser billboards (rear screen projection billboards)

Convenience stores	Ads attached to waste containers in stores Convenience store media (from ceilings, above coolers, etc.)
Golf advertising	Colored posters framed behind plexiglass featuring golf subjects in clubhouses Ads on golf carts Colored ads on redwood tee-markers on courses Ads on front and side of golf carts
Grocery stores	Ads on grocery carts inside stores Checkout channel: Ads on TV sets mounted above checkout aisles P.O.P. Radio: Ads interspersed with music and information that can be heard throughout store Aisle ads: Posters in aisles or ads on shelf (shelf talkers)
Health clubs	Full color ads displayed on wallboards in general traffic areas and/or locker rooms
Movie theater	Colored ads displayed in lobbies of movie theaters On-screen slide show during intermissions
Phone booth	Ads on/in phone booths
Physician's waiting rooms	Integrated multi-media system consisting of TV, magazines, wallboards, and take-home booklets
Schools	Newspaper dispensers with ads on them Campus media boards: poster framed and shown in cafeterias, residence halls, etc.
Channel One	TV sets installed in high schools with 12 minute programs featuring news and teen interests plus ads
Shopping malls	In mall and store TV advertising is shown in between feature clips
Stadium/arena	Use of giant, color TV quality matrix. Has instant replay of sports and provides commercials
Advertising in motion	Full colored decals and signs applied to sides and rear of trucks Mobile ad units

Each of these specialized media have their own advantages and limitations, but in general, the advantage of place media is that advertising can be seen in areas relevant to the products or services offered. Therefore, these media may have more meaning for audiences than ads seen out of context. Often consumers are already motivated to buy. But these ads may provide added impetus.

In general, a disadvantage of place media is that they may not be available whenever wanted as traditional media are. Timeliness of the message may suffer. Furthermore, when consumers are tired, the message is not always seen or heard as when audiences are at rest. Also, sometimes the advertisements may be seen as intrusions rather than as helpful product information. There are probably some consumers who simply do not want to see these media and ignore them whenever they can, no matter what kind of information and entertainment are offered.

Intermedia Comparisons for Nonmeasured Media

Almost every medium in existence has some qualities that are useful for one or another advertiser. There are times when nonmeasured media are useful. A nonmeasured medium is one that is not measured regularly to find precisely who is exposed to it. Such media include car cards, telephone book advertising pages, theater or concert program advertising pages, and others. A planner who wants to use such media may have to rely on much more subjective judgments about audience sizes and/or demographics, especially when comparing nonmeasured to measured media.

Sometimes nonmeasured media will conduct research that may help the media planner in making intermedia comparisons. Unfortunately, most research is suspected of being biased in favor of the company that pays for it, because it has a vested interest in the outcome. As a result, it is difficult to make intermedia comparisons even on a subjective basis for nonmeasured media except in simple, obvious areas.

Recall Scores

One way to approach the dilemma of noncomparable measuring techniques for intermedia comparisons is to use response functions as a criterion of effectiveness. If it could be shown that an ad in one medium generates more recall than an ad in another medium, then one might assume that the medium with the higher recall is better. However, the ad or ads used for comparative purposes cannot be indiscriminately chosen. Nor can average recall of many ads be used in measuring recall of one medium versus another. The reason is that some products or brands may be inherently more interesting than others and therefore generate higher recall scores.

To prevent such bias, the same ad is usually measured in two different media. As a result, researchers hope that any variation in the recall scores is due to the effect of the medium rather than the ad. Although this procedure attempts to solve the problem, it is still questionable whether dual measurement represents a valid means of intermedia comparisons.

The reason is much the same as mentioned earlier: Comparing the differences in print and broadcast is like comparing apples and oranges. If a cola product were being tested on television and a similar ad were tested in a print medium, it would be difficult, if not impossible, to keep the copy and creative elements constant. A commercial for a cola drink usually features an announcer's voice, whether on or off camera. Most of the time the message features action and music rather than still scenes. Then, too, the audience sees the message on many different-sized televisions screens, some in black and white, but most in color.

If a similar cola ad were placed in print, the size of the ad would probably be constant from magazine to magazine, and there would be no sound of a well-known personality's voice and no music. Furthermore, if the print ad were placed in a magazine, there would be competition for attention from other ads, while the television program in which the commercial was placed would have no competition for attention at the same time (unless the viewer zapped a commercial while recording the program on a VCR).

Therefore, any results of recall measurements could not be considered unbiased. Any one of the variables exclusive to the ad in a given medium could account for the greater or lesser recall scores. Although such techniques may be helpful for other purposes, they may not be entirely valid for use in intermedia comparisons.

Often a medium in one class, such as magazines, will spend a great deal of money to prove that it is better than a medium in another class. Although the results are interesting, they cannot be considered valid for intermedia comparative purposes because of the vested interest problem.

Finally, the overall subject of recall scores is a controversial one within the research community. The question is whether a high recall score indicates that product sales will increase. Does high recall necessarily relate to changing the consumer's attitude in a positive way toward the product? Does recall relate to persuasion? There are many research professionals who believe that recall does not relate to sales effectiveness.

The Media Mix

In planning strategy, the planner may decide to use a single medium or a number of media. When more than one medium is used, the result is called a *media mix,* meaning that the plan mixes a number of media classes to reach certain target audiences. The planner must consider whether to use a single medium or a mix. Is one strategy better than another?

Generally, a planner uses a media mix because a single medium such as television cannot reach the target market in sufficient numbers or with sufficient impact to attain a media objective. When a planner does not define the target market narrowly, the targets represent such a broad spectrum of consumers that the only way to reach them is through multiple vehicles. Most planners narrow the definition of targets to reach *only* those with the best potential. Another situation that might call for a media mix strategy occurs when a planner has segmented targets into two key groups, each of which is about equal in importance.

A question that a media planner ought to raise when trying to decide whether to use a media mix is, What part of the market *cannot* be reached with a single medium? Generally, vehicles within one media class can reach a substantial part of a market, perhaps 90 percent. The percent of the market not covered may not be worth the extra cost of employing an additional medium. If 20 percent of the population accounts for 80 percent of product consumption, and this 20 percent is within the reach of a single medium, it may be inefficient to try to reach more with additional, but different, media. *Inefficiency* means that the additional media have substantially higher costs per thousand than the original medium.

John J. Meskill, senior vice president and director of media at Warwick, Welsh & Miller, Inc., has pointed out another consideration in the media mix question: There are times when a medium covers a market, but heavy users are only lightly exposed to the medium.[3] Generally, it is assumed that it is better to reach heavy users who are heavily exposed to a given medium under consideration.

When to Use a Media Mix

The following are some important reasons for using a media mix:

1. To extend the reach of a media plan. By doing so, the plan adds prospects not exposed by using a single medium.
2. To flatten the distribution of frequency so that there is a more even distribution of those who are exposed to a medium.
3. To add gross impressions, assuming, of course, that the second or third medium is cost efficient.
4. To reinforce the message—or help audience members remember the message by using different kinds of stimuli.
5. To reach different kinds of audiences, perhaps differentiated by life-style as well as demographics.
6. To provide unique advantages in stressing different benefits based on the different characteristics of each medium.
7. To allow different creative executions to be implemented.

---

3. Meskill, John J., "The Media Mix," *4A Media Letter*, January 1979, pp. 1–2.

FIGURE 10-1. An Evaluation of Traditional Media for Different Uses

Kind of use	Least value	Little value	Some value	More value	Best value
Authority	Outdoor	Radio	TV	Newspapers	Magazines
Beauty	Radio	Newspapers	Outdoor	TV	Magazines
Bigger than life	Radio	Magazines	Newspapers	TV	Outdoor
Demonstration	Outdoor	Radio	Newspapers	Magazines	TV
Elegance	Newspapers	Radio	TV/Outdoor	TV/Outdoor	Magazines
Entertainment	Outdoor	Magazines	Newspapers	Radio	TV
Events	Outdoor	Magazines	Radio	Newspapers	TV
Excitement	Newspapers	Outdoor	Radio	Magazines	TV
Features	Radio	Newspapers	TV	Magazines	Outdoor
Humor	Outdoor	Magazines	Newspapers	Radio	TV
Imagination	Outdoor	Newspapers	Magazines	TV	Radio
Information	Outdoor	Radio	TV	Magazines	Newspapers
Intimacy	Newspapers	Outdoor	TV	Magazines	Radio
Intrusion	Radio	Newspapers	Magazines	Outdoor	TV
Leadership	Newspapers	Outdoor	Radio	Magazines	TV
News	Outdoor	Magazines	Radio	TV	Newspapers
One-on-one	Outdoor	Newspapers	Magazines	Radio	TV
Package I.D.	Radio	Newspapers	TV	Radio	Outdoor
Personal	Outdoor	Newspapers	TV	Magazines	Radio
Prestige	Outdoor	Radio	TV	Newspapers	Magazines
Price	Outdoor	Magazines	TV	Radio	Newspapers
Product-in-use	Radio	Outdoor	Newspapers	Magazines	TV
Quality	Newspapers	Radio	Outdoor	TV	Magazines
Recipes	Outdoor	Radio	TV	Newspapers	Magazines
Sex Appeal	Newspapers	Radio	Outdoor	TV	Magazines
Snob Appeal	Outdoor	Radio	TV	Newspapers	Magazines
Tradition	Outdoor	Newspapers	TV	Radio	Magazines

*Evaluations are subjective

Meskill, however, felt that the idea of using a media mix ought to be challenged more often than it has been, and that many times one medium will do the job.

Criteria for Media Selection beyond the Numbers[4]

Media selections usually are made by examining quantified data showing the abilities of alternative media to reach select target audiences. But comparisons are also made on an objective and subjective basis covering materi-

---

4. This illustration adapted from DDB Needham Worldwide promotion piece, ''Which Media Do It Best?''

als cited in this chapter. The latter two criteria deal with the strengths of media to do certain things better than others.

Unfortunately, these latter criteria are subject to debate, and sometimes are simply the perceptions of either a planner or the client who sees things a certain way.

DDB Needham Worldwide presents the criteria in Figure 10–1 on the previous page as a means of promoting the message and the medium in making selection decisions. If a planner disagrees with these decisions, at least the chart will encourage more thought about just what it is that makes one more useful than another for achieving a client's objectives.

QUESTIONS FOR DISCUSSION

1. What are the differences between direct mail and direct marketing?
2. The volume of cable advertising has grown tremendously in the last 10 years. Discuss the main reasons for its growth.
3. Explain the advantages and disadvantages of using Sunday supplements over magazines.
4. National magazines and network television both provide broad reach. Explain the marketing situations that would require such reach.
5. Which media provide a high level of brand visibility over the summer months?
6. Which medium is the most ''selective'' of all? Explain when this medium is not as selective as assumed?
7. Explain how database media planning offers advantages that traditional media usually do not have?
8. Discuss the manner in which cross-media plans offer advantages to advertisers.
9. Explain why local radio typically has relatively low ''reach.'' How can radio be used to build higher reach?
10. Explain the reasons some planners object to comparing a CPM from television with a CPM from magazines.

SELECTED READINGS

Alexander, Suzanne, ''Whittle News Program Has Little Effect on Students' Knowledge, Study Shows,'' *The Wall Street Journal*, April 24, 1992, B4.

Boehlert, Eric, ''Cable Rep Offers New DATABASE,'' *Inside Media*, November 6, 1991, 34.

''Cable Television Special Report, Fit to Be Tied,'' *ADWEEK*, April 6, 1992, 1–30.

''Dawn of the Brand Analyst,'' *Food & Beverage Marketing*, October 1991, 18–21.

Donaton, Scott, ''More Turbulence for Channel One,'' *Advertising Age*, May 18, 1992, 48.

Donaton, Scott, ''Second Whittle Sponsor Out,'' *Advertising Age*, September 30, 1991, 52.

Donaton, Scott, ''Whittle Shifts Focus to Boost Profit Margins,'' *Advertising Age*, May 18, 1992, 3.

Fahey, Alison, ''Area Sports Cable Scores Ad Deals,'' *Advertising Age*, March 30, 1992, 56.

Fahey, Alison, ''Dogged Determination: Ralston, Cable Make 'Value-

Added' Come to Life," *Advertising Age*, July 22, 1991, S–22.

Fahey, Alison and Scott Donaton, "Downsizing Likely for Cross-Media Deals," *Advertising Age*, March 9, 1992, S–12.

"Fragmentation in TV: Old Media versus New Media," *Chicago Advertising & Media*, August 16–31, 1991, 10–12.

Horton, Cleveland and Raymond Serafin, "Car Marketers Drive Hard Bargain," *Advertising Age*, June 24, 1991, 16, 51.

Hume, Scott, "Special Report: Non-Traditional Media, Steady Diet of Basics," *Advertising Age*, August 19, 1991, 27.

Hume, Scott, "Sponsorships Up 18%, Whittle Says Event Spending Will Supplant Net TV," *Advertising Age*, March 23, 1992, 4.

"In-Store Insider Spots Growth Areas. Act Media Chief Chastises Marketers Who Are Putting Heads in Sand," *Advertising Age*, August 19, 1991, 28.

Lawrence, Jennifer, "In-flight Gets Above Turbulence," *Advertising Age*, August 19, 1991, 32.

"One More Spoke on the Wheel: (Cross-Media)," *MediaWeek*, February 4, 1991, 18–19.

Retailers Launch 'Place-Based' Magazines," *Folio's Publishing News Magazine*, March 15, 1992, 10.

Schrader, Martin, "Magazines 'Partnering' with Retail Just New Label for an Old Practice," *Advertising Age*, October 14, 1991, 28.

"The Insertible Advertisement," *CableAvails*, December 1991, 17.

Winkleman Michael, "Alternative Media," *PROMO*, January 1991, 10 +.

Winski, Joseph M., "Multimedia 'Multi-Mania'," *Advertising Age*, July 22, 1991, S–20.

11
Planning Media Strategy

This chapter explains how media strategy is developed. Readers should already understand the general background for strategy planning (found in Chapters 7, 8, and 9) including target market definition, target locations, target market identification, and reach and frequency concepts. This chapter discusses how to plan actions that will eventually become a media plan.

All media strategies are preceded and affected by media objectives—the goals that are derived from the marketing plans of a company. Each objective concentrates on a specific aspect of a marketing plan. Strategies then, are simply actions that need to be taken to attain a specific objective. Most of this chapter deals with strategies. But objectives also are covered bcause they too are important parts of a media plan.

Important Media Strategy Ideas

A Complete Definition Is Needed

Earlier in this book, media strategy was defined as a series of actions that planners take to attain media objectives. Now a description should also include the idea that media strategies are supposed to be actions that achieve an advantage over competitors (just as military strategy is supposed to gain an advantage over the enemy). If media objectives are achieved, it is because optimum strategies were employed. Thus it is necessary to first state the objectives and follow with correct media strategies.

Will media strategies that have advantages over competitors always be successful? The answer is: not necessarily. This is because other factors may play a larger role in determining success. Lower prices, good distribution, or a better quality brand could offset advantages. However, media strategies that have higher reaches, higher frequencies, spend more money, and have better creative messages, are examples of what gaining an advantage over competitors means. This idea assumes that most other factors in the media plan are equal between competitors and the advertiser. It is hard to see how a plan with less reach, less frequency, and so on can make much difference in a competitive battle.

A Brand's Presence in Media Should Be Large

A common practice in planning is buying small amounts of media, presumably to save money. The result is that audiences may not notice advertisements. In other words, small bits of media rarely accomplish much. It is better to combine media units into a few large media units to achieve presence.

Usually, "being big" in media is better. However, being dominant, or spending more money than a competitor doesn't always guarantee success. The "big" idea is to be visible and have a noticeable presence. This gives advertising a chance to be seen.

Advertise When Consumers Are Buying

There is a general belief by the uninitiated that advertising—at any time— can "make" people buy a given product or brand. This belief is not supported by experienced advertisers. For seasonal products like tire chains, lawn mowers, or Christmas trees, it is almost impossible to sell out of season. Occasionally, fur coats are sold in the summer when drastic price reductions are made. However, when the competition's brand is being purchased by large numbers of consumers at a certain time of the year, it is usually a good time for you to sell your brand. Most advertisers have track records of sales by month, and these will show the optimum times for advertising. The strategy is to find these time periods and heavy-up (or increase) media weight to take advantage of the natural opportunity that exists.

Creative Strategy Strongly Affects Media Strategy

Creative strategy is one of the most significant considerations in planning strategy. In fact, it is often the starting place for all media planning. "Creative" indicates that some media are much more appropriate to the message than others. For example, when full color is needed, then print media is best because there is little variation from the appearance of an ad in one medium to another. Consider the differences in color appearance from one television set to another. Despite the great advances made in television set technology, there are some differences. For advertisements that require controlled color, such as an ad featuring appetite appeal, then creative strategy can play an important role in its success.

Sometimes, creative can be written so that it will be effective in all media. At other times, creative may be restrictive or may be designed for a small market segment that will run in new, or non-traditional media.

In some situations, media planners may work more closely with creative people in an advertising agency than ever before. The reason is that they may be planning integrated communication tactics, which requires different creative for different communication techniques. Obviously, the media will also be somewhat different, so planners should check early with creative people in the planning process.

Many Alternative Media Strategies Should Exist

It should always be assumed that in choosing a suitable strategy there is usually more than one available. There are many strategies available to a planner. Some alternative courses of action are equally viable and a few are usually better than others. Table 11–2 lists alternative media strategies that might be used to achieve a given media objective.

One of the problems with planning strategies, however, is finding the best from among the alternatives. Sometimes it is necessary to prove that the best one was chosen by writing a rationale in the media plan that explains why one was chosen over others. If it isn't written, someone in the client's organization may ask for an oral explanation of why it was chosen.

What Media Planners Should Know Before Starting to Plan

Know the Marketing Problems

Although planners may want to start writing a media strategy from the moment they are assigned to a product and brand, they should first have a full understanding of the marketing problems. Marketing solutions to these problems directly affect the choice of media strategy.

Almost all marketers have one or more marketing problems that require relatively quick solutions. These problems could be national, regional, or local in scope, and may deal with many different aspects of business, such as advertising, sales, manufacturing, and sales promotion. However, marketing or advertising problems usually include the advertising message (or creative), sales volume, market share, and profits.

The marketer is responsible for devising solutions to these problems. Solutions are usually marketing mix elements (product, price, place, and pro-

TABLE 11–1. Alternative Media Strategies

National coverage (buying all stations in a network television lineup)
Large national reach
Buying different dayparts to reach women at home and women who work
Buying national magazines or national newspapers
Buying local advertising in top 100 markets
Buying network radio
Buying national cable (e.g., ESPN)

motion, which includes advertising, sales promotion, public relations, and direct marketing). When a solution calls for advertising, then media automatically become an important ingredient in the solution.

A careful and complete analysis of the problem often helps make a proposed solution obvious. On the other hand, a loose or careless definition may provide a bare minimum of direction. The media planner should know precisely what the marketing problem is—including a history of the brand that is relevant to the present problem—and the solutions that have been proposed. Part of the job of writing strategies is to show how media fits into the total marketing plan and the role it can perform in the solution.

Know the Recommended Actions

The marketer who uses advertising recommends courses of actions (strategies) to solve the problems. Shown in Table 11–2 are alternative solutions to a marketing problem of declining sales. Each solution may require a different media strategy. If, for example, one solution to the problem of declining sales is reducing prices, then the media planner may recommend large target reach *and* high frequency as two strategies. Reach will provide broad dissemination of advertising messages—the marketing strategy cannot work well if few consumers know that prices have been reduced. Thus, more consumers are more likely to take advantage of the offer. Furthermore, high frequency may be necessary to help the message overcome the clutter of commercials that appear on television and radio.

Know the Complexities of a Strategy

Strategy decisions are usually not very simple and have effects that occur in many different ways. Neither of the two media strategies mentioned above, however, may be totally feasible and could require a different strategy if they require more money than the client is willing to spend. Now a strategy may have to be created to fit the budget. One way to do this is to limit the high reach and frequency to only the three or four months when sales responses for the product have traditionally been high. Beer advertising, for

TABLE 11–2.   Declining Sales: Possible Marketing Solutions

Reduce prices
Get wider and/or larger or better product distribution
Reduce price and use advertising to publicize
Use advertising to announce
Use innovative advertising messages to attract attention and communicate offer
Use sales promotion incentives
Use integrated marketing communications
Improve product quality
Use more attractive packaging
Choose new target segments (with different demographics and/or lifestyles)

example, could require a strategy that limits advertising to only summer months or that uses a flighting strategy.

If the situation is more complex—consumers who regularly bought a certain brand but now have switched brands—the solution would require an explanation of just how these consumers are supposed to respond to advertising communication. Now the marketer should try to motivate the consumer to switch back to the original brand.

Marketing situations requiring the use of different media—public relations, sales promotion, *and* advertising—now have a unique problem: all of the communications objectives may not appear to be "seamless" to consumers. This situation occurs when media planning for integrated communications has too many communication objectives. First the media strategist should remind creative personnel that multiple communications objectives can be confusing to consumers because each was produced with a different communication technique. The goal should be to help the advertising speak with one voice in its use of various media.

Know How the Product Will Be Sold

A media planner should know how the product will be sold and which marketing mix elements will be used. The term "how" refers to the creative personnel department's perception of the proposed advertising: will it communicate with consumers? Generally, this is part of what is known as "creative strategy." Specifically, it uses applied consumer behavior principles and research to explain how consumers are supposed to react to advertising.

Know How Advertising Sells a Product to One Customer

Gus Priemer, former marketing and media manager of Johnson's Wax, urged media planners to first *understand how to sell a product to one customer* before planning large-scale media. Priemer also noted that planners should be able to describe how advertising communication is expected to work to influence the consumers' behavior toward a brand. The failure to do both is often the cause of unsuccessful strategies because no one is sure about how the consumers will respond to marketing efforts. If a planner cannot perceive how one person buys, how can he or she know what will happen when the advertiser is dealing with millions of consumers?

When a product's price is reduced, there are three elements that can affect the consumer: price, communication method, and media choice. Simply telling consumers that a product's price is reduced often has little or no effect. Sometimes this is because the price is obtuse, such as when advertising features only the percentage discounts given. This type of information makes the consumer work to figure out the dollar value of the discount and may create doubt that the offer is genuine and not a "come-on." Sometimes the price reduction is so insignificant that it has no motivational impact for the consumer.

The second factor in determining the success of the communication is the way the offer is announced. If the ad is dull, or unnoticeable among more interesting ads, or lacks audience appeal, then the communication may fail. Even the personality of a presenter may make a difference in getting communication through.

The third element of a successful communication is media choice. Television probably has the best chance of getting a message to consumers because it provides emotional and factual presentation techniques to help it sell. Media works best when combined with a motivating force—like price reduction—and an attractive message placed in a strong medium.

Sometimes the solutions are so obvious that no written rationale is needed. If, for example, the selling technique is to lower prices, the consumer motivation will be that because prices are lower (perhaps lower than all competitors) the consumer will buy the product in order to save money, and get a good or superior product value at the same time. Therefore the motivation does not really require that someone write every strategy statement about selling.

Know How to Neutralize the Competition's Strategy

Media strategies take place in a dynamic, active, marketing environment in which competitors typically want to outsell each other and gain a larger market share. In planning media strategy, these competing strategies cannot be ignored, especially when any one of them are directly attacking your brand. Is there any way that the media planner can neutralize the competition's strategy? In the past, this was accomplished by: (a) spending more money than the competition on advertising in geographic markets where brands were likely to do better, (b) using more and better advertising messages, coupled with more or better promotion, (c) making better use of any marketing communication mix, and (d) modifying or creating a product that better met consumers' needs. The "more and better" idea, however, proved to be ineffective in many situations. In fact, it seemed to have little or no effect when the economy was poor, or when a given brand was perceived to be equal to or even poorer than competitors' product quality.

Today, the use of truly dynamic innovation in creative messages is one technique that only works some of the time. In the area of media planning, however, certain strategies can be devised that do succeed. Here are some examples:

1. Reach more members of a target market than competitors.
2. Reach a different demographic target market.
3. Use higher average frequency.
4. Reach targets in new and different media formats. For example, use cable television if the competition uses network television. Or, buy spot television exclusively if competitors use network.
5. Run a special promotion in conjunction with a medium.
6. Use media creatively.

Know the Cost of Strategies

An important media strategy is determining how much money it will take to accomplish any or all media objectives. The planner will probably make a cost estimate of all the strategies and decide how much money is in the media budget. If the advertiser has already given the planner a number that represents the most the client will spend, then the solution has to be devised with strategies that do not go above that amount.

At times, a planner might devise two different strategies. One strategy will cost about the same amount the client wanted. Another strategy, called an investment spending strategy, will cost more because the planner feels that more money will return more in sales than the smaller budget.

Other Elements of Media Strategy

Media Targets

To whom will advertisements be directed—users, persons who influence users, or both? The more specific a planner is in identifying targets by demographic or other means, the easier it will be to find media that will reach those targets. Most media targets are defined demographically. Occasionally, some other description such as psychographics (the psychological descriptions of targets) is used. The goal, however, is to be as specific as possible because a vague description may mean exposures wasted on individuals who never buy a given product or brand under any circumstances. Once media targets have been specified, then all subsequent decisions can be checked to see whether the correct targets are being reached by the media selected.

Media objectives usually include a statement indicating where targets are located geographically. Sometimes this information is stated in the strategy portion, rather than the objectives portion, of the plan.

The Creative Strategy

The creative strategy and creative executions are the heart of an advertising campaign, whether one is planning a national campaign or a local campaign for a retail store. The reason should be obvious: copy and art are the communication that drives advertising. They sell! Media may or may not sell, depending on the marketing situation, but unless the copy has been well planned and written, it is highly unlikely that the product will sell. Copy (meaning words, pictures, sound, color, white space) are motivating forces. They are the things that that get into the minds of consumers and in many ways affect sales.

Because of the creative importance, planners should not proceed until they know what the creative is, and in which media creative people think the message would be best suited. In fact, creative personnel should discuss their strategies beforehand with media personnel. If they do not, then it is up to media planners to seek out creatives and learn which media would be best suited. In fact, media planners have worthwhile suggestions for creatives and lead to a closer relationship that exists in actual practice.

The creative strategy affects the choice of media classes, and individual media. It also affects the degree of creative media planning that can result (discussed later in this chapter). It is inconceivable that a planner would ignore the creative plan.

Budget Constraints

Even though the relationship of marketing objectives to media objectives is clear, a number of constraints often temper the planner's decision. The size of the budget, if known ahead of time, is one such constraint. Many times, the marketing budget is set before any media planning takes place. In such a situation, the media objectives will have to be written with the budget in mind.

If no budget is available, then media objectives may well serve as a guide to setting a budget, at least as far as the cost of time or space is concerned. Once planners have a general idea of their goals, they are in a position to estimate what it will cost to achieve them. Sometimes, a budget cannot be set at the media objectives stage, but must wait until the strategy has been worked out. In such cases, media objectives may have to be rewritten later to accommodate the size of the budget. Perhaps a series of marketing/media priorities may have to be set so that the planner achieves those goals that are most pressing, while secondary goals may have to wait for another day. The size of a budget recommended by a media planner might be reduced by the client after examining marketing/media objectives and strategy.

Cost Efficiency

Cost-per-thousand maximum levels may or may not be a part of media objectives. Usually, cost-per-thousand targets are needed to discriminate between media. In past years, when media planning was often based on large audience figures (sometimes called *box-car figures*), representing crudely identified media audiences, maximum cost-per-thousand levels were usually stated in media objectives. For example, one media objective might have been written to warn buyers not to buy any medium that had a cost per thousand over $5 for total audiences. But at the present, and most likely in the future, maximum levels of cost per thousand may be meaningless, because cost-efficiency formulas are now used mostly to help discriminate between the ability of various media to deliver prospects at the lowest unit cost. But even the lowest CPM among all alternatives may be high.

Reach and Frequency

When planners select media they are, in effect, choosing those that will deliver a given number of target audiences. Delivery, however, is nothing more than exposures. Because all research data represent measurements taken in the past, the data therefore represent only "estimates of exposures." The future may be somewhat different.

But the number of estimated exposures contracted for in a media plan may be patterned in such a way as to maximize either reach or frequency, or to attain effective reach and frequency. Media objectives should be set so as to obtain whichever goal is sought. Brown, Lessler, and Weilbacher called this pattern the "message basket."[1] They meant that, without clear-cut, deliberate planning, all of the potential exposures planned may produce only a confused basket of numbers, some of which may even represent contradictory goals. Therefore, media objectives should be written in such a way as to bring control and order out of the chaos in the basket.

More explicitly, media objectives should state whether reach or frequency is to be the goal, and explain why each is or is not needed. In addition, the levels of reach and frequency should become part of the strategy. Here, too, an explanation is needed to justify, logically, why any given level is desired.

Continuity

It should be apparent that media objectives will affect the kinds of strategies that later evolve. One important goal that will affect the timing of advertising during weeks and months of a year is continuity. *Continuity,* as previously described, is the consistency of advertising placement. Like reach and frequency, continuity may result in many contradictory patterns of placement if not controlled.

One placement pattern, for example, may consist of advertising appearing every day of the year; another may be limited to placing ads once a week. Which is better? The answer depends on a number of factors. What are the brand marketing goals and strategy? Do they require a given pattern? Does the creative strategy require a different pattern? (For example, if the creative strategy includes a very complex message in television commercials, will audiences be able to grasp the meaning if the commercials are shown once a week or will a pattern of frequent showings be required?)

Therefore media goals will have to be based, to some extent, on continuity. (See discussion on scheduling, page 256.)

---

1. Brown, Lyndon O., Lessler, Richard S., and Weilbacher, William M., *Advertising Media,* Ronald Press, New York, 1957, p.118.

Creative *Media* Strategy

In Chapter 1, we discussed the *creative media plan* as a problem to be solved. In this chapter, we make suggestions on how to implement a creative media strategy that will help solve this problem to a great extent.

Our first recommendation is that the media planner understand what is meant by the term *creative media strategy.*

It must first be pointed out that there is no universally agreed-upon definition of this term. However, in general, we believe a creative media strategy to be one that is innovative enough to secure for an advertised brand some advantage over competitors' brands. Such a strategy may accomplish this by helping the advertising stand out against competitors' advertising, giving the messages a better chance of being absorbed. Many advertised brands in product categories (margarines, or TV sets, for example) tend to use similar media strategies. If all brands in a category are also similar, then consumers may have difficulty distinguishing one brand from another. Perhaps a creative media strategy will help solve the problem.

More specifically, however, we offer five guidelines for implementing a creative media strategy:

1. *Be sure that the media strategy is different from and more innovative than competitors' media strategies.* It is very important to realize that simply being different is not enough. There is no evidence that a plan that is different from competitors' plans will accomplish anything. But, there is the testimony of media and marketing planners that truly innovative plans can accomplish key goals and attain competitive advantages.

   The key elements in the *innovative* are ideas that make a brand's advertising stand out from the competitors' advertising. This assumes that advertising messages have something to say that is meaningful to consumers. What this also means is that the creative media dollars are supposed to return more than a typical brand's media strategy.

2. *The ability to be creative should not depend on additional dollars spent for media.* Innovative strategies that could cost more than what is considered normal are not considered valuable unless there is evidence that the increased spending will result in superior returns.

3. *Media strategy should start with quantitative proofs of the best media choices and usages . . . but then go beyond numbers.* A creative media strategy is not a substitute for quantitative proof that the best media have been selected and used. Without measures of reach, frequency, effective frequency, and other kinds of useful numerical data, a planner would have to rely on gut instinct. It is difficult to convince clients who are spending large amounts of money for media to rely on gut instincts as proof. But

when a plan is built on good quantitative proof, and a good creative strategy, the combination may be just what is required.

4. *A good creative media strategy should be dramatic rather than ordinary.* It is the drama of the innovation that can make a strategy stand out from all the others and secure special benefits for a brand.

5. *A creative media strategy should be relevant to the problems that the advertised brand has.* Being creative is sometimes interpreted as being "offbeat" or "new." It is important to make a creative media plan relevant to the marketing situation and not just "different."[2]

It is important to understand that a media planner should be the person to make contributions to the overall marketing plan with creative media strategies. Planners typically are thought of as "number crunchers," or "people with only quantitative skills." Both stereotypes ought to be dismissed. When given an opportunity to be creative, a media planner should be able to think of innovative ways to solve problems.

Examples of Creative Media Strategies

Listed below are some examples of creative strategies used by various advertisers to achieve special attention to their messages:

Problem: Xerox Corporation was about to sponsor the U.S. Open golf tournament in Rochester, New York. Rochester is also the home of Kodak, a competitor in the copier field.

Solution: On the first day of the tournament, Kodak's agency printed an ad in *USA Today* that looked just like the newspaper's real front page, except that it only carried stories about Kodak's copiers. The single page ad appeared in a special section on the Open, and wrapped around the front page so that the first thing readers saw was the Kodak copier line. The real front page was underneath. The Kodak page appeared only in the Rochester area but was circulated at the tournament site, airports, and hotels. Kodak's planners were creative because they saw an opportunity that had not been apparent before.

Problem: How to use media *and* promotion in local radio to help increase distribution of a food product in a number of markets.

Solution: The agency created several alternative promotions and went to local radio stations in different markets and asked them to choose which they wanted, since the promotion also benefited the sta-

---

2. Recommendations (1), (2), and (5) were made by Prof. Ron B. Kaatz, in various speeches and lectures on Creative Media Planning. (Medill School of Journalism, Northwestern University, 1987)

tion. The alternative chosen most often was a contest in which the prizes were a trip to a major league baseball park of their choice. The agency created a 60-second program called *Mystery Ballpark,* which was used with the voice of a local announcer. The 60-second spot was equally devoted to the food product and to the participating retailer.

Problem: The Kodak Company needed a "big media event" without taxing the advertising budget.

Solution: The advertising agency suggested that the client buy and be the sole sponsor of a special issue of *Time* magazine. The issue had a "theme" that fit with the client and the medium: "150 years of Photojournalism." This special issue went to subscribers free, as a bonus. It was also supported with a special ad campaign that appeared in key markets. It was a traveling photo exhibit that worked as a public relations event and received extra publicity from the local press.

Problem: The agency had a problem in finding enough money to communicate with consumers in 10 of the client's key markets. The budget was only $250,000. Among those markets were Cincinnati, Cleveland, and Detroit.

Solution: The agency found an hour-long TV program that had been produced by a station in Seattle on art in ancient China. It bought the rights to that program and scheduled it in the 10 markets. The agency localized the program to fit each market separately. It then got most stations in the markets to broadcast the show for free, arguing that it had a strong cultural affairs type of appeal.

Media Strategy Is Not A Science

In practice, planners have to remember that media strategy is not a science in the same manner as physics or medicine. Its outcomes cannot always be predicted with great accuracy. One significant reason for this is that the marketplace may be constantly changing as competitors use many different tactics to gain an advantage over each other. In addition, the original marketing problem may not be solved after strategies have been implemented.

The outcomes of *some* media strategies can be achieved quite well, such as "reaching 70% of a target market by placing ads in a certain group of vehicles." However, it would be incorrect to assume that everyone reached will see an advertisement in the selected medium, or that they will respond appropriately. So part of the practice of planning strategy is knowing precisely what each strategy means and implies.

For the most part, planners learn what each individual strategy will accomplish from personal experiences. When planners have worked with a given product category or a brand for many years, they learn what a strategy will accomplish under certain marketing conditions. As time goes by, they modify their findings to develop a body of knowledge that enables them to make better predictions of the results.

The following is a list of questions that covers typical basic media strategies. They should be included in a typical media plan, and for complex strategies, should be accompanied by a rationale.

Relationships among Reach, Frequency, Continuity, and Number of Markets

In planning strategy, there are usually four elements that are closely related: reach, frequency, continuity, and number of markets to be used. A person cannot plan for one of these elements without simultaneously considering the others, because of their close relationship. The relationship grows out of

---

Questions to ask in planning media strategies

Marketing questions:
1. What are the marketing problems that require media?
2. What marketing objectives and strategies have been planned?

Media questions:
1. What is the creative strategy and recommendations for best use of creative?
2. What are the media objectives?

Strategy questions:
1. Who should targets be? (Demographic and lifestyle description of prospects.)
2. Which media classes are recommended?
    a. What percent of the budget should go to each media class? (Example: 60% network TV; 20% spot TV; 10% cable; and 10% magazines)
3. How much reach and frequency do we need? Effective Reach and/or frequency? Why?
    a. How much reach, frequency, and GRPs are needed per quarter?
4. How large is the media budget?
    a. What percent spending per month and quarter is required? Why?
5. What is the best timing and scheduling for this year?
    a. What pattern of continuity is recommended?
    b. Is there an introductory period? For how many weeks? Why?
    c. How heavy should introductory weight be compared to sustaining parts of the plan?
    d. Is there a heavy-up period? When? Why?
6. Geographical concentration:
    a. In which media should it occur? Why?
    b. What are the criteria for selecting markets?
    c. What are the importance of BDIs–CDIs?
    d. How many markets should we be in?
    e. What are the names of individual markets?
    f. How much weight should we plan for in each market?
    g. What are the seasonal variations in weighting?
7. Which daypart selection for broadcast media?
8. Media units:
    a. Sizes needed? 30 seconds or 15 seconds? Page or partial page units?
    b. Use of special color or treatment (gatefold, etc.)?
9. Miscellaneous

a fixed budget size, which means, in effect, that if any one of these elements is strongly emphasized, the others will, of necessity, suffer.

Each of these elements costs a considerable amount of money to attain. Reach, for example, usually means that advertising messages must be dispersed widely so that many different persons in the target audience will have an opportunity to see the messages. Generally, one single media vehicle, such as one television program or one magazine, will not deliver a high reach. Multiple vehicles are usually required, and the more that are purchased, the greater the cost. As the cost for reach goes up, the amount of money available for the other three elements becomes more limited.

The same holds true for continuity. If an advertiser wants to plan continuous advertising over 52 weeks, the cost will be high, leaving minimal amounts of money for the other three elements. Often as much as six or more months of advertising must be sacrificed in order for the reach to attain a high enough level in the remaining six months.

Likewise, the number of individual markets in a plan, where national media may be used in conjunction with local media, clearly affects overall costs. Even if only local media are used, the same concept prevails. The more markets used, the higher the cost, and the less money available for the other elements.

Figure 11–1 shows to some extent what happens when a planner tries to manipulate the four elements within the constraints of a fixed budget. The

FIGURE 11-1.   Alternative Strategies within a Fixed Budget

A

| Reach | Frequency |
| Continuity | Number of Markets |

Strategy A is a balanced strategy—reach, frequency, continuity, and number of markets were deliberately given equal weight.

B

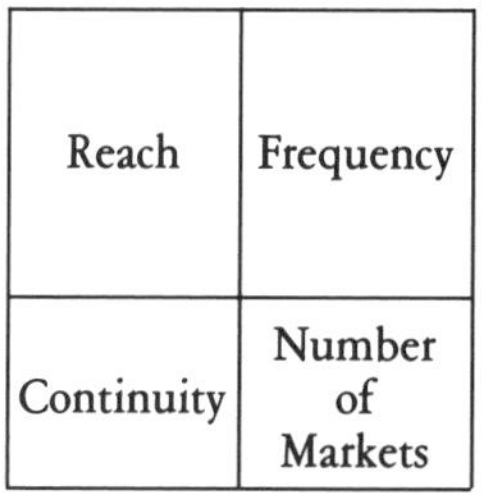

| Reach | Frequency |
| Continuity | Number of Markets |

Strategy B was planned to emphasize reach and frequency at the expense of continuity and number of markets.

C

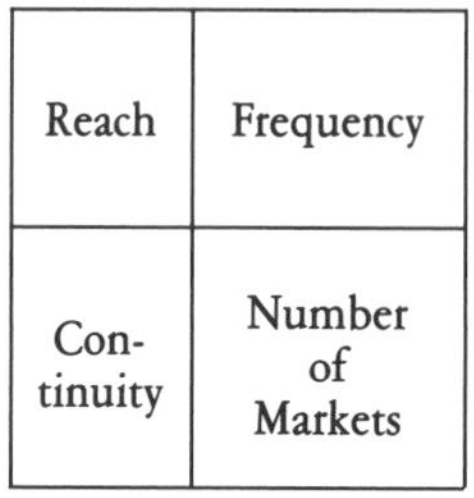

| Reach | Frequency |
| Continuity | Number of Markets |

Strategy C emphasizes frequency and number of markets, but reach and continuity have been reduced.

D

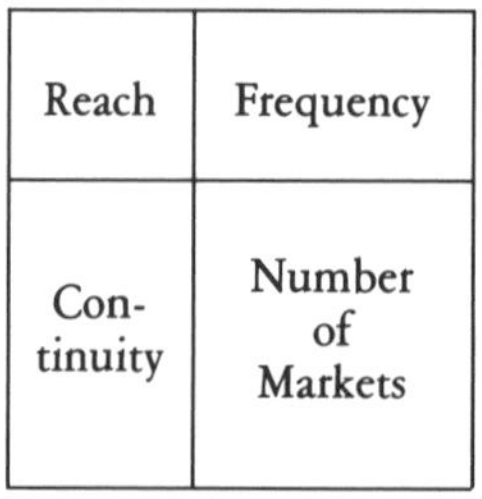

| Reach | Frequency |
| Continuity | Number of Markets |

Strategy D shows most emphasis on the number of markets with the others being downplayed.

figure shows some ways to vary the weights of reach, frequency, continuity, and number of markets. Other possibilities, not shown, also exist. One part of a planner's job is to weight each of the four alternatives and decide which of the four needs more emphasis (usually at the expense of the others). Of course, if the budget size can be increased (unfortunately, it usually can't), then different emphases can be achieved. As a consequence of this dilemma, the planner needs some criteria for weighting the alternatives.

Weighting Alternatives

Reach and frequency are the two most important elements of a media plan. Because they occupy such an important position in a plan, they are usually considered before continuity or number of markets. When a media budget is very high, it may be possible to achieve both high reach *and* high frequency levels. But most often, the cost is too high to do both.

If high reach is planned, it will probably cause the frequency level to decline somewhat because reach and frequency are inversely related. If, however, reach is very high (at the 90 percent level), then frequency can be increased by extra dollar expenditures because most of the money will go into building frequency and a very small increment will go to building reach. This is the natural consequence of trying to reach new persons who have not already been reached by some other mass vehicle.

Higher reach will be necessary when the media plan calls for anything new: new prices, etc. Reach is also needed for building brand awareness at significant levels. If a brand awareness level is now at 25 percent and an objective is to raise it to 75 percent, then higher reach will probably be required, and frequency will be sacrificed. Also calling for higher reach is the announcement of various kinds of promotions such as cents-off deals, special coupon promotions, or refund offers. Such promotions need to build a great deal of awareness so that consumers will take advantage of the offer. Still another high-reach situation occurs when changes in the brand or changes in the creative strategy are important. Finally, more reach may be needed when it becomes necessary to meet or exceed competitive reach levels. One goal could be to steal customers from a competitor by showing them that the advertised brand better meets their needs, in which case enough reach might be needed to equal or better the competitor's reach.

More frequency, at the expense of reach, may be needed when the brand awareness levels are already high due to the cumulative effect of past advertising. At that point, more frequency may be needed to meet or surpass frequency levels of competitors. When the advertising noise level of all competitors is already high, then more frequency also may be needed to meet or surpass frequency levels of competitors. There are certain marketing situations where a minimum frequency threshold must be passed before consumers start paying attention to the message. The effectiveness of the media plan may be directly related to high frequency. Sometimes a frequency level from three to ten must be achieved for the campaign to be considered effective.

Although brand awareness may be a campaign or creative objective, it may be necessary to advertise in a pattern that matches the purchasing cycle of a product class. Some products are not sold to any great extent at certain times of the year. Calculators, for example, require heavy media usage in spring, early fall, and at Christmas time. Reach levels also will probably be high at those times. On the other hand, in the case of beer—sold all through the year with summer peaks—reach levels may have to be sacrificed at some times of the year in order to have enough money to cover the year and, at the same time, spend heavily during summer. When high reach is necessary, it is sometimes necessary to sacrifice continuity. In some situations, advertisers may drop out of advertising for as long as six months, allowing the product to keep selling at lower volume levels in order to have sufficient money to advertise at high levels during peak volume seasons.

The final variable affecting the budget allocation is the number of markets to be used. There are two methods of arriving at this number. The older method consisted of creating national media plans in which the number of markets would not be considered until after other strategies were decided. A newer technique starts with a market-by-market analysis and sets strategies for each market. Once communication goals are set for each market, then reach and frequency levels may be set after the number of markets has been decided. Still another approach is to determine the number of markets and minimum communication goals simultaneously—meaning that reach and frequency levels and degree of continuity are also determined simultaneously.

Setting Priorities

An important step in weighting the four elements is that of setting priorities. A planner should do this early so that it will be easier to decide which of the four elements is most or least important. Priorities come from media objectives, and some objectives are obviously more important than others. If there is any doubt, then a planner must not only state the priorities, but also explain why one objective is more important than another and how much more important. Once the priorities are clear, then the allocation of a budget to the four variables should be relatively clear.

Choosing Media Strategies from Among Alternatives

The discussion in this chapter to this point has been on elements that affect the planning of media strategies. Now the question arises: which strategy from among the alternatives should be selected as the most appropriate? Since many strategies can be used in one media plan, there should be guidelines to studying alternatives. This section discusses a select group of strategies that media planners are often confronted with, in order to help answer the perennial question: Which one should be chosen?

In offering these explanations, the reader should already know that "media strategy is *not* a science." There is little evidence that one can refer to in trying to make the best decision. Many of what are called "best strategies" have not been proven to be best, objectively, but are judged to be best by a planner based on the facts available. Many times, however, strategists speak with so much conviction that it is assumed they must be correct. On the other hand, many strategists have learned by experience what works best, and they use this learning in future decision making. In these cases, they are using their experience as a different form of research.

Recently, the advertising industry conducted major research about strategy that has confirmed what most experienced planners already believed. This research was conducted by Information Resources, Incorporated, through their BehaviorScan measuring device, and was sponsored by Leo Burnett, DDB Needham, Nobel & Associates, and J. Walter Thompson advertising agencies. Other sponsors included the three television networks and 16 major manufacturers, many of whom are in the packaged-food business. The findings were presented to the marketing and advertising industry on November, 6–7, 1991, in a presentation called "How Advertising Works." In some cases, the findings of this research were new. But in many cases, the findings turned out to confirm what planners had already learned by experience.

One must realize that the effects of some strategies cannot be measured. As an example, it is almost impossible for most marketing and media planners to prove how many sales were actually delivered as a result of a media strategy's contribution because the strategy cannot be parsed out separately. What seems to be working may instead be the product of other variables that are difficult to measure. Furthermore, media responses are mostly affected by advertising's creative efforts. Media's effectiveness is probably the most difficult of all advertising variables to measure. Ads are responded to, but mostly as a result of creative efforts. We can find out how many magazines were subscribed to, how many were sold on newsstands, how many readers there were, and even whether audiences saw a given ad in certain magazines. But how many sales did the magazine produce? That isn't known, and it is probable that we will never know precisely this kind of information. The exception to this is direct response advertising. With the use of toll-free and "900" telephone numbers, or business reply cards, it is possible to directly attribute sales to a distinct media vehicle.

Strategy Trade-offs

Another way to look at the problem of strategy planning is that there may be a trade-off involved. In other words, with every strategy decision there are advantages and disadvantages. The strategist's problem is finding which advantage is the best trade-off. Sometimes the decision is one of common sense; however, frequently there is an equal number of advantages and disadvantages when compared to another option. Trading off is giving up one strategic option for another because one offers more advantages. An example of a media strategy trade-off would be to buy advertising only in the top five U.S. markets at a high average cost, versus buying advertising in markets six to 20, but at a much more modest average cost.

Typical Media Strategies and Alternatives

The following discussion covers selected marketing or media problem situations, and the prevailing strategy opinions about them. Let's examine some of these major strategies that planners have to deal with and show how and why they are used. Alternatives will also be discussed.

Scheduling. When the market for a brand seems very flat during the entire year (meaning that sales are approximately even during all 12 months), the scheduling strategy suggests that advertising should be done every month. This implies that because consumers buy a product category evenly, the scheduling should reflect this evenness. This kind of scheduling therefore would call for even continuity during all 12 months.

What is missing from a high continuity strategy is the effects of all competitors' advertising. "Even continuity" means that spending is approximately the same amount of money during each month. But this strategy ignores the competition, unless the competition is also supporting its brand throughout the year. The net effect of even spending is to have lower reaches and frequencies (communication opportunities) each month unless a huge amount of money is spent.

Flighting. If the competition concentrates its advertising support during certain times of the year, a better scheduling strategy may be to sacrifice even continuity to concentrate money at certain time periods during the year, so that our brand can be more prominent (compared to competitors' brands). This strategy is called *flighting*. Now, a schedule may concentrate advertising into bursts of four to six weeks at a time, with a two or three week hiatus between each burst. The effect of this strategy is that (assuming the budget is a fixed amount) more money is available to be spent during the bursts, with the accompanying effect of greater reach and frequency when the bursts occur. As a consequence, continuity is not as close as it was, but it is there to a lesser degree.

Heavy introductory effort. If a brand is just being introduced, it has the problem of breaking through consumers' mental sets that have endured without this new brand. Competitive brands may have a strong hold on the market, making it difficult for the new brand to establish a foothold. A strategy here would require heavy spending at the beginning of a campaign, and sacrificing advertising during the latter part of the year to have the money to finance the upfront idea. The introductory period may run anywhere from one to three months.

The Information Resources, Inc. study confirmed that "the concentration of higher TV weight into fewer weeks is related to an increase in sales.'' While the study concentrated only on television advertising, the same concepts would apply for other advertising media with the exception that television is more dynamic than most others.

In most new product introductions, the client is willing to spend more money to get the product launched in the marketplace. But this additional money may not be enough. Beginning media planners are often surprised to learn that as much as 70 percent of an advertising budget is recommended to be spent in this introductory period. The student will often ask: ''what happens to advertising in the remainder of the year since there is very little money left?'' The experienced planner will usually respond by saying that ''if we can't make it upfront, the remainder will be wasted anyway.'' One of the principles of strategy planning is to make advertising appear as large as possible for maximum effect. So the upfront strategy for a new product introduction is the best alternative.

Heavy-up scheduling. Most planners spend more on advertising when consumer buying is heaviest, and spend less at other times. Many brands have two to four months a year of heavy buying activity. The opportunity to get competitors' customers to switch brands during these heavy buying seasons may be greater at this time if something worthwhile is said in advertisements. Advertising should show a brand's superiority over others. These heavy buying seasons are usually the best times to advertise because consumers may be more responsive to advertising for a product category than at other times. It cannot be assumed that by ''heavying-up'' for two or three months, sales automatically will increase proportionately. Most consumers are looking for good values to meet their needs and wants.

However, a planner can have an advantage over competitors who also recognize that the buying season is the time to advertise. If all competitors are spending more at the same time, they may nullify each other. This could require a strategy for one competitor to start a month or two before all the others start heavy spending, and thereby ''get a jump'' on the market.

Geographical market weighting. Weighting geographical markets means adding either dollars, GRPs, or a large number of advertisements in a geographical market because that market has greater sales potential than others. Each of these dollars, GRPs, or ads represent the same idea to some extent. When any of them are added, it is assumed that advertising has a better chance of being more effective than the same markets with lesser weights.

The need for extra weighting in certain markets is based on market potential, which is usually very uneven nationally. A brand may be selling very well in some markets, and poorly in others. The assumption is that adding weight to low volume sales markets represents a bigger risk than adding weight to markets that have already been producing good sales. (See Chapter 7 for more information on the use of BDIs and CDIs in evaluating market potential).

One of the general principles of weighting then, is to add extra weight to a market equal to its realtive sales contribution. This is called *pro rata budgeting.* This suggests that a market that produces 6 percent of a company's sales should receive at least 6 percent of the advertising budget. If this is followed, then the weighting of markets can be on the basis of relative sales volume it has already produced. It has established a positive track record that serves as a guideline for weighting. When there are some markets that haven't done well, and there is reason to believe that one of the reasons for its sales limitations is the lack of advertising weight, then the pro rata technique may not be adequate. A planner may experiment with added weight to see what will happen. Without evidence that sales would increase with more advertising weight, the pro rata technique is a low risk alternative.

Combining media and/or vehicles. Another strategy deals with how many different vehicles or media are optimum in achieving a media goal. The nature of the goal is a consideration in answering this question. However, if the goal is building reach (perhaps a reach of about 70 percent of a target market), then the media and dayparts or vehicles should be selected with consideration for the diversified audiences they reach. There are many ways to achieve the desired 70 percent reach, both within an individual medium and across media. For example, the use of multiple media may mean that there is less duplication in the media mix, which is one way to build reach.

The use of multiple media is also used by planners to build concentrated reach of a demographically defined target market. Each medium will bring new audience members to a plan. But, as each additional vehicle is added to a list, more weight goes into building frequency than reach because the latest added medium target audiences have already been reached by those selected first.

Conversely, if the media goal is to build frequency, then it may be correct to use as few vehicles as are reasonable. The more weight added to vehicles already in use, the more duplication (or frequency) will occur. The more TV comedy programs that are bought, the more frequency will likely occur. On the other hand, the more differences in program types one buys, the more likely it is that broader reach will occur.

One of the strange things about the inverse relationship of reach to frequency is that it is possible to buy high frequency and have reaches that are so small as to be of questionable value. A media mix that produces an average frequency of 20 may only have a very small reach, such as 12 percent. The value of high frequency may be lost on such a small market reach size. This is something a planner has to watch carefully in planning.

Share-of-voice. One of the questions raised in planning a competitive media strategy is the goal of having a higher share-of-voice than key competitors. If, as explained in Chapter 7, the share-of-voice is made on a comparison of dollars spent, then it has very little meaning because some competitors who are spending about the same amount of money for advertising may be receiving more or less communication for the same amount of dollars. The brand that receives the most communication power should have the best advantage. Communication power consists of target rating points (target GRPs). Those with more TGRPs should have an advantage. But products that are inherently better than competitor's, or meet more consumer wants and needs, are the ones that can benefit most from heavier share-of-voice. Share-of-voice based on dollars spent is the poorest way to evaluate communication power. So the answer to using this kind of strategy is to identify the brand that has the most communication power, not the one that spends the most money for advertising.

The strategies discussed above are just a sampling of those that arise in a media plan. But they give the reader an idea of the thinking that goes into planning and hopefully show the importance of exploring alternative strategies.

How I Might Plan A Cross-Media Strategy—By Louis Schultz*

The following are recommendations of how a cross-media strategy would be planned for an artifical sweetner using Time-Warner facilities. The recommendations are made by Louis Schultz, executive vice president and director of media services at Lintas, USA. The material comes from an interview by John McManus, of Mediaweek.

"Here's how it would work, If I had an artificial sweetener, it would make a lot of sense to start with a magazine, *Cooking Light*. Why wouldn't I start by running four spreads in *Cooking Light?* Now I also want to create, with your editors, a book on cooking light that's sponsored by my artificial sweetner.

I will use that as a premium giveaway—for a purchase—and I will mail that as a fulfillment. By the way, if you happen to have a production house, you will write it and produce it, because you can print all this stuff [inside your company]. While we're at it, since my consumers are interested in health, why don't I create a 30-second vignette, "How to cook better, sponsored by *Cooking Light*," and the artificial sweetener will be the other 30-second partner.

Now I've got the vignette; where do I run it?

Why don't I go to your cable properties and I'll buy your local cable interconnects, or I'll buy cable television of which you'll get a part. Or, why don't I run a promotion or a sweepstakes on HBO and Cinemax, that I will partner up with somebody like an automotive company with a car.

We'll have a *Cooking Light* take-care-of-yourself sweepstakes and promotion tied in with HBO to bring in more subscribers. And you get an opportunity to win a week or two at a spa, cars, and such.

Why don't I also create an on-pack premium—knowing these people who are very active—with videotapes that I will offer from the Warner stable. They can write for them and can make it a self-liquidating item at a discount.

Why don't I take the vignette series I have and tie it in with Warner Brothers releases, and run this commercial on the front of that and create that whole program?

And continue on: You can build a whole marketing program within an organization like Warner. And by the by, when I do my vignette series, I'll have it produced by Sunset Fliks, or Warner. I will look at their syndication properties, like *Jenny Jones.* Maybe I can cut a deal with them as part of it. Maybe I'll have my commercial shot at their production facilities rather than using somebody else's, all of which can be discounted. All of which is additional money that the parent group would not have gotten."

---

*McManus, John, "Lou's Laws of Multimedia," in *Mediaweek*, July 8, 1991, p.12–14.

QUESTIONS FOR DISCUSSION

1. Will a media strategy that gains an advantage over competitors' brands always be successful?
2. Can an advertiser sell his seasonal brand out of season?
3. Why should planners consider alternative media strategies as an important part of contemporary media planning practices?
4. Explain the value of knowing how to sell a brand to *one customer* before selling to mass target audiences in media planning?
5. Where in a media plan is it necessary to provide as rationale for the decisions recommended?
6. Should media planners try to follow the budget limitations determined by the client before starting to plan?
7. What is the main value of using "new or non-traditional" media in a plan?
8. Why would a media planner generally not want to advertise in every one of the 52 weeks in a year?
9. What are the major strengths of cross-media planning?
10. What are the dangers of adding public relations, sales promotion, and direct marketing to advertising plans in order to accomplish objectives?

SELECTED READINGS

Lubetkin, Beth, *Additional Major Findings from the "How Advertising Works Study,"* Information Resources, Inc., Marketplace Advertising Research Workshop, New York, Nov. 6–7, 1991.

"The 1989 Creative Media Awards," *Adweek,* November 20, 1989.

Priemer, August B., "New Alternatives to Effective Frequency in Media Planning," *Journal of Media Planning,* Evanston, Illinois, Fall 1986, 28.

12

Evaluating and Selecting Media Vehicles

After selecting media classes, the media planner is ready to select media vehicles within classes. To some extent, previous strategy decisions will spell out criteria for this selection. These criteria grow out of an evaluation of relative media values. The discussion in this chapter covers the most important considerations.

Determining Media Values

An elementary principle for selecting media stated in Chapter 1 was to select those vehicles that reach a large number of targets at a cost-efficient price. Although this principle seems to suggest that this is all there is to the selection process, nothing could be further from the truth. A more advanced principle is to determine the full extent of each vehicle's value in terms of the desired criteria *and then* select from among those that best meet the criteria. Some of these criteria may be measured quantitatively and the numerical values of various criteria can be combined into a single number. Others are qualitative, and it is more difficult to assign numerical weights to these. But both should be considered in the selection process. Table 12–1 lists the most important objective and subjective criteria usually considered in magazine selection.

Target Reach and Cost Efficiency

The most important criterion in determining media values is a combination of two principles: (a) finding vehicles that reach a large number of targets, and (b) selecting from among these only those with the lowest cost per thou-

TABLE 12-1. Criteria for Determining Media Values

Primary objective criteria
- a. Delivery of demographic targets
- b. Cost efficiency of delivered targets
- c. Delivery of product-class user targets
- d. Delivery of strategic targets
- e. Delivery of psychographic targets

Secondary objective criteria
- a. Primary vs. pass-along readers
- b. Editorial features/content related to brand's image
- c. Special editions/issues/sections in print
- d. Media imperatives
- e. Color reproduction
- f. Circulation trends in print vehicles
- g. Geographic flexibility
- h. Production flexibility
- i. Positioning opportunities within print vehicles

Subjective (or qualitative) criteria
- a. Writing tone
- b. Reader respect
- c. Leadership in media class
- d. Believability

sand. The logic of using these two principles in combination should be obvious. Advertising and marketing today are directed to certain demographic targets. Assuming that these targets can be identified precisely, it follows that media vehicles should be selected to reach the largest number of targets efficiently.

It should be noted, however, that the decisions to select or reject alternative vehicles do not always rest *only* on finding vehicles that reach large numbers of targets. Another variable in the decision process occurs when a given media strategy calls for high frequency. When frequency is needed, vehicles with less reach (and more duplication) may be preferred. Because reach and frequency levels are inversely related, the selection process may result in sacrificing some reach for more frequency. However, most planners have minimum levels of reach below which they will not go even to attain high frequency. For example, reach may not be allowed to go below 50 percent of a target base, such as women aged 18–34.

Some media planners tend to use the two criteria of high reach and low cost almost exclusively to define media values. Others, however, see that the selection process requires much more input on what constitutes value. Shown in Table 12–2 are four print vehicles compared on the basis of target delivery and cost per thousand. In the table it is obvious that the vehicle that delivers the largest number of prospects (targets) also has the lowest cost per thousand. Such is not always the situation, however. Note that the term *coverage* as used in this context is sometimes called *selectivity percentage*. Both terms mean essentially the same thing, but one company may prefer to use one term rather than the other.

TABLE 12–2. Comparison of Four Print Vehicles on Targets Delivered and Cost per Thousand

Vehicle	Cost per Insertion	Targets Delivered Men 18–49 (thousands)	Selectivity or Coverage (%)	Cost per Thousand
A	$54,849	13,992	31.8	$ 3.92
B	25,641	2,772	6.3	9.25
C	10,696	484	1.1	22.10
D	15,382	3,344	7.6	4.60

If computer capability is available, it is possible to cross tabulate demographic segments to make composite analyses. For example, a computer makes it possible to find the best media vehicles to deliver women, aged 18–49, with over $25,000 annual income, who live in households of five or more persons.

Occasionally, a planner will find that the vehicles that deliver demographic targets most efficiently do not deliver the most users efficiently. When that situation occurs, the planner will have to decide whether demographic targets or users are the more valuable criterion. The planner may also compromise and select vehicles that deliver both kinds of targets.

Strategic Impressions

In evaluating alternative media vehicles, it may be necessary to reach different targets in certain proportions. In other words, a planner evaluating media vehicles in terms of ability to deliver certain kinds of targets does not want these targets delivered in a capricious pattern. If, for example, the planner felt that most advertising messages ought to go to women aged 18–49 and a much smaller number ought to go to men aged 18–49, then the desired proportions for each should be determined and appropriate vehicles selected to deliver these proportions. If the planner wants 60 percent women and 40 percent men, it would not be logically sound to have the delivery total reversed.

To decide on the relative proportions, a planner studies product usage and demographic data, then uses judgment to arrive at the desired proportions. If women are the primary decision makers in the purchase of a product, then they should be allotted a larger percentage than men.

In selecting media, then, the planner tries to select vehicles whose audiences are divided in roughly the same proportions as the desired target audience. Because media vehicles may not deliver audience segments in precisely the same percentages that the planner feels desirable, the division of gross impressions may not be precise, but approximate. For example, if the planner decides that women aged 35–49 should constitute 70 percent of targets delivered and women aged 18–34, 30 percent, then either a 65 percent/35 percent split or a 75 percent/25 percent split might be acceptable.

TABLE 12-3.   Impressions Delivered by a Simulated Schedule

	Gross Impressions Delivered by Each Vehicle*		
	Men	Women	Total
Magazine A	1,500	15,000	16,500
Magazine B	1,500	14,000	15,500
Network TV Program C	5,540	7,000	12,540
Network TV Program D	4,000	9,000	13,000
Total Gross Impressions	12,540	45,000	57,540
Percent Total Impressions	21.8	78.2	100

*Goal: 75% women, 25% men.

Table 12-3 shows strategic impressions from a media plan that delivers targets close to the proportions of 75 percent women and 25 percent men, aged 18–49. In studying Table 12-3, one should remember that the desired division of impressions was 75 percent/25 percent. But because of the difficulty of finding media vehicles with precisely the desired proportions, those vehicles that come close are usually accepted as satisfactory, as long as the impression proportions are not equal, or reversed.

The planner should also keep in mind that the same type of vehicle need not be used consistently in order to deliver the desired division of impressions. In Table 12-3, for example, all four media vehicles provide audiences that are concentrated among women (women account for the majority of adult delivery for each vehicle). A combination of male-oriented vehicles and female-oriented vehicles, combined possibly with dual audience vehicles, could also produce a net effect that divides total impressions according to objectives.

Other Media Values

Secondary Audiences

Secondary (or pass-along) audiences also must be considered in evaluating media vehicles. Because the primary audiences have a regular opportunity to see a given magazine and secondary audiences do not, then primary audiences should be more valuable to the media planner. *A Study of Printed Advertising Rating Methods* (PARM), conducted by the Advertising Research Foundation and Alfred Politz, Inc., found that primary readers were more valuable than secondary readers—because they had a better opportunity to see the magazine, and because they paid more attention to advertisements than did secondary readers. Furthermore, the PARM study showed that, for the Gallup-Robinson (Aided Recall) Measuring Technique, fewer of the out-of-home pass-along readers were able to recall ads than other secondary readers. Table 12-4 shows some of the findings that support the conclusion that primary readers are more valuable than secondary readers. Although there were differences between Starch and Gallup-Robinson, each

TABLE 12–4. Recall of Ads Using Starch and Gallup-Robinson

Type of Audience	Recall Using Starch (%)	Recall Using Gallup-Robinson (%)
Primary	20.0	3.2
Out-of-home pass-along	17.9	2.5

Source: Advertising Research Foundation and Alfred Politz Research, Inc., *A Study of Printed Advertising Rating Methods*, Vol. III, N.Y., 1956.

method found less recall among pass-along audiences than primary audiences. Audits and Surveys Research Company also conducted a study for *Look* magazine and found the differences between primary and secondary audience recall as shown in Table 12–5. Here again, fewer secondary readers were able to recall ads than were primary readers.

These research studies provide some clues about the value of secondary, pass-along audiences. If the secondary audiences are deemed less valuable, then it seems reasonable to discount them in some way. But few media planners would ignore them entirely.

Dr. Seymour Marshak, formerly manager of advertising and distribution research of the Ford Motor Company, felt that simply discounting the secondary audience was not correct.[1] Instead it would be better to determine the value of a secondary reader on the basis of how important that individual was in the target audience and then determine what opportunities he or she had to see a given advertisement in a given medium. For example, secondary readers may be even more important than primary readers when they receive only one or two exposure opportunities compared to primary readers who might receive over twenty opportunities. This assumes that high frequencies (or many exposure opportunities) are not automatically good media strategy. Each marketing/media situation may be different. Foremost in this kind of evaluation is the assumption that secondary readers are the most important target audiences and have to be reached if the advertising message is to have the proper effect.

One method that could be used for discounting the pass-along secondary audience is simply to cut their numbers in half. If Medium A has a total audience of 37 million of which 75 percent is primary and 25 percent is secondary (out-of-home) readers, then the latter is discounted 50 percent.

Table 12–6 shows an example that first treats the secondary audience at full value and then at a 50 percent discounted value. The example is based on the total audience. Typically, media planners discount only the demographic group that comprises the target audience, such as men aged 18–34, or women who graduated from high school, for example.

Marshak cited examples of two different ways to determine the value of a pass-along reader:

1. Marshak, Seymour, "Forum Question: Generally Speaking, What Value Do You Place on the Secondary or Pass-along Reader?" *Media/Scope*, February 1970, p. 26.

TABLE 12-5. Percent of Respondents Who Were Able to Recall Advertisements

Type of Audience	Verified Recall Average (%)
Subscribers (primary)	27.4
Nonsubscribers (secondary)	17.8

Source: Roth, Paul, "Why We Discount Out-of-Homes by 50%," *Media/Scope*, March 1967, p. 64.

1. The product is advertised in only one medium. The secondary reader has a regular source for obtaining the medium and he is a member of the target group. His value should be equal to the value of a primary reader.
2. The product . . . is advertised in many small circulation magazines (e.g., camping and fishing magazines plus others). The secondary reader, by chance, sees the ad for a product in medium Z while waiting in a pizza parlor. The reader has already seen, or had the opportunity to see, the ad in 20 other media. The value of this 21st exposure within a short time period may be very low.[2]

Marshak, therefore, felt that the value of the secondary audience depends on a number of things: (a) whether it is possible to reach the target audience entirely through primary readers; (b) the relative importance of targets where, perhaps, one demographic group may be as much as three times as important as some other demographic target; and (c) whether the planner needs some other measurement on which to base a decision.

In conclusion then, there seems to be good evidence for not using secondary audience data at full value. The method of discounting the secondary audience should be based on logic and research evidence rather than on subjective judgment alone.

Editorial Environment

It is conceivable that vehicles that reach targets efficiently may not be well-suited to an advertiser's messages because the editorial environments of the vehicles under consideration are incompatible with the ad message. This concept is related to the need for psychographic data to fit demographic data discussed earlier. Two college graduates may be the same age and in the same income class, but lead radically different lives. Similarly, two media

TABLE 12-6. Two Bases for Analyzing the Audiences of Magazine A

Full Value Basis	Number (millions)	Out-of-Home Audience Discounted 50% Basis	Number (millions)
Primary audience	27.75	Primary audience	27.75
Out-of-home audience	9.25	Out-of-home audience	4.63
Total audience	37.00	Total audience	32.38

---

2. Ibid.

TABLE 12–7. Index of Editorial Environments for Salad Dressings

Magazine	Four-Color Food Pages	Food Photo-graphs	Number of Recipes	Editorial Lines Dealing with Salads	Average of Four Scores
Better Homes & Gardens	127	255	107	135	156
Good Housekeeping	138	56	89	192	119
Woman's Day	84	29	212	108	108
Sunset	12	165	102	121	100
Family Circle	136	83	105	59	96
Ladies Home Journal	115	85	81	51	83
McCall's	104	70	57	53	71
American Home	86	56	48	81	68

Source: Kaatz, Ronald B., *Dr. (un)Strangeperson, or, How I Learned to Stop Worrying (about Some Numbers) and Love My Magazine Plans!* Paper presented to the American Academy of Advertising Convention, April 1975, Knoxville, Tennessee.

vehicles can reach the same demographic targets with about the same cost efficiency, but each may feature editorial material of interest to different kinds of readers. This difference may be important in determining a media vehicle's advertising value.

An example might occur when an advertiser for salad dressings is considering eight potential vehicles, each of which may reach the demographic targets fairly well. But the editorial environments may differ widely, as Table 12–7 shows. The editorial environment criteria in the table are: number of food pages printed in four colors, number of food photographs, number of recipes, and number of editorial lines dealing with salads. These criteria were arbitrarily selected by the planner, so others could be substituted or added to provide a composite evaluation of the media alternatives. If this evaluation is combined with criteria of target reach and cost efficiency, a better approach to evaluating media may be found. Based on the criteria shown, the data show that *Better Homes & Gardens* was found to be the best vehicle.

The only problem with this kind of evaluation is that the planner must have someone available to do the research, because it is not always readily available for every product class. Such research can be very expensive and time-consuming to collect. Furthermore, the research would have to be repeated year after year to determine whether or not any changes in editorial policies were taking place.

Special Opportunities in Magazines

Media planners who want to reach special or limited markets may find that magazines can be adapted to meet their needs. This is because special demographic or geographic editions have been devised by some media for just that purpose. Table 12–8 lists some of the demographic breaks that are available in major consumer and business magazines.

In addition to offering special demographic and geographic breakouts,

TABLE 12–8.   Some Demographic Editions of Magazines

Publication	Name of Edition	Target
Better Homes & Gardens	Super Spot	Upper income homes
Newsweek	Women	Women
Time	Campus	Students and educators
Time	B	Business executives
Time	Top Management	Top management
Sports Illustrated	Homeowners	Homeowners
U.S. News & World Report	Blue Chip	Top management
Prevention	Over 55	Adults 55 +
Reader's Digest	Power Plus	Households $50,000 +

most of the larger circulation magazines offer two-way (and in some cases even four-way) copy splits. *Reader's Digest*, for example, can distribute special copy to one out of every four subscribers across the nation through the use of zip coding and block coding. This trend toward increased flexibility and specialization is expected to continue.

Media Imperatives

A planner considering media vehicle alternatives must be aware that although some vehicles reach target audiences very well, the data on reach can sometimes hide important facts. For example, the planner may find that television best reaches a given target audience, but those reached may be light television viewers and heavy magazine readers. In other words, reach figures do not indicate the degree of exposure to a given medium. *Media imperatives* is a form of research that provides information on the degree of exposure to television and magazines. It is supplied by SMRB.

   Television imperatives show that some targets are heavy television viewers and light magazine readers, while *magazine imperatives* show that some persons are heavy magazine readers and light television viewers. In addition, media imperatives can also show dual audiences (or heavily exposed individuals in both media, and lightly exposed individuals in both media).

   So media imperatives are a means of comparing magazines and television based on the degree of exposure to each medium. It also shows how much of various product categories are purchased by the four groups measured. Table 12–9 provides a general analysis of heavy versus light exposure to magazines and television on the basis of the media imperative's data.

   A study of media imperatives, then, may motivate a planner to shift spending into or away from either television or magazines. The data do not answer all questions, but add another quantitative dimension to help solve the selection problem, as well as the problem of allocating money.

Position Alternatives

Some print vehicles offer advertisers selected positions, such as front-of-book or next to editorial material, which, if accepted, may turn out to be

TABLE 12–9. General Findings of Media Imperatives

Group	Population (%)	Magazine Reading (%)	Television Viewing (%)
Heavy Mag/Light TV	33	47	16
Heavy TV/Light Mag	39	20	57
Dual (Heavy TV/Heavy Mag)	15	29	23
Neither (Light TV/Light Mag)	13	4	4
Total	100	100	100

Source: Ogilvy & Mather.

advantageous in reaching the targets with more impact. Sometimes premium rates are charged for position, but other times, the cost may be relatively low. So the planner may consider the availability of favored positions as a factor in weighing one vehicle against another. Those that offer selected positions may be a better buy than those that do not.

Advertising Clutter and Product Protection

In both television and print media, it is possible to measure the amount of clutter that occurs. Presumably, the medium that reaches the maximum number of targets at the best cost efficiency, and at the same time is the least cluttered, would be the most desirable. There are, however, exceptions to this assumption. For example, in certain magazine classes, such as fashion and shelter, readers look for many ads and they buy the magazine to shop through advertising. But, if all competitors are in the same magazine, and there are also many other ads in the magazine, it may be questionable whether that vehicle is the most desirable for a specific advertiser. Brands with a clear-cut competitive advantage over other brands should prosper when placed in close proximity to competitors. Other brands, perceived as less desirable, may suffer from such competition. Generally, clutter is undesirable and product protection is something to be sought. This means keeping competitive ads within the vehicle at a reasonable distance from the advertised brand.

In evaluating the effect of clutter in a print medium, one should consider the Starch studies that show that the readership of the average advertisement in a magazine declines as the number of ads in the vehicle increases.

In television and radio, product protection, although desirable, is no longer affordable for most advertisers.

Circulation Trends

An objective measurement of a medium's value is the trend of circulation over a period of at least a year or two. Because advertising is sometimes planned more than a year ahead of time, media planners might want to study the latest Audit Bureau of Circulation (ABC) circulation figures for the last twelve to twenty-four months to see what has been happening. If a magazine under consideration has shown a decline, it may be dropped from the list. On the other hand, magazines with increasing circulation trends may be considered valuable.

New Product Editorial Features

Some magazines are known for their editorial features on new products. It is assumed, therefore, that readers know this and when they want to learn about the existence of new products they turn to such a magazine in preference to another magazine.

Advertising Copy Checking

Some media have a reputation for examining the veracity of all advertising copy and claims and annually reject many dollars of advertising. They publicize this fact regularly. The assumption here is that readers, knowing of this practice, will prefer to read ads in such a vehicle in preference to others that do not publicize their censorship efforts. *Good Housekeeping*, many newspapers, and network television organizations are among those that check copy carefully.

Response to Coupons, Information, or Recipes

Measurements of the number of audience members who send in coupons or ask for information or recipes may provide a planner with the type of qualitative data that would allow him or her to differentiate one magazine from another. This is not public information, however, and may be difficult, if not impossible, for all magazines to obtain. In situations where an advertiser runs the same ad in more than one magazine, it is sometimes possible to learn which magazine pulled best.

Available Discounts

Sometimes the value of a medium is directly affected by the nature of the discounts that it offers. If a number of ads are planned for a calendar year in several vehicles that are otherwise about equal, that vehicle offering a substantial discount may represent the best value of all. However, it would seem obvious that discounts rank relatively low on the scale of criteria. Target reach and target cost efficiency, for example, are more important than discounts. Likewise, the vehicle with the larger number of product users is usually more important than the vehicle with a large discount potential.

Flexibility

Two kinds of flexibility can affect media value. One is the degree to which a medium can be used to reach geographically superior markets precisely, while at the same time avoiding relatively weak markets. Generally, local media such as newspapers, spot radio, spot television, and outdoor are considered flexible media in the geographic sense. Magazines have some flexibility with their regional and local market issues. But often there may not be a local edition for a market that the planner deems necessary, or a regional edition that covers an advertiser's sales divisions with much precision. A media vehicle that has the potential for geographical flexibility may be more valuable than one that is not flexible.

A second kind of flexibility concerns the ability of the medium to make quick changes in copy, that is, production flexibility. There could be many reasons why an advertiser might need to change an advertising message quickly. In some media, this is a relatively easy job; in others, it is not. Black and white ads in print media can usually be changed quite easily and quickly in many vehicles. When a print ad is to be run in four colors, however, it becomes more difficult to make changes because it may be necessary to re-make four-color printing cylinders. Generally, print media printed by offset are easier to change than those printed by gravure. Gravure-printed media take a long time to change, especially if the printing cylinders have already been prepared and are ready for printing. In broadcast, it is easier to change live or videotaped commercials than filmed commercials. So production flexibility may be a consideration in determining media value if changes in the advertising message are contemplated.

Color Quality

In print media, color quality can be important in determining media values. The problem of color quality is twofold. First, there is the problem of simply achieving the color quality of the original artwork planned for an advertisement. Some publications may find it difficult to attain this quality because of the kinds of ink and paper they use. A second problem concerns the maintenance of consistent color quality during the entire press run. Printing presses running at high speeds sometimes wear out printing plates because of the friction of metal on paper; certain colors will print heavier or lighter than required. The planner should know the printing abilities of the publishing organization. Some vehicles have a distinct production control advantage over others.

The Qualitative Values of Media

As stated earlier, media selection is based mostly on the ability of specific media vehicles to reach precise target audiences with high cost efficiency and little waste. Other considerations in planning include the total cost of the medium plus the reach and frequency to be generated. Before a final decision for or against any medium is made, however, the planner may want to consider the qualitative values of each medium and how important these values are for the plan.

What Is a Qualitative Value?

A *qualitative value* is some characteristic of a medium that enhances the chances that an advertising message carried within it will be effective. It is based on the assumption that media are not simply passive carriers of advertisements; they are active carriers. A media vehicle is an environment with a personality of its own which may rub off on its advertisements and make them more effective in disseminating their messages. Social Research, Inc., defined this environment as follows:

> Think of a magazine as similar to a geographic location, a neighborhood, or a section of town. There are certain meanings that are generally associated with the location, and these meanings usually are known and taken for granted by most people living in the community. When an advertiser buys a lot in that location, it automatically buys whatever connotations the neighborhood carries. The building erected on this site (or the ad placed in this magazine) is responded to in terms of its own merits. But the edifice is also thought of in connection with its location, and this will either add to or detract from the impression the building makes.[3]

A medium's environment, therefore, may represent a qualitative value that could affect each advertisement carried within it. William Weilbacher, former vice president of Dancer-Fitzgerald-Sample, defined a qualitative value more specifically, as follows:

> Qualitative media value is the total increment to advertising message effect contributed by the medium or media vehicle. This qualitative medium value includes such individual contributors . . . as the special characteristics of the audience attracted to the medium or vehicle, and whatever personality characteristics are attributed to it by its audience members.

> Implicit in this usage of the term qualitative value is the notion, that, beyond individual and definable sources . . . such as demographic and attitudinal characteristics, the medium may also con-

---

3. Social Research, Inc., *Advertising Impact and Business Magazines*, Chicago, 1959, p. ii.

tribute completely undefined, even unanticipated, values to the advertising process.[4]

Weilbacher warned, however, that his concept of a qualitative value did not include such general media characteristics as the image and prestige of each medium because these, although easily measured, did not necessarily add to advertising effectiveness. He preferred to deal with qualitative values that specifically affect individual advertisements.

Weilbacher's warning, however, focuses attention on the kinds of problems planners face in using the concept of qualitative values in media planning. Because it is so easy to measure the image of a magazine, it is often done. One way to measure the image is to compile a list of adjectives that could describe a magazine and ask respondents in a study which best represents the medium being studied. Such adjectives might include interesting, learned, dynamic, timely, modern, and alert.

The problem with studies of magazine images is: What does one do with the results? Because one magazine has a different and presumably better image than another magazine, does this have anything to do with advertising effectiveness? There is very little evidence to suggest such a relationship. Therefore image studies, though a form of determining a qualitative value, have little importance in media planning.

Measuring Qualitative Values

The kind of research needed to prove that media have qualitative values is that which tests the effectiveness of the same advertisement in two or more media. If all variables are held constant, then differences in reactions to the same advertisements may be due to qualitative values.

Alfred Politz studied responses by women to twelve advertisements appearing in *McCall's* against responses to the same twelve advertisements placed in *Life* and *Look* magazines. In order to isolate the qualitative media effects of each vehicle, he first solicited responses from his sample with no exposure to the ads to determine what respondents knew about the brands without having seen the ads.

Then he exposed the ads to the respondents in all three magazines, after which he measured responses again. Any differences between no exposure and one exposure were attributed to the qualitative differences of the medium as they affected readership of ads within them.[5] Shown in Table 12–10 are some of Politz's findings. Not only were there differences in responses with no exposure between *McCall's* and *Life/Look*, but there were greater

4. Weilbacher, W. M., "The Qualitative Value of Advertising Media," *Journal of Advertising Research*, December 1960, p. 14.

5. Politz, Alfred and *McCall's*, "A Measurement of Advertising Effectiveness," November 1962, p. 11.

TABLE 12–10.   Some Findings from the Politz Study

Respondents who:	McCall's (%)	Life/Look (%)
1. Were familiar with the brand		
a. With no exposure	16.3	15.0
b. With one exposure	20.6	18.2
2. Believed claims found in ads		
a. With no exposure	17.0	16.5
b. With one exposure	19.4	17.8
3. Considered advertised brand to be one of the "very highest quality"		
a. With no exposure	17.6	17.8
b. With one exposure	21.4	18.8
4. Were interested in buying the brand		
a. With no exposure	10.3	10.1
b. With one exposure	13.2	11.6

Source: Politz, Alfred, and *McCall's*, "A Measurement of Advertising Effectiveness," November 1962, p. 11.

differences after one exposure between the two magazine measurements. Presumably these differences were the effect of the magazine.

Using Qualitative Values

Notwithstanding Politz's and others' research on qualitative values, there is still little consensus about the matter. The tendency in most companies is to rely very little on such evidence of qualitative values in media planning. When they do use such values, they are apt to prepare the following kind of statement for their plans: "We feel that Medium A reflects greater authority and prestige than other media and therefore recommend that we purchase X number of ads in it."

Other terms that are used in the same manner are impact, mood, believability, atmosphere, excitement, and leadership. In addition, print media are sometimes judged on the following qualitative values:

> **Reputation of media for attracting ads of only the highest quality products.** It is assumed, therefore, that readers knowing this fact will be more favorably inclined toward products and brands advertised in these media than they would for products and brands advertised in other media.
>
> **Reading days.** How many days, totally, are alternative magazines read? If a magazine is opened at any time on a given day, this constitutes a reading day. If, for example, there is evidence that Magazine A is read more total days than Magazines B, C, D, and E (all under consideration) then the planner has one more qualitative reason to select A. More reading days represent more opportunities to see ads.
>
> **Reading time.** In a similar manner, it is possible to measure the total or average number of hours spent reading magazines. These mea-

surements may indicate that the magazine with the largest number of reading hours is more attractive than others. It may be assumed that audience members have more opportunities to see ads if they spend more time reading.

Page openings. It is possible to measure the number of pages opened in alternative magazines. A technique in which a tiny spot of glue is applied to pages containing ads may be used. Respondents may be given specially glued magazines on a given day. On the next day (or two) the interviewer may return and pick up the special copies. The number of pages pulled open are then counted. Another variation of page-opening measurements is simply to count page traffic on all ad pages. Using a "recognition measuring technique" researchers count the number of pages where any ads on the page were noted by audience members who comprise a sample. Page traffic data is a measure of the net potential audience size of a magazine and may play a role in the final selection decision.

The above list is by no means complete, but it does show how media planners might use the qualitative values of various media in planning.

Probably the most misused of all media qualitative value terms is that of "impact." Print media executives often claim their magazine has more impact than other magazines. If they mean that an ad in their magazine will sell more of the product than an ad in any other magazine, this cannot be proved and is, therefore, conjecture on the part of the executives. It is generally not possible to determine the effect of a media vehicle and an advertisement on sales.

Conceivably, there could be a careful testing program conducted for one advertiser, with strict controls, to prove that more people recalled a given ad in one magazine than in any other. But recall and sales are quite different. How can one prove that it wasn't the price, the packaging, the distribution, or the sales promotion that sold the product? Some vehicles are better than others, but not on the basis of impact, which is too vague a concept to be used in media planning. Only when a clear-cut cause-and-effect relationship can be established for the brand and the vehicle on sale can the concept of impact be used.

Qualitative rationales for selecting media have a place in planning procedures. But there are some reasonable guidelines that ought to be kept in mind if they are used:

1. Qualitative, or subjective, rationales should never be a total replacement for quantitative substantiation.
2. Qualitative consideration should be used *after* quantitative analysis has been made and thereby modify numerical relationships.
3. If possible, more than one person should contribute to making the subjective analysis in order to reduce the possibility of individual bias.

4. Media sponsored research concerning qualitative values such as high impact, "liked most," and so forth, should be considered suspect. Much of this kind of research tends to be highly promotional rather than objective. It is very difficult to transfer the findings from one medium to another.

In conclusion then, qualitative values of media do exist, but they can't be used as the main criteria in media planning. They are simply not objective enough to be used alone for decision making. Perhaps ways will be found to prove that one medium indeed has more impact than others, but at present it cannot be proved. Experts can only agree that media are not passive carriers of ads. They do have qualitative values, and some can be used for planning purposes.

Ad Positions within Media

Assuming that media vehicles have been selected, the budget allocated, and a schedule worked out, in theory, media planning could end at this point.

In practice, however, there are still questions that are often asked by planners themselves and others interested in media. Is there nothing else that can be done to help in the advertising communication process? Are reach, frequency, and cost efficiency all there is? The problem is to find ways for the media planner to go beyond delivery and not only get vehicles exposed, but get ads within those vehicles exposed, and finally, get the ads read.

To a great extent, this last responsibility belongs to the creative people: planners, writers, and art directors who have special talents for getting advertising communication "through" to the reader. The copy people, for example, can write scintillating headlines and meaningful words. The art director can devise fascinating layouts. The creative people can ask for four-color ads, bleed pages, reverse printing, gatefold-size ads, two-page spreads; they can print ads on unusual stock such as acetate or aluminum foil; they can use unusual inks such as day-glo or perfumed inks. These are but a few of the many options open to the creative personnel in getting ads noticed and read.

What, then, can media planners do to help the situation? They can ask for certain positions within media that are felt to be better than other positions. This, however, leaves them open to questions about positioning research and strategy.

Problems of Positioning Research

There are a number of media positions that appear to be better than others. For example, the fourth cover of a magazine is generally conceded to be the best place in a magazine for an ad. In fact, research confirms that the fourth cover is one of the best positions. But many media experts question the research. Nonetheless, there is some logic, even without research, to suggest that a fourth cover position is a valuable position. There is not much agreement among experts about other media position. The research tends to be weak, and therefore inconclusive.

Perhaps the foremost problem of position research is that it is difficult to separate measurements of position from copy effects. Most research techniques that are used to establish the effects of position are really a mixture of copy and position. In some research studies, another dimension, that of size, is added. Then, too, averaging data for position effects that contain widely varying degrees of copy effectiveness may not truly represent the effects of position. Averaging tends to be unduly affected by extreme copy-effect scores. Some media experts question whether there is any copy measuring device that is totally valid. But assuming that most are valid, there is still no way, through present-day measurements, to know the effect of position alone.

A solution would be to design experiments involving ad copy that is held constant with the only variable being position. Because the same ads would be measured in different positions in different media vehicles, the effects of position alone could be found. However, there still is dissatisfaction with much research devised to measure position because it is not carefully controlled to eliminate bias. Research designs are often poor or nonexistent. Samples are often nonrandom and selected haphazardly. Questionnaire design and interviewing controls are not always the best. As a result, much position research is suspect.

Some Position Effects

What follows is a brief summary of position effects that some media planners accept. The reader is cautioned about accepting them as valid evidence. They are presented to show a sample of the kinds of positions that *may* affect the communication power of advertisements placed in vehicles.

Position in Magazines. (a) Fourth cover positions are usually considered better than any inside positions if Starch Adnorm data are used as a guide; (b) second cover and page one positions are about equal and are the next best to fourth cover positions; (c) front of the magazine positions (from page 3 to about page 20) are the next best positions; (d) righthand pages are somewhat better than lefthand pages, with some exceptions. Keep in mind that these are generalities based on the research findings across many different magazines. Specific magazines, which might have uncommon editorial layouts, might produce different readership patterns.

Position in Newspapers. (a) Ads near the front are considered better than those near the back, but the differences are small; (b) there is no significant difference between righthand and lefthand pages; (c) inside a newspaper section is better than the last page of the section; (d) there is little difference between ads above or below the fold; (e) editorial environment affects the readership of ads (ads for male products prove better on sports pages and ads for female products do better on women's pages); (f) preprint stuffers, while they cost about 4.6 times as much as ROP color, do about 3.8 times better in responses.[6]

Position in Television. (a) Attention to programs is greatest during late fringe and poorest in early fringe times; (b) mysteries, spy adventure programs, and movies do a little better than varieties and western programs in recall of messages; (c) daytime is about 50 percent to 80 percent as good as nighttime recall; (d) a thirty-second commercial has about 60 percent to 75 percent the recall value of a sixty-second commercial, and a fifteen-second commercial has about the same relative recall value as a thirty-second commercial; (e) high-rated programs have higher attention levels than low-rated programs; (f) in-program commercials do better in recall than between-program commercials. According to SMRB's *Television Attentiveness and Special Events Study,* attention levels are greatest during late fringe and prime time, and poorest during early morning.

Cost Considerations

A major consideration in deciding whether to use a special position in a vehicle is the premium cost. Some positions may not be worth the extra cost. Even if it seems to be worth the cost, it may be difficult to support a decision one way or the other because the research is questionable.

QUESTIONS FOR DISCUSSION

1. How important is editorial quality in media planning?
2. What are strategic impressions and how are they used in media planning?
3. Why do some media planners believe that the primary audience is more important than the secondary audience of print vehicles?
4. Explain how product protection is given to ads in a print vehicle. In a broadcast vehicle.
5. What kinds of marketing situations would require a media plan to have good geographic flexibility?
6. What is the value of having special demographic editions of print vehicles?
7. If a vehicle charges more for a special position, is it worth the extra cost? Discuss.
8. Suppose salespeople for a given publication point out that their vehicle has a better image than competitors. Is this fact alone enough to make a difference in the decision to buy or not buy that vehicle?

---

6. Jain, Charman L., "Newspaper Advertising: Preprint vs. R.O.P.," *Journal of Advertising Research*, August 1973, p. 32.

9. Are there significant differences in the position of ads placed in print media?
10. Why isn't editorial environment used more often as a criterion in making vehicle selections?

SELECTED READINGS

Banks, Allen, "How National Is National Network Television?" *Marketing and Media Decisions*, January 1986, 86–88.

Carter, David, "Newspaper Advertising Readership: Thick vs. Thin Issues," *Journal of Advertising Research*, September 1968, pp. 39–42.

Davis, Laurie, "Sunday Comics: Not to Be Taken Lightly," *Marketing and Media Decisions*, December 1985, 95–96.

Hamilton, Jerry, "15-Second Effectiveness," *Marketing and Media Decisions*, November 1986, 90–93.

Jain, Charman L., "Newspaper Advertising: Preprint vs. R.O.P." *Journal of Advertising Research*, August 1973, 30–32.

Joyce, Timothy, "Target Weighting Gives Boost to Consumer Studies," *Advertising Age*, July 15, 1974, 27.

Martin, Stephen H., "Fear of Radio," *Marketing and Media Decisions*, June 1986, 98–99.

McGuire, Dennis F., "Buying Radio: A Primer," *Marketing and Media Decisions*, January 1986, 92–93.

Media Decisions, "When JWT Picks Magazines, Numbers Aren't Everything," June 1975, 65–69.

Media/Scope, "Forum Question: Generally Speaking, What Value Do You Place on Secondary or Pass-along Readers?" February 1970, 26.

Newspaper Advertising Bureau, Inc., and the *Minneapolis Star and Tribune* (Facts), *The Influence of Position, Size, Color, Creativity on Newspaper Advertising Readership,* 1972.

Papazian, Ed, "Qualitative Comparisons—a Necessary Ingredient in the Planning Process," *Media Decisions*, January 1979, 16–18.

Papazian, Ed, "TV's Qualitative Values," *Marketing and Media Decisions*, December 1985, 89–90.

Rice, Roger, and Severance, Dick, "Who's Winning the War of Imperatives?" *Media Decisions*, December 1978, 64–65.

Weilbacher, William, "The Qualitative Values of Advertising Media," *Journal of Advertising Research*, December 1960, 12–17.

13

Putting a Media Plan Together: The Mechanics

The last four chapters have dealt at length with the important decisions that go into media planning. This chapter explains how to pull these elements together into a document, the *media plan*.

A Graphical Overview of the Media Planning Procedure

Shown in Figure 13–1 is a graphical overview of the entire media plan. Because of the limited amount of space, it does not show every detail of planning. But it covers the most important categories, and what each is about.

The Mechanics of Preparing a Media Plan

Since a media plan is a blueprint for action, it is necessary to organize it so that each set of actions flows smoothly in the readers' minds. There are two main audiences for the plans: the clients (including the account persons) and the media buyers. Most likely the client will be the first person outside the agency to see the plan. The clients will probably pay most attention to determining whether the chosen media do what they are supposed to do in solving the original marketing problem.

The plan should also enable the buyers—who eventually have to implement the strategies—to proceed quickly and accurately. Good organization can help all this by being well written and simply presented. The following discussion covers the more important details that should be considered in the plan's organization.

FIGURE 13–1.   An Overview of the Media Planning Process

Problem	Marketing Solutions		Media Planning Solutions			Implementing the Plan	7. Post-Analysis
A. Marketing problems	1. Marketing Objectives	2. Marketing Strategies	3. Media Objectives	4. Media Strategies	5. Decisions Implementing Strategies (Tactics)	6. Media Buying	
The brand's sales have been eroding because competitors have created superior products. This analysis is a historical perspective (or the situation analysis).	A number of marketing goals for a given brand, presumably, based on best opportunities for sales or solving other marketing problems.	A number of broadly conceived marketing decisions, organized into a unified plan of action aimed at attaining marketing objectives.	A number of media goals, all related in some way to helping attain marketing objectives, or related to marketing strategy.	A number of broadly conceived media decisions, organized into a unified plan of action aimed at attaining media goals.	A number of very specific decisions that implement the media strategy. In many instances, these decisions serve as a basis for media buying.	Actual purchasing decisions involving the selection and use of media.	Did the strategy work? Or, what parts worked or failed? Find reasons for both.
			Examples				
Questions should be raised about why and how the problem arose. Is the brand really inferior? Are there other marketing problems such as poor distribution? Overpricing? Better competitive advertising? Better promotions? A marketing plan will grow out of this investigation.	Goal: increase brand share of market by 5 percent over last year, nationally.	Concentrate on taking customers from competitors by using ads that show ways in which our brand is better than theirs.	Goal: plan media selections so as to deliver at least 80 percent of target markets, ours and competitors'. Targets are defined demographically.	Frequency goal: 4.5. Use network TV, day and late fringe, spot TV in top 30 markets. Use: 30s. Buy 600 GRPs in spot markets.	Eliminate newspapers, spot radio, spot TV, and billboards from consideration. Use network TV or magazines. Find which gives 80 percent net reach of targets at lowest CPM.	Make purchase of best alternative media according to the specifications laid down in strategy and tactical plans, and according to any other specifications (such as creative requirements).	Make notes of which strategies succeeded and why others failed. These notes provide keys to more success in the future.

Organize the Plan in Steps

Create a list of procedures in order of importance. Here is what should be covered:

1. **State the marketing problem quickly and succinctly.** It often helps everyone involved if they are reminded of the original problem, and what the entire plan is about. This will also usually cover the marketing mix elements plus other marketing decisions that help in solving the problem.

2. **State the most significant marketing objectives and strategies,** especially if the media plan has to implement them.

3. **Write media objectives.** There are two elements of objectives that should be remembered: (a) each objective should relate to a marketing objective and/or strategy; and (b) each media objective should be stated as completely and detailed as possible. The more detail, the more likely the objectives will serve as guides for media strategies. Many times objectives are hard to understand because they are written with little or no details in them.

   An objective may be written that states: "we need large reach and modest frequency." The terms "large" and "modest" ought to be explained. But the strategies should be written to spell out at what level reach should be, such as that a 70 percent target reach and an average frequency of at least 5 should be attained. These levels can be as high or as low as the planner wishes, but they are alternative actions—not goals. This point is often violated by many planners who list both the reach and frequency levels in the objectives.

   Remember the differences between media objectives and media strategies. Media objectives are goals that are related to marketing objectives and strategies, while media strategies are actions that can fulfill these objectives. Also, there are usually many alternative strategies that can fulfill one objective. The planner has to choose the best—or most effective—strategy from all the other possibilities. Of all the errors that beginners make in preparing objectives and strategies, the failure to discuss alternative strategies is the one that is most often made. Sometimes, the client—in a planning meeting—will ask a planner, "Why didn't you consider the use of newspapers (or some other medium) in this plan?" Newspapers, therefore, could have been an alternative.

4. **Write media strategies.** (See the outline of strategy questions in Chapter 11 for a guide of which strategies should be listed). Sometimes planners will list two or three alternative strategies and show why the one recommended is better than the other two. Every strategy should refer to at least one media objective.

5. **Write rationales when necessary.** There are times when the strategies are self-explanatory and no defense for a decision need be made. But at other times, it may be necessary to explain why the decision was made, and/or why the decision was the best of all alternatives. At other times, presentation of data such as costs, dayparts, and production treatments need no explanation, as long as they are listed for the plan's readers to know. If an idea is stated with no data to support it, it may be difficult to understand and a rationale is necessary.

6. **Some agencies require that media plans start with an executive summary.** This is a short presentation that shows only the main details of the plan so that a busy executive can quickly know the essence of the plan. Others omit this feature.

7. **Show numerical data in table form.** Where data is placed in the plan is a matter of agency style. Many planners prefer data next to the text so that the reader can quickly find the numbers that the text refers to. Other agencies want most large tables placed in the Appendix.

8. **Present an overview of competitive activity and the effects on your strategies.** Some agencies and/or planners hardly mention competitors, but most brands are fighting for competitive volume and market share. Therefore, competitors' budget, plans, and strategy may be very important. If the data is available, it should be shown. If it is not available, then estimates of significant strategy parts should be made and discussed. Rough estimates of which media are used most, and how they are used (reach and/or frequency) help support your plans.

9. **Spot television decisions.** When spot television is recommended for a plan, explain how decisions were made for the following: (a) How many markets are to be chosen? (b) Which markets? (c) How much weight should be used in each? (d) Explain how weight is to be allocated. Provide a list of all markets chosen and the weight for each. These details are sometimes called media tactics, but because they can vary so much, they are often properly included within the strategy section of the plan organization.

10. **Remember not to confuse creative strategies with media strategies.** Many times, beginners will ask in the objectives that the plan build brand awareness. That is not a media objective—it is a creative objective. Getting consumers to use more of a brand—or to switch brands—are also creative objectives, and *not* media objectives.

11. **Remember not to confuse marketing strategies with media strategies.** Marketing strategies deal with elements of the marketing mix, such as price, distribution, and so on. These can be mentioned anywhere in the plan, but they are not media strategies.

12. **Provide a flow chart** (also called a media calendar schedule sheet) in the plan.

13. **Historical information usually belongs in the appendix.** Historical data, if provided at all, should not impede the understanding of what is happening today. Often, historical data is not presented at all in a media plan.

14. **Make the plan interesting.** A media plan should also be exciting and innovative, if at all possible. When an advertising agency presents its entire campaign to the client, the creative section tends to get the attention because it is the most interesting part of the campaign. Media—with all of its numbers and details—tends not to be as interesting. Since media plans have to be sold—just as creative is sold to the client—the presentation should avoid dullness. Creative media planning not only helps sell the brand in question, but helps make the plan more interesting to look at. Innovative ways of presenting data should be sought.

Assembling Elements of a Plan

What information belongs in a media plan, and in how much detail? Where do various kinds of information belong? These questions can best be answered by using checklists that serve as the planner's reference. Checklist 13–1 will help the reader understand what belongs in a media plan and where it should appear. It is an operational checklist showing how to proceed in the actual planning process.

CHECKLIST 13–1. Media Planning Operational Checklist

Some elements in the subject checklist often are not pertinent for a given media plan. The *operational* checklist shows what is most likely to be required for a typical media plan and in about what order items should appear.

    I. Marketing Objectives and Strategies That Relate to Media
These are usually summarized rather than being presented in detail. Presumably, they already have been explained in detail in another document, the marketing plan.

    II. Copy Strategy Statements and How Media Will Support or Relate to Them
A copy strategy is not always a part of a media plan. If there is any special reason for including it, such as to clarify decisions of media selected, or media used in a certain way, then it belongs here.

    III. A Summary of the Entire Plan (optional)
This section allows an executive a quick overview of what actions are recommended so that the full scope of the plan is visible. Often the details occupy so many pages that it is difficult to get an overview of the plan easily.

    IV. Media Objectives
        A. A clear statement of each objective is necessary, using enough words to make them meaningful

    B. Statements should show precisely how media objectives relate to marketing objectives and/or strategies

    C. Objectives should cover the following topics as a minimum:

       1. Specification of target audiences (in demographics and psychographics if pertinent)

       2. Budget available and any restrictions on its use

       3. Reach and frequency needed

       4. Effective reach levels needed

       5. Continuity needed

       6. Pattern of monthly and yearly continuity

       7. Special geographic weighting needed

       8. Merchandisability of media if necessary

       9. Flexibility needed

      10. Degree to which media will have to support promotions

      11. Creative strategy implications

    D. A rationale for decisions must be included

V. Media Strategy

    A. Each strategy must be stated clearly

    B. Each strategy should be related to one (or more) media objectives

    C. Why certain other obvious strategies were *not* used should be explained

    D. Strategies should include (as a minimum):

       1. Media classes selected (e.g., network television, magazines, or telemarketing)

       2. Strategy for allocating the budget to geographic areas (roll-out vs. national introduction; spot only or national plus spot heavy-up)

       3. Allocation of budget to media classes (dollars and percentages of total)

       4. Allocation of budget by months and/or quarters of year; introductory vs. sustaining period strategy

       5. Reach and frequency levels desired by months and/or quarters of the year

       6. Effective reach and frequency levels per typical month

       7. Size of the primary and secondary target markets

       8. Weighting of strategic targets

       9. Geographical weighting requirements that must be used

      10. Cost-per-thousand standards, if required

      11. Explanations of why a strategy is different from previous ones

      12. Specifications of the size of media units to be used (15-, 30-, or 60-second commercials; full or fractional pages)

      13. Criteria to be used for selecting or scheduling media (need for flighting)

      14. Relationship of strategy to that of competitors, with special emphasis on certain key brands that must be dealt with specifically

      15. A rationale for each strategy statement

VI. Media Plan Details (and Documentation)

    A. A statement of criteria for determining media values

    B. Proof that vehicles selected are the best of all alternatives (using media value criteria) and for the budget (data plus words)

    C. Data showing net reach and frequency for targets reached by a combination of all vehicles, including frequency distributions

    D. Data showing gross impressions for a combination of all vehicles, especially for target audiences

    E. Costs per thousand shown for all vehicles selected or considered

    F. Cost summary tables showing each vehicle, number of times used per month, cost per insertion, and total cost per month

      G. Yearly cost summary

      H. Yearly flow chart (or schedule) showing vehicles, weeks of insertions, reaches, frequencies, and costs per month for the year

      I. Any other data that will help buyers implement the plan

VII. Overview

      A. Is the plan well organized? Is it easy to find specific information desired?

      B. Are topics delineated with appropriate headings?

      C. Are all tables of data headed properly so as to explain precisely what the data are about?

      D. Is there a Table of Contents with page numbers?

      E. Is there a review of key marketing objectives and/or strategies?

      F. If data are voluminous, have some been relegated to a special documentary section?

      G. Are there any weaknesses in the logic or reasoning of the plan?

The Media Flowchart

Special consideration ought to be given to the flowchart (also called a media calendar, or schedule sheet) of a media plan. A *flowchart* is a graphic presentation of all major actions that comprise a media plan. It is presented in notation form (or a form of shorthand) enabling the planner to place a great deal of information in a small amount of space.

The most important purpose of a flowchart is to provide everyone involved—the planner, the media buyer, the account executive, the client—with a bird's-eye view of the entire plan of action. Elsewhere in the plan are myriads of details explaining what actions are to be taken and why, but the flowchart places all actions in a single, easy-to-see frame of reference showing the flow of media purchases throughout the year. Some planners refer to this flow as a *pattern* of media delivery. The pattern is clearly discernible and makes it relatively easy to compare one part with another.

It is important, then, to make this flowchart understandable and not to omit anything that is essential to this bird's-eye view. For example, it would overly complicate a flowchart to list the number of targets reached in raw numbers, but it is useful to show the reach and frequency in percentages. It is not necessary to show the dollars spent in media each week of the year, but it is useful to show how much will be spent by each month or quarter of the year. If quarterly figures are not important, then monthly figures should be shown.

Essentials of a Flowchart

Although different advertising agencies may organize their flowcharts differently, there are some basic elements that are common to almost every flowchart:

1. The name of the brand and the year the plan covers should be at the top.
2. All months of the year should be aligned across the top of the page, usually placed horizontally on the page so that more space will be available. Some media planners prepare their flowcharts on large sheets of paper and reduce them photographically to an $8^{1}/_{2}$'' x 11'' size so that they can be assimilated easily in a bound document.
   a. The month that is shown first is usually the first of the fiscal, or financial, year. Some companies have fiscal years that begin with months other than January. At times, the first month listed may be the month in which the first media vehicles are to be bought. This is purely a matter of judgment.
   b. The months may be divided by quarters if the planning is done on a quarterly basis. If not, each of the months is listed next to each other across a page.
3. Each week of the year should be given a separate column under each month. Months with five weeks should contain five columns instead of four. It is debatable whether or not each week should be numbered from 1 to 52, or numbered on the basis of the first day of each week. Some media plans do not show any week numbers.
4. The left side of the page should contain media information.
   a. Each medium class used (by daypart if pertinent).
   b. Length of commercial or size of page and color (for example, thirty-second commercial, or $^{1}/_{2}$ page/four color).
   c. If spot television is used, each market group should be shown, and the number of markets in each group. (This number will refer to a market list that appears elsewhere in a plan.)

    d. If market groups receive different GRPs or TRPs (target rating points), this fact should be listed at the left or in a prominent place.

    e. A row labeled *reach*, and one underneath labeled *frequency*, should appear somewhere, often placed at the left side, bottom. If gross rating points or target rating points are important, then this information should appear below reach and frequency rows. If different geographic areas are to receive varying weights, then each area should be listed with a row underneath for reach, another for frequency, and another for the appropriate gross rating points (if important).

    f. At the bottom there usually is a row showing media expenditures by month and/or quarter of the year. At the extreme right side, these should be summed.

    g. At the very bottom, percentages of total media expenditures are usually shown by month and/or quarter with a 100 percent total at the extreme right.

5. Each week of advertising should be blocked-in. Some agencies eliminate all the column lines from their flow chart, so their flowcharts would show the number of weeks of advertising as a rectangle. Inside the rectangle should be the number of GRPs or TRPs to be used per average week. The length of the rectangle should cover the number of weeks of advertising required. Some planners place a small numeral above the rectangle to show how many weeks of advertising will occur. Such a numeral is not needed if the length of time covers the entire year.

The reader should study Figures 13–2, 13–3, and 13–4 for examples of different kinds of flowcharts prepared for different kinds of media plans. No matter which format is used, it should contain all the essential details. Above all, it should be easy to read and understand without the use of excessive explanatory symbols or other notations.

FIGURE 13–2.   A Sample Media Plan Flowchart for Television

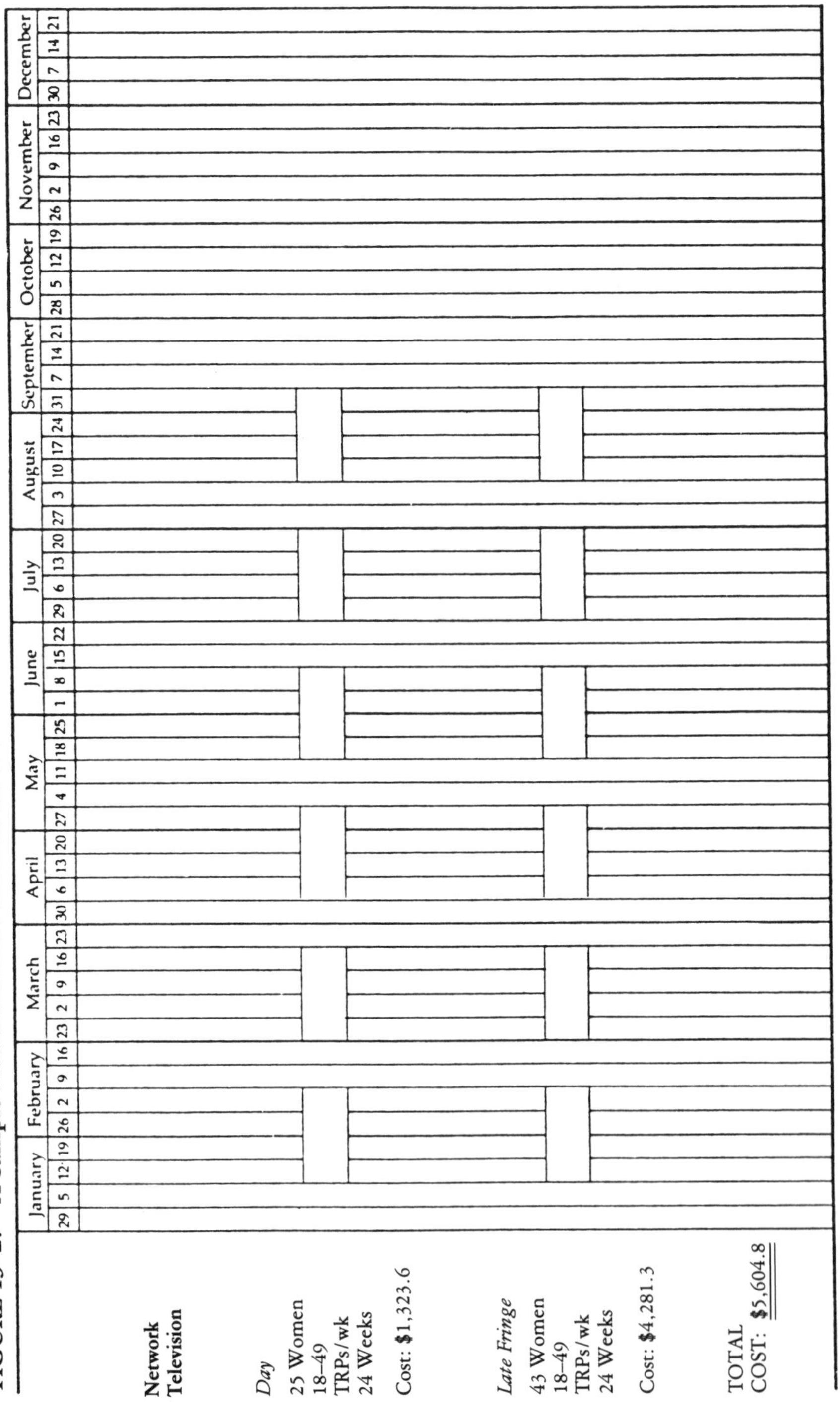

Network
Television

Day

25 Women
18–49
TRPs/wk
24 Weeks

Cost: $1,323.6

Late Fringe

43 Women
18–49
TRPs/wk
24 Weeks

Cost: $4,281.3

TOTAL
COST: $5,604.8

FIGURE 13–3. A Sample Media Plan Flowchart for Magazines

Olympics		February		March		April		May		June		July		August		September		October		November		December		January	
		3 10 17 24		2 9 16 23 30		6 13 20 27		4 11 18 25		1 8 15 22 29		6 13 20 27		3 10 17 24 31		7 14 21 28		5 12 19 26		2 9 16 23 30		7 14 21 28		6 13 20 27	

Winter ██ 2/12 2/24

Summer ██ 7/8 8/5

Magazine Schedule

Magazine		Feb	Mar	Apr	May	Jun	Jul	Aug	Sep	Oct	Nov	Dec	Jan
Life	4x			█	█	█		█		█			
Newsweek	4x		×	×	×	×	×	×	×	×	×		
People	5x		×		×	×	×		×	×			
Sports Illustrated	4x		×		×	×	×		×				
Reader's Digest	4x				█	█		█			█		
Ebony	4x					█	█		█	█			
Nuestro	4x					█	█		█	█		█	
Senior Scholastic	3x				×				×		×		
Young Athlete	4x											█	

Target R/F

	July Issue	May Issue	Sept. Issue	Nov. Issue

| Per Month | 17/1.0 | 24/1.2 | 36/1.3 | 24/1.2 | 40/1.4 | 16/1.0 | 36/1.3 | 24/1.2 | 36/1.3 | |

Total Year 75/4.2

*Adults 18–49 with household income $15,000 +

FIGURE 13–4. A Sample Media Plan Flowchart for Specialized Publications

	October	November	December	January	February	March	April	May	June	July	August	September
	6 13 20 27	3 10 17 24	1 8 15 22 29	5 12 19 26	2 9 16 23	2 9 16 23 30	6 13 20 27	4 11 18 25	1 8 15 22 29	6 13 20 27	3 10 17 24 31	7 14 21 28

Business Publications

Wall Street Journal
(5 1,480-line ads)

Forbes
(2 spreads, 3 pages)

Dun's Review
(4 spreads, 4 pages)

Harvard Business Review
(2 spreads, 2 pages)

—Nov. issue

—Mar. issue

—May issue

Specialty Publications

Oil & Gas Journal
(2 spreads, 3 pages)

*Engineering and
Mining Journal*
(3 pages, 1 spread)

*Bay Hill Citrus Classic
Gold Program* (1 page)

NBAA Daily News
(3 spreads)

3x

× – 1,480 ll
× – Page 4/C-bleed
– Spread 4/C-bleed

QUESTIONS FOR DISCUSSION

1. Why would it be a good idea to show media plan data such as tables of reach, frequency, dollars spent, etc. arranged by quarters of the year?
2. What are the negative consequences of writing very short, general statements of media objectives in a plan?
3. Explain the most significant function of a media flow chart.
4. Why is it important to show and discuss alternative media strategies somewhere in a plan?
5. What information belongs in a media plan concerning the use of spot television?
6. What is wrong with the following statement that appeared in a media plan: "We need a 70% reach in this plan."?
7. Why is it generally conceded to be bad form to list all statistical data in an appendix?
8. Why is it not a good idea for a planner to make sure that all data in a flow chart fall within some monthly column?
9. What is meant by the "merchandisability" of a media plan?
10. Why would we want to make sure media plans flexible? Explain.

SELECTED READINGS

Advertising Age, "Pulsing Schedules of Ads an Effective Technique," October 20, 1969, 270.

Hays, Henry, "How to Have More Fun Writing a Media Plan," *Marketing and Media Decisions*, December 1986, 91–94.

Krugman, Herbert, "What Makes Advertising Effective?" *Harvard Business Review*, March–April 1975, 96–103.

McCann–Erickson, *A Point of View on Advertising Strategy* (White Paper I) October 1972.

Papazian, Edward, "Structuring Media Plans for Maximum Effect," *Media Decisions*, March 1974, 12–14.

Papazian, Edward, "Bottom Up Planning," *Media Decisions*, August 1978, 16–18.

Roth, Paul, *How to Plan Media,* Media and Market Decisions (Publisher), 1974.

Surmanek, James, "Let Reps in on Media Planning," *Advertising Age,* September 11, 1978, 78.

14

An Annotated Media Plan

This chapter is intended to help readers visualize a media plan as created by a professional planner in a large advertising agency. It is assumed by this time that the reader will know the concepts and terminology used in planning and therefore be able to easily follow and understand the plan. Because this plan was made for a brand product in a highly competitive market, a number of changes were made in it to keep certain proprietary information confidential: the brand is called X, the product category is not identified, and certain pieces of information have been eliminated, such as a creative strategy statement.

All other essentials are included and explained in annotated remarks on the corresponding facing pages. The plan has been divided into more parts than the original plan contained, but these parts should help the reader more easily understand the underlying thinking that went into the planning. In addition, each notation has been coded with a number which refers back to the same number in the plan.

PLAN

[1] **PART 1**
Brand X Media Plan (Next Year) Summary

[2] **A. TASK**
   1. Maintain the current strength of Brand X franchise

[3] **B. AVAILABLE FUNDS**

Total advertising budget	$18,370,000
Less production	1,420,000
Working media budget	$16,950,000

[4] **C. MEDIA PLAN**
   1. Objectives
      a. Direct advertising toward current users to increase loyalty
      b. Maintain current share
      c. Encourage ongoing use of the brand
[5] **2.** Strategy
      a. Direct impressions toward all women proportionate to their Brand X volume contribution, with emphasis on the primary targets: women aged 35-plus, living in $15,000-plus households, in A counties.
      b. Allocate media dollars in proportion to current Brand X sales volume by market, while maintaining competitive levels in high-volume Brand X areas.
      c. Achieve at least a 75 reach with an average frequency of 5 among total women in key areas. Concurrently, seek a reach of 50 among women exposed at least three times within any given four weeks of advertising.
      d. Distribute advertising pressure according to quarterly volume contribution.

NOTES

Notes on Part 1—Summary

(Numbers refer to same numbers in plan)

[1] This summary is a quick overview of the entire plan. In a typical media plan, the exact year (calendar or fiscal) would appear in place of the phrase "next year."

[2] This states one important marketing objective: to maintain the current strength of the Brand X franchise. The term *franchise* is not used here to mean a franchising business, such as McDonald's hamburgers. Rather, it means "the brand's usage or financial position in the marketplace."

[3] The available funds statement breaks down the budget into media and production costs. Production costs can be estimated before media costs, if the creative strategy has been devised and the numbers of broadcast commercials and print ads have been spelled out. Television production costs normally include cost of studio time, sets, crew, director's fees, special effects, casting, editing, music, as well as initial talent fees and residual talent payments. It should also be noted that the budget is one of the most significant constraints on media objectives and strategy and therefore must be discussed early in the planning process.

[4,5] Objectives and strategies have been reduced to simple declarative statements here. Later on, however, more will be said about each.

[4] It is important to note the nature of objectives. User demographics have been spelled out earlier. Although it usually is a part of marketing objectives, market share here is listed as a media objective, which is acceptable. Likewise, the encouragement of ongoing use of the brand (item C1c) is related to creative objectives and therefore might appear in a different place in other media plans.

[5] Strategies C2a to C2g are very specific and cover parts of the recommended media strategy.

[5] C2a. Media targets are identified first. Two kinds of targets are to be reached: one target is broadly based and consists of all women. A second target consists of those demographic segments that have greater sales potential because they purchase more. They will be given special treatment.

[5] C2b. While the targets in C2a were based on personal demographics, this category considers geographic demographics. The identification of both types of targets is usually necessary for media planning. Advertising impressions are to be delivered proportionately to sales potential in each area.

[5] C2c. Reach and frequency requirements in key market areas are spelled out here. A 75 reach and a 5 average frequency are to be attained. Although the planner did not specify the time period for such reach and frequency, it is presumed to be for a four-week period. The planner did specify an effective reach goal in a four-week period of 50 with a frequency of 3 or more. It is important to remember that this reach is for women targets only.

[5] C2d. This is an allocation strategy and explains that the budget is to be proportionately distributed according to the volume of sales made in each quarter of a year. If the first quarter of the year accounts for 27 percent of sales, it would receive about 27 percent of the advertising budget.

PLAN

    e. Maintain financial and geographic flexibility.

    f. Provide continuous support within the quarterly investment allocation once the reach/frequency goals are met.

3. Plan

	Dollars	Percent
Day Network TV	$ 3,960,000	23.4
Late Network TV	3,869,000	22.8
Fringe Spot TV	6,121,000	36.1
Direct Mail/Postage Production	1,061,000	6.3
List Rental	111,000	0.7
Fulfillment	307,000	1.8
In Store Targeted Couponing	980,000	5.7
Redemption	541,000	3.2
TOTAL	$16,950,000	100.0

[7] D. DELIVERY

1. Demographics—Slightly underdeliver upper income category as a result of concentrating in television.
2. Geographics—Overspend spot TV markets by 11 percent in order to maintain competitive posture in key franchise areas.
3. National Effort—Network television represents 46 percent of total media budget.
4. Reach/Frequency—Delivery achieves goal in key markets.
5. Allocation Requirements—Generally follows the quarterly sales volume.

[8] E. TASK ACCOMPLISHMENT

1. The plan accomplishes the task of providing support to maintain current franchise of the brand.
2. Minor deviations from demographic and geographic targets result from optimizing total plan delivery.

PART 2
Marketing and Copy Background

[9] A. OVERVIEW

For the preceding year, Brand X had a severe business decline. Brand performance showed loss of momentum and was characterized by market share erosion, volume misses, and weakened distribution.

[10] B. OBJECTIVE

Stabilize the franchise in key marketing areas.

    National share and volume objectives:

        Share: 6.0

        Volume: 3,606

NOTES

[5] **C2e.** The need for flexibility influences the strategy. Although reasons for wanting it are not given, presumably flexibility is needed to make quick media changes if sales opportunities or problems develop. Competitors' activities often cause a company to make changes in media plans after the plan has been devised. When the plan is flexible, it can be changed more easily.

[5] **C2f.** Employ media vehicles that are compatible with the copy requirements and overall brand image.

[5] **C2g.** Implement loyalty program directed to heavy current users.

[6] This is an expenditure analysis in both raw dollars and percentages. Media plans must show expenditures in both forms to enable easy analysis.

[7] **D1.** Delivery analysis explains how well the plan's statistical data prove that the plan reaches the objectives set out for it. For example, D1 explains that the plan will slightly underdeliver upper-income targets. Slight underdelivery is not considered to be an error.

[7] **D2.** It also points out that the budget will be overspent by 11 percent in spot TV markets and why.

[7] **D3.** Network television accounts for 56 percent of the media budget.

[7] **D4. D5.** Reach and frequency are attained as planned, and expenditures follow sales volume by quarters, also as planned.

[8] This is an evaluation statement based on judgment. It explains that the plan accomplishes the tasks set for it and why there are minor deviations. It is important to note that the planner tries to anticipate questions and answer them before they can be asked.

Notes on Part 2—Marketing and Copy Background

[9] This is a brief overview of the marketing situation of Brand X for the past three years. Its market share was declining, its sales volume was not reaching goals set for it, and the number of stores distributing the product was declining.

[10] This is a marketing objective in terms of market share and sales volume. The number 3,606 refers to millions of units sold.

PLAN

[11] C. MARKETING STRATEGY
   1. Allocate marketing funds according to the brand's consumption.
   2. Continue to place heavy emphasis on promotion, especially consumer.
   3. Implement a program of case rates designed to put Brand X back in the feature cycle.

[12] D. COPY STRATEGY
   (Omitted for reasons of confidentiality)

PART 3
Marketing Objective/Rationale

[13] Objective: Direct advertising toward current users to capitalize on current strengths.

Rationale: The goal is to maintain share and encourage ongoing use of the brand.

Next year is expected to be a year of intense competitive pressure when Brand A (Brand X's main competitor) dominates the product category with its key selling features and Brand B dominates consumer promotion activity.

At this time, no product improvements for Brand X are planned for next year.

[14] PART 4
Media Strategy/Rationale

[15] Part 4A—Prospect Definition

Direct impressions toward all women proportionate to their Brand X volume contribution, with emphasis on the primary Brand X targets.

Primary targets are women with the following characteristics:
   1. Age 35–plus
   2. In $15,000-plus households
   3. Living in A counties

Demographic details are provided in Table 14–1.

NOTES

[11] Marketing strategies are stated here. Strategies C1 and C2 are obvious. Marketing strategy C3 is to build distribution and will be accomplished by giving retailers a higher mark-up on cases purchased as an incentive for stocking the brand.

[12] The copy strategy has been omitted here because it would have revealed the name of the brand. But the categories in the copy strategy may be stated. They were: copy objective, definition of prime prospects, competitive stance, key benefits, support, copy tone, and manner of presentation. These are components of creative strategy.

Notes on Part 3—Marketing Objective/Rationale

[13] The main objective is to retain present users. Ordinarily, such an objective is listed as a creative responsibility or perhaps a marketing responsibility. Essentially, all that media can do to keep present customers is to deliver the message to the correct targets with a certain amount of frequency. However, because media do at least play some role in helping attain this objective, it may be considered appropriate here.

Another media objective is to capitalize on current strengths. The comment made earlier applies here as well. Media cannot capitalize on current strengths, but copy can.

The reader, therefore, has to recognize that the planner from this particular advertising agency is not following the recommendations of writing objectives as presented in this text. The planner's objectives are communication-oriented, and as such they are copy objectives rather than media objectives. An expected increase in competitive pressure is also mentioned here. Although detailed analysis is not provided, it is assumed that the media planner has completed a detailed competitive brand and category media/promotion spending analysis, and found sufficient data to warrant projected increase pressure from Competitor A.

Notes on Part 4—Media Strategy/Rationale

[14] This part of the plan consists of strategy details and rationale, much of it fairly obvious statistical data.

Notes on Part 4A—Prospect Definition

[15] This definition first appeared in the summary [5] but is spelled out in greater detail here. There are two bases for selecting media targets (prospects): (a) the volume of Brand X that was purchased (as shown in percentages in [19]), and (b) the index numbers that relate volume-usage to population distribution by demographics (as shown in [20]).

PLAN

TABLE 14–1. [17] Demographic Targets

		U.S. Women[18] (%)	Brand X[19] Volume (%)	[20] Index
Total Women		100.0	100.0	100
Age: Total		100.0	100.0	100
	18–24	18.0	13.9	77
	25–34	20.4	17.9	88
	35–49	23.0	21.3	93
	50-plus	38.6	46.9	122
Nonworking		56.6	60.4	107
	18–24	8.4	6.0	71
	25–34	10.4	9.7	93
	35–49	11.1	11.0	99
	50-plus	26.7	33.7	126
Working		43.4	39.6	91
	18–24	9.6	7.9	82
	25–34	10.0	8.2	82
	35–49	11.9	10.3	87
	50-plus	11.9	13.2	111
Household Income	Under $8,000	38.1	28.6	75
	$8,000–$14,999	34.5	33.0	96
	$15,000-plus	27.4	38.4	140
Household Size	1–2	39.9	38.0	95
	3–4	35.8	37.7	105
	5-plus	24.3	24.3	100
County Size	A	40.9	51.0	125
	B	26.2	24.1	92
	C	19.4	17.3	89
	D	13.5	7.6	56

[16] Source: MRCA Demographic Analysis.

[21] Part 4B—Media Allocation

Allocate media dollars in accordance with the current Brand X sales volume of each market.

The media budgets of the individual markets will be prorated to the estimated volume contribution of each area. However, in the interest of strengthening the Brand X franchise in key markets and also recognizing the competitive spending environment, additional weight will be placed in the following areas. To the degree affordable, the following minimum spending versus Competitor A will be sought:

Eastern Region	+ 85%
Detroit District	+ 85%
Chicago District	+ 65%
Los Angeles District	+ 65%

NOTES

[16] The source of statistical data is at the bottom of Table 14–1.

[17,18,19,20] A study of demographic usage and index numbers shows some interesting data. The largest index of users is for women, aged 50-plus, with income of $15,000-plus, who live in A counties. Why, then, did the planner select women aged 35-plus instead of only those aged 50-plus? The reason is that the target market would have been too small (only 38.6 percent of U.S. women are age 50 or over). By increasing the primary target segment to all women over 35, the population base has now been increased to 61.6 percent (23.0 + 38.6 = 61.6 percent) and brand volume to 68.2 percent. Why also were *all* women considered a target? It is probable that the client wanted a very broad target rather than a narrow one, and all Brand X users are to be reached, even though there are proportionately fewer Brand X users in the younger demographic segments.

Notes on Part 4B—Media Allocation

[21] This part of the media plan deals with strategies for weighting advertising by geographical area. The main strategy is to allocate the media budget proportionately to the sales volume contributed by each of four sales regions: Eastern, Central, Southern, and Western.

However, another part of the strategy is to add extra weight in those geographical markets that have done best in sales. A study of [25] shows that all markets in the Eastern Region have indices over 100 and therefore are among the best in the country. Detroit also has an index over 100. Chicago and Los Angeles do not have exceptionally high index numbers but do have large volumes of sales as shown in [24]. The planner, therefore, wants to add extra weight in these key markets. The goal is to add 85 percent more dollars than Competitor A in the Eastern Region and Detroit and 65 percent more in Chicago and Los Angeles. Although the planner does not show competitors' media expenditures, it is assumed that estimates are available. Also note that the extra spending depends on ''the degree affordable.'' This means that the extra money can be spent if it is available after other priorities have been met.

PLAN

Table 14–2 shows in detail the geographic targets based on Brand X volume.

TABLE 14–2. [22] **Geographic Targets**

	U.S.[23] Women (%)	Brand X[24] Volume (%)	Brand X[25] Development Index (BDI)
Eastern Region			
Boston	5.28	6.60	125
New York	9.42	13.04	138
Philadelphia	7.75	13.34	172
Syracuse	3.38	5.91	175
Youngstown	4.78	6.55	137
Total Eastern	30.61	45.44	148
Southern Region			
Charlotte	5.55	3.83	69
Atlanta	4.03	3.24	80
Jacksonville	3.89	3.08	79
Detroit	4.76	8.52	179
Cincinnati	5.44	4.42	81
Total Southern	23.67	23.09	98
Central Region			
Chicago	6.44	5.35	83
St. Louis	3.57	2.91	82
Memphis	4.65	2.89	62
Kansas City	3.92	2.46	63
Dallas	6.46	3.60	56
Total Central	25.04	17.21	69
Western Region			
Minneapolis	4.15	2.01	48
Denver	2.40	1.30	54
Portland	2.77	1.80	65
San Francisco	4.01	2.67	67
Los Angeles	7.35	6.48	88
Total Western	20.68	14.26	69
Total U.S.	100.00	100.00	100

Source: A. C. Nielsen Company.

Part 4C—Performance/Delivery Goals

[26] **A.** Total Reach/Average Frequency
Provide at least 75 reach with an average frequency of 5 among total women in the key areas.

B. Effective Reach
Concurrently, seek a four-week reach goal of 50 among women who have been exposed at least three times.

	Four-Week Reach/Frequency Goals
Total Reach/Average Frequency	75/5.0
Effective Reach	50/3 +

NOTES

[22,23,24,25] These figures show sales volume and Brand Development Indices. Such data provide the basis for the decisions in [21].

Notes on Part 4C—Performance / Delivery Goals

[26] Communication goals are listed in A as reach / frequency and effective reach.

In determining communication goals, it is important to note estimated competitive delivery levels that should be taken into consideration. Here again, category confidentiality prohibits explicit details, but it is assumed that the planner has a good understanding of competitors' delivery activity.

The use of the term *communication goals* tells the reader how the planner perceives reach and frequency. Both serve as controllers of message distribution: reach controls dispersion, while frequency controls the degree of repetition.

The reader should note that a reach of 75 and a frequency of 5 is for total women, in certain parts of the country only. It is for women in the key marketing areas mentioned in Part 4B—''Media Allocation.'' The levels of 75 and 5 have been arrived at on the basis of experience and judgment.

The *effective* reach and frequency is different: 50 and 3 + . These levels come from an analysis of a frequency distribution (see [37]). The reader should note that an effective frequency of three is based on a judgment about the specific needs of Brand X. So the reach percentages at a frequency of 3 + were determined (from the frequency distribution) to be 50.

PLAN

[27] C. Distribute Advertising Pressure according to Quarterly Volume Contribution

Quarter	Volume (%)
April–June	24
July–September	23
October–December	26
January–March	27
Total	100

[28] D. Maintain Flexibility

It is recommended that all media activity be scheduled to run at the same time and that a substantial portion of the budget be placed in flexible media so the Brand can quickly react to:

1. Competitive activity
2. Key promotional events

[29] E. Continuous Support within the Quarterly Investment Allocation Will Be Sought Once the Reach/Frequency Goals Are Achieved.

Continuous advertising is desirable for the following reasons: (a) there is sufficient evidence of advertising recall erosion among consumers during nonadvertising periods; (b) the daily traffic in stores includes Brand X purchases; (c) pressure against competition should be maintained. Therefore, as soon as reach/frequency goals are achieved, advertising periods will be extended within the boundaries of the quarterly investment allocation. A total of thirty-six weeks of advertising has been set as the minimum.

[30] F. Employ Media Vehicles That Are Compatible with the Copy Requirements and Overall Brand Image.

A balance of highly efficient and effective media will be sought to ensure the most desirable combination of copy and media.

[31] PART 5
Description of Media Plan

[32] Next year, the Brand X media plan will use television as the primary medium for the following reasons:

1. The intrusive nature of the medium makes it the most effective vehicle for communicating the Brand X message.
2. It is highly efficient in reaching the target audience.
3. On judgment, at the current budget level, concentrating efforts on the primary medium should maximize the effectiveness of communication.

NOTES

[27] Quarterly distribution of sales volume is shown. Media planners use sales volume data by month or by quarter of the year in making budget allocation decisions. Most planners use both.

[28] The need for flexibility is explained here. Flexible media are usually local media such as spot television, spot radio, newspapers—media which can be purchased or cancelled quickly.

[29] This part of the strategy discusses the use of continuity in relation to reach and frequency *per quarter*. The planner sets reach and frequency as a higher priority than continuity. But once the reach and frequency levels have been reached, good continuity should be attained within a thirty-six-week period. The flow chart located at [37] shows a flighting pattern of continuity in which there are five time periods in which a hiatus occurs, not counting the weeks before advertising starts and after it ends. These are brief, two-week hiatuses. So the pattern of continuity is fairly extensive within the thirty-six-week period, from May to the middle of March the following year.

[30] The requirement for the kinds of vehicles to be selected in the plan is clear: Use only those that best convey the copy and the brand image.

Notes on Part 5—Description of Media Plan

[31,32,33,34,35,36] The description of the media plan consists of statements about which classes of media and kinds of vehicles should be selected and the rationale for selecting each. Essentially, television—network and spot—is recommended as the primary vehicle with network being restricted to daytime and late night (fringe time). Two direct vehicles—mail and targeted couponing—will be used for Brand X heavy user loyalty program.

PLAN

33 Daytime network television will provide the base upon which other national and local media efforts will be structured. This medium is the most efficient vehicle for reaching a broad national base of adult women.

34 Late night network television will be used to extend reach nationally and increase the delivery of women in the higher income category ($15,000-plus).

35 Fringe spot television will be implemented to align media to targets and, tactically, to furnish additional support for Brand X's markets against competitive pressures.

36 With the objective of retaining present users, a targeted marketing campaign is planned. Two targeted media will be purchased to reach Brand X's heavy users:

1. Direct mail
2. In-store targeted couponing

Through these two media, we will be able to select Brand X's heavy users and send our loyalty purchase program to them. The program will be tested prior to national roll-out to determine payout potential. The direct programs will be scheduled to run at the same time as the network and spot television in order to maximize advertising pressure.

PART 6
Recommended Plan

Part 6A—Flowchart

The major recommendations of the media plan are summarized in a yearlong flowchart, as shown in Figure 14–1.

NOTES

PLAN

FIGURE 14–1. [37] Recommended Plan—Flowchart

Television	June Quarter				September Quarter			December Quarter			March Quarter		Total Year
	Apr.	May	June	July	Aug.	Sept.	Oct.	Nov.	Dec.	Jan.	Feb.	Mar.	
		9		1	4	4	5	4	4	5	4	4	
Day Network :30		35 WGRP/Wk.			35 W	35 WGRP/Wk.			35 W	35 W		35 W	
Late Network :30		14 WGRP/Wk.			14 W	14 W	25 W		25 W	25 W	25 W		
Combination Fringe :30 / 45.8% U.S. Women / 62.2% Target		82 WGRP/Wk.			82 W	82 W	98 W		98 W	98 W	98 W		
Direct Mail 1MM Mailing / Targeted Couponing / 2MM circulation		XXXXXXXX			XXXXXXXX			XXXXXXXX			XXXXXXXX		
Reach/Frequency													
Spot Area													
Total Women		81/5.1			81/5.1			84/5.9			85/5.8		
3 +		53			53			59			60		
$15M +		77/4.5			75/4.3			80/5.3			80/5.2		
3 +		47			44			53			52		
Remainder U.S.													
Total Women		57/3.4			57/3.5			61/3.8			63/3.7		
3 +		27			27			32			33		
$15M +		51/2.9			51/2.8			56/3.5			56/3.4		
3 +		21			21			27			27		

continued on next page

PLAN

FIGURE 14–1. (continued)

Television	June Quarter			September Quarter			December Quarter			March Quarter			Total Year
	Apr.	May	June	July	Aug.	Sept.	Oct.	Nov.	Dec.	Jan.	Feb.	Mar.	
Day Network		$965.0M*			$867.1M			$1,069.0M			$946.2M		$3,847.7M
Late Network		718.3M			662.1M			1,471.0M			1,079.8M		3,931.2M
Combination Fringe		1,399.7M			1,400.3M			1,686.5M			1,684.6M		6,171.1M
Direct Mail		326.9M			310.6M			448.1M			393.4M		1,479.0M
(Includes list rental, postage production, fulfillment)													
Targeted Couponing		336.1M			319.4M			460.9M			404.6M		1,521.0M
(Incluces production and redemption)													
Total		$3,746.0M			$3,559.5M			$5,135.0M			$4,508.6M		$16,950.0M
Percent		22.1%			21.0%			30.3%			26.6%		100.0%

*M = 000.

NOTES

Notes on Part 6A—Flowchart

[37] Note carefully how this flowchart has been arranged. It is the source of a great deal of important information. These are its key components:

1. The year has been divided into fifty-two weekly segments, which in turn have been divided into quarters, with the first fiscal quarter (April–June) coming first. This first fiscal quarter could start in January or any other month, depending upon the client's fiscal year.

2. Vehicles that are to be used are shown at the left hand side, followed by the lengths of commercials, which are all :30s (or thirty-second commercials). The terms "Day Network," and "Late Network" mean that commercials will be purchased in these dayparts. "Combination Fringe :30" means early and late fringe daypart placements of commercials.

 The 45.8 percent (underneath "Combination Fringe :30") refers to the percent of total U.S. women in primary markets, and 62.2 percent refers to the sales volume that these women account for. The reason these two percentages are listed is to remind those who read the flowchart that the planner wants to concentrate advertising in primary markets as a means of stimulating more sales. In other words, "sell where the product already has sold well." (See these data in their marketing context, on Table 14–6[54,55], No. 2, which follows.)

3. Next on the left, geographical targets have been divided into key markets and the remainder of the U.S. Then key target markets are indicated: total women and women with incomes of $15,000-plus a year and 3 + effective reaches.

4. The dollar expenditure per quarter is listed at the bottom for each category of vehicles used, and at the very bottom a percentage of the total is shown.

5. Advertising is shown by number of consecutive weeks followed by the number of "women gross rating points" (WGRP). The number of weeks during each flight is shown. For example, Day network (:30s) starts in the last week of April and continues for nine weeks in the June quarter plus one week in the September quarter. Then there are two more four-week schedules in the September quarter, and so on. The number of weeks per month is shown on the top of each rectangle as follows: 9, 1, 4, 4, 5, 4, 5, 4 = 36 weeks.

6. In the category of reach and frequency levels, note that the designation for total women in the June quarter is shown as 81/5.1 (81 reach and 5.1 frequency for total women). Reach of women with $15,000-plus income is shown in the same manner (77/4.5). But the designation for 3+ , referring to effective reach, comes from frequency distributions where the effective reach is 53 for total women for the average four weeks in the first quarter for spot area and 27 for the remainder of the U.S. See next section (Part 6B).

7. Note that the direct mail and the targeted couponing are not referenced with a GRP/week nor are they included in reach and frequency levels. Rather, the flowchart indicates how large the mailing and coupon circulation and flighting are for both events.

NOTES

PLAN

Part 6B—Frequency Distribution Analysis

Going beyond the summary flowchart, the media planner has also provided a frequency distribution analysis (see Tables 14–3 and 14–4) that breaks down the reach and frequency, and total exposures, among all women in the selected spot TV markets and secondarily in the remainder of the United States.

TABLE 14–3.   [38] Total Women Frequency Distribution Analysis–Spot Area

	June Qtr. May	Sept. Qtr. Sept.	Dec. Qtr. Oct.	Mar. Qtr. Jan.
Reach/Frequency	81.1/5.1	81.0/5.1	84.3/5.9	84.7/5.8
No. of Exposures				
1+	81.1	81.0	84.3	84.7
2+	65.8	65.7	70.8	71.1
3+	53.2	53.2	59.2	59.5
4+	43.0	42.9	49.5	49.5
5+	34.6	34.6	41.2	41.1
6+	27.8	27.8	34.2	34.0
7+	22.3	22.3	28.4	28.0
8+	17.8	17.8	23.5	23.0
9+	14.1	14.2	18.8	18.0
10+	11.2	11.2	15.9	15.4
11+	8.9	8.9	13.1	12.6
12+	7.0	7.0	10.7	10.2
Weekly Women Gross Rating Points				
Day Network	35	35	35	35
Late Network	14	14	25	25
Spot TV	54	54	65	65
Total	103	103	125	125

TABLE 14–4.   [39] Total Women Frequency Distribution Analysis–Remainder U.S.

	June Qtr. May	Sept. Qtr. Sept.	Dec. Qtr. Oct.	Mar. Qtr. Jan.
Reach/Frequency	56.8/3.4	56.5/3.5	61.4/3.8	62.6/3.7
No. of Exposures				
1+	56.8	56.5	61.4	62.6
2+	38.5	38.5	43.5	44.4
3+	27.3	27.4	32.0	32.5
4+	19.7	19.8	23.9	24.2
5+	14.3	14.5	18.0	18.1
6+	11.5	10.7	13.6	13.5
7+	7.6	7.8	10.3	10.2
8+	5.5	5.7	7.8	7.6
9+	4.0	4.2	5.9	5.7
10+	2.9	3.1	4.4	4.2
11+	2.1	2.2	3.3	3.1
12+	1.5	1.6	2.5	2.3
Weekly Women Rating Points				
Day Network	35	35	35	35
Late Network	14	14	25	25
Total	49	49	60	60

NOTES

Notes on Part 6B—Frequency Distribution Analysis

[38,39] These are frequency distributions for determining effective reach. Since effective frequency is felt to be three or more impressions, the corresponding reaches are shown by quarter for the spot area [38] and the remainder of the U.S.[39]. The data come from computer analysis of television programs and time periods that were selected.

Note also that the weekly women gross rating points are shown at the bottom. This comes from the planner's desired GRP levels as shown in the bars on the flowchart.

PLAN

[40] **PART 7**
Gross Impression Analysis

Gross impression analysis, as detailed in Table 14–5, shows the duplicated weight of advertising to each target audience member.

TABLE 14–5.   Gross Impression Breakdown (thousands)

	Day[40,41] Network	Late[42] Network	Fringe[43] Spot	Plan[44] Total	% of[45] Plan	% of[46] Target	[47] Index
Total Women	929,464	531,122	722,917	2,183,503	100.0	100.0	—
Age							
18–24	156,150	86,573	108,438	351,161	16.0	13.9	115
25–34	177,528	104,631	137,354	419,513	19.2	17.9	107
35–49	198,905	142,872	170,608	512,385	23.5	21.3	110
50+	396,881	197,046	306,517	900,444	41.3	46.9	88
Household Income							
Under $8,000	448,002	195,984	261,696	905,682	41.5	28.6	145
$8,000–14,999	310,441	198,108	234,225	742,774	34.0	33.0	103
$15,000+	171,021	137,029	226,996	535,046	24.5	38.4	64
Household Size							
1–2	370,856	215,104	329,650	915,610	41.9	38.0	110
3–4	340,184	182,175	166,271	688,630	31.5	37.7	84
5+	218,424	133,843	226,996	579,263	26.6	24.3	109
County Size							
A	308,582	246,972	471,342	1,026,896	47.0	51.0	92
B	276,980	151,370	153,981	582,331	26.7	24.1	111
C	187,752	72,764	78,798	339,314	15.5	17.3	90
D	156,150	60,016	18,796	234,962	10.8	7.6	142

NOTES

Notes on Part 7—Gross Impression Analysis

[40] While the frequency distribution analysis shown in Part 6B gives the client an idea about how many different target members were reached an average number of times, gross impression analysis enables everyone to see whether or not advertising is distributed to these various targets in the correct proportions. Some planners may be inclined to call such data strategic impression analysis, implying that the distribution of impressions is not haphazard, but rather part of the strategy.

[41,42,43,44] The numbers shown in these columns are the duplicated impressions delivered by the various media. They are calculated by multiplying the average ratings for the vehicles by the audience base times the number of commercials telecast during the plan, or simply by multiplying the annual GRPs by the audience universe.

[45] This column indicates the strategic impression proportions. For example, women aged 18–24 are to receive 16.0 percent of total impressions for the age category, and households with incomes under $8,000 a year are to receive 41.5 percent of all impressions for that income level.

[46] This column, however, shows what proportion of impressions these demographic segments actually received.

[47] This is simply an index rating targets to delivery. For example, in the category of women aged 18–24, the index is calculated as follows: $16.0 \div 13.9 \times 100 = 115$, or 15 points higher than the goal.

A careful investigation of the impression analysis reveals that the percent of delivery for the three key target groups (women aged 35 + , in households with $15,000+ income, and in A counties) is slightly less than desired. As shown in Part 8 of the plan, the planner opted to purchase more impressions overall (through the purchase of daytime network) than to purchase fewer impressions but in the desired proportions. Also see Part 9 of the Media Plan.

PLAN

[48] PART 8
Media Rationale

[49] **A.** Daytime Network Television :30s

Daytime network television at a level of 35 WGRPs per week will be scheduled for thirty-six weeks beginning in April of next year.

1. It delivers the Brand X target audience more efficiently than other television dayparts.

	Television Efficiency Comparison (:30)			
	Daytime Network	Prime Network	Late Night Network	Combined Fringe
Households	$2.78	$7.69	$4.43	$4.48
Total Women	3.25	9.59	6.94	6.63
Women 35 +	5.08	14.50	10.23	9.76
Women $15,000 +	7.85	16.94	12.73	12.55

2. It furnishes efficient national coverage while supporting the Brand X high-development areas. At comparable rating levels, the cost of daytime network is 3 percent less than day spot and delivers 34 percent more audience than using spot in the top sixty U.S. markets.

	:30 Cost	U.S. Women (%)
Day Spot		
10 WGRPs Top 60 Markets	$30,036 (100)	73 (100)
Daytime Network		
10 WGRPs	$29,280 (97)	98 (134)

3. Daytime television offers the greatest concentration of women viewers compared with the other television dayparts.

		Women Audience Composition					
	% U.S. Adults	Daytime %	Index	Prime Time %	Index	Late Night %	Index
Total Women	52	81	(156)	57	(110)	56	(108)

In addition, on an equal dollar basis, daytime television furnishes the greatest absolute number of the Brand X target audience members.

NOTES

Notes on Part 8—Media Rationale

[48] This is an explanation (or rationale) for the decisions about which media are recommended. Although the rationale provided does not include reference to other daypart combinations, it is important to note that in the early stages of media planning, several alternatives are considered, the best of which is shown here. Further detail is provided in Table 14–6.

[49] Note that 35 women gross rating points (WGRPs) were chosen for daytime network television. Why 35 and not more or less? The answer is based on the planner's judgment that with a given budget and with the given goals, 35 WGRPs a week for thirty-six weeks are adequate, as explained in A4 of the plan.

A1. This section shows relative cost per thousand for the three key targets for alternative television classes. The plan consists of daytime network and a combination of late night and fringe network times. But the cost-per-thousand figures also show primetime and late night television alone as alternatives. The latter two alternatives are shown to be fairly efficient in reaching some targets, but on balance, the selected alternatives are better.

A2. The planner is trying to show in this paragraph that another alternative to daytime network TV might be considered. Is this alternative better? The planner proves that daytime network TV, when compared to an alternative of daytime spot TV in sixty markets, would deliver more targets at a lower cost. The method employed was to take 10 WGRPs in each alternative, cost them out, and see which delivered the most women. The proof is that daytime network TV both costs less and delivers 34 percent more women (100 vs. 134 index numbers).

A3. The purpose of this section is to compare deliveries of primetime and late night television with daytime network television in reaching target groups. Index numbers for daytime are all 100, while alternatives are shown to be less capable of reaching targets (with index numbers less than 100).

PLAN

	Women Delivery (Equal Dollars)					
	Daytime		Prime Time		Late Night	
	Millions	Index	Millions	Index	Millions	Index
Total Women	43.4	100	18.6	43	24.9	57
Women 35 +	27.8	100	12.1	44	9.1	33
Women $15,000 +	8.0	100	4.8	60	6.6	83
Women in A Counties	14.4	100	7.1	49	11.7	81

4. Thirty-five women gross rating points weekly are judged to be a desirable level of daytime network for Brand X. That level provides adequate women delivery nationally and also serves as a strong base upon which to build other national and local advertising efforts.

	Total Women
Reach	42.0
Average Frequency	3.2

50 **B.** Late Night Network :30s

Late night network television will be implemented for thirty-six weeks at a level of 14 WGRPs per week for the first two quarters of the fiscal year. This will provide one announcement a week on each of the three networks. For the balance of the year, 25 WGRPs weekly will be used in recognition of the brand's quarterly volume contribution.

1. Late night network extends the reach nationally among the $15,000-plus household income group.
2. Late night television usage is not affected by seasonal variations as much as other dayparts. This gives the daypart excellent reach opportunities even during the summer months.

	Index of Homes Using TV				
	Average	Spring	Summer	Fall	Winter
Daytime	100	96	96	100	107
Prime Time	100	95	89	107	111
Early Evening	100	92	85	110	113
Late Evening	100	100	100	96	104

51 **C.** Combined Fringe/Spot Television :30s

A combination of one-third early and two-thirds late fringe will be implemented at varying levels for thirty-six weeks in thirty-two Brand X markets.

1. This permits the opportunity to align the allocation of expenditures in accordance with the anticipated business opportunities in these markets.

NOTES

[50] This explains why late night network television was selected.

[51] This explains why a combined early and late fringe pattern for spot television was recommended.

PLAN

2. The use of this medium further increases advertising pressure in key markets.
3. The flexibility of spot TV allows quick reaction to competitive activity.
4. Spot television improves the delivery of the Brand X target audience in A counties.

		Total Audience Delivery		
	Day Net	Prime Net	Late Night Net	Spot TV
A Counties	33.2%	38.1%	47.0%	65.3%
Index	100	115	142	197

[52] **D. Direct Mail Program**

A direct mail program will be implemented in various waves four times during the fiscal year. The program will target Brand X's heavy users for a usage/frequency loyalty program.

1. Several lists exist with names and addresses of heavy purchasers of Brand X. We will rent these names and mail the loyalty program to them.
2. Direct mail allows us to target our best customers and reach them with a compelling message directly to them.
3. We will mail to one million names and with a projected 10% response rate, estimate 100,000 active participants in Brand X loyalty program by the end of the year.

[53] **E. In-Store Targeted Couponing**

In-store targeted couponing will be used to reward Brand X's heavy purchasers during four cycles of the year. After meeting a pre-established purchase requirement, the Brand X heavy purchaser will receive a cents-off coupon for Brand X. The coupon will have space for name and address so that when coupon is redeemed there will be the opportunity to capture this information for the Brand X direct mail loyalty program. Subsequently, the direct mail program will be mailed to the respondents of the in-store targeted couponing.

1. The use of this medium allows us to reward Brand X's best customers at the store where the product is purchased.
2. Targeted coupons offer the added benefit of name/address capture that allows database/direct mail program to grow.

NOTES

[52,53] This explains why direct mail and in-store targeted couponing were used.

[52] Note that this portion of the plan came from a database that showed actual names and addresses of prospects. This portion of the plan, when added to the traditional media portion, makes the plan more powerful.

[53] Note that when consumers respond to targeted couponing, the data can be added to the existing database as an update.

PLAN

[54] PART 9
Comparison of Plan with Strategy

This section explains how the proposed media plan meets the designated strategy and objectives. Table 14–6 outlines this comparison in detail.

TABLE 14–6. Comparison of Plan with Strategy

Strategy				Plan		
[55] 1. Concentrate impression delivery among the primary Brand X demographic targets.				1. The recommended plan furnishes the best delivery among the target audience (women 35-plus, living in A counties) than alternative plans investigated.		
	Total U.S. Women (%)	Target (%)	Index	Impressions (%)	Indices Women	Target
Age						
18–24	18.0	13.9	77	16.0	89	115
25–34	20.4	17.9	88	19.2	95	107
35–49	23.0	21.3	93	23.5	102	110
50-plus	38.6	46.9	122	41.3	107	88
Household Income						
Under $8,000	38.1	28.6	75	41.5	109	145
$8,000–$15,000	34.5	33.0	96	34.0	99	103
$15,000–plus	27.4	38.4	140	24.5	89	64
Household Size						
1–2	39.9	38.0	95	41.9	105	110
3–4	35.8	37.7	105	31.5	88	84
5-plus	24.3	24.3	100	26.6	109	109
County Size						
A	40.9	51.0	125	47.0	115	92
B	26.2	24.1	92	26.7	102	111
C	19.4	17.3	89	15.5	80	90
D	13.5	7.6	56	10.8	80	142

In terms of absolute impressions delivered, the recommended plan furnished about 10 percent more impressions than Alternative III delivers (day net, prime net, fringe spot plan).

Women	Recommended (thousands)	Prime Net Alternate (thousands)	Index
35–plus	1,412.8	1,318.9	107
$15,000–plus	535.0	481.3	111
A Counties	1,026.9	932.4	110

NOTES

Notes on Part 9—Comparison of Plan with Strategy

[54] This part of the plan explains how the plan as outlined achieves the objectives set for it. The strategies are listed at the left and the proof that the strategies were fulfilled is shown at the right in statistical form. For example, look at women aged 50-plus. The plan delivers 41.3 percent of its impressions to women 50 years and older. This is less than desired as shown by the index of 88 to the target (41.3 ÷ 46.9) but more than needed to concentrate among older women in the population (41.3 ÷ 38.6).

[55] Note that at the end of the demographic analysis of delivery there is a statement about a plan titled Alternative III. Alternative III was one of three media plan alternatives devised for the client to provide other options in media strategy. The manner in which these options are compared is through gross impression analysis. In [52] the planner points out to the client that the recommended plan (Alternative I) delivered about 10 percent more gross impressions than Alternative III, which consisted of a strategy of day network television, prime network, and fringe spot. The big difference between Alternatives I and III was the use of late night network in I and prime network in III. Alternatives II and III were omitted from this text, since much of both plans consisted of similar kinds of data and strategies as Alternative I.

PLAN

2. Allocate dollars according to current Brand X sales volume while trying to stimulate development in high volume areas.

	U.S. Women (%)	Volume (%)	Index
Primary Markets	45.76	62.16	136
Remainder U.S	54.24	37.84	70
Total U.S.	100.00	100.00	100

2. The recommended plan provides a 111 index of investment among the primary Brand X markets.

Investment (%)	Index (Vol. = 100)
69.06	111
30.94	82
100.00	100

3. Provide at least a 75 reach with an average frequency of 5 among total women in key areas. Concurrently, seek a reach goal of 50 among women who have been exposed at least three times.

	R/F Goals
Total Reach/Frequency	75/5.0
Frequency Distribution	50/3 +

3. The reach/frequency goals were achieved in the key areas that provide Brand X with 62 percent of its volume.

	Volume (%)	Low	High
Key Markets	62		
Reach/Frequency		81/5.1	85/5.8
Frequency Distribution		53/3 +	52/3 +
Remainder U.S.	38		
Reach/Frequency		57/3.4	63/3.7
Frequency Distribution		27/3 +	33/3 +

4. Distribute advertising pressure according to quarterly volume contribution.

Quarter	Contribution
June	24
September	23
December	26
March	27
	100

4. The plan follows the contribution pattern.

Quarter	Contribution
June	22
September	21
December	30
March	27
	100

5. Flexibility should be maintained.

5. The plan is sufficiently flexible to permit a reallocation of funds from one geographic area to another or from one quarter to another. About 45 percent of the budget is invested in spot TV.

6. Provide as many weeks of activity as affordable within the quarterly investment allocation once the reach/frequency goals are met.

6. The plan provides for thirty-six weeks of activity in flights ranging from four to ten weeks in length with short (two weeks) durations of nonadvertising periods after an initial hiatus of four weeks.

7. Employ media vehicles that are highly compatible with the copy requirements and overall brand image.

7. The plan uses television primarily, capitalizing on the effectiveness of the medium in communicating the taste appeal of the product. Direct mail and in-store targeted couponing are used to reach Brand X's heavy users with a sales building loyalty program.

NOTES

PLAN

PART 10
Spot Television: Market Selection Methodology

As stated in the strategy sections, media dollars are to be allocated to current Brand X sales volume by market while maintaining competitive levels in high-volume areas. The allocation of delivery to each market is on a dollar basis, following the philosophy of spending in those areas where business is best.

The dollar allocation is based on the brand's total budget, not just the spot television budget. By using the total budget (national and local), the contribution made in each local TV market by network television is included in the allocation.

The market selection procedure employs a computer system that allocates media budgets to each TV market based on a target percentage. Adding all of the targets for all markets in the U.S. equals 100 percent. The target is obtained by weighting various factors in each market: sales, Nielsen county size consumption indices, and population. Once the targets are obtained, the computer system then calculates delivery of the network television portion of the media plan as well as the amount of money to be spent in spot television.

The following explains how markets were selected to receive spot TV and how much spot TV is to be used in each market.

1. District sales are put into the computer. Example: Boston District sales = 6.6% of total U.S. sales.
2. Nielsen county size consumption indices are put into the computer (note that each Sales District has a different consumption index):

A counties	128
B counties	128
C counties	150
D counties	150

3. Each market's total women population by county size is weighted by (multiplied by) the brand's regional Nielsen county size consumption index:

   Example: Boston TV Market

	Population (thousands)	Index	Weighted Population (thousands)
A counties	1,195.4	128	1,530.1
B counties	434.4	128	556.0
C counties	215.9	150	323.9
D counties	23.3	150	35.0
Total	1,869.0		2,445.0

NOTES

Notes on Parts 10 and 11—Spot Television Market Selection and Buying Strategy

[56] Whenever a media plan calls for the use of spot television, there must be some statement explaining how the markets that are part of the spot plan are to be selected. There are many ways to make market selections. The criteria for this plan are listed here.

[56] More detail was shown in this media plan than usual for the benefit of readers who have little or no background in selecting spot TV.

PLAN

4. The weighted women populations are totaled by District and each market is assigned a percentage of the District total. These percentages are then applied to the appropriate District sales volume contribution of each market.

Boston District

Market	Weighted Women Population (thousands)	% of Total	% of Sales Target*
Bangor	159.1	3.17	0.20
Boston	2,445.0	48.79	3.22
Hartford	896.9	17.89	1.18
Portland	401.1	8.00	0.53
Presque Isle	43.5	0.87	0.06
Providence	770.0	15.38	1.02
Springfield	295.6	5.90	0.39
Total	5,012.1	100.00	6.60

*Obtained by multiplying the percentage of weighted women population in each market by the District sales percentage total of 6.6%.

5. In order to concentrate dollars in the most productive markets, a judgment was made to eliminate from spot television consideration any market that had less than 0.35 percent of U.S. sales. In the Boston District, two markets (Bangor and Presque Isle) were eliminated.

6. Network television expenditures are allocated to each TV market based on the local rating point delivery of the network programs that will be purchased. Total network dollars and specific dayparts have already been determined.

   (Note: As discussed in Table 9–1, a national medium such as network television does not produce the same level of gross rating points in each market. To allocate network TV dollars to each market, therefore, local GRP delivery of programs must be obtained. Local GRPs are then multiplied by a local market's population to yield impressions. Impressions are multiplied by the national cost per thousand of network TV, which results in the prorated local market dollar allocation of network TV. These calculations can be done by hand. For this media plan, the computer system automatically makes all these calculations.)

	Network Budget	% of Total TV Budget
Boston TV Market	$ 157,645	1.13
Total Network Budget	7,829,000	
Total TV Budget	13,950,000	100.0

NOTES

PLAN

Note that the network delivery in the Boston TV market comprises 1.13 percent of the total TV budget of $13,950,000. An additional 2.09 percent investment is required to align the expenditures with the target percent of the total budget.

7. Supplementary spot television weight is added as required to align total market expenditures with market targets.

	Boston TV Market	
	Dollars	% of Total TV Budget
Network TV	$157,635	1.13
Spot TV	291,255	2.09
Total	$448,890	3.22

8. Insofar as markets with less than 0.35 percent of sales contribution were eliminated from spot television consideration, the total spot TV budget of $6,121,000 was not completely allocated. The remaining spot TV budget is therefore re-allocated proportionately to each selected TV market based on the target percentage. This results in an increase of spot TV expenditures in each market.

	Boston TV Market	
	Dollars	% of Total TV Budget
Network TV	$157,635	1.13
Spot TV	309,690	2.22
Total	$467,325	3.35

9. Spot TV dollars are converted to gross rating points per week by using individual market cost per rating point data. It had been predetermined to schedule a minimum of thirty-six weeks of activity with spot television:

Boston Market	
Spot TV Budget	$309,672.00
Cost per GRP	158.04
Total Affordable GRPs	1,959
Weekly GRPs (for thirty-six weeks)	54

10. Adjustments in spending were made after the initial computer calculations to recognize both competitive pressures and minimum GRP levels:

   a. It was decided, in light of competitive pressures and the brand's development, to further increase support in spot TV markets in the Chicago and Los Angeles districts.

NOTES

PLAN

b. Four markets—Hartford, Johnstown, San Diego, and Phoenix—were scheduled to receive less than a minimum amount of weekly GRPs (over thirty-six weeks). Rather than construct a separate spot TV market group for these four markets (with less than thirty-six weeks of activity), it was decided to increase spending in these areas until a full thirty-six weeks of activity was affordable.

Table 14–7 shows the spot TV market list for Brand X that shows GRP delivery for network TV and spot TV, as well as the dollar allocation to each TV market.

Note: Let's take a closer look at how we convert from GRPs to dollars in the Boston market. First, each daypart's weekly women ratings points are cumed. For daytime, 32 WGRPs are multiplied by 36 weeks for a cume of 1,152 WGRPs (or 11.52 percent of the target population). The cume GRPs are then multiplied by the local market's target population to yield impressions. For daytime, 11.52 percent is multiplied by the Boston women population of 2,445,000 for a total of 28,166,000 women impressions. Impressions are multiplied by that daypart's national CPM, resulting in the dollar allocation seen in Table 14–7. Daytime's 28,166,000 women impressions are multiplied by the women national daytime CPM of $3.25 for a total of $91,540.

	Boston TV Market			
	Local WGRPs (cume)	Women Population	Impressions (000)	National Women CPM	Budget*
Day Network	1,152	2,445,000	28,166	$3.25	$ 91,540
Late Network	360	2,445,000	8,802	6.94	61,086
Spot TV	1,944	2,445,000	47,531	6.63	315,131
Total					$467,757

*Differences versus Table 14–7 due to rounding.

NOTES

PLAN   TABLE 14-7. Spot TV Market List—Brand X

District/DMA	Pop. (%)	Tgt. (%)	BDI	36 Week Average WGRP/Week			
				Day Net.	Late Net.	Spot TV	Total
Boston							
Boston	2.61	3.22	123	32	10	54	96
Hartford/N.H.	.95	1.18	125	32	12	45	89
Portland	.39	.53	132	39	12	85	136
Providence	.83	1.02	123	35	20	75	130
Spgfld./Holyoke	.32	.39	123	39	8	53	100
Total Markets	5.10	6.34	124	33	12	55	100
Total District	5.28	6.60	125				
New York	9.42	13.04	138	32	20	160	212
Syracuse							
Alb./Sch./Troy	.60	1.10	182	32	14	103	149
Buffalo	.89	1.58	178	35	18	109	162
Burlington	.25	.37	149	46	10	58	114
Rochester	.44	.77	175	35	20	73	128
Syracuse	.60	1.10	183	35	10	130	175
Total Markets	2.78	4.92	177	35	15	98	148
Total District	3.38	5.91	175				
Philadelphia							
Baltimore	1.12	1.91	170	32	8	82	122
Harr./Lanc./York	.60	1.03	172	32	18	104	154
Philadelphia	3.47	5.91	171	39	18	113	170
Washington, D.C.	1.86	3.22	174	28	8	114	150
Wilkes-Barre	.62	1.09	176	46	22	67	135
Total Markets	7.67	13.16	172	35	14	102	151
Total District	7.75	13.34	172				
Youngstown							
Cleveland	2.01	2.82	140	35	14	130	179
Johnstown	.52	.41	79	49	18	50	117
Pittsburgh	1.67	2.30	138	42	22	69	133
Youngstown	.33	.46	139	35	20	65	120
Total Markets	4.53	5.99	132	39	18	88	145
Total District	4.78	6.55	137				
Detroit							
Detroit	2.33	4.35	187	35	14	156	205
Flint	.56	.95	171	42	14	191	247
Fort Wayne	.29	.48	170	35	16	67	118
Grand Rapids	.64	1.11	174	39	10	126	175
Lansing	.26	.46	176	39	8	89	136
Toledo	.48	.83	173	46	28	84	158
Total Markets	4.56	8.18	179	38	15	130	183
Total District	4.76	8.52	179				
Chicago							
Chicago	4.07	3.48	86	32	32	84	148
South Bend	.37	.43	117	39	18	141	198
Milwaukee	.90	.69	77	32	26	54	112
Total Markets	5.34	4.60	86	32	30	82	140
Total District	6.44	5.35	83				

TABLE 14–7. (continued)

District/DMA	Pop. (%)	Tgt. (%)	BDI	36 Week Average WGRP/Week			
				Day Net.	Late Net.	Spot TV	Total
Los Angeles							
Los Angeles	4.98	4.81	97	25	18	59	102
San Diego	.67	.57	86	21	10	30	61
Phoenix	.71	.55	78	28	12	31	71
Total Markets	6.36	5.93	93	25	16	47	88
Total District	7.35	6.48	88				
Total Key Markets	45.76	62.16	136	33	18	90	141
Total Key Districts	49.16	65.79	134				
Rem. U.S. Key Markets	54.24	37.84	70	37	22	—	59
Rem. U.S. Key Districts	50.84	34.21	61				
Balance U.S.	100.0	100.0	100	35	20	—	—

TABLE 14-7. (continued)

Budget				Dollars	
Day Network	Late Network	Spot TV	Total	(%)	Index
91,872	65,773	309,672	467,317	3.35	105
33,660	27,856	124,848	186,364	1.34	114
16,632	10,059	50,796	77,487	.56	105
31,680	35,981	80,784	148,445	1.06	105
13,464	5,803	37,944	57,211	.41	105
187,308	145,472	604,044	936,824	6.72	106
196,812	148,182	604,044	949,038	6.80	103
325,512	430,617	1,145,440	1,901,569	13.63	105
23,364	20,118	117,504	160,986	1.15	105
35,640	35,594	157,896	229,130	1.64	105
9,504	4,642	39,780	53,926	.39	106
17,028	18,958	74,664	110,650	.79	110
21,384	11,993	126,684	160,061	1.15	105
106,920	91,305	516,528	714,753	5.12	105
135,828	115,296	516,528	767,652	5.50	93
40,392	21,666	217,260	279,318	2.00	105
21,384	22,827	104,652	148,863	1.07	105
144,540	135,028	578,952	858,520	6.15	105
58,212	34,821	373,320	466,353	3.34	105
31,284	30,178	96,084	157,546	1.14	105
295,812	244,520	1,370,268	1,910,600	13.70	105
297,792	246,455	1,370,268	1,914,515	13.72	104
76,032	59,195	274,176	409,403	2.93	105
21,780	14,702	26,316	62,798	.95	110
75,240	76,606	182,988	334,834	2.40	105
12,276	14,702	39,780	66,758	.48	105
185,328	165,205	523,260	873,793	6.26	105
197,604	180,295	523,260	901,159	6.46	98
90,288	76,606	463,896	630,790	4.52	105
25,344	16,249	97,308	138,901	1.00	105
10,692	9,285	48,348	68,325	.49	102
28,116	15,089	118,728	161,933	1.16	105
10,296	5,029	51,408	66,733	.48	105
22,572	27,856	69,768	120,196	.86	105
187,308	150,114	849,456	1,186,878	8.51	105
198,792	156,694	849,456	1,204,942	8.64	101
138,600	277,794	364,752	781,146	5.60	161
12,672	11,220	72,216	96,108	.69	161
34,056	48,749	74,052	156,857	1.12	162
185,328	337,763	511,020	1,034,111	7.41	161
232,848	394,251	511,020	1,138,119	8.16	153

TABLE 14–7. (continued)

Budget					
Day Network	Late Network	Spot TV	Total	Dollars (%)	Index
140,976	195,384	438,192	774,552	5.55	115
16,632	14,315	89,964	120,911	.87	150
19,800	17,023	72,828	109,651	.79	144
177,408	226,722	600,984	1,005,114	7.21	123
208,296	248,002	600,984	1,057,282	7.58	117
1,650,924	1,791,718	6,121,000	9,563,642	68.56	110
1,793,484	1,919,792	6,121,000	9,834,276	70.50	107
2,309,076	2,077,282	—	4,386,358	31.44	83
2,166,516	1,949,208	—	4,115,724	29.50	86
$3,960,000	$3,869,000	$6,121,000	$13,950,000	100.00	100

PLAN

PART 11
Spot Television: Buying Strategy

Target audience	Primary—women aged 35-plus Secondary—total women Other—$15,000-plus household income A counties
Fringe Mix	$1/3$ early fringe $2/3$ late fringe
Buying Goal	Spend to budget
Spot TV Objectives	Spot television is being implemented to align impressions in accordance with the anticipated business opportunities in these markets. Spot TV is also being used to extend reach among the brand's target audience in key markets.

In general, high-rated shows with an above average concentration of women aged 35-plus are the most desirable. Implicit in high-rated shows are higher than average levels of attentiveness. In addition, in-show positions are preferable to those during the break.

The $1/3$ early, $2/3$ late dispersion of WGRPs is designed to place additional pressure among upper income women who are available in late fringe. It is also an attempt to capitalize on the higher attentiveness levels generated during late fringe. This dispersion, however, is directional and should not be construed as being inflexible.

A Final Note

Some readers may wonder why the names of individual television programs were not mentioned in this plan. The reason is that the selection of individual programs is part of the buying strategy. The buying strategy is always to select those programs which best fulfill the demographic profile stated in the media objectives. The plan shown on the preceding pages clearly specifies the kind and the number of television programs that need to be selected. After the plan has been approved, buying will begin through negotiation with network and spot time sales representatives.

NOTES

57 When the media plan has been approved, it will be necessary for the spot television buyer to buy spots as the plan recommends. To make the buyer's job easier, specific criteria for buying have been listed here.

QUESTIONS FOR DISCUSSION

1. Why should this planner want to "direct impressions toward all women proportionate to their Brand X volume contribution?"
2. What media planning principle is not specifically stated in this chapter, but is obvious in the following statement from the plan: "Why then did the planner select women 35 + instead of only those aged 50 + "?
3. Why was it necessary to buy flexible media in this plan?
4. How will the media planner probably justify advertising for only 36 weeks out of 52, when the product is sold in every week of the year?
5. Although the case does not explain why market share for Brand X has eroded, what is a probable answer (use only the information from the case)?
6. In studying Table 14–2, you will find Detroit listed in the "Southern Region." Is this a mistake? Explain.
7. In Table 14–5 you will find that women targets in the $15,000 a year income class had an index of 64. Is this acceptable for the plan? Why?
8. Explain why the planner deliberately did not try to reach non-users of this brand.
9. Quarterly sales volume is shown in Part 4–C. If this was your plan, what strategy would you try to follow as a result of this data?
10. Part 8: Media Rationale shows how well network TV delivers the target audience. Explain then, why spot TV was also recommended in this plan.

15

Media Costs and Buying Problems

One of the major tasks of a media planner is to match markets with the best media for reaching those markets at the most favorable cost to the client. Earlier chapters have discussed how markets are defined in terms of people and their product consumption, geographic distribution, and demographic characteristics. Those chapters also noted that individuals are exposed to media in varying degrees. On one hand, for example, full-time home-makers are more likely to watch daytime television shows and read women's service magazines than are teenagers or working men and women. On the other hand, men are more likely than women to read sports magazines or watch sports television programs.

Each of these media alternatives has a different cost. The final media plan emerging from the marketing strategy should effectively maximize the delivery of the designated marketing target in the most cost-efficient manner. Therefore, the media planner must be familiar with market definition, and be fully versed in how people utilize various media. In some instances, as is the case with television time, the cost of media varies with supply and demand. Other media, such as magazines and newspapers, tend to remain fairly constant in cost, thereby providing a high degree of predictability as planners develop costs for the media plan.

The costs that go into the final media plan are always in a state of flux. Estimating such costs is as much an art as a science; it depends heavily on the experience and professionalism of the media planner and the media buyer. If a plan is based on costs that are way out of line with marketplace realities, it can result in faulty media plan delivery. For example, if a planner estimates that 100 gross rating points of prime-time television can be purchased for $200,000, and the actual cost of that time is $300,000, the deliverability of the plan is seriously impaired. The client can then justifiably question the value of that media plan as well as the competence of the planner.

Estimating media costs is a complex task. In addition, different media have different problems connected with the buying process. This chapter will identify the importance of the planner's involvement in the media buying process and explain why this involvement requires familiarity with both the cost of media and the problems associated with purchasing different media types.

Some Considerations in Planning and Buying

The value of a media plan is related to how well it delivers the designated marketing targets at the lowest cost with the least amount of waste. The criteria for determining how well the plan accomplishes its mission are related to such concepts as reach, frequency, and target market impressions delivered. The gross number of target market impressions, coupled with the reach and frequency associated with those impressions within the designated budget, form the nucleus of an effective media plan. The media planner must go through a calculated process of matching the cost of various media alternatives with the delivery of the plan to arrive at the optimal relationship between cost and delivery.

For example, let's assume the cost per thousand of women 18 years of age and over for daytime network television is about $4.46 (:30 basis) while the cost per thousand for the same audience segment in nighttime network is approximately $12.87. A set budget—placing all dollars in daytime network—will deliver three times more impressions to women 18 + than will nighttime network based on these costs per thousand. For a $5 million budget over a one-year period of time allocated to thirty-second commercials, it is estimated that the average four-week reach and frequency for nighttime would be lower than the same budget in daytime, as is illustrated in Table 15–1. However, the reach of nighttime will be higher than the daytime reach over the total fifty-two-week period. Conversely, the frequency in daytime will be higher than the frequency in nighttime over the total fifty-two-week period.

Two ways most often used to analyze media costs are to calculate cost per thousands on the basis of either gross impressions or net reach. Whichever method is used, the cost efficiency of media delivery is important. It may be found that the medium with the largest reach or the most gross impressions is not necessarily the best buy because its cost efficiency is somewhat poorer. Table 15–2 shows a rough comparison of alternative media deliveries and cost efficiencies.

An examination of the table shows that different coverage levels are achieved by different media vehicles, with certain cost-per-thousand implications. The media planner's task is to fully combine a familiarity with me-

TABLE 15-1. Average Four-Week Delivery Estimated for a $5 Million Budget

	Night Network	Day Network
Commercial unit	30 seconds	30 seconds
Total affordable GRPs		
Households	547	1,826
Women	427	1,480
Total fifty-two-week R&F		
Households	86/6.4	76/24.0
Women	76/5.6	59/25
Average four-week GRPs		
Households	42	140
Women	33	114
Average four-week R&F		
Households	34/1.2	43/3.3
Women	30/1.1	36/3.

dia costs and delivery dynamics with the goals of the marketing plan to reach designated audiences. The planner must be careful to employ correct media cost assumptions in the development of the plan. Table 15–2 shows that, if inappropriate cost assumptions are used in estimating the costs of daytime network versus women's service magazines, it would be possible to include one media type in the plan to the exclusion of the other.

There are several ways media planners can help ensure correct and current media cost estimates. It should be noted that although we refer to media planners here, it is common for many companies to have media buyers, professionals trained in purchasing, make these decisions.

First, the planner must maintain close contact with media marketplace cost mechanisms. For example, for many years pricing for print media such as magazines, newspapers, and newspaper preprints tended to be related to the cost of producing the product. As paper, ink, wage, and postal costs increased, magazine and newspaper publishers passed these costs on to the reader, to some degree, and to the advertiser.

During these years, magazine costs tended to grow at a relatively modest annual rate compared with broadcast. However, with the advent of negotiated rates in the print media in the early 1980s, print increases have tended to parallel broadcast increases as shown in Table 15–3.

Today, both the broadcast media and magazines are influenced not so much by the cost of the product as by the law of supply and demand. The media planner assesses supply and demand in these media by maintaining constant contact with suppliers, that is, the media representatives. These contacts give the planner a feel for what is transpiring in the market and thus enable the forecasting of changes (upward or downward) in pricing.

Second, intelligent media planners will include media buyers in the development of media cost estimates. Many agencies and advertisers employ media buying specialists whose sole responsibility is the purchase of media. Such media buyers are in regular contact with the media suppliers with

TABLE 15–2.   Alternative Media—Cost and Delivery

	Advertising Unit	National Equiv. Cost $ (000)	Women 18+			Men 18+		
			# (MM)	%	CPM	# (MM)	%	CPM
Night Network	:30	$ 108.1	8.3	8.7	$13.02	5.7	6.6	$18.96
Day Network	:30	15.6	3.6	3.4	4.33	1.1	1.3	14.18
Sports Network	:30	40.9	2.0	2.1	20.45	3.1	3.6	13.19
Late Night Network	:30	17.6	1.9	2.0	9.26	1.4	1.6	12.57
Early Network News	:30	50.5	6.5	6.9	7.77	5.0	5.8	10.10
General Magazines (5 Mag. Avg.)	1P4C	120.9	19.2	20.3	6.30	15.6	18.1	7.75
Women's Magazines (6 Mag. Avg.)	1P4C	92.4	18.8	19.8	4.91	2.3	2.7	40.17
Newspapers (Top 100 Mkts.)	Full P B/W	3,661.1	56.9	60.0	64.34	55.3	64.0	66.20
Network Radio	:60	5.2	0.3	0.3	17.33	0.4	0.5	13.00
Outdoor (Top 10 Mkts.)	100 Showing	1,591.4	26.8	N/A	59.38	24.9	N/A	63.91

Sources: Nielsen Media Research, NAD Reports; Leo Burnett 1991 Media Costs and Coverage; Marketer's Guide to Media; RADAR, Full Bureau, Standard Rate & Data Service; and Mediamark Research Bureau, Institute of Outdoor Advertising.

TABLE 15-3. Media Cost and Cost-per-Thousand Trends Index

	Prime		Daytime		Consumer Magazines		Newspaper		Net Radio	
	Unit Cost	CPM	Unit Cost	CPM	Unit Cost	CPM	Unit Cost	CPM	Unit Cost	CPM
1980	100	100	100	100	100	100	100	100	100	100
1981	116	113	109	105	104	106	110	109	109	108
1982	120	126	114	110	113	116	121	121	121	115
1983	140	160	133	120	123	125	133	132	133	123
1984	151	176	148	140	128	132	100*	100*	144	132
1985	155	178	146	140	135	141	111	112	157	141
1986	164	200	138	140	139	149	116	118	172	154
1987	167	211	123	120	144	155	116	117	184	162
1988	176	221	107	110	149	162	132	134	193	169
1989	191	253	113	121	156	171	134	136	201	176
1990	169	230	112	125	162	183	140	142	210	184

Sources: A. C. Nielsen *NIT Planner's Report; Marketing & Media Decisions, RADAR; SRDS;* and *Editor and Publisher Yearbook,* 1991.
*Conversion from line to inch rates in 1984 makes indexing to 1975 impossible. Therefore, indices after 1984 are indexed in 1984 costs and CPMs.

whom they do business on behalf of the agency/client. During the course of the numerous media buyer–seller transactions, the buyer acquires a familiarity with what is occurring in the marketplace. Such familiarity can assist the media planner in forecasting media price changes. Media buyers are expected to maintain good media supplier relations to facilitate this flow of information. Media planners should make it a point to maintain close communications with the media buyers so as to tap this source of media cost information.

Third, agencies develop expertise in estimating media cost changes based on the agency's total experience. Over a period of time, the agency can compile media cost information in various markets, or nationally, by generalizing from various specific buying experiences. It is not necessary to breach security within an agency in order to develop this information. Generalized experience is one of the reasons many agencies have gone to buying media by market as opposed to buying by brand. The individual responsible for buying an individual market (or markets) is intimately acquainted with the media cost picture in those areas.

Once the media plan has been implemented and the schedules completed, the media planner should examine how closely the media cost estimates compare with actual costs. This is called a postbuy analysis. By conducting a postbuy analysis, the planner can sharpen the capability to forecast costs by reviewing what went into the original estimates. Such trial-and-error devices assist the media professional in developing the personal art of media cost forecasting. Major variations between cost estimates and actual plan delivery cost may uncover flaws in understanding or thinking, or may be the consequence of significant media marketplace cost changes that could not have been anticipated. In any event, the media planner, in check-

TABLE 15–4.   National Advertisers Media Expenditures (1985)

Media	Dollars Spent (MM)	Portion of Total (%)
Newspaper	3,867	11%
Spot TV	7,788	21
Network TV	9,383	26
Spot Radio	1,635	4
Consumer Magazine	6,803	19
Business Magazine	2,875	8
Cable TV	1,393	4
Syndicated TV	1,589	4
Outdoor	640	2
Network Radio	482	1
Farm publications	215	1*
	36,670	100%

Source: *Advertising Age*, May 1991.
*Less than 1 percent.

ing back over the implemented plan, should consider the exercise an important learning experience.

A Discussion of Media Costs

Table 15–4 shows national media expenditures by major consumer media
types for 1990. The chart identifies the major media to which national advertisers direct their dollars. Note that newspapers and television comprise
nearly 75 percent of national expenditures. The magnitude and complexity
of planning and buying these media require close attention to cost implications.

Within these broad media types, there are numerous alternatives available with which the media planner must be acquainted. In addition to understanding general media cost relationships, for example, between television and magazines, the professional media planner must be familiar with
costs of network versus spot, and the different availabilities within the general broadcast medium as well as the changes over time—a complex and difficult assignment, but a necessary one.

Television Costs

Table 15–4 showed that combined television expenditures accounted for 55
percent of total advertising dollars spent in 1990. Most of the television investment was for consumer goods and services. However, there has been a
growing use of the medium by industrial and business-related advertisers.
In view of the magnitude of the investment in television, a media planning
professional must be fully conversant with all phases of the medium. The
major characteristic of television, insofar as media costs are concerned, re-

FIGURE 15-1. Daypart Programming Available for Network Use

6 7 8 9 10 11 12 1 2 3 4	5 6 7 8 9 10 11	12 1 2
AM PM		AM

L O C A L	Network	L O C A L	Network Daytime Programs	L O C A L	N E T W O R K	L O C A L	Network Prime-time Programs	L O C A L	Net- work Late Night Progs.	L O C A L

lates to the "perishability" of the inventory. Generally speaking, there is a fixed amount of television time available for sale. Unlike a magazine or newspaper that can expand or contract the number of advertising pages available for sale in any given issue, a commercial minute that is unsold can never be recovered. The sellers of television time must contend with this perishability concept in selling the medium.

Although marketplace pricing conditions prevail at any given time, these prices are subject to change as advertisers' demand for that time increases or decreases. The stronger the demand and the earlier the sale in relationship to the program air date, the more likely that pricing will be higher. Less advertising demand close to air date can create lower pricing, assuming inventory availability. These interrelated conditions of perishability, demand, and inventory create a dynamic marketplace. The buyer of television time must, therefore, be alert to these changes by maintaining close contact with the marketplace.

Under the broad heading of television, there are basically four subcategories, national network, local spot, syndication, and cable.

Network Television. Certain parts of the broadcast day are programmed by the national networks: the American Broadcasting Company (ABC), the Columbia Broadcasting System (CBS), the National Broadcasting Company (NBC), and the Fox network. Figure 15-1 illustrates the dayparts when network programming is usually made available to *affiliates* (the individual stations that comprise a network lineup). The number of stations serviced by a given network can vary from 150 to 210, depending on the strength of the network programming available. The networks sell commercial time to advertisers to run within specific programs. These programs can appear throughout various parts of the day—for example, daytime network series, prime-time network, or late night (post-prime-time) segment.

Prime time (8:00 P.M. to 11:00 P.M. EST), because of the high HUT (homes using television), generally provides the highest ratings. This time period tends to deliver a family audience with high reach levels of most viewing segments. Media costs for prime time are generally the highest per :30 second commercial of all network time segments available for sale. The cost for thirty seconds in prime time, as indicated in Table 15-2, can be in the area of $108,100 (or higher for certain programs). Individual program costs will vary depending on rating level and the amount of inventory available for sale. As discussed earlier, the less inventory, generally, the higher the cost.

Daytime network (10:00 A.M. to 4:30 P.M. EST) is normally the least costly of the network dayparts. An average cost for thirty seconds will be somewhere in the vicinity of $15,600 with an average household rating of approximately 4.6. This results in an extremely efficient cost-per-thousand delivery of homes and women.

Late night (11:30 P.M. to conclusion EST) network programming tends to vary from network to network and over time. This time period is generally programmed with talk shows, movies, and different types of entertainment including drama, rock concerts, and comedy. Pricing for this time period, since fewer sets are in use than during prime time, tends to be about $17,600 for thirty seconds with an average household rating of 3.0. Although the rating levels for late night are comparable to daytime, there is a dual audience (both men and women) included in late night that is not generally the case in daytime. Thus, pricing for that dual audience tends to be somewhat higher than daytime.

Most network programming on weekends is in the sports and children's areas. Sports programming, for the most part, is the domain of the male-oriented advertiser. Such products as beer, male grooming aids, investment counseling, and automobiles are heavily represented on weekend sports programming. In general, there is a limited amount of broadscale sports programming compared with other network program time. Therefore, pricing tends to be relatively high on a cost-per-thousand basis for the higher interest sporting events. However, the value of identifying with a major high-interest sports event has distinct rub-off effects on brands associated with such programming.

Children's programs, often referred to as "kid TV," are the primary fare on Saturday mornings. Nearly all of this programming are cartoons, but there are some live-action shows, especially in the action/adventure and sports areas. The predominant audience is children, and the advertising, therefore, is highly child-oriented. Cereal, toy/game, fast food, and candy advertisers concentrate a significant portion of their advertising budget in kid TV.

The diversity of programming provided by the networks ranges from the all-family interest generated in prime time to highly selective shows of interest to perhaps relatively few households. Such diversity provides the media planner with rich opportunities for reaching broad national markets with programming aimed specifically to target market interests. Costs for such programming will change as marketplace demand changes so that the media planner must be ever alert to the buying implications of the programming selected for inclusion in the media plan.

Local Stations. Announcements can be purchased on local television stations, which are either affiliated with a network and carry network programming at certain times of the day or are independent stations, which do not have any network affiliation and thus must program the entire day on their own.

Costs for local announcements vary from market to market based on audience delivered and advertiser demand for the available commercial time. Generally speaking, the costs for scheduling announcements in markets like New York, Los Angeles, and Chicago are higher than those for smaller markets because of the amount of circulation delivered by these stations. Time is made available for sale, whether the station is network-affiliated or independent, across almost the entire day. Even within daypart programming by the networks, such as in prime time, there are certain segments of time set aside for local sale. This means that it is possible for a local advertiser, for example in Chicago, to purchase a thirty-second announcement (if available) in a network-originated program, or between programs at the station break.

Because independent stations program for the entire day, there are numerous opportunities for the advertiser to select specific dayparts and programming to reach the target audience. In addition to adjacencies next to and, at times, within network programming, commercial time can be selected in what is termed *fringe time*. Generally speaking, the fringe dayparts and the programming contained therein might look something like the following:

Sample Schedule

Station	Local Time (EST)	Program
A	6:00 P.M.–6:30 P.M.	Local news
	6:30 P.M.–7:00 P.M.	Local news
	11:00 P.M.–11:30 P.M.	Local news
	11:30 P.M.–Conclusion	Movie
B	5:00 P.M.–5:30 P.M.	"M*A*S*H"
	5:30 P.M.–6:00 P.M.	"Three's Company"
	6:30 P.M.–7:00 P.M.	"Night Court"
	10:30 P.M.–Conclusion	Local movie

Pricing for dayparts and specific programs within dayparts will again vary based on audience delivery and availability of commercial time. It is difficult to generalize about pricing and relationships between dayparts, stations within a market, and between markets because of the diversity associated with purchasing local announcements. However, in general, spot television is a highly cost-efficient media vehicle for reaching specialized geographic markets. Such geographic selectivity enables the advertiser to concentrate dollars in markets representing the greatest sales potential.

Syndication. Syndication is the development or packaging of programming that is sold directly to the advertiser and/or cleared on a market-by-market basis by the syndicator. Clearances for a syndicated property can range from a program run one time in a few markets to weekly series clearing in 70–90 percent of the U.S. for extended periods of time. Syndicated properties include first-run talk shows, specials, sports events, entertainment, information, and game shows as well as off-network reruns of sitcoms and serials. Table 15–5 lists the top ten syndicated properties in the 1990–1991 broadcast year. Nationalized ratings, percent coverages, and time period clearances are also listed.

There are four types of syndication deals: Straight Barter, Part Barter/Part Cash, Cash, and Scatter. *Straight Barter* involves the local station receiving the program and a percentage of the commercial time within the program for local sale in return for airing the show. *Part Barter/Part Cash* requires the local station to pay a license fee to broadcast the program. This arrangement allows local station control of most of the commercial time with a smaller percentage of the commercial minutes being sold to national advertisers by the syndicator. In a pure *Cash* syndication deal the local station pays cash for the syndicated property and can sell all the commercial time to both local and national advertisers on a market-by-market basis. *Scatter* syndication is a unique situation in which the stations are obligated to run national commercial spots for a specific syndicator. The local station can drop or retain the syndicated show, but if the station elects to run the show, it must run the program in a predetermined period of time. The time period restriction provides the syndicator with the means to guarantee national coverage by daypart for its national advertisers.

The costs and efficiencies of the best syndicated properties are comparable to network program costs and efficiencies. However, overall syndicated cost efficiencies generally run 15–35 percent better than network cost efficiencies.

Cable Costs

Cable TV can be purchased on either a national or spot basis. Although each cable network schedules programming differently, there are general dayparts that mimic traditional network TV—dayparts such as early morning, daytime, prime time, and late night.

Today, cable TV is considered by most major advertisers and their agencies to be a viable media option. However, until recently, cable was considered a "new medium," one that played only a minor role, if any, in most media plans. With cable penetration reaching nearly 62 percent in 1991 and with 24 measured cable networks currently on the air, cable TV is becoming an increasingly important element in most media plans.

There are three main benefits of including cable TV in a media plan. First, each cable network targets selective audience groups. For example, the Arts & Entertainment network targets upscale, educated individuals; the ESPN net-

TABLE 15-5. Top 10 Syndicated Properties: 1990–1991

Rank	Program	Nationalized Ratings	No. of Markets	Percent of U.S. Coverage	M-F Daytime		M-F Fringe		M-Sa Access		S/S Prime		S/S Latenight		S/S Daytime		S/S Fringe	
					# Mkts.	% U.S.	# Mkts.	% U.S.	# Mkts.	% U.S.	# Mkts.	% U.S.	# Mkts.	% U.S.	# Mkts.	% U.S.	# Mkts.	% U.S.
1	"Wheel of Fortune"	15.5	195	98	—	—	92	50	103	49	3	2	—	—	1	N/A	3	1
2	"Jeopardy"	13.0	185	97	6	4	106	53	77	44	3	2	1	1	—	—	—	—
3	"Oprah Winfrey"	12.0	198	99	11	13	188	86	—	—	1	N/A	—	—	—	—	—	—
4	"Entertainment To-night"	7.8	161	93	—	—	—	—	—	—	3	1	108	58	22	13	38	26
5	"A Current Affair"	7.7	176	95	1	1	107	53	60	44	3	2	9	6	1	1	1	1
6	"The Golden Girls"	4.4	98	55	1	1	68	38	26	13	4	3	12	8	2	N/A	3	8
7	"Cheers"	7.4	170	95	—	—	53	35	46	25	20	14	92	55	9	4	18	12
8	"The Cosby Show"	7.4	187	96	3	2	119	75	59	14	10	10	5	6	4	3	2	1
9	"Donahue"	7.3	202	99	114	54	88	45	—	—	—	—	—	—	—	—	—	—
10	"Inside Edition"	5.6	119	77	8	2	76	50	23	18	1	N/A	16	9	—	—	—	—

Source: Nielsen Media Research, NSI Report, May 1991.

work primarily reaches men; and Nickelodeon attracts children aged 2–17. This type of selectivity is referred to as *narrowcasting* and allows advertisers to be extremely focused in their targeting efforts. Secondly, cable tends to be more cost efficient than other TV options. By including cable in their plan, an advertiser can add exposures to a national network TV plan. Finally, homes wired for cable in the United States tend to not watch as much network television as unwired homes because of the numerous cable choices available to them. Therefore, advertisers' national broadcast network schedules may underdeliver their planned GRPs to these cable households. Placing a portion of their media budget in cable can make up the network underdelivery in cable homes in a relatively efficient and inexpensive way.

Magazine Costs

The two major print advertising categories are magazines and newspapers. Advertising pricing for print space tends to be slightly more stable than for broadcast media because magazines and newspapers can adjust upward or downward the number of pages they print on an issue-to-issue basis. Thus the cost of printing is somewhat variable in contrast to the fixed commitment of television and its resultant commercial time perishability. Newspapers and magazines generally issue rate cards that cover future costs, although they are no longer reliable due to negotiated rates and package deals. A media planner constructing a plan for a year in advance must be careful in projecting magazine rate increases during the course of the year, particularly if the magazines the buyer plans to use are among those negotiating their rates. In those cases, the buyer must make judgment calls as to the rates to be used in the future media plan.

There is considerable diversity within the broad category of magazines. Some of the categories include the following:

General Interest (Dual Audience). Such publications as *Reader's Digest, TV Guide*, and perhaps to some degree *People, Time,* and *Newsweek*, are viewed as general interest magazines in view of the diverse audiences they reach. Their editorial content by nature does not exclude any potential reading group. Along with the large circulation delivered by these publications goes a commensurately high cost per page. As such, the costs per page for these dual-audience magazines take into account the audience they reach though their circulations vary.

	Cost per Four-Color Page	Circulation (000)
Reader's Digest	$141,300	16,306
TV Guide	117,350	15,354
Time	134,400	4,249
Newsweek	114,535	3,420
People	97,090	3,235

Women's Service Magazines. More editorially selective publications, such as *Ladies' Home Journal, McCall's, Good Housekeeping, Family Circle, Woman's Day,* and *Redbook* gear their interest primarily to women. The editorial content of these publications is designed to be informative and entertaining. However, male readership, as a percentage of total readership, is not very high compared with the general interest magazines. Following are sample costs for these selected magazines.

	Cost per Four-Color Page	Circulation (000)
Ladies' Home Journal	$92,100	5,003
McCall's	83,315	5,009
Good Housekeeping	122,035	5,028
Family Circle	96,990	5,151
Woman's Day	84,320	4,752
Redbook	75,820	3,842

Home Magazines. Other magazines segment their editorial target in a different way, namely by environmental considerations such as the home. Such magazines as *Better Homes & Gardens* speak to the interests and concerns of homeowners. By their editorial nature, these magazines tend to be adult and dual-audience oriented. Here again, selectivity of editorial content as well as audience gives the advertiser an opportunity to position a commercial message in a highly compatible environment. The costs for some of these magazines are as follows:

	Cost per Four-Color Page	Circulation (000)
Better Homes & Gardens	$136,500	8,003
House & Garden	36,770	629
House Beautiful	51,290	1,002
Decorating Remodeling	31,700	668
Sunset	40,510	1,393
Southern Living	63,400	2,385

Categorization of these magazines is somewhat arbitrary. One could argue that *Better Homes & Gardens* is a general interest publication based on the duality of the readership. In the final analysis, categorization is not nearly so important as the quantity and quality of the readership, compatibility of editorial with the sales message, and the cost of running the insertion—all of which must be taken into account by the media planner. A cost delivery relationship, however, is a good starting point in categorizing magazines from which to select those that then can be qualified based on the editorial content within which the message will appear.

Newspaper Costs

In 1990, there were 1,611 daily newspapers in the United States, in addition to 7,550 non-daily newspapers (weekly, bi-weekly, and so on). Newspapers provide the distinct benefits of flexibility in adjusting efforts from market to market, quick closing dates, strong local market coverage, and individual market identification. As with other media, newspapers are also highly diverse in the ways they can be bought and the advertising units available for sale. The major categories include the following:

ROP (Run of Paper). ROP advertising can be purchased in virtually any size unit from full page down to just a few lines in both black and white and color. If one color is added to black and white, the premium runs about 10–15 percent. Four-color (where available) cost premiums run 20–40 percent; however, it may be possible to package certain groups of newspapers to reduce the cost premium or to eliminate it entirely.

Supplements. Preprinted newspaper distributed supplements can be purchased either on a syndicated basis (*Parade, USA Weekend*) or on an independent basis such as the *Chicago Tribune Magazine*. Preprinted supplements provide all the benefits of newspapers in today's market coverage with four-color magazine-type reproduction when desirable. Costs for independent supplements vary from market to market. Costs and circulation levels for the syndicated supplements are as follows:

	Cost per Four-Color Page	Circulation (000)
Parade	$264,100	35,314
USA Weekend	212,599	15,591

Custom Inserts. In addition to ROP and magazine supplements, newspapers provide for advertising inserts printed outside the paper and stuffed inside. These inserts may be used in many different forms. They may be printed on fine quality or inexpensive papers, in many different sizes, used as single sheets or booklets, and printed in many different ways. All of these alternative production techniques allow advertisers to create unique advertising that will communicate whatever they want and can afford. Costs for custom-tailored inserts obviously vary depending on how elegant they are. Each newspaper also may charge different prices for stuffing and carrying the inserts.

Radio Costs

Radio is offered both on a national network and individual local market spot basis.

Network Radio. Network radio programming available for advertiser sale includes news, music, sports, and drama. Costs are comparatively low for a network radio announcement. The average network charges $3,600 for a thirty-second announcement and delivers an average rating of 1.2 to men, 1.1 to women, and 0.9 to teenagers.

Spot Radio. Spot radio programming formats vary widely from market to market. In major markets, such as New York, Los Angeles, and Chicago, there are numerous radio formats appealing to a wide variety of listener interests. Programming ranges from talk shows to various kinds of music formats to total news.

As is the case with spot television, it is extremely difficult to generalize about costs because of the diversity of the medium. In overall terms, however, spot radio selectively purchased against designated target audiences can be an exceptionally cost-efficient medium for reaching these audiences.

Many station groups have developed and make available computerized reach and frequency programs that help planners measure the effect of different combinations of stations in delivering both gross impressions as well as reach and frequency estimates against selected audience segments.

Out-of-Home Media Costs

Out-of-home media come in a wide range of availabilities that differ dramatically in size and location. Out-of-home media are the most local of all media forms, inasmuch as one advertising unit can be purchased in one very specific location geographically. The more popular varieties of out-of-home media are the following.

Poster Panels. A *poster panel* is an outdoor advertising structure on which a preprinted advertisement is displayed. The most widely used poster sizes are standard, junior, and three-sheet. The *standard poster,* or *thirty-sheet poster,* measures approximately 12 feet high by 25 feet long, but dimensions vary from one location to another. The *junior panel,* or *eight-sheet poster,* is about one-fourth the size of a standard poster. The *two-sheet poster* is used extensively at transit or train stop. It is 60 inches by 46 inches.

Poster panels are generally sold in packages of gross rating points. For example, a 100–GRP package will deliver in one day exposure opportunities equal to 100 percent of the population of the market. The cost for posters varies tremendously from one market to another, and often from one location to another in a given market. The cost to purchase a 100–GRP package for one month in standard posters in the top ten markets of the U.S. is approximately $1,480,000. The same purchase encompassing the top 100 markets is about $4,300,000.

Painted Bulletins. A painted bulletin is an outdoor advertising structure that is painted with the advertising copy. ''Paints'' are generally larger than posters and measure, on average, 14 feet high by 48 feet wide. ''Paints'' are sold both individually and in packages. There are basically two types of paint availabilities: permanent and rotary. In the case of a *permanent paint*, the advertiser buys the specific location for one or more years and the units may vary in size. A permanent paint is usually bought for the specific location's desirability and is priced accordingly. *Rotary paints* are sold individually or in packages. The rotary bulletin is moved from location to location within a market on a set schedule (either 30-, 60-, or 90-day cycles, depending on the market).

The cost for one painted bulletin can range from as low as $2,000 in smaller markets to more than $15,000 in larger markets for an average month.

Transit. Transit advertising is available on buses, taxi cabs, trains, and in carrier terminals (train stations, airline terminals, etc.) in selected cities. There are numerous sizes and shapes that can be purchased, with advertising costs varying depending on the market, the medium, the size of the advertisement, the length of the purchase, and the scope of the purchase.

Media Buying Problems

As indicated earlier, audience delivery and cost estimating represent major considerations in the development of a media plan. Once the plan has been approved, it becomes necessary to implement the budgeted effort in the most effective manner possible. Knowledge of how media sell their product is vital both for the development of the plan and its ultimate implementation. This section discusses some of the timing and buying implications associated with various media. Here again, as in the case with cost estimating, the major distinction rests between broadcast and print.

Network Television

Network television is a negotiated medium; it is bought and sold somewhat like a commodity on the commodities exchange. The network television market is a supply and demand market whose goods are highly perishable. A minute not sold is a minute wasted, and it results in lost revenue for the network. Consequently, the first problem the network television buyer must consider is timing. Incorrect timing and wrongly assessing when to buy can lead to severe implementation problems. For example, if the network buyer waits too long before committing the designated budget, all of the availabilities could be exhausted, thus leaving nothing to buy. Generally, the earlier the network buy is initiated, the more likely it is that desired programming in terms of audience delivery and stability will be obtained. The longer the buyer waits before committing to a buy for a specified period of time, the less likely it is that the most desirable programming will be available. There is, however, the increased possibility of lower pricing for the inventory that remains if demand is low. The ideal time to buy is when sellers are anxious to sell, just before others enter the market. In general, in a seller's year, an advertiser should buy early before prices rise and quality inventory is gone. In a buyer's year, an advertiser should buy as late as inventory is available and prices are likely to be favorable.

Network television time can be purchased in packages of shows or by the individual program. Packages, multiple programs with a few commercials per program during the course of the advertising schedule, provide maximum programming dispersion and thus tend to generate broader reach for the available budget. In addition, the risk of not delivering the specified weight levels is reduced because the outcome of the buy is not based on one or two programs achieving their audience levels. Conversely, networks also make individual programs available for sale on a continuity basis. Commercials regularly appearing on one or two shows can be highly effective when the planner can identify the specific audience values in those shows that achieve the objectives of the media plan.

Three factors are key in determining network costs: (a) demand by advertisers, (b) estimates by both buyer and seller of audience delivery and cost per thousand, and (c) network overhead and expenses in doing business. By far, advertiser demand is the most important determinant of network costs. Seasonal demand and the strength of the network and its programming best illustrate the effect of supply and demand on the network television marketplace. During the time of the year when an advertiser's sales are expected to be greatest, advertising time is in great demand and as a result, network prices are high. For example, for toymakers, the pre-Christmas season, the fourth quarter of the year, is a time of great seasonal demand. In addition, advertisers generally prefer high-rated, popular programming in any given daypart. Such programming enables them to reach a large audience in a good commercial environment. This preference increases the price for that particular programming and in many cases increases pricing for an entire daypart on a network if that particular program dominates the daypart.

Estimates by both buyer and seller of audience delivery and cost per thousand are also key determinants of network pricing. In most major agencies, network TV buyers estimate delivery for all network programming prior to starting the negotiation process. These estimates are based on consistent tracking of audience shares from week to week to determine audience trends. Network buyers are also aware of any network scheduling changes, new programs, and program cancellations. The networks also project audience delivery. Network projections are usually higher than agency projections. If a substantial long-term network buy is made using the network projections, the delivery is normally guaranteed by the network. If the network does not meet its guaranteed projections it then must "make good" by offering compensatory units.

Finally, the network's expenses also affect network pricing. For example, the network will try to cover the cost of programming and business overhead. An expensive production may be priced at a premium to offset its costs. In addition, there are mechanical charges for national and regional advertisers. An integration fee is charged to place the commercial into its proper pod within the program reel. Additional mechanical fees are also charged to regional advertisers for regional feeds, program cut-ins, and regional blackouts.

Three Ways to Buy Network TV

There are three primary ways to purchase network television: upfront (or long-term), scatter (or short-term), and opportunistic (or last-minute) buys.

An *upfront network television buy* is the purchase of inventory for all four quarters of the coming broadcast year. Advertisers' dollars are committed upfront in the spring/summer for the following television season, which begins in September. Upfront network buying is also called long-term buying. Upfront buying usually involves a guaranteed audience delivery which is expressed as a guaranteed cost efficiency and consists of premium inventory. By committing dollars in the upfront market, the advertiser has insurance against sellouts but has little flexibility with regard to possible cancellation (contingencies out with ninety days notice). At best, networks will generally grant cancellation options on a portion of the last half of a long-term buy.

Scatter buying is the purchase of inventory within a specific quarter made prior to the start of that quarter. Scatter buys are negotiated on a quarterly basis and give the buyer a better fix on the marketplace, that is, the buyer knows pricing from the upfront market as well as pricing from the previous quarter. Scatter buys offer the advertiser more financial flexibility with dollar commitment required only one to two months prior to the air date. There are, however, inventory and efficiency risks involved in buying scatter, because the best inventory may be depleted and scatter has historically tended to be less efficient (priced higher) than the upfront market. Finally, scatter buys are usually not guaranteed by the networks.

Opportunistic buying involves the purchase of inventory on a last minute basis if the networks have any remaining inventory to sell. Although there is a high risk of sellout in opportunistic buys, these buys can sometimes be very efficient because the networks are trying to get rid of last minute inventory just prior to air date.

Network television programs are also occasionally purchased on a full or partial sponsorship basis. A full sponsorship involves purchase of all of the commercial time available in one or more telecasts of a program. Partial sponsorship requires purchase of at least three or four thirty-second units of commercial time in one or more telecasts of a program. In the early days of television, sponsorship was common. Today, however, very few hours of network television are sponsored. The advantages of sponsorships include the identification the sponsor has with the program, the additional exposure in the form of opening and closing billboards, use of the cast in commercials, and participation in high-quality programming. However, sponsorships are generally very expensive, and the advertiser takes a chance that the program will not do well. In addition, audience reach is limited with a single program as compared to spreading the buy over a variety of programs.

Special event network programming can also be purchased unit by unit or as program sponsorship. Specials provide a good environment for new product introductions and for seasonal advertisers because they frequently have mass audience appeal and high visibility. In general, special event programming carries a premium price.

Finally, network regional time is also available. In a regional network buy an advertiser buys only a portion of the country, with another advertiser or advertisers buying the remainder. Regional network availabilities can be beneficial to advertisers who seek certain types of programming identification, for products with less than national distribution, or for introducing new products to specific regions. Regional network time purchases are generally difficult to execute and involve considerable planning and discussions with the network sales departments.

Spot Television

There are 211 Designated Spot Television Markets with 1,098 commercial television stations in the United States. The number of stations per market, which directly influences spot inventory, ranges from a high of 11 in Los Angeles to many markets with only one or two stations.

Major markets with multiple stations offer a considerable spot inventory from which to select. The multiplicity of spot commercial availabilities in such markets allows the buyer to be somewhat selective as far as programming and timing are concerned. Spot schedules are generally purchased two weeks to two months in advance of the start date of the schedule. Spot time can be bought for specified flight periods or on a continuing basis until canceled. Most station contracts call for cancellation notice to be given four weeks prior to the end of a schedule.

Buying Syndication

Syndication is bought much like network television—the advertiser makes one national buy. However, unlike network television, syndication buys can include either packages of time on several shows or time purchased on one program. Here again, the percent of national coverage varies by syndicated property and pricing varies according to coverage, projected performance, and demand. Audience delivery guarantees are often available.

Cable TV

Cable TV is negotiated the same way as network TV—the buy is negotiated on a cost-per-thousand efficiency basis with a guaranteed audience delivery. Like network TV, the cable networks are pitted against each other during negotiations to obtain the best possible pricing. The cable marketplace is unique because it has limited mass appeal. Except for the cable networks that program like network TV (i.e., USA), most target specific demographic groups. Therefore, it may not be possible to pit these niche networks against each other in negotiations.

Magazines

Once the planner has designated which magazines (or magazine types) will carry the approved schedule, the plan implementation has tended historically to be relatively mechanical. This situation changed dramatically in the early 1980s when magazine rates began to be negotiated. Negotiating magazine rates is now common practice in the U.S. as it has always been in many countries around the world. Most national publications accept space reservations guaranteeing that advertising space will be available in the desired issues. Space reservations can be made almost any time in advance of the issue. The final date for contracting to appear in a given issue is called the *closing date,* which varies by publication. Closing dates for monthly magazines will generally be from sixty to ninety days in advance of issue. Closing dates for weekly publications normally fall about three to seven weeks prior to issue.

National magazines provide regional and test market circulation breakouts for achieving coverage in specified geographic areas. The regional availability can include multiple states or just a limited area such as New York City. The remainder of the circulation carries either another advertiser or editorial material. Magazines also make available test market circulation breakouts that conform closely to television market coverage patterns, thus permitting test translations of national plans into local test areas. Costs and availabilities of such special breakouts must normally be secured from the magazines prior to order since they are subject to change.

Many magazines also make available what are called A and B *copy splits.* This means two different blocks of copy can appear in alternate copies of the magazine in the same issue. These copy splits provide opportunities to test alternative copy approaches or they can be used by different brands when national coverage is desired and half of the circulation is considered adequate for each brand. Some magazines also make available demographic breakouts. Such demographic breaks might include space only in copies going to physicians, or businessmen, or some other breakout provided by the publication.

Media planners, in the course of continuing their education, should keep abreast of the flexibilities provided by the ever-changing publishing industry.

Newspapers

Space closing for ROP space is only a few days before the actual issue. If a special unit is desired, such as a two- or four-color half-page, then additional time in ordering such space is generally required. However, the advance notice time to the newspapers is still relatively short compared with the longer closing dates of national magazines.

Newspapers have been very aggressive in developing special sections geared to various audiences and issues. For example, many food advertisers look for what is called the Best Food Day. Best Food Day in most markets is Wednesday or Thursday, the days that major food chains schedule their advertising. The advertiser is positioned adjacent to the special editorial sections that the consumer is likely to read before going to market. Positions within these sections are generally available at no extra cost.

Other sections that can be advantageous in reaching selected audiences include sports, business, and special features on fashion, good grooming, and home care. In addition to such regular opportunities for positioning, newspapers offer availabilities for special preprints such as hard stock inserts. In most cases, the advertiser provides the particular preprint to the newspaper. Such advertising units have to be ordered well in advance to ensure space availability.

Network Radio

Network radio programming tends to offer relatively few format types such as news and sports and some special events. Network radio is purchased in the same way as network television, that is, a contractual obligation for a specified number of commercials over a designated period of time.

Spot Radio

Spot radio provides different buying problems in view of the tremendous selectivity and diversity of programming and stations in many major markets. Rating information is available in most markets, but does not provide the total picture in buying radio. The number of men, women, and teenagers listening at various times to specific radio stations can be identified. However, the format, whether it be contemporary music, country western, stock market reports, music/weather, or sports, can be an important factor influencing station selection. The planner must rely heavily on the buyer's experience in executing a local market radio buy and ensuring a close match between the commercial copy, audience, and station format.

* * *

This chapter has examined the essential elements of media costs, accuracy, and related problems in implementing the media plan. There is a high degree of art in good media planning because the audiences of media and the pricing of advertising time/space are in a constant state of change. The professional media planner never stops inquiring and learning. The ability to form sound judgments about alternative media values requires intense concentration on the part of the planner. In the final analysis, those judgments are what distinguish a qualified media professional from a competent numbers manipulator.

QUESTIONS FOR DISCUSSION

1. Explain the main bases upon which broadcast and print media set their prices.
2. What is the value of analyzing costs *after* a media plan has been implemented?
3. What is meant by the term ''perishability of the inventory'' in selling television broadcast time?
4. About how much more does it cost to print a four-color ad in newspapers than it does a black-and-white ad? Explain why color costs more.
5. What information belongs in a media plan concerning the use of spot television?
6. What is wrong with the following statement that appeared in a media plan: ''We need a 70% reach in this plan.''?
7. Why is it generally conceded to be bad form to list all statistical data in an appendix?
8. Why is it not a good idea for a planner to make sure that all data in a flow chart falls within some monthly column?
9. What is meant by discussing the ''merchandisability'' of a media plan?
10. Why would we want to make some media plans flexible? Explain.

16

Setting and Allocating the Budget

One of the most difficult tasks facing advertising and agency planners is that of determining the optimum amount of money to spend for advertising. This is a problem that seems to defy solution despite the time and thought that have been given to attacking it. This amount is called the *appropriation* or the *budget*. We will use the latter term in this book. The main difficulty in determining the budget size is that no one knows precisely how a given amount of money spent for advertising will affect sales or other marketing goals. Media expert Herbert D. Maneloveg summarized the problem as follows:

> Our major problem, I believe, is that we really don't know how much advertising is enough. And we haven't done much about trying to find out. Not until lately. When someone asks about the amount of advertising pressure needed to make a potential consumer aware of the merits of a brand, we fumble and grope. When asked to justify an increase or decrease in advertising budget, we are lost because of an inability to articulate what would happen with the increase or decrease: if sales go up, we credit advertising; if sales go down, we blame pricing, distribution, and competition.[1]

In other words, there is no simple cause and effect relationship between the amount of money spent and the sales results that are supposed to occur because of the expenditure. Some manufacturers have been able to learn from experience how much money they should spend to obtain a desired

---

1. Maneloveg, Herbert D., "How Much Advertising Is Enough?" *Advertising Age*, June 6, 1966, p. 130.

share or sales volume at a given time. But even these manufacturers do not assume that the relationship will remain constant at all times. At some time or other, they and most other advertisers are in the same quandary about how much to spend on advertising.

What further complicates the matter is that each brand usually has a number of competitors whose changing activities make it difficult to anticipate correctly what they will do. The dynamic marketplace situation makes the task of budget setting—including having to estimate probable competitors' activities and allow a portion of money for contingencies—a difficult task for most advertisers.

Finally, advertising is not the only factor that contributes to the sale of a product. Other elements of the marketing mix, such as pricing, sales promotion, personal selling, and packaging, also play a role. But who can separate the precise contribution of advertising from the effects of the other marketing mix elements? Few, if any.

Despite these problems, advertising budgets must be established, and the task is performed based on as much knowledge as is available at the moment. This chapter outlines some of the major methods and problems of setting budgets, along with their advantages and disadvantages.

Setting the Budget

Ogilvy & Mather's Approach to Budgeting

The following, prepared by Ogilvy & Mather as an in-house presentation, is a brief introduction to the subject of advertising budgeting. It presents a frame of reference for thinking about budgeting and serves as a preparation for studying the various techniques of budgeting that follow.

> One of the most important and perplexing questions confronting advertisers is how much to spend on advertising. If too little is spent, the most brilliant campaign can fail. Conversely, if too much is spent on advertising, money will be wasted no matter how effective the campaign is.

> How much to spend on advertising is a strategic decision. The budget must be viewed as a function of the marketing and selling objectives of the brand or company. Modest budgets and ambitious goals are irreconcilable. Ambitious budgets for modest goals are inexcusable. One must clearly define the role of advertising and its task must be decided before settling on the budget.

> Until planners have positioned the advertising task, they cannot apply the necessary discipline and available techniques to determine how much money is required.

Here are some factors to consider in determining an advertising/spending strategy:

1. In what market will the brand compete?

   In the U.S., Mercedes-Benz decided to compete with the $10,000-plus luxury cars as well as luxury imports. This required an advertising budget many times greater. Had Mercedes decided to compete with the top-of-the-line Buicks, Chryslers, etc., even this budget would have been insufficient. Here are some points to remember:

   a. Expanding a market usually requires higher advertising expenditures than gaining competitive share. The reason? It is usually far more difficult to induce consumers to switch to or try another brand.

   b. The broader the market the brand competes in, the larger the advertising budget required. The reason? The brand must talk to more people and its competitive world is more diverse.

   c. Precise definition of a marketing target can save the advertiser money. For example, advertising just to children requires less expenditure than reaching children plus parents; reaching women only can be done more efficiently than reaching all adults.

2. What is the brand's current market position?

   When an advertiser has decided upon the market to compete in, the advertiser will know the product's relative strength compared with competitors. This will help define the planner's task. While all brands seek growth, the difficulty of achieving specific goals relates very importantly to a brand's position in a clearly defined market.

3. How does the advertiser evaluate the competition?

   In evaluating a brand's requirements versus competition, the planner should bear in mind that the market leader can usually retain business by spending relatively less than the brand rated second, third, or fourth. A low-rated brand must spend proportionately more to stay in business. To increase competitive position, a planner should be prepared to spend proportionately more than the brands he or she wants to overtake.

4. Where will the brand be advertised?

   Invariably, all brands have pockets of strengths and weaknesses across the country. Spending decisions must take these variations into consideration. The same rate of spending in every city or region will not produce the same results. Determining local spending policies requires a great deal of marketing homework. It is not sufficient to simply know the share of market. The planner must try to determine why that share of market exists. Quite often, poor share areas are a result of distribution deficiencies, pricing policies, or sales force weaknesses. Knowing the whys will help the planner judge the contribution that can or cannot be made by advertising. This in turn will help the planner determine spending policies. So it is important to determine the importance and ability of advertising to effect sales change.

Traditional Methods of Setting Budgets

There are a number of widely used methods of determining the budget. Those used most often tend to be simple to understand and quick and easy to compute.

Percent-of-Sales. In the *percent-of-sales* method, an advertising budget is determined by multiplying projected sales revenue for the year by a given percentage. The amount of money available for advertising purposes, therefore, is based directly on the sales achievement of the brand. As sales increase, so does the advertising budget. But as sales decline, the budget also declines.

The heart of this method is the *multiplier,* the percentage by which the sales base is multiplied. In determining which percentage to use, one must consider the cost of goods and the pricing policy of each industry. If a brand costs 15 cents to manufacture and distribute and sells for $1.25, a considerable margin is available for advertising, promotion, and profit.

The first step in setting a budget based on percent of sales is to determine the expenses incurred in manufacturing and distribution. The difference between this cost and the selling price helps determine the margin available for advertising, promotion, and profit. (There are, of course, other costs to be factored in, such as overhead.) Smaller margins may mean a smaller percentage available for advertising.

The key to this method of setting budgets is that of finding the best multiplier. Many times this multiplier is determined arbitrarily. At other times, industry standards may be used as a base.

Textbooks that discuss the percent-of-sales method of budgeting often give the impression, however, that the method is totally inflexible. This is not true. Often the percent of sales may be only the starting point. After the percentage is multiplied by gross sales, the total may be adjusted to compensate for special marketing situations. When there are special marketing needs, extra dollars are added. Some companies, instead of adding to the total, will raise the multiplier when they are introducing a new product or when they are faced with very heavy competition. In some instances, however, the percentage multiplier remains constant year after year no matter how much sales may vary. When this happens, the multiplier tends to become a historical figure that is rarely questioned.

The multiplier is also affected by product pricing. Sales of low-ticket products such as drugs or supermarket items depend heavily on advertising, while high-ticket items such as appliances, cars, and home furnishings are less dependent on advertising. A rule of thumb for determining whether the multiplier should be large or small is that the more advertising is used as a substitute for personal selling, the higher the multiplier (or the higher the margin to advertising).

Among the advantages of this method are that it is easy to manage and easy to understand. It is self-correcting as sales volume changes, and it may maintain a consistent profit margin. It also is suitable for both financial and marketing group needs.

However, there are many criticisms of the percent-of-sales method. It may well be illogical because advertising is based on sales rather than the other way around. When sales decline, less advertising money will be spent when perhaps more money should be spent. Also, unless the advertising-to-sales ratios are analyzed by area, better sales areas will tend to get better and weaker sales areas will get little relief. This technique also assumes that there is a direct linear relationship between advertising and sales, which is not always true.

Another criticism of this method is that it does not encourage companies to provide the research money needed to find the relationship between advertising and sales. Marketing expert Alfred A. Kuehn offered this comment:

> Perhaps the best of these rules [methods of setting budgets] for an established brand is "budget a percentage of expected sales equal to the industry average." This rule is of particular interest since it is self-adjusting over time, and appears to be a low-risk policy for a firm which does not have a better understanding of the effects of advertising than does its competitors.[2]

On the other hand, if all competitive brands used this method and employed about the same percent multiplier, advertising budget sizes would be approximately proportional to market share, thus limiting investment spending for advertising warfare among competitors.

Competitive Spending. The *competitive spending* method depends on setting the budget in relation to the amount of competitive spending. The amount to be spent need not be precisely the same as that of competitors, though at times it is. At times, a brand that has a smaller market share than its competitor may be given an amount to spend equal to or greater than the competitor, as a means of improving the share position.

A major criticism of this approach is that it assumes that competitors know what they are doing or that competitors' goals are the same as one's own. It also assumes, incorrectly, that a simple increase in advertising expenditures will automatically increase sales and/or market share. The products of competitors may be different, or at least consumers may perceive

---

2. Kuehn, Alfred A., "A Model for Budgeting Advertising," *Mathematical Models and Methods in Marketing,* Homewood, Ill.: Irwin Publishing Company, 1961, pp. 315–16.

them as different, so that a company's advertising may have to work much harder to make sales than competitors' advertising. Certainly, the marketing goals of one company are not the same as another, and the ability of advertising to create sales also is not the same.

Objective and Task. The *objective and task* method starts with someone setting specific marketing and/or advertising objectives that are then costed out. The total cost represents the budget. Objectives may be sales, share volume levels, revenues expected, income, or profit.

There are two main criticisms of this method. First, it is not always possible to determine how much money it takes to attain any given objective. Second, the method does not consider the value of each objective and the relationship to the cost of obtaining it. Is it really worth all of the money necessary to achieve any given objective?

Expenditure per Unit (Case Rate). This system is a variant of the percent-of-sales method. In the *case-rate* method, the budget is generated as a result of sales, but units sold, not dollar sales, are used as the base. Many of the same advantages and disadvantages of the percent-of-sales method apply also to this method. However, there are two additional disadvantages:

1. Unless the method is properly handled, there is a possibility that the control of profits may be lost. This is particularly true if the product or brand has a wide range of sizes or prices. Shell Oil Company, for example, has four types of gasoline ranging from Super-Regular (premium price) to Regular (lowest price). Profitability varies for each. Spending on a cents-per-gallon basis must take into consideration the mix of the line.
2. Working with units and fixed rates of expenditures will not take inflation into account. To overcome this, the case rate must be adjusted from year to year.

Subjective Budgeting. These budgeting systems involve decisions made on a subjective basis. Essentially, the executive whose responsibility it is to determine the budget size uses experience and judgment as a basis for decisions. This is not to say that such executives would not consider some objective factors as well, such as first determining the minimum job that advertising will be required to do, or perhaps considering available profit margins as a basis. But after such considerations, the final figure is decided upon rather subjectively.

One subjective budgeting method is known as "All We Can Afford." Although at first glance, this approach may seem illogical or crude, it may be quite realistic if the subjective decision is accurate. This method generally starts by setting a profit percent or dollar figure, then systematically analyzing the costs of doing business. The remaining figure, after all other costs are accounted for, is spent in marketing, a portion of which is advertising. A budget made on such a basis may be difficult to defend, especially when there is reason to believe that if more money had been appropriated, the result then would be higher sales and higher profits.

Newer Methods of Setting Budgets

Experimental Methods. A number of marketing and advertising professionals feel that the best way to determine the size of an advertising budget is by testing various levels of expenditures to see which will produce the most sales at the lowest total cost. The experimental designs for this purpose may range from a simple before-and-after test in one market to elaborate designs in which many markets are tested and compared with control markets. Although the details of such experiments are usually kept secret, occasionally some are publicized.[3,4]

Essentially, experimental tests involve trying different advertising expenditure levels in different markets. In one example, Anheuser-Busch used three sets of markets (each set consisting of nine individual markets) to test alternative expenditure levels and measure the effects on sales. In one set of markets, advertising expenditures were reduced from 50 percent to 100 percent below the level that ordinarily would have been used in those markets. In another group of markets, the budget was increased by 50 percent to perhaps as much as 300 percent. A third group of markets were control markets where there was no increase or decrease in normal advertising expenditures to provide a base of comparison with the other market groups.

In some experimental situations, advertisers discover that they can reduce advertising expenditures without any effect on sales. In other situations, increases in advertising produce varying degrees of sales increases.

If the experimental method is indeed as effective as some individuals assume it to be, why then is it not used more often to determine budget size? There are a number of reasons. George H. Brown, former director of the U.S. Census Bureau and a marketing expert, cited two problems involved with this method. The first is the relatively high cost of conducting the experiment, which involves finding and measuring a fairly large sample. The second problem is the long time span, perhaps a year or more, that is required. By the time the experiment is completed, the marketing situation may have changed, making the final figures irrelevant. Brown also pointed out that, although the cost may not be considered too high if the payoff is accurate and valuable, the payoff may not be worth the cost.

At present, not many companies use the experimental method, though some who have used it are quite content with it. Unfortunately, most of

---

3. McNiven, Malcolm A., "Choosing the Most Profitable Level of Advertising" (case study), in *How Much to Spend for Advertising,* Association of National Advertisers, Inc., 1969.

4. Newell, Thomas M., "What Is the Right Amount to Spend for Advertising?" in *Papers from the 1968 American Association of Advertising Agencies Regional Convention,* Palm Springs, California, Oct. 6–9, 1968.

TABLE 16-1.   Methods 100 Executives Use to Set Advertising Budgets *

Methods	Consumer Product Companies		Nonconsumer Product Companies	
	Averages (%)	Rank	Averages (%)	Rank
Percent of anticipated sales	50	1	28	2
All that is affordable	30	2	26	3
Others (not specified)	26	3	10	5
Percent of past years' sales	14	4	16	4
Arbitrary approach	12	5	34	1
Unit anticipated sales	8	6	10	5
Objective and task	6	7	10	5
Unit past years' sales	6	7	4	6
Quantitative models	2	8	0	7
Don't know	2	–	2	–
Total**	156		140	

Source: San Augustine, A. J., and Foley, W. F., "How Large Advertisers Set Their Budgets," *Journal of Advertising Research,* October 1975, p. 12.
  *Sample consisted of two executives from each of 25 nonconsumer product companies, and 25 consumer product companies. One was a financial executive and the other an advertising executive. The averages are of two percentages representing two executives per company.
**Adds to over 100 percent because of multiple responses.

these companies have not revealed the details of their methods so that no outside evaluation is possible.

Which Methods Are Used Most Often?

Table 16-1, compiled by Andre J. San Augustine and William Foley, gives some indication of the prevalence of methods currently in use.

Factors in Determining the Size of an Advertising Budget

Although it may not be possible to determine a budget size scientifically, it may be advisable to approach the task by weighting a number of factors that might affect the budget size. Setting a budget in this manner might be called "atomistic" in that one could think about each factor separately (like a collection of atoms), then assemble these factors into a final budget figure.[5]
    In weighting each factor, some will be found to be more important than others, suggesting that priorities for marketing the brand must be determined first. Furthermore, each factor must be judged on the basis of whether one should spend more than, the same as, or less than the previous

5. Kershaw, Andrew, "How to Use Our Media Dollars as a More Effective Marketing Tool," speech given to the Association of National Advertisers Workshop on Media Planning, New York, Sept. 30, 1971.

year. Again this is a subjective decision, but it may help the executive arrive at a final figure more easily.

A brief discussion of these factors follows.

Assessing the Task of Advertising. Before deciding on any figure, it is reasonable to determine what role advertising is to play. Must it do the selling job alone, or will it be added to other marketing mix elements such as reduced prices and sales promotion? If advertising must do the selling job alone, the size of the budget may have to be substantial. If it works with other marketing mix elements, the size of the budget may be less.

Important in this consideration is an understanding of the power of advertising to sell the brand. Some brands simply are not sensitive to advertising; perhaps because they are so much like other brands on the market, because they do not have a unique selling proposition, or because it is difficult to be creative in presenting the message through print or broadcast media.

Long- and Short-Term Goals. To some extent advertising may have long- and short-term goals set for it, but when the objective is to build an image, then the budget should be treated as an investment rather than an expense (as one would treat the budget for short-term goals). If both goals are required at the same time, then more money may be required because advertising has been given a dual function. The advertising copy for immediate sales may differ markedly from the copy whose goal is to build an image.

In a sense, however, the concept of dividing an advertising budget into an expense for immediate sales and an investment for long-term image building may be invalid. The reason is that image-building advertising may not consist of special ads that are designed for that purpose. If the brand image is thought of as a "long-term investment in the reputation of a brand," then every ad that is run, no matter whether it opts for immediate or future image, contributes to the long-range goal.

The goals of the company and advertising's relationship with them, then, affect to some degree the amount of money to be spent. Companies may perceive this relationship somewhat differently, so no general principle can be extracted.

Profit Margins Affect Budget Size. There is an assumption in the industry that where there are larger profit margins there will be larger advertising budgets, and the converse is also assumed to be true. Profit margins may be a limiting factor in setting marketing and/or advertising goals—what one would like to do cannot be done simply because there isn't enough money available to do it. It may be ironic that when profit margins must be increased, advertising expenditures also should be increased, but there is little or no money available to do the job.

Degree of Product Usage. Products that are used widely throughout the country may require more money for advertising than those whose usage is limited to a relatively small geographic area. However, some local and regional advertisers may find it necessary to invest heavily in their marketing area due to heavy competitive spending, e.g., fast-food firms and automobile dealers.

Difficulty in Reaching Target Markets. Some markets are so unique that no single medium reaches them well, such as the market for expensive yachts. A number of different media may have to be purchased, requiring more money. Many times, targets are so spread out geographically that mass media may have to be purchased, resulting in enormous message waste. When this occurs, more money is needed to do a reasonable job.

Frequency of Purchase. It is assumed that brands and/or products purchased frequently will require more money for advertising than those that are purchased infrequently. However, an exception occurs when the advertising goals of infrequently purchased brands are such that they require more money to be spent for other reasons than frequency of purchase.

Effect of Increased Sales Volume on Production Costs. If there is a danger of demand exceeding supply because of advertising's power, the consequence may be that a new plant must be built. In that situation, the amount of money spent for advertising may have to be limited until the factory is built or a decision is made to the contrary. The advertiser may want to reduce advertising expenditures for a while until it is possible to supply the demand.

New Product Introductions. It is widely held that new product introductions take a great deal of additional money to break into the market. How much more depends on the size of the market, the degree of competition, and the desirable qualities of the new brand. A rule of thumb is that it takes at least one-and-a-half times as much as is spent on established brands to introduce the new brand.

Competitive Activity. In markets where competitors are very active in advertising and sales promotion, it may be necessary to match, or even exceed, their expenditures, depending on the marketing goals of the brand in question. While the preceding factors do not indicate exactly how much to spend on advertising, they do serve as decision-making guidelines.

Allocating the Advertising Budget

Once the size of the advertising budget has been determined, then it must be allocated, or apportioned, in some reasonable way. When relating advertising to source of sales, advertising budgets are allocated to geographic areas. Many advertisers, however, particularly on a national level, allocate their budgets on the basis of national media selection with relatively little concern for geographical business skews.

Geographic Allocations

Perhaps the most often used budget allocation technique is to allot at least equal portions to the amount of sales produced by a geographical area. The reasoning behind this method is that one takes a minimal risk in allocating the most dollars to areas where sales are known to have been good. If previous budgets were successful in producing or at least contributing to sales, why would not more money (or an equal amount relative to sales) be equally effective? The concept is not only to keep the risk low, but to optimize whatever monies are available.

If a geographical area contributed 15 percent of total sales, then it may be assumed that it would get 15 percent of the budget. Of course, there may be a problem here. It is possible that it took much more than 15 percent of the previous year's allocation to produce 15 percent sales. In such a case, a different method of allocation could be used, one based on the amount of profit produced by the area in proportion to total profit nationwide. Allocating on the basis of profit is simply another method of distributing effort.

Other methods could be based on the market share contributed by each area, the anticipated sales produced by each area, or some number that would be a composite of a number of marketing variables, such as population, income, retail sales of the product class, plus other related variables.

In practice, formula methods of allocating budgets tend to be only the starting point, rather than the endpoint, of the allocating procedure. Adjustments usually have to be made to take into consideration special marketing problems. One such problem could be that the media in a particular area may cost much more, proportionally, than in any other part of the country. More money may have to be added to the initial allocation figure to compensate for this problem. Another problem could be that competitors have started to promote more heavily in areas that have been most profitable for the brand in question. Again special adjustments will have to be made to the original allocation.

Example of a Geographical Allocation Formula

To illustrate how a computer formula can solve the problem of allocating an advertising media budget among 212 geographical markets, the following formula program of Interactive Marketing Systems (IMS) is shown. It is called the PAL System.

The problem: A national advertiser wants to allocate a budget of $650,000 to both network and spot television in 212 markets. The total budget was determined by one of the alternatives discussed at the beginning of this chapter.

IMS ....P A L S Y S T E M* ....IMS
Television Allocation Analysis

TABLE 1
TVHH   Over 4 weeks

RANK MARKET	(1) TV HOMES (%)	(2) BDI	(3) IDEAL DOLS (000)	(4) NETWK DOLS (000)	(5) SPOT DOLS UNADJ	(6) SPOT DOLS (000)	(7) TOTAL DOLS (000)
1 NEW YORK	8.44	80	43.9	46.4	– 2.5	0.0	46.4
2 LOS ANGELES	5.34	107	37.2	29.4	7.8	5.9	35.3
3 CHICAGO	3.76	105	25.7	20.7	5.0	3.8	24.5
4 PHILADELPHIA	3.17	126	25.9	17.4	8.5	6.5	23.9
5 SAN FRANCISCO	2.49	106	17.1	13.7	3.5	2.6	16.3
6 BOSTON	2.38	118	18.3	13.1	5.2	3.9	17.0
7 DETROIT	2.11	103	14.1	11.6	2.5	1.9	13.5
8 WASHINGTON, DC	1.84	113	13.5	10.1	3.4	2.6	12.7
9 CLEVELAND	1.78	125	14.5	9.8	4.7	3.5	13.3
10 DALLAS–FT WORTH	1.55	100	10.1	8.5	1.6	1.2	9.7
10 MKTS: TOTAL	32.87	103	220.3	180.8	39.5	32.0	212.7
212 MKTS: GRAND TOT	100.00	100	650.0	550.0	100.0	100.0	650.0

RANKED ON: HOMES (000)   COST PRO-RATE: TVHH

Column 1 The basis for allocating dollars is the number of households in the market. Presumably, the product being advertised has adult family appeal. The number of TV households in each market is recorded in this column as a percent of the total United States.

Column 2 are the BDIs of each market. This information comes from the client's own records.

Column 3 is called "ideal dollars" and represents:
Number of TV households × BDI × the total U.S. budget, or
.0844 × .80 × $650,000 – $43,900 for the New York market

Column 4 represents the cost of network programs in each market. To find this information, the gross impressions of all TV programs that a client intends to buy can be added for each market and converted into a percentage. So for the New York market, the network dollars would be $46,400. The sum for the top 10 markets is shown as $180,800, and for the entire United States, it is $650,000.

Column 5 shows the subtraction of network dollars from ideal dollars. In the New York market, the amount of network dollars is greater than the ideal dollars, so the amount is shown as a negative number (– 2.5). But in Los Angeles, the differences between network and ideal dollars is positive and is the amount (unadjusted) to spend for spot TV in that market.

Column 6 shows that only the New York market has no dollars to spend for spot television among the top 10 (because of the negative dollars). (*Note that data for the remaining 212 markets are not shown.*) The sum of all negative numbers—like those of New York—is 31.3. (Note that other negative numbers in markets beyond first 10 are not shown.) This repre-

---

*Reprinted with permission of Interactive Marketing Services (IMS).

sents overspending and must be deducted proportionately from all other markets.

The formula that is used for the adjusting for the 31.3 is the following:

$$\frac{\text{Total spot dollars}}{\text{Total spot overspending}} \quad \frac{100}{131.3} = 76.2\%$$

Therefore each unadjusted spot dollar is multiplied by .762 to arrive at the final amount of dollars to be allocated in each market. In Los Angeles, 7.8 unadjusted spot dollars × .762 = 5.9 dollars. This multiplication is done for every market until the 31.3 overspending is totally reduced. Some markets like New York received only network advertising messages, while most others received both network and spot.

Is this end of the allocation process? No; adjustments now have to be made again, perhaps on a subjective basis on whether each local market receives an adequate amount of dollars for spot advertising. (See Chapter 9 for a further discussion of weighting techniques, and Chapter 14 for the allocation technique used in the sample media plan.)

Payout Planning

The Concept. Another kind of budgeting operation that media planners may be involved with is called payout planning. A *payout plan* is a budget used in new product introductions where more money than usual is needed to launch a brand. The extra dollars come not only from the sales made by the brand, but also from allocating the brand's profits to advertising, for a limited time.

The following data may be helpful in explaining the situation before studying the formal portions of a payout plan. A new brand may have the following costs and pricing:

	Per case
Selling price of brand by factory	$12.00
Costs of manufacturing, overhead, and selling the brand	7.00
Amount available for promotion and profit	$ 5.00
Normal amount available for promotion	$ 2.50
Normal amount available for profit	2.50
Full amount available for introducing the new brand: promotion + profit	$ 5.00

So, in new product introductions, the manufacturer may be willing to forego profits for a limited time and invest them in advertising, in addition to the usual advertising investment. This practice of investing both promotion and profit funds is called *full available*.

What is important to understand about this investment is that in the very first months, the brand does not earn enough money to pay for the extra heavy advertising investments that it needs. Therefore, the company, in a

TABLE 16–2.   A Three-Period Payout Plan

(1) Time Periods	Period 1	Period 2	Period 3	Total
(2) Size of total market in millions of cases	10	11	12	
(3) Average share for the brand	12%	18%	25%	
(4) Year-end total share for the brand	15%	25%	25%	
(5) Cases (millions) purchased by pipeline	0.4	0.2	0.1	
(6) Cases (millions) purchased at consumer level	1.2	2.0	3.0	
(7) Total shipments from factory (millions of cases)	1.6	2.2	3.1	
(8) Factory income @ $12 a case*	$19.2	$26.4	$37.2	
(9) Less cost @ $7 a case	$11.2	$15.4	$21.7	
(10) The budget (dollars available for promotion and profit)	$ 8.0	$11.0	$15.5	$34.5
(11) Reallocation of budget to place heavier weight in first period	$14.9	$11.7	$ 7.9	$34.5
(12) Percent of reallocated budget	43%	34%	23%	100%
(13) Allocation of budget to advertising and sales promotion				
To advertising (85%)	$12.7	$ 9.9	$ 6.7	$29.3
To sales promotion (15%)	$ 2.2	$ 1.8	$ 1.2	$ 5.2
Total	$14.9	$11.7	$ 7.9	$34.5
(14) Profit (or loss)	($ 6.9)	($ 0.7)	$ 7.6	—
(15) Cumulative investment	($ 6.9)	($ 7.6)	0	—

*All dollar figures are in millions. Thus 19.2 = $19,200,000.

sense, invests money (or pays out of its own pocket) to the brand during the early periods of selling. But, as the brand begins to sell more and earn more money, it begins to be in a position to start paying back the investment that the company made. Finally, if everything goes well, the brand will be selling enough of the product to pay back the entire investment and stand on its own as a profit center. When that happens, the full available is divided so that part goes for profits and a portion for advertising.

Explanation of a Payout Plan. Following is an explanation of the payout plan shown in Table 16–2. Each paragraph is keyed to the number at the beginning of each row on the plan. Although payout plans are not generally calculated by media planning personnel, the media planner should be aware of the mechanics insofar as they bear on the final advertising budget.

1. **Time periods.** Although three time periods are shown on the payout plan, more or fewer could have been used. Furthermore, these time periods could have varied from one to three years in length, or they could have been one to three six-month periods. The timing, therefore, is a matter of judgment and experience on the part of the planner who must estimate how long it will take to pay back the money necessary to get the brand launched in the marketplace.

2. **Size of total market in millions (MM) of cases.** A market may be described in any way most suitable to the advertiser. Some prefer to use cases. Others use pounds of the product, packages, or dollars. The data for the number of cases that will be sold is an estimate, based on trend analysis, modified by the judgment and experience of the advertising executive. If these estimates are wrong, then the payout plan will have to be adjusted accordingly.

3. **Average share for the brand.** As a new product is introduced and begins to be purchased by wholesalers, retailers, and consumers, it is obvious that the share of market could vary considerably from month to month. So this percentage represents the average for the year rather than the total. Either could have been used, but the more modest percentage is probably safer. Again, this is a crucial estimate which, if incorrect, would require the plan to be adjusted immediately.

4. **Year-end total share for the brand.** This figure is shown only as a guide to what the executive hopes to achieve at year end. It is not used in the calculations, though it could be substituted for average share, as previously mentioned.

5. **Cases purchased by pipeline.** The first factory sales could be to pipeline companies such as wholesalers and distributors (depending on how the product is distributed). This group of companies represents a portion of total sales. The amount in the pipeline at any time can be estimated from past experience with similar types of products.

6. **Cases purchased at the consumer level.** This figure is calculated by multiplying the average share expected times the number of cases expected to be sold in the total market: (10,000,000 × 12% = 1,200,000 cases).

7. **Total shipments from factory.** Pipeline and consumer purchases are added here: (400,000 + 1,200,000 = 1,600,000 cases for Period 1).

8. **Factory income @ $12 a case.** Since the decision was to price a case at $12 each, then this figure is multiplied by the number of cases expected to be sold for each period. Period 1: (1,600,000 cases × $12 a case = $19,200,000 income).

9. **Less cost of $7 a case.** Here $7 (the total manufacturing cost) was multiplied by the estimated number of cases that will be sold: (Period 1: 1,600,000 × $7 = $11,200,000 cost).

10. **The budget.** Since the budget is composed of dollars allocated both for promotion and for profit (or full available) it is necessary only to subtract the cost of cases sold per period from the selling price to learn what amount of money is available for promotion. Period 1: ($19,200,000 – $11,200,000 = $8,000,000). The term promotion as used here does not mean sales promotion, but more broadly, advertising and sales pro-

motion. As a result of the subtraction in each period, there is a given amount of money available in each, which when added together equals $34,500,000.

11. **Reallocation of budget.** Although $34,500,000 would be available for advertising and sales promotion, the budget as it is shown in paragraph (10) is allocated in a strict mathematical fashion, rather than with an understanding of advertising investment needs. Most of the budget occurs in the third period. On the other hand, most of the money is needed in the first period, where extra heavy expenditures usually are needed to launch the brand.

12. **Percent budget.** So the executive has reallocated the budget total ($34,500,000) in the manner felt necessary. As a result, the executive allocated 43 percent of the $34,500,000 to the first period instead of the 23.2 percent that would have been available if the budget were accepted as shown in paragraph 10: ($8,000,000 ÷ $34,500,000 = 23.2%).

13. **Allocation of the budget to advertising and sales promotion.** This is an arbitrary allocation based on what the executive thinks is needed for each. Some other executive with a different marketing situation and product might think the proportions should be different.

14. **Profit or loss.** At this point, an investment in the brand must be made. Since the amount of money available for promotion in Period 1 is only $8,000,000 (paragraph 10) and dollars needed for the same period are $14,900,000 (paragraph 11), it will be necessary for the company to invest an additional $6,900,000, which represents a loss for the brand for Period 1. The brand now owes the company $6,900,000 for Period 1.

In Period 2, again the reallocated budget is more than the brand would earn for that period, $11,700,000 vs. $11,000,000. Again the brand loses money; only this time not so much, $700,000. If this amount is added to the amount already owed to the company from Period 1, the cumulative total for Period 2 is now $7,600,000. This means that the company has to give the brand $7,600,000 for the extra amount needed above sales dollars up to the end of Period 2.

However, in Period 3, the brand earns enough money ($7,600,000) to pay back the amount given to it by the company. At this point it has made a profit, paid back the money given to it by the company, and presumably will make a profit to keep it going in Period 4. When the brand makes a profit, it *pays out* money to the company. Not shown in this example, but what obviously should be included in real situations, is the inflation factor. Money "loaned" to a brand in Year 1 is worth more than face value in succeeding years.

Conclusion

Although media planners have begun to use more scientific tools in budgeting, many areas still require judgment. The area of planning that most seems to defy solution is how to determine the optimum size of an advertising budget. Methods described in this chapter have been used for many years. Though they are considered relatively crude, they are easy and quick to compute, and for that reason they have maintained their popularity over many years. Allocation techniques, on the other hand, can be characterized as logical and reasonable. Some involve decisions based on subjective judgments of what will happen in the marketplace, as the payout plan indicates. But in any case, allocation procedures are more advanced than previous budget-setting methods have been. Perhaps the greatest advances have come in theoretical model building on the relationship between advertising, sales, and share of market. None of these have found their way into everyday use, though the Hendry method may be the one most operational at this time.

QUESTIONS FOR DISCUSSION

1. What is the difference between setting and allocating a budget?
2. Why is it so difficult to devise an advertising budget using scientific methods?
3. Why is the percent-of-sales method probably the most widely used method of budgeting, considering the fact that it has many limitations?
4. Discuss the question of whether a company that wants larger profit margins should increase or decrease its advertising budget.
5. Often markets are assigned budgets in direct proportion to the volume of sales or market share they produce. Under what conditions might this practice not be advisable?
6. Although the objective and task method of budgeting is often considered to be one of the best methods, what limitations does it have?
7. What is the underlying concept of a payout plan?
8. Discuss the question of whether a planner with the third-rated brand on the market ought to copy a leading competitors' budgets.
9. Where, in a payout plan, is it possible to make a judgmental error that could affect the outcome of the plan?
10. On what is the budgeting technique called "All I can afford" used?

SELECTED READINGS

Blasko, V. J., and Patti, C. H., "The Advertising Budgeting Practices of Industrial Marketers," *Journal of Marketing,* Fall 1984, 104–110.

Canter, Stanley D., "Exposition of the Hendry Advertising Analysis Model," speech presented to the Association of National Advertisers Workshop on Media Planning, New York, September 30, 1971.

Cheek, Logan M., *Zero-Based Budgeting Comes of Age,* Amacom (American Management Association), New York, 1977, 314.

Kelly, Richard S., and Ahlgren, Herbert A. (eds.), *The Advertising Budget,* New York: Association of National Advertisers, 1967, 289.

Kershaw, Andrew, "How to Use Our Media Dollars as a More Effective Marketing Tool," speech presented to the Association of National Advertisers Workshop on Media Planning, September 30, 1971.

Kropp, H. R., Ehrenberg, A. S. C., Butler, Ben, Sr., and Gross, I., "Setting Budgets and Allocating Advertising Efforts," *Advertising Research Foundation 19th Annual Conference Report,* New York, 1973, 29–38.

Mason, Kenneth, "How Much Do You Spend on Advertising? Product Is the Key," *Advertising Age,* June 12, 1972, 41–44.

McCabe, Thomas B., "How Much to Spend for Advertising," *Perspectives in Advertising Management,* Association of National Advertisers, New York, 1969, 113–23.

Newell, Thomas M., "What Is the Right Amount to Spend for Advertising?" *Papers from the 1968 Regional Conventions,* American Association of Advertising Agencies, New York.

Parrish, T. Kirk, "How Much to Spend for Advertising," *Journal of Advertising Research,* February 1974, 9–12.

Pyhrr, Peter A., *Zero-Based Budgeting,* John Wiley & Sons, New York, 1973, 231.

K. Weeks, "How to Plan Your Ad Budget," *Sales and Marketing Management,* September 1987, 13–14.

17

Testing, Experimenting, and Media Planning

Most of this book deals with the statistical data and subjective judgment that a media planner uses to decide among strategy alternatives. Most of such data comes from syndicated research companies whose services are widely available. This chapter, however, deals with the use of custom-made research to help the planner in making decisions. Such research usually is not under the direct supervision of a media planner, but there are some important facts about research that every media planner should know.

Tests and Experiments

Most of the research used to evaluate alternative media strategies falls under the general heading of tests and experiments. Briefly defined, a *test* is a simple field study of some advertising variable. An *experiment* is a carefully designed study in which the researcher controls and manipulates conditions to see how an experimental variable may affect audience behavior. A more comprehensive explanation of the two kinds of research will be given later.

Why Test or Experiment?

There are a number of reasons why testing or experimenting is necessary. The most important reason was stated earlier: to help the planner make decisions. Often the planner is faced with alternatives that are seemingly equal, and there might be differences of opinion between the planner and others (such as account executives or clients) about whether to use a given alternative. A way to resolve these differences is through custom-made research.

Another reason for testing or experimenting is to avoid making costly errors; the rising cost of media time and space, plus the proliferation of many new media alternatives, makes this more necessary than ever. Furthermore, clients want more and better proof that they are getting their money's worth in media, and that optimum media strategies are being used.

Finally, although media planners use numerical data in making decisions, they often modify the data with their own judgment, based on personal experience. But often such personal experience may not be broad enough, or the current situation may be vastly different from what it was in the past. Research is needed to answer the question of which strategy may work best.

Tests and Experiments: How They Differ

Because both tests and experiments usually involve field studies, they may seem to be alike. But tests are quite different from experiments.

In advertising or marketing, a test is a simple piece of research in which one measures a variable (or treatment) introduced into the market to see what effect it has. Although advertising can be tested in one market, most often it is tested in at least two; each market is given a different treatment. For example, in one market $500,000 could be spent for advertising, while in the other $1 million could be spent, using the same medium in both markets. Results could be measured on the basis of which dollar amount produced the greatest sales.

When the test was over, it might be seen that the $1 million produced 10 percent more sales than did the smaller figure. Which treatment was better? The answer depends on the decision maker who, on the basis of experience, judgment, or a payout calculation, says one expenditure is better than another. The most important characteristic of the test is its simplicity and its minimal controls. Although some attempts may have been made to see that the two test markets were alike, the nature of testing is such that it is simple and not too much trouble is exerted to control extraneous factors that could affect its outcome. Such rough testing provides guidelines for decision making rather than yielding definitive and projectable results.

An experiment resembles a test in that similar markets are selected for treatments, but great care is exerted to make sure that the markets are equivalent in nature. Usually the same treatments are assigned to two or more test markets, and usually two or more treatments are used. Finally, the treatments must be assigned at random, by using a table of random numbers or, perhaps, in simple cases, the toss of a coin. Furthermore, in measuring the results that occur because of the different treatments, a random sample must be drawn from each test marketing unit, and two or more replications may be made of each advertising treatment.

Once a random sample has been drawn from each of the test markets, the samples are measured through normal survey techniques to determine the effects of the various treatments. Results from experiments are analyzed, however, in a much different manner than in test results. In tests, the percentage of change from one market to the other is probably the most sophisticated analysis made; in experiments, data are cast in the form of analysis of variance, or some other statistical technique that helps tell the experimenter whether there is a cause and effect relationship between the treatment and the result.

The difference between the test and the experiment is that a better basis for decision making exists in the experiment, as noted by Dr. Seymour Banks, former vice president at the Leo Burnett Company, Chicago, when he wrote:

> The importance of experimental design versus mere testing lies in the fact that the existence of an experimental error permits use of a whole system of logical inference about the meaning of the data. It may well be the case that a test will produce empirically useful information, but there exists no logically defensible system for evaluating results. A test may come up with the true answer, it may not; nobody really can tell which condition is true.[1]

Which Is Better: Test or Experiment?

There are advantages and limitations to both testing and experimenting. The experiment is preferable when the highest degree of objectivity is needed. In evaluating one against the other, the following should be considered:

Experiments are better controlled than tests. This means that special efforts usually have been taken to exclude from the study any extraneous variables that could seriously bias the findings. In addition, experiments are designed or planned to allow statistical inference to be used in making decisions, whereas tests usually are based on some one person's (or group's) judgment. Statistical inference is usually more valid than personal judgment. As a consequence, the results of an experiment may be projected to a large universe, whereas the results of a test usually are restricted to the areas where the test was conducted.

On the other hand, a test may be less expensive than an experiment. Many companies that cannot afford the cost of an experiment still have some way of finding answers to their problems by conducting tests. Furthermore, tests usually take less time to conduct than experiments. Often there just isn't enough time for an experiment, but something needs to be learned. A test may provide this. Then, too, although the test design promises less than an experiment, often what is promised is enough. For example, a planner may simply want some clues, rather than a complete rationale, for a decision. Finally, a test is analyzed on the basis of relatively simple logic and

---

1. Banks, Seymour, "Using Experimental Design to Study Advertising Productivity," in *How Much to Spend for Advertising*, New York: Association of National Advertisers, 1969, p. 77.

reasoning that can be understood by everybody. Those who use experiments often err by substituting the elegance of their statistics for good, common-sense reasoning. The formulas of statistics are means to an end—not the end.

Yet both experiments and tests have limitations. For example, neither may be able to detect small changes that have occurred. Furthermore, when testing alternative advertising expenditure levels in a number of markets, the total sales of a brand may decline because a control market has received no advertising for a period of time. Both tests and experiments may also be so visible that competitors not only know they are going on, but they may deliberately foil the research by reducing the price of their own brands or by introducing another product similar to the one being tested. Sometimes, the sales force of a company can ruin either a test or experiment by working either for it or against it—rather than letting the research commence naturally. When salespeople deviate from their normal handling of a brand, their actions can distort the outcomes of research.

One final consideration about both testing and experimenting: Neither may produce results that are projectable across the country. As Professor Roy H. Campbell of Arizona State University noted, "Research has shown the projection error from three markets to national market shares ranges from 22 percent over-projection to 22 percent under-projection."[2]

Even an experiment may be inadequate, because it does not take competitive action (or reaction) into consideration, a concern expressed by Benjamin Lipstein, senior vice president for research at the advertising agency Sullivan, Stauffer, Colwell & Bayles:

> There is serious question as to whether this classical experiment is valid in the social and economic sciences. The experimental design inference process implies that we can draw conclusions from the experiment which will have application in the larger world. If we arrive at some optimum level of advertising expenditures from test marketing situations, these results when applied to the larger environment of the total economy could well lead to serious error since they do not anticipate competitive reaction to our presumed optimum level of expenditures. The experiment in no way makes provision for the independent intellectual life of competition.[3]

Lipstein also noted that, although it may be possible to anticipate competitive reactions to a strategy, statistical theory could give no rules on when and how competitors would really react. He concluded that competitive reactions would have to be assessed on the basis of judgment, something the

2. Campbell, Roy H., *Measuring the Sales and Profit Results of Advertising*," New York: Association of National Advertisers, 1969, p. 54.

3. Lipstein, Benjamin, "Advertising Effectiveness Measurement, Has It Been Going Down a Blind Alley?" in *Papers from the American Association of Advertising Agencies Regional Meetings*, New York, 1969, p. 2.

experiment was supposed to have eliminated. Lipstein's alternative to classical experiments was a call for nonmanipulative experiments in marketing and advertising, using mathematical model building to estimate what is likely to happen in the real world. These mathematical theories involve the use of nonstationary Markov chains, stability theory, simulation, and adaptive control theory.

What the Media Planner Should Know about Test Marketing

What Is Test Marketing?

Test marketing is the use of controlled tests or experiments (depending on how they are done) in one or more geographical areas to gather certain kinds of information or to gain experience in marketing a brand. In actual practice, test marketing may mean different things to different people. Consultant Alvin Achenbaum pointed out that to research-oriented people, test marketing means a precise method for gaining information or experience.[4] At the other extreme, test marketing can mean to some entrepreneurs: "Let's try something out in the marketplace." Between these two extremes exist many other possibilities.

Test marketing is most often done for new brands in existing product categories or for extensions of a product line. Even in new product testing, the media portion of the test is usually not the first consideration because the brand first has to be developed, packaged, and priced; selling strategies must be determined; and starting dates must be decided upon. In a sense, then, media planning assumes the same relationship in test marketing that it does in an existing brand strategy: Marketing considerations must be decided first.

It is important for a media planner to have a good basic understanding of test marketing because the planner may be involved in it when translating national media plans to a local level. Although it is beyond the scope of this book to provide all the details of test marketing, the following discussion covers the more essential facts for planners.

Purposes of Test Marketing

Because most market testing deals with new products, it should be obvious that the risks of making a wrong decision in introducing a new product could be costly. The number of new products that fail each year always is assumed to be high. Essentially test marketing is conducted to reduce the risk of fail-

---

4. Achenbaum, Alvin A., "Market Testing: Using the Marketplace as a Laboratory," in *Handbook of Marketing Research,* Robert Ferber (ed.), New York: McGraw-Hill, 1974, pp. 4–32.

ure by providing top management with knowledge gained from advertising in a limited geographical area. Management then can project test findings to a larger geographical area. The major objectives of test marketing are to estimate the brand market share that is likely to occur once the brand is introduced nationally and to evaluate alternative marketing and advertising strategies that also may be effective on a national basis.

Specifically, the purpose of test marketing is to help planners work out the mechanics of a market introduction while learning the local market share and effects of various strategies. If problems exist, then it is better to learn them ahead of time and solve them before national introduction. By spending a relatively small amount of money in a local market, one has less to lose than after national introduction. Once top management learns the local brand shares, then it may try to project those findings to the national market, using local shares as a predictive device. At that point, management may decide not to go ahead because there is not enough profit in the brand. In such a case, the investment in the test is considerably less than it would have been had the brand been introduced nationally without test marketing.

Despite the fact that a brand's local share can be learned from test markets, a growing number of marketing experts feel that the data cannot be projected nationally, because a few markets simply cannot accurately reflect the national market. Because the number of test markets used tends to be no more than three, the populations found in those markets may not be representative of the national universe. As a consequence, statistical inference usually cannot be used to analyze results. Furthermore, biases of many kinds tend to creep into test marketing operations. For example, in some tests higher distribution levels are present in test markets than could be expected on a national level. Or extra sales efforts are used locally that could not be expected nationally. Sometimes the expenditure of dollars for advertising is excessive at the local level and could not be duplicated nationally. Finally, markets change, people's attitudes change, and the economy may change so that, by the time a test marketing operation has been completed, the national universe, as well as the local universe, is far different than it was in the initial findings.

One must not conclude, however, that test marketing results can never predict national shares and/or profits. A sizable number of experts still feel that test marketing is here to stay and believe firmly in its underlying concepts. Their attitudes toward test marketing are based on the following arguments.

1. It is possible to improve the projectability of local market shares to national shares if better controls are exercised and more than just a few markets are used.
2. Market testing is better than no testing at all. It helps reduce the odds of failure, and it is the best that is available.
3. It has been successful in predicting market shares many times.

The track records for some companies using market testing in predicting national share have been excellent.

A study made by Market Facts, Inc., and reported by Verne B. Churchill, Jr., showed that 52 percent of the respondents said their test marketing results were "very predictive"; and in controlled test marketing, the percentage saying results were very predictive was even higher.[5] So it would be incorrect to state that test marketing is totally invalid as a means of predicting national share, although almost all marketing experts agree that there is room for improvement in the degree of control that could be exercised to produce more meaningful results.

On the other hand, there is less disagreement about the use of market testing for determining alternative strategies. The test market seems to be a laboratory that can help the planner decide which courses of action to use nationally. However, most of the same limitations that apply to market share prediction should also apply to alternative strategy prediction.

Number of Test Markets to Use

Although most marketing experts would agree that more markets should be used in testing, few actually are used. In Churchill's research, 67 percent (or 36 out of 54) used no more than three markets.

The reason more markets are not used is the prohibitively high cost. Even though management can be shown that the results of an experiment might be considerably enhanced through the use of more markets, there is still a great deal of reluctance to spend the extra money. Using fewer than three markets could be considered inadequate for predicting national share, but some kinds of information may be learned from two or even one market. But the results usually are not representative of the entire country. Cost and degree of accuracy are considerations in determining the number of markets that should be used. No simple rules exist for deciding on a number of markets.

Kinds of Markets to Include

There are a number of criteria used in selecting test markets. The primary one is that a market should be representative of the universe. Because the markets selected are really samples from the universe, the more they are like the larger area, the better. This would mean that the markets selected should have the same demographic distribution of population as the country (if the universe is the entire country).

5. Churchill, Verne B., Jr., "New Product Test Marketing—An Overview of the Current Scene," an address before the Midwest Conference on Successful New Marketing Research Techniques, March 1971, p. 4; report published by Market Facts, Inc., Chicago, 1971.

TABLE 17-1.   Peoria Compared with the National Population (1971)

Population	Metro Peoria	Total U.S.A.
Male	49.2%	49.2%
Female	50.8%	50.8%
Children under 18 yrs. of age	35.5%	35.8%
Age Brackets:		
Under 5 years	11.5%	11.3%
5–19 yrs.	26.6%	27.2%
20–34 yrs.	19.1%	18.7%
35–44 yrs.	13.1%	13.4%
45–64 yrs.	20.4%	20.1%
65 & over	9.3%	9.3%
Employment:		
Employed Males	53.1%	49.2%
Employed Females	21.8%	23.2%
Unemployed Males	46.9%	50.8%
Unemployed Females	78.2%	76.8%
By occupation:		
Business and Professional	9.6%	11.2%
Salaried and Semiprofessional	7.8%	8.4%
Skilled	63.7%	59.6%
Unskilled	18.9%	20.8%
Median Family Income	$5,998	$5,660
Median School Years		
(males, 25 yrs. & over)	10.2 yrs.	10.6 yrs.
Median Age (total population)	29.4 yrs.	30.3 yrs.

Source: Sederberg, Kathryn, "The Anatomy of a Test Market: How It Works in Peoria," *Advertising Age,* November 1, 1971, p. 147.

Peoria, Illinois, is among those markets that have a population distribution that closely matches the population distribution of the entire country, as shown in Table 17–1. Because of this similarity, Peoria is often used as a single test market. At times, it is used in combination with others. Yet, despite this similarity, there should be some question about the life-style of Peoria inhabitants compared with life-styles in other areas of the country.

Other criteria for a test market are:

1. Its economy should be independent rather than dependent on a nearby market.
2. Competition in the market should be similar to what a brand would expect nationally, and distribution opportunities in the number and kinds of retail outlets should be similar to the national level.
3. There should be diversification of industry in the community, and there should not be a strong franchise for other brands.[6]

---

6. Sederberg, Kathryn, "Anatomy of a Test Market: How It Works in Peoria," *Advertising Age,* Nov. 1, 1971, p. 147.

Media availability should be investigated to ensure that the market is representative of the average market in the universe. There is one other requirement: Markets should be randomly dispersed so that, in conjunction with large-sized markets, the competitors would find it difficult to disrupt the effects of the test.

Market Sizes

There is a difference of opinion about the optimum market size for test markets. One expert feels that the range should be from 100,000 to 1,000,000 population. Another expert employs a rule-of-thumb that the size should be about 2 percent to 3 percent of the national population. Achenbaum feels that the total population involved in test marketing should be not less than 20 percent of the United States because anything less would affect the amount of statistical sampling variance.[7] Probably the size of each market is not as important as the kinds or numbers of markets used. Size, however, may be an important consideration controlling the cost of the test. Larger markets could be expected to have relatively higher media costs.

What to Test

A number of marketing variables can be tested in addition to sales volume or share at a profitable level. These include tests of advertising media weights, various price levels, store promotion plans, trial and repeat buying rates, creative approaches, package sizes and assortments, brand names, brand awareness and/or attitude changes, and alternative media strategies.

Research Designs Used in Test Marketing

Research design refers to a plan of actions to be taken in the testing. This plan, or design, is carefully worked out in such a way so as to obtain certain kinds of information. Most often research design refers to experimental situations where the test data results will lend themselves to statistical manipulation.

Research design can be very simple, for example, observing a market, introducing an experimental variable, and then observing it again to learn what effects the variable had on the market. Or, the design can be simple to the extent that two or more markets, presumably similar in demographic characteristics, are tested at the same time, with each one getting a different treatment. However, more complex designs sometimes are used in test marketing experiments.

---

7. Achenbaum, Alvin A., "Market Testing: Using the Marketplace as a Laboratory," in *Handbook of Marketing Research,* Robert Ferber (ed.), New York: McGraw-Hill, 1974, pp. 4–32.

FIGURE 17–1.   How Test and Control Markets Are Used

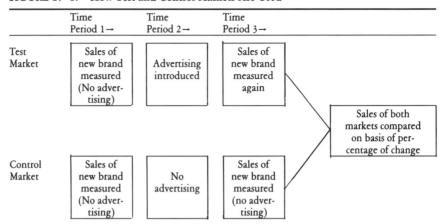

Use of Control Markets. Before conducting test marketing, the planner must design the test in such a way as to guarantee its validity. *Validity* means that the test measures what it is supposed to measure and not something else. If, for example, advertising is introduced into a test market as an experimental treatment, the planner will want to know to what extent advertising had any effect on the outcome.

One method of assuring the planner of the internal validity of the test is to use a control market along with a test market. A *control market* is one that does not receive any experimental treatment while the test market does. The control market, therefore, must be selected carefully so that it shares all the demographic and economic characteristics of the test market. If the research objective is to measure advertising's effect on sales, then advertising will be used in the test market only. Sales then are measured in both kinds of markets. If sales rise higher in the test market than in the control market, one may conclude that advertising had a significant effect on sales. But if sales rise to about the same degree in both markets, then advertising had little or no effect.

The design of a test and control market for a new brand is shown in Figure 17–1. This kind of test can involve more than a single variable. For example, different spending levels may be tested in different test markets and compared with the control group. In addition, market shares of all groups may be tested simultaneously for the total of all test groups and compared with the control group.

Randomized Block Design. A *randomized block design* is one where subjects to be measured are first grouped together into blocks. Each subject is carefully chosen so that he or she will be much like every other subject in that block. The selection process, however, is done on a random basis so that every person with the same characteristic has an equal chance of being chosen. Randomized blocks are designed to prevent situations in which differ-

TABLE 17-2. A Latin Square Design Applied to a Test Marketing Situation

Degree of Competitive Spending	Regions of the United States		
	East	Central	West
Low spending levels	A	C	B
Medium spending levels	C	B	A
High spending levels	B	A	C

Source: Lipstein, Benjamin, "The Design of Test Market Experiments," *Journal of Advertising Research,* December 1965, p. 6.

Treatments: A = high spending level for Brand X; B = medium spending level for Brand X; C = low spending level for Brand X.

ences within the sample affect the outcome, rather than differences due to the treatments.

The matching or grouping of subjects can be on the basis of age, for example, people aged 18–34; or income, people earning $15,000 or more a year; or store volume, grocery stores with less than $500,000 income. Once subjects are placed into blocks, the experimenter can compare the results of treatments among the blocks. If subjects are not combined into blocks, then the experimenter may not be able to find significant results because the differences might be too small to be measured. This problem may be overcome if the experiment uses a very large number of subjects, but randomized blocks aid the experimenter in reducing the number of subjects to be used in an experiment.

Latin Square Designs

A *Latin square* is a block divided into a number of cells containing coded letters and so arranged that a letter appears only once in each row and column. This design technique is more precise than the randomized block because it helps control the problem of two rather than one source of variation within markets that could not be controlled by careful selection.

An example of a Latin square used in a marketing experiment is shown in Table 17-2, within which two variables were controlled, and three different treatments were applied. The two variables were geographic variation and competitive expenditures. It is assumed in this design that each control or treatment is independent of the others and therefore will not affect the others in any way.

The problem illustrated in Table 17-2 is: If Brand X should spend three varying amounts of money for advertising, which would produce the most sales, or brand awareness, or other marketing variable? In order to make the experiment projectable to the entire country, different expenditure levels were tried in different parts of the country, and also in areas where different competitive spending levels took place. By controlling for both variables, the experiment thereby eliminated them as possible reasons for variations in sales that were found through the experiment.

The method of eliminating the effects of both variables is to add the rows and average out the effect of regions. By adding the columns, it is possible to average out the effects of competitive spending levels. By adding the expenditure levels for Brand X (or treatments), it is possible to average out the effects of both regions and competitive activity to obtain a determination which Brand X spending level was best.

Factorial Design. A *factorial design,* based on a factor as an independent variable, is one in which it is possible to measure the effects of different kinds of treatments, with the added value of determining whether the factors interact, or whether they are independent of each other. In conceptual terms, experiments may be designed to determine the influence of two or more independent variables on a dependent variable. *Independent variables* are those which the experimenter controls, manipulates, or varies. *Dependent variables* are the yield, or the effect variables; they vary depending on the independent variable.

An example of differing treatments in an experiment could be the effects of old versus new packaging, or an old package price versus a new price. The goal is to determine whether price and package changes are related to each other or are independent.

Other Test Marketing Designs

Achenbaum suggested a *checkerboard design* as a valid means of obtaining data in test marketing.[8] He described this design as requiring three basic elements:

1. Dividing a universe into groups of markets. These markets should be randomly selected and be about equal in size; for example, select three television market groups from each of Nielsen's ten geographical areas.
2. The use of alternative strategies in groups of three. Perhaps one group would receive 80 percent of a current spending level while the second group would receive 100 percent and the third group might receive 120 percent. Achenbaum would also use local media such as newspapers, spot television, and local magazines as the testing media. Three complete media plans at each spending level would then be produced.
3. Then, through syndicated retail auditing services, measure results over a period of a year. The key to the success of this plan is representativeness, good control, and ease of measurement (because it uses Nielsen areas).

---

8. Achenbaum, Alvin A., ''Market Testing: Using the Marketplace as a Laboratory,'' in *Handbook of Marketing Research,* Robert Ferber (ed.), New York: McGraw-Hill, 1974, pp. 4, 47, 48.

Other testing designs are *minimarkets*, where a test is conducted in a very small area, usually for testing a new product introduction; or *in-store tests*, used to test marketing variables within a store. Stores may be divided into two groups with each group being given a different treatment. And finally, there are Cable TV *tests*, in which two randomly matched groups of homes that have cable television can receive different treatments. At present, about one in two homes have cable television. But if expectations are correct, the number will be significantly larger in the future.

Media Testing

Media play an important role in most test marketing operations. Although the objective of a market test may be to learn whether certain marketing actions will result in a given level of sales or profits, usually other parts of a test are directly related to the selection and use of media. These other parts may have different objectives, such as learning which spending levels or which media mixes to use.

How Planners Test the Plan

A media planner's initial responsibility in test marketing is to create a national media plan, then reduce this plan in size to fit the individual markets that are to be tested. (The reduction process is called *media translation,* and will be explained in detail later.) Meanwhile, the planner may have a number of different objectives to test, which are described in the following sections.

Testing a Complete Media Plan. A national media plan may be developed for a new product that has not been marketed before. While the objective of the marketing part of a test is to learn a brand's sales or the market share that may be developed on a national scale, alternative forms of the national media plan may be tested to see which will best fulfill the brand's media needs later on.

Testing Alternative Spending Levels. A special part of media planning information is testing how much money should be spent on media. The following kinds of spending plans could be tested:

1. High spending versus current spending levels
2. Low spending versus current spending levels
3. High spending versus low spending levels
4. Allocation spending tests to determine how much to allocate, either by dollars or gross rating points, to various geographic markets and/or media. In testing allocation weights, the tester may use various kinds of weighted BDIs and CDIs to help arrive at spending levels.

Testing Alternative Schedules. At times, it is important to know whether a media plan should use flighting, continuity, or pulsing. Although experience provides planners with some basis for judgment, there are times when a test may provide more objective information than that based on experience.

Testing Alternative Media Mixes. One could test the results obtained from any single medium or any combination: television versus magazines, television versus newspapers, national versus local media, etc. Media mix testing could also include the comparison of various dayparts in broadcast media: Should a media plan use an exclusive daypart, such as prime time, or a combination of dayparts, such as daytime and early or late fringe? These are only a few of the possible combinations that could be tested.

Testing Alternative Commercial Lengths or Ad Sizes. In these tests, one could test 60-second versus 30-second commercials, or 30-second versus 15- (or 10-) second commercials, or 60-second commercials versus a full page print ad.

It should be noted that there are times when media tests are made for reasons other than that of predicting sales share. It may be important to learn how media and advertising work, and media may play an integral role in such learning experiences.

Requirements for Media Testing

There are a number of criteria for selecting test markets that apply specifically to media. For example, there should be enough media options available in the test markets to replicate the national media that will be used later. As a result, certain very small markets may be unsuitable for testing purposes. But there are other considerations as well.

Media Availability. A test market must have a balance of media alternatives available. For example, if television is to be part of a national media plan, then there ought to be at least three TV stations in the test market because there probably will be at least three TV stations in most major markets when the plan is implemented nationally. In the same manner, if radio is to be used in the national plan, then one radio station in the test market should not dominate the market, because it is highly unlikely that, when translated nationally, most markets will be dominated by a single radio station.

Spill-in and Spill-out. One of the qualities of a test market medium is the degree to which it is isolated from other markets. Media from markets outside the test area often *spill into* the test market, that is, people in the test market are exposed to media originating from another market. Sometimes it works the other way, when media from the test market *spill out* into adjacent markets.

The degree to which media in a test market spill out messages to markets outside the test area can be a serious problem. Spill-out is generally undesirable for a number of reasons. Consumers who live outside the test market area may hear or see advertising for a product but may be unable to buy it because it does not yet have national distribution. These consumers may become irritated at their inability to buy the advertised brand, and may not respond to later advertising because of their annoyance at not being able to find the brand on store shelves during the testing period.

A marketer can attempt to avoid the problem by distributing the brand in the broader spill-out area, but this in turn may cause another problem: Will the supply of the brand be adequate? At times, only a limited amount of a brand is available for testing purposes, perhaps just enough for the test, but not for spill-out.

There is another way to get around the problem of poor distribution in spill-out areas: Print and broadcast advertisements can specifically tell consumers where to purchase the brand, thereby averting the animosity that could occur when there is no distribution in a spill-out area.

The reverse problem to spill-out is *spill-in*, which occurs when media originating in another market spill into the test market. The more that people in the test market are exposed to media from another market, the greater is the variation in the reach and frequency pattern from the pattern ordinarily expected. For example, if a schedule of 100 GRPs produces a 50 reach and a 2.0 frequency in an *average* market, it will produce lower reach and higher frequency in a market where there is a proportionately high level of spill-in.

Some areas of the United States have more spill-in markets than others. Markets in the Northeast, for example, tend to have large spill-in (although Portland, Maine, is an exception). Meanwhile, Phoenix and Tucson (southwestern markets) have relatively little spill-in.

Recently, the growth of cable TV has added a complicating factor to the problem of solving spill-ins and spill-outs in testing. Adjustments for cable TV should be made by using local cable systems or over-the-air stations to deliver proper test weight.

Media Costs. When a market becomes known as a good test area, the local media may sometimes raise their advertising rates to take advantage of their popularity, making it more expensive to test media in such a popular area. Some experts feel that persons responsible for the media portion of testing should not worry about higher media costs in certain markets because there are other more important considerations to watch for—spill-in, spill-out, quality, availability, etc. In translating a national media plan to a test market, the objective should be not to translate costs downward from a national plan, but to translate the delivery (e.g., reach and frequency) into the test market regardless of the cost. If a test market cannot generate the kinds of reach and frequency effects that are necessary, then some other market should be selected.

Test Area Coverage. In selecting test markets for media planning, enough markets (whether ADIs or DMAs) should be used to cover at least 95 percent of the test areas (sales districts, territories, etc.) that the company typically uses. This assumes that the test is being made to correspond to a specific company's sales area. At times, this correspondence is not necessary, depending on what the client wants to learn from the test.

Network Delivery. Another consideration for test market selection, especially when the test is supposed to represent the entire United States, is that the daypart usage in the test market should closely match the planned national daypart usage of television or radio.

Number of Markets. As discussed previously, the number of markets used in testing should be more than two or three. Yet despite consensus that as many as five, six, or more are desirable, only one is often used. When a single market is used, it is assumed that the "one" is a Little U.S.A. market (to be discussed later). Dangers of projecting from one market are well recognized.

Some advertisers find it advantageous to test in very large markets such as New York, Los Angeles, or Chicago, on the assumption that these markets are more representative of the United States than smaller markets. A marketer might also try a test in an entire geographic region, such as the West Coast, where a number of various-sized population centers exist. The regional approach could be much easier to use than a single isolated market because the planner can more easily simulate the national media plan in the area. Regional editions of national magazines may be available, whereas in a single market no local editions of a national magazine may exist. The regional test would be less likely to be affected by local strikes, bad weather, or high competitive reactions to the test. Sometimes network buys in a region such as the West Coast may be relatively inexpensive and flexible, but for most regions regional network buys may be difficult, if available at all, especially with the advent of satellite-delivered network programs to affiliates.

Other reasons why regional test markets may be preferred to individual and isolated markets are that it may be easier to obtain distribution in a region as well as easier to compare market data with media coverage. In local test markets, the media coverage may far exceed market coverage measurements. Finally, in auditing sales, it may be easier and less costly to audit sales in large regions than in isolated markets.

On the other hand, there are three good reasons for not using regional tests: the cost may be prohibitive; there could be a large amount of wasted media impressions because not everyone in the region is being tested; and a regional test is not really a laboratory or sample test, but a small-scale introduction. If the product is not well accepted, the risks of large-scale failure have not been eliminated in the testing procedure.

Sometimes media considerations are not an important part of test marketing. Although media usually are an important part of test marketing, there are occasions where the purpose of the test does not involve media. As one media planner noted, "our client was interested only in finding out if he could sell the product to the trade. In this instance, the actual media schedules were not important."[9]

Media Translations

Media translation was defined earlier as a process for reducing national media plans to fit the needs of individual test markets. This is an adjustment technique, and there are several ways to make such adjustments. Each technique is based on a different philosophy of operations.

Little U.S.A. versus As Is (or Take It As It Falls) Philosophy

There are at least two philosophies regarding media translations in test marketing. One is the *Little U.S.A.* concept; the other the *As Is* concept. The *Little U.S.A.* concept is based on the idea that some test markets are so much like the country as a whole, that what one finds in one market can easily be projected to the National market. Therefore, if a media plan calls for the use of one prime-time network minute per week with a 20 national rating, the test market translation would be a 20 rating on some local program, or a number of spot commercials with 20 gross rating points in that market, regardless of the local rating for that network vehicle in the test market. Another way of using the Little U.S.A. concept would be to translate it in direct proportion to the weight that would be delivered on a national basis. The measurement could be the average number of impressions to be delivered per household nationally, translated to a proportion the local market should have received.

In the *As Is* concept, the exact media weight of the national plan is delivered into specific markets. Using the same example as above, with a prime-time network program rated 20, the planner might find that this program delivers a higher or lower rating in the test market, since national media deliver varying levels of advertising weight from market to market. If the prime-time program happens to deliver, for example, an 18 rating in the chosen test market, then 18 GRPs should be purchased in the test market.

The decision to use Little U.S.A. or As Is is generally related to how representative the test area is relative to the national plan. If the As Is translation method would result in delivering an abnormally high (or low) level of media weight, some adjustment toward the Little U.S.A. should be considered.

Table 17–3 shows how a Little U.S.A. media translation would be made. A national media plan has been devised in which network and spot television and national magazines would be the only media used. The spot televi-

9. Yovovich, B. G., "Quality of Local Media Can Be a Determining Factor," *Advertising Age*, Feb. 4, 1980, p. S–2.

TABLE 17-3. National Media Plan—Little U.S.A. Method

Media Used	Spot Markets (Women GRPs)	Total U.S. (Women GRPs)	Test Market Translation (Women GRPs)
Network TV		400	400
Magazines		100	100
Spot TV (60% of U.S. covered)			
Average spot*	100	60**	60 (National average)
Total		560	560

*A markets received 150 GRPs, B markets 100 GRPs, and C markets 50 GRPs, but the average for all markets is 100.

**Average calculations are as follows: 100 GRPs in 60% of U.S. = 60
0 GRPs in 40% of U.S. = 0
Weighted average = 60

sion plan covers markets that include 60 percent of U.S. households. In order to make a Little U.S.A. translation, average delivery is scheduled in local test markets as shown in Table 17-3.

Using the same data, the As Is translation would first require the planner to determine how many GRPs were to go into individual markets. Whereas the Little U.S.A. technique used the average delivery, this technique requires much more detail planning in order to know what local delivery might be. In making this translation it may not be possible to buy GRPs precisely as planned, so some media get more and others less than the national plan, as shown in Table 17-4.

Note that, under the As Is approach, only 380 GRPs were purchased in network TV while 120 GRPs were purchased in magazines in the test market. The reason is that this combination of national media delivers the desired levels of GRPs in the test market. Although the difference between the two-translation techniques may not seem like much, it is the difference between average and actual plan deliveries.

Translations in Radio and Television

There are a number of ways to translate a national media plan in radio and television. One way is the *cut-in,* in which a local commercial is inserted in a network or transcribed program in place of some other commercial originally scheduled in a market for the same advertiser. This is possible when the client already has purchased a commercial on a network, and simply replaces it with the test market commercial by cutting in only in the test market. The remainder of the country would see the national commercial. A cut-in is considered an excellent way to translate for broadcast media because it keeps the program environments the same as in the national plan, and it provides the exact national weight in a local market. Local stations, however, charge high fees for mechanically inserting substitute commercials. Also, national

TABLE 17–4.   National Media Plan—As Is Method

Media Used	Spot Markets (Women GRPs)	Total U.S. (Women GRPs)	Test Market Translation (Women GRPs)
Network TV		400	380
Magazines		100	120
Spot TV (60% of U.S. covered)			
Average spot*	100	100	
A markets	150		
B markets	100		
C markets*	50		50
Total		600	550

*The GRPs of C markets were used because test markets were C markets in character.

advertising for some other product may suffer because it was replaced with the cut-in.

If a cut-in is not feasible, then the planner will have to substitute local announcements for the network commercials. This may be a problem because the spot announcement times chosen must provide the same kind of target audience and the same audience sizes that the network program in that market would provide. In order to use spot television, the only times available at a reasonable cost may be fringe times. Although fringe time spots do not produce as high ratings as would prime-time network programs, some kind of compensation might be used. Planners add gross rating points to those of the theoretical plan level as a form of compensation. The degree of additional spot weight over the theoretical plan level is usually determined by the research experience of each advertiser. There is no single set of industry standards that applies to such translation methods.

When a prime-time spot is used (instead of a prime-time network program) then the additional gross rating point compensation may not be as high as the amount of compensation used with fringe spot. In deciding on any compensation, two factors should be considered: compensation for loss of reach, and compensation for loss of program environment. Of course, it is assumed that any spots used will aim for a selected target audience.

Compensations will vary in different markets, depending on the relationship of audience sizes between prime-time and fringe times. Daytime spots, on the other hand, may be used in lieu of daytime network programs without compensation since they may be purchased either within or next to the kinds of network programs used in the national media plan.

When a national media plan calls for spot television, no compensation may be necessary; spots are simply scheduled in the same number, same number of gross rating points, length, placement, reach, and frequency called for in the national plan.

In translating network radio, the method is identical to that used for translating daytime network television. For spot radio, the translation method would be identical to spot television.

TABLE 17-5.   Translation of National Magazine Impressions to Sunday Supplements

Problem: How many Sunday supplement ads are needed to deliver the same number of national magazine impressions that would be delivered by a national magazine in Test Market X?

Solution: 1. Find the number of target audience members of a national magazine delivered into Test Market X (either from published data or by estimate). Suppose the magazine delivers 100,000 readers in Market X.

         2. Assume that the national media plan called for 6 national ads in that market for a year. Find the total number of impressions in Market X: (100,000 impressions × 6 ads = 600,000).

         3. Find the number of target audience members delivered by one ad in a Sunday supplement in Market X. Assume it would be 75,000 readers.

         4. Calculate the number of Sunday supplement ads that would be needed to deliver 600,000 target impressions: 600,000 ÷ 75,000 = 8 ads.

         5. If the media planner judges that supplements have a lower ''value'' than magazines, the number of insertions needed in the test market can be increased to compensate: For example, scheduling 9 or 10 insertions in supplements rather than 8.

Translations in Print

Translation of newspapers is direct and simple, because the national media plan would spell out all details for local markets.

Magazines may or may not require special translations. If regional, metropolitan, or special test market editions of a magazine exist, then there is little difficulty in making a translation.

But if a national magazine has none of the above editions, three alternatives exist for translation: using Sunday supplements adjusted to deliver the same number of impressions in a local market that a national magazine would have delivered, using local magazines that are similar to those in the national plan and adjusting differences through compensation, and using ROP color in newspapers with some kind of compensation. The last alternative may be the poorest choice because the reproduction of ROP color in newspaper advertisements is not the same as color printed in most national magazines. But it would be possible to make some kind of compensation for the differences if that were the only viable alternative.

The first alternative, using Sunday supplements in lieu of national magazines, may be relatively easy to translate. An example of how this could be done is shown in Table 17-5. If the data on target audience delivery is not known in any given market, it could be estimated by working from known data. The number of circulation units delivered into Market X can usually be obtained from the publisher, who also can furnish the national number of readers per copy for the magazine. Multiply circulation by readers per copy to find the readers in Market X. However, these would be total audience readers, not target audience members. The same could be done for readers of Sunday supplements or similar magazines, and a translation then could be worked out. At times, the audience data could be further reduced by multiplying it by known recognition scores for a product category and comparing it with the substitute medium's noted score projection.

If a national media plan calls for Sunday supplements in a select group of test markets, then translation is easily done by using the local supplement or test insertions in the nationally syndicated supplements. On the other hand, if there is no Sunday supplement in a given market, then one could buy ROP color ads in the local newspaper. In the latter situation, some form of compensation would be required. In some markets, syndicated national supplements make test market breakouts available.

In summary, whenever a direct translation can be made, it is preferable to simulating a national medium in a local market. Almost any simulation will require some kind of compensation based at times on arbitrary rather than empirical means.

Conclusions

Testing and experimenting to find the best media strategy is a reasonable and relatively objective way of finding answers, as opposed to using simple judgment and experience. Yet there are countervailing forces that work against them. The high cost of research, the pressure of time, and the failure to control extraneous factors that could bias the outcomes all affect the continued use of these methods. But it is likely that as time progresses, more companies will pay the cost, take the time, and place competent persons who understand experimental research in positions of authority so that experiments will be used more for solving problems. At present, the number of persons engaged in this kind of research is not large compared with the number of companies for whom media strategies are being devised in a single year.

QUESTIONS FOR DISCUSSION

1. Generally, what is the difference between testing and experimenting?
2. What is test marketing?
3. Does an experiment, even if carefully designed and conducted, guarantee an answer that will solve a problem?
4. Why are the results of test marketing sometimes not projectable to the entire country?
5. Although Peoria, Illinois, may have demographics similar to the demographics of the entire country, why are there still some questions about its population being representative of the country?
6. What is the value of using statistical inference in market testing?
7. What are the main differences between the "Little U.S.A." and the "As Is" philosophies of media translation?
8. What are the main reasons for not using an entire geographic region, such as the West Coast, for a media translation?

9. Why may it be important to test in very large metropolitan centers such as New York, Los Angeles, or Chicago, apart from other testing?
10. Explain the purposes of media translations.

SELECTED READINGS

Achenbaum, Alvin A., "Market Testing: Using the Marketplace as a Laboratory," *Handbook of Marketing Research,* Robert Ferber (ed.), New York: McGraw-Hill, 1974, 4–47.

Advertising Age, "Test Marketing Full of Inconclusive, Contradictory Evidence, Berdy Says," November 16, 1964, 37.

Advertising Age, "Test Marketing," February 4, 1980, S–1, 5–28.

Banks, Seymour, *Experimentation in Marketing,* New York: McGraw-Hill, 1965.

Banks, Seymour, in "Using Experimental Design to Study Advertising Productivity," *How Much to Spend for Advertising?* Malcolm A. McNiven (ed.), New York: Association of National Advertisers, 1969, 72–89.

Becknell, James C., Jr., "Use of Experimental Design in the Study of Media Effectiveness," *Media/Scope,* August 1962, 46–49.

Brown, George H., "Measuring the Sales Effectiveness of Alternative Media," *Advertising Research Foundation, 7th Conference Report,* 1961, 43–47.

Campbell, Roy H., *Measuring the Sales and Profit Results of Advertising,* New York: Association of National Advertisers, 1969.

Canter, Stanley, "The Evaluation of Media through Empirical Experiments," *Advertising Research Foundation, 11th Conference Report,* 1965, 39–44.

Casey, Richard F., "Tests for Test Marketing," *Papers from the 1962 Regional Conventions,* American Association of Advertising Agencies, Western Region Meeting, October 22, 1962.

Cohen, R. J., "Computer Enhanced Qualitative Research," *Journal of Advertising Research,* June/July 1985, 48–52.

Edwards, Allen L., *Experimental Design in Psychological Research,* New York: Holt, Rinehart and Winston, 1960.

Giges, Nancy, "Advertisers Take Harder Look at Test Market Ways," *Advertising Age,* October 12, 1972, 3.

Hajek, F., "Testing," *Marketing and Media Decisions,* July 1987, 132.

Hardin, David K., "A New Approach to Test Marketing," *Journal of Marketing,* October 1966, 28–31.

Honomichl, Jack J., "'Market Facts' Success with Controlled Market Tests Attracts Nielsen," *Advertising Age,* October 8, 1973, 3.

Keshin, Mort, "Media Planners' Role in Test Marketing," *Media/Scope,* December 1967, 14–17.

Kroeger, Albert R. (ed.), "Test Marketing: The Concept and How It Is Changing," Part I, *Media/Scope,* December 1966, 63; Part II, January 1967, 51.

Lasman, L. L., "Determining the Proper Advertising Mix for a Consumer Product," *NAEA 1964 Summer Meeting Digest,* 21–25.

Lipstein, Benjamin, "The Design of Test Marketing Experiments," *Journal of Advertising Research,* December 1965, 2–7.

Lipstein, Benjamin, "Advertising Effectiveness Measurement: Has It Been Going Down a Blind Alley?" *Papers from the 1969 American Association of Advertising Agencies Annual Meeting,* April 25, 1969, White Sulphur Springs, W. Va.

Marketing Insights, "Test Marketing, The Most Dangerous Game in Marketing," published by *Advertising Age*, October 9, 1967, 16–17.

Media Decisions, "The Media Testers," September 1971, 52.

Orman, Allen, "Which Marketing Alternative Should We Test in the Market?" *Marketing Insights,* published by *Advertising Age*, January 22, 1968.

Ribstein, D. J., "Overcontrol in Advertising Experiments," *Journal of Advertising Research*, June/July 1984, 37–42.

Sederberg, Kathryn, "Anatomy of a Test Market: How It Works in Peoria," *Advertising Age*, November 1, 1971, 144.

Sherak, Bud, "Controlled Sales and Marketing Tests," paper delivered to the Advertising Research Foundation Conference, March 15, 1967.

Sponsor, "Testing! Anywhere, U.S.A.," March 8, 1965, 28–34.

18
The Future

It has been said that the future belongs to those who plan for it, and in this spirit we will speculate on changes that may occur in the marketplace and how they will impact on media planning in the future.

Everything you have read in the preceding chapters applies to the state of the art of advertising as it now exists. The future of advertising is shaping up as something quite different from what we have been accustomed to. There will be enormous changes in the years ahead—in our society as a whole, in media availability, and in media consumption patterns. Moving at great speed is technological evolution that will affect how people consume various media and how advertisers reach consumers with their advertising.

Former New York Yankee manager Casey Stengel once said, "Predictions are a very tricky business. Especially if they involve the future." But predictions must be made so that advertisers and media planners can cope with change and pave the way for a better understanding of what might happen. All media plans are written for the future, even if that future is only three months to a year away. The astute media planner is constantly trying to foretell what will happen—what costs will be, which TV programs will be viewed and at what levels, which radio stations will garner what kinds of audiences, which magazines will perform as they have in the past, and on and on. Therefore, attempting to predict what media will be like ten years from now can only be an aid to the media planner, as the planner can anticipate the potential changes and harness the opportunities these changes might present.

Population Changes

Let's first make some predictions about people. America is undergoing substantial changes. Inflation, escalating energy costs, economic uncertainty,

TABLE 18-1.   U.S. Population Projections by Age (millions)

Age	1980	1990	2000	Increase from 1980	
				Millions	Percent
Total	228	249	277	49	18
65+	26	31	35	9	35
45–64	45	47	62	17	38
25–44	64	81	83	19	30
Under 25	93	90	97	4	4

unemployment, and the international skirmishes in which our government finds itself frequently embroiled are making people wonder what kind of future they and their children face. All of these events affect the fundamental values of Americans, and to a great extent affect the demographic composition of the population.

The U.S. Census indicates that the population did not grow much in numbers in the 1980s, but it grew older. The total U.S. population increased by only 21 million from 1980 to 1990—a 9 percent increase, compared with 13 percent from 1960 to 1970. Table 18-1 compares predicted population bulges for the year 2000 with those existing in 1980. Only a slight change is expected in the number of people under the age of 25. With a decreasing birth rate and people living longer, the population profile will be older. The 1970 median age was 28. For 1980, it was 30.3, and for 1990 the projected median age was 32.9. For the year 2000, the median age is projected to be 35.7.

In coming years, there will be smaller family units, but more of them. While the total population will not increase much, and the number of persons per household will actually decline (from more than 3 to around 2.6) the number of people living alone will grow.

Minority populations will increase, especially the Hispanic population. The United States is now experiencing a wave of immigration from Mexico, the Caribbean, and South America. According to the U.S. Census, there are now over 22,000,000 Hispanic Americans. Since 1980, the U.S. Hispanic population has grown by 53 percent at a rate eight times faster than the general population. (Total Anglo population grew by 6 percent; total African-American population grew by 13.2 percent.) Furthermore, these census estimates only include a portion of the illegal population which is conservatively estimated to include more than 4,400,000 undocumented Hispanic immigrants. By the year 2000, Hispanics will represent 11 percent of the U.S. population—and a much higher proportion in certain geographic centers, such as the Southwest. The Census Bureau projects that by the year 2010, Hispanics will comprise the largest minority group in the United States, surpassing African-Americans.

The population will continue to shift geographically. More and more Americans are moving to the Sunbelt states. During the 1970s, two-fifths of the U.S. population growth occurred in three states: California, Florida, and Texas. The South and West together accounted for 89 percent of national population growth in the 1980s. Their combined share of the national population increased from 48 percent in 1970 to 52.3 percent in 1980 and to 55.6 percent in 1990. There is no evidence that this trend will change. Big, overcrowded, cold northern cities will lose population to the warmer climate cities.

The economic pie will be sliced differently in the years ahead. The 1980s will usher in a period of economic extremes. The now comfortable middle class will have to strive to stay ahead of inflation and the tax collector. Disposable income will erode as income and sales taxes continue to inch up. And the real income left after these deductions will buy less and less as inflation raises prices at a faster rate than real income increases. Although the tax reform of the mid–1980s has paralleled an easing of the country's inflation rate, history indicates that income and sales taxes will probably start to rise during the 1990s, with a corresponding erosion of disposable income. However, if the inflationary spiral continues to abate, we will see an easing that should stimulate the economy.

Energy costs will take a bigger bite. How big, no one knows. But the past trend is indicative: In 1970, the average fuel cost per BTU was 30.4 cents; in 1973, it was 41.9 cents; in 1977, $1.08. Energy costs have a ripple effect on much of the economy: industrial production, home heating, and transportation are all affected. Food scientists at Cornell University estimate that the 240 percent increase in American corn yields between 1946 and 1970 was accompanied by a 310 percent increase in the cost of energy used to produce that corn.

So, in the coming years we will see an older population, smaller family units, a higher percentage of minority population, a continuing geographic movement to the Sunbelt, and less disposable income for the masses. All of these factors will have a marked effect on what people will be like, and the population will move from a *basically* poor/middle-class/upper-class structure to a new market segmentation.

Table 18–2 provides a picture of what American consumers will be like during the 1990s. People will fit into one of four segments.

The younger haves. These are people who are essentially now in college—for the most part the readers of this textbook. The college student today is looking at a world in which it will be far more difficult to make a living—especially one that is considered a good living. "Me" is becoming increasingly more important: my career, my future, my possessions, my body, my health. The younger haves, skeptical of tomorrow, will favor going into debt today for what they want tomorrow. They will expect more from life, from relationships, and from themselves. And this demand for more will make this group very careful—reading the specs, looking for performance and value.

The younger have-nots. This group exists now. It is the same group that challenges the economic and social status quo. It is a group that will live in a

TABLE 18-2.   The Market Segmentation of 1990

	Younger	
Affluent		Underclassed
Educated		Disenfranchised
Careful		Disillusioned
Cautious		
Haves ——————————————————————————— *Have-nots*		
Affluent		Poorest of the poor
Free-spending		Need more government
Less cautious		assistance and
Less careful		intervention
	Older	

society with moral and political commitments to social welfare programs. The younger have-nots will continue to be an underclassed, disenfranchised, and disillusioned segment of the population. There could well be negative social consequences as a result of this group's actions.

The older haves. The focus on "me" will not be limited to the younger haves. The older haves will be more concerned with themselves than with their children and grandchildren. They will not especially be concerned with building an estate for their heirs and retiring into a moderate-expense way of life.

In 1990, those 50 and older were the same people who were the free spirits of the 1960s. Their outlook on life was formed in a relatively optimistic social environment. As such, the older haves tended to be self-indulgent spenders, less cautious about spending than the younger haves. This assumes that those now approaching this age category are preparing for it. If the economy sputters there could be a dramatic change in how the "older haves" view money.

The older have-nots. This group will be the most economically disenfranchised in America during the 1990s.

Advertising in the 1990s and Beyond

Advertising and marketing will confront a changed consumer, and increasingly complex, specialized, and expensive media. The great technological advances now becoming operational, especially in television, coupled with changes in the family, the economy, and society as a whole, will usher in a decade of media selectivity never known before. The remainder of this chapter will explore the changes in the major media (magazines, newspapers, out-of-home, radio, and television) and demonstrate how media planning must adapt to these changes.

Magazines

It is predicted that magazines will grow during the 1990s at a slow but steady pace. Circulation, in general, will keep pace with population increases. Right now the average adult spends about half an hour a day reading magazines. There is no evidence that time spent reading will decline. But *what* is read will change.

The greatest growth in magazines is expected in special interest magazines and special editions of existing magazines. We've seen much evidence of this already. Magazines such as *Lear's, Cooking Light, Victoria, Men's Health, Elle,* and *Decor* have debuted in just the last few years. These, and other "lifestyle" publications, are cutting a unique slice from the total circulation pie. Mass audience publications are losing circulation. Many large circulation publications are producing more and more demographic and geographic editions that appeal to specific segments of the population. The result of all of this change is an increasingly fragmented medium in which a specific publication will reach only a specific, and oftentimes small, audience.

Costs are increasing. Production and editorial costs, ink, paper, and postage are problems that all publishers must deal with. Publishers have the advantage of being able to increase advertising costs and cover prices to offset production costs. Cover and subscription prices will continue to increase. By the end of the decade it will not be uncommon for single issue cover prices to reach $5 and even $6, which appears extraordinarily high relative to today's family income level, but which will be commonplace in the 1990s. The higher prices will limit circulation levels and help maintain magazine profitability levels.

In the last decade, in order to maintain a more competitive edge over broadcast media, publishers did not increase advertising costs in the same proportion as production costs. Readers helped absorb a substantial amount of the production cost. But advertisers will see a change in this pattern. In order to maintain circulation at a level that allows the publication to be a viable alternative for advertisers, publishers will have to balance carefully the cost of advertising and the cost to the reader. Advertisers may be in a better position than readers to absorb most of the cost. (Remember, inflation is biting into consumers' real income and consumers must make careful decisions about their discretionary income and how much they will pay for the privilege of reading magazines.)

The 1991 Russell Hall editorial reports show that the average national consumer magazine has an advertising to editorial ratio of about 49/51. This ratio reflects a 6 percent change from 1985 when the ad/edit ratio reached 52/48. It is believed that this ratio will remain fairly constant in the future.

There is no research showing the perceived value of a magazine with a preponderance of advertising. Some magazines, such as *Seventeen* and *Vogue*, are in fact often purchased by readers very much for their advertising. But whether or not readers think they are getting a better, or worse, value when advertising makes up the majority of pages is not important. What is important is the idea of "clutter." Will an advertisement be read in a cluttered environment? If readership of advertising declines, will more pages of advertising in a given magazine be necessary to effectively communicate with the reader? These questions have not been answered, and unfortunately, there is no research on the drawing boards right now that addresses the issue. The astute media planner, however, must keep these questions in mind when evaluating magazines in the future.

Newspapers

As with magazines, consumers spend about half an hour a day reading a newspaper. This will continue. Circulation will increase in a fairly direct proportion to population increases. And as people move around geographically, newspaper circulation will follow—from the central city to the suburbs to the Sunbelt.

Newspaper publishers will continue to develop special interest and geographic sections. The *Chicago Tribune* coined the phrase "Sectional Revolution" to describe all the new sections of many large daily newspapers that were created to attract new readers, to better serve the readers' interests in specific subjects, and to offer advertisers an opportunity to position ads in a specific editorial environment.

By the year 2000, it is probable that major newspapers will develop regular suburban editions. The editing would occur on location in suburbs and be relayed to the center city operations for make-up. The totally made-up newspaper would then be relayed back to the suburban printing facility using cathode ray equipment. The suburban editions (suburban section plus the center city portions) would then be printed and distributed in the outlying areas. Big city news would be incorporated into suburban editorial. These localized sections and editions will serve to target consumers in an even more precise manner than now—and, of course, will also fragment audiences further.

Newspapers will also be troubled by the rising costs of paper, printing, distribution, and editorial. Publishers will continue to raise advertising rates to pay for these increased production costs, and they will also increase cover prices to the readers.

Newspapers will continue to be an important medium for advertisers, because of their immediacy in delivering advertising, their retail orientation, and schedule flexibility. They are now the second most local of major media (out-of-home being the most local) and with the advances in sectional and geographic editions, newspapers will become more local in nature and therefore more efficient in reaching small segments of the population.

In addition, the emergence of *USA Today* has added a fresh element to the newspaper advertising industry for national advertisers. Traditionally, national advertisers have been charged higher rates than local advertisers, and they found local newspaper advertising too expensive and difficult to execute. *USA Today* now offers an efficient, one-buy, four-color newspaper medium for national advertisers desiring to reach a national audience.

The printed newspaper is now available on your TV set. Two techniques, now in operation, make this possible.

Teletext printed messages are carried along with the normal broadcast signal. The subscriber is supplied with a key-pad and a decoder attached to the TV set. This equipment enables the user to access the Teletext signal and receive specifically requested data, such as classified advertising, airline schedules, theater reviews, restaurant listings, etc.

Viewdata or **Videotex** takes Teletext a step further and allows the viewer to interact with the TV set (not unlike QUBE). With Viewdata, the subscriber requests specific information (using specialized equipment), such as a catalog listing, and then can order the merchandise directly from the TV set by punching certain codes on the TV attachment. The advertiser then sends the merchandise and the invoice directly to the consumer.

Clearly, the viewer who subscribes to the Teletext or Viewdata systems can preempt programming or commercials at any time to use the systems—a real threat to broadcasting.

The Electronic Newspaper

Such publishers as the *New York Times* and the *Wall Street Journal* have been supplying professional and business customers with data electronically through news-retrieval services. As the cost for computers declines, general-interest newspapers are testing the viability of having all their news broadcast on TV. Many newspapers have already converted their production operations to electronics, with computers and display screens in newsrooms and press rooms. Extending the technology to delivering news to homes would be relatively simple.

There were a number of experiments in operation in the United States during the late 1970s and early 1980s. The *Ledger & Times* in Murray, Kentucky, fed its text onto a cable TV screen that could be seen by any cable viewer tuning in. *Knight-Ridder* newspapers aggressively tested Viewtron, a Viewdata system. Gannet Company, the nation's largest circulation newspaper chain, planned to establish a satellite network to transmit new information services. The *New York Times* and the *Times Mirror* were among the publishers buying cable TV systems—for investment and for possible transmission of news directly to viewers.

The use of electronic information services has been increasing as more and more Americans purchase computers for their homes. Accessed through a modem and a standard IBM or Macintosh computer, electronic information services provide their customers with features like home shopping, travel booking, electronic news, sports, stock quotes and even computer games.

Prodigy Services—a joint venture of IBM and Sears—began testing in 1984 and went national in 1990 and today has about a million and a half subscribers. Already using Prodigy's information services as an ad medium are a blue-chip roster of marketers including BMW, Panasonic, Sharp, and USA Today. Ads for various products and services appear on the screen along with general Prodigy information.

H&R Block's CompuServe is Prodigy's main rival and offers similar services. Though older than Prodigy, CompuServe has fewer members—about a million. To compete better with Prodigy, CompuServe recently replaced its hourly fee with a monthly usage fee, similar to Prodigy.

Other videotex companies include General Electric's GEnie and America Online. The Videotex Industry Association estimates that there are 40 such services.

Electronic newspapers and information services are obviously in a volatile market primarily due to the players involved and the assessment of future consumer needs and ready acceptance of information services. In the near future, the telephone companies will join the other expert companies in the areas of retail, computers and computer communications, finance, and entertainment/publishing that have entered the electronic information service market. A recent U.S. Supreme Court decision to allow the regional Bell companies to enter information services means even more rivals. The regional Bells have the one trump card other videotex entrants lack: universal access. Nynex is the first regional Bell company to introduce an electronic information service: an on-line electronic Yellow Pages directory that will eventually carry display ads. The service allows customers to search listings by product category, location, or name throughout Nynex's six-state region. It also offers UPI news, stock quotes, financial and travel information.

Currently, Viewdata is available in less than 1 percent of households. With the entrance of such big players in the marketplace, Viewdata's growth could follow the growth of computers; it could be available in 50 percent of U.S. homes by the year 2000. Its success, however, will depend on how well it meets a given consumer need at an affordable cost and/or its ability to demonstrate its usefulness.

In general, Americans are increasingly more video conscious, but it would appear that the newspaper (in the printed form) will continue to be published and read at breakfast and on the commuter train. Any reduction in printed circulation probably will not surface until cable penetration reaches extraordinarily high levels, and the consumer becomes accustomed to ''reading'' TV.

Out-of-Home Media

Several facts suggest that demand for out-of-home media will increase in the 1990s. Advertisers will continue to feel the pressures of government restrictions on broadcast copy. There will be lower billboard capacity due to attrition. Land development and construction will eliminate some portion of existing locations, while local zoning laws will limit deployment of new boards. The result of all this interplay will be a net loss of available units.

Some new technology will make out-of-home more attractive and more effective. Computerized painting of painted boards, for example, will serve to speed up production, ensure uniformity of design across multiple showings, and help control production costs. Panographics, which are billboards illuminated from behind the design, will be available on a broadscale basis. In addition, outdoor big screen video boards, health club boards, and restroom advertising are available.

Other forms of outdoor in existence today show signs of significant growth. Advertising displays in shopping malls, at bus shelters, on trash cans, on top of taxi cabs and the sides of buses, and around stores and other gathering places are all increasing in number.

The out-of-home media are changing and will continue to change, shifting from the traditional billboard medium to a great variety of unique and localized options. This fragmentation of the creative unit will provide new opportunities for reaching very selective markets with even greater effectiveness.

Radio

People will have a continuing need for radio, especially when TV viewing is impractical, such as when getting ready in the morning, going to and from work and the store, while working, studying, relaxing. But, as stated earlier, the population is getting older, and this graying of the population could have an adverse effect on overall radio listening levels. The heaviest listening segment is comprised of people under 30 years old, and this segment is declining as a percentage of the population.

Broadcasters will have to adapt to the population changes in order to retain the nearly three and a half hours a day each individual spends with radio. Different formats must be developed to hold the 30- to 40-year-olds. The possibility of specialized programming for those over 50 also exists, as does possible programming for the sick and those with poor vision.

Radio is now the most fragmented of the major media. To reach large numbers of people, it is necessary to purchase a long list of stations in a given market. This is considered by some media planners as a disadvantage. Planners often characterize radio as a frequency medium (as opposed to reach) because budgets are often too slim to purchase a significant number of announcements on each radio station *and* a long list of stations to increase reach. But what now works for radio will work even harder in the future. What works is radio's fragmentation—its ability to attract very selective audiences that have specific demographic and life-style patterns.

Advertising rates will increase, but at a slower rate than the other major media. This will give radio a relative cost advantage over other major media forms.

TABLE 18–3.   Historical Network Prime-Time Ratings and Shares

Year	Average Three-Network Prime-time Rating	Index to 1978–79	Three-Network Share	Index to 1978–79
1978–79	17.2	100	89	100
1979–80	16.8	98	86	97
1980–81	16.5	96	83	93
1981–82	15.5	90	80	90
1982–83	15.3	89	77	87
1983–84	15.0	87	75	84
1984–85	14.6	85	73	82
1985–86	14.9	87	73	82
1986–87	14.2	83	71	80
1987–88*	13.1	76	68	76
1988–89*	12.7	74	64	72
1989–90*	11.8	69	62	70
1990–91*	11.4	66	59	66

*Peoplemeter

Television

The most dramatic changes in media are happening in television. The popular TV medium that was born in the 1950s has matured considerably. Currently, 98 percent of the reported TV households have color sets. Sixty-five percent of all homes have two or more sets and 25 percent of homes have three or more sets. It is conceivable by the end of the century that half of all homes will have three or more TV sets—75 percent of homes will have two or more sets.

The television public appears to have an insatiable appetite for more and better viewing options. It is this hunger for programming that is encouraging the development of imaginative systems for delivering greater diversity and choice. Syndication, new independent networks, cable, the VCR as well as new technologies like stereo television and remote control devices offer the viewer more choice of programming and more control over viewership.

The lesson learned in the 1970s is that consumers are willing to pay to satisfy their appetite. The emergence of pocket-size units has made television a portable medium making it reasonable to project that, like Dick Tracy, the comic book detective, we could have TV sets the size of a watch snapped to our wrists.

Network Decline. Historically, the three networks have held a dominant share of the television audience. However, network ratings and shares have experienced a steady decline. Table 18–3 details the 34 percent decrease in average prime-time ratings and shares the networks have experienced since the 1978–79 broadcast year.

The decline in network ratings and shares is largely attributable to the rapid changes that have occurred in the television environment over the past several years. Four major events have accounted for the changing network

TABLE 18–4. Prime-Time Viewing Shares

| | Broadcast Year | | |
	1984/85	1991/92	2000/01
Network	73%*	59%	50%
Fox	—	10	16
Independent	12	9	9
PBS	4	4	3
Superstations	5	6	6
Basic cable	11	20	25
Pay cable	7	5	5

Note: Figures add to more than 100 percent due to multiset viewing.

television environment. First, the 1970 FCC decision which ended network-controlled program production and re-run syndication, fostered the development of independent program producers, independent syndicators, and local independent stations without network affiliation. Second, the 1974 FCC Prime Access Rule which prohibited network originated programming in the 7:00 P.M.–8:00 P.M. time slot further encouraged independent re-runs and first run syndication and gave local independent stations an opportunity to compete with off-network re-runs. Third, the emergence of satellite delivery systems during the mid–70s enabled the rapid growth of pay cable (HBO, Showtime), superstations (WTBS, WGN), and basic cable networks (ESPN, CNN). Fourth, and finally, the emergence of VCR technology at ever-decreasing prices allows viewers to take control of the TV schedule and watch noncommercialized tapes instead of over-the-air network programming.

In summary, although television viewing is becoming more fragmented and the choices offered increase, the networks continue to hold the dominant, albeit declining, share of viewing. As illustrated in Table 18–4, it is estimated that network shares of prime-time viewing will continue to decline from 59 percent in 1991–92 to 50 percent in the broadcast year 2000–01.

Syndication and Independent Stations. Many of the same factors that contributed to the decline in network shares have also contributed to the growth of syndication and independent television stations. Syndication evolved in the 1970s and has boomed in the 1980s. The number of syndicators increased from 143 in 1975 to 226 in 1985, with the greatest increase, +51% from 1980 to 1985. Major companies such as Columbia, Paramount, 20th Century Fox, and Disney Studios now offer quality syndicated programming. Due to the mergers of some syndicators, the number of syndicators has decreased to 108 in 1992. The number of syndicated properties has shown a steady increase. For example, in 1975 approximately 306 properties were available; by 1992, the number of properties available had increased to over 350.

Along with the increase in the number of syndicators and the number of syndicated properties has come a dramatic increase in the amount of advertiser's dollars in syndication. All of the top 100 advertisers use syndication.

TABLE 18–5.   Advertising Dollars in Syndication

	Dollar Amount (Millions)	Percent of Increase
1983	$300	—
1984	400	+ 33%
1985	N/A*	N/A
1986	600	50
1987	762	27
1988	901	18
1989	1,288	43
1990	1,589	23

*N/A because spot/local TV dollars combined with syndication dollars.

Further, syndication generally consists of more than 10 percent of a major advertiser's network budget. Table 18–5 details the dollar growth syndication has experienced since 1983. As more and more quality syndicated properties and original programming become available, it is likely that the advertiser commitment will increase to an estimated two billion dollars by the year 2000.

The number of local independent television stations and their percentage of U.S. coverage has also increased dramatically. In 1975, there were seventy-two independent stations that provided 63 percent U.S. coverage. By 1985, there were 294 independent with 82 percent U.S. coverage. In 1991, the Association of Independent Television Stations reports there are 424 independents providing 93 percent coverage of U.S. TV households. Independent television stations are also increasing share in almost all dayparts at the expense of network affiliate shares. However, the greatest competition for share in most markets is between the independent stations within that market, not between independents and networks.

One of the most interesting recent developments in independent television is the emergence of the "Fourth" network, Fox Broadcasting Company, under the control of Rupert Murdoch. The initial offering of Murdoch's fourth network was a late night talk show originally starring Joan Rivers which premiered in October of 1986 (no longer on the air). Original prime-time programming on Saturday and Sunday nights followed in the spring of 1987, with later expansion to three additional nights. As of the 1992–93 season, Fox will have prime-time programming seven nights a week, competing with ABC, CBS, and NBC. Currently, Fox provides 94 percent coverage of U.S. TV households.

Cable Television. Let's review the history of cable TV. Community Antenna Television (CATV, now referred to simply as *cable*) began in the late 1940s as a means of providing a television signal, or an improved signal, to households in areas unable to receive "over-the-air" signals. These households were generally located in mountainous regions where the topography interfered with normal transmission. The cable operator built a high an-

TABLE 18-6. Growth of Cable Television

Year	Cable Systems	Total Subscribers (thousands)	U.S. TV Households (%)
1952	70	14	—
1970	2,490	4,500	7
1975	3,506	9,800	12
1979	4,150	14,100	18
1981	4,375	29,300	36
1990	9,575	55,900	60

Source: *Television Digest's Cable & Station Coverage Atlas;* A. C. Nielsen; Turner Communications; Leo Burnett Media Costs and Coverage, 1991.

tenna designed to receive signals from the closest television stations. These signals were then transmitted via coaxial cable to households subscribing to the service. One cable system was capable of transmitting a maximum of twelve channels (approximately 24 percent of the systems in operation today still offer no more than twelve channels).

Early cable operators were rarely involved in television programming. They were entrepreneurs and engineers who seized the opportunity to provide a needed service and enjoy a handsome return on their investment. Some of the more innovative cable operators broadcast local community events. Nearly all systems provided a twenty-four-hour weather channel. Advertising on the weather channel took the form of a printed reminder to shop at the local grocery store or drug chain.

In November 1975, Home Box Office (HBO) began using a satellite to transmit first-run movies to cable operators across the United States Cable operators received the signal via a disc antenna ("Earthstation") and retransmitted it to their subscribers. The cable industry learned that satellites could be used to distribute quality programming over great distances faster and more efficiently than transmitting the same program over land. The ready accessibility of quality programming was rapidly changing the cable industry from a transmitter of signals (with an emphasis on engineering) to a transmitter of television programming (with an emphasis on entertainment and information).

This change in industry emphasis stimulated growth in the number of cable systems and cable subscribers. As shown in Table 18-6, households subscribing to cable represented seven percent of households in 1970. By 1981, the percentage of households with cable TV more than quintupled. Currently, approximately six out of ten homes have cable capacity, which is not likely to increase substantially. (Technology employing fiber optics permits each household to receive a limitless number of channels. Of course, each household pays for this chance to view additional channels, and most of these homes pays an extra subscription fee for at least one pay channel.)

Cable programming can be divided into two basic segments: basic programming and pay programming. Basic programming is the standard service available at the normal subscription rate. In addition to installation charges, there is a basic monthly rate each subscriber pays to the cable operator. Basic programming consists of local television signals and two types of additional programming:

News/Community Programming. This programming consists of 24-hour national and international news, state news, community news, live coverage from the House of Representatives, stock market reports, coverage of the local school system, comparative shopping information, and classified advertising.

Information/Entertainment Programming. This programming includes sports, "superstation" news, children, special audience, and religious programs.

Pay programming is an option available to subscribers for an additional monthly fee—on top of the basic fee. It normally consists of movies, specials, and sports. Pay networks do not currently accept advertising. Table 18–7 lists the fifty-nine cable networks in operation in 1991, all of which are transmitted to cable operators via satellite, and which are, in turn, transmitted to television households subscribing to basic and/or pay programming. (All this increased programming availability, especially recently released movies, could have an adverse effect on the local movie theatre. It's conceivable that movie house attendance will decline, or change in demographic composition to exclude many of those able to afford a pay cable package.)

Once HBO and its competitors began generating ratings at the expense of the networks and WTBS succeeded in getting distribution all over the U.S., many observers adopted a "pie-in-the-sky" perspective on the growth of cable. They expected that cable network shares would eventually overtake the networks, creating a ratings free-for-all among a wide variety of program outlets. Many thought most minority tastes would be served by 100 or more cable networks, and that interactive cable systems would become the norm, facilitating all sorts of two-way communications like polling, security monitoring, and fire alarms.

The reality of cable thus far has turned out to be considerably less grand than what was anticipated. Only a few operators built as many as 100 channel systems, and they are full of unused channels. As noted, only about sixty networks exist today, and while new ones are coming on board all the time, network failures occur just as fast. No single cable network has come close to catching any of the networks in the ratings race—only HBO approaches a 10 household rating, which is only about 2 percent of total U.S. homes in its cable universe. Two-way services have also fallen by the wayside as costs relative to the demand have not been efficient enough to ensure their survival.

Nonetheless, a number of networks will survive and continue to grow, albeit in a limited fashion. Pay services that offer uninterrupted movies, or movies and specials, will probably survive in the long term, despite inroads made by the release of movies on videotape and disc immediately after their theater release. Basic services—those supported by advertising—will also

TABLE 18–7. Cable Networks

Network	Systems	Homes (000)	Percent of U.S. TV HH	Percent of U.S. Cable HH	Advertising Supported
Basic Services					
ACTS Satellite Network	478	9,500	10.2%	16.9%	Yes
American Movie Classics	2,621	34,000	36.5	60.6	Yes
America's Disability Channel	238	14,200	15.3	25.3	Yes
Arts & Entertainment Network	6,500	50,000	53.7	89.2	Yes
Black Entertainment Network	2,400	31,200	33.5	55.6	Yes
Bravo	455	6,000	6.4	10.7	Yes
CNBC	3,000	40,000	43.0	71.3	Yes
Cable News Network (CNN)	10,877	58,892	63.3	100.0	Yes
Channel America	12	471	0.5	0.8	Yes
C-SPAN	4,038	54,000	58.0	96.3	Yes
C-SPAN II	783	23,400	25.1	41.7	Yes
Comedy Central	1,282	18,250	19.6	32.5	Yes
Country Music Television	1,974	13,100	14.1	23.4	Yes
Courtroom Television Network	N/A	4,800	5.2	8.6	Yes
The Discovery Channel	8,989	54,500	58.5	97.2	Yes
E! Entertainment Television	777	18,750	20.1	33.4	Yes
ESPN	23,300	57,200	61.4	100.0	Yes
EWTN	774	23,300	25.0	41.6	Yes
The Family Channel	9,500	53,500	57.5	95.4	Yes
Fox Net	250	1,000	1.1	1.8	Yes
Galavision	249	1,750	1.9	3.1	Yes
Headline News	5,506	46,500	49.9	82.9	Yes
Home Shopping Network	1,502	18,000	19.3	32.1	Yes
Home Shopping Network II	400	7,000	7.5	12.5	Yes
The Inspiration Channel	810	7,600	8.2	13.6	Yes
International Channel	35	2,200	2.4	3.9	Yes
KTLA	292	4,800	5.2	8.6	Yes
KTVT	481	2,200	2.4	3.9	Yes
Learning Channel	1,401	21,000	22.6	37.5	Yes
Lifetime	5,300	52,000	55.9	92.7	Yes
Mind Extension University	254		0.0	0.0	Yes
The Monitor Channel	242	3,500	3.8	6.2	Yes
MTV	6,405	55,000	59.1	98.1	Yes
The Nashville Network	11,776	53,000	56.9	94.5	Yes
National College Television	380	5,983	6.4	10.7	Yes
Nickelodeon	8,635	55,400	59.5	98.8	Yes
Nick at Nite	3,837	50,250	54.0	89.6	Yes
North American Television	8	513	0.6	0.9	Yes
Nostalgia Television	602	12,300	13.2	21.9	Yes
Prevue Guide	835	24,526	26.3	43.7	Yes
QVC Network	3,900	41,000	44.0	73.1	Yes
SCOLA/News of all Nations	35	2,800	3.0	5.0	Yes
Silent Network	238	14,200	15.3	25.3	Yes
Sportschannel America	58	2,320	2.5	4.1	Yes
TBS Superstation	11,105	56,586	60.8	100.0	Yes
Telemundo	36	1,362	1.5	2.4	Yes
TNT	6,958	53,733	57.7	95.8	Yes

TABLE 18-7. (continued)

Network	Systems	Homes (000)	Percent of U.S. TV HH	Percent of U.S. Cable HH	Advertising Supported
The Travel Channel	735	17,000	18.3	30.3	Yes
Trinity Broadcasting Network	1,015	13,300	14.3	23.7	Yes
Univision	814	11,063	11.9	19.7	Yes
USA Network	10,100	54,500	58.5	97.2	Yes
VH-1	3,985	41,800	44.9	74.5	Yes
Video Jukebox Network	96	9,050	9.7	16.1	Yes
VISN	500	7,700	8.3	13.7	Yes
The Weather Channel	4,500	49,063	52.7	87.5	Yes
WGN	13,969	34,900	37.5	62.2	Yes
WPIX	641	9,200	9.9	16.4	Yes
WSBK	73	2,000	2.1	3.6	Yes
WWOR	3,013	13,500	14.5	24.1	Yes
Pay Services					
Cinemax	5,458	6,400	6.9	11.4	No
The Disney Channel	7,000	5,665	6.1	10.1	No
Encore	854	25	0.0	0.0	No
Home Box Office (HBO)	8,833	17,300	18.6	30.9	No
The Movie Channel	3,250	2,800	3.0	5.0	No
Showtime	6,000	7,400	7.9	13.2	No
TV-Japan	5	N/A	0.0	0.0	No

Source: Cablevision, August 12, 1991.

survive, and it appears that many will be successful over the long term. Today cable TV networks program to reach a wide variety of audiences. Some, like WTBS and USA, function more like a broadcast station or network, offering a smorgasbord of programming for all demographics. Others, like CNN or the Weather Channel, reach more selective audience segments by breaking out the same program type around the clock. There are a few true ''narrowcast'' cable networks, like MTV (rock video), Nickelodeon (kids), and Discovery Channel, that target selective audiences with custom-tailored programming. Of these three types, broad appeal networks attract the largest audiences.

Years of speculation about direct satellite-to-home broadcasting (DBS) resulted in several companies' aborted development of such a service. The widening availability of cable, the discount pricing of VCRs, and proliferation of backyard satellite receiving dishes designed to receive cable-only signals spelled doom for one company (USCI) that actually marketed a DBS service, and scared several others away from start-up. In fact, the easy availability of satellite dishes in rural areas led to a sort of de facto DBS; essentially, the dish owner was pirating pay and basic cable feeds. This led to computerized scrambling of pay and some basic signals, which resulted in direct marketing of descrambling devices and collection of program fees from dishowners not unlike the fees cable customers pay.

VCRs. The biggest news in the 1980s has been the advent of the low-priced VCR, and the resultant proliferation of video software which is available in video rental stores, record stores, bookstores, supermarkets, and convenience marts. Currently, 79 percent of all homes have VCRs. Many have their own video cameras, and many have digital audio/video disc technology which will enable them to record and play back audio and video software.

The impact of all this on the media plan is already being felt. The popularization of VCRs has introduced remote control, and these remote controls are being used to, among other things, avoid commercials while watching television (zapping), and to fast-forward through commercials while replaying taped television programs (zipping). These phenomena are expected to increase as penetration of remote controls increases. Currently, 77 percent of all homes have remote controlled television sets and/or remote controlled VCRs.

New Technologies. In addition to the many changes the television environment has already experienced, new and better technologies that will change the face of the television medium have been and will continue to be developed. Stereo television, high definition television, satellite technology, and the home computer are but a few of the technologies that we know will contribute to the changes in media.

Stereo Television. Currently, over 400 television stations broadcast in stereo, covering 85 percent of U.S. homes. General Electric's purchase of RCA, and its subsidiary NBC, sparked the growth of stereo television. NBC became the first network to broadcast in stereo, and RCA introduced its deluxe line of stereo television sets. ABC began transmitting in stereo shortly thereafter, followed by CBS. Although the sale of stereo television receivers has been slow (due primarily to $100 difference between mono and stereo), it is estimated that stereo will soon be available to all homes. Currently, 31 percent of all households have stereo TVs.

High Definition Television (HDTV). HDTV—currently available only in Japan—is expected to be available in the United States by 1995. HDTV sets have wider screens, much sharper pictures than today's television, and sound as good as compact disc players. They sell for at least $15,000 in Japan.

HDTV is slow in coming to America in part because there are no real advantages for broadcasters. It costs more and does not compensate by providing more income. However, if all goes according to plan, the Federal Communications Commission (FCC) will decide on the first completely new television transmission standard in America in more than 50 years. Zenith Electronics Corporation and American Telephone and Telegraph are currently testing systems for an all-digital version of HDTV that could give America the best TV system overall.

Satellite Technology. Since 1975, when SATCOM I, the first domestic communications satellite, was launched, satellite technology has changed the communication paths between senders and receivers. It is estimated that well before the end of the century, all network audio and video signals (radio, broadcast, and cable) will be delivered via satellite. This would eliminate all land-line distribution and facilitate stereo sound.

In addition, satellite technology is and will continue to be used by the print media. National print editorial and advertisements are being sent by satellite uplinks and downlinks to regional and local printing plants to improve the timeliness of content and delivery. In addition, clients and their agencies may use satellite transmission to beam copy executions from office to office, reducing time spent on the road and in meetings.

Home Computers. Estimating home computer penetration is more difficult than estimating VCR penetration. SMRB states that 21.4 percent of all adults own home computers. Although initial home computer sales were sluggish, advances in technology will lower prices and the maturing of a new generation of computer-literate children should increase sales. By the end of the century, at least 50 percent of all homes should have a computer. Ultimately, home computer usage for business and pleasure may impact on TV viewing.

Technology Summary

Over the next twenty-five years, technology will continue to grow and provide the media environment with more choices, more consumer control, as well as the capability to interact with information and entertainment sources. Satellites, video recorders, and computers will dominate the media world. Consolidation will be a key trend, not only in the ownership of media sources themselves, but in the technologies which access them. Electronic component systems, which incorporate TV monitors, cable tuners, videocassette players and recorders, computer keyboards, stereo receivers and speakers, compact disc players, and computer modems are available now. Stereo sound will soon be commonplace. Video enhancements, such as digital signal transmission, will make the channel switcher's life easier by displaying two channels simultaneously. More people, with more leisure time, will spend that time at home in their "media rooms"; they will have more opportunities to work at home, and more reasons to be there.

Media Planning

Media planners will have their hands full trying to come to grips with a bigger total audience that will be more and more splintered. As an outgrowth of rapidly developing marketing sophistication and an increasingly personalized media environment, marketing and media planning goals will become more precise, with consumers being defined in much greater detail than we have today.

In addition to more and better traditional consumer data, research will have to provide a greater understanding of who the best prospects are and how to reach them. For example, women aged 25–54 who are working and in a household with a total income of $25,000 are good prospects if they characterize current Brand Z users. But women currently using a category brand, or intending to buy, are even more descriptive of a prime prospect. Research will provide greater insight into media usage patterns to reach these individuals and others who will influence a purchase.

An increasingly fragmented audience, coupled with a media inflation spiral that appears to have no end, will make it more important than ever to get every ounce of effectiveness out of each advertising dollar by developing new media techniques and applications. A vast amount of testing and trial of new media will occur in the 1990s and beyond. The new technologies will enable advertisers and agencies to measure alternatives and concepts with greater precision than ever. Two-way interactive communication systems can be employed for many purposes. Measurements of attitudes or actual purchases may occur instantaneously.

Each component of a media plan might be scheduled as part of a unique pattern to achieve a designated effective reach goal against each specialized segment of the target audience. The average media plan could have a very unorthodox appearance when it includes some daytime serials, pay cable adult movies, sports cable network, demographic editions of magazines and newspapers, some syndicated network radio, in-store media, and direct response.

A new generation of sophisticated computerization will permeate media planning and media buying. There will be more research, more media outlets, more complex analyses to conduct, more extensive tracking of results—more details than ever. All media professionals will have to have a greater understanding of computer technology, while not losing touch with basic tools and responsibilities.

Changing Dynamics

The first important consideration is that current solutions to the problems of the future will not work. All media dynamics must be reassessed: reach, frequency, frequency distribution, audience accumulation, target audience, etc.

Average Rating

If you buy Kansas City spot TV in late fringe now, you will be purchasing one or more of the five TV stations in the market and delivering, on average, a 4.4 household rating, as shown in Table 18–8.

TABLE 18–8.   Late Fringe TV—Kansas City

Station	DMA/HH Rating
WDAF	5
KCTV	6
KMBC	8
KSHB	2
KSMO	1
Total	22
Average	4.4

Now consider the ratings report of the future. As Table 18–9 shows, it will contain many more stations.

The media planner in 2000 might find eighteen different stations broadcasting in the Kansas City market. Perhaps ten to fifteen of these stations will accept advertising. The planner will have to choose among programs that will be delivering an average of a 1.4 rating. Four programs (or announcements) will have to be purchased to equal the 4.4 gross rating points one can now buy with one program.

Reach/Frequency

If 400 gross rating points are planned today, it can be anticipated that it would be necessary to purchase twenty-five announcements with an average of a 16 rating each. These twenty-five announcements, on the average, will

TABLE 18–9.   Representative TV Market in the Future

Station	DMA/HH Rating
A	0.1
B	3.1
C	1.3
D	1.3
E	2.2
F	0.5
G	0.1
H	0.7
I	1.2
J	1.8
K	2.3
L	0.7
M	0.9
N	1.7
O	0.4
P	3.2
Q	2.0
R	2.7
Total	26.2
Average	1.4

TABLE 18–10. Reach/Frequency

	Now	Future
Number announcements	25	200
Average rating	16	2
Gross rating points	400	400
Reach/frequency	87/4.6	87/4.6 (?)
		90/4.4 (?)
		80/5.0 (?)

reach 87 percent of the designated audience an average of 4.6 times each. In the future, that viewing audience will be splintered across 10, 20, 30, or more channels with each channel delivering a smaller average rating than today. To deliver 400 gross rating points, more announcements will have to be purchased, and probably more stations, as shown in Tables 18–9 and 18–10.

This raises the following questions:

- Will the reach/frequency be the same?
- Is it conceivable that reach could be higher because new programming will attract light and non–TV viewers?
- Is it possible that reach will be lower because there will be more viewers watching pay TV?

Audience Accumulation

When one thinks of audience accumulation, one generally thinks of magazines because it takes time for magazines to build their total readership through pass-along. Television and radio are now thought of as "instantaneous" media vehicles. This will probably change. Reach accumulation in the future could be the same over a long period of time, but it is possible that it could take longer to accumulate a total broadcast audience because many people will record a program for later viewing. If the advertiser plans a sale that ends June 30, it should anticipate that some viewers will see the commercials in July, August, or even later. Table 18–11 illustrates the problem.

TABLE 18–11. Audience Accumulation in TV—100 GRPs per Week

Week	Now	Future	
		Same (?)	Longer (?)
1	59	59	50
2	78	78	65
3	85	85	75
4	87	87	80
5	—	—	85
6 Mos. later	—	—	87

Target Audience

Many advertising people have historically subscribed to a viewing theory that might be called "least objectionable program"—viewers first decide to watch TV, then tune in a specific program. In the future, the program will be the first decision made. People will seek out programs they really want to watch, and there will be many more programs available. Programs will appeal to very specific segments of the population based both on demographic characteristics and life-style orientation. When broadcast media are purchased now, audience information is available only for certain demographic breaks. In the future, research will have to provide not only narrower demographic breaks, but also life-style and, quite possibly, product consumption information.

Direct Response

Another media/marketing vehicle that has received increased attention by national advertisers is direct response or direct mail advertising. As noted in an earlier chapter, direct response is a very selective, targeted, personal medium that offers great geographic and production flexibility and response is easily measurable. Direct mail promotions, catalogs, and home shopping vehicles are receiving increased usage by both national advertisers and their agencies. According to the Direct Marketing Association, marketers who utilize catalogs most frequently express positive feedback regarding their intent to continue utilizing direct mail/catalog advertising. More importantly, these catalog leaders reported strengthened unit sales and higher profits as a result of their direct mail/catalog efforts.

The emergence of home shopping television broadcasts (such as Home Shopping Network) have also contributed to the increase in interest in direct response advertising. Advertisers now have the ability to sell products directly to the consumer simply by providing a toll-free phone number and an operator standing by to take the credit card number and the order. As the popularity of this medium increases, it is probable that media planners will utilize direct response advertising as an integral part of their media plans.

Integrated Marketing Communications

Traditional advertising has been an overwhelming choice of marketers for years, though it now seems other kinds of communication may be required *in addition to advertising* in order for advertisers to effectively reach their targets. As discussed in an earlier chapter, included here are communication elements such as public relations, direct marketing, sales promotion, and event marketing. Essentially, marketers are using a wider variety of communication tools today than ever before.

This concept of broadening an advertiser's communication mix to include a wide array of tools is part of the concept known as *integrated market-*

ing communications. Integrated marketing communications entails coordination of all marketing efforts into a single, unified plan, with one cohesive message for consumers to understand. Additionally, integration suggests that the blending of all marketing efforts be perceived by consumers as "seamless." In other words, the messages coming from any or all of the communication tools should appear to be part of the total picture and not as separate entities.

Some professionals believe that integrated marketing communications will impact all aspects of marketing and advertising. Still others call it a buzzword that will fade into obscurity as soon as the next fad appears. However, this is not the belief of John O'Toole, president of the American Association of Advertising Agencies. He is an industry leader who not only believes in the concept of integrated communications, but has called for ad agencies to change their operations to accommodate other forms of marketing communications. O'Toole believes so firmly in the concept of integration that he has warned, "the future success of the advertising agency business will belong to those who can make that change."

New Media Jargon

Media planners certainly will have new challenges in the decades to come. There will be bigger audiences, but they will be more splintered. *When* a person will be exposed to advertising will become as important as *what* they are exposed to. There will be greater selectivity in television, magazines, newspapers, radio, out-of-home, and direct response.

Media jargon will have to keep pace with these changes. Planners will have to shift from *average quarter hour rating* to *accumulated program rating. Homes using TV* will be antiquated and eventually will be replaced by *homes using electronic media. Cost per thousand* may change to *cost per hundred* or *cost per user* because there will be smaller target audiences to reach. *Reach* will change to *eventual reach* and eventually to *reach when needed. Frequency* will become divided into *initial frequency* (when the commercial is first seen), *eventual frequency,* and *repeat frequency* (for those who record a program and view it a second time). Will part of a newspaper's or magazine's delivery be called *electronic delivery* for those subscribers who view the periodical on their TV screen? If *Time* magazine's experiment of creating a "talking magazine," which uses an electronic device reacting to an electronically treated page, is successful, will these readers need to be called *reader/listeners?*

Media Planning Summary

The future offers advertisers both opportunities and obstacles. A more fragmented media world results in greater audience selectivity, and greater selectivity results in less waste. In light of the increasing cost of media, the less waste in a media plan the better.

More viewing, reading, and listening options should inevitably lead to higher interest, deeper involvement, and higher attentiveness—to both the media and the advertising within the media. There is a good chance that if advertisers react to this segmentation with personalized and localized advertising messages, their media budgets can be used with greater discrimination and far more effectiveness.

The key to all is research. With more precise research, the media planner can make better decisions.

QUESTIONS FOR DISCUSSION

1. How will population change affect media planning?
2. Does high-definition television advertising (HDTV) have advantages for advertisers, stations, and audiences?
3. How are magazines expected to change in the future?
4. What new kind of media may change the buying process somewhat in the future?
5. Will the decline in network television viewing cause this medium to go out of business?
6. What is the main value of *USA Today* for advertisers?
7. What, from the point of view of print media publishers, are some of the major problems they face in order to stay in business?
8. Which research technologies now being developed may have the most effect on media planning?
9. Although the topic was not elaborated, what skills will media planners probably need more of in the future?
10. What is one of the most notable advances and limitations for media planners in cable television operations?

SELECTED READINGS

Chook, Paul H., "The Need for a New Media Model," *Journal of Media Planning,* Fall, 1989, 11–15.

Cohen, Stanley E., "The Dangers of Today's Media Revolution," *Advertising Age,* Aug. 26, 1991, 18.

Frank, Betsy, "When VCR Meets NBC," *Marketing and Media Decisions,* October 1986, 106–10.

Heeter, Carrie, and Greenberg, Bradley S., "Profiling the Zappers," *Journal of Advertising Research,* April/May 1985, 15–20.

Kaplan, Barry M., "Zapping—The Real Issue Is Communication," *Journal of Advertising Research,* April/May 1985, 9–14.

Poltrack, David F., "Good Media Planning Will Have To Go Beyond Numbers to Qualitative Analysis," *Journal of Media Planning,* Fall 1989, 25–28.

Zeller, Joseph P., "Interactive Media—Media Playthings of the '90s or Path to Better Media Plans?" *Journal of Media Planning,* Fall 1990, 25–30.

Glossary

A **A.B.C. (Audit Bureau of Circulations)**—An organization that provides certified statements of net paid circulations of magazines and newspapers, supported jointly by advertisers, agencies, and media.

A.B.P. (Associated Business Publications)—A trade association of business (industrial, trade, and technical) publications.

Accordion Insert—An advertisement not printed by the publisher, but inserted in a magazine, folded in such a way as to appear as an accordion fold.

Accumulation—A method of counting audiences wherein each person exposed to a vehicle is counted once, either in a given time period such as four weeks for broadcast, or for one issue in print.

A Counties—As defined by A. C. Nielsen Company, all counties belonging to the 25 largest metropolitan areas. These metro areas correspond to the *MSA (Metropolitan Statistical Area)* and include the largest cities and consolidated areas in the United States.

ADI (Area of Dominant Influence)—Geographical market definition wherein each county is assigned exclusively to only one television market as defined by Arbitron.

Adjacencies—The specific time periods that precede and follow regular television programming, usually two minutes. These are commercial break positions between programs that are available for local or spot advertisers. There is no such thing as a network adjacency; only spot adjacencies are available.

Adnorm—A term used by Daniel Starch & Associates to indicate readership averages by publication, by space size and color, and by type of product for ads studied by Starch in a two-year period. It is used to provide a standard of comparison for individual ads against averages of similar types of ads.

Advertising Allowance—Money paid under contract by the manufacturer or his representative to a wholesaler or a retailer for the express purpose of being spent to advertise a specified product, brand, or line. Usually used for consumer advertising. (See *Cooperative Advertising, Promotion Allowance*.)

Advertising Appropriation—A company's estimated dollar figure for an advertising effort of a short-term flight, seasonal campaign and/or total marketing year. Usually reflects general categories for media, production, promotion, and reserve and is based on projected business volume.

Advertising Checking Bureau (ACB)—A service organization that supplies advertisers and agencies with tearsheets of advertisements run in publications and with other information, in order that client and competitor advertising impact can be assessed.

Advertising Impression—One person or home exposed to a single advertisement: on a gross basis, the sum of all impressions to the ads in a schedule. This includes duplication, for some of those exposed may be exposed more than once. In some instances, advertising impression refers to those persons or homes that are exposed to a media vehicle (magazine, television show, etc.) and is developed by multiplying the audience of each vehicle (on a household or person basis) by the number of advertisements or commercials carried by each vehicle and obtaining the total. In other cases, it refers to the number of persons or homes exposed to an advertisement or commercial within the carrier. In these cases, data on ad/commercial exposure are applied to the carrier audiences.

Advertising Page Exposure (APX)—A measurement of physical opportunity to observe a print ad. Defined as the act of opening a spread of facing pages wide enough to glance at any advertising.

Advertising Weight—The amount of advertising planned for, or used by, a brand. Al-

431

though it is not limited to a particular measurement, it is most frequently stated in terms of the number of messages or impressions delivered or broadcasts/insertions placed over a period of time.

Affidavit of Performance—A notarized statement from a television or radio station that verifies that a media schedule ran as ordered.

Afternoon Drive—Radio daypart between 3:00 P.M. and 7:00 P.M.

Agate Line (usually simplified to Line)—A unit of space by which newspaper and other print advertising space is sold. One agate line represents a space 1 column wide and $1/14$ of an inch high. This is a measure of area, not shape—a 210 line ad can be 1 column $\times$ 210 lines, 2 columns $\times$ 105 lines, or 3 columns $\times$ 70 lines.

Agency commission—A commission that an advertising agency receives for media it has placed. Traditionally, this fee is a 15 percent discount on the gross advertising rate billed to the client by the agency. However, this form of agency compensation is being reevaluated by many in the industry, and some are now billing clients on a straight fee basis, with each agency function assigned a set fee.

Agency of Record—An agency that purchases media time or space for another agency or a group of agencies serving the same client.

Aided Recall—A measurement technique in which respondents are helped to remember portions or all of ads by having an interviewer provide clues. (See *Unaided Recall*.)

Algorithm—A computer term referring to processing rules: a defined process that leads to an assured development of a desired output from a given input.

Alternate Week Sponsor—An advertiser who purchases full or participating sponsorship every other week of a network program for a full fifty-two-week broadcast year. Each sponsor purchasing at least two minutes in a given program episode will receive billboard commercial time on his week of sponsorship.

AM (Amplitude Modulation)—AM is the standard broadcast transmission system used by the majority of licensed radio stations. The term is commonly used to differentiate between AM and FM radio.

Animatic—(a) Noting or pertaining to mechanical animation. (b) A television commercial produced from semifinished artwork, generally used only for test purposes.

Announcement—A commercial message between or within programs. Announcements may be live, or recorded, or a combination of both. Common lengths in television are 60, 30, 20, 15, and 10 seconds.

Annual Discount—A discount given to an advertiser by a media carrier based on the number of advertising insertions or units run during an established contract year.

Arbitron—A television and radio rating service used to measure viewing/listening audiences. Arbitron publishes both a monthly radio network rating report and TV and radio reports for selected individual markets (no network TV).

Area of Dominant Influence (ADI)—An exclusive cluster of counties in which the originating or home market station reflects the largest share of total viewing hours. This term is used by Arbitron.

Arrears—Subscribers whose subscriptions to a periodical have lapsed, but who are retained temporarily on active subscription lists to boost that periodical's circulation. It is an industry standard that arrears must be dropped from circulation figures after three months.

Audience—The number of people or households who are exposed to a medium. Exposure measurements indicate nothing about whether audiences saw, heard, or read either the advertisements or editorial contents of the medium.

Audience Accumulation—The total net audience exposed to repeated periodical, outdoor, television, or radio advertising.

Audience Composition—The demographic makeup of people represented in an audience with respect to income group, age, sex, geography, etc.

Audience Duplication—In broadcast, a measurement of the number of listeners or viewers reached by two or more programs, or by the same program over repeated telecasts, sponsored by the same advertiser. In print, the measurement of the overlap of potential exposure between different issues of the same magazine or among issues of different magazines.

Audience Flow—Changes in audience of broadcast programs. May be reported on a minute-by-minute basis, by five-minute intervals, or from show to show.

Audience Holding Index—A measurement of the retentive power or audience loyalty of a given program. A. C. Nielsen, for thirty-minute programs, uses an index based on the percentage of homes tuned to the same program twenty-five minutes after the first measurement. It is a simple measure of the ratio of average audience rating to total audience rating of a given program.

Audience, Potential—In broadcasting, the number of sets in use in the time period to be studied, or the number of set owners. In print, the total audience of an issue.

Audience, Primary—In a study of audience accumulation, the noncumulative potential audience of an advertising message. In print, all readers who live in households where someone subscribes to, or purchases, the magazine. May be called primary readership.

Audience Profile—The characteristics of the people who make up the audience of a magazine, TV show, newspaper, radio show, etc., in terms of age, family size, location, education, income, and other factors.

Audience, Secondary—Pass-along readers who read a publication they did not purchase. These readers should be taken into account in determining the total number of readers of a particular publication.

Audience Turnover—The average number of times that a television program receives new audience members in a four-week period. Calculated by dividing reach by the average rating.

Audilog—The diary that members of Nielsen's local rating panels fill out to show what they are viewing on television.

Audimeter—An electronic device developed by the A. C. Nielsen Company that records set usage and tuning on a minute-by-minute basis. Nielsen used a national sample of approximately 1,200 Audimeter homes which are used to measure television usage and program audiences.

Audit Bureau of Circulations (ABC)—A tripartite, nonprofit, self-regulatory organization of advertisers, agencies, and magazine and newspaper publishers, which verifies the circulation figures of publishers and members and reports these data to advertiser and agency members.

Audit Report (White Audit)—Official document issued by the A.B.C. detailing its findings as a result of an audit. (Printed on white paper to differentiate it from semiannual publisher's statements printed on colored paper.) Audit reports are issued annually covering the twelve-month period of the two previous publisher's statements. (See *Pub-*

lisher's Statement.) If the auditor's findings differ from the information in the publisher's statements, the discrepancies are reported and explained in the audit report.

Availability—A specific period of broadcast commercial time offered for sale by a station or network for sponsorship.

Average Audience (AA)—In broadcasting, the number of homes/persons tuned in to a TV program for an average minute (a Nielsen network TV measurement). In print, the number of persons who looked into an average issue of a publication.

Average Frequency—The number of times the average home (or person) reached by a media schedule is exposed to the schedule. This is measured over a specific period of time, e.g., four weeks in broadcast media.

Average Net Paid—Average circulation per issue arrived at by dividing the sum total paid circulation for all the issues of the audit period by the total number of issues.

B   **Back of Book**—The section of a magazine following the main editorial section.

Back-to-Back Scheduling—Two or more commercials run one immediately following the other.

Banner Advertising—A unit of advertising space that runs above a number of columns of advertising or editorial material.

BAR (Broadcast Advertisers Reports)—An organization that monitors network and spot TV activity and spending by brand as well as non-network activity in selected markets and reports to subscribers the position, length, and advertised brand of all announcements broadcast during a given week. Also reports network radio.

Barter—Acquisition by an advertiser of sizable quantities of spot time or free mentions at rates lower than card rates from broadcast stations in exchange for operating capital or merchandise. Although direct negotiation between the advertiser and station is possible, it is more common for barter to be arranged through a middleman, a barter agency, or a film producer or distributor, who may have procured the time through an exchange of film or taped shows.

Base Rate—See *Open Rate*.

Basic Cable—A service that transmits television signals by wire (cable) instead of through the air. This allows for improved reception and increased availability of retransmitted local and distant stations. Available at a basic monthly subscription fee.

B Counties—As defined by A. C. Nielsen Company, all counties not included under A that are either over 150,000 population or in a metro area over 150,000 population according to the latest census.

BehaviorScan—A technique for measuring product and brand purchased through use of Universal Product Code at checkout counters.

Best Food Day—A day on which a newspaper runs editorial material on food, making that day's edition the most advantageous for retail grocers' advertising and hence, for the advertising of food manufacturers; usually Wednesday evening or Thursday editions.

Billboard—An identifying announcement of sponsorship at the beginning, end, or breaks of radio and television sponsored programs. Billboards are not sold, but usually are a bonus, based on the advertiser's volume or commitment with the program or the broadcaster. Usually 5 to 10 seconds in length. Also, an outdoor poster.

Billing—(a) A charge made to an advertiser by an advertising agency, based on the listed or gross charges of the media from which space or time has been purchased, along with any other charges and fees incurred by the agency that are passed on to the advertiser. (b) Loosely, the money spent by an advertiser through an agency. (c) The actual charge made by a medium of communication to an advertising agency; the gross charge less the agency discount.

Black & White (B&W, B/W)—Printing with black ink on white paper (or vice versa); no color. Also known as monotone.

Blanket Coverage—Total coverage by television and radio of a given geographic area.

Bleed—An advertisement in which part or all of the illustration or copy runs past the usual margins out to the edge of a page. Bleed insertions are generally sold at a premium price, usually 15 percent over the basic rate.

Bonus Circulation—Circulation delivered by a publication that is above and beyond the circulation on which an advertiser's rate is based.

Brand Development Index (BDI)—The number of cases, units, or dollar volume of a brand sold per 1,000 population. It is calculated by dividing the percentage of sales in a market by the population percentage in the same market.

Brand Extension—A line extension or flanker item marketed under a single brand name.

Broadcast Calendar—A calendar used for accounting purposes in the radio and TV industry which contains months of four or five whole weeks, each month beginning on a Monday. Each quarter in the broadcast calendar contains 13 weeks.

Broadsheet—A newspaper size approximately 15 inches wide and 22 inches high.

Broadside—A promotion piece consisting of one large sheet of paper, generally printed on one side only.

Brochure—An elaborate booklet, usually bound with a special cover.

Bulk Circulation—Sales in quantity lots of an issue of a magazine or newspaper. The purchases are made by individuals or concerns and the copies are usually directed to lists of names supplied by the purchasers. In the A.B.C. report, bulk circulation is listed separately from single-copy sales.

Bulk Sales—Sales of copies of a publication in quantity to one purchaser to be given free by him. Many advertisers do not consider bulk sales to be a valuable part of a publication's circulation.

Bulldog Edition—An edition that is issued and on sale earlier than regular editions. Usually applies to morning newspapers. There are also Bulldog Sunday editions that go on sale Saturday night.

Burke Test—A test service of Burke Marketing Research, Inc., that measures recall of an advertisement among those persons exposed to it the preceding day.

Business Building Test—A test run by a specific brand designed to determine if a marketing or advertising plan change will produce enough additional business for the brand to pay the required costs of the change.

Business Paper—A publication directed to a particular industry, trade, profession, or vocation. A *horizontal* business paper is designed to reach all groups in a broad trade or industry regardless of location or occupational title. A *vertical* publication is for a specific profession, trade, or occupational level within or across various industries.

Buyout—A one-time payment to television or radio talent for all rights to performance.

C   **CATV**—Community Antenna (or cable) TV services that deliver high-quality TV signals to homes via coaxial cable. Also called *cable television*.

C.C.A. (Controlled Circulation Audit)—An organization that audits the circulation statements of publications that are sent free to selected lists.

Cable TV—A system of broadcasting television whereby programs are first tuned-in by a Community Antenna and then distributed to individual homes by cables. Cable operators often receive programs transmitted by satellites and then transmit by cable to their subscribers.

Cancellation Date—The last date on which it is possible to cancel advertising. Such dates occur for print, outdoor, and broadcasting.

Cannibalize—To draw sales away from another product of the same manufacturer in a manner diminishing the maker's profit; said of new products, flanker items, or line extensions.

Car Card—A standard 11-inch-high siderack card, generally with posterlike design, placed in buses, street cars, and subways. Common sizes are 11″ × 28″, 11″ × 42″, and 11″ × 56″.

Card Rate—The cost of time and space quoted on a rate card.

Case Allowance—An allowance or discount a manufacturer or wholesaler gives to a retailer on each case of product purchased in return for which the retailer is to use the money to advertise the product.

Cash Discount—A deduction allowed by print media (usually 2 percent of the net) for prompt payment (e.g., within 15 to 30 days), generally passed along by the agency to the advertiser to encourage collections.

Cash Refund Offer—A type of mail-in offer used by a brand, or group of brands, which offers cash to the consumer upon providing proof of purchase.

Category Development Index (CDI)—Means the same as *Marketing Development Index*. Essentially, the percentage of total U.S. sales of a product category related to population percentage in a geographical market.

C Counties—As defined by A. C. Nielsen Company, all counties not included under A or B that either have over 40,000 population or are in a metropolitan area of over 40,000 population according to the latest census.

Center Spread—An advertisement appearing on the two facing center pages of a publication.

Chain Break—(a) The time between network programs during which a station identifies itself. (b) A commercial appearing in a chain break.

Checking Copy—A copy of a publication sent to an advertiser and agency as proof that the advertisement appeared as ordered.

Circulation—In print, the number of copies of a vehicle distributed based on an average of a number of issues. In broadcast, the number of television or radio households that tune in to a station a minimum number of times within a specified time period (such as once a week or once a day). In outdoor, the total number of people who have an opportunity to see a given showing of billboards within a specified time, such as a twenty-four-hour period.

City Zone—A geographic area that includes the corporate limits of the central city of the market plus any contiguous areas that have substantially the same built-up characteristics of the central city. This provides a method of reporting newspaper circulation according to A.B.C. standards.

Class A, B, C Rates—Rates for the most desirable and costly television time, usually between 6 P.M. and 11 P.M., are called Class A rates; the next most costly is Class B; and so on. Each station sets its own time classifications.

Class Magazine—A publication that reaches select high-income readers in contrast to magazines with larger circulations, generally referred to as *mass magazines*.

Clear Channel Station—An AM radio station allowed 50,000 kilowatts, the maximum power allowed, and priority in the use of frequency band. At sunset, other stations on this frequency sign off, because broadcasting range is extended after dark and stations on the same frequency tend to interfere with one another.

Clear Time—Process used by an advertiser to reserve a time period with a local station and by a network to check with its affiliates on the availability of a time period.

Clearance—Obtaining a time period for a program or commercial on a station or obtaining approval to use advertising from clients, legal and/or medical counsel, or network continuity departments.

Clipping Bureau—An organization that examines newspapers and magazines and clips articles from them; references and allusions of interest to its clients are sent to them.

Clock-Hour Delay—A delay in the broadcasting of a program originating in another time zone in order that the program may be aired at the same clock time in both time zones.

Closed Circuit TV—The transmission of television signals by cable or other nonbroadcast means to connected locations. Often used to transmit special events to theaters or for educational purposes.

Closing Date—The final date to commit contractually for the purchase of advertising space. Generally, cancellations are not accepted after the closing date, although some publications have a separate cancellation date, which may fall before the closing date. Also used in connection with supplying ad material to the publication.

Clutter—Excessive amounts of advertising carried by media vehicles, both print and broadcast. Term refers to both the total amount of advertising time and space and to its scheduling—long strings of consecutive commercials for broadcasting and solid banks of advertisements in print.

Coaxial Cable—Usually abbreviated to *cable*. The mechanical facility used by broadcasters for the transmission of programming from city to city or from a cable organization to individual homes. The cable is actually owned by A.T.&T. and, in turn, is rented to the user. Sometimes, microwave broadcasting operations are utilized instead of these cables. More generally, coaxial cable is any electrical cable capable of carrying large information loads with minimal distortion. (See *CATV, Cable TV*.)

Color Separations—A set of negative or positive films in which each color of a picture (plus black) are copied on a single film. Individual printing plates are made for each color. The four color plates, when printed in the proper relationship appear as a complete, lifelike colored picture.

Column Inch—A newspaper space measurement that is one column wide and one inch deep.

Combination Rate—A discounted rate offered to encourage use of two or more stations, newspapers, magazines, etc., having common ownership. Occasionally, an advertiser has no choice but to buy the combination as space/time may not be sold separately.

Commercial Audience—The audience for a specific commercial as determined by a survey that elicits information about what program viewers were doing just before, during, and after the commercial. The commercial audience is operationally defined as those people who were physically present in the room with the TV set at the time the commercial was on.

Commercial Break—In broadcasting, an interruption of programming in which commercials are broadcast.

Commercial Delivery—That part of the audience actually exposed to a particular commercial.

Commercial Pool—The selection of television or radio commercials that an advertiser has available for airing at any one time.

Commercial Protection—The amount of time that a network or station provides between the scheduling of competitive commercials.

Commission—Compensation to a salesperson, agency, etc., as a percent of their sales. (See *Agency of Record*.)

Competitive Parity Method—A method of establishing a marketing or media budget based on matching anticipated competitive expenditures.

Competitive Separation—An agreement between advertisers and a medium to separate competitive ads.

Concentration Campaign—One in which a small number of media vehicles is used to carry a relatively heavy amount of advertising.

Confirmation—Broadcast media statement that a requested time slot is available to a prospective client.

Consecutive Weeks Discount—A discount granted to an advertiser who uses a minimum number of weeks of advertising on a station or network without interruption.

Consumer Magazine—A magazine whose editorial content appeals to the general public, or a specific segment or layer of the public. Differentiated from trade or business magazines.

Contemporary Format—The format of radio stations which play mostly single records (usually country, pop, or middle-of-the-road styles) currently being sold at record stores, rotating them on the basis of popularity. Also called top-40 and rock formats.

Continuity—A method of scheduling advertising so that audiences have an opportunity to see ads at regular intervals. There are many patterns that could be used, from advertising once each day of the year to once a month.

Controlled Circulation Publications—Publications that confine or restrict their distribution to special groups on a free basis. Some controlled circulation is solicited, although most is nonsolicited.

Cooperative Advertising—Advertising run by a local advertiser in conjunction with a national advertiser. The national advertiser usually provides the copy and/or printing material and also shares the cost with the local retailer. In return, the national advertiser receives local promotion for its product. The name of the local advertiser and its address appear in the ad.

Co-Sponsorship—The participation of two or more sponsors in a single broadcast program where each advertiser pays a proportionate share of the cost.

Cost Efficiency—The effectiveness of media as measured by a comparison of audience, either potential or actual, with cost and expressed as a cost per thousand.

Cost per Point—In broadcast, the cost of one household or demographic rating point in a given market. Used in media planning and evaluation, it is calculated by dividing the cost per spot by the rating, or, in the cost of a number of spots, their total cost by the total ratings or GRPs.

Cost per Thousand (CPM)—A figure used in comparing or evaluating the cost efficiency of media vehicles. CPM is the cost to deliver 1,000 people or homes and is calculated by dividing the cost by the audience delivery and multiplying the quotient by 1,000.

Cost Ratio—Term used by Daniel Starch & Associates. The cost ratio is an adjustment made to the score obtained on each readership measure. The score is translated into per dollar terms (based on the magazine's reported primary circulation and the cost of the ad in terms of size, color, etc.) and then stated as a percentage of the average per dollar scores of all ads studied in the same issue. (See *Noted, Starch Method*.)

Counterprogramming—A technique used by networks to regulate audience flow by offering a program of a different type from that broadcast by a strong competitor in the same time period.

Coupon Insert—An IBM-type coupon attached to a carrier unit that is bound into the subscription copies of a magazine much like a normal page is inserted. Several configurations are available depending on the size of magazine, the manner in which it is bound, and the number of coupons to be carried.

Couponing—Distribution of coupons by a manufacturer through the mail, by household calls, or through media, offering a price reduction at the store on a product.

Coverage—A term used to define a medium's geographical potential. In newspapers, the number of circulation units of a paper divided by the number of households in a given area. In magazines, the percentage of a given demographic market reached by a magazine. In radio/television, the percentage of television households that can tune in to a station (or stations) because they are in the signal area. In outdoor, the percentage of adults who pass a given showing and are exposed in a thirty-day period. In previous years, coverage meant the same as reach. Today, the meaning will depend on which medium is being discussed.

Cover Positions—Premium-priced cover space for magazine or business publication advertisements: 1st cover—outside front cover; 2nd cover—inside front cover; 3rd cover—inside back cover; 4th cover—outside back cover. The first cover of consumer publications is seldom used for advertising.

Cowcatcher—A commercial occurring at the beginning of, and forming a part of, a television or radio program, advertising a product of the sponsor that is not mentioned again in the program.

Cume—A broadcast term that is Nielsen's shorthand for net cumulative audience of a program or of a spot schedule (radio or TV) in four weeks' time. Based on total number of unduplicated TV homes or people reached.

Cumulative Audience—The net unduplicated audience of a campaign, either in one medium or a combination of media. Sometimes called *reach* or *cume*.

Cut-In—Different broadcast copy or format that is used to replace an originating commercial in a network program in a specific market or region. Frequently used in test markets.

Cycle—An interval within a contract year at the end of which, upon proper notice, an advertiser may cancel network stations and/or facilities. Weekly and multiweekly program cycles usually are thirteen weeks in length, while co-sponsored program cycles usually encompass thirteen major broadcasts. Also refers to the thirteen-week periods used as a base for talent and use fee payments.

D   **Daily Rate**—The rate a newspaper charges for space in its weekday editions as opposed to the rate for the Sunday or weekend editions.

Day-After Recall—Probably the most common method used to test television commercials. Test commercials are shown on the air in the normal fashion. Approximately twenty-four hours later people are phoned and asked about their previous day's viewing. Only those who viewed the program carrying the test commercial are further questioned. The test score consists of that proportion of the commercial audience who are able to provide specific correct audio or video details from the test commercial. (See *Burke Test, Commercial Audience*.)

Daypart—A part of the broadcast day, so designated for analytical purposes. In TV, the dayparts are usually daytime (morning and afternoon), early fringe, prime time, and late fringe. In radio, they are morning, daytime, afternoon, evening.

D Counties—Essentially rural counties in the Nielsen classification system of A, B, C, D counties.

Decoder—An electronic device used for converting a scrambled TV signal into a viewable picture.

Delayed Broadcast—A program broadcast by a station at a time or day later than its original broadcast. The delay can range from hours to weeks.

Demographic Characteristics—Physical characteristics, such as sex, age, education, occupation, used to describe a population. Standard definitions, established by the 4A's, are used by many research companies.

Demographic Edition—An edition of a national publication circulated only to individuals with known demographic characteristics. Usually these editions differ from the national edition only in different advertisements.

Designated Marketing Area (DMA)—Nonoverlapping TV market coverage as defined by the A. C. Nielsen Company. (ADI is the equivalent term used by Arbitron.)

Diary Method—A research technique in which a sample of respondents record in diaries specific viewing behavior within a given period of time. This method is commonly used to measure the consumption of both media and products.

Differential (Newspaper)—The difference in newspaper rates charged local and national advertisers. Most newspapers continue to charge higher rates to national advertisers.

Direct Broadcast Satellite (DBS)—A satellite transmission system that delivers a signal directly to a home via an earth station or a receiver dish.

Direct Mail Advertising—Letters, folders, reprints, or other material sent through the mails directly to prospective purchasers.

Direct Response Advertising—Advertising material reproduced in quantity and distributed directly to prospects, either by mail, house-to-house delivery, bag stuffers, magazines and newspapers, or television. Allows prospect to respond directly to the advertiser rather than going through a retailer or other middleman.

Directory Advertising—Advertising in a directory. Popularly used to signify any advertising that consumers may deliberately consult, i.e., department store or food advertisements.

Discount—A reduction from regular rates when an advertiser contracts to use quantities of advertising. Discounts in print may consider amount of space bought and frequency of insertion. Discounts in network broadcasting may be based upon number of dayparts used, frequency or weight, and length of contract; in local broadcasting, discounts will consider number of spots per week, length of contract, or purchase of plans or packages.

DMA (Designated Market Area)—Geographical market definition wherein each county is assigned exclusively to only one television market as defined by Nielsen.

Double-Carding—A transit advertising term specifying two displays in each vehicle.

Double Truck—A two-page spread in newspapers where the editorial or advertising runs across the gutter of the spread.

Downlink—Programming delivered from a satellite to the ground.

Downscale—A general description of a medium's audience of lower socioeconomic class members.

Drive Time—The times of day (both morning and afternoon) when most people drive to or from work (about 6 to 10 am and 3 to 7 pm).

Duplication—The number or percentage of people in one vehicle's audience who also are exposed to another vehicle. Also audiences who are counted more than once in measurements, such as those who view the same TV program more than once a month.

Dutch Doors—In magazines, vertical half-page gatefolds which fold inward on both sides of a two-page spread.

E   **Earned Rate**—The rate that an advertiser has earned based on volume or frequency of space or time used to obtain a discount.

Earth Station—Communications station used to send or receive electronic signals from or to a satellite (seldom both). Usually employs one of a variety of dish-type antennas used by television stations and cable operators.

Effective Reach / Frequency—The reach of a medium or media schedule at a predetermined level of frequency (as opposed to total reach).

Efficiency—See *Cost Efficiency*.

Eight-Sheet Poster—See *Junior Panel*.

Elasticity—The degree to which demand for a product varies, depending on price or marketing support.

Electronic Newspaper—The use of a home CRT to receive newspaper-type textual material such as news, stock listings, and sports.

Entertainment and Sports Programming Network (ESPN)—An advertiser-supported twenty-four-hour cable service covering professional and amateur sporting events and sports talks. The primary owner is Getty Oil.

Ethnic Media—A catch-all term for those newspapers, magazines, and radio and television stations that direct their editorial and/or language to specific ethnic groups.

Exclusivity—Freedom from competing advertising within a given communications medium enjoyed by one advertiser; requires major space or time purchases.

Expansion Plan—An outline of the media to be used and timing thereof for a brand that plans to apply a theoretical national plan to portions of the country subsequent to testing and prior to actual national application. The expansion areas are the geographical units in which the product is to be sold.

Exposure—"Open eyes facing a medium." Practically, however, measurements are based on respondents who either say with assurance that they have looked into a given magazine, or that, after looking at a list of magazines, say that they have looked into those they checked on the list. In broadcast, those who are sitting in the room while a television or radio program is being broadcast.

Exposure, Depth of—The value credited to an increased number of broadcast commercials or multipage spreads in the form of heightened consciousness of an advertisement. While the audience for such media usage generally does not increase proportionally with the amount of additional investment made, the depth of exposure tends to provide adequate compensation.

Exposure, Opportunity of—The degree to which an audience may reasonably be expected to see or hear an advertising message.

F   **Facing**—Used in outdoor advertising to refer to the number of billboards used in one display. A single facing is one billboard. A double facing is two billboards either joined or with less than twenty-five feet between them. A triple facing is three billboards, etc. Also, the number of packages in a store facing out from the front row of a shelf.

Farm Publication—A publication devoted to general agricultural topics edited for farm families or farmers.

Fiber Optics—The use of very thin and pliable tubes of glass or plastic to carry bands of broadcast frequencies.

Field Intensity Map—A broadcast coverage map showing the quality of reception possible on the basis of signal strength. Sometimes called a *contour map*.

Field Intensity Measurement—The measurement of a signal delivered at a point of reception by a radio transmitter in units of voltage per meter of effective antenna height, usually in terms of microvolts or millivolts per meter.

Fifteen and Two—The same terms on which advertising media is ordered by advertising agencies for their clients, i.e., 15 percent commission is allowed by the media on the gross cost, plus 2 percent discount on the net amount for prompt payment.

Fifty-Fifty Plan—In cooperative advertising, the equal sharing by a manufacturer and a dealer of the cost of a manufacturer's advertisement appearing over a dealer's name.

Fixed Position—A specific period of station broadcasting time reserved for an advertiser and sold at a premium rate.

Fixed Rate—Station's price for a time slot which guarantees that the advertiser's announcement will run in that position without preemption.

Flat Rate—An advertising rate that does not include any discounts.

Flighting—A method of scheduling advertising for a period of time, followed by a period of no advertising, followed by a resumption of advertising.

Float—In periodical advertising, to run an advertisement within a space which is larger than the ad.

Flowchart—A system-analysis tool, either computerized or manual, that provides a graphical presentation of a procedure. Such charts present data flows, procedures, growth, equipment, methods, documents, machine instructions, etc.

FM (Frequency Modulation)—FM is a radio broadcast band in the broadcast spectrum different from that used by AM stations. There is no static in FM radio reception.

Folio—(a) A size of paper measuring 17″ by 22″. (b) A book with signatures formed of a single sheet of paper folded once, and thus of four pages each. (c) Loosely, any book with very large pages. (d) Any of the numbers that identify the successive pages of a book.

Forced Combination—Morning and evening newspapers owned by the same publisher that are sold to national advertisers only in combination. Some forced combinations are morning and evening editions of the same newspapers.

Four-Color (4/C)—Black and three colors (blue, yellow, red). Standard color combinations used by practically all publications offering color advertising.

Fourth Cover—The outside back cover of a magazine.

Fractional Showing—In outdoor, a showing of less than 25, offered in certain areas.

Franchise Position—A specified position in a publication (e.g., back cover, inside front cover) for which an advertiser is granted a permanent franchise (or right to use) as long as he continues to use it. Franchise positions are sometimes specific locations such as "opposite punched hole recipe page" in *Better Homes & Gardens*. Some positions are negotiated for specific issues, while others may be granted by frequency of use (i.e., six out of twelve issues). If a given position is not used one year, it usually must be renegotiated to regain it.

Free Publication—A publication sent without cost to a selected list of readers. Circulation may or may not be audited by C.C.A., but cannot qualify for A.B.C. audit unless at least 70 percent of circulation is paid.

Free-Standing Insert (FSI)—A preprinted advertisement in single or multiple page form that is inserted loose into newspapers, particularly Sunday editions.

Frequency—The average number of times an audience unit is exposed to a vehicle. Usually referred to as *average frequency*.

Frequency Discount—A discount given for running a certain number of insertions irrespective of size of advertisement within a contract year. Similar discounts are available in broadcasting, but may be of two types: frequency per week as well as total number of announcements in a contract year.

Frequency Distribution—An array of reach according to the level of frequency delivered to each group.

Fringe Time—Time periods preceding and following peak set-usage periods and adjacent network programming blocks. Usually represents for television, Class B or C time— 4:30–7:30 P.M. or after 11 P.M. EST.

Front-End Display—An outside transit advertising display placed on the front of vehicles. Also known as headlight display.

Full Position—Preferred position for a newspaper advertisement, generally following and next to reading matter, or top of column next to reading matter. When specifically ordered, it costs more than a run-of-paper (ROP) position.

Full-Program Sponsorship—A regular program sponsored by only one advertiser.

Full-Showing—In car card advertising, usually denotes one card in each car of a line in which space is bought. In New York subways, a full showing consists of two cards in each car; a half showing is two cards in every other car. In outdoor poster advertising, a full or 100-intensity showing indicates use of a specified number of panels in a particular market.

FY—Fiscal Year.

G **Gatefold**—A special space unit in magazines, usually consisting of one full page plus an additional page or part of a page that is an extension of the outer edge of the original page and folds outward from the center of the book as a gate.

General Editorial Magazine—A consumer magazine not classified as to specific audience.

Geographic Split Run—A split run where one ad is placed in all of the circulation which falls within a specified geographic area and another ad is placed in other geographic areas or the balance of the country.

Grade A and B Contours—Areas in a television station's coverage pattern in which the transmission signals should have specific levels of strength according to FCC requirements. Grade A service is defined as providing a picture expected to be satisfactory to the median (average) observer at least 90 percent of the time in at least 70 percent of the receiving locations within the contour, in the absence of interfering co-channel and adjacent-channel signals. Grade B service is satisfactory at least 90 percent of the time in at least 50 percent of the receiving locations.

Grid Card—A rate card in which a broadcast station's spots are priced individually, with charges related to the audience delivered.

Gross Audience—The combined audience of a combination of media or a campaign in a single medium. For example, if Medium A and Medium B have audiences of 7 million and 6 million respectively, their gross audience is 13 million. To go from gross audience to net audience, one must subtract all duplicated audiences.

Gross Impressions—The sum of audiences of all vehicles used in a media plan. This number represents the message weight of a media plan. The number is sometimes called the ''tonnage'' of the plan, because it is so large. (See *Gross Audience*.)

Gross Rate—The published rate for space or time quoted by an advertising medium, including agency commission, cash discount, and any other discounts.

Gross Rating Points (GRP)—A measure of the total gross weight delivered by a vehicle (or vehicles). It is the sum of the ratings for the individual announcements or programs. A rating point means an audience of 1 percent of the coverage base. Hence 150 gross rating points means 1.5 messages per average home. Gross rating points are duplicated ratings. Also, reach times frequency equals GRPs.

Guaranteed Circulation — The circulation level of a print vehicle on which the advertising space rate is based. Similar to *rate base circulation* except that an advertiser is assured of an adjustment if the circulation level is not achieved.

Gutter—The inside margins of facing pages; the point at which a saddle stitched publication is bound.

H   **Half-Page Spread**—An advertisement composed of two half-pages facing each other in a publication.

Half Run—In transportation advertising, a car card placed in every other car of the transit system used. Also called a *half service*. Can also apply to publications that offer advertising in half of their circulation.

Half Showing—One half of a full showing of cards; a 50-intensity showing of outdoor posters or panels.

Hiatus—A period of time during which there is no advertising activity.

Hi-Fi Preprinted Insert—A full-page, four-color gravure advertisement printed by a supplier on coated newsprint and furnished to a newspaper in roll form for insertion in lieu of a page of standard newsprint. As the roll is fed into the newspaper, the newspaper prints normal editorial/advertising matter on the reverse side and, in some cases, a column of type next to the advertisement itself. The advertiser pays the supplier for producing the ad and the newspaper for distributing the ads (usually B&W space rates plus an insertion charge). Generally, the cost is twice as expensive as ROP color. Because there is no accurate cut-off on Hi-Fi pages, the copy and illustration has a repeating "wallpaper" design in order to insure full ad exposure.

High Definition TV (HDTV)—A television system that can provide a sharper picture than the current U.S. standard (or 525 lines per frame).

Hitchhike—An isolated commercial for a sponsor's secondary product (not advertised in the main body of the show) which is given a free ride following the end of the program.

Holding Power—The degree to which a program retains its audience throughout a broadcast. It is expressed in a percentage determined by dividing the average audience by the total audience.

Holdover Audience—The audience a program acquires from listeners or viewers who tuned to the preceding program on the station and remained with the station.

Home Box Office (HBO)—The first pay cable service. Began satellite distribution in December 1975 and ushered in a new era in cable television. Currently programs movies and specials reaches about 25 percent of U.S. households.

Home Service Magazine—A publication with editorial content keyed to the home and home living. Examples of this are *Better Homes & Gardens* and *House Beautiful.*

Horizontal Cume—The cumulative audience rating for two programs in the same time period on different days.

Horizontal Half-Page—A half-page advertisement running horizontally across the page. (See *Vertical Half-Page.*)

Horizontal Trade Publications—A business publication editorially designed to be of interest to a variety of businesses or business functions.

HUT (Households Using TV)—A term used by Nielsen and referring to the total number of TV households using their television sets during a given time period. Can be used for the total U.S. or a local market.

Hyping—Intense activity on the part of a broadcaster to increase rating during a rating survey.

I   **ID**—Any short-length "identification" commercial on radio or TV (i.e., a 10-second ID).

Impact—The extent and degree of consumer awareness of an advertisement within a specific medium, and the degree to which a medium and an ad within that medium affect the ad's audience.

Illuminated Panel—See *Panels.*

Impressions—See *Gross Impressions.*

Impression Studies—Starch provides studies of print ads and TV commercials called, respectively, "Starch Reader Impression Studies" and "Starch Viewer Impression Studies," which try to evaluate the kind of impressions made by the ad.

Imprint—Used in cooperative poster advertising programs. Sometimes the local dealer pays a portion of the cost of the poster space and the parent company pays the remaining portion. The dealer's name—the imprint—is placed on the bottom portion of the poster design (about 20 percent of the total copy area) so that his store is listed as the place to buy the product advertised.

Index—A percentage that relates numbers to a base. Used to show what is above average (101 or greater), average (100), or below average (99 or less).

Industrial Advertising—Advertising of capital goods, supplies, and services directed mainly to industrial or professional firms that require them in the course of manufacturing.

Informercial—A long commercial (2 to 7 or more minutes) that provides more information than thirty-second commercials.

Inherited Audience—The carry-over from one program to another on the same station of a portion of the preceding program's audience. (See *Holdover Audience*.)

In-Home—Refers to that portion of media exposure (reading, listening, or viewing) done in the home.

Ink Jet Printing—A technology for an advertiser to print a personalized message in a print advertisement. This message can be specifically tailored to each individual reader.

Insert—A special page printed on superior or different paper stock by the advertiser and forwarded to the publisher to be bound into the publication or to be inserted loose. Usually used for fine color work.

Insertion—An advertisement in a print medium.

Insertion Order—Authorization from an advertiser or agency to a publisher to print an advertisement of specified size on a given date or dates at a definite rate. Copy instructions and printing materials may accompany the order or be sent later.

Instantaneous Rating—The size of a broadcast audience at a given instant expressed as a percentage of some base.

In-Store Media—These are ads that appear in stores and can be either print or broadcast. Print options include shopping cart, billboards, shelf talkers, and aisle posters. TV options include end-of-isle monitors, and shopping cart and check-out monitors. For the most part, these media options are still in their infancy stages. Major companies providing these services are ActMedia and Turner Place-Based Media.

Integrated Commercial—A commercial that features more than one product or service in the form of a single commercial message.

Integrated Marketing Communications—Integrated marketing communications brings a holistic perspective to marketing in that it entails coordination of all marketing efforts into a single, unified plan with one cohesive message for consumers to understand. It also involves reaching customers and prospects through targeted messages through a strategic mix of advertising, direct marketing, telemarketing, sales promotion, public relations, and retail marketing.

Integration (or Origination or Networking) Charge—An extra cost charged to an advertiser by a TV network for integrating a commercial into a program and for the distribution of the commercial from origination and other points, including the preparation of prints for delayed broadcast.

Intensity—In outdoor advertising, the strength of combinations of poster locations throughout a city in terms of coverage or repetition opportunities. A 100 showing has a 100 intensity. A 100 showing (therefore, a 100 intensity) varies from city to city.

Interconnect—Two or more cable systems joining together to create a larger subscriber base for advertising sales purposes.

Interactive Cable—A system where audience members respond to messages on a TV screen by pushing buttons that send responses back to the station.

Interim Statement—Sworn circulation statement of a publisher made quarterly to the

A.B.C. at the publisher's option and issued unaudited but subject to audit. A situation that might call for an interim statement would occur when a community served by more than one newspaper loses one of them through consolidation or discontinuance and its circulation is absorbed by the other newspaper. (See *Publisher's Statement*.)

Island Position—A newspaper or magazine advertisement entirely surrounded by editorial matter or margin.

Isolated 30—A thirty-second commercial surrounded only by programming.

Issue Life—The time during which a publication accrues its total readership. For a weekly, this is generally five weeks; for a monthly, three months.

J **Junior Page**—In print, a page size that permits an advertiser to use the same printing materials for small and large page publications. The ad is prepared as a full-page unit in the smaller publication, appears in the larger publication as a junior page with editorial around it.

Junior Panel—A small-scale version of the thirty-sheet poster. Also called *eight-sheet poster*.

Junior Spread—An advertisement appearing on two facing pages that occupies only part of each page.

K **Keying an Advertisement**—Identification within an advertisement or coupon that permits inquiries or requests to be traced to a specific advertisement.

Keyline—An assembly of all elements of a print ad pasted on a board. It is camera-ready art that is photographed in order to make the negative that in turn is used to make the printing plate. Also called *mechanical*.

L **Lead-In**—Words spoken by announcer or narrator at the beginning of some shows to perform a scene-setting or recapitulation function. Also a broadcast program positioned before another program.

Lead-Out—In relation to audience flow, the program following an advertiser's program on the same station.

Life-Style targeting—A target audience classification system which allows categorization of people into groups based on their activities, interests, and opinions.

Lift—The increase in basic cable penetration brought about by the introduction of a new service or program.

Limited Time Station—A station that usually shares its channel with another station in the same area.

Linage—A newspaper term denoting the number of (agate) lines in an ad or an ad schedule. Also, amount of total space run by a publication in certain categories, e.g., retail grocery linage.

List Broker—In direct mail advertising, an agent who rents prospect lists, compiled by one advertiser, and sold by the agent to another advertiser. He receives a commission for his services.

List House—In direct mail advertising, an agent who sells prospect lists compiled by the organization to an advertiser.

Listener Diary—Method of TV or radio research whereby audience keeps continuing record of viewing or listening in a diary.

Listening Area—The geographic area covered by a station's signal, usually divided into primary and secondary areas.

Little America (or Little U.S.A.) Concept—A test market media plan translation method that equalizes the media weight in the test area with the weighted average of the media weight that will be delivered by the national plan in all areas of the country.

Live Time—The time that the actual performance of a program is transmitted by interconnected facilities directly to the receiving stations at the moment of performance.

Live Time Delay—A delay that coincides with the local live time. Usually occurs when the station is noninterconnected and thus unable to take a live feed.

Leading National Advertiser-Broadcaster Advertiser Reports (LNA-BAR)—A monthly analysis for network television, national spot TV, local spot TV, TV syndication, cable TV, and network radio. It covers competitive spending in these media, plus other related data.

Lloyd Hall Editorial Analysis (now called Russell Hall)—A study of the number of editorial pages a magazine devotes to various categories of product interest over a period of time. For example, the number of pages a magazine devotes to articles on food, home furnishings, fiction, news. This information is frequently used in analyzing the editorial content of a magazine before advertising is placed in it.

Local Advertising—Advertising by local retailers (as opposed to national advertisers advertising in local markets), usually at a lower rate than that charged national advertisers.

Local Channel Station—A radio station that is allowed just enough power to be heard near its point of transmission and is assigned a channel on the air wave set aside for local channel stations (usually 250 watts).

Local Media—Media whose coverage and circulation are confined to or concentrated in their market of origin. Usually, they offer different sets of rates to the national advertiser and the local advertiser.

Local Rate—Rate charged by a medium to the local retail trade.

Local Time—Availabilities or times of broadcasting quoted in terms of local time rather than Eastern Standard Time.

Locally Edited Supplement—Sunday magazine supplement similar in character to syndicated magazine supplements but owned and edited by the newspaper distributing it. Such supplements are available in most of the larger cities throughout the country. Certain of them have banded together into groups for purposes of more efficient soliciting of national advertising and they offer group rates to advertisers who buy all the papers.

Low Power Television (LPTV)—A mini television station whose broadcast signal is limited to ten to twenty miles to better serve smaller communities.

Loyalty Index—Frequency of listenership to a particular station.

M **Magazine Supplement**—A magazine section of a Sunday or daily newspaper distributed either locally or nationally.

Mail-In Premium—A premium offered at the point of sale in a retail store to be obtained by the consumer by mailing a box top, coin, or label to the manufacturer.

Mail Order Advertising—Type of advertising in which the complete sales transaction is handled through advertising and by mail.

Mail Survey Map—A broadcast coverage map prepared by tabulating cumulative, unsolicited mail received during a certain period or by tabulating listener response to a special order or contest run during a certain period.

Makegood—An announcement or advertisement run as a replacement for one that was scheduled but did not run, or that ran incorrectly.

Market-by-Market Allocation (MBM)—The MBM system of media/marketing planning, which allocates a brand's total available advertising dollars against current and/or potential business on an individual TV market basis. MBM spends all advertising dollars (national and local) available in each market in proportion to current and/or anticipated business in the market. The result of MBM planning is to spend more accurately against anticipated sales and thereby generate greater business for a brand.

Market Development Index—See *Category Development Index, Market Index.*

Market Index—The factor chosen to measure relative sales opportunities in different geographic or territorial units. Any quantitative information that makes it possible to estimate this might be used as a market index. A General Market Index is a factor developed that influences the purchase of a specific product or groups of related products. Sometimes called *Market Development Index* or *Category Development Index.*

Market Outline—The measurement of the share of market based on total purchases of a particular brand or groups of similar brands with a product category during a specific time period.

Market Pattern—The pattern of a product's sales in terms of the relation between the volume and concentration either by total market or by individual market. A *thick market pattern* is one in which a high portion of all people are prospects for a product. A *thin market pattern* is one in which a low portion of all people are prospects for a product.

Market Potential—That portion of a market that a company can hope to capture for its own product.

Market Profile—A demographic description of the people or the households in a product's market. It may also include economic and retailing information about a territory.

Market Segmentation—A strategy of implementing different kinds of marketing programs to various segments of the total consumer market based on demographic or lifestyle characteristics.

Market Share—A product's share of an industry's sales volume.

"Marriage" Split—Occurs when more than one advertiser buys the total circulation of a magazine and each of the advertisers runs its ad in only a portion of that circulation. For example, an advertiser with distribution in the western U.S. and one with distribution in the eastern U.S. may split an ad in a magazine that permits this. In this case, the advertiser with distribution in the West would use only that part of the magazine's circulation which reaches the West and the other advertiser would use the remainder.

Masked Identification Test—A method of assessing an ad's effectiveness by finding the percentage of respondents who can identify the advertiser or brand when all identifying marks are concealed.

Mass Magazine—Magazine of a general nature that appeals to all types of people in all localities.

Maxiline—The maximum milline rate for a newspaper. (See *Miniline.*)

Maximil/Minimil—Milline rates for newspapers offering sliding scale discounts. The maximil is the milline computed on the maximum line rate. The minimil is computed on the lowest line rate available.

Mechanical—See *Keyline*.

Mechanical Requirements—The physical specifications of a publication that must be met by advertising material to be reproduced in the publication. Such requirements are brought about by the physical requirements of the vehicle and the characteristics of its printing process. Broadcast media have similar requirements governing the physical characteristics of material acceptable for broadcast.

Media Consortia—A group of advertisers or advertising agencies who pool their media budgets to obtain maximum buying discounts through their greater combined negotiating leverage.

Media Records—A detailed report of advertising volume by selected brands in selected daily and Sunday newspapers in selected cities.

Media Strategy Statement—Prepared by an agency, outlining the specific media that it believes best accomplish the brand's marketing objectives (as outlined in the market strategy statement) within the funds available.

Media Translation—The process of reducing a national advertising media plan to local level in order to test a product or campaign locally. It also can mean the expansion of a local advertising campaign to a national level.

Media Weight—The total impact of an advertising campaign in terms of number of commercials, insertions, reach and frequency, advertising dollars, etc.

Medium—Any media class used to convey an advertising message to the public, such as newspapers, magazines, direct mail, radio, television, and billboards.

Metropolitan Statistical Area (MSA)—An area that consists of one or more entire counties meeting specified criteria pertaining to population, metropolitan character, and economic and social integration between outlying counties and the central county, determined by the Bureau of the Budget with the advice of the Federal Committee on Standard Metropolitan Areas composed of representatives of major federal government statistical agencies.

Message Weight—Refers to the gross number of advertising messages delivered by a vehicle or group of vehicles in a schedule.

Metro Area—A well-defined county or group of counties comprising the central core of a geographical market (usually based on governmental lines).

Microwave—A way of interconnecting cable systems with a series of high-frequency receiving antenna transmitters mounted on towers spaced up to fifty miles apart.

Middle Break—Station identification at about the halfway point of a show.

Milline Rate—A means of comparing rates of newspapers. It is the cost of one agate line per million circulation. The milline rate is computed by multiplying the line rate by 1 million and then dividing by the circulation. The factor of 1 million is used merely to provide an answer in convenient terms of dollars and cents rather than in fractions of a cent.

Miniline—The milline rate for a newspaper at its minimum rate. (See *Maxiline*.)

Minimil Rate—This represents the minimum cost of one line of advertising per million circulation at the lowest rate available after deducting all space or frequency discounts. (See *Maximil/Minimil*.)

Minimum Depth—Most newspapers have minimum depth requirements for advertising. In general, an ad must be at least one inch high for every column it is wide. For example, if an advertiser wants an ad to run that is eight columns wide, it must be at least eight inches high.

Minute-by-Minute Profile—Nielsen minute-by-minute program audience data. Used to study audience gains and losses during specific minutes of the program and to aid in placing commercials at times in which they receive maximum audiences.

Monitor—To check timing, program, and commercial content of individual broadcasts of radio and/or television shows.

Morning Drive—Radio daypart from 6:00 A.M. to 10:00 A.M.

MRI—Mediamark Research, Inc. A company that measures magazine audiences using the recent-reading technique.

Multichannel Multipoint Distribution System (MMDS)—A wireless (over-the-air) cable network providing entertainment, information, and sports for a fee.

Multi-Network Area Rating—This rating, which is tabulated by Nielsen, measures a program's performance in seventy cities with three or more TV stations.

Multiplexing—A technique that allows cable operators (using satellite multiple feeds) to show the same program at different times and in different formats. It makes it possible for cable operators to expand the number of channels from an average of 40 to over 150 channels.

Multipoint Distribution Systems (MDS)—A pay television system that transmits programming via microwave for short distances to subscribers who pick them up with special equipment.

Multistation Lineup—Buying more than one station in a market.

N   **NAB Code**—The National Association of Broadcasters promulgates radio and television codes to assist its members to meet their mandatory obligation to serve the American public. Such codes deal with both program and advertising standards. Included in the advertising standards are sections dealing with presentation techniques, contests, premiums and offers, and time standards. These codes are extended by other documents dealing with interpretations and guidelines, e.g., Children's Television Advertising Guidelines and Alcoholic Beverage Advertising Guidelines. Disbanded in 1982.

Narrowcasting—Describes a cable system's service to a small community. It is the delivery of programming that addresses a specific need or audience.

National Advertising Rates—Rates for newspaper space charged to a national advertiser as distinguished from local rates applying to local retailers. National advertising rates are generally higher than local rates.

National Media—Media that are national in scope.

National Plan—A media plan that is national in scope, as opposed to a local plan covering less than the entire U.S.

National Rating—A rating of all households or individuals tuned in to a program on a national base. Sometimes the base is all television or radio households in the country. Other times, the base is only those households that can tune in to the program because they are in the signal area of a station carrying the program.

Net Controlled Circulation—The number of purchased and unpurchased copies of a controlled-circulation publication that are actually distributed to its intended readership.

Net Paid Circulation—A term used by A.B.C. audit reports and publishers' statements referring to circulation that has been paid for at not less than 50 percent of the basic newsstand or subscription price.

Net Plus—The net cost of a print ad, commercial, or program with an earned discount added on.

Net Unduplicated Audience—The combined cumulative audience for a single issue of a group of magazines or broadcasts.

Net Weekly Audience—In broadcast research, the number of families tuned in at least once to a program aired more than once a week.

Network—Two or more stations contractually united to broadcast programs, e.g., network programs.

Network Affiliate—A broadcast station that is part of a network and therefore offers network programs.

Network Franchise—A brand's right to retain the sponsorship of a program at the sponsoring brand's discretion. This right is acquired by agreeing to sponsor a program on a continuing basis.

Network Identification—Acknowledgment of a network affiliation at the end of a network broadcast.

Network Option Time—Time on network affiliates for which the network has selling priority. Also called *network time*.

Newspaper Distributed Magazine—A supplement inserted into a Sunday newspaper.

Newspaper Syndicate—A business concern that sells special material (columns, photographs, comic strips) for simultaneous publication in a number of newspapers.

Newsstand Circulation—Copies of publications which are purchased at outlets selling copies. May include hotels, vending machines, newsboys, drug stores, and supermarkets in addition to the traditional newsstand or kiosk.

Nielsen—The A. C. Nielsen Company is the world's largest research company, with worldwide operations. It operates a wide variety of syndicated services: NTI—a national television rating service using people meters to collect set-tuning data; Food & Drug Index—a service collecting information on retail sales movement by means of store audits; NMS—a service collecting audience data by personal interview and diaries for television programs, publications (magazines and newspapers); NSI—a local television rating service. Nielsen is a division of Dun & Bradstreet.

Nielsen Clearing House (NCH)—A company that handles the administrative work associated with processing coupons.

Nielsen Coverage Service (NCS)—This provides broadcast station coverage and circulation information rather than program audience measurements. The data are reported for each station in terms of total daytime and total evening audiences over the span of the day, week, and month, on a county-by-county basis.

Nielsen Market Section Rating—A Nielsen report on television ratings by zone breakdowns. The rating breakdowns are: Territory; County-size Groups; Age of Housewife; Age of Household Head; Size of Family; Time Zone.

Nielsen Rating—TV program rating that uses set-tuning data from Audimeters. The Nielsen rating is used to refer to households who have viewed a program five or more minutes. This audience definition is to the *average audience*, which is the audience of the average minute of a program.

Ninety-Day Cancellation—All poster advertising is cancellable on ninety days' notice to the plant. This means that the advertiser or his agency must notify the poster plant owner of cancellation ninety days prior to the contract posting date.

Noted—The basic measure of the Starch method for testing print ads. The Noted Score represents the percentage of respondents (claimed readers of the issue) who say they saw the ad when they first read or looked into the magazine issue, i.e., claimed recognition of the ad.

O **O & O Station**—A station owned and operated by a network. The FCC allows networks to own five VHF stations and two UHF stations.

Obtained Score—This is a Gallup-Robinson term for the actual percentage of respondents who prove recall of a print ad before the score is adjusted for color and size or converted to an index score. It is the basis for the final score.

Off Card—The use of a special rate not covered by a rate card.

Offensive Spending—Advertising activity intended to secure new business.

On-Air Test—A test of a commercial that uses a real broadcast response prior to using that commercial on a larger scale. An on-air test generally measures audience response to the creative executions, such as recall, attitude, or purchase interest for that product.

One-Time Rate—The highest rate charged by a medium not subject to discounts. Sometimes called *open* or *transient rate*.

Open End—A broadcast that leaves the commercial spots blank to be filled in locally.

Open End Transcription—A recorded program usually sold on a syndicated basis in various cities and produced so that local commercial announcements may be inserted at various points throughout the show.

Open Rate—In print, the highest rate charged to an advertiser on which all discounts are placed. Also called *base rate*, or *one-time rate*.

Option Time—Network option time is that time reserved by the networks in contract with their affiliates and for which the network has prior call under certain conditions for sponsored network programs. Station option time is that time reserved by the local stations for local and national spot shows.

Orbit—A scheduling method used by stations that consists of rotating an advertiser's commercial among different programs and/or time periods.

O.T.O.—One-time-only, a spot that runs only once; bought outright or as a makegood.

Outdoor Advertising—Display advertising (billboards, posters, signs, etc.) placed out-of-doors, along highways and railroads, or on walls and roofs of buildings.

Outdoor Advertising Plant—A company that builds, maintains, and sells space on outdoor displays consisting of painted bulletins and/or poster panels.

Out-of-Home Audience—Listeners to auto and battery-operated radios outside their homes. Also the audience of a publication derived from exposure that occurred outside the reader's own home. (See *In-Home Audience*.)

Overlapping Circulation—Duplication of circulation when advertising is placed in two or more media reaching the same prospects. Sometimes desirable to give additional impact to advertising.

Overnights—Nielsen household ratings and shares provided to NSI Metered Market clients the morning following the day or evening of telecast.

P **P4C**—Abbreviation for Page/Four-Color. Other abbreviations are P2C (Page/Two-Color), PB&W (Page/Black and White), 3/5P4C (3/5 Page/Four-Color), 2C (Second Cover), BC (Back Cover), etc.

Package—A combination of programs or commercials offered by a network for sponsorship as an entity at one price. Spot TV is sometimes sold as a package. Also, a program property in which all elements from script to finished production are owned and controlled by an individual or organization, commonly known as a *packager*.

Packaged Goods—Mostly food, soap, and household products that are marketed in the manufacturer's package, wrapper, or container.

Package Enclosure—A premium enclosed in a package.

Package Insert—Separate advertising material included in packaged goods.

Package Plan—A plan by which an advertiser purchases a certain number of TV or radio announcements per week, in return for which he receives a lower rate per announcement from the station. The advertiser agrees to run the specific number of announcements each week and cannot split them up over a period of time.

Package Plan Discount—In spot television, a discount based upon frequency within a week, e.g., "5-plan," "10-plan."

Packager—An individual or company producing a broadcast program or series of programs that are sold as complete units.

Painted Bulletin—This structure is approximately 48' long by 14' high with the copy message painted on the face of this structure as contrasted to the poster panel.

Painted Display—In outdoor, a display painted on a bulletin structure or wall, which may be illuminated, and sold as an individual unit. The standard size is 48' × 14'.

Painted Wall—An outdoor advertising unit, purchased individually, usually situated on a high-traffic artery or in a neighborhood shopping area.

Panel—A fixed sample of respondents or stores selected to participate in a research project who report periodically on their knowledge, attitudes, and activities. This is in contrast to the technique of using fresh samples each time. (See *Store Panel*.) Also a master TV or radio control board, usually in a master control room.

Panels—Regular and illuminated units of outdoor advertising. A *regular panel* is a billboard that is not lighted at night. An *illuminated panel* is a billboard that is lighted from dusk until midnight.

Panographics—An outdoor bulletin that is lit from behind the display.

Pantry Audit—A consumer survey to tabulate brands, items, and varieties of grocery store products in the home.

Parallel Location—An outdoor advertising location in which the poster panel is parallel to the road.

Participation—A station or network may program a segment of time to carry *participation announcements* sold to various advertisers for commercial use. The announcements are usually :10, :30, or :60, but may be longer. Participations are announcements inside the context of programs as opposed to sponsorship or to chain or station breaks which are placed between programs.

Participation Program—A commercial program co-sponsored by a number of advertisers. Or, a program in which the audience participates, e.g., a quiz show.

Pass-Along Reader—A person who reads a publication that he or a member of his family did not purchase. These readers must be taken into account in determining the total numbers of readers of a particular issue or a particular publication. (See *Audience, Secondary*.)

Pay Cable—Any of a number of program services for which cable subscribers pay a monthly charge in addition to the basic cable subscription fee.

Pay-per-View Television—Pay TV for which subscribers pay on a program basis rather than on a monthly subscription basis.

Pay TV—A television system providing programs available only to subscribing homes. Signals are generally transmitted via coaxial cables or telephone lines, and the subscriber is usually charged on a sliding scale for the number of channels the subscriber can receive.

Penalty Costs—In test market and expansion operation, this refers to the premium paid for local replacement media compared with the national media that the brand would be using under their national plan.

Penetration—The percentage of total homes in a specified area owning at least one TV set.

Penetration Study—The study of the effectiveness of advertising on the public.

Peoplemeter—An electronic device that measures viewership of a given program. Present meters require TV audiences to push buttons when they are viewing. Passive meters may not require button pushing.

Percent Composition—The percentage of a medium's total audience that is part of a specific demographic group. Example: If there are 10 million women who read Magazine A, and 5 million are 18–34 years old, then 50 percent of the total audience is composed of women 18–34.

Percent Coverage—In print media: the total audience of a publication as a percent of the total population. Or, the circulation of a publication as a percent of total homes. In broadcast media: the number of homes that are able to receive a signal of specific strength, but which do not necessarily tune to the station(s). Or, all homes in counties which meet a minimum circulation criterion (e.g., 50 percent).

Per Inquiry Advertising (P.I. Advertising)—An agreement between a media owner and an advertiser in which the owner agrees to accept payment for advertising on the basis of the number of inquiries or completed sales resulting from advertising, soliciting inquiries, or direct sales.

Persons Using Radio (PUR)—The percentage of an area's population (over age 12) listening to a radio at any given time.

Piggyback—The back-to-back scheduling of two or more brand commercials of one advertiser in network or spot positions.

Pilot (Pilot Film)—A sample of a proposed TV series used for demonstration.

Plan Rate—The rate paid by an advertiser who purchased a TV or radio package plan. The rates are lower than if the spots were purchased individually since the advertiser agreed to run a specific number of spots each week.

Plant Operator—The company that owns and maintains poster panels in any given market. The plant operator rents space on its poster panels to advertisers in thirty-day units. It leases or owns the land on which the poster panel is erected.

Pod—A commercial position within a network television program whose length varies according to daypart and program. A pod is usually comprised of more than one commercial.

Position—An advertisement's place on a page and the location of the page in the publication. A preferred position is an especially desirable position obtained by paying an extra charge, or granted to an advertiser who has placed a heavy schedule in a publication, occasionally rotated among advertisers who have contracted for space above a specified minimum. In broadcast, programs or time spots considered most desirable by advertisers.

Posttest—Study of the response to finished advertising after it has been published and telecast in media. Posttests rely on normal patterns of behavior to expose respondents to advertising.

Poster—A product sign intended to be displayed on a store window, or on an inside wall, large enough to be legible at a reasonable distance.

Poster Frame—In point-of-purchase advertising, a frame holding a blowup of an advertisement or poster. Layers of advertisements may be mounted on one frame, and the top one torn off to reveal a new one.

Poster Panel—A standard surface on which outdoor advertisements are mounted. The poster panel is the most widely used form of outdoor advertising. The standard panel measures $12' \times 25'$ long, is usually made of steel with a wood, fiberglass, or metal molding around the outer edges. The twenty-four-sheet poster is actually posted on this structure.

Poster Plant—The company that builds and services poster panels and hangs poster sheets on them displaying illustration and/or message of advertiser.

Poster, Regular—A nonilluminated poster.

Poster Showing—Poster advertising is sold in packages called *showings*. A 100 showing (synonymous with *Gross Rating Points*) produces an advertiser circulation in one day that is equivalent to the total population in the market.

Potential Audience—See *Audience, Potential*.

Preemption—Recapture by the station network of an advertiser's time in order to substitute a special program of universal value. For example, when the President speaks, the show regularly scheduled at that time is preempted.

Preemptible Spot—A spot announcement sold at a reduced rate because the station has the option to sell that same spot to another advertiser willing to pay full rate.

Preferred Position—A position in a magazine or newspaper which is regarded as excellent in terms of its ability to generate a large readership. Preferred position is usually located next to editorial material that has a high interest among the publication's readers.

Premium Offer—Supplementary items accompanying a product sold either to consumers or the trade as an inducement to buy that product.

Pre-priced Packs—Product packages printed with lower than usual prices used to produce an immediate increase in sales for that product. Sometimes pre-priced packs are shipped to retailers in special containers that convert into display stands.

Preprint—A reproduction of an advertisement before it appears in a publication.

Pretest—Study of advertisements or commercials prior to distribution via regular media channels. Advertising may be studied in rough or finished form; pretesting relies on some special means of exposing respondents to the advertisement other than the regular media planned—portfolios, dummy magazines, etc.

Primary Audience—See *Audience, Primary*.

Primary Households—Households into which a publication has been introduced by purchase, either at the newsstand or by subscription, rather than by pass-along.

Primary Readers—The readers of a publication who reside in primary households.

Primary Research—Research that is conducted for a specific client or to meet a specific agency need.

Primary Service Area—In AM or standard broadcasting, the area in which a station signal is strongest and steadiest. Defined by Federal Communications Commission rules as the area in which the ground wave (the primary wave for broadcast transmission) is not subject to objectionable interference or objectionable fading. No similar term is officially used in TV broadcasting, although television engineering standards recognize three zones of signal service existing in concentric rings from the transmitting tower: City Grade Service, A Contour, B Contour.

Prime Time—The period of peak television set usage—between 7:30 P.M. and 11 P.M. in Eastern and Pacific Time zones and 6:30 P.M. to 10 P.M. in the Central and Mountain Time Zone.

Prime Time Access Rule (PTAR)—The Federal Communications Commission has mandated television stations to put on a required amount of their own programming during prime time. Under PTAR III, regular network programming starts at 8 P.M. NYT Monday through Saturday and 7 P.M. on Sunday.

Product Protection—Protection that an advertiser wants and sometimes gets against adjacency in a medium to advertising of a competitive product. Has special interest in television advertising.

Program Basis—A Nielsen cost estimate of a television show that takes into consideration the length-of-commitment discount as determined by whether the program is normally telecast every week, less-than-weekly, more-than-weekly, or one-time-only. This discount is determined by the number of telecasts of the show and not the number used by a specific advertiser. Also, this basis disregards other programs sponsored by an advertiser that affect its discount structure.

Program Coverage—The number (or percentage) of television households that can receive a program over one or more stations, because they are in the signal area of some station carrying the program.

Program Delivery (Rating)—Percentage of sample contacted who tuned to a particular program at a particular time.

Program Lineup—A listing of stations carrying a program either on a live or delayed basis. Stations are as supplied by the network or as received directly from their affiliates.

Program Station Rating—A rating based on the television homes located in the area in which a program was telecast that permits an unbiased comparison of different programs regardless of variation in the number of homes capable of receiving the programs.

Promotion Allowance—Money received by a wholesaler or a retailer from a manufacturer or his representative for sales promotion other than advertising. (See *Advertising Allowance*.)

Psychographic—A term that describes consumers or audience members on the basis of some psychological trait, characteristic of behavior, or life-style.

Public Access—FCC rule that requires any cable system with 3,500 or more subscribers to have at least one noncommercial channel available to the public on a first come nondiscriminatory basis.

Public Broadcasting Service (PBS)—Distributor and representative organization of public TV. Similar to network but does not produce programs or have control over station schedules.

Public Service Announcement (PSA)—Promotional material for a non-profit cause, usually prepared at no cost to the service advertised, and carried by vehicles at no cost.

Publisher's Information Bureau, Inc. (PIB)—PIB Service is a monthly analysis of both advertising space and revenue in general magazines, national farm magazines, and newspaper sections. It is designed to give convenient summaries of national advertising expenditures by advertisers and by media.

Publisher's Statement—A notarized statement made by the publisher regarding total circulation, geographic distribution, methods of securing subscriptions, etc. These are often issued between audited statements, especially when market conditions have changed.

Pulsing—A media scheduling technique which produces alternating periods of heavy activity followed by lower activity periods.

Pure Program Ratings—A measurement of audience size in which estimates are made excluding program preemptions that have occurred during the survey period.

Q   **Qualified Issue Reader**—A respondent who qualifies to be interviewed about advertisements in a magazine on the basis of having read the study issue of a magazine. Requirements for such qualification vary: for Starch interviews, readers have merely to claim they looked into the issue when shown the cover; for Gallup & Robinson studies, respondents must prove reading by correctly describing some article when shown the cover and Table of Contents.

Qualified Viewer—Respondent who has demonstrated viewing of a TV program (on the basis of recall of at least one part of the episode), thus becoming eligible or qualified for interview about commercials aired on that show.

Quantity Discount—A graduated discount on quantity purchases scaled to the number of cases in a single order; or, a periodic refund based upon the value of purchases over a period of time.

Quintile—The division of any sample of respondents into five equal-sized groups ranging from the heaviest to the lightest amount of exposure to the medium. Samples may also be divided into tertiles, quartiles, deciles, etc.

Quota—A predetermined media goal in a market. Goals can be established in dollars spent, number of spots to be purchased, or GRPs to be achieved. Used as a target for the agency time buyer in implementing a media plan.

R   **Radio Rating Point**—One percent of the homes in the measured area whose sets are tuned to a station, used for making comparisons of spot stations.

Rate Base—The circulation level of a print vehicle used in setting rates for advertising space charge.

Rate Card—A listing put out by a medium containing advertising costs, mechanical requirements, issue dates, closing dates, cancellation dates, and circulation data. Rate cards are issued by both print and broadcast media.

Rate Class—In broadcast media, the time charge in effect at a specified time.

Rate Differential—Among newspapers, the difference between the national and the local rates.

Rate Holder—A minimum sized advertisement placed in a publication during a contract period to hold a time or quantity discount rate. Also, an ID spot bought by the advertiser for the same reason.

Rate Protection—A guarantee that an advertiser's current rate under the old rate card will be protected for a period, usually from three to six months, should a new rate be introduced.

Reach—The number of different persons or homes exposed to a specific media vehicle or schedule at least once. Usually measured over a specific period of time, e.g., four weeks. Also know as *cume, cumulative, unduplicated,* or *net audience*.

Reach, Cumulative—The total number of homes reached by a medium during a specific time period.

Reader Impression Studies—Studies carried out by Starch over and above their regular Readership Study to find out something of what the advertisement meant to respondents who "noted" the ad.

Reader Interest—Expression of interest by readers in advertisements they have read. Sometimes evaluated by unsolicited mail. Sometimes evaluated by the numbers of people who can remember having read material with interest. Also, an evaluation of the relative level of general interest in different types of products.

Reader Traffic—The movement from page to page by readers of a publication.

Readers—People who are exposed to a print vehicle.

Readers per Copy—The average number of readers of a magazine per copy of circulation. When multiplied by a magazine's circulation, the result equals its audience.

Readership—The degree to which print vehicles have been seen (not necessarily read) by members of the publication's audience.

Readership or Audience—The total average number of persons who are exposed to a publication as distinguished from the circulation or number of copies distributed.

Read Most—Starch ad readership measurement term referring to magazine or newspaper readers who read 50 percent or more of the copy of a specific advertisement.

Rebate—A refund that reduces the contract price for merchandise. A term frequently used for advertising allowances. Also given to advertisers by a certain media vehicle as a result of an advertiser's exceeding the contract minimum and earning a greater discount.

Recent Reading—A measurement technique for magazines in which survey respondents check a list of magazines they have read recently.

Recognition—The technique used to determine whether a person saw or heard a given print advertisement or broadcast commercial by actually showing the ad or commercial (or playing it) and inquiring whether he or she saw or heard it at a previous date in a specific medium. This technique was pioneered and is still being used by Starch.

Recordimeter—An electromechanical device utilized by the A. C. Nielsen Company in conjunction with the *Audilog*. It measures the amount of time that a radio or TV set is turned on during the day, but cannot distinguish among stations as does the *Audimeter*.

Regional Edition—A geographical section of a national magazine's circulation that can be purchased by an advertiser without having to purchase the rest of the magazine's circulation (as is required in a split run). A higher premium is usually paid for regional editions and demographic editions.

Regional Network—A network of stations serving a limited geographic area.

Regular Panel—See *Panels*.

Remnant Space—Magazine space sold at reduced price to help fill out regional editions.

Remote—A broadcast originating outside the regular studio. Also called *remote pickup*.

Remote Control—Broadcasting a program from a point removed from the regular studios of the station.

Renewals—In print: refers to magazine or newspaper subscriptions which people extend past their expiration dates. In outdoor advertising: extra posters over and above the quantity actually needed to post the exact number of panels in a showing. They are shipped to the plant operator and, if one of the posters on display is damaged, the plant operator has a complete poster design on hand to replace immediately the damaged poster.

Representative (or Rep)—A general term used to describe sales representatives for media vehicles. A representative firm usually handles several vehicles, serving as their sales agent and taking commissions on the sales they make; salespersons may also be directly employed by stations or publications.

Replacement Media—Local media that are being used to replace national media in a test market or expansion area, e.g., local rotogravure supplements, comic sections, black-and-white daily newspapers.

Resale Samples—A trade promotion device used to generate trial of a new product. Retailers are offered a shipper-display containing samples priced low enough to allow retailers a much higher than normal markup.

Response Function—An effect of an ad in a medium, sometimes called *impact*. These effects may be attitude change, degrees of brand awareness, or sales.

Retail Trading Zone—The area beyond the city zone whose residents regularly trade to an important degree with retail merchants in the city zone. These are defined by the Audit Bureau of Circulation.

Returns per Thousand Circulation—A gauge of the effectiveness of media used in support of promotions computed by dividing the total number of returns by the circulation of the publication to which the returns are attributable. (See *Keying an Advertisement*.)

Roll-Out—A marketing strategy technique in which a brand is introduced in a limited geographical area. If it succeeds in that area, it is then introduced in adjacent areas and, if successful, in other adjacent areas until the entire country is covered.

Roster Recall—Method of research in which a list of radio or TV programs is submitted to respondents for recall.

Rotating Painted Bulletins—Moving the advertiser's copy from one painted bulletin to another, usually every sixty days. This service is available in most major cities. Offers advertiser an opportunity to cover a large area or a given market (over a long period of time) with a limited number of painted bulletins.

Rotation—The practice in store management of moving the older stock forward when restocking shelves or cases. The practice, in retail advertising, of scheduling a branded product or group of products to be featured at intervals throughout the year to maintain a desired stock balance. Also, the process of continuing a series of advertisements over and over again in a regular order.

Rotogravure (Roto or Gravure)—Printing process where an impression is produced by sunken or deep etched letters or pictures in a copper printing plate. The ink is held in indentation in the plates, not on the surface as in offset, or on the tops of dots or letters as in letterpress.

Run of Press (ROP)—A newspaper advertisement for which a definite position is not specified is inserted as run of press (or run of book), but usually in the general news sections. The term is also used in connection with color newspaper advertising to distinguish color advertising in the main portion of the paper from that placed in the magazine section (*Sunday supplement*).

Run of Schedule (ROS)—A broadcast commercial for which a definite time is not specified. For example, a nighttime commercial during prime time may be run at any time during this period. Also, the time at which an announcement runs may vary from week to week, depending upon other requirements.

Runs—In television film syndication, the number of times a film has been telecast in a given area. The number of times a film may be run according to an advertiser's lease. A rerun among television film syndicators is an available program previously telecast in an area.

Russell Hall—See *Lloyd Hall*.

S   **Sales Promotion**—Those sales activities that supplement both personal selling and advertising, coordinate the two, and help to make them effective, for example, sales incentives.

Satellite-Fed Master Antenna Television (SMATV)—A small cable system for apartment buildings which provides video for many viewers within the buildings.

Satellite Station—A station that rebroadcasts the signal of the parent television station to an area that would not otherwise be covered. Also it may originate some local programming of its own.

Saturation—A level of advertising weight several times above normal coverage and frequency levels standard for the market or product involved. Saturation implies simultaneous achievement of wide coverage and high frequency designed to achieve maximum impact, coverage, or both.

Saturation Showing—In outdoor, a showing of maximum intensity, designed to surpass complete coverage (the 100 showing) with repeat impressions. Often a 200 showing.

Scatter Plan—The placing of announcements in a number of different network TV programs.

Schedule—A list of media to be used during an advertising campaign. A list of a product's advertising to be included in a media vehicle during a specific time. The chronological list of programs broadcast by a station. Also called a *flowchart*.

Scrambler—A device used to electronically alter a broadcast signal so that it can only be viewed on a receiver equipped with a special decoder.

Secondary Audience—See *Audience, Secondary*.

Secondary Research—Research information contained from a published study by another person or group.

Secondary Service Area—The distant area in which a broadcast station's signal is subject to interference or fading, but can still be received.

Sectional Magazine—A magazine that is distributed only sectionally and not nationally (such as *Sunset*, which is confined to the western states). Also called a *regional magazine*.

Selective Magazine—A magazine which, because of its nature and editorial content, appeals only to a certain type of audience.

Self-Liquidating Point-of-Purchase Unit—One for which the retailer wholly or partially pays.

Self-Liquidating Premium—A premium whose total cost is recoverable in the basic sales transaction.

Self-Mailer—A folder, booklet, or other direct mail piece that provides space for addressing, postage, and sealing, and therefore requires no separate envelope for mailing.

Semi-Liquidator—Premium offered to the consumer whose cost is partially recovered by the manufacturer or merchant offering the inducement.

Sets in Use—The total number of sets tuned in to some program at a given time of day and day of week. At one time *sets in use* was equivalent to HUT, but today, its meaning is limited to sets, not households. (See *HUT*)

Share or **Share of Audience**—The audience for a program as a percentage of all households using the medium at the time of the program's broadcast.

Share of Market—The percentage of the total sales of a specified class of products that is held by or attributed to a particular brand at a given time.

Share of Mind—The percentage of relevant population (or a sample of that population) who indicate awareness of, or preference for, the various brands within a product group. Specific meaning varies considerably with the method of measurement. It may be a test of salience or a test of total recall, aided or unaided. Usually refers to consumer awareness of brands in comparison with like measures of awareness for competing brands.

Share of Voice—A brand's share of the total advertising for a product or commodity classification.

Shelf Talkers—In-store printed ads that are located on the actual store shelf next to or hanging down from a shelf with products on the top shelf. Also known as shelf screamers.

Shelter Magazines—Magazines dealing editorially with the home such as decorating, maintenance, gardening, etc. Additionally, these magazines carry a considerable amount of food editorial matter. An example is *Better Homes & Gardens*.

Shop-at-Home—Cable TV networks that allow subscribers to view products and order them by phone.

Shopper—A newspaper published in a local community and containing mainly local news, shopping hints and suggestions, and advertisements. Sometimes called a *shopping newspaper*.

Short Rate—The additional charge incurred when an advertiser fails to use enough media time or space to earn the contract discount envisaged at the time of the original order.

Showing—In outdoor advertising, the number of posters offered as a unit in terms of 100 intensity and variations thereof. In transit advertising, the number of cards included in a unit of sale. (See *Poster Showing*.)

Significantly Viewed—According to the FCC definition, a station is "significantly viewed" in a given county if (a) it is a network affiliate and achieves among noncable households a share of total viewing hours of at least 3 percent, and a net weekly circulation of at least 25 percent; or (b) it is an independent station and achieves among noncable households a share of total viewing hours of at least 2 percent and a net weekly circulation of at least 5 percent. A station which is significantly viewed becomes "local" for regulatory purposes, that is, it can demand carriage on cable systems, and the systems are no longer required to delete the duplicate programming of a significantly viewed station at the request of a higher priority (local) station.

Simmons Data—Print and broadcast media audience exposure and product-usage data reported by the Simmons Market Research Bureau.

Simmons Market Research Bureau (SMRB)—A media and marketing research firm providing syndicated data on audience size, composition, turnover, and duplication of approximately 100 publications using the "through the book" technique to determine readership for selected types. Also provides broad measures of broadcast exposure and data on ownership and usage of consumer products.

Sliding Rate—A space or time rate in a medium that decreases as the amount of space or time used by an advertiser increases over a period of time.

Space Position Value—In outdoor, an estimate of the effectiveness of a particular poster location. The factors considered are the length of approach, the speed of travel, the angle of the panel to its circulation, and the relation of the panel to adjacent panels.

Space Schedule—A schedule sent to the advertiser by the agency, showing the media to be used, the dates on which advertising is to appear, size of advertisements, and cost of space.

Special—A one-time TV show generally employing known talent and usually running an hour or longer. Also called *spectacular*.

Spectacular—(a) Can be a large and elaborate outdoor advertising display with vivid color, special lighting effects, animation, or the like. (b) A television, motion picture, or stage show elaborately cast and produced.

Spill-In (or Spill-Out)—The degree to which programming is viewed in adjacent ADI (or DMA) areas. Depending on the perspective, this is either spill-in or spill-out. Milwaukee television programming spills out of the Milwaukee DMA and spills into the Madison, Wisconsin, area, and vice versa.

Spinoff—A line extension of a magazine on a short-term basis. Also called a "one-shot" annual edition.

Split Run—The running of two or more versions of an ad in alternate copies of the same magazine or newspaper. There are also split runs in which one version of the ad appears in newsstand copies and one in mail subscription copies. Splits may also occur geographically.

Split Run Test—Research designed to test the effectiveness of various copy elements, prices, or types of offers by placing them in alternate copies of an issue. The various forms of the advertisement are evaluated by means of coupon or inquiry returns, or by orders placed for trial offers.

Sponsor Identification (SI)—The extent to which a program's sponsor is identified or its product or service remembered. The percentage of listeners or viewers who correctly associate a program with the sponsor or his product is the Sponsor Identification Index (SII).

Sponsor Rating—A rating determined by applying the Sponsor Identification Index to the total audience rating.

Sponsor Relief—Occurs when an advertiser on a regular television program wishes to suspend activities for an off-season period, and requests contractual relief from the TV networks.

Sponsorship—The purchase of more than one announcement in a program (usually a majority of commercials) by one advertiser.

Spot—A time period filled entirely by a commercial or public service message and sold separately from the adjacent time periods. Such announcements may be placed between network programs or within local programs. Also, to buy time (programs and/or announcements) on a market-by-market basis from stations through their representatives.

Spot Announcement—Commercial placed upon individual stations, radio and TV. Often referred to as *spots*. Technically, spots should be referred to as *announcements*.

Spot Programming—The process by which an advertiser secures the rights to a television program and places it on stations in selected markets without regard to network affiliation. The advertiser may own the television program outright, have rights to the program for a specific length of time, or have the rights to the program in only a certain part of the country.

Spot Radio—The use of stations in selected markets without regard to network affiliation. May involve spot announcements or complete programs.

Spot Schedule—A local spot announcement buy or a standard form that agencies submit showing specific times, adjacencies, etc., of a brand's current spot announcements in a market.

Spot Television—The use of stations in selected markets without regard to network affiliation. May involve spot announcements or complete local programs.

Spread—An advertisement appearing on any two facing pages of a publication.

Staggered Schedule—Several advertisements scheduled in two or more publications, arranged so that the dates of insertion are alternated or rotated.

Standard Activity Unit (SAU)—The fifty-six advertising units in broadsheet, and thirty-three units in tabloid newspapers that are fixed sizes in depth and width and are measured in standard column inches.

Standard Industrial Classification (SIC)—A classification system set up by the U.S. Bureau of the Budget to define business establishments by type of activity. Used to facilitate the analysis of business paper markets.

Standard Rate & Data Service, Inc. (SRDS)—A service that publishes the rates and discount structures of all major media. It also publishes market research studies, often on media or market areas.

Standby Space—An order accepted by some magazines to run an advertisement whenever and wherever they wish, at an extra discount. Advertiser forwards plate with order. Helps magazine fill odd pages or spaces.

Starch Method—A term that refers to the recognition method used by Daniel Starch & Associates in their studies of advertising readership.

Station Break—A time period between two programs when a station announces the call letters, channel number, and also broadcasts commercials.

Station Log—The official, chronological listing of a radio or television station's programming and commercial announcements throughout the day.

Station Rep—A sales organization or person representing individual stations to national advertisers. Short for station representative.

Store Check—An in-the-field personal review of merchandise movement conducted in retail outlets by nonstore personnel.

Store Distributed Magazine—Any one of several magazines (e.g., *Family Circle, Woman's Day*) whose primary channel of distribution is retail grocery stores.

Store Panel—A selected sample of stores used repeatedly for market research to collect data on retail sales movement, e.g., A. C. Nielsen Company's food store panel. (See *Panel*.)

Strip Programming—(a) Running of a television or radio series at the same hour on each weekday. (b) Similar but different programs telecast at the same time throughout the week. (c) The same program, but different episodes, broadcast several times weekly at the same time.

Subscription TV (STV)—A pay television system by which programming is transmitted over the air and must be picked up by a special unscrambling decoder apparatus.

Sunday Newspaper Supplement—Any printed matter that is inserted in a Sunday edition of a newspaper on a continuing basis and is not part of the newspaper itself. Two main publications fitting into this category are magazine supplements and comic sections. A supplement may be either syndicated nationally or edited locally.

Superstation—A term originally coined for and copyrighted by WTCG (later WTBS) Channel 17, Atlanta. Now generically, a station whose signal is available to cable systems across the country via satellite transmission. Other superstations currently "on the bird" are WWOR-TV, New York, and WGN-TV, Chicago.

Sweeps—Both Arbitron and Nielsen survey all television local markets four times yearly (November, February, May, and July). These are called *sweep months*.

Syndicated Program—A method of placing a TV or radio program on a market-by-market basis as opposed to the line interconnected network system of program transmission.

Syndicated Sunday Magazine Supplement—A magazine supplement that is distributed through a group of newspapers and is owned by a single publisher. The distributing newspapers pay the publisher for the privilege of distributing the supplement which in turn helps to build circulation for the distributing newspapers. There are only two nationally syndicated supplements: *Parade* and *U.S.A. Weekend*.

Synergy—The mutual strengthening of various elements of an integrated advertising campaign. A synergistic campaign is said to be greater than the sum of its parts.

T **Tabloid**—A smaller than standard-sized newspaper, with five columns and about 1000 lines per page.

Tag Line—A final line of dramatic scene or act that is treated to give point or impact to the preceding dialogue.

Target Audience—The desired or intended audience for advertising as described or determined by the advertiser. Usually defined in terms of specific demographic (age, sex, income, etc.), purchase, or ownership characteristics.

Targetcasting—Another term for narrowcasting, where cable programming is created to meet special demographic audience interests.

Tear Sheets—Actual pages of advertising as they appear in an issue of any publication, used to serve as proofs of insertion.

Telecast—A broadcast, program, or show on television.

Teleconferencing—Live conferences involving participants in two or more separate locations, with audio, video, and data transmission via satellite to television monitors at each location.

Telemarketing—The sale of goods and services through the use of a telephone. There are two classes of telemarketing: in-bound telemarketing—consumers initiate the call to ask questions or order a product, and out-bound telemarketing—calls are initiated by a telemarketing firm to consumers' homes.

Telephone Coincidental Survey—In research, the interview method in which telephone calls are made while a particular activity, usually a broadcast program, is in progress.

Teletext—A transmission system of text information, by which viewers with special adapters can retrieve wanted signals such as news, weather, etc.

Test Market—A given marketing area, usually a metropolitan census region, in which a market test is conducted. Sometimes used as a verb to refer to introduction of a new product.

Test Market Translation—The use of local media that are available in a specific market to replace the national media included in a brand's national plan. The theoretical national plan must be reproduced as carefully and as accurately as possible in the test market since sales results will be used by company management to determine whether or not the product should be expanded to national distribution.

Thirty-Sheet Poster—An outdoor poster that is approximately 12' by 25'. In the early days of advertising, the poster consisted of twenty-four individual panels pasted together to form an advertisement. Today about ten to twelve panels are used, depending on the type of artwork and copy used.

Through-the-Book—A technique of determining a print medium's audience size by having respondents go through a stripped-down issue with an interviewer to learn which articles are most interesting. After this preliminary examination, respondents are asked whether they are sure they looked into the magazine. Only those who answer positively are counted as readers.

Tie-In—Advertisement run by retail outlets in a newspaper referring to or associating with another ad in the same newspaper. Tie-ins are paid for by the retail outlets running them.

Tiering—Different amounts or levels of cable services that can be ordered by subscribers at different fees.

Time Shifting—Programming that is copied off the air and played back at a different time.

Total Audience—Audience viewing all or any part of a program in excess of five minutes. For programs of less than ten minutes duration, households viewing one minute or more are included. Also total number of unduplicated readers of a magazine.

Total Audience Rating—The sum of all exposures to several issues of the same publication or several issues of different publications.

Total Net Paid—Total of all classes of a publication's circulation for which the ultimate purchasers have paid in accordance with the standards set by the Audit Bureau of Circulations' rules. Includes single copy sales, mail subscriptions, and specials.

TPT (Total Prime Time)—A television research project of Gallup & Robinson evaluating all paid commercials aired during the evening period when national network programming is shown, i.e., both program commercials and station breaks. Offers data both on percentage of commercial audience able to recall the commercial, plus an estimate of actual audience in station coverage.

Traceable Expenditures—Published reports on advertising expenditures by media for different advertisers. Currently, traceable expenditures are available for consumer magazines, farm publications, supplements, newspapers, spot TV, network TV (gross time only), and outdoor.

Trade Advertising—Advertisements of consumer items directed to wholesalers and retailers in the distribution channel.

Trade Magazine—See *Business Paper*.

Trade Paper—Publication covering the commercial activities of wholesale and retail outlets, but many reach the sales departments of manufacturers. Trade papers include all publications that offer a manufacturer the opportunity to reach those who will sell the product for him, either from the standpoint of the retail or wholesale level.

Trading Area—The area surrounding a city set up by the Audit Bureau of Circulations whose residents would normally be expected to use the city as their trading center.

Traffic Audit Bureau (T.A.B.)—An organization sponsored by outdoor advertising plants, advertising companies, and national advertisers for the purpose of authenticating circulation as related to outdoor advertising.

Traffic Count—The evaluation of outdoor poster circulation by an actual count of traffic passing the poster.

Traffic Flow Map (Outdoor)—An outline map of a market's streets scaled to indicate the relative densities of traffic.

Traffic Pattern—Comparisons of customer count to establish averages. How customers behave as to shopping time, hour of day, day of week, frequency.

Transient Rate—Same as *one-time rate* in buying space.

Transit Advertising—Advertising on transportation vehicles such as buses, subways, street cars, etc. Uses poster-type ads.

Translator—An independent TV station that picks up programs from a given station and rebroadcasts them to another area on the upper 13 UHF channels (chs. 70–83). Translators serve from several hundred to, in several instances, up to 50,000 TV homes.

Truline Rate—A rate concept sometimes used at the local level. It is computed by multiplying the agate line rate by 1,000,000 circulation and dividing it by the retail trading zone circulation.

Turnover—The ratio of a weekly rating to a four-week reach. This ratio serves as an indication of the relative degree to which the audience of a program changes. The greater the turnover in the audience, the higher the ratio.

TVAR (TV Advertisers Report)—A bimonthly report from Trendex that gives indices of TV audience characteristics in three categories: audience composition, program selection, and sponsor identification.

Two-Sheet Posters—Outdoor posters placed at transit or train stops. They are 60″ × 46″.

U **UHF (Ultra High Frequency)**—Television channels 14–74.

Unaided Recall—The process of determining whether a person saw or heard a given ad or commercial or brand sometime after exposure with only minimal cueing such as mention of product class (not brand).

Upscale—A general description of a medium's audience indicating upper socioeconomic class membership.

V **VCR**—Video tape recorder that copies programming off the air.

Vehicle—A particular component of a media class, e.g., a particular magazine or broadcast program.

Vertical Cume—In broadcast research, a cumulative rating for two or more programs broadcast on the same day.

Vertical Discount—Broadcast media discount earned through maintenance of specified frequency during given time period, e.g., six spots per week.

Vertical Half-Page—A half page where the long dimension of the ad is vertical. (See *Horizontal Half-Page*.)

Vertical Publication— A business publication that appeals to a specific trade, industry, business, or profession.

VHF (Very High Frequency)—Television channels 2–13. Generally, VHF stations have the greatest range of coverage, whereas UHF stations cover a much smaller area.

Video Compression—A technique for doubling the number of TV channels a cable operator can send his signals on. At present, the average number of channels operators can use is about 40. With compression, the number may increase to 150 or even 200 channels.

Video Discs—A machine that plays pre-recorded programming from a special disc to a special player. It cannot record programming.

Videotex—A two-way interactive cable system that can be retrieved on home TV screens through special terminals. Audiences can request information or data.

Viewer Impression Studies—A service of Daniel Starch & Associates that provides qualiative data about TV commercials. It is based on interviews with respondents who have seen a commercial in the context of normal at-home viewing. Viewers are asked probing questions about the communication of the commercial and its meanings.

Viewers per Set (VPS)—The average number of persons watching or listening to a program in each home.

Viewers per Viewing Households—The average number of persons viewing a television program per total viewing households at that time.

Volume Discount—A discount given for running a certain volume of space in a publication. An advertiser might use many small insertions to make up the required number of pages.

W Waste Circulation—The audience members of a magazine or newspaper who are not prospects for a particular advertised product. Circulation in an area where an advertiser does not have distribution of his product.

Women's Service Magazine—Magazine appealing directly to women (housewives specifically), and whose editorial contents are designed to further their knowledge as homemakers.

Z Zapping—Using a remote control device to change television channels from across the room. This technique is usually applied to commercial avoidance.

Zipping—Using a remote control device to skip ahead of any portion of a television or VCR program. Usually applied to skipping over commercials.

Index

TITLES OF INTEREST IN
PRINT AND BROADCAST MEDIA

For further information or a current catalog, write:
NTC Business Books
a division of *NTC Publishing Group*
4255 West Touhy Avenue
Lincolnwood, Illinois 60646-1975 U.S.A.
800-323-4900 (in Illinois, 708-679-5500)